Family-Style Devotions

Other books by David Servant

Christ's Incredible Cross

Forever Rich

Forgive Me for Waiting so Long to Tell You This

God's Tests

HeavenWord Daily

Modern Myths About Satan and Spiritual Warfare

The Disciple-Making Minister

The Great Gospel Deception

Through the Needle's Eye

Family-*Style* Devotions

A Six-Month Focus on Jesus' Amazing Life

David Servant
ETHNOS PRESS
Pittsburgh, Pennsylvania

Family-Style Devotions
A Six-Month Focus on Jesus' Amazing Life
First Printing: November 2012

Printed in the United States of America
International Standard Book Number: 978-0-9827656-4-7

"How can a young person stay on the path of purity?
By living according to Your word."
(Psalm 119:9 NIV)

Introduction

As a home-schooling family, we've enjoyed many daily devotions with our children. But as we surveyed Christian resources that were available for family devotions, it seems that most focused solely on teaching ethics or life lessons, whereas we wanted to teach our kids about the Lord Jesus and Scripture (which certainly includes a lot of ethics and life lessons, but also a whole lot more.) So I set myself to the task of writing a daily devotional for families that centered on the life of Christ, touching most everything written about Him in the four Gospels. It ended up being a 147-day devotional, which your family can now use each day as well. Each day there is an application and questions to provoke discussion with children. I recommend that parents read my introduction first, which contains some practical ideas on how to hold daily family devotions.

I've had the privilege of serving in vocational ministry for the past twenty-four years, much of which I've served as a pastor. God-called pastors are preeminently concerned with the spiritual health of the people they serve, thus they "keep watch over the flock," always looking for signs of spiritual weakness or sickness. They are usually astute observers, because they care about their people, both young and old. As a pastor, I've observed a phenomenon in many, if not most churches, which troubles me more as each year passes. It's one that can be detected only by someone who observes a congregation very carefully for several years, which is probably why many "laypeople" have missed it.

What have I noticed that concerns me so deeply? The fact that many children, who are raised by good Christian parents and who regularly attend church, slowly grow cold toward God. These children, upon "leaving the nest," give no evidence of possessing any real relationship with Jesus Christ. I'm not speaking of children raised by hypocrites and counterfeit Christians, but of children whose parents love the Lord, parents who faithfully attend and support their church and who sincerely want their kids to know and serve God.

Because of many factors, few believers realize the frequency with which this happens. One of those factors is the general mobility of Americans, who are always changing jobs, homes and churches. They just aren't in one location long enough to realize what is happening with so much regularity in so many places.

It's also true that most Christian married couples tend to associate with other married couples who have children about the same ages as their own children. Consequently, like the proverbial frog in the boiling kettle, they and their married friends don't realize what's happening until it's too late.

Are parents the ones to blame? As difficult as it is for me to say it, I think God would point His finger first at pastors. Too many are failing to tell their flocks the truth and, at the same time, are promoting a lie. Specifically, they aren't teaching that God has given responsibility to the *parents* to teach their children about God. Moreover, they're promoting a system of spiritual education for children that leaves the impression in the minds of most church members that *the church* has been given that responsibility.

How many times have you heard a pastor promote from the pulpit his church's "fun-filled" children's church or "dynamic" youth ministry? Any church hoping to grow or even survive in 21st-century America is almost forced to offer an exciting cradle-to-diploma Christian education program that "your kids will just love." If we hope to compete with every other church in our city for a larger share of the church shoppers and hoppers, we must heed the bottom line of the church-growth surveys: "People are attracted to churches where there is exciting ministry for their kids." And so the message we send is clear: "Come to our church, and you can rest assured that your kids will grow up to love church and serve Christ. The only part you need to play in your children's spiritual growth is to make sure they're here to participate in our exciting program."

Unfortunately, by the time parents realize that the church can't deliver on its promise, it's too late. Their kids are adults who are heading down the wrong road. (Praise God for those who eventually turn back to the Lord, but how much better it is for kids to find and keep their parents' faith their entire lives.)

But the fault doesn't fall entirely on the shoulders of pastors. Pastors often promote the lie because they believe it themselves. At a recent prayer gathering for pastors only, the one prayer request I heard more than any other was for wayward children. Pastors, like laypeople, are victims of a lie built upon tradition. "We've always done it this way," and so our church programs continue as always, and only occasionally does a pastor wonder why there are no examples or instructions for children's Sunday school or special kids' ministry recorded in the New Testament. Following the lead of modern society, the church contributes to the fragmentation of families and the abdication of parental responsibility through a customer service policy that says, "leave the driving to us."

Please understand that I'm not discounting the value of church Christian education programs and the many wonderful people who serve in those programs. Certainly there is fruit for their labor. I am saying, however, that church Christian education programs, if they exist, should only serve to supplement and reinforce what children should be learning at home all the time from their parents. The problem is not Christian education programs *in* themselves, but Christian education programs *by* themselves. The solution is not the elimination of children's Christian education programs; the solution is the parental reclamation of their God-given responsibility. They should be teaching their children about God, as Scripture directs:

"Hear, O Israel! The Lord is our God, the Lord is one! And you shall love the Lord your God with all your heart and with all your soul and with all your might. And these words, which I am commanding you today, shall be on your heart; and you shall teach them diligently to your sons and shall talk of them when you sit in your house and when you walk by the way and when you lie down and when you rise up" (Deut. 6:4-7, NASB, emphasis added).

And, fathers, do not provoke your children to anger; but bring them up in the discipline and instruction of the Lord (Eph. 6:4, NASB, emphasis added).

Probably the most well known verse in the Bible about raising children is Proverbs 22:6: "Train up a child in the way he should go, even when he is old he will not depart from it" (NASB). Christians have been known to disagree on whether this verse is a guaranteed promise of salvation for properly-trained children or just a general principle that is true much of the time, but not always.

Regardless of which interpretation is correct, a much more important issue is the definition of the phrase, *Train up a child in the way he should go.* The understood subject of the sentence is *you*, indicating that parents have the responsibility of training their children. Can it be said that parents who play no active role in teaching their children the Word of God, leaving it all to the church, are training their children in the way they should go? No, they're expecting someone else to play a major part in their children's training. Those parents who consider Proverbs 22:6 to be a promise have no reason to expect the promise to be fulfilled unless they are doing their part to train their children. They can't claim the benefit unless they meet the conditions. And for those parents who think Proverbs 22:6 is a general principle, there isn't much difference. They've no reason to hope that the general principle will hold true for their kids unless they fulfill their God-given responsibility to train their children.

Parents often need help to teach God's Word to their kids, and that's where this daily devotional comes in. I've written it to assist parents who desire to teach their children the Bible. During the next 147 days, you and your children will be reading a small but significant portion of God's Word. We'll cover the life and ministry of Jesus. For each day's reading, I've provided a short commentary that highlights the most important spiritual truths. Also, I often pose a few questions that parents might want to ask their children.

The important thing is that you and your kids talk about what you've read. As your family grows more comfortable doing daily devotions, your kids will spontaneously instigate discussion. That is when it becomes fun.

"But what happens if my kids ask a question for which I have no answer?" you ask? Simply tell them you don't know the answer. That in itself can serve as a wonderful example of humility to your kids and a lesson about telling the truth. If it's any consolation, there are scores of questions about the Bible for which no one has yet come up with a truly satisfying answer. Honest theologians admit they are often stumped. If our daily reading raises an obvious question that I don't attempt to answer in my commentary, it's probably because I'm stumped as well.

What about those passages that contain sexual terminology or describe violence? As a parent, you are the most qualified to make a decision regarding what to do. You may just want to skip over certain verses if you think your children are too young. Or you may want to supply age-appropriate definitions, such as explaining adultery to young children as "when someone who is married falls in love with another person."

We must face up to the fact, however, that the Bible describes life as it is on planet Earth. Unregenerate people have the capacity for incredible acts of wickedness, and our children will discover it sooner or later. Exposure to such things within the moral framework of the Bible is much better than through the polluted rivers that spill out of TV sets into our living rooms. We want our kids to be trained regarding what is right and wrong, and the Bible doesn't conceal either. Your daily devotions will be springboards to life-directing conversations, many of which you'll cherish.

There will be other challenges you'll face, but which will pay rich dividends in your life and the lives of your family. Your first challenge might occur when, after reading a clear command in Scripture, one of your children asks you, "Why didn't you do that the other day at the grocery store when that lady ran her shopping cart into our shopping cart?" That is another positive benefit of family devotions---you'll grow spiritually and your kids will have the benefit of watching God work in your life. No longer will they be exposed only to the apparent perfection of Sunday morning Christianity contrasted with rest-of-the-week application, which otherwise appears as hypocrisy to younger minds. They'll learn what it means to "work out your salvation with fear and trembling" (Phil. 2:12, NASB) by observing you.

Here's how I suggest you conduct your daily family devotions: Gather your family together and pray a short opening prayer, such as, "Lord, help us to understand Your Word and apply it to our lives. In Jesus' name, Amen." Then read the day's portion(s) of Scripture out loud. I suggest that you use the *New Living Translation*, which is one of the easiest translations to understand. Then, either read my commentary, or explain the scriptures yourself in your own words if you've read my comments previously. The idea is to help your kids understand what you've read.

When you finish reading, ask them questions about spiritual principles that surfaced in what you just read. I've usually included a few questions (with the answers) that you might want to ask to provoke dialogue. Work toward a discussion about how you and they can apply what you've learned in your own lives. Allow your kids to interrupt at any time with questions. When they do, you'll know they're interested.

Then spend a few minutes praying together. The idea is to get your kids comfortable with praying sincerely, out loud. Prayer can easily become a meaningless ritual, and the quickest route to ritualistic prayer is to pray the same thing every day. Don't let that happen. I suggest that you model your daily family prayers after this sequence: God, Others, Us. Give each member of your family a different part of the sequence to pray each day. Begin by praising and worshipping God, expressing thankfulness or affirming something about one of His attributes that surfaced in the Bible chapter you just read. The person who is assigned this sequence might simply say, "God, You are really powerful" or, "Thank You for Your great mercy." Next, pray for others. You could pray for a ministry in your church, a missionary you support or know, a sick friend or an unsaved neighbor. Finally, pray for your own needs. These could be material, emotional or spiritual needs among your family. ("Lord, help us to become more like You" or, "Lord, I request Your help on my English test today.")

When you first begin praying as a family, you may want to solicit ideas from the whole group for specific prayers for each category and then assign each member one item on your list. Once everyone grows more comfortable praying together, your prayer time will probably grow more spontaneous. Keep your prayer time short. One-sentence prayers are just fine. If they grow longer, let it happen naturally. Make sure that your prayer time is always meaningful and fresh, never just a time of "going through the motions." Your total time spent in family devotions can be as short as 15 minutes or as long as your schedule permits. If your kids are asking questions, keep going as long as you can!

I suggest ending each gathering with a short song and hugs all around. You'll need to set a regular time for devotions each day, depending on your family's schedule. Right before or after breakfast, right after dinner or just before your youngest child goes to bed are possibilities. Very young children who can't really participate will benefit by realizing that family devotions are something that is done every day. And they'll love the singing and hugs at the end. Curb your children's silliness during your time together but don't be too serious. Enjoy yourself. If you do, your kids are more likely to enjoy themselves too.

You've made a great decision that will pay off in this life and the next. My prayer is that your family will grow closer to the Lord and each other as you fulfill your God-given responsibility to teach your children God's Word.

The Preexistence and Deity of Christ
John 1:1-3; 17:5, 24

The story of Jesus begins long before He was born as a baby in Bethlehem. Because Jesus is and always has been God's Son, He existed before anyone or anything was created. John wrote that Jesus was with God "in the beginning" (John 1:2), which means before the world was created and before time began. When Jesus was conceived in Mary's womb, He was not created—He just moved from heaven to earth and changed His form into a tiny human being inside Mary's belly. It would be something like shrinking and transforming yourself into an ant in order to visit an ant colony.

Not only was Jesus *with* God in the beginning, but John also said that Jesus *was* God. There are three persons who, according to the Bible, can be called God: God the Father, God the Son (Jesus) and God the Holy Spirit. Jesus is just as much God as God the Father is God. We learned today that Jesus helped create everything that exists (see John 1:3).

We also read that Jesus prayed to God the Father just before He died, "Father, bring me into the glory we shared before the world began" (John 17:5). Before the world was created, Jesus lived in heaven, a place filled with God's glory, with His Father. What is God's glory? It is something like sunshine, only much brighter. It radiates from God.

The best part is that everyone who is a follower of Jesus will one day see God's glory in heaven, because Jesus requested that we would. He prayed, "Father, I want these whom you've given me [that includes us] to be with me [in heaven], so they can see my glory" (John 17:24). When we see Jesus one day in heaven, He'll be brightly shining with God's glory. The Bible tells us that His face will shine like the sun (see Matthew 16:27-17:2)!

Q. Where did God the Father, Son and Holy Spirit come from?
A. The answer is that They have always existed. They have no beginning and no end. That is hard for us to understand, but that is the answer. The reason we have difficulty understanding it is because most everything we know has a beginning and an end.

Q. Why did John call Jesus "the Word"?
A. The word *word* sometimes means "a message." For example, your teacher might say, "I have a word from our principal," meaning a message from the principal. Or you might hear someone on a TV show say, "And now a word from our sponsor," which means a commercial is coming with a message from an advertiser. Jesus is given many symbolic titles in the

Bible, such as "Lamb," "Cornerstone" and so on, which all describe something He has done for us. Perhaps He is called "the Word" (or "the Word of God"; see Rev. 19:13) because Jesus was God's message to all people of the world. Isn't it amazing that God had a message prepared for all the people of the world even before He created anyone?

> Application: *Because we will one day live with Jesus in heaven and see His glory, we should live "in a manner worthy of the God who calls [us] into His own kingdom and glory"* (1 Thessalonians 2:12, NASB).

The Deity and Humanity of Jesus Christ
John 1:14; Isaiah 7:14; 9:6

Yesterday we read what John wrote about Jesus being called "the Word." A few verses later in his Gospel, John said, "the Word [who is Jesus] became human and lived here on earth among us" (John 1:14). John was talking about when the glorious God Jesus was transformed into a baby in Mary's womb, lived there for nine months, was born, grew up, and lived for about 33 years on the earth as a human being. It was a really big miracle for God to become a man, but nothing is too hard for God!

It's very important for us to understand that Jesus was a very special person. He was God transformed into a man. He wasn't one-half human being and one-half God. He was 100% of both. That has not been the case with any other person who has ever lived. Jesus was one-of-a-kind! He wanted us to know that He was both human and divine, calling Himself the *Son of God* and the *Son of Man.*

Hundreds of years before Jesus became a man, God told Isaiah the prophet what He was planning to do. He promised that a special baby would be born through a woman who had never been married. People often have special names that they call their babies, such as "sweet pea," "little guy" or "chubby cheeks." But the special baby that God told Isaiah about would be called "Immanuel," a name that means "God is with us" (Isaiah 7:14). That is what Jesus was. He was no longer the God in heaven—He was God living with us.

Through Isaiah, God the Father helped us understand how His Son, who had no beginning, would have a beginning as a human being. He promised, "For a child is born to us, a son is given to us" (Isaiah 9:6). It was a human being, a *child*, who was born in Bethlehem, but the Father's *Son* was not born because He always existed. Thus, He was *given.*

Finally, notice Jesus was born *to us* and given *to us*. It was *for us* that He came because God loves us.

 Q. Let's pretend that you wanted to show the dogs in your neighborhood how much you loved them. What would you do? If you had the power, would you be willing to change yourself into a baby dog inside its mother, live there for nine months, be born as a puppy and live for 33 years as a dog when you could have been enjoying life as a human being? You would really have to love dogs to do that! Jesus becoming a man was a bigger step down than for us to become dogs. Does that give you an idea of how much Jesus loves us?

A. Yup!

Q. Are there any other major religions in the world besides Christianity that can truly say they were begun by a human being who was actually God?

A. Nope!

 Application: *Since Jesus is God, we should pay careful attention to what Jesus said and obey Him.*

3

One Reason Why Jesus Became a Human Being
John 1:18; Hebrews 1:1-3

Many people have wondered what God is like. They've looked at flowers, snowflakes, hummingbirds and rainbows and realized that God must be *very* smart and *very* powerful. The things He's made are amazing! And when people eat a crisp apple, sit by a warm fire on a cold day, or listen to musical instruments, they realize that all those wonderful things are made possible by God, and so He must also be very kind.

But knowing God through what He's made is somewhat like knowing an artist only through his paintings. How much more could you learn about that artist if you could actually meet him in person and be friends for a few years?

God wants us to know Him personally, and not just through what He has created. That is one reason that God sent Jesus to the earth. We read today, "No one has ever seen God. But his only Son, who is himself God, is near to the Father's heart; he has told us about him" (John 1:18). Nobody knew God the Father better than Jesus. They had lived together forever! In the original language in which John wrote, he said something like, "Jesus and God the Father were bosom buddies!"

Not only did Jesus know more than anyone else about God the Father, He also *acted* more like God the Father than anyone else. Have you ever heard the expression, "Like father, like son"? That was certainly true concerning Jesus and His Father. Jesus once said, "Anyone who has seen me has seen the Father!" (John 14:9). If we want to learn what God the Father is like, all we have to do is learn about Jesus. We read today, "Everything about [Jesus] represents God exactly" (Heb. 1:3). If God the Father had become a human being instead of Jesus, He would have said and done the same things.

Before Jesus came, there were only two ways to learn about God: through looking at His creation, and through studying the words of the people who wrote the Old Testament. Some of those people had experiences with God from which we can learn, and some of them (the prophets) actually spoke God's words. But ever since Jesus came, we now have three ways to learn about God! As we study the life and ministry of Jesus in the weeks ahead, we'll be learning about God, the creator of everything, a person with whom we'll be friends forever. What could be more exciting than that?

Q. Perhaps your parents are like most parents: one is a little more strict than the other. If you have to get a spanking, you probably would prefer to get it from your mother, because she doesn't spank quite as hard as your father! Do you think God the Father is more strict than Jesus is since He's the Father?

A. No. Both the Father and Son are equally loving and equally strict. They become equally angry over the same things and care about you the same.

Application: *Since God has put forth so much effort to help us to get to know Him, we should study His creation, His Word, and the life of Jesus so that He will become our closest friend.*

4

Another Reason Why Jesus Became a Human
1 Timothy 1:15; Hebrews 2:14-15

Yesterday we learned one reason why God's Son became a human being: to teach us about God. But there was a second reason that is even more important. Jesus became a human being so our sins could be forgiven, as we just read: "Christ Jesus came into the world to save sinners" (1 Timothy 1:15).

Why did Jesus have to come into the world in order for sinners to be saved? If God wanted to forgive sinners, why didn't He just do it from heaven? Why did God have to become a human being?

To answer those questions, we first have to understand something about God. He is perfect. He always does the right thing, and it wouldn't be right for God to simply forgive people who continually do bad and evil things. What would you think of your parents if they never punished a brother or sister who beat you up every day? You would think that they didn't love you and weren't fair.

If God didn't punish people when they did bad things, He would be unloving toward people who were hurt by other people's sins. And He would be acting unfairly. So God couldn't just decide not to punish people for their sins, or He would become a sinner Himself!

However, God loves the people He's created, and He needed a way to forgive them without becoming a bad person Himself. So God decided to become a human being who would face every temptation that anyone ever faced. He, however, would never sin. Then, as a substitute, He would take the punishment for everyone's sins! As an example: Perhaps you were about to be spanked for disobeying your mother or father, and your sister or brother volunteered to be spanked in your place! (Pretty slim chance of that happening, right?)

That is why God had to become a human being. God, of course, can't die, but humans can. So God became a human being in order to die. And His painful death was the payment for our sins. Jesus Himself said, "I... came here...to give my life as a ransom for many" (Mark 10:45). A ransom is a payment to set free someone who is a prisoner. Jesus gave His life as a payment to God's justice so He could set us free from our sins.

 Q. Why couldn't some other human being have died for our sins instead of Jesus?

A. Because all of us have sinned, we all deserve to be punished. So none of us could serve as a substitute to die for the sins of others. It would be like two convicted murderers who become friends in prison. If both were sentenced to die in the electric chair, it would be silly for one to say to the prison warden, "I will sacrificially volunteer to die in place of my friend." The warden would reply, "You can't die for him because you are going to die for your own crime."

We needed someone who was sinless, who didn't deserve any punishment for his own sins, to be punished in our place. Jesus was the only person who has ever lived without sin.

Q. How could the painful death of only one person be enough payment for the many sins of everyone who has ever lived?

A. It was not the *amount* of suffering that made Jesus' death sufficient payment for everyone's sins; it was the fact of *who* did the suffering. Let's say, for example, that your dog attacked and killed your neighbor's dog. Your neighbor might demand that your dog be killed so that your dog suffers just as much as his did. That could be considered fair. But what if he demanded that *you* die for what your dog did? That would be unfair, because you are worth a lot more than a dog. You have more value than an animal!

In the same way, God has much more value than all the human beings put together. If Jesus had been *just* a man, His sufferings would have been sufficient payment for only one other person who deserved to die. But because God's value is infinitely higher than all human beings combined, His painful suffering was more than sufficient to be able to pay fairly for everyone's sins.

Application: *Since God loved us enough to die as our substitute, we should show Him love in return by doing what He says. Jesus said, "If you love me, obey my commandments"* (John 14:15).

The Birth of John the Baptist Foretold
Luke 1:5-25

This story happened about 2,000 years ago in Jerusalem, Israel. The Jewish people had a big building something like a church that was called the Temple. God had said that all the men who were descendants of Moses' brother, Aaron, were supposed to work at the Temple doing various jobs. They were called priests. One of their jobs was to burn incense, something that smelled very nice, in an inner room of the Temple, called "the holy place."

There were so many descendants of Aaron at the time of this story that they took turns doing the various jobs. It just happened that Zechariah was chosen to be the one to burn incense inside the Temple, and it was a once-in-a-lifetime opportunity for him. He was probably really excited to go in the Temple into a special room that few people ever got to see! Imagine how shocked he was when an angel named Gabriel suddenly appeared before him! Have you ever been scared in your own house when you suddenly saw a family member whom you didn't know was in the same room with you? Think of how you'd feel if it was someone you didn't recognize. What if it was someone who looked like an angel? No wonder Zechariah was "overwhelmed with fear" (Luke 1:12).

The angel told Zechariah some amazing news: In answer to his prayer, his elderly wife would have a special baby. Zechariah's son would be a great prophet and preacher, and by the Holy Spirit's power, he would persuade many people in Israel to quit sinning. That way, they would be prepared for another very special person who was about to come: God in the form of a man!

Zechariah didn't believe what he heard because he thought he and his wife were too old to have a baby. They were as old or older than your grandparents! But nothing is too hard for God, and Zechariah should have believed what he heard. It was an angel who spoke to him, and that angel had just come from heaven to deliver the message from God.

God was a little bit angry with Zechariah's unbelief, so He took away Zechariah's ability to talk for about nine months! God expects us to believe what He says because He never lies. A lesson we can learn from Zechariah is that it is better to say nothing at all than to say something that disagrees with what God has said. God is always right in what He says.

Q. We learned today that many of the Israelite fathers weren't very good fathers, but when they heard John's preaching they repented and started to really show their kids that they loved them. What is the most important thing your father or mother could do to show you how much they love you?

A. Teach you about God and the Bible! (So you must have good parents!)

Q. When do you think Zechariah prayed to have a son?

A. Probably many years before when he was a younger man, since he didn't believe it was possible for his wife to have a baby even after hearing the angel's message. Our prayers are not always answered as soon as we'd like.

Application: *God's Word is always true, so we should never say anything that contradicts what God has said.*

Jesus' Birth Foretold to Mary
Luke 1:26-56

Back in the days of Elizabeth and Mary, people got married at a younger age than people do today, often when they were teenagers. Mary may have been only sixteen or so when the angel Gabriel appeared to her and told her she would have a child. Imagine God coming to the earth through a teenager!

Because she was not married to Joseph yet, Mary wondered out loud how she would be able to have a baby. Gabriel explained to her that although the baby would be *her* son, the child would not be Joseph's son. He would be *God's* son, conceived by the Holy Spirit. He would be the first and only God-man, 100% human and 100% God.

Gabriel told Mary that her son would be given the throne of His ancestor David and that He would "reign over Israel forever" (Luke 1:33). His kingdom would have no end. David was a great king who had ruled over the nation of Israel about one thousand years before the time of Jesus. When David was still alive God had promised him, "When you die, I will raise up one of your descendants....and I will establish the throne of His kingdom forever. I will be his father, and he will be my son....Your dynasty and your kingdom will continue for all time before me, and your throne will be secure forever" (2 Samuel 7:12-16). After David died, his descendants did rule after him for about five hundred years, but since then there has been no descendant of David ruling over Israel.

When Jesus lived on the earth He never did rule over Israel. In fact, the people of Israel killed Him. But God's promises are true. The Bible tells us that Jesus will one day live in Jerusalem, and from there He will rule the entire world! There won't be any United States of America then or any other countries—Jesus' kingdom will be the only kingdom. And His kingdom will never end! Everyone should want to be in that kingdom.

Gabriel told Mary that her relative Elizabeth had also experienced a miracle: she was pregnant in her old age. So Mary journeyed to Elizabeth's house and stayed with her for three months, probably until John was born. Elizabeth probably appreciated having someone to chat with during those three months since her husband couldn't talk!

When Mary arrived at Elizabeth's house, John, who was probably already filled with the Holy Spirit (see Luke 1:15), "jumped for joy" inside his mother. The Holy Spirit in John knew who was inside Mary, and was quite happy about it! So what is the key to being joyful? Being close to Jesus!

Elizabeth may have heard about what Gabriel had told Mary, because when Mary arrived at her door she already knew that Mary was pregnant with a very special child. Or it's possible that the Holy Spirit inspired her with a gift of prophecy, because we read that she was filled with the Holy Spirit upon Mary's arrival. Regardless, Elizabeth knew that Mary's baby was even more special than her own. She called Mary "the mother of [her] Lord" (Luke 1:43), so she knew that God was living inside Mary's womb.

It seems that Mary was suddenly filled with the Holy Spirit then as well, because she responded to Elizabeth's greeting by speaking a beautiful poem. It was all about God's goodness toward her and to everyone who fears Him. The best thing God did for us was to send Jesus! Like Mary, we're blessed!

Q. Because Mary and Elizabeth were somehow related, we know that Jesus and John the Baptist were distant relatives. Do you know of anyone who is alive today who is related to Jesus?

A. Everyone who believes and follows Jesus is a brother or sister of Jesus!

Q. Jesus lived inside of Mary for nine months. Has He ever lived inside of anyone else?

A. Yes! If you believe in Him, Jesus lives inside of you! He doesn't live inside you physically, like a baby inside its mother, but spiritually, because the Holy Spirit lives in everyone who believes in Jesus, and the Holy Spirit is just like Jesus and the Father. That is why Jesus once promised everyone who loves Him that both He and His Father would come to live inside them (see John 14:23).

Application: Since Jesus lives in us by the Holy Spirit, we should always remember that He is with us to direct our thoughts, words and deeds.

John the Baptist is Born
Luke 1:57-80

When new babies are born, people always make a fuss over them. If you've ever had a baby brother or sister born into your family, you may have felt like your mom and dad forgot about you for a little while. However, the fuss that was made over your baby brother or sister was nothing compared to the one that was made over John the Baptist when he was born. *Everybody* was talking about it for miles around—a baby had been born to an old woman! Plus, an angel had appeared to the baby's father, who had been unable to speak for nine months! Everyone who heard about it knew that Zechariah and Elizabeth had a special son for whom God had a special plan.

The people of Israel had been given many laws by God, one of which concerned baby boys. All of them were supposed to be circumcised on the eighth day of their lives. To be circumcised means to have a little piece of skin removed from a boy's private parts. It hurts for a little while, but quickly heals like any other cut. All the Israelite boys were supposed to be circumcised in order to mark them as being God's people. It showed that they belonged to God.

Like all other baby boys in Israel, John the Baptist was circumcised on the eighth day of his life, and that is when he was given the name *John* according to the instructions of the angel who appeared to his father. *John* means "God is very kind."

On the day of John's circumcision, his father was suddenly able to speak once again, and the first thing he spoke was praise to God. Soon after, the Holy Spirit spoke through him in a beautiful prophecy. If you listened to it closely, you probably noticed that the prophecy was more about Jesus than John. That's because Jesus was a million times more important than John. John was only a man made great by God. Jesus *was* God. Zechariah's prophecy revealed that it was God's plan for John to prepare the way for Jesus to begin His ministry.

What did Zechariah's prophecy say regarding Jesus? It revealed that Jesus was God. It said that *God* would *visit* His people (see Luke 1:68).

When He visited, God would redeem His people (see Luke 1:68). In the New Testament, the word *redeem* means to purchase someone's freedom from being a slave. Before we were born again, we were slaves to selfishness, sin and Satan.

Zechariah's prophecy also revealed that Jesus would be a mighty Savior (see Luke 1:69). We needed someone to save us from the penalty for our sins: eternal separation from God in hell. Through our Savior, our sins have been forgiven because of God's wonderful mercy (see Luke 1:77-78).

That Savior would be a descendant of King David, just as God had promised David a thousand years before (see Luke 1:69b-70).

Jesus would also save God's people from their enemies. Through Jesus, we've already been saved from our spiritual enemies: Satan and his evil spirits. They can't control us as they used to. Now, as Zechariah said, we can serve God without fear of them (see Luke 1:74). And one day, all of God's people will be saved from their physical enemies, when we live in

God's eternal kingdom. There won't be anyone there who hates us.

The truth that Jesus would bring to the people of the earth would be like light coming down from heaven. No longer would we have to stumble around in darkness, not knowing where we are going. His truth would guide us into peace (see Luke 1:79). Aren't you glad that Jesus came?

 Q. Is there any evidence in today's reading that Zechariah was not only temporarily mute, but also temporarily deaf?

A. Yes. Read Luke 1:62 closely. If Zechariah had been able to hear, his friends and relatives wouldn't have needed to communicate to him "by making gestures."

Q. If you were unable to speak for nine months, what would be the first words out of your mouth when your speech was restored? Why?

Application: Isn't it amazing that God had a plan for John's life even before he was born? Did you know that, according to Ephesians 2:10, God also had a plan for our lives even before we were born? All of God's children are somewhat like John the Baptist. Like John, our main job is to get people ready to meet the Lord.

Matthew Tells the Story of Jesus' Birth
Matthew 1:18-25

When two people are engaged, that means they've promised to marry each other but are not yet actually married until their wedding. In our day, engaged people sometimes get "disengaged," and when they do, it's usually because one of them has discovered something about the other person that wasn't known previously. (That's why it's a good idea to get to know a person as much as you can before promising to marry him or her.)

That was the situation for Mary and Joseph. When Joseph discovered that Mary was pregnant, he figured that she had fallen in love with someone else. That greatly alarmed him for several reasons. First, Mary undoubtedly told Joseph that she would marry him because she loved him. But the baby in her belly indicated that she loved another man, and so she had lied to him. No one wants to marry a liar.

Second, in order for Mary to become pregnant, she must have had a sexual relationship with that other man. That meant she had broken one of the Ten Commandments, and so she was also an adulteress (or more technically, a fornicator). No one wants to marry an adulteress.

Third, in her defense, Mary surely explained to Joseph that the baby in her belly was conceived by the Holy Spirit. If she did, Joseph obviously didn't believe her. He must have thought she was going crazy, claiming to have seen an angel who told her she would give birth to God's Son! No wonder Joseph decided to break their engagement! He was a wise man.

Joseph was also a very good man. Even though he was surely very hurt by what he discovered, he knew that everyone would think badly about Mary if they also knew what he did. So he decided to break his engagement quietly, so as not to embarrass her. The Bible says that when we love someone, we won't want to advertise his or her sins, but keep quiet about them.

God, who knows everything, knew what Joseph was planning to do, so He had an angel appear to Joseph in a dream. The angel explained the truth about Mary's baby, and instructed him to name the child Jesus, which means "the Lord saves." Jesus would save us from our sins, and that was the main reason He came into the world. Joseph was greatly relieved to learn the truth, and he did what the angel told him.

Q. There were probably many people who passed judgment on Joseph and Mary when they saw that Mary was pregnant but not yet married to Joseph. It must have really hurt them. Have you ever had someone believe something bad about you that wasn't true? What should you do when that happens?

A. You should try to explain the truth to those who have passed judgment on you, hoping that they'll realize their error. But, even if they don't, you can be thankful that God knows the truth and trust that He will eventually clear you, just as He did Mary.

Q. Have you ever believed something bad about someone else that you later discovered wasn't true? Why did you believe it at first? What did you learn from that experience?

Q. Do you think you will ever get married? How long do you think you should be friends with a person before agreeing to get married? What are the most important traits you should look for in a person to marry?

A. Obedience to God and unselfishness.

Application: We should always believe the best about people until we know differently, and when we do, if we love them, we will hide their sins, not tell everyone about them.

Luke Tells Us More About the Birth of Jesus
Luke 2:1-20

Through the Old Testament prophet Micah, God had foretold that the Messiah would be born in Bethlehem: "But you, O Bethlehem...are only a small village in Judah. Yet a ruler of Israel will come from you, one whose origins are from the distant past" (Micah 5:2). So it was no accident that Mary and Joseph were in Bethlehem when Jesus was born. Before the world was created, God knew that around the year 6 B.C. the leader of the Roman Empire would decree that a census be taken of all the people in his domain. For that reason, Joseph and Mary had to journey about 65 miles to register in the town of Joseph's ancestor, David.

When we think about Jesus being born, we often imagine a picture similar to what we've seen on the front of Christmas cards: a soft golden glow surrounding a beautiful mother with a baby in her arms, as her husband and the animals of the manger scene adoringly watch. But Jesus' birth was not such a pretty picture. First, giving birth to a baby is not an easy thing to do—just ask your mom about when you were born! Then ask her how she would have enjoyed delivering you in a stinky barn, right on the floor, after several days of traveling! That is probably how Jesus was born. Mary laid him in a manger, which is a nice word for an animal feeding trough. How would you like to sleep in a box where animals had eaten and slobbered? Jesus went through a lot of trouble to become a human being, and that shows us how much He loves us.

I wonder if Mary and Joseph complained to each other about all their troubles. Just to register their names in Bethlehem, they had to make a long journey when Mary was very pregnant, and Mary had to give birth in very unpleasant surroundings. They probably didn't realize that they were right in the center of God's will, fulfilling an ancient prophecy. We often grumble about circumstances in our lives when we don't see God's plan. But if we could see our circumstances through God's eyes, we would rejoice. And so we should!

God's perspective of Mary and Joseph's plight was revealed to the shepherds of today's reading. The multitude of angels that God allowed them to see were praising God because the Son of God, the long-awaited Messiah, the Savior, had been born! At that time, it was the greatest event of history! Those angels had been sent from heaven to tell them the wonderful news because God was so excited about the birth of His Son. Just like when you were born, your dad wanted everyone to know about it!

Q. Why are we certain that the prophet Micah, in his prophecy about a ruler coming from Bethlehem, was talking about Jesus, and not some other ruler of Israel?

A. We are certain because Micah identified that ruler as being someone "whose origins are from the distant past" (see Micah 5:2). The Jewish leaders in Jesus' time knew that Micah could have only been speaking of the Messiah, even if they didn't understand that the Messiah would be God Himself, who existed from eternity (see Matt. 2:3-6).

Q. Looking back at your life, do you think that anything has happened to you that you complained about at the time, but that God was excited about because He could see the whole picture? Could that be true of anything you are complaining about right now in your life?

Application: The Bible says, "God causes everything to work together for the good of those who love God and are called according to His purpose for them" (Romans 8:28). God doesn't cause all things, and not all things are good, but God does cause all things to work together for good. Since that's true, we should maintain a good attitude, even when things don't go the way we want them to.

10

The Records of Jesus' Ancestors
Matthew 1:1-17 Luke 3:23-38

What long lists these are! Aren't you glad you don't have to memorize all those names for your history class?

Why are these two lists of Jesus' ancestors not identical? Probably because Matthew recorded Jesus' ancestry through His stepfather, Joseph, and Luke recorded Jesus' ancestry through His mother, Mary. Also, Matthew's list goes back to Abraham, whereas Luke's list goes all the way back to Adam. If you'll compare the lists closely, you'll discover that both Mary and Joseph were descendants of King David, but through two different sons. On both lists, the people from Abraham to David are the same, except that Matthew left out one name, perhaps to make his list easier to remember as three segments of fourteen generations, as he mentioned (see Matthew 1:17).

Did you know that some of the people on Luke's list are your ancestors? The reason is because they're everyone's ancestors! All of us are descendants of Adam, Seth, Enosh, Kenan, Mahalalel, Jared, Enoch, Methuselah, Lamech and Noah, so all of them are your great, great, great, great (and so on) grandfathers! You'll get to meet at least some of them in heaven some-day!

To the Jewish people, keeping track of their ancestry was very impor-tant. All of them were descendants of Abraham, Isaac and Jacob. Jacob was renamed *Israel* by God, and that is why all his descendants are called "the people of Israel" or "the Israelites." Jacob had twelve sons who became twelve tribes, and all their descendants knew from what tribe they came.

There are two main reasons why these two lists are so important to us. First, because they prove that Jesus was a real person of history. Some peo-ple foolishly think that the story of Jesus is just a myth or fairy tale (like Santa Claus) that someone made up. But Jesus was a person who really was born just like everyone else. He was a person of history just as much as George Washington or Abraham Lincoln.

Second, these lists are important because God had promised in the Old Testament that the Messiah would be a descendant of Abraham, Isaac, Ja-cob, Judah, Jesse and David. If Jesus had not been a descendant of those men, we could be sure that He was not really the Messiah. Matthew and Luke's lists prove, however, that Jesus was in the lineage of all six of those men through both His mother and stepfather.

Q. Luke recorded 76 generations from Adam until Jesus. If each gen-eration was twenty-five years apart, how long ago could we conclude that Adam was created?

A. About 3,900 years [(25 x 76) + 2000]. If we use a high estimate for the average rate of growth of the world's population over the past centuries (.5%) and work backward from that, we can conclude that the earth's popu-lation consisted of just a few people around 4,000 years before Jesus, about the time of Noah's flood.

Q. Then why do some scientists say that the fossilized human bones they discover are millions of years old?

A. Because the dating methods of those scientists are very questionable. They try to determine the age of the bones based upon their location in the layers of rock, and the dates of those layers of rocks is a guess. Many scientists assume the rock layers were laid down gradually, over billions of years, underneath ancient oceans. They don't consider the fact of a world-wide flood during Noah's time, when rock layers could have formed very quickly. Nor do they seem to consider the fact that dead bodies don't nor-mally turn into fossilized bones. The average dead dinosaur didn't fossil-ize—it rotted away. Only under catastrophic circumstances do living things fossilize, which is what may have happened during the worldwide flood of the Bible. People and animals may have been buried quickly under tons of sediment that is now exposed thousands of years later through the process of erosion.

Q. From which tribe of Israel was Jesus descended?
A. Judah

 Application: Since Jesus was a real person of history who was also the Son of God, we should want to learn all we can about Him and do what He says.

11

Baby Jesus Presented in the Temple
Luke 2:21-40

When Jesus was just a newborn, He was like any other baby. He couldn't walk or talk, He cried when He wanted to be fed, and He dirtied His diapers regularly. Isn't it funny to think that God dirtied His diapers? More than making us chuckle, however, it should make us realize how much God must love us—He humbled Himself that much in order to save us from our sins.

In the Law that God gave to the descendants of Israel, there were several rules relating to the birth of children. Those rules revealed that God wanted His people never to forget how special it was to have a baby. All babies are made in God's image and are His own potential children, and parents should never forget that. Becoming a parent is a very serious and important thing. God required Israelite parents to bring their first-born sons to the Temple in Jerusalem to present them before Him there. Perhaps one reason for this law was to help new parents understand how valuable their children were and how important their responsibility was in His eyes. It was a way of saying to God, "This is not as much *my* child as it is *Your* child. Therefore, I will raise this child as You want me to."

Mothers were also required to offer a sacrifice at the Temple several weeks after their babies were born (see Lev. 12:1-8). This was a way of expressing thanks to God for giving them their babies, and it also served as a reminder to them of how good God had been to them in spite of their sins. They shouldn't think that having a baby was a sign of God's approval of their lives. Sometimes people think that God's blessings are proof that they are holy and fully pleasing to God, but it often only means that God is merciful and good. He is good to everyone, even to bad people! Anyone who has a baby should be thankful for God's goodness.

Simeon must have been a very spiritual man who studied the Scriptures closely. He knew God would keep His many promises to send the Savior, and must have hoped and prayed that he would live to see that day. God revealed to him that he would not die until his desire was realized. The Holy Spirit led him to baby Jesus the day that Mary and Joseph brought Him to the Temple. Simeon also knew that because God had sent His Son into the world, every human being would be faced with a decision: Would they reject or receive Him? Jesus' coming into the world would reveal what was in people's hearts. Because of the hardness of their hearts, many people of Israel would reject Jesus, and it would be "their undoing" just as Simeon predicted. That means they would go to hell. But to those who receive Jesus, it is their "greatest joy," because they know their sins are forgiven and they are going to heaven one day.

The Bible doesn't tell us much about the childhood of Jesus. We did learn today that He grew up in the town of Nazareth. We also read that He was "filled with wisdom beyond his years" (Luke 2:40), so He wasn't like a normal child in that respect. We'll learn in two days that when He was twelve years old, He had more spiritual wisdom than your parents probably do right now!

 Q. What do you think Simeon meant when he told Mary that a "sword would pierce [her] very soul"?

A. She would be convicted by what Jesus would say and have to make a decision to obey or disobey Him.

Q. What do you think it means to have Jesus be your "greatest joy"?

A. It means that Jesus is the most special person in your life. Your relationship with Him is the most valuable thing you possess. Thinking about Him and what He has done for you should make you very happy on the inside.

Q. Has Jesus become your "greatest joy" yet?

Application: Jesus was the most special person ever to have lived because He was the Son of God. Therefore, He should be more important than anything in our lives, and it should show by how we live our lives.

The Wise Men Visit Jesus
Matthew 2:1-23

Mary and Joseph remained in Bethlehem for at least a few weeks after Jesus was born, and it may well have been during that time when the wise men visited Him. They had seen a star appear in the sky about two years earlier that led them to Jerusalem. Unfortunately, we don't know much about those wise men. We can assume that the new star they saw was placed in the sky by God, and that He somehow revealed the significance of the star to them. We don't know, however, which country they came from or how long they traveled. If they departed from their home country soon after they first saw the star, they started on their journey almost two years before Jesus was born! It's quite obvious that they knew Jesus was worth traveling a long way to see, and that He was worthy to be worshipped and given expensive gifts appropriate for kings. He was God!

Wicked King Herod didn't like hearing the news that a baby had been born who was destined to be king of the Jews, because at that time, he was a king over the Jewish people. (Herod hadn't been elected by the Jewish people to be king, but was appointed to be king by the Roman government that then controlled Israel.) Herod wanted to kill the new baby, but all he knew about the child was that He had been born in Bethlehem (as the prophet Micah had predicted), and that His special star had appeared in the sky about two years before. So Herod told the wise men that once they found the child, they should return and tell him so that he could go to Bethlehem and worship Him also. He was lying of course, and was really planning to kill Jesus. Herod was so evil that when he realized that the wise men weren't going to return to him with the details he requested, he ordered that every boy two years old and younger in the region of Bethlehem be killed by Roman soldiers. It was just as horrible as you can imagine, and Jeremiah had predicted it about 600 years earlier in a prophecy about Rachel, the wife of Israel, weeping for her dead children. The murdered boys were perhaps some of Rachel's descendants through her sons Joseph and Benjamin. Rachel herself had died in Bethlehem.

We are blessed to live in a nation where no one has the kind of absolute power that Herod had. No one in the United States has the authority to order the mass killing of people he doesn't like. But no matter where injustice exists, we know that God will ultimately bring justice because He is loving and fair. Did you notice that it wasn't long after the slaughter of the little boys in Bethlehem that Herod died? (see Matthew 2:19). People always "reap what they sow," which means that God will treat them like they treat others. Unless Herod repented of his horrible sins and believed in Jesus, when he died he went to hell and has been suffering there ever since.

Q. The wise men from the east brought Jesus some very expensive gifts, including gold. Can you think of a reason why Jesus may have needed those expensive things?

A. It's possible that Mary and Joseph used those gifts to support their little family during their flight to Egypt. If that was the case, God used the wise men to provide for their needs until they could return to Nazareth. There Joseph could support his family as a carpenter.

Q. What makes murder wrong?

A. Murder is wrong for several reasons. First, because every human being is created in God's image, and when a person is murdered, it is the killing of one who looks something like God. When someone angrily destroys or defaces a photograph of another person, it is an offence against the person in the photograph. If for no other reason, we should respect other human beings because they're created in God's image. Second, murder is wrong because every person is loved by God, so no one has the right to take the life of another person. When someone commits a murder, he has taken the life of someone who was loved by God. Murder is the highest form of selfishness.

Application: Wise people know that Jesus is worth traveling to see, even if it takes months. He deserves to receive their best gifts, and is worthy to be worshiped. We are a wise family!

Jesus as a Young Boy
Luke 2:41-52

One of the many laws that the Israelites were required to obey was to observe the yearly Passover festival in Jerusalem. It was a time to remember when God delivered the Israelites from slavery in Egypt over a thousand years before Jesus was born. God's destroying angel had killed all the firstborn Egyptians, but he didn't harm the firstborn Israelites because they had obeyed God's instructions to kill a lamb and mark their doors with its blood. When the destroying angel came to a house that was marked with the blood, he "passed over" it. The Egyptians were so afraid of the Israelites' God that they released them from slavery, and all the people of Israel left Egypt to journey to a new land God would give them.

God had said that from then on, the Israelites should kill a lamb every year on that same day to remind them of what He had done for them in Egypt. He also wanted them to understand that their sins could be forgiven only through a sacrifice that served as a substitute. Of course, an animal can't really serve as a substitute for a human being, so we know that the animal sacrifices only served to reveal what Jesus would do for us when He died as our substitute on the cross. That is why Jesus is referred to as "the Lamb of God" in the Bible. Jesus died on the cross during a Passover festival.

When Jesus was young, He journeyed every year to Jerusalem to celebrate the Passover with Mary, Joseph and many other people who lived in Nazareth. The festival lasted for one week, and then everyone returned to their home towns. Mary and Joseph, probably knowing that Jesus was responsible enough to take care of Himself, didn't worry that He wasn't with them when they departed from Jerusalem. They assumed He was with their friends and relatives traveling back to Nazareth with them. Once they discovered He was missing, however, they went back to Jerusalem and frantically searched for Him, finally finding Him three days later talking to the religious leaders in the Temple. Mary and Joseph were probably very angry with Jesus at first, but they could hardly remain angry since He was amazing everyone in the Temple with His deep understanding of spiritual matters. (If you were missing for three days, your parents would be very angry with you, but if they found you at school teaching your teachers and the principal, they would probably cool down quickly!)

Jesus was surprised that Mary and Joseph had searched for a whole day in Jerusalem before they found Him. He thought they should have known right where He'd be, in His "Father's house," the Temple. But Mary and Joseph didn't understand what He meant, which is often the case with parents and their children!

 Q. At twelve years of age, Jesus was most interested in spiritual matters. Does that mean He was a nerd?

A. No, it means that He was a very wise boy with whom God was pleased. Kids are often very interested in sports, hobbies and other fun activities, and there is nothing wrong with those interests. However, wise young people are most interested in learning more about their relationship with God. Knowing and obeying God should be the most important thing in everyone's life, young and old.

Q. Because Jesus remained in Jerusalem when His parents left for Nazareth, does that mean He was disobedient to His parents?

A. Although it may seem that way, it couldn't be that way because disobedience to parents is a sin, and Jesus never sinned. Mary and Joseph apparently departed from Jerusalem without being certain Jesus was with them, assuming that He was with others who were also departing. It could be considered a case of negligence on their part. Perhaps when Jesus discovered that His parents had departed without Him, He assumed they would soon return upon discovery of His absence. And the best place to wait for them was at the Temple, as that would surely be the first place they would look for Him, knowing who He was. One other possibility is that Jesus' heavenly Father had instructed Him to remain at the Temple. If that was the case, Jesus had to obey regardless of how Mary and Joseph reacted. The only time it is acceptable to disobey parents is when obeying them would mean disobeying God.

 Application: Since we are followers of Jesus, we should obey our parents just as Jesus obeyed Mary and Joseph.

John the Baptist Prepares the Way for Jesus
Luke 3:1-20

John the Baptist was the greatest evangelist who has ever lived, and today the world needs more evangelists who will imitate him. An evangelist's job is to preach the gospel, and that is what John did. He told people that the Messiah whom they had been waiting for was about to appear. They should get ready for Him by repenting, which means to stop doing what they knew was wrong and start doing what they knew was right.

John was called by God to do his job, and he was specially anointed by the Holy Spirit to preach powerfully. John told the people the truth, and he didn't water it down. First, he told them not to trust that they were saved just because they were descendants of Abraham. Sometimes people think that they are saved because their parents are saved, but God has no grandchildren, just children!

Second, John warned the people that they were sinners who were in danger of suffering God's judgment. If they didn't repent, they would perish in hell. That is the truth, and truthful evangelists will warn people about hell.

Third, John told them that if they truly believed and repented, their lives would show it. People who didn't change weren't really saved. People who keep on sinning just as they did before their so-called conversion won't get into heaven.

John used examples that the people he was preaching to could understand. Most of the people were farmers, so John compared Jesus to a farmer separating the chaff from the grain. The farmers in John's day used a tool that looked like a big fork, which they would shove into a pile of wheat cuttings and then throw them up into the air. The wind would blow the chaff away (the part that couldn't be eaten), and the heavier grain would fall into one pile below. John said that Jesus would be doing the same thing, only with people instead of grain. He would separate believers from nonbelievers, and just like the farmer who burns up the chaff, Jesus would cast the unbelievers into hell. The believers, however, Jesus would gather into His "barn," bringing them into heaven. Everybody is in one of only two categories: grain or chaff, believers or nonbelievers, hell-bound or heaven-bound.

John didn't preach using only general terms that people could interpret any way they liked. He told people specifically what they should do. If they were sincere about repenting, they would quit acting selfishly and start considering others, treating them just like they wanted to be treated. John told the people to share their belongings and food with the poor, to do their work honestly and to be content with their wages.

John was also a very humble man. Although God used him in a mighty way, and Jesus later stated that he was the greatest man who ever lived, John considered himself unworthy to be even a slave of Jesus. He knew that Jesus was a million times more important than he, and it was his job to point people to Jesus. If only every evangelist today was like John!

Many people who heard John preach were convicted of their sins, and John told them that they should be baptized in the Jordan River as a public testimony of their repentance. When someone believes in Jesus, he should be baptized as soon as possible, and he should do it in front of other people. Jesus commanded those who believe in Him to be baptized (see Matthew 28:19), and so when someone who claims to be a believer in Jesus refuses to be baptized in obedience to what Jesus commanded, we know he really doesn't believe that Jesus is the Son of God. When new Christians are baptized, they are making a public declaration that they have become followers of Jesus and that they are turning away from sin. Have you been baptized yet? If you are a believer in Jesus, you should be baptized as soon as you can.

Q. We read today that Herod had John the Baptist put in prison. Could that Herod have been the same Herod who ordered the killing of the baby boys in Bethlehem?

A. No, he died when Jesus was very young. This Herod was one of his sons, and he was evil like his father.

Q. Have you become a follower of Jesus yet? Becoming a follower of Jesus begins with repentance, and if you have never yet repented of sin, you haven't begun following Jesus. If you have already become a follower of Jesus, what changes were evident in your life after you repented?

⊙ Application: As followers of Jesus, we should be living lives that are different than those who are not saved. The things we say and do should make us stand out from people who are not followers of Jesus.

Jesus is Baptized by John the Baptist
Matthew 3:13-17; John 1:29-34

John had baptized many people who had repented and believed his message that the Messiah would soon appear. When Jesus came to be baptized, John didn't yet realize that He was the Messiah, so it wasn't for that reason that he was hesitant to baptize Jesus. He must have been hesitant because, when he compared himself to perfect and sinless Jesus, his own sinfulness was evident. That is why John suggested that Jesus baptize him! This reveals to us that Jesus had a reputation of being a very holy person, which we would have expected anyway since we know Jesus never sinned.

It was right after John baptized Jesus that John saw the Holy Spirit descend upon Him in the form of a dove. God had foretold John that when he saw that happen, it would reveal the person who was the Savior. Can you imagine how John felt at that moment when Jesus came up out of the water? His own relative, the most holy person he had ever met, was actually God's Son! For thirty years Jesus had kept it a secret! From then on John began to tell everyone that Jesus was the Son of God. The secret was out!

John also understood something about the main reason why Jesus became a man, because he began referring to Jesus as "the Lamb of God who takes away the sin of the world" (John 1:29) For thousands of years the people of Israel had sacrificed lambs during every Passover, just as God had commanded. But those lambs only served to prefigure Jesus, who would die for everyone's sins, not just covering them, but, as John said, taking them away. If you are a believer in Jesus, you should know that He has taken away your sins. In God's eyes, you aren't just a sinner who was found guilty and then forgiven, you are a new person who has been declared "not guilty"! Wow!

Q. Why didn't John call Jesus "Lord" when he objected to baptizing Him?

A. Because John didn't know at that point that Jesus was Lord.

Q. Why do you think Jesus wanted to be baptized by John like everyone else?

A. It couldn't have been because Jesus needed to repent like everyone else, because He was sinless. Jesus told John that He should be baptized in order to "do everything that is right" (Matthew 3:15). Some people (including myself) think that Jesus was baptized as a way of foreshadowing His death on the cross. Picture it this way: Thousands of sinful people being baptized in the Jordan River, washing their dirty sins into the water, and then Jesus, who was clean and sinless, going down into the water and coming up with everyone's sins on Him. That is what happened on the cross, when Jesus took the sins of the world on Himself and suffered as our substitute.

Application: Once we realize and believe, just as John the Baptist did, that Jesus is the Son of God, we need to tell other people, especially those who are searching for the truth.

Satan Tempts Jesus
Luke 4:1-13

In order for Jesus to die on the cross bearing our sins, it was necessary that He have no sins of His own. If He had committed any sins, then He couldn't have taken our sins and died as our substitute. Therefore, Jesus had to be sinless, and in order to be proven sinless, He had to be faced with temptation (it's easy not to sin when there's no temptation). That is why the Holy Spirit led Jesus out into the desert to be tempted by the devil.

Jesus' temptations in the desert, however, were not the only times Satan tempted Him, because the Bible tells us that Jesus "faced all of the same temptations we do, yet he did not sin" (Hebrews 4:15). Jesus was tempted to do wrong throughout His entire life. He was tempted to lie, cheat, steal, disobey His parents and act selfishly, but He never gave in to those temptations even once.

We read today that Satan twice tried to get Jesus to doubt what God the Father had told Him just a few days before: that He was the Son of God. Satan always tries to make people doubt what God has said. That is how he got Adam and Eve to disobey the Lord. Anytime we hear something that does not agree with what God's Word says, we should realize that it is a lie from Satan. Satan can only fool people who don't know or don't believe what God has said. But once you know and believe the truth, you can't be tricked into believing one of Satan's lies. People who know and believe what God has said don't have to be scared of Satan. He can't hurt them at all.

Knowing that Jesus was hungry after fasting for forty days, Satan tempted Him to change a stone into a loaf of bread so He would have something to eat. But Jesus responded by quoting what God had said, "People need more than bread for their life" (Luke 4:4). When the devil tempts us, we overcome him by knowing, believing, saying and obeying what God has said.

According to the Bible, Satan is "the god of this evil world" (2 Corinthians 4:4). That means he is controlling all the people in the world who are not submitted to Jesus, and also controlling all the evil spirits who rule over those unsaved people. Since most people are unsaved, Satan has power over the majority of people in the world in practically every country. God has allowed him to rule over that domain, called in the Bible, "the kingdom of darkness." Satan offered Jesus the second-in-command position over his worldwide kingdom if Jesus would join his side, proving His allegiance by bowing down before the devil and worshiping him. Again, Jesus responded by knowing, believing, saying and obeying what God had said: "You must worship the Lord your God; serve him only." Jesus knew that one day He would be ruling over the entire earth and that Satan would one day be banished to hell forever.

Finally, Satan tried to twist some Bible verses to make them mean something that they really didn't say. He quoted from Psalm 91, saying that it promised Jesus protection if He jumped from the highest point of the Temple. But Jesus knew what the rest of the Old Testament had to say, and He knew that it would be wrong and foolish to jump off a high place and expect God to protect Him. That would be testing God. Again Jesus overcame the devil by knowing, believing, saying and obeying God's Word.

Aren't you glad Jesus didn't give in to any of Satan's temptations? If He had, you and I couldn't have been saved!

Q. What temptations have you faced in the last week? Did you give in or resist? What can you do the next time you face the same temptation?

Q. When you are tempted, does that mean that the devil himself is in your presence, right beside you, suggesting that you do the wrong thing?

A. No, the devil can only be in one place at one time. One of Satan's evil spirits might be present who is tempting you. However, the Bible says that temptation comes "from the lure of our evil desires" (James 1:14). That means we can be tempted without the help of Satan or one of his evil spirits.

Application: When we face a temptation to do wrong, we should think of what God has said to do. If we don't know, we should find out what God has said to do. Then we should do it.

Jesus' First Disciples
John 1:35-51

John the Baptist had a group of disciples with whom he was very close. They were men who were very excited that the Messiah was about to appear, and John shared with them everything he knew about spiritual things. Together, they were anticipating that they would soon meet the Savior of the world.

When John saw the Holy Spirit come upon Jesus, he knew that Jesus was the one they'd been waiting for, and he undoubtedly told his disciples soon after. Jesus, however, departed for the desert immediately after He was baptized, where He spent forty days. Thus John never had the opportunity to point at Jesus and tell anyone who He was. After the forty days, Jesus returned to a place where John was baptizing, and John began pointing Him out as "the Lamb of God." Two of John's disciples were the very first people who learned this wonderful news. One of those two was Andrew, and the other is unnamed in today's reading, but many people think he may have been John, who became one of Jesus' twelve disciples and who wrote the Gospel of John.

When people find out that Jesus is the Son of God, they naturally want their friends and families to know also, and so Andrew went and told his brother, Simon. Then he brought Simon to Jesus, and amazingly, Jesus already knew his name! Jesus also told him that one day people would call him a different name, Peter, which means "rock." Jesus knew the Holy Spirit would change Simon into a man who would be firm in his faith and hard to move, like a rock. God would use him in a mighty way to lay the foundation of the early church.

When Philip brought his friend Nathanael to meet Jesus, Nathanael was surprised that Jesus also knew some things about him. Jesus knew he was a very honest man, and He apparently had a vision of Nathanael sitting under a fig tree where Philip found him. Because of this, Nathanael was immediately convinced that Jesus was the Son of God. Jesus promised him that he would one day be in heaven and see angels. That's something to which everyone who believes that Jesus is the Son of God can look forward!

Q. As we learned from reading about Peter and Nathanael, God knows everything about you, including your personality, your past, present and future. How should that affect your relationship with Him?

A. It should motivate you to obey Him, trust Him, and want to get to know Him better. It should encourage you to seek His direction for your life.

Q. All the men we read about today, except Nathanael, became members of Jesus' band of twelve disciples. Many people think that Nathanael was also called Bartholomew, and if he was, then he, too, became one of the twelve. Can you think of any reason why Jesus may have chosen those men rather than others?

A. One obvious reason Jesus chose them was because they were very interested in Him. God chooses and uses spiritually hungry people.

Application: Like Peter, the more we get to know Jesus, the more we'll be changed to become like Jesus. We can trust that Jesus is going to complete the good work He's begun in us.

Four Fishermen Become Fishers of Men
Luke 5:1-11

As we learned before, Andrew and his brother Peter had already met Jesus through John the Baptist. Both Andrew and Peter were from the Galilean village of Bethsaida, and worked together as fishermen on the Sea of Galilee with their friends, James and John, who were also brothers.

One day shortly after Peter and Andrew had met Jesus, Jesus was preaching to great crowds of people along the shore of the Sea of Galilee. They were probably sitting on the steep banks as Jesus preached by the water's edge. But there were so many people who wanted to hear what He was saying that the crowd kept pressing in to get closer. Jesus didn't have a sound system to amplify His voice, so if people wanted to hear Him, they had to get close. As a result, they were forcing Jesus out into the water! So Jesus stepped into Peter's boat and asked him to push it out a little way from shore so He could continue teaching while sitting in the boat.

When we give or lend something to Jesus, He always pays us back, and so He did for Peter after borrowing his boat. Peter and his partners had worked hard all night but hadn't caught a single fish. (The reason they had fished at night was because that was the best time to catch fish. Perhaps they used a lantern to attract the fish at night to their nets.) Even though Peter had already cleaned his nets and was probably ready to head home to get some sleep, Jesus instructed him to put down his nets in the deep water during the daylight, promising him that he would catch a lot of fish. It certainly didn't seem like a very good idea to an intelligent fisherman. It sounded like it would be a waste of time, but Peter had already witnessed the fact that Jesus knew things supernaturally, and so he did what Jesus said.

Amazingly, Peter's net was soon so full of fish that it began to tear. So Peter yelled to James and John on the shore to bring their boat out, and when they did, they filled both boats with so many fish that they were close to sinking! Imagine how funny it must have been to watch them try to row their heavy boats successfully to shore without sinking or losing any fish!

It was a *huge* catch of fish, more than anyone had ever caught before, and Peter and his partners knew it was miraculous. They were stunned when they looked at the big piles of fish in their boats. Peter, realizing how much money all those fish were worth at the market, couldn't believe how good God had been to him. He knew he didn't deserve such a blessing, and so he fell at Jesus' feet, confessing his sinfulness. But Jesus told him not to be afraid, and told him he would soon have a new job: catching people instead of fish!

Q. When Peter realized how kind God had been to him, even when he didn't deserve it, he became a changed man. He was saved. What evidence is there in what we just read that indicates Peter repented and believed in Jesus?

A. First, Peter humbled himself by falling at Jesus' feet. Not many people, especially grown men, and especially tough fishermen, would fall at someone's feet unless they truly believed that person was very special. Second, Peter called Jesus *Lord*. That indicates Peter believed Jesus was worthy to control his life. Third, Peter admitted that he was a sinner. Before anyone can be saved, they must admit that they are guilty sinners who need a Savior. And fourth, Peter began following Jesus from that day on, leaving everything behind. He made obeying Jesus the most important thing in his life.

Q. How was it, do you suppose, that Peter, Andrew, James and John were able just to quit their jobs to follow Jesus? How did they have money to live?

A. If they sold the great quantity of fish that Jesus just blessed them with, that probably provided their needs for quite some time. There's a proverb that says, "Where God guides, God provides." Also, many people supported the ministry of Jesus by giving Him money, so Jesus was able to take care of all His disciples. Finally, it is quite probable that some of the four fishermen we read about today were not yet married, so they didn't have families to support.

Q. Can you find any evidence in today's reading that Jesus was in the boat with Peter when they caught all the fish?

A. We read that Peter fell at Jesus' feet when he realized what had happened (see Luke 5:8-9). If Peter was in the boat (which he apparently was), then Jesus must have been there also. Additionally, Jesus told Peter that he would be catching men before the boats landed (see Luke 5:10-11).

Application: It is always smart to do what Jesus said and trust His promises, even when others might think we are foolish. Jesus can't lie, and He knows what He's talking about!

Jesus Changes Water into Wine
John 2:1-11

If you've ever been to a wedding reception, you probably remember having lots of food to eat and wedding punch to drink. Can you imagine how embarrassed the bride and bridegroom would be if people were standing in line to get punch and were told the punch had run out? The wedding guests would know that the hosts hadn't planned properly, and in a hot climate like Israel, their thirst would certainly aggravate the situation. This is what occurred at this wedding in the village of Cana that Jesus, His mother and disciples attended.

When Mary told Jesus about the wine running out, Jesus responded with words we wouldn't have expected. "How does that concern you and me?" Jesus asked. "My time has not yet come" (John 2:4). If we read through the whole Gospel of John, we discover that Jesus spoke often about His "time" coming, and it becomes obvious that He was always referring to the time when He would die for the sins of the world. So when Jesus responded to Mary's statement about the lack of wine, He must have been thinking about people lacking, not wine, but something that wouldn't be provided until He died. It's possible that Jesus was referring to His own blood, which was symbolized by wine at the Last Supper. Or He may have been speaking about the Holy Spirit, who is sometimes symbolized by wine in the New Testament. Everyone needs to have his sins forgiven through the shedding of Jesus' blood and be born again by the Holy Spirit. Both of those are much greater needs than wine running out at a wedding feast. Jesus was concerned about *much* more important things than Mary was.

Jesus, however, must have been somewhat concerned about the lack of wine at the wedding feast because He performed a miracle to solve the problem. That miracle may also have had a deeper spiritual meaning, because Jesus didn't change just *any* water into wine—He changed water that was used by the Jews for the purpose of purification rites into wine. Because of the many laws that God gave the Jews to keep, they were very conscious (or aware) of their sinfulness, and they were always trying to keep themselves symbolically purified by various washings with water. But since Jesus died for us, cleansing us from all the guilt of our sins, we don't need any other way of getting spiritually clean. Knowing that we're cleansed, we can now enjoy ourselves, drinking Jesus' good wine. Now we can really celebrate!

But isn't it wrong to drink anything that is alcoholic? If so, why did Jesus change water into wine that day?

Historians tell us that the Jews always diluted their wine with water, so the amount of alcohol in their wine was very small. It was more like what we today call "grape juice" than what we today call wine. We must also remember that, other than water, wine was practically the only beverage people could drink back in Jesus' day, and the water that was available was often contaminated and undrinkable in the villages and cities. We have many choices of beverages today, so no one *has* to drink wine. Christians don't all agree if it is wrong for them to drink alcoholic beverages, but one thing all true Christians agree on is this: the Bible very clearly says that it is a sin to get drunk. Getting drunk starts with one drink, and if that one drink begins to cloud a person's thinking, he might more easily yield to the temptation for another drink and then another. The safest thing to do is completely abstain from all alcoholic drinks.

Alcohol has caused a lot of heartaches to multitudes of people. Many babies have been born with deformities because their mothers drank alcohol when they were pregnant. Many innocent people have been killed by drunk drivers. Many families have been ruined by parents who became addicted to alcohol. Because alcohol is responsible for so much that is evil and sinful, my advice to Christians is to abstain from drinking it at all. John certainly didn't record this miracle of Jesus changing water into watered-down wine for the purpose of encouraging Christians to drink modern alcoholic beverages. He recorded this miracle to prove that Jesus was the Son of God and to remind us of the wonderful salvation He's provided for us!

Q. Did you notice that the wine Jesus made was described by the master of ceremonies as being better than the first wine that ran out? Does this teach us anything about God?

A. Perhaps it does. It shows us that when God does something, He does a quality job, and He wants us to enjoy the best He has to offer us. He has provided a wonderful salvation for us that includes loads of benefits for all eternity, not just a temporary fixer-upper salvation that puts a band-aid on our problem. He doesn't want us to have mediocre families, but quality families, with truly loving relationships. Are you enjoying all the benefits of what God has to offer us?

Q. Does this miracle of Jesus' changing water into wine teach us anything about God's power?

A. Yes, it shows us that God can change anything into something else. If you believe in Jesus, He has changed you from a child of Satan into His own child. One day God will change your physical body into a brand new body that glows with His glory.

Application: Because of this first miracle, Jesus' disciples believed in Him. For us, this miracle is one more proof that Jesus truly is the Son of God, and because we believe He is, we should trust and obey Him.

The First Time Jesus Cleans Out the Temple
John 2:13-25

Many people like to hear about God's love, but they aren't interested in hearing about God's anger with sin and wrongdoing. Today's reading reveals that side of God. Jesus was obviously very angry about what was taking place in the Temple, and He reacted furiously.

What was Jesus so mad about? Of course, there's nothing sinful about buying or selling animals or exchanging money. Jesus was angry over the fact that the Temple in Jerusalem, a sacred place where His Father was supposed to be honored and worshipped, had been turned into a marketplace. The Temple was the place where the priests offered sacrifices to the Lord, and in the innermost part of the Temple, called "The Holy of Holies," God's presence resided. But in Jesus' day, the people around the Temple weren't focused on God or serving the people who came to worship God, but on making money. Not only that, but they were taking advantage of people who came from far away places to worship at the Temple, charging them very high prices to purchase animals and exchange their foreign currency. In another Gospel, the writer records Jesus saying to the merchants at the Temple, "'My Temple will be called a place of prayer,' *but you have turned it into a den of thieves*" (Matthew 21:13, emphasis added). There was dishonesty in their dealings, and God doesn't like that, as Jesus so clearly revealed.

What we've read today contains a lot of proof that Jesus was the Messiah and was God in the form of a human being. First, we learned that a verse in the Old Testament book of Psalms foretold that the Messiah would have very strong emotions about God's house, or Temple. That same Psalm also predicted that the Messiah would be given sour wine to quench His thirst, just as Jesus was when He hung on the cross (see Psalm 69:21 and Matthew 27:34, 48).

Second, if Jesus wasn't God, then He had no right to chase out the oxen and sheep or overturn the tables of the moneychangers, spilling their money all over the ground. Any person who was not God and who did such a thing would be guilty of not showing respect for the private property of other people. God created everything and owns everything, so *everyone* and his property belongs to Him! He can do what He wants with anyone's property, and Jesus, being God, knew He had that right.

Some of the Jewish leaders thought Jesus had no right to do what He did, and they asked Him to justify His actions. He responded by telling them about His resurrection, although they didn't understand what He was talking about. This is a third proof to us that Jesus was God. Not only did He come back to life after being dead for three days, He predicted it would happen three years before it did!

Q. Jesus told the Jewish leaders who questioned Him, "Destroy this temple, and in three days I will raise it up" (John 2:19). He was speaking of the temple of His body, but His listeners thought He was speaking about the Jerusalem Temple building. How was Jesus' body even more of God's temple than the Jerusalem Temple?

A. Because Jesus was actually God in the form of a human being, His body was much more a temple of God than the Temple building, which only contained God's presence in the innermost parts.

Q. In the final verses of today's reading, we read that Jesus didn't trust everyone who said they believed in Him. Why didn't He?

A. Because Jesus knew that people are often liars, and just because someone says he believes in Jesus doesn't prove he actually does. A person's actions speak louder than his words, and so the true proof that someone believes in Jesus is his obedience to the Lord.

⊙ Application: Because Jesus has come into our temples, and because we are now temples of God, we should keep our temple clean from sin and anything that is not pleasing to Jesus.

A Jewish Teacher Visits Jesus at Night
John 3:1-16

The Pharisees of Jesus' time were a very strict sect of Jews. They tried to follow all of God's laws fully as well as many laws they made up themselves, thinking they could earn their way to heaven. Nicodemus was not only a Pharisee, but also a member of the Jewish ruling council and a very well known religious teacher. He was amazed by the miracles Jesus performed, and was convinced that Jesus was sent from God. However, he didn't yet know that Jesus was actually the divine Son of God. So Jesus knew He needed to explain some very important things to Nicodemus.

He began by telling Nicodemus that, in order to get into heaven, he had to be born a second time. Nicodemus didn't understand what Jesus meant. He couldn't imagine how he could ever go back inside his mother and be born another time! So Jesus explained that He wasn't talking about his *body* being born again through his mother, but his *spirit* being reborn through the Holy Spirit. The Bible says that every person is three parts: spirit, soul and body (see 1 Thess. 5:23). Your body is what you can see in the mirror. Your soul is your mind and emotions. Your spirit is the real you that lives inside your body. It is not made of bones or blood, but of spiritual material. It has a shape and form, just like your body. When your body dies, you, as a spirit, will leave your body and go to heaven if you are a follower of Jesus.

It is people's spirits that need to be reborn in order for them to get into God's future kingdom because if a person is not born again, his spirit has a sinful, satanic nature that has no relationship with God. He is spiritually dead. But when a person repents and believes in Jesus, the Holy Spirit comes into his spirit and removes the old sinful nature and gives that person a new nature, making him a child of God. Before a person is born again, the devil is his spiritual father. After he is born again, God is his spiritual Father.

As Jesus said, none of us can see the wind, and neither can we see people's spirits being born again nor the Holy Spirit that makes people's spirits new. However, just as we can see the effects of the wind, for example, leaves moving in the trees, so we can see the effects of the Holy Spirit when He moves inside a person's spirit. When He does, people start loving God and serving Him.

Jesus also explained to Nicodemus what he had to do in order to be born again. He told Nicodemus that He would be lifted up on a pole, meaning the cross, and that anyone who believed in Him would then forever have the new life that the Holy Spirit gives. It was just like the story of Moses and the people of Israel in the desert. One time God became very angry with them because of their sins, so He sent snakes into their camp, and anyone who was bitten, died. Moses prayed for God to have mercy, and so God told Moses to make a snake out of bronze and attach it to a pole. Moses then sent news to the people, "If anyone who is dying from a snake bite will come and look at the bronze snake on the pole, he will live."

The people who believed the news came, looked, and were healed. In the same way, all people have been filled with the venom of sin. Their spirits are dead and their bodies are dying. But if they will believe in the Lord Jesus who hung on the cross, bearing our sins, their dead spirits will be made alive and their bodies will one day live again forever. Have you believed that good news? If you have, you've been born twice! (Maybe you should try to convince your mom that you deserve two birthday parties every year!)

 Q. Jesus said that people must be born of "water" as well as the Spirit. What do you think He meant?

A. Different Christians have different answers to that question. Some say Jesus was talking about when a person is born as a baby. When babies are inside their mothers, they are enclosed by a sac of water. Just before they're born, that water sac breaks, so water comes out before the baby does.

A second interpretation is that Jesus was referring to people being baptized. Everyone who believes in Jesus should be baptized in water soon after they first believe. However, you don't have to be baptized in order to be born again. Baptism represents what has already happened the moment a person first believes in Jesus: He was dead but now has come back to life. Being under the water symbolizes being buried, and coming out of the water symbolizes being raised from the dead.

A third interpretation is that water is symbolic for God's Word. Truly, in order to be born again, a person needs to first hear the good news of Jesus' sacrificial death. Then, if he believes it, the Holy Spirit causes his spirit to be born again. People need both the Word of God and the Holy Spirit to be reborn.

Q. We read the most famous verse in the whole New Testament today, John 3:16. It tells us why God gave us His only Son. Why did He?

A. Because He loves us.

⊙⁄ Application: Since our spirits have been born again, we should follow the inward leading of our new nature to obey God, and not the evil leading of the old nature that we also still possess. We're thankful that one day that old sinful nature will be completely done away with when we get brand new bodies.

Jesus Continues His Conversation with Nicodemus
John 3:17-21

Jesus really wanted Nicodemus to understand how he could have his sins forgiven and be born again. Nicodemus needed to know that salvation is not something that *he could earn*, but something that *was earned for him* by Jesus Christ and is therefore a free gift from God. It is only through Jesus that anyone can be saved. That is why Jesus told Nicodemus that God sent His Son into the world, not to condemn it, but to save it. God wants everyone in the world to be saved because He loves us all.

If God wants every person to be saved, then why isn't everyone saved? The reason is because people have a part to play in their salvation. As Jesus explained to Nicodemus, every person must individually, by himself, believe that Jesus is the Son of God.

But why doesn't everyone believe that Jesus is the Son of God? Jesus explained the answer to that question by using the words *darkness* and *light*. Darkness represents ignorance (which means not knowing the truth). Light is symbolic of knowing the truth. When you turn out the lights in your bedroom at night, you are somewhat ignorant of where things are. You can't see where you're going and might stub your toe on your bed. But when the light is on, you can clearly see your path. Now you know what you didn't know when you were in darkness.

Jesus said that light from heaven came into the world. He was speaking of the truth that He brought from God the Father and shared with people on earth. Jesus said that people love the darkness and hate the light. They stay away from the light. That is, they don't want to know the truth that Jesus brought.

But why don't people want to know the truth? Jesus also explained that. The reason is because people don't want to stop sinning, and they know that if they come to the light and believe the truth, they will have to change the way they live. So they remain in the darkness, purposely believing all kinds of lies from Satan so that they can continue rebelling against God.

That is the reason, for example, that some people believe that there is no God. Even though it is obvious from looking at all God has made that He must exist, people don't want to believe it because they know that if there is a God, He has a right to tell them how to live. They want to control their own lives and keep sinning, so they believe the lie that God doesn't exist.

Thankfully, *some* people come out of the darkness into the light. Those are people who willingly repent of their rebellion against God because they believe the good news that Jesus is the Son of God who freely offers them salvation. This is why it is necessary to repent, or turn away from sin and selfishness, in order to be saved. Repenting of sin doesn't earn us our salvation—but repenting is the proof that we really believe that Jesus is the Son of God.

Some people think they are saved even though they have never repented of sin, but they are mistaken. True Christians, although not perfect, are trying to please God and obey Him. People who are constantly sinning aren't really saved. They are still living in darkness, believing the lie that they can have a relationship with God while they continue a lifestyle of disobedience to Him. They will go to hell when they die. But those who have truly believed in Jesus, as proven by how they live their lives, don't have to worry about going to hell. As Jesus said, "There is no judgment awaiting those who trust" Him (John 3:18).

Q. Nicodemus heard everything he needed to know in order to be saved, but our reading today doesn't tell us if he believed it. Do you think Nicodemus ever "came to the light"?

A. According to other scripture verses, we know that he did. He helped another man, Joseph of Arimathea, bury Jesus' body after He was crucified (see John 19:38-42). By doing so, because he was a ruler and well-known teacher of the Jews, Nicodemus risked being rejected by many people who hated Jesus. But it is better to believe in Jesus and be rejected by others than not to believe in Jesus and be rejected by God and cast into hell!

Application: Sometimes kids who are raised in Christian homes and who have always been taught to do the right thing have a hard time remembering when they first believed in Jesus and repented of their sins. Perhaps you are one of those kids. If you are, don't let it concern you. The important thing is, do you believe in Jesus right now? And is your faith in Jesus evident by how you live your life? Are you trying to obey God? Perhaps your parents, if they were not raised in a Christian home, can tell you about when they first believed in Jesus and repented.

John's Final Testimony About Jesus
John 3:22-36

Today we realize even more what a humble man John the Baptist was. We can learn a lot about humility by considering his words and deeds.

Although John was, according to Jesus, the greatest person to have ever lived (see Matthew 11:11), John knew that Jesus was far superior to himself, since Jesus was God from heaven. Pride sneaks into our lives when we compare ourselves with others. If we know we're better at doing something than someone else, we can become prideful. If, however, we will compare ourselves with Jesus, as John did, we won't be able to become proud.

Most often, we compare ourselves with people who have similar abilities and talents. If I'm a basketball player, I don't care how good another person might be at playing the piano—I'm only interested in other basketball players. For a while, John was the most famous preacher around. Multitudes traveled great distances to hear his anointed sermons and to be baptized. But then Jesus started doing the same things as John, preaching and baptizing, and Jesus' popularity began to grow. Additionally, God gave Jesus the Holy Spirit "without measure" (John 3:34), something He didn't do for John. Thus Jesus was able to perform miracles, something John never did, and those miracles really attracted large crowds. God the Father gave Jesus "authority over everything" (John 3:35), including sicknesses and demons. Before long, hardly anyone was coming to hear John, and some of his own disciples became jealous for him.

John, however, realized his place and time in God's plan. His job was to prepare the way for Jesus. The whole idea from the beginning was that *Jesus* would be exalted, not John. John knew his ministry would be temporary and said of Jesus, "He must become greater and greater, and I must become less and less" (John 3:30). Proud people don't want to ever let go of something God has given them, even when it's obvious that God's plan for them is that they move on to do something else because God has anointed another person to take their place. Proud people want to be recognized and appreciated more and more. Christians, however, should want Jesus to become greater in people's minds, not themselves. They should be interested in building God's kingdom and not kingdoms for themselves. They should want to be servants, not rulers.

John also knew that Jesus was the only way to heaven, and that only Jesus could give eternal life to people who believed in Him. John clearly understood that those who truly believe in Jesus obey Him. John said, "Those who don't *obey* the Son will never experience eternal life, but the wrath of God remains upon them" (John 3:36, emphasis added). This doesn't mean that if we commit a sin that we will go to hell, because no Christian is perfect and we all do sin at times. We know from reading the rest of the New Testament that John was talking about people who *never* obey Jesus, living a lifestyle of sin and selfishness. They are not submitted to Jesus at all, which proves they don't believe in Him.

Q. Could God ever be guilty of the sin of pride?
A. No, it would be impossible for God to think too highly of Himself. When He speaks of His own wonderful attributes, He isn't bragging—He's only telling the truth.

Q. Is there something that you do better than others? (Parents, this would be a good time for you to compliment your kids for things they do well, as they may think they're being proud if they respond.) Could that talent be an inroad for pride? What can you do to keep pride out?

Q. Is it prideful to say, "I'm a good swimmer" if you are a good swimmer?
A. No. Pride is having an inflated or unrealistic opinion of yourself. To say that you are a good swimmer when you *are* a good swimmer is simply telling the truth. But, to say that you are the world's best swimmer (unless you are) would be prideful. It's best to talk as little as possible about yourself, your abilities and your accomplishments, because even if you are just telling the truth, some people might think you are pridefully boasting. As the proverb says, "Don't praise yourself; let others do it!" (Proverbs 27:2).

Application: The Bible says that God humbles those who exalt themselves and exalts those who humble themselves. In which of these two categories do you fall?

The Bad Samaritan
John 4:1-26

The people who lived in the region of Samaria came from a mixed ancestry of Jews *and* Gentiles. Because of that, the Samaritans were hated by the Jews who considered themselves of purer ancestry, and the Samaritans hated them in return. It was the same as it is today, when people of different races or cultures hate each other only because they're different.

But God isn't prejudiced. He loves everybody, no matter what color their skin is or what language they speak. Today's reading provides additional proof that Jesus was God, because He loved a Samaritan whom an ordinary Jew would have hated. This woman was very surprised when Jesus spoke to her, because usually, Jews didn't even speak to Samaritans!

Jesus told her that if she knew who He was and what He could give her, *she* would have been the one to initiate the conversation, asking Him for some very special water. Obviously, when Jesus offered her living water, He was speaking symbolically of something else. What was it? Let's look at how Jesus described it.

First, it was something that only He could give. It wasn't available from any other source. Second, it was a free gift, not something that could be purchased or earned. Third, like water, it would go inside people, forever satisfying their spiritual thirst. And fourth, when the living water went inside, it would give people eternal life. Jesus must have been speaking about receiving the Holy Spirit and being born again. He was offering the Samaritan woman salvation.

She, however, didn't understand what Jesus was talking about, and she probably began to wonder if He was a little crazy. So she jokingly requested some of His living water so she wouldn't ever be thirsty or have to haul water again from the well to her house. She was probably thinking to herself, "How can I get away from this oddball?"

But Jesus knew how to make her seriously consider what He was saying. Before she could see her need for a Savior, she had to acknowledge she was a sinner. So Jesus told her to call her husband, and she replied that she didn't have a husband. By telling a partial truth, she was trying to hide a big secret of which she was very ashamed. And that is when Jesus really got her attention, telling her He knew that she had been married and divorced five times and that now she was living with a man who was not her husband. Now she knew she was talking with Somebody special! He must be a prophet to know things about her past, and she wanted to change the subject in a hurry before He began talking about anything else of which she was ashamed! So she quickly brought up a religious question about the proper place to worship.

Jesus downplayed the importance of what was at that time a big dispute between Jews and Samaritans. It doesn't make any difference *where* a person worships. What matters is *how* he worships. Just because a person is worshipping in Jerusalem or at Mount Gerizim doesn't mean his worship is acceptable to God. The important thing is the condition of a person's heart. The only kind of worship that is acceptable and pleasing to God is worship that is done by people who worship "in spirit and in truth" (John 4:23). That is, their worship has to originate from their spirits, or hearts, and it must be sincere, not just a ritual. They worship God with their lives, living obediently to Him all the time. Only people who are born again can worship that way, and that is exactly what this Samaritan woman lacked.

Still hoping to end their conversation, she tried an argument that guilty people have always used to evade their accountability before God: "People will always disagree about religious issues, but someday God will straighten us all out. So there's no sense in us discussing it now." This woman, however, made the mistake of saying that she figured that when the Messiah came, He would explain everything. So Jesus dropped the bomb, telling her that He was the Messiah! And He *was* explaining to her what she needed to know, so she had no more excuses! Now she was faced with the biggest decision of her life, but we'll have to wait for tomorrow to find out what she decided. (This is what is known as a "cliff-hanger devotional"!)

 Q. Is it OK for Christians to be prejudiced against people of other races or cultures?

A. No. Christians should reflect the love that God has for all people. Jesus died for everyone, and the greatest act of love we can show anyone is to tell them about Jesus.

Q. Have you ever tried to convince someone of his or her need for Jesus, but, like this Samaritan woman, he or she keeps trying to evade the issues? What did you learn from Jesus about how to deal with people like that?

A. Don't let them direct the conversation onto what is really not important. Keep it centered on two things: their sinfulness and need for a Savior, and the Lord Jesus Christ, who is the only way anyone can be saved.

Application: Am I a person who worships "in spirit and truth," or am I just a religious person who practices certain rituals? Is worshipping God something I do just because I'm in church, or something I do because I love God with my heart? Is my daily life an act of worship to God?

Revival in Sychar
John 4:27-42

When Jesus told this woman at the well of Sychar that He was the Messiah, she had to make a decision that everybody must make: to believe or not to believe. We can't be *absolutely* certain from what we've read today, but it seems this woman at the well was convinced that Jesus was the Messiah. Soon after Jesus told her who He was, she left her water jar and went back into her village, telling everyone to come and meet a man who knew her past. "Can this be the Messiah?" she asked them. Perhaps she was sincerely uncertain at that point and wanted to hear the opinions of the people of her village. Or, perhaps she was already convinced about Jesus, and her apparent uncertainty was just a means of wise persuasion by a woman with a bad reputation in her village. Regardless, after Jesus stayed with the people of Sychar for two days, many of them believed that He was the "Savior of the world" (John 4:42). Though they had previously hated all Jews, these Samaritan people now loved a Jewish man who had first loved them.

While the woman was back in her village telling people what had happened to her, Jesus' disciples returned from the village with food. They urged Him to eat something, and, not surprisingly, Jesus saw the opportunity to convey a spiritual lesson. He responded, "No...I have food you don't know about" (John 4:32). They thought someone else had brought Him food, but Jesus was talking about His spiritual hunger being satisfied by doing the will of His Father. Just as they had a physical hunger that could only be satisfied with food, He had a spiritual hunger that could only be satisfied by obedience. And, just as we feel much better after eating a good meal (especially if we were really hungry beforehand), Jesus was enjoying the good feeling that came from sharing God's truth with the woman at the well.

Comparing them to harvesters, Jesus then encouraged His disciples to get involved in telling people the good news of who He was. They didn't need to wait for the harvest to ripen as do those who harvest wheat or apples. Jesus' followers were hired to harvest people, and there are always people who are ready to receive the gospel. When Jesus told His disciples this, they were just minutes away from being crowded by spiritually hungry people from Sychar who would soon be saved!

Q. Is there a spiritual hunger inside of us to do God's will?

A. Yes, if a person is born again, Jesus lives inside him by the Holy Spirit, and Jesus wants to obey God the Father. When we obey God by telling people His truth, we'll get a good feeling on the inside, because our spiritual hunger will be satisfied for a while.

Q. Is leading people to Jesus the only thing that we can do that contributes to the spiritual harvest that God desires?

A. No, Jesus said that some people plant seeds, while others harvest. We can plant seeds by loving unbelievers, living rightly before them and by sharing the good news. Although they might not believe in Jesus immediately, hopefully our good influence will lead to their eventual conversion, even if someone else gets the privilege of actually seeing them repent and become a follower of Christ. However, Jesus said that there is joy awaiting both planters and harvesters. When we get to heaven and see the people there whom we helped come to Christ, we will be very happy!

◎ Application: We should live our lives in such a way that people are attracted to Jesus. The most important thing that we can do is tell someone else about Jesus.

Jesus Visits His Hometown
Luke 4:14-30

After spending two days in Sychar (where Jesus met the woman at the well) Jesus and His disciples continued journeying to the region of Galilee. When they arrived, Jesus preached in many places, telling people to repent and believe the good news. He often taught on Saturdays, the Sabbath day of the Jews, in their small church buildings, called synagogues.

One of the places Jesus visited in Galilee was Nazareth, the town in which He had grown up. Because He never sinned, Jesus probably had a good reputation there. However, when He had lived among them, none of His friends or acquaintances realized He was God's Son. He had never told them who He was or worked any miracles. To the people of Nazareth, Jesus was just a good man, a carpenter by trade, one of the five sons of Mary and Joseph (see Matthew 13:55-56; Mark 6:3). Since they had last seen Him, however, He had received the power of the Holy Spirit, and they had heard He was performing miracles in other parts of Galilee. Now it was time for Jesus to tell them who He was, and so He joined the people of Nazareth at their synagogue one Saturday.

On this occasion, Jesus was given the scroll of the book of Isaiah to read before the congregation. He opened it to some verses that described the Messiah's ministry, hoping they would realize that He was the one of whom Isaiah had written. The word *messiah* means "anointed one," and the portion of Isaiah's prophecy from which Jesus read, spoke of a person who would be anointed by God's Spirit to preach, deliver and heal. That is exactly what Jesus had been doing. In fact, the first thing the people of Nazareth noticed was Jesus' ability to speak. They were all "amazed by the gracious words that fell from his lips" (Luke 4:22).

Even though the people of Nazareth had heard the report of His miracles in other towns, most of them refused to believe that one of their hometown boys was the anointed person Isaiah had predicted would come. They wanted to see some miracles right before their eyes before they would believe in Him. Their hearts were hard, and Jesus responded to their unbelief by saying that prophets are usually not received in their hometowns.

Even though Jesus wasn't surprised by their unbelief, He was saddened by it, because He knew it would hinder God's work in their midst. Then He cited two other prophets who weren't received by their own people, and as a result, those people missed out on blessings that other people, even foreigners, enjoyed. Once during the time of Elijah the prophet, there was a three-and-one-half year famine in Israel. Jesus said that there were many Israelite widows who suffered during that famine, but God sent Elijah only to a foreign widow to provide food supernaturally for her. And during the time of the prophet Elisha, there were many Israelites who needed to be healed of leprosy, but God used Elisha to heal only one leper, and he also was a foreigner.

Jesus' message to the people of Nazareth was clear: because they rejected Him, an anointed man of God and the Messiah, they would forfeit God's blessing, just like the Israelites of Elijah and Elisha's day. When the people in the synagogue realized what Jesus was saying, their mood quickly changed. At the beginning of His sermon, "all who were there spoke well of him" (Luke 4:22). By the end of His sermon, they wanted to kill Him, revealing the wickedness within their hearts. As they often do, desires turned into deeds, and they attempted to kill Him by throwing Him over a cliff. Jesus, however, was somehow supernaturally delivered. Perhaps God the Father made Him temporarily invisible! Wouldn't that be fun if God did that to you?

Q. According to the Bible, Jesus had four younger brothers and at least two younger sisters. He knows what it is like to live as part of a family. What kind of an older brother do you think Jesus was?

A. He was the *perfect* older brother! That means He always thought first of His younger brothers and sisters before thinking of Himself. He assisted them whenever they needed His help and shared with them what was His. Because Jesus lives in you by the Holy Spirit, you have the potential to be the kind of brother (or sister) that Jesus was as He grew up.

Q. Just as the people who knew Jesus before He was anointed by the Holy Spirit found it difficult to believe that He was the Messiah, often the people who knew us before we were born again by God's Spirit have a difficult time believing that we've been changed. What is the best way to convince them that you're not the person they knew before?

A. By our daily lives. As they listen to us and observe our actions, they'll see that we've changed. Then they'll be more open to hearing the good news about Jesus.

Application: People who reject Jesus reject God's blessings. Because
we believe in Jesus, God is going to bless us forever!

Jesus Demonstrates His Authority Over Evil Spirits and Sickness
Mark 1:21-39

For a while Jesus lived in Capernaum, a village on the coast of the Sea of
Galilee, and He frequently taught in the synagogue there. The people who
heard Him were amazed at His teaching because He taught "as one who
had real authority" (Mark 1:22). That means Jesus came across as if He was
absolutely certain of what He was saying. This is another proof that Jesus
was God in the form of a human being. Naturally, God knows what He is
talking about. Jesus never said, "I may be wrong, but let Me tell you how I
feel about that subject" or, "Your opinion is as good as Mine." If He had said
those things, we'd know He really wasn't God.

Once, right as Jesus was teaching in the synagogue in Capernaum, a
man who was possessed by an evil spirit began shouting at Him. The evil
spirit was actually the one speaking, using the man's mouth, and he said,
"Why are you bothering us, Jesus of Nazareth? Have you come to destroy
us? I know who you are-the Holy One sent from God!" (Mark 1:24). Jesus,
to whom God the Father had given authority over everything, including
evil spirits (see John 3:35), commanded the evil spirit to come out of the
man, and it did. From this incident, we can learn several things about Jesus
and evil spirits.

If you're born again, you don't have to worry about evil spirits getting
inside you or possessing you, because Jesus lives inside you by the Holy
Spirit. This man who was possessed by an evil spirit wasn't born again. The
Bible tells us, "The [Holy] Spirit who lives in you is greater than the spirit
who lives in the world [the devil]" (1 John 4:4). Evil spirits are no match for
Jesus. The evil spirit we just read about was afraid that Jesus was going to
completely destroy him and all his fellow evil spirits.

This evil spirit also knew who Jesus was, calling Him "the Holy One
sent from God" (Mark 1:24). Evil spirits like to brag about what they know,
but in doing so, this particular demon showed how stupid he was. He said
something in the synagogue that his boss, the devil, didn't want *anyone*

to know! I wonder if he got in trouble with the devil for shooting off his mouth!

Regardless, when the demon-possessed man was delivered, the news spread quickly in Galilee. God the Father was advertising His Son because He wanted people to listen to what Jesus was telling them. Believing Jesus' message was the only way people could have their sins forgiven.

Next we read about Jesus healing Peter's mother-in-law who had a very high fever. The news of that miracle also spread quickly, and when evening arrived, many sick and demon-possessed people came to Peter and Andrew's house seeking help. According to Matthew and Luke's Gospels, Jesus healed and delivered every single one of them (see Matthew 8:16; Luke 4:40-41). This not only again proves that Jesus was the Messiah sent from God, it also shows us that Jesus loves everyone who is sick or possessed by evil spirits. He loves them enough to heal and deliver them.

Q. In the final verses of our reading today, we read that Jesus arose early in the morning and went out into the wilderness to pray. Why would God need to pray? What do you think Jesus prayed about?

A. While Jesus was on earth, He was following His Father's orders. One reason He prayed was to receive those orders. From what we read today about Jesus' prayer time, it seems He received direction to leave Capernaum to preach in other towns (see Mark 1:38).

Q. We know that no true Christian could be possessed by a demon. But why is it that only some unsaved people become possessed by demons?

A. No one knows for sure. However, it is quite likely that many unsaved people who become demon-possessed open the door to possession by continually thinking wrong thoughts and giving in to temptation. An evil spirit can't get inside any person it wants. Becoming demon-possessed is normally a gradual, progressive thing that begins when a person yields to the suggestions of a demon.

Application: Just as elephants shouldn't be afraid of mice, we shouldn't be afraid of the devil and evil spirits. They're afraid of Jesus who lives in us!

Jesus Heals a Man With Leprosy
Mark 1:40-45

If you live in the United States or any other developed nation, you will probably never see a person with leprosy. It's a horrible skin disease that actually eats away at the parts of the body it has infected. People who are afflicted with leprosy watch their fingers and toes slowly dissolve. Eventually, they die from the disease. To make matters worse, leprosy is easily spread to other people, so no one wants to be near a leper. When a person gets leprosy, he soon loses all his friends. In the Old Testament, God made a law that required all leprous people to cry out, "Unclean! Unclean!" whenever they were in a public place where other people might be infected (see Leviticus 13:45).

The Greek word translated *leprosy* was used to describe various skin diseases in Jesus' time, so it's possible that this man whom Jesus healed was not suffering from the disease we refer to today as leprosy. However, there's no doubt he had a very serious physical problem, and his situation was desperate. He fell on his knees before Jesus, begging to be healed. From the reports he had heard of others being healed, he knew Jesus was *able* to cure him. But he didn't know if Jesus *wanted* to heal him. Jesus, however, was moved with pity for the distraught man, and assured him that He did want to heal him. A second later, the leprous man felt something he hadn't felt in a long time: the touch of another person. As Jesus put His hand on him, instantly his leprosy was gone. Imagine how he felt as he looked at his new skin!

Some people think that Jesus healed people only to prove that He was the Son of God. Certainly Jesus' healings did prove that. Because God the Father had given Him authority over all things, including disease, Jesus simply spoke and the leprous man was instantly healed. We read today, however, that Jesus was "moved with pity" over the leprous man's situation. Jesus healed this man because He loved him, not just to prove that He was the Son of God.

For *all* Christians, this healing story, along with the many others in the Bible, affirms that God cares about our health and will one day give us brand new bodies that will not be subject to sickness and disease. For *some* Christians, like myself, the stories of people whom Jesus healed inspire us to trust that we don't have to wait until heaven to experience physical healing. Jesus never told anyone who came to Him requesting healing, "Rejoice, because in heaven you'll be healthy." In every case, He healed sick people, often crediting their faith. When we remain ill, we often claim that it must not be God's will for us to be healed, but more likely, our own lack of faith is to blame. Jesus said, "Anything is possible if a person believes" (Mark 9:23). Praise God that we can trust God for healing, and praise God that even if we fail to trust God for healing, He doesn't condemn us.

According to the Old Testament law, the priests were responsible to determine whether or not people had leprosy. If a person thought he might have contracted the disease, he was supposed to be examined by a priest. If the priest declared him a leper, he had to obey the laws of leprosy, removing himself from contact with non-leprous society. Likewise, if a leprous person was healed, only a priest could make the official determination and allow the former leper reentry into normal society.

Jesus commanded this leper to obey that law and show himself to the priest, taking along the required offering, as a testimony of his healing. It was probably the first time that priest ever performed that part of his job, declaring a leper to be cleansed! I wonder if he had to look up the appropriate scriptures just to find out what he was supposed to do!

 Q. Why did Jesus tell this man He healed not to talk to anyone on his way to the priest?
A. Because Jesus didn't need any more advertising. If the former leper started spreading the news of what happened, Jesus knew He would soon be mobbed with people, and it would actually hinder His ministry. Sure enough, the man didn't obey Jesus, telling everyone what had happened, and Jesus was then unable to publicly enter any nearby towns. Several days later, Jesus did sneak back into Capernaum where He had been living, but was soon discovered. Within a short time, the house where He was staying was crammed with people, inside and out (see Mark 2:1-4).

Q. Wouldn't it be horrible never to be touched by anyone? Sometimes parents feel like they must have leprosy, because their kids never hug or kiss them (especially when their kids are with friends). Have you hugged your parents today?

Application: In one way, we were like this leper. We had a spiritual disease that prevented us from ever hoping to enter the society of heaven. But Jesus cleansed us! Now we can look forward to enjoying eternal life with the many others like us whom Jesus has cleansed of sin.

Jesus Heals a Paralyzed Man
Mark 2:1-12

Can you imagine what it would have been like to witness this miracle? Four men brought their paralyzed friend on a pallet to a house where they heard Jesus was staying. Upon arrival, they discovered that the house was jammed with people, and many others were standing outside looking in, blocking all the doors and windows. There was no way to get their friend close to Jesus.

But they would not be discouraged. The roofs of the houses in Capernaum were flat, and many of them had stairs that went from the outside of the house up to the roof. So they carried their paralyzed friend to the roof of the house, dug an opening through the clay, and then lowered him on his pallet by ropes right in front of Jesus. It must have taken a lot of time and effort to dig through the hardened clay roof and caused some commotion inside the house when the clay dust began falling from the ceiling. I wonder what the people inside were thinking as they coughed, wiped dust from their eyes, and watched a hole slowly form in the ceiling above their heads.

What was Jesus thinking then? He was thinking about the faith of the men who were going to so much trouble. The Bible says that it is "impossible to please God without faith" (Hebrews 11:6). Because of their faith, the paralyzed man was forgiven and completely healed within seconds. If they hadn't believed, they would never have gone to so much trouble, and their friend would have remained unforgiven and paralyzed, even though it was obviously God's will for the man to be forgiven and healed.

Why did Jesus first tell the paralyzed man that his sins were forgiven? No one knows for sure, but perhaps the paralyzed man was coming to Jesus both for healing *and* forgiveness. Certainly being forgiven of sins is even more important than being healed. Or, perhaps the paralyzed man, because of all his sins, had doubts that he would be healed, so Jesus removed his doubts by assuring him of forgiveness. Or, possibly the man had become paralyzed as a direct result of some sin he had committed. In that case, Jesus took care of the cause before giving the cure.

Regardless, when Jesus told him that his sins were forgiven, it caused quite a stir among the religious teachers who were present. They knew that only God could forgive sins, so Jesus was claiming to be God! They thought He was guilty of blasphemy (saying something that was very offensive to God).

Jesus knew what the religious teachers were thinking, so He proved, right before their eyes, that He had the right to forgive sins, also proving His deity. Anyone could pretend to have the authority to forgive sins because there would be no visible result. But no one can convincingly pretend to have authority to heal paralysis, because the result would be plain for everyone to see. When Jesus instantly healed the paralyzed man, it proved He had authority to heal, and it gave credibility to His claim to be able to forgive sins.

To us, this is one more proof that Jesus was the Son of God. If an average sinful human being claimed to be able to forgive sins, we would know he was blaspheming. But when a virgin-born, sinless, miracle-working person forgives someone's sins, it's just one more proof of what we would already suspect: God had become a man!

 Q. We read that Jesus actually saw the faith of the four men and their paralyzed friend. How can faith be seen?

A. By actions. The Bible says, "faith is dead without good deeds" (James 2:26). Many people say that they believe in Jesus, but only those who have corresponding actions really do. Sometimes, Christians say they believe certain promises in the Bible, but their contrary actions prove that they really don't.

Q. Just like this man whom Jesus healed, our sins have been forgiven by Jesus. If we truly believe our sins are forgiven, we will act like forgiven people. How do forgiven people act?

A. At the minimum, they would be happy and grateful to God for their forgiveness, and would show their gratitude by obedience to God.

Application: There has never been another person in history like Jesus. Other people in history may have claimed to forgive sins, but their lives proved they were phony. Any honest person who examines the evidence will be convinced that Jesus was God in the form of a human being.

Jesus Dines With Matthew and His Sinful Friends
Luke 5:27-32

Apparently Levi, also known as Matthew, had been touched by Jesus' ministry in Capernaum. Perhaps he had listened as Jesus taught by the Sea of Galilee or heard the testimonies of people who had been healed. When Jesus called Matthew to be His disciple, he didn't hesitate for a minute, but left everything behind to follow his new Lord.

What was so amazing about Matthew's calling is that he was a very sinful man—at least until he met Jesus. Matthew was a tax collector, which meant that he worked for Rome, the country that occupied and controlled Israel at that time. The Israelites hated the Romans, and naturally they had no respect for any fellow Israelite who worked for them. Tax collectors were considered traitors by their countrymen.

Beyond that, tax collectors had a reputation for being very dishonest, forcing their fellow Israelites to pay more in taxes than Rome required and then keeping the extra money for themselves. In so doing, they became rich at the expense of their own neighbors. Thus, the only type of people who would have been Matthew's friends were fellow tax collectors and other people of very low moral character. Those were the type of people who came to Matthew's banquet.

Matthew, however, had become a disciple of Jesus, repenting of his sins, and as is the case of anyone who is a true follower of Jesus, he wanted his friends to meet Jesus also and be saved. That is the reason he held a banquet in Jesus' honor. It was a low-key evangelistic meeting, and Jesus, who loves everyone, gladly accepted the invitation to spend some time eating with Matthew's sinful friends.

Because He did, He was criticized by the Pharisees and religious teachers, who would never associate with such people. Jesus responded by informing them that the purpose of His coming was to "call sinners to turn from their sins" (Luke 5:32). In order to do that, He had to spend time with sinners, and that is exactly why He attended Matthew's banquet. Jesus didn't spend His time at that banquet talking about sports or the weather! He was telling sinners that they needed to repent and follow Him, just as their friend Matthew had!

Q. The Pharisees and religious teachers we read about today didn't understand two important things. First, they thought holy people shouldn't associate with sinful people. But just the opposite is true. If people are truly holy, they will associate with sinful people, because holy people are motivated by love to share Jesus with those who need to be saved.

That should give you a clue concerning the second thing about which the Pharisees and religious teachers were mistaken. What was it?

A. They thought they were holy, but actually they were themselves sinners who needed to be saved. Jesus referred to this fact when He said, "I have come to call sinners to turn from their sins, not to spend my time with *those who think they are already good enough*" (Luke 5:32, emphasis added). Jesus was speaking of the Pharisees and religious teachers.

Q. What would you think if your pastor accepted an invitation to a party that was hosted by a newly-converted drug pusher for his drug pusher friends?

Application: *Jesus in us loves evil and sinful people. Do we? Or are we like the Pharisees who considered themselves too holy to spend time with sinners?*

New Clothes and New Wine
Luke 5:33-6:5

The Pharisees were a sect of Jews who prided themselves in their holiness. They thought they were fully obeying God's laws and were certain that God especially favored them because of it. Surely God, impressed by how they had kept their religious duties, would welcome them into His kingdom. But now they had a big problem, and His name was Jesus. He claimed to be an authority on spiritual matters, and His popularity as a religious teacher was rapidly growing as He traveled about teaching and healing. To the Pharisees' alarm, Jesus' teaching about holiness was much different from theirs. Some of those differences surfaced in today's reading, as the Pharisees vainly tried to find fault with Jesus.

The first fault the Pharisees found in Jesus was that He and His disciples didn't fast. When someone fasts, he stops eating food for a while for some religious purpose. Not eating for a day or two is not an easy thing to do, and the Pharisees prided themselves that they fasted often. They thought they were earning points from God for their self-sacrifice.

Of course, skipping meals is foolish and pointless unless it is something God wants a person to do. And if it is, you can be certain God has a good reason for wanting a person to fast, since He obviously created people with a need to eat food regularly in order to live! So why would God want someone to fast? Probably the most valid reason for fasting is to have more time to spend in God's Word and prayer. This was especially true in ancient times, when the preparation of meals took much more time than it does today.

Jesus didn't say that fasting was wrong. He only said that, because the Pharisees and religious leaders didn't understand who He was, they were fasting during a time when it wasn't necessary. The main reason to fast is to spend more time in prayer to God. *But God was right in their midst!* Why would they ever fast to try to get closer to God when they had direct access to Him in Jesus? Jesus said that people don't fast during someone's wedding simply because that is not an appropriate time to fast. It's a time to celebrate. Likewise, it was now a time to celebrate and enjoy God's presence! When Jesus returned to heaven, then they could intelligently resume their practice of fasting.

Then Jesus shared two illustrations that explained the heart of His problem with the Pharisees and religious leaders. Both illustrations present the folly of mixing new and old things.

Jesus said that people don't tear a piece of cloth from a new piece of clothing in order to patch a hole in an old piece of clothing. If they did, the new clothing would be ruined, and the old clothing would look bad with a patch that didn't match. The understanding of the Pharisees and religious teachers was like an old, worn-out garment that needed patching. But Jesus' teaching was like new clothing. It would be foolish to try to take a small part of Jesus' teaching and make it fit with the old ideas and traditions of the Pharisees. The only intelligent thing to do would be to simply discard the old, worn-out clothes and put on the new ones.

In His second illustration, Jesus mentioned wineskins. They were bottles made out of animal skins for the purpose of holding wine. Nobody would pour brand new wine into old wineskins, because as the grape juice fermented and released gas, the old, hard, inflexible wineskins would burst, and all the wine would be lost. People only put new wine into new wineskins that were more flexible and wouldn't burst as the grape juice fermented. The Pharisees and religious leaders were like the old, hardened, inflexible wineskins and Jesus was like the new wine. It was impossible for them to accept His new teaching because they were so set in their ways. They were satisfied with just holding the same old wine, and were unable to receive anything new and fresh from God. In fact, they considered their old understanding of spiritual matters to be superior. How wrong they were!

The second fault the Pharisees found with Jesus was His disregard of the law of the Sabbath. God did say in the Old Testament that the Sabbath should be a day of rest, and, therefore, no one should work on the Sabbath. The Pharisees, however, had taken that law to the extreme, claiming that Jesus and His disciples were sinning when they prepared a low-budget meal by breaking off heads of wheat in a field. It would be like claiming that you sinned by working on the Sabbath if you exerted effort in pouring milk over a bowl of breakfast cereal!

Jesus responded to their criticism by proving from the Old Testament that God was not opposed to what He and His disciples were doing. Once David had broken the law, eating bread that was supposed to be eaten only by the priests. David normally would not have eaten that consecrated bread, but he did it out of necessity because there was nothing else to eat, and he and his companions needed nourishment. God certainly understood, and He wasn't angry with David. The same was true concerning Jesus and His disciples. They needed to eat, and God wasn't angry with what they were doing. He gave the law of the Sabbath because He loves people and doesn't want them to work at their jobs seven days a week. He wants them to enjoy a day of rest. Picking a little grain to eat on the Sabbath is OK. Jesus said, "The Sabbath was made to benefit people, and not people to benefit the Sabbath" (Mark 2:27).

Beyond that, Jesus was God, and He is the One who gave the commandment about the Sabbath! So He certainly knew how to interpret His own law! Jesus' claim to be "master even of the Sabbath" (Luke 6:5) was equivalent to claiming to be God. The one who gives the law is greater than the law he gives. God can do anything He wants to do on the Sabbath, because He doesn't have to answer to anyone! On this occasion, Jesus acted like we would expect God to act, adding additional proof that He was who He claimed to be.

Q. Is it wrong to rake leaves in your yard or ride your bike up a steep hill on Sunday afternoon since God said the Sabbath should be a day of rest?

A. Only if you rake leaves for a living, and had raked leaves Monday through Saturday, then it might be wrong to rake leaves on Sunday! (And especially not if you are planning to jump in the pile of leaves you rake!) And only if you are a professional bike racer who had ridden his bike Monday through Saturday might it be wrong to ride your bike on a strenuous course on Sunday afternoon.

Additionally, the real Sabbath is not Sunday, but begins Friday evening and ends on Saturday evening! And the Sabbath commandment was not carried over into the New Covenant, proven by the fact that it is not found in any of the letters to the churches in the Bible.

Application: Aren't you glad that your heart and mind are not closed, like the Pharisees', to Jesus' teaching? Some people's minds are like concrete: thoroughly mixed and well set! Ask God today to open your mind and heart even more, and show you if you are like an old wineskin in any way.

Jesus Heals on the Sabbath
Matthew 12:9-21

What a wrong idea the Pharisees held about keeping the Sabbath holy! They were hoping to catch Jesus healing someone on the Sabbath so they could bring charges against Him for breaking the fourth commandment. Their spiritual blindness is almost beyond our comprehension. No wonder that Mark wrote about Jesus' reaction, "He looked around at them angrily, because he was deeply disturbed by their hard hearts" (Mark 3:5). Because they classified healing as doing work, they actually thought God would be displeased if Jesus healed someone on the Sabbath day! They didn't know very much about God, did they?

Jesus exposed their hypocrisy by asking them what they would do if one of their sheep fell into a well on the Sabbath. Certainly they would work to pull it out, even on the Sabbath day. Jesus stated that a person is much more valuable than a sheep, and thus He was only doing for a man what they would do for their sheep. As Jesus so accurately pointed out, the Pharisees were actually claiming that it was wrong for Him to do good on the Sabbath!

Amazingly, even after Jesus exposed the error of their thinking and then instantly healed the man before their eyes, their reaction was not one of repentance. Rather, they called a meeting to discuss plans to kill the One God had sent to be their Savior.

Even though Jesus knew their plans, He was not afraid, but kept right on healing "all the sick among them" (Matthew 12:15). He knew He wouldn't die until His Father decreed it was time. Knowing the truth and trusting in God will make us courageous, too.

Q. Jesus said that a person is much more valuable than a sheep. Can you think of any modern examples of people placing more value on animals than people?

A. When it is a federal crime to kill a whale or some endangered species but it is lawful to kill unborn babies, it reveals how mixed up people's minds have become.

Q. Our reading today ends with Matthew quoting one of Isaiah's prophecies that was fulfilled by Jesus. How can we be sure that Isaiah was speaking of Jesus and not someone else?

A. Because the entire prophecy fits Jesus perfectly. Jesus was God's chosen servant. What God said through Isaiah about His servant being His beloved and that He was very pleased with Him also fits Jesus perfectly. The Father said of Jesus at His baptism, "This is my beloved Son, and I am fully pleased with him" (Matthew 3:17). Also, just like the person Isaiah wrote of, we know that Jesus had God's Spirit upon Him, because the Holy Spirit descended upon Jesus in the form of a dove at His baptism. Finally, we know that Isaiah's prophecy which Matthew quoted could only apply to Jesus, because it could only be said that in "his name will be the hope of all the world" (Matthew 12:21). No other person of history could make a similar claim.

Part of what God said through Isaiah is yet to be fulfilled, but it will be fulfilled one day when Jesus rules the entire world. Then He will bring "full justice with his final victory." Until that day, the world will be full of injustices.

Application: Praise God that He is not mixed up in His thinking as are the majority of people. Praise God that He has opened our eyes to see things His way, which is the only right way.

Jesus Chooses Twelve Apostles
Mark 3:7-19

As time went on, Jesus' fame spread far and wide. Curiosity seekers and spiritually hungry people journeyed as far as one hundred miles to see Him, which was quite a distance at a time when there were no cars, trains or airplanes. People had to walk or ride a donkey. But it was worth their effort to see the Son of God, especially for those who needed healing or deliverance from demons. Lots of those kinds of people sought Jesus. One day, there were numerous sick people trying to touch Jesus as He taught along the shore of the Sea of Galilee. So many of them were pressing their way through the crowd that Jesus instructed His disciples to have a boat ready—just in case He was forced into the water by the mob of people! Imagine what that must have been like!

We have to wonder why Jesus would need a boat in such a situation, when we know that on another occasion He walked on the water of the Sea of Galilee. The answer is that, although Jesus was the Son of God, when He became a man, He emptied Himself of some of the qualities that God possesses. For example, Jesus was no longer omnipresent (present everywhere), omniscient (all-knowing) or omnipotent (all-powerful). He didn't know everything about everybody, and He couldn't work a miracle at any time, but only as the Holy Spirit willed. That is why Jesus had to be anointed by the Holy Spirit before He began His ministry, and why He did no miracles until after He was baptized in the Holy Spirit. Although Jesus was God, in His ministry He operated as a man anointed with the gifts of the Holy Spirit, which operate as the Spirit wills (see 1 Corinthians 12:11; Hebrews 2:4). Therefore, we shouldn't doubt Jesus' deity when we read about Him relying on a boat to keep Him above water or asking questions to obtain knowledge.

Today we read about Jesus choosing twelve men to be apostles. The word *apostle* means "one who is sent," and that is why Jesus chose His apostles—to send them out to preach the gospel. Jesus never could have, by Himself, preached the gospel to everyone who needed to hear it. These twelve men would be His helpers. Notice that there were two sets of brothers in the list: Simon Peter and his brother Andrew, and James and John, the sons of Zebedee. There were also three sets of people with the same name: Simon called Peter and Simon the Zealot, James son of Zebedee and James son of Alphaeus, and Judas son of James (here called Thaddaeus) and Judas Iscariot.

Q. Jesus gave authority to cast out demons to the twelve men He chose to be His apostles. Why do you think He did that?
A. To help them in their task of spreading the gospel. When people were delivered from demons by the apostles' command, it would advertise their ministry and draw more people to hear the gospel.

Q. Why do you think Jesus nicknamed James and John the "sons of thunder"?
A. To be a "son of thunder" would mean to be the product of something powerful and loud that startles people and gets their attention. For example, you may have heard the expression, "son of a gun." It's not a compliment to call someone the offspring of something that kills. Jesus would never have given James and John a nickname that would have been a continual criticism, so it must have been either a compliment or an encouragement. Probably it was an encouragement that God would transform them both into powerful preachers who would startle people like thunder and arrest their attention.

Application: Just as Jesus chose twelve apostles to help Him reach more people with the gospel, so Jesus is still choosing people for the same task. Everyone who is a believer in Jesus is given some kind of ministry that contributes to the expansion of His kingdom.

34

Jesus Describes His True Followers
Matthew 5:1-16

Many people came to Jesus seeking to be blessed, wanting to see a miracle or receive healing or deliverance. But Jesus didn't come to earth simply to attract large crowds of curiosity seekers or provide temporary blessings. He came to "call sinners to turn from their sins" (Luke 5:32), so people would be *eternally* blessed. Although it's certainly a blessing to see a miracle or be healed of a sickness, people who are blessed by God *only* to that degree will still spend eternity in hell when they die. Truly blessed people are those who are eternally blessed.

One day as the curious and blessing seekers were gathering, Jesus took the opportunity to explain what kind of people are eternally blessed of God. In short, they are people who have repented of their sins and have been born again. They are those who have made Jesus their Lord and are destined to spend eternity in God's kingdom. They can be recognized by how they live their lives, and Jesus described them in the first portion of His sermon on the mountainside. These are the people who are eternally blessed. Let's consider how Jesus described them.

First, Jesus said that the person who is eternally blessed of God is one who realizes his spiritual poverty apart from God (see Matthew 5:3). Before anyone can be saved, he must see his need for salvation and the impossibility of saving himself.

Second, Jesus said the person who is eternally blessed of God is one who mourns. What did He mean? Possibly Jesus was referring to the mourning a person experiences during the first stages of his repentance, when he realizes how he has offended God. Jesus taught that unless a person is sorrowful for his sins and repents, he would not get into heaven.

Perhaps Jesus was speaking of the sadness that all true Christians feel when they view the world around them, a world that is in rebellion against God and is so far from His original plan. One day those of us who mourn will be comforted, when God creates a new heaven and earth, a place where everyone will do God's will.

Third, people who are truly and eternally blessed by God are those who are gentle and lowly. One version of the Bible uses the word *humble* to describe these blessed people. In order to be saved, a person has to humble himself, admitting his helplessness to save himself and depending solely on God's mercy for salvation. True followers of Jesus continue on the path of humility throughout their lives, recognizing their own inadequacy and complete dependence upon God for everything. As Jesus said, one day "the whole earth will belong to them" (Matthew 5 5). Those humble followers of Jesus will one day be the only people who live on the earth, eternally blessed, because God will have condemned everyone who is proud.

Fourth, truly blessed people are those who long for everyone to be obedient to Jesus. True followers of Jesus hate all the disobedience that exists in the world, but they can look forward to the time, according to Jesus' promise, when worldwide righteousness will be a reality. That will happen when Jesus rules the world.

Fifth, truly blessed people are merciful. Born-again people can't help but show mercy to others, because they realize how much mercy God has shown them. They will one day experience the fullness of God's mercy when they enter into God's heavenly kingdom, knowing how unworthy they are of such blessings.

Sixth, truly blessed people have pure hearts. Jesus promised that they would one day see God! All true Christians will experience that indescribable blessing, so Jesus must have been describing another characteristic of all His true followers. They have repented in their hearts of wickedness and evil, and now their hearts' desire is to obey their Lord. People who aren't born again have impure hearts and are motivated by selfishness.

Seventh, people who are truly blessed of God are "peacemakers." Jesus must have been describing another characteristic of all true believers, because He promised that the peacemakers would be called children of God, something that all true believers are. True Christians love people with the love God has deposited within them, and thus they hate discord and strife. They work to maintain harmony in their relationships. People who are full of hatred and are always involved in strife are not really saved. Paul wrote that people whose lifestyles are characterized by hostilities, quarreling, jealousy, outbursts of anger, divisions and envy will definitely not inherit the Kingdom of God (see Galatians 5:20-21).

Eighth, the truly blessed person is one who is persecuted because he lives for God. Once again, it's clear Jesus must have been describing another characteristic of all His true followers, because He promised them that the Kingdom of Heaven is theirs. Anyone who truly believes in Jesus will be persecuted. That doesn't mean he will be put in jail or tortured, but it at least means that he will be hated and talked about by others. Jesus once said, "Woe to you when all men speak well of you" (Luke 6:26, NASB). When we are persecuted, Jesus said we should be happy about it, because it indicates we're among the blessed group of people who are going to heaven. Peter wrote, "If you are reviled for the name of Christ, *you are blessed*, because the Spirit of glory and of God rests upon you" (1 Peter 4:14, NASB, emphasis added).

Finally, Jesus described His true followers as being the "salt of the earth" and the "light of the world." In Jesus' time, salt was used primarily as a preservative—to keep foods from going rotten. If it weren't for the followers of Jesus, the world would surely become completely rotten and everything about it would be evil. However, our job is not only to keep the world from going completely rotten, but to work to improve the world by letting our lights shine. We should bring the light of God's truth to people who are living in the lies of darkness so that they can join us and be eternally blessed as well!

Q. Did you notice that most, if not all, of the blessings Jesus promised in today's list are future blessings? And that those who will enjoy those future blessings might suffer some in this life? What does that tell you about God's perspective of our present lives?

A. It tells us that this life is not as important as our future lives. Our present lives are temporary and will end someday, but our future lives will be eternal. Therefore, it is very wise to make temporary sacrifices in this life to enjoy eternal blessings in the next life. A well-known missionary once wrote, "He is no fool who gives up what he cannot keep to gain what he cannot lose."

Q. As you read through Jesus' description of a truly blessed person, did you think about your own life? Was Jesus describing you?

Application: Although people who are not saved might think we're foolish for following Christ, and even though we might suffer temporarily because of it, we know we're truly blessed by God, because we will be citizens of God's kingdom forever.

Jesus Explains God's Standards of Holiness
Matthew 5:17-30

As people listened to Jesus' new and authoritative teaching and heard Him frequently debate the Pharisees and religious teachers, some may have thought He had come to introduce a brand new religion, abolishing the Law of Moses and the writings of the prophets. But nothing could be further from the truth. God was the author of the Old Testament, and Jesus, being God, certainly wouldn't invalidate even one small part of it. There was no contradiction between Jesus' teaching and the teaching found in the Old Testament. He wanted everyone to know that obeying God's commandments was still of utmost importance and therefore said, "If you break the smallest commandment and teach others to do the same, you will be the least in the Kingdom of Heaven. But anyone who obeys God's laws and teaches them will be great in the Kingdom of Heaven" (Matthew 5:19).

Jesus wants our complete obedience, but from what we just read, He obviously wants us to know that we don't have to be perfect to get into heaven. He said that people who break small commandments and even teach others to do the same can still make it into heaven. However, Jesus made it clear that our degree of obedience in this life will affect our standing in the next life. There will be people in heaven who are lesser and greater than others who are there. And, lest anyone thinks Jesus was saying that it doesn't make *any* difference how people live their lives, He went on to say, "But I warn you—unless you obey God better than the teachers of religious law and the Pharisees do, you can't enter the Kingdom of Heaven at all!" (Matthew 5:20).

Jesus disagreed very much with the way the Pharisees and religious teachers had interpreted and twisted what God had said in the Old Testament. Many of their interpretations of God's laws allowed them to sin. They thought, for example, that they could be filled with hatred, anger and bitterness, and be embroiled in cursing, name-calling, strife and lawsuits with one another, but as long as they didn't murder any of the people they hated, they figured they were OK. But Jesus explained that those kinds of people are going to hell just as much as any murderer! God expects much more of us than that, and all true heaven-bound Christians will do better than that. Jesus taught that *if our relationships with others aren't right, our relationship with God is not right.* God expects us to love others, to be patient and kind, and to work toward reconciliation when we do have disagreements.

(Note: Parents should preview this paragraph before reading it to their children.) The Pharisees and religious teachers thought that as long as they kept clear of committing adultery, they were OK in God's eyes, even if they were full of lust or sexually involved, short of adultery, with a person to whom they were not married. God, however, expects much more than that! Jesus explained that a person who imagines having a sexual relationship with a person to whom he is not married has sinned in God's eyes. The one who continually dwells upon impure sexual thoughts or is involved sexually with someone with whom he is not married is in danger of hell—just as much as the person who constantly commits adultery.

This is serious stuff, and Jesus wanted to make His point unforgettable since it involved eternal consequences—heaven or hell. So He used a figure of speech we call a *hyperbole*, which is exaggerating to make a strong point. When your mother says, "I must have called you a thousand times to come home for dinner," that's a hyperbole.

Jesus said that if our eye or hand causes us to sin, we should cut them from our bodies, because it would be better to lose one part of our bodies than spend eternity in hell. We know, of course, that Jesus doesn't actually want us to cut off any parts of our bodies to keep from sinning. What He meant was that we should remove from our lives whatever is causing us to stumble into sin. Of course, cutting off a hand or gouging out an eye will not stop a person from lusting or committing acts of immorality. The problem is with people's hearts. However, once they repent of their sins, believe in Jesus and are born again, they will want to obey God from the inside.

They will still be tempted to sin, but they will have the power not to give in to sin through the Holy Spirit within them.

 Q. Was the point of Jesus' sermon saying that people could earn their way to heaven if they are holy enough?

A. No. Jesus clearly taught at other times that people are saved by believing in Him and being born again. In the sermon we've begun reading, Jesus was speaking to people who already were His disciples (see Matthew 5:1), and was revealing the standards of holiness He has set for them. He didn't want anyone who only held to the standards of the Pharisees to think they were actually saved. Jesus concluded this sermon by saying, "Not all people who sound religious are really godly. They may refer to me as 'Lord,' but they still won't enter the Kingdom of Heaven. The decisive issue is whether they obey my Father in heaven" (Matthew 7:21). True believers in Jesus live obedient lives according to God's standards.

Q. (For teens only) Regarding sex, people often ask, "How far can I go sexually with someone I'm not married to before I'm sinning?" Based on what we've read today, how do you think Jesus would respond to that question?

A. He might first ask us why we are asking such a question. Does our question reveal that we are like the Pharisees, looking for an excuse to gratify our sexual desires by using a person to whom we are not committed as a lifetime partner? Sex is a sacred experience designed by God to be enjoyed only within the marriage relationship. God also designed that sex would be a progressive thing, one thing leading to another. It begins with thinking about it, which leads to physical contact. Even when a man and woman are just kissing, their bodies are preparing for intercourse. If, according to Jesus, thinking about sex with a person with whom you are not married is a sin, then it is safe to say that doing the things that lead to more intimate sex is also a sin. Additionally, when you are kissing someone to whom you are not married, you are kissing someone who may well be someone else's future husband or wife! For these reasons and others, most Bible-believing pastors strongly recommend to the single people that they avoid any and all sexual involvement with anyone to whom they are not engaged. Engagement, unlike marriage, is not a license for sex.

Application: God's standards for holiness are high when compared to what human beings normally expect from themselves. But, thanks to God, it is possible for us to attain His standards once we are born again. Then the Holy Spirit changes us, and we are no longer captive to sinful living.

Jesus Continues to Explain God's Standards of Holiness
Matthew 5:31-48

During His sermon on the mountainside, Jesus continued to explain the difference between God's standard of holiness and the Pharisees' and religious teachers' standard of holiness. Today the first subject in our reading is divorce. Many of the religious teachers of Jesus' day misinterpreted, for their own convenience, what Moses had said about divorce. The Law of Moses made provision for divorce only in cases when adultery had been committed. However, the divorce had to be done legally, and it was required that an official divorce certificate be given by the husband to his wife. Many of the religious teachers, however, twisted what the Law actually said, teaching that a man could divorce his wife for any reason, as long as he gave his wife a certificate. As a result, men were divorcing their wives for reasons other than adultery and thinking that they were OK in God's eyes.

Jesus, however, said they were very guilty before God. In fact, they were triply guilty, because they were not only responsible for their own sin of divorcing their wives, but they were held accountable by God for the "adultery" of their divorced wives (who often had to remarry to survive) and the "adultery" of the men whom their divorced wives married! (I've put quotation marks around the word *adultery* because it was adultery only because the first man had no right to divorce his wife. Thus it was equivalent to his forcing her to have a sexual relationship with another man while he was still married to her.)

Next in His sermon on God's standards of holiness was the subject of making vows, something else the Law of Moses spoke about which had been conveniently altered by the religious teachers of the day. They taught that if a person swore by the temple, the altar, or by heaven, he was not obligated to keep his vow, but if he swore by the gold of the temple, the offering on the altar, or God in heaven, he was obligated (see Matthew 23:16-22). Apparently there were other items by which a person could vow and not be obligated as well, such as the earth, Jerusalem and his own head (see Matthew 5:35-36). In short, the religious teachers had devised a way by which they could lie, supposedly without being guilty of sin.

Jesus said that God's standard is much higher than that. People should say what they mean and mean what they say. When someone says, "I swear to God that I'm telling the truth," he's admitting that he's usually a liar. Jesus said His followers should have no need to swear or make vows because they should always tell the truth. Their "yes" and "no" should be trustworthier than anyone else's most convincing vow.

Next was the subject of revenge. The Law of Moses said that when a person is found guilty in court of injuring another person, his punishment should be equivalent to the harm he caused. If he knocked out someone's tooth, in fairness and justice, his tooth should be knocked out. This was a commandment to insure that justice would be served in court cases.

However, once again, the religious teachers had twisted this scripture, making it into a commandment for getting personal revenge, something God's Word forbids (see Deuteronomy 32:35). Obtaining due justice in court is one thing, but getting revenge is another. Additionally, the religious leaders of Jesus' day had conveniently overlooked the fact that the Old Testament taught they should show kindness to their enemies (see Exodus 23:4-5; Proverbs 25:21-22). That was God's standard of holiness, and Jesus endorsed it further by telling us to turn the other cheek and go the extra mile when we are dealing with evil people. God wants us to be merciful, not revengeful, when we are wronged.

Finally, we read one more God-given commandment that the religious teachers of Jesus' day had changed to accommodate their hateful hearts. In the Old Testament, God had said, "Love your neighbor," but the religious teachers had conveniently assumed that if God wanted them to love their neighbors, then He must have meant for them to hate their enemies. But, according to Jesus, that is not at all what God meant! Jesus would later teach in the story of the Good Samaritan that we should consider *every* person to be our neighbor. God wants us to love *everyone*, which includes our enemies. That is God's standard for His children, a standard to which He Himself lives. He sends crop-growing sun and rain not only on good people, but also on evil people. We should follow His example, showing kindness to undeserving people. As Jesus said, if we only love people who love us, we are doing no more than wicked unbelievers. God's standard of holiness is perfection, and that is what we should be striving for in our lives.

Q. When Jesus commanded us to turn the other cheek and go the second mile when dealing with evil people, does that mean He wants us to allow people to take advantage of us, allowing them to ruin our lives if they desire?

A. No. Notice that Jesus did not say that we should kill ourselves when someone slaps us on the cheek, give someone our house and furniture when they sue us for our shirt, or walk a thousand miles with a soldier who demands that we carry his gear for a mile. Jesus was simply telling us to be merciful, not revengeful, when dealing with selfish, evil people.

Q. Under Roman law, a Roman soldier could demand that any person carry his gear for one mile, and the Roman soldiers took advantage of that law whenever they could. What did that reveal about the average Roman soldier? What kind of effect do you think it had on a soldier when he forced a Christian to carry his gear, and that Christian gladly accepted and then carried his gear two miles?

Application: Too often, Christians are known for their snobbery or their doctrine. God wants us to be known for our love and servanthood. What do unbelievers think of when they think of you?

Jesus Continues to Explain God's Standards of Holiness
Matthew 6:1-18

During the first part of His mountainside sermon, Jesus told His disciples that they had to obey God better than the Pharisees and religious teachers, or else they wouldn't enter the kingdom of heaven (see Matthew 5:20). After that, He began explaining the difference between what God expects and what the Pharisees and religious teachers practiced. One of the many faults that Jesus found with them is that they did their good deeds to be admired by other people. When they gave money to the poor, they announced what they were doing with trumpets! When they prayed, they did so on the street corners and in the synagogues where everyone could see them. When they fasted, they adjusted their appearance so everyone would know they were fasting and admire them. *Their good deeds were really evil deeds because their motives were selfish.* Jesus said that the only reward they would ever receive would be the praise of people.

God expects more from His children than that. When we give, we should be motivated by love for the person we're helping. As much as possible, we should give and serve in secret. If we will, Jesus promises that God will reward us. The same is true for our secret praying and fasting. Although our salvation is received purely through God's grace (undeserved mercy), many of God's blessings are bestowed because we earn them through our obedience.

In this part of His sermon, Jesus gave further instruction about prayer. He said that people of other religions pray the same thing over and over again, continually repeating the same requests. They think their god will hear them if they just pray long enough. But we are praying to a God who knows everything! He knows what we need before we ask Him, so it would be foolish for us to think we need to keep saying the same things over and over again! Continually repeating the identical prayer is insulting to God. We should converse with Him as we would with our most respected and trusted friend. He's listening to us, not ignoring us, and we don't need to pray long prayers to be heard.

Jesus gave us an example of a model prayer we could pray. Notice that it isn't a long prayer. Don't think that short prayers are a waste of time or that you don't have enough time to pray. You can pray short prayers all the time and any time!

We should begin by realizing that we are praying to our heavenly Father, which means we have a special relationship with the One we're addressing. We're not talking to a stranger! We're talking to someone who loves us dearly!

Beginning our prayers with worship is appropriate. "May your name be honored" (Matthew 6:9) is an example of a worshipful statement we could make, but there are many others.

After worship, we can begin with our requests, and the first ones should be for things that concern God. We should want, more than anything else, for God's kingdom to expand and for His will to be done on the earth. Many people want *their* desires to become God's desires, and they try to change His will by their prayers. But God wants His desires to become everyone's desires, because His desires are best. More than anything, He wants people to hear the gospel and be saved. So we should pray first for things that relate to the spread of the good news of Jesus. We should pray for missionaries, the people of our church, and for opportunities to spread the gospel ourselves.

Next, we can pray for our own needs. Later in this same sermon, Jesus assured us that God will take care of our need for food, clothing and other material things, but *only if we are living for Him and making the Kingdom of God our primary concern* (see Matthew 6:33). If our prayers are only for our own needs, that's a good indication that God's kingdom is not our primary concern.

One of our foremost needs is for forgiveness when we've sinned. Jesus said we can be assured that our requests for forgiveness will be answered as long as we forgive people who have sinned against us. Of course, God doesn't expect more of us than He does of Himself, and we know that He doesn't forgive people unless they admit their sin and ask for forgiveness. When people request our forgiveness, admitting their wrongs against us, then we must forgive them, or else God will not forgive our sins when we ask. This does not give us the right, however, to hate people who sin against us but who never ask our forgiveness. Jesus still expects us to be merciful and kind to such people, loving them and praying for them, as we have already learned from this sermon (see Matthew 5:43-47), and to even confront them if they are Christians. But forgiveness is impossible to give unless it's first requested.

Finally, we should pray that God will help us during times we are tempted to do the wrong thing, delivering us from giving in to the devil. This prayer request also indicates that our primary concern should be with pleasing God. We need His help to be obedient, and He will help us when we're tempted if we'll ask Him to help us.

Q. We read today what is commonly known as "The Lord's Prayer." Many people have memorized this exact prayer and pray it, word for word, all the time, without even thinking about what they are saying. Do you think that is what Jesus had in mind when He first taught this prayer?

A. No, because Jesus said in the verses preceding the prayer that our prayers shouldn't be meaninglessly repetitious. Of course, we can pray the Lord's prayer with meaning if we concentrate, and we are not limited to just praying this one prayer! It is a wonderful model for all prayers, however.

Q. If you had to summarize with one word what we've read so far of Jesus' sermon on the mountainside, what one word would you choose? Does this tell us anything about what is most important to Jesus?

A. I would choose the word "holiness." What is most important to Jesus is how we live our lives. Obedience to God is what should be most important to all Christians.

Application: Do I act differently when I'm in public than when I'm alone? If I do, what does that reveal about me? What should I do about it?

Jesus Teaches About Material Possessions
Matthew 6:19-34

For many people, money is their god. Just like a god, money controls their lives, consuming all their energy, thoughts and time. Money is the main source of their joy, and they're never satisfied with how much they have but are always wanting more. This is often true for rich and poor people, and Jesus addressed both groups among His followers during His sermon on the mountainside. He explained how God expects His children to view money and material things, making it very clear that we can't serve both God and money. It's one or the other, but not both.

Wealthy people often reveal that money is their god by hoarding their riches, continually accumulating more and more for themselves, amassing much more than they really need. Jesus said, however, that we shouldn't store up treasures on earth. It's foolish to do so, because everything on this earth is destined to perish ultimately. In fact, most of it is slowly perishing right before our eyes. This was even more obvious to the people in Jesus' day, who didn't have the benefits of moth balls, rust-proofing paint or padlocks! But what Jesus said then is still true today.

For those of us who are saved, hoarding riches on earth is even more foolish, because there's a way we can convert our temporary riches into eternal riches. Jesus said that we should lay up our treasures in heaven. How can we do that? Jesus once told a very wealthy young man that if he sold his possessions and gave the money to the poor, he would then have treasure in heaven (see Matthew 19:21). We can do the same thing. When we give money on earth, it's like making a deposit into our bank accounts in heaven.

Rich people aren't the only people who often make money their god. Poor people frequently become just as consumed with material things. Their concern, however, is not with hoarding more and more riches, but with the simple necessities of life. They become worried about whether or not they are going to have enough food and clothing. Just like many wealthy people, their focus is on material things.

But God expects His children, even those who are poor, to be focused on Him and His kingdom. Jesus promised that if we will live for Him and make the kingdom of God our primary concern, then God will supply all our daily needs. He cares about us, so there's no need for us to worry. Look how well God takes care of all the birds, providing them with food. If you ever see the birds gathered in your yard having a prayer meeting for food, then you might begin to worry about God supplying your needs!

Q. Today we read something that is difficult to understand, when Jesus said, "Your eye is a lamp for your body. A pure eye lets sunshine into your soul. But an evil eye shuts out the light and plunges you into darkness. If the light you think you have is really darkness, how deep that darkness will be!" (Matthew 6:22-23). What do you think He was talking about? Hint: Look at the context of those statements.

A. Jesus was talking about two kinds of people, the saved and unsaved. People whose god is money are not saved, because Jesus said it is impossible to serve both God and money. His comments about the eye allowing light into the soul or shutting it out also describe the saved and unsaved. A person with a "pure eye" is a person who is looking for the truth (often symbolized by light), and when he finds it, he lets it into his soul. He then has God's truth within him. A person with an "evil eye" is a person who does not want God's truth, and when the light of God's truth shines in his face, he shuts his eyes because he doesn't want it to get inside him. Many people shut their eyes to God's truth because they think they already have the truth, but really they've believed only lies. Consequently, they are full of darkness even when they think they have light inside them. That kind of darkness is the worst kind.

Q. Can we rightly conclude from what we read today that it is wrong for us to work hard to make money, or save some of the money we earn?

A. Certainly not. We can't give any money away unless we first have some ourselves. Jesus was warning us that money cannot be our main priority in life if we are going to be His followers. Our primary concern should be with His kingdom and living for Him. We should guard ourselves against greed, and shouldn't worry about having enough, but rather, should trust in our heavenly Father's care.

Application: Many kids don't have a lot of money, but nevertheless, like poor people, money can become their god. Is there evidence in your life that God is your god and not money? Do you give away a portion of what you do receive?

Jesus Teaches about Being Critical of Others
Matthew 7:1-6

As Jesus continued teaching about God's standards of holiness, He told His followers to stop judging other people. What did He mean? A judge is someone who looks for faults in people who are brought to court. That's his job, and there is nothing wrong about what he does, as long as he judges according to proven facts. Judges are *supposed* to judge people, measuring them by the standard of the law of the land. If there were no judges, criminals would never go to jail.

However, many people seem to think that they have been appointed as judges, and thus they are always looking for faults in others. That is wrong. Furthermore, they often judge people without considering all the facts, jumping to wrong conclusions. For example, they see a mother spank her child in the grocery store and conclude she must be a child abuser. They don't stop and think that perhaps the child deserved a spanking!

To make matters worse, these self-appointed judges usually measure other people by standards that they themselves fall short of, making themselves hypocrites. Jesus' funny illustration about trying to remove a speck from someone else's eye while you have a log in your own eye is a perfect example of this. Imagine trying to help someone get a little speck out of his eye with a big log sticking out of yours!

What would you think if you saw two little children sitting in a mud puddle, covered with mud, and one pointing his finger at the other and saying, "You are filthy!" That is how we look to God when we criticize others.

What right do imperfect people have to find faults in others? Absolutely none. As followers of Jesus, we should be more concerned with correcting our own faults.

Q. When brothers and sisters are constantly "telling" on each other, that makes them "tattletales." Do Jesus' words about judging others have any application to tattletales?

A. Occasionally telling your parents about a sin of a brother or sister can be OK, if it is done out of love and concern for that brother or sister. For example, telling your parents that your brother is not wearing his seat belt in the car is a good thing. But when you tell on your brother just because you want to see him get in trouble, that is wrong, especially if you are guilty of the same sin. Then you are a hypocrite. When brothers and sisters are *always* telling on one another, constantly getting revenge for being told on, they demonstrate exactly what Jesus said about others treating you as you treat them. Like Jesus said, others will judge you by the same standard you use to judge them. People who are always finding fault aren't liked by the people with whom they find fault. Consequently, those people look for faults in the people who find fault with them!

Q. What if you see a fault in another person of which you are not personally guilty? You see the speck in his eye but don't have a log in your own eye. Should you speak to him about his fault?

A. Only if you know that the person is open to receive your constructive criticism. Otherwise, you would be giving your "pearls to a pig" (see Matthew 7:6). That is, he won't appreciate or receive what you have to tell him. A proverb says, "Don't bother rebuking mockers; they will only hate you. But the wise, when rebuked, will love you all the more" (Proverbs 9:8).

Constructive criticism offered by one who has a right to offer it is a holy thing. Jesus said we shouldn't give what is holy to unholy people.

Application: Are people always finding fault with me? Could it be because I'm always finding faults with others, and thus I'm being measured by the same standard by which I measure others? If so, I determine to be less critical and more merciful. As a result, people will be less critical and more merciful with me.

Jesus Teaches About Persistence and Prayer
Matthew 7:7-11

This portion of Jesus' sermon on the mountainside is commonly considered teaching about prayer. However, I think Jesus had more in mind than prayer in what we've just read. I think He was also talking about laziness and persistence.

Jesus first talked about asking for things, which could certainly apply to prayer. However, He then mentioned *looking* and *knocking*. Do those terms also refer to prayer? Perhaps, yet as we continue to read, we have to wonder. Jesus went on to say that everyone who asks, receives, everyone who seeks, finds, and to everyone who knocks, the door is opened. We know that is not always true concerning prayer. Although there are scores of examples of answered prayer in the Bible, there are also examples of unanswered requests, and certainly it is not true that *everyone*, non-Christians included, receives what he asks for in prayer.

For this reason, I wonder if Jesus was simply encouraging His followers to be askers, seekers and knockers in every area of their lives. It *is* true that the only people who receive their requests are those who make requests, the only people who find are those who seek, and the only people who have doors opened to them are those who knock. Those who wait around for things to happen or improve without any effort on their part are usually disappointed. As one Chinese proverb says, "Man stand for long time with mouth open before roast duck fly in."

Many people are lazy. Even Christians sometimes try to make excuses for their laziness by saying things such as, "Well, if God wants me to have a certain thing, He'll just get it to me." But that isn't true according to what Jesus said. People who get jobs are those who seek for employment, asking employers. People who go to college are those who knock on doors and fill out applications. People who get married are those who seek for a potential mate. If you want things to improve, you have to work at it and be persistent, never giving up. Everyone who puts forth that kind of effort is rewarded. But lazy people who refuse to ask, seek and knock never make any progress in life.

This concept also applies to prayer. Christians who assume that God will automatically give them whatever He wants them to have are wrong. According to Jesus, our heavenly Father wants to give us good gifts, but we *must* ask (see Matthew 7:11). Furthermore, we shouldn't be satisfied, as many Christians often are, with receiving something other than what we've requested. Jesus said that if a child asks his parents for bread, they won't give him a stone. And if he asks for a fish, they won't give him a snake! Our heavenly Father loves us even more than any parents love their children. We should expect that He is not going to give us something other than what we request, and when it appears as if He has, we should not be discouraged, but continue to persevere in faith until we possess what we desire. Strong faith never quits!

 Q. Have you ever become discouraged and given up on reaching a goal? What do you think Jesus would say about that?

A. If your goal is a good one, He would encourage you to keep asking, looking and knocking. With God on our side to help us, there is always good reason to persevere.

Q. Proverbs 22:13 says, "The lazy person is full of excuses, saying, 'If I go outside, I might meet a lion in the street and be killed!'" Can you think of any other funny excuses that lazy people use to avoid work? Are there any excuses that you use to avoid work?

 Application: Proverbs 26:14 says, " As a door turns back and forth on its hinges, so the lazy person turns over in bed."

Jesus Summarizes His Sermon on the Mountainside
Matthew 7:12-29

Jesus was the greatest teacher who ever lived, and what we've read today adds proof. He illustrated the truths He taught with examples His hearers could relate to easily. Today we've read about narrow gates and broad highways, wolves pretending to be sheep, trees producing good and bad fruit, houses built upon rock and sand, and winds and floods. All these things make it easy for us to remember what Jesus wants us to do.

The easiest way to remember how God expects us to treat other people is to recall what is called *The Golden Rule*: "Do for others what you would like them to do for you" (Matthew 7:12). Jesus said that one rule summarizes the teaching of the Old Testament. How would you like other people to treat you? That's how you should treat them. Let's apply this to you and your brothers and sisters. Do you want your sister to share a favorite music CD? Share what you have with her. Do you want your brother to remember you before he eats the last piece of pizza, saving some for you? When you have the opportunity, save some pizza for him. One of the nicest things about following the Golden Rule is that when you treat others nicely, they will probably treat you nicely in return. It's hard being mean to someone who's nice to you!

Jesus told His followers early in this sermon that they had to obey God better than the religious teachers and the Pharisees did, otherwise they wouldn't get into heaven. Just like today, there were many religious people in Jesus' day who weren't really saved. The majority of people are on "the highway to hell," and it's the minority who are on the true narrow path to heaven. Jesus wanted those who were following Him to make sure they were His true disciples, and that they were following leaders who were also on the right path. The way they could tell if they or a religious leader were on the narrow path was by looking at how they lived their lives.

Jesus first talked about phony religious teachers by calling them false prophets and wolves in sheep's clothing. Outwardly they look harmless, but their inward motivation is selfish. They want to take advantage of those they lead. The way to identify them is to look at their "fruit," or their actions. Good people act good. Bad people act bad.

Also, we should be careful not to follow someone just because he does miraculous things. Jesus said many people would stand before His judgment seat, listing the miracles they did and hoping to convince Him to let them into Heaven. If they lived sinful lifestyles, however, they would be refused entrance. Jesus said that those who don't produce good fruit will be "chopped down and thrown into the fire" (Matthew 7:20). That means they will be cast into hell.

Jesus was not saying that we can earn our way into heaven by doing good things. Our salvation is a gift from God's grace, offered to anyone who will believe in Jesus. However, those who truly do believe in Jesus will produce good fruit, just as a good, healthy apple tree naturally produces good apples.

Q. When Jesus finished His sermon on the mountainside, the people were amazed at His teaching, because He taught as one who had real authority. That means Jesus spoke knowing exactly what He was saying, and no one had a right to disagree with Him. What does this tell us about Jesus?

A. It either indicates that He was a very proud, opinionated, bold and self-centered human being, or else He was God, pure and holy, telling the truth.

Application: Have you ever built a sand castle close to the water along the seashore? If you have, you know what can happen to a house built upon sand when a big wave comes in. Anyone who is not doing what Jesus said is just like a person building his house on sand—he's heading for a big disaster. That's why we should take very seriously all that Jesus had to say, including everything He said in this sermon on the mountainside. Are you building your house on a rock, doing what Jesus said?

A Roman Soldier's Faith
Matthew 8:5-13; Luke 7:1-10

Because Jesus ministered in Israel, a nation predominantly inhabited by Jewish people, most of the people He helped were Jewish. However, during Jesus' time, Israel was controlled by the Roman Empire, so there were also Roman governmental leaders and soldiers living there. This Roman soldier of whom we just read was called a centurion, which meant he was an army officer in charge of one hundred other soldiers.

According to Luke's account, the centurion was a good man who loved the Jewish people, and he even helped them build a synagogue. These facts, along with what we've read about his words and actions as he related to Jesus, indicate to us that he was a godly man. He even considered himself unworthy to personally meet Jesus, sending some respected Jewish leaders to take his request for his servant to be healed.

Upon learning of the centurion's desire, without hesitation, Jesus began heading toward his house. However, when the centurion heard the news that Jesus was coming, he realized that the Jewish leaders he'd sent had partially misunderstood his request. He wasn't expecting Jesus to actually come to his house, but if He would just speak a word where He was, that would bring healing to his servant. He considered himself unworthy to have Jesus in his home, again revealing his high regard for Jesus. Perhaps he even realized that Jesus was God in the form of a human being. So he quickly sent another messenger, hoping to convey to Jesus before He arrived that it was not necessary for Him to come. Just as he had authority over other soldiers who obeyed his commands, he believed Jesus had authority over all sickness, and that He didn't have to be physically present to heal his servant.

Jesus was amazed by the Roman centurion's faith, a faith that was stronger than what He had yet encountered among Jewish people. He then seized the opportunity to tell everyone present that the kingdom of heaven is wide open to non-Jewish people who have faith. In fact, He said that many people who aren't Jewish will feast in heaven with Abraham, Isaac and Jacob, while many Jewish people who don't believe in Him will be cast into hell, where there will be "weeping and gnashing of teeth" (Matthew 8:12). That was shocking news for the Jews, who prided themselves as being God's special people. They despised anyone who was not Jewish, calling them "dogs." Praise God that anyone who believes in Jesus can be saved! If you believe in Jesus, you'll get to eat one day with this centurion in heaven, along with Abraham, Isaac and Jacob!

For the centurion, his faith in Jesus not only paid off for eternity, but also during his earthly life, as his dying servant was healed "that same hour" (Matthew 7:13).

Q. You probably noticed that Matthew and Luke's versions of the same story were slightly different. Matthew said that the centurion personally made his request of Jesus, whereas Luke said that the centurion sent some Jewish leaders on his behalf. Some people claim that this contradiction proves that this story is just a myth, making the Bible unreliable. Does it?

A. No. There are *numerous* details in this story that are identical, and only one apparent contradiction. Matthew must have either not known the detail of the Jewish leaders' involvement, or he simply chose not to include it, purposely condensing the story a little bit. When two people report the same incident, it's not unusual for one to omit details the other might include.

Q. Jesus talked about people eating in heaven, so there must be people who will have mouths and stomachs there. He also talked about people weeping and gnashing their teeth in hell, indicating that there will be people there with eyes and mouths. How can this be true if, when people die, they leave their bodies behind, and only their spirits go to heaven or hell?

A. The answer is that everyone, saved and unsaved, will one day receive new bodies. Those bodies will be somewhat different than what we have now, because they will never die, but will also be similar to our present bodies in some ways. Christians will receive their new bodies when Jesus comes back. The unsaved people now in hell will not receive resurrected bodies until after Jesus reigns for one thousand years on the earth. Then they will stand before the final judgment and be cast bodily into the lake of fire (see Revelation 20:5-6, 11-15).

Application: Although some Christians don't want to face up to this fact, it is entirely scriptural: Those who trust Jesus receive blessings in this life that aren't received by those who don't believe. Jesus said the centurion had greater faith than any Jewish person He'd met. How do you think He would evaluate your faith?

Jesus Heals a Royal Official's Dying Son
John 4:46-54

Yesterday we read about Jesus healing a young man whom He did not see or touch. Jesus was perhaps several hundred yards away from the centurion's young servant when He spoke His healing word. But today's story even tops yesterday's, because Jesus was about *ten miles* away from the governmental official's son when He healed him! Distance does not limit God's healing power. He can heal people from as far away as heaven!

This governmental official received the blessing he desired because he "believed Jesus' word" (John 4:50). Notice that he believed his son was healed before he had any evidence of it, other than Jesus' promise. It wasn't until the next day that he learned from his servants that his son had recovered. The Bible says that "faith...is the evidence of things *we cannot yet see*" (Hebrews 11:1, emphasis added). When we have a promise from God, that's all the evidence we need, because it's impossible for God to lie. We don't need to see something to believe it.

For example, although we can't see, feel, or hear them, we can be certain that there are TV waves in the air all around us, otherwise our TV sets wouldn't work. We can also be sure that there are angels all around us even though we've never seen them, because God's Word says, "The angel of the Lord encamps around those who fear Him, and rescues them" (Psalm 34:7, NASB).

When we read this story closely, the faith of this governmental official becomes even more evident. His son was dying in Capernaum, but hearing that Jesus was back in Judea, he had to travel about ten miles to track Him down in Cana. Jesus pronounced his son healed around one o'clock in the afternoon (see John 4:52-53), so the man could have journeyed the ten miles back to Capernaum that same day. But it wasn't until the *next* day, before he arrived home, that he met some of his own servants who told him the good news about his son. So obviously, the governmental official trusted Jesus enough that he didn't rush home to see *if* His promise had actually come to pass! Resting in Jesus' promise, he apparently stayed overnight in Cana, and departed the next day for his home in Capernaum.

This is a good lesson for us to learn as well. People who trust God don't worry. They know the outcome of their present problems in advance, so they can rest in God's promises. God doesn't want us to be worrywarts!

 Q. Is there anything you are worried about? If so, is there a promise in the Bible that you can believe so you can stop your worrying?

Q. Yesterday we read about Jesus healing a servant who belonged to a man who had several servants (see Matthew 8:9; Luke 7:8), which tells us that the man was wealthy enough to have servants. Today we read about Jesus healing the son of a man who was also wealthy enough to have several servants (see John 4:51). Why do you think Jesus helped people who had so much money?

A. Because God loves everyone, rich and poor. Additionally, we shouldn't assume that God is holding something against a person just because he's rich. There are many rich people in the Bible of whom God approved. They obeyed God with their money by blessing others. The centurion we read about yesterday apparently used some of his money to help the Jews build a synagogue.

Application: The final outcome of this healing miracle was that the official "and his entire household believed in Jesus" (John 4:53). Naturally, all of them were convinced that Jesus was the Son of God after witnessing the official's son being suddenly healed at the exact time when Jesus, ten miles away, said he would live. That ought to be enough to convince anyone!

Jesus Raises a Widow's Son From the Dead
Luke 7:11-17

O how I would love to have been present to see this miracle in person! How about you? If we use our imaginations, however, picturing in our minds what happened that day outside the gate of Nain, we can still share in some of the thrill of the eyewitnesses.

A weeping woman, who had already suffered the tragedy of her husband's death, is now following the funeral procession of her only son, trudging to the place where a fresh grave has been dug in the ground, right beside the place where her husband's body lay. Carried on a pallet in front of her is her son's lifeless body, cold, still and white, a child who once walked, laughed and held her hand. She has no other children of her own to comfort her, but her relatives and neighbors are walking with her, weeping out loud, sympathetic to her adversity, but helpless to do anything to reverse her misfortune. Many are wondering why God would allow their friend to face such anguish, and at the same time, secretly thankful that they are not wearing her shoes. Her future looks bleak with no husband or son to support her. How could things be worse?

That day the Holy Spirit led Jesus to the village of Nain, with a plan to turn mourning into joy and to glorify the Son of God. When Jesus saw the funeral procession, His "heart overflowed with compassion" (Luke 7:13), and He walked over to the coffin bearers and stopped them. Then, with the same spoken power He used to create the universe, Jesus commanded the dead boy to get up, which he instantly did! Shock waves of astonishment rippled through the crowd as the boy began speaking. He was dead, but now is truly alive! As the stunned crowd tried to make sense of what their eyes had just witnessed, Jesus helped the boy off his funeral pallet and gave him to his mother. No doubt they embraced with tears of joy and praise to God.

Although Jesus doesn't intervene every time people face similar tragedies, this story should remind us that He does deeply care when we suffer. Additionally, it proves that Jesus has power over death, and strengthens our faith that He is certainly the Son of God. There are no other religions in the world that claim that their founder raised people from the dead!

 Q. Can you think of a reason why someone being raised from the dead is a greater miracle than someone being healed?

A. When a person is raised from the dead, he also has to be healed of whatever killed him, otherwise he'd immediately die again. Additionally, every cell in his body is healed, because all of them die once he's dead.

Q. What do you think would have been your reaction if you had seen Jesus perform this miracle?

Application: Our Savior is master over death, and we've been delivered from our fear of it (see Hebrews 2:15). One day Jesus will resurrect every person who has died, and one day we will be united with our loved ones who have died in Christ. The joy this widow experienced when her son came back to life is nothing compared to the joy we'll have in heaven!

John the Baptist Questions Jesus
Luke 7:18-35

While John the Baptist was imprisoned by Herod (see Matthew 11:2), it was apparent that he began to doubt that Jesus actually was the Messiah, even though he had seen the Holy Spirit descend upon Jesus at His baptism. Just as we often do, John began to battle doubts when he faced adversity. This shows us that John was an ordinary person like the rest of us.

Jesus replied to John's questions by speaking of His authenticating miracles. The blind, lame, deaf and leprous were being healed. Even the dead were being raised. Only the Messiah sent from God could do such things.

John's doubts may have also stemmed from his misunderstanding of God's Word, just as our misunderstanding of God's Word sometimes fuels our doubts. Perhaps John was expecting the Messiah to set up the long-awaited kingdom, as the Old Testament promised He would. John's problem is that he didn't sufficiently understand all that the Old Testament promised concerning the Messiah. With His reply, Jesus may have been pointing him back to Scripture, specifically to a messianic prophecy in the book of Isaiah. Jesus knew John realized that Isaiah 40:3 was a reference to his own ministry. John had once quoted it, explaining his identity to some Jewish priests: "I am a voice shouting in the wilderness, Ô Prepare a straight pathway for the Lord's coming.'" In His reply to John, Jesus may very well have been quoting from Isaiah 61:1, a passage that refers to the Messiah's healing and preaching ministry.

Although John experienced temporary doubts about Jesus, Jesus still called him the greatest man who ever lived. This indicated that John wasn't great because of anything _he_ did, but because of what God did through him. He was chosen before conception in his mother's womb to be a prophet, a prophet who would prepare the way for the Messiah. His ministry had been foretold in the Old Testament. God made him into a bold, anointed preacher, and multitudes of people repented as a result.

The amazing thing that Jesus said is that "even the most insignificant person in the Kingdom of God" will be greater than John the Baptist. John was the greatest person who ever lived because of what God did through him, but every one of us will one day be able to rightly consider ourselves greater, because of what God will do through us in His kingdom! Wow! Perhaps it will be then that Jesus' amazing promise of John 14:12 will come to pass: "The truth is, anyone who believes in me will do the same works I have done, and even greater works..." John the Baptist never performed any miracles, but, speaking of His miracles (see John 14:12), Jesus said all believers would do the same works and even greater works! Can you imagine being used by God to heal the blind, lame and deaf, or raise someone from the dead? The Bible says that we will one day rule with Jesus for a thousand years over the whole earth, and perhaps it is then that we can look forward to being used by God so greatly!

 Q. When we are tempted to doubt that Jesus is the Messiah and Son of God, what would be the best way we could eradicate our doubts?

A. By re-examining the evidence for these facts in the Bible. God's Word builds faith within us.

Application: In the final part of today's reading, Jesus compared those who rejected Him to children arguing with one another, who, no matter what, can't be pleased. Jesus' enemies found fault with John the Baptist for his fasting and abstinence, and criticized Jesus for His feasting and drinking. It wasn't that they couldn't believe; it was that they didn't want to believe, and so they used any and every excuse they could think of to remain unbelieving and disobedient. As sad as it may seem, there are some people whom we will never convince to believe the gospel.

A Forgiven Woman Shows Her Faith and Gratitude
Luke 7:36-50

This woman who kissed Jesus' feet probably had a reputation as a prostitute. Although the Bible contains no such record, it seems likely that Jesus had previously ministered to her, accepting her repentance and forgiving her many sins. Now, at Simon the Pharisee's house, she returned to show her love and gratitude for her Savior. It's quite obvious she believed that Jesus was God in the form of a human being: How many people's feet would you wash with your tears and dry with your hair? How many people's feet would you repeatedly kiss and perfume? Hopefully only God's!

This story, for several reasons, also affirms that Jesus was who He claimed to be. First, because Jesus allowed the woman to do all those things to His feet, and there's no evidence that He was the least bit uncomfortable with it. Why? Because He was God, and God deserves to be worshipped. Would you allow someone to do that to you? Hopefully not! Any other human being who allowed another person to perform such a worshipful act would be guilty of great pride.

Second, Jesus told the woman that her sins were forgiven, something that only God has a right to do, as those present that day realized. If Jesus wasn't God, then He was one of the most evil people who ever lived, because He knowingly deceived people into believing that He was God and accepted worship of which only God is worthy. If you don't love Jesus, then you hate Him! But nobody should be neutral about Him, because He wasn't, as some think, "just a good man." Simon the Pharisee thought that what he was witnessing proved that Jesus wasn't even a God-sent prophet.

Simon assumed that a God-sent prophet would automatically know how immoral the woman was. It hadn't occurred to him that Jesus was God and that the woman had repented and had been forgiven by Him. So Jesus explained to him what was happening before his eyes. He was witnessing a redeemed person worshipping God with humble gratitude. Because she had been forgiven of so many sins, she was especially thankful, and it showed.

Then Jesus compared her actions with Simon's. Simon hadn't even offered Jesus the common courtesies of that day which any dinner guest should have received. No doubt Simon had a servant wash the feet of his other guests when they arrived, but he hadn't even offered Jesus water to wash His own feet! Yet the forgiven woman washed His feet with her tears and wiped them with her hair. Simon hadn't greeted Jesus with a common kiss of greeting as he had his other guests, but the forgiven woman repeatedly kissed His feet, an act of adoration. Neither had Simon extended to Jesus the common courtesy of anointing His head with olive oil as he probably had done for his other guests, but the forgiven woman anointed Jesus' feet with rare and very expensive perfume.

Simon's discourtesy revealed that he didn't invite Jesus to his house for dinner in order to get to know Him or ask Him honest questions, but to set Him up before his other Pharisee friends, so they could have a close-up chance to find fault with Him. They hated Jesus, and wanted to prove He wasn't even a God-sent prophet. How sad! If they had known and believed the truth, there would have been no room for the forgiven woman near Jesus' feet, because they would have all been on their knees there, weeping for their sins and asking for His forgiveness!

Q. How was the forgiven woman able to perform her act of worship while Jesus was eating with Simon and some other Pharisees? Do you think that she crawled under the table or did she stick her head under His chair?

A. That was a trick question! In Jesus' day, people ate their meals lying on their sides around a very low table, their legs pointed outward like spokes on a bicycle wheel. The woman in today's story knelt behind Jesus' feet and legs, where she was easily able to wash His feet with her tears and dry them with her hair.

Q. According to Jesus, what was it that channeled salvation from Him to the immoral woman?

A. Her faith in Him.

Q. How can we be certain that she did possess saving faith?

A. Her humble act of worship revealed her faith. She publicly, without shame, demonstrated that she believed Jesus was God. All true Christians possess a deep gratitude to God for the forgiveness of their sins, and it shows by how they live their lives.

Application: Jesus said that a person who has been forgiven much, loves much, and a person who has been forgiven of little, loves little. Actually, all of us who are saved have been forgiven of much more than we realize. Does your love and gratitude for Jesus show by how you live?

A Few Good Women
Luke 8:1-3; 10:38-42

The United States Marines often advertise for recruits, saying they are looking for "a few good men." Jesus, however, found a few good men *and* women as the first recruits for His growing army. They loved Him because He first loved them. According to what we just read, some of the female recruits had been previously ill or demon-possessed. Mary Magdalene, whom you will one day meet in heaven, had been delivered of seven demons, which tells us that she had been in a horrible condition before she met Jesus. Unsaved people can allow the entrance of demons into them by practicing wicked things, and so it's quite possible that Mary Magdalene was formerly a *very* sinful person. But Jesus delivered and forgave her, and now she was following Him closely. She was the very first person to see Him after He had risen from the dead!

Another one of Jesus' female followers was Joanna, the wife of Herod's business manager. She, along with Mary Magdalene, was one of the first people to see Christ's empty tomb. She also helped to support Jesus and His disciples financially. Since Joanna's husband made his living working for Herod, it was actually some of Herod's money that was used to buy food for Jesus.

People who are true followers of Christ, male or female, want to support

His cause, and one of the ways they do that is with their money. Today, Christ's followers financially support His cause by giving money to their church, missionaries and mission works. Anyone who claims to be Christ's follower (and who makes money) but gives no money to Christ's cause is only fooling himself. Do you give a portion of the money you receive to Christ's cause?

Joanna and her husband, who worked for the occupying Roman government's ruler were probably looked upon by most other Jews as traitors. But Jesus gladly accepted her as a member of His band of disciples, right along with a number of other people even though their reputations might hurt His. But Jesus was motivated by pure love, and He was unconcerned what judgmental people might think of Him because of those with whom He associated. We should follow His example.

Today we also read about *another* Mary and her sister Martha, two women who were very good friends of Jesus. Jesus visited their home one day, and as Martha diligently worked to prepare dinner, Mary sat at Jesus' feet, listening to His teaching. Martha was trying to be a good hostess, worrying about every little detail, and she became angry that her sister wasn't helping her with all the preparations.

Under most other circumstances, her anger might have been justified, because her sister should have been helping her. But that day, *God* was visiting their house! That doesn't happen often! Jesus commended Mary for her right priorities. Spiritual food is more important than physical food, especially when it is being served by God Himself!

Q. If there is work to be done at your house by you and your brother(s) and/or sister(s), based on what Jesus told Mary, is it OK if you don't help carry your share as long as you grab your Bible and start reading it?

A. Sorry! You can read your Bible any time, and you certainly shouldn't use Bible reading as an excuse to get out of acting like a Christian! Mary's case was different because Jesus was physically present and was teaching. I suppose if He had been taking a nap, He would have agreed with Martha.

Q. What do you think Jesus would say to the person who skips church on Sunday morning because he or she has so much to do to prepare for the church picnic on Sunday afternoon?

A. He would tell them that their priorities were mixed up.

Application: God loves women just as much as men. Therefore, no Christians should think of themselves as being superior to the opposite sex.

Jesus is Accused of Working for the Devil
Matthew 12:22-37

Today we realize even more how wicked the Pharisees were. After witnessing the instantaneous deliverance of a man who had been both blind and unable to talk, they claimed that Jesus got His power to cast out demons from Satan. Most of the other witnesses whose hearts weren't so hard began wondering out loud if Jesus was the Messiah.

Jesus easily exposed the lie of the Pharisees' accusation. Why would Satan empower someone to cast out his own evil spirits that he had commissioned? He would be undoing his own work, and if he continued, his kingdom would be doomed to self-destruction.

Jesus also mentioned that some of the Pharisees' own followers were casting out demons. Were they empowered by Satan as well? The Pharisees would of course deny such a thing, showing their double standard.

Jesus then explained that He cast out demons by the power of the Holy Spirit, who is much stronger than any evil spirit. The Bible says that Jesus came to "destroy the works of the devil" (1 John 3:8, NASB). Jesus explained that by using greater power, He was able to "tie up the strong man," Satan, and rob him of his possessions, the people he'd held captive. He then went on to warn the Pharisees that they were guilty of a sin that could never be forgiven: blasphemy against the Holy Spirit. What is that? The Pharisees were saying that the marvelous works of the Holy Spirit were actually works of the devil. That is blasphemy, aimed specifically at the Holy Spirit. When someone's heart is so hard that he can see the power of the Holy Spirit instantly heal a blind and mute man, and then call it the work of Satan, there is no hope for him to be saved. The condition of his heart is so bad that forgiveness is out of the realm of possibilities.

Sometimes the devil convinces young Christians that they have somehow blasphemed the Holy Spirit by something they've thought or said. But no true Christian could commit this sin. In fact, if you're even concerned that you've committed this sin, that proves you haven't, otherwise you wouldn't be concerned.

Referring to the Pharisees, Jesus said that the condition of their hearts was revealed by their words, just as fruit reveals whether a tree is good or bad. A bad tree can't produce good fruit, and likewise, evil men can't say "what is good and right" (Matthew 12:34). When people one day stand before God to be either allowed into heaven or thrown into hell, the words they spoke on earth will be used as evidence to prove whether they are saved or unsaved. People who have truly believed in Jesus will have spoken kind words, forgiving words, words about God and Jesus, words from the Bible, and words of praise and thanksgiving to God. People who have never believed in Jesus will have spoken many hateful, selfish words, words that mocked the Bible and Christians, and even used God's name as a swear word. Do your words prove that you're a believer in Jesus?

 Q. How do you suppose some of the Pharisees' own followers were able to cast out demons?

A. We can read in another Gospel something that John once reported to Jesus, "Teacher, we saw a man using your name to cast out demons, but we told him to stop because he isn't one of our group" (Mark 9:38). Jesus replied, "Don't stop him!...No one who performs miracles in my name will soon be able to speak evil of me" (Mark 9:39). So we learn that other people, even those who weren't followers of Jesus, *were using His name* to cast out demons. They had discovered a way to cast out demons that worked: tell the demons to come out *in Jesus' name*! That shows us that there's a lot of power in the name of Jesus! It also indicates that the followers of the Pharisees who were casting out demons must not have been too devoted to the Pharisees. Their hearts were obviously more open to Jesus, and they were on the verge of believing in Him.

Q. Jesus said that any city or home divided against itself is doomed. Can that same principle be applied to a church?

A. Yes. God wants His people to be unified, but when Christians in the same church start fighting with one another, it can ruin their church. The more unified we are, the stronger we are.

Application: The Holy Spirit is a million times more powerful than any evil spirit from Satan. That's why the Bible says, "The Spirit who lives in you is greater than the spirit who lives in the world" (1 John 4:4).

The Pharisees Request a Sign from Jesus
Matthew 12:38-45

One day some religious teachers and Pharisees asked Jesus to show them a miraculous sign to prove that He was from God. Jesus had performed many miracles already, healings in particular, and the Pharisees had surely heard the reports and even witnessed some themselves. So they were probably asking for something even more spectacular, like fire falling from the sky or the Sea of Galilee being divided in two.

Jesus replied that their request showed how evil and faithless they were, but then promised them a spectacular miraculous sign: Just as Jonah was in the belly of a great fish for three days and nights and came back to life, so He would spend three days and nights inside the earth and come back to life! That would prove beyond all doubt that Jesus was from God, because He was dead and only God could bring Him back to life! No magician could pull that off!

Jesus knew, however, that even after He was resurrected, the Pharisees and religious teachers would not believe in Him. Hoping to bring them to their senses, He told them what would happen when they stood before God's judgment seat. God would assemble the people of Nineveh who repented at Jonah's preaching, and they would condemn those who rejected Jesus. Additionally, God would bring before His judgment seat the Queen of Sheba, who was so spiritually hungry that she journeyed hundreds of miles to hear Solomon's God-given wisdom. She also would condemn the Pharisees and religious teachers for rejecting Christ. Both she and the people of Nineveh demonstrated an openness to the truth, and were convinced of the truth with much less proof than that which God had granted to those to whom Jesus was speaking.

Finally, Jesus compared the people of His time to a demon-possessed person who was temporarily delivered. After the demon had gone out, the person's condition improved and he was temporarily clean. But he then allowed the demon to come back into him, and this time that demon brought with him seven other more wicked demons. Consequently, the man became more wicked than he was previously.

This comparison has been proven universally true. Our own nation has experienced several periods of national repentance and revival, however, the effects are short-lived. After a period of years the nation slides back into sin, and the people become more sinful than those who lived before the last revival. We are praying for another revival in our nation, but there will be no lasting righteousness until God's kingdom comes.

 Q. Did you notice that Jesus claimed to be greater than both Jonah and Solomon? Isn't that an indication that He was prideful?

A. No, it's another indication that Jesus was God in the form of a human being. It would be prideful for any other human being to make such a claim. God, however, can't think too highly of Himself, because He is by far the greatest person ever. It would be impossible for Him to be guilty of pride.

Q. If a person is possessed by a demon or demons, but then becomes born again and delivered, according to what we just read, does he have to worry about becoming demon-possessed again?

A. A person who is born again has the Holy Spirit living inside him, and so he could never be demon-possessed and Spirit-born at the same time. The demons that formerly possessed him may come back to tempt him, but he can use God's Word, believing and obeying it, to resist them, and they will flee (see James 4:7). In the passage we just read, Jesus was making a comparison to describe the deteriorating spiritual condition of His generation. He wasn't trying to convey that every demon-possessed person who is delivered eventually becomes more demon-possessed.

Application: Today we learned about the varying receptivity of people to the truth. Entire cities sometimes collectively repent, while other, more spiritually privileged groups of people harden their hearts. How would you rate your city's or country's receptivity to the truth? Do you think the people are becoming more or less receptive?

Jesus' Mother and Brothers
Matthew 12:46-50

This short section in Matthew's Gospel serves as additional evidence that Jesus was God in the form of a human being. Although He had a mother, four half-brothers and at least two half-sisters, He did not think of them like you or I think of our mother, brothers, or sisters. We consider our relationships with them as special, and unlike what we share with any other people on earth. They're our own "flesh and blood." Jesus, however, considered Himself to be more closely related to those who, as He said, do the will of His Father in heaven. Had He been *only* a human being and not God, His reaction to the request of His mother and brothers to see Him could be considered thoughtless, uncaring, and even sinful. But because He was God, He spoke the pure truth, testifying that He had a closer, more important relationship with those who obeyed God than He did with His own mother and brothers.

At least two other points could be made about this short passage. When Jesus declared that His disciples had a relationship with Him that could be best compared to the relationships between family members, He endorsed the fact that family relationships ought to be the closest relationships among human beings. Again, notice that when He wanted to make a point about the closeness of His relationship with His disciples, He used a comparison of relationships within a family. He did not say, "Who are My favorite neighbors?" or, "Who are My best friends at school?" but, "Who is my mother? Who are my brothers?" (Matthew 12:48).

In our perverted and ungodly culture, many families are fragmented. Parents and children are alienated from one another; brothers and sisters hate each other. Families slowly drift apart as individual members seek deeper relationships elsewhere. That which God has intended to be an institution for building our closest relationships is often just a dormitory at best or a battleground at worst. But Christian families shouldn't be like that. God wants your closest relationships to be with your father, mother, sisters and brothers. It may sound hard to believe if you and your brother(s) and/ or sister(s) are enemies, but *God wants you to be very close friends*. Are you?

There is, however, one possible exception to this, also made clear in this short passage in Matthew's Gospel. Just as Jesus acknowledged that His relationships with His spiritual brothers were higher than His relationships with his physical brothers, the same is true for all followers of Christ. As Christians, we can and should have relationships with one another that transcend the best relationships that non-Christians have with their own family members. If some or all of your family members aren't Christians, you may well have closer relationships with people outside your family, people who are believers like you. This doesn't mean, however, that you should neglect your relationships with unsaved members of your family. Rather, you should love them with God's love, attempting to win them to Christ. And if all of your family members are saved, then you are doubly blessed to have such special relationships with people who are your physical *and* spiritual brothers and sisters!

Q. How would you describe your family and the relationships between members? Are you very close, close, not so close, drifting apart, or splintered? What could you do to improve the relationships within your family?

Q. How much time does your family spend doing things together? Do you think the amount of time you spend together is sufficient to build your closest relationships? Do the things you do together as a family truly contribute to drawing you closer to one another, or are they non-productive things, such as watching TV?

Application: As believers in Jesus, we are members of the most wonderful family in the world. We've got millions of brother and sisters in heaven and on earth, an awesome big brother named Jesus, and a Father who cares for us like no other!

Jesus Tells a Story About Different Soils
Matthew 13:1-23

The best way to teach is to take what a person already understands and relate it to what he needs to understand. For example, if a person didn't know what a donut was, you could explain it by saying that donuts are round with holes in the middle, like car tires, but small enough to hold with one hand. They taste something like bread, and often have sweet-tasting icing on top, and so on.

Jesus wanted His followers to understand certain spiritual principles, and He explained those principles using parables, stories that compared natural things with spiritual things. Jesus' parables were not only meant to help His followers understand spiritual concepts, they were also designed to hide those same truths from those who were not His followers. Jesus, of course, wants *everyone* to be His follower, but only those who *decide* to become His followers receive certain privileges, such as going to heaven in the future and understanding spiritual truths right now. Jesus said, "To those who are open to my teaching, more understanding will be given, and they will have an abundance of knowledge" (Matthew 13:12). But those people who weren't open to His teaching would be cursed to remain ignorant of wonderful spiritual truths.

This particular parable we just read explains why so many people who hear God's truth are not changed by it. Speaking to people who understood about planting seeds, growing plants and harvesting a crop, Jesus compared God's Word to seeds and people to four different types of soil. Just as a seed planted in good soil sprouts, grows and bears fruit, so God's Word planted in a receptive heart will produce a changed life. But the same seed planted in poor soil will never produce fruit. It's important to realize that in Jesus' story, the seed and the sower, unlike the soils, didn't change. The reason that some people are never saved has nothing to do with God and everything to do with people's receptivity.

Jesus first spoke of seeds falling on a footpath. The soil there was packed hard from people always walking on it, so the seeds couldn't penetrate. Jesus said that this soil represents people who don't understand the good news. The reason they don't understand it is not because they can't understand it, but because they *don't want to* understand it. Anyone, even a child, can understand that Jesus is the Son of God who died on the cross for his sins. And God certainly wouldn't hold someone responsible to understand something that is impossible for him to understand.

God's Word can't penetrate hardened hearts, and like the exposed seed that is quickly eaten by birds, so God's Word is snatched from hardened hearts by the devil. When that happens, a person who could have been born again remains unchanged.

The second type of soil Jesus spoke of was a shallow, thin layer over rocks. If you've ever planted anything in shallow soil, you can understand exactly what Jesus was talking about. The seed sprouts and the plant begins to grow, but when the sun shines, the shallow soil quickly dries, and the young plant withers and dies. This soil represents the person who enthusiastically receives the gospel at first, but when he faces trouble or persecution because of his new belief, his faith quickly dies. Most pastors and evangelists have seen a lot of people like that. Saving faith is a faith that perseveres no matter what. Every Christian will have his faith tested in difficulties and persecution, so hold fast to your faith.

In Jesus' third example, the seed fell on ground where thorn seeds had also been sown. The thorns ultimately dominated, and the little shoots from the good seeds were choked by the thorns and died. This represents a person who receives God's Word but doesn't make it his highest priority. Other things become more important, like making money. The good news about Jesus demands our utmost attention, because through it, Jesus calls us to be His devoted followers. You can't have a casual relationship with the Lord.

Finally, Jesus talked about the good soil where the seed sprouts, grows and produces fruit. Of the four types of soil, only this kind represents a person who is saved in the end. Only this kind produces fruit. Those fruits would include the fruit of the Spirit listed in the book of Galatians: love, joy, peace, patience, kindness, goodness, faithfulness, gentleness and self-control (see Galatians 5:22). It would also include the fruit of obedience.

If you've become a true follower of Jesus, you can rejoice that you are good soil! Aren't you glad you are?

 Q. According to this parable, will every Christian produce the same amount of fruit?

A. No, some produce thirty, some sixty, and some one hundred fold. Additionally, fruit is something that gradually ripens, and every Christian can grow in the fruit of the Spirit. Some of us still have some green apples, but at least they're apples!

It is also important to understand that if a person has no fruit at all, he is not really saved. Every true Christian will bear some fruit.

Q. Even though all true Christians could be classified as good soil, do you think there's any possibility of our soil becoming like any of the other three kinds?

A. Yes, there is that possibility, and we should guard ourselves from allowing it to happen. The writer of the book of Hebrews said, "Take care, brethren, lest there should be in any one of you an evil, unbelieving heart, in falling away from the living God" (Hebrews 3:12, NASB). This warns us that good soil can become bad soil.

Application: The most wonderful thing is when we meet an unsaved person who is receptive, like the good soil of this parable. Let's pray today for God to direct us to encounter people like that, so we can share the good news with them.

Mustard Seeds and Satan's Weeds
Matthew 13:24-43

The people who weren't Jesus' followers heard Him tell many parables, but they didn't understand what He was talking about. Jesus, however, would always explain the parables to His followers later on because they were open to the truth (see Mark 4:34). Aren't you glad that the Bible records many of Jesus' explanations so that His modern-day followers can also understand His parables?

Today we read the parable of the wheat and the tares. Tares are weeds that look very much like wheat, but when the wheat begins to produce grain, the tares produce nothing. From God's perspective, there are only two categories of people in the earth: "the people of the Kingdom" who are the followers of Jesus, and "the people who belong to the evil one" who are not followers of Jesus. Although saved and unsaved people look a lot alike, what differentiates them is their fruit, or lifestyles. True believers in Jesus act like it, just as true wheat produces grain.

At present, God is allowing both saved and unsaved to live side by side. But that will not always be the case. At the end of the world the two categories will be separated, and the unsaved will be gathered by God's angels and thrown into hell where there will be "weeping and gnashing of teeth" (Matthew 13:42). The godly people, however, will live together forever in God's kingdom with brand new glorified bodies. Perhaps Jesus was literally referring to those new bodies when He said we will "shine like the sun" (Matthew 13:43). (And you thought you were a bright kid now!)

Two other parables we read today illustrate the future outcome of what Jesus began two thousand years ago. Both parables are about things that grow large after a small start. A mustard seed is so tiny that it's difficult to see without a magnifying glass, but it grows into a huge plant. So God's kingdom began very small, with just Jesus and a few disciples. But it has been growing ever since then, and one day there will be nothing other than God's kingdom. And, only a little bit of yeast is added to bread dough to make it rise, but that little yeast permeates the entire lump, ultimately affecting the whole loaf of bread. So, too, one day Jesus' influence will affect the entire world. That is the day we're waiting for!

Q. Can you imagine living in a world where everyone is obedient to God and has a glorified body? Can you think of some things people now use that won't be necessary in God's kingdom?

A. Door locks, guns, burglar alarms, band-aids, and deodorant to name a few!

Q. Jesus never once referred to people as Christians and non-Christians. In what we read today, He defined people as either being "people of the kingdom" or people "who belong to the evil one," evildoers or godly (see Matthew 13:38,41,43). What do these terms tell us about who really is a Christian and who is not?

A. They tell us that people who are evildoers and claim to be Christians are not really Christians.

Application: Most people think that things will always be the way they are right now. But what we read today from the lips of God's Son indicates that is not the case. The wisest thing anyone can do is to get ready for the eternal future, regardless of what anyone else thinks. Although Christians may be in the minority right now, one day we'll be a 100% majority.

Hidden Treasures, Priceless Pearls and Fishing Nets
Matthew 13:44-50

In the ancient land of Israel where Jesus lived and taught, on occasion, people accidentally found hidden treasures that had been buried hundreds of years beforehand by some wealthy member of a forgotten civilization. Naturally, if the fortunate finder didn't own the land where he found the treasure, he would attempt to buy it, thus gaining the land and, more importantly, the treasure. If the purchaser thought the treasure was valuable enough, he might sell everything he owned to have enough money to purchase the field. It would be worth it, however, because he would regain all he sold and more, once the treasure was in his hands.

A place in the kingdom of heaven is like that because it is the most valuable thing anyone could possess, and it would be worth giving up anything and everything else to gain it. People who truly believe the gospel, who believe there is a place in heaven to gain, value their salvation above all else, and it shows in their lives. They repent of their sins and will give up anything that they know might keep them out of heaven. Their relationship with Jesus is the most important thing. It is their hidden treasure and their priceless pearl!

I'm sure you easily understood the parable of the fishing net, so there's no need for my explanation. However, this would be a good time to learn something about interpreting Jesus' parables. Usually, each parable serves to illustrate one primary point, and to try to find spiritual significance in every detail of a parable is dangerous. The point of the parable of the fishing net is that there are two categories of people in the world: the wicked and the godly. One day they will be separated, and the wicked will be cast into hell. That's what Jesus wanted to teach through this parable. There is no spiritual significance to the net, the beach or the crates mentioned by Jesus, and we shouldn't look for any.

Q. What would you be willing to take as a trade for your salvation?
A. If you answered, "A billion dollars," or named anything else, you probably don't really believe the gospel. True believers value their salvation above all else. There is nothing they would take in trade for it.

Application: When the men of the first two parables realized what could be theirs, they did whatever it took to gain their desire. Following Jesus does cost us something, and many people decide not to follow Jesus because they value other things more highly than eternal life, like respect from other people, or their wealth that they don't want to share. We should value what God values, because He knows what is truly valuable.

Jesus Calms a Storm
Mark 4:35-41

This story is a good illustration of what it means to trust God's Word. Jesus told His disciples, "Let's cross to the other side of the lake" (Mark 4:35), speaking of the Sea of Galilee. At that point, they knew it was His will to go to the other side, and Jesus expected them to believe what He said.

However, after they launched out, they soon found themselves in a fierce storm, and waves were breaking over the edge of the boat, filling it with water. Amazingly, Jesus was taking a nap! He obviously believed, unlike His disciples, that they were going to make it to the other side of the lake.

Little children are often scared over things that their parents, who have a higher knowledge, aren't the least bit concerned about. We are often like those fearful little children and God is always like the confident parent. Like little children, we should look at our Father's confidence and have faith. When we trust Him, we can sleep even when things are going badly, because we know God has everything under control. Fear and anxiety are what keep people up all night long.

Jesus' disciples should have followed His example, believing His Word in spite of their predicament. They should have realized that if Jesus was asleep, He must not have been worried, and so there was no cause for them to be concerned either. They were, however, petrified over what was happening to them, and finally woke Jesus, who immediately calmed the wind and waves with a rebuke. Can you imagine seeing such a violent storm immediately stop?

After rebuking the wind and waves, Jesus then rebuked His disciples, asking why they were so afraid and why they had no faith in Him. *God expects us to trust Him.*

Jesus' disciples were too stunned by what they'd just seen to attempt to answer Him, and probably missed what He was hoping they'd learn. But they would soon have another chance to use their faith against some wind out in the middle of the Sea of Galilee, only next time, Jesus wouldn't be in the boat with them! God is a great teacher!

Q. Certainly Jesus was always in the center of His Father's will, and was surely led by the Holy Spirit to cross over the Sea of Galilee that evening. And certainly God knew there would be a violent storm that would threaten their lives as Jesus and His disciples crossed. So why do you suppose God led Jesus to cross the Sea of Galilee when He did?

A. We don't know for sure, because the Bible doesn't say. However, we can read other stories in the Bible where God led His own people into difficulties with the purpose of delivering them. He wants us to learn to trust Him, and times of trial are great times to trust God! God may have been teaching the disciples a lesson about faith, as well as glorifying His Son before them.

Q. When you face difficulties that you can't control, what do you think God would want you to do?

A. He wants us to trust Him, taking Him at His Word. Of course, unless we know what He has said, we have nothing to trust. That is why it is so worthwhile to know the Bible. That is the only place we can find God's promises.

 Application: The only time we should worry about our circumstances is when God is worried about them. But since God never worries, we should never worry either!

55

Jesus Delivers a Demon-Possessed Man
Mark 5:1-20

As we read yesterday, not only did Jesus have authority over the wind, commanding it to stop, He also had authority over evil spirits. Remember John the Baptist said that God had given Jesus "authority over everything" (John 3:35). The demons that possessed the man we've just read about were obviously very powerful, to the point of being able to empower the man with the strength to break chains. However, they were no match for Jesus. In fact, all the evil spirits in the world together don't have a fraction of the power that God has.

The demons who inhabited this man drove him to do strange things. He lived in a cemetery, wandering through the tombs night and day without any clothes, screaming and cutting himself with stones. That shows us how wicked the devil and his evil spirits are. Because people are created in God's image, Satan loves to see that image marred. If you've ever had an enemy draw a mustache on a photograph of yourself, you have some idea what I mean. Satan would love it if every person would become demon-possessed and act like that man did.

Notice how afraid the demons were of Jesus. When Jesus came ashore, the demon-possessed man ran to meet Him and fell down before Him. Was that act the man's own doing or was he being motivated by the demons? Probably it was the demons, because it's unlikely the man had any idea of who Jesus was. The main demon, however, named Legion, knew Jesus was the Son of God, and confessed it through the man's shrieking voice, begging Jesus not to torture him. Later, all the demons repeatedly begged Jesus not to send them "to some distant place" (Mark 5:10). Those demons were scared to death of Jesus, because they knew who He was and what He could do! They were bowing before Him hoping for some mercy!

Also notice that Jesus asked the main demon inside the man what his name was. This is another indication that although Jesus was God, when He became a man He laid aside His attribute of omniscience, or knowing everything. God the Father, of course, knew what the demon's name was.

I don't know why Jesus gave the demons permission to go into the nearby herd of pigs. Perhaps it was just to display God's great power. Can you imagine seeing a herd of 2,000 serenely grazing pigs suddenly going crazy, stampeding to their deaths down a hill into a lake? This also seems to indicate that at least 2,000 demons were previously living inside one man. Either demons can squash really close together, or, more likely, there is no such thing as space in the spiritual realm.

This story should fill us with awe at the mercy, goodness and power of the Lord. One day in heaven we'll meet the man who was delivered, and rejoice with him for all that God has done for us. Not all of us were demon-possessed before our salvation, but all of us have been delivered from Satan's power over our lives.

Q. Should Christians be afraid of demons?

A. Absolutely not, because demons are afraid of Jesus who lives in all Christians.

Q. Wasn't it wrong of Jesus to allow the demons to go into someone else's pigs? Surely the owners were upset over the loss of 2,000 pigs.

A. Actually, Jesus' allowing the demons to enter the pigs serves as another proof that He was God, because God owns everything, including those 2,000 pigs. God can do anything He desires with people's private property, because it's more His property than theirs! Additionally, the Jews were forbidden in the Law to eat pork, and so perhaps the owners of those pigs were breaking God's law, and what Jesus allowed was an act of judgment.

Finally, this story also teaches us the value that God places on people, who are created in His image, compared to animals, who are not. One man is worth much more than 2,000 pigs! This is a message to our perverted society, which allows the killing of baby humans but forbids the killing of certain animals.

Application: The people of the region who saw the formerly-possessed man were filled with fear, and rather than bowing before the Son of God and requesting forgiveness for their sins, they begged Him to leave them alone. Jesus sadly granted them their request, but instructed the delivered man to return to his friends with his testimony. This is a picture of the whole world today. They really don't want Jesus around, but Jesus, hoping that they will soften, has sent us, those He's delivered from Satan's power, to tell others what God has done for us.

Jesus Raises a Dead Girl and Heals a Sick Woman
Mark 5:21-43

In both of the healing stories we read today, faith was a factor. Jairus believed that if Jesus would lay His hands upon his dying daughter, she would live. His faith was evident from his actions. First, he journeyed to Jesus who was by the seashore. And second, he made his way through a crowd, fell at Jesus' feet, and publicly begged Him to come and lay His hands on his daughter, stating that she would live if He would. Only someone who had faith would do what Jairus did.

Also, when messengers from Jairus' house told him that his daughter had died, we read, "Jesus ignored their comments and said to Jairus, O Don't be afraid. Just trust me'" (Mark 5:36). Luke's Gospel records Jesus saying, "Don't be afraid. Just trust me, and she will be all right" (Luke 8:50). Naturally, Jairus was tempted to be afraid that his daughter would not be raised, but Jesus encouraged him to keep on believing. Obviously, Jairus' faith played a key part in his daughter's being raised from the dead.

The faith of the woman who had suffered for twelve years with internal bleeding also played an important role in her healing. Jesus plainly told her that it was her faith that had made her well (see Mark 5:34). Her faith was also evident by her actions. She, too, pressed through a crowd in order to touch Jesus. She had been thinking to herself, "If I can just touch his clothing, I will be healed" (Mark 5:28).

This helps us to understand better why more people aren't divinely healed today. If more of us truly believed, more of us would be healed. But we have been brain-washed (or better said, "brain-dirtied") to believe that God only chooses to heal some and not others. As a result, we doubt that we are among those whom God wants to heal, and our lack of faith stops our healing.

But this idea is proven to be biblically unsound by what we've just read. Obviously, healing is available to all who will believe, because the woman with internal bleeding was healed by Jesus *even before He knew who had touched Him*. He realized that power had gone out of Him for healing, but didn't know *who* had been healed. Faith drew His healing power out, and it was available for anyone and everyone! The reason that woman believed Jesus would heal her was because she heard He never turned anyone away who came to Him requesting healing. She had heard that everyone who touched Him was healed.

This same story also disproves the idea that if it is God's will for someone to be healed, He will automatically heal that person. It was obviously God's will for the woman we just read about to be healed, but she wasn't healed until she did something: she put her faith into action. It was and is Jesus' will for everyone to be healed, but they have to do something. They have to put faith into action. It is just the same as salvation. God wants everyone to be saved, but not everyone is automatically saved. People have to believe the gospel.

One reason more preachers in America don't teach this truth is because they know it offends proud people who refuse to acknowledge that their lack of faith stops them from being healed. They would rather put the blame on God and His supposed will not to heal everyone.

Even people who believe that God wants them to be healed aren't always healed, because their faith is often very weak. I've personally experienced weak faith. But I would rather admit my weakness than say that God wants me to remain sick, contradicting His many healing promises. And I would rather have a weak faith that can grow stronger than be stuck with no faith for the rest of my life. And finally, I'm sure God would prefer weak or wavering faith over no faith at all!

Divine healing is a subject upon which we need to remain balanced. We shouldn't think that God condemns us for our lack of faith, or that He is opposed to our seeking a doctor's help. Jesus didn't condemn the sick woman in today's story for previously going to a doctor. But praise God that Jesus can fix *anything* doctors can't! Let's trust Him more!

 Q. According to something we've read today, is there any time when we should ignore people's comments?

A. Jesus ignored the negative reports that the messengers brought from Jairus' home. When anyone says something that contradicts what God has said, it's good to ignore it. We don't want to be influenced to doubt. Perhaps that is also the reason why Jesus cleared all the mourners from Jairus' house before He raised Jairus' daughter. Their weeping and wailing could have influenced Jairus and his wife to doubt, drawing their attention away from Jesus' promise to change their sad situation.

Q. Why do you suppose that Jesus commanded Jairus and his wife not to tell anyone what had happened?

A. Because Jesus already had more publicity than He needed. This also indicates that Jesus didn't raise and heal the little girl to prove that He was God's Son. He did it because He loved that family and wanted to help them.

Q. Why did Jesus instruct the parents to give their daughter some food?

A. Because her body needed nourishment, and Jesus was concerned that her parents, in their excitement, might overlook her need. Jesus really cares about people.

⊙ Application: Today we read about a man who had something restored that he'd cherished for twelve years (see Luke 8:42) but lost. And we read about a woman who had something removed that she wanted to be rid of for twelve years. Jesus intervened in both situations at the same time, restoring and removing, according to the need. He is wonderful!

The Blind and Mute are Healed
Matthew 9:27-34

According to Matthew's Gospel, these two miracles occurred right after the miracles we read about yesterday. Perhaps within the space of only one hour, Jesus healed a woman who had bled internally for twelve years, raised a young girl from the dead, opened the eyes of two blind men and cast a demon out of a man who had previously been unable to speak! No wonder the crowds who were with Him that day marveled. Yet the Pharisees, unable to improve upon their old explanation, continued to accuse Jesus of using Satan's power to cast out demons.

As we read yesterday's two miracles, we learned that faith was a key ingredient in both instances. Today's first miracle, the instant healing of two blind men, was also credited to faith. Jesus asked the blind men, "Do you believe I can make you see?" and they responded, "Yes, Lord, we do" (Matthew 9:28). What do you think would have happened if they had said, "No, Lord, we doubt it"? Obviously they would not have been healed, because Jesus then said, "*Because of your faith*, it will happen" (Matthew 9:29, emphasis added). If they had not had faith, they would not have been healed, even though it was obviously God's will for them to be healed, because they *were* healed.

This proves again that God's will doesn't always automatically come to pass. As I mentioned yesterday, this truth makes proud people angry, because they would rather put the blame on God, claiming that it's not His will for them to be healed, rather than admit that their faith is weak or nonexistent. However, Jesus said, "If you believe, you will receive whatever you ask for in prayer" (Matthew 21:22). There are scores of examples in the Bible of people doing just that and receiving healing.

The faith of the two blind men was not only evident by what they said, it was evident by what they did. When they heard that Jesus was passing by, they followed along behind Him, shouting, "Son of David, have mercy on us!" It wouldn't have been easy to follow along behind Jesus without sight. Perhaps someone was guiding them. Notice also that, before crowds of people, they kept shouting to Jesus for mercy. They were obviously convinced He could open their eyes, and weren't ashamed to publicly and repeatedly ask Him. They were bold and persistent in their faith, to the point of going right inside the house where Jesus was staying! They would not be denied! True faith is always determined, and when people have strong faith, they don't quit.

Q. Nothing is mentioned in today's reading about the man who was mute having any faith. Is there any indication of his faith in the story?

A. Yes. The man must have possessed some amount of faith, or he wouldn't have cooperated with his friends who brought him to Jesus. It is also true that Jesus did sometimes heal people who apparently didn't demonstrate any outward signs of faith. Those cases could be categorized as "gifts of healing" mentioned in 1 Corinthians 12:9 (NASB). They operate as the Holy Spirit wills, and are sovereign acts of healing by God that don't necessarily require faith on the part of the person being healed.

Application: You may not need to receive healing, but perhaps you are facing some other difficulty in which you could apply faith in God's Word. If so, imitate the faith of the two blind men we just read about. Be bold and persistent, and your faith will bring the miracle you need!

Jesus Finds Little Faith in His Hometown
Mark 6:1-6a

After reading the past two days about people who received miracles from Jesus through their faith, today we read about an entire town that, for the most part, missed out on receiving any miracles from Jesus because of their lack of faith. This once again proves that God's will coming to pass in our lives is dependent on our faith. Naturally, Jesus wanted to bring blessings to the people in the town where He had spent most of His life. The Bible, however, said that He couldn't do any mighty miracles there because of the people's unbelief (see Mark 6:5). This clearly indicates that He desired to do mighty miracles there. Notice also that the Bible said Jesus *couldn't*, not *wouldn't* do any mighty miracles there. It wasn't because He didn't want to perform mighty miracles for them, it was because He was actually limited by their unbelief.

All Christians know this is true concerning salvation, so why don't they realize that it's true concerning anything else we receive from God? It is God's will for everyone to be saved, but God's will doesn't come to pass in a person's life unless that person believes the gospel. That means there are people in hell right now whom God wanted to be in heaven. Likewise, if a person is ill, we should not conclude that it's God's will for that person to remain ill. God expects us to believe His Word, but so few do when it comes to healing because they've been wrongly taught that it may not be God's will for them to be healed. Thus they have no faith for healing, and Jesus is hindered by their unbelief.

Even when they pray for healing, many Christians confess their unbelief, saying, "Lord, if it is Your will, please heal me." They are admitting that they aren't sure what God's will is, which makes it *impossible* for them to have faith. Faith can only be born from God's promises. Only when God's will is not revealed is it appropriate to say, "If it is Your will." Otherwise, we're saying to God, "Lord, I know what You've promised, but in case You were lying about it, I don't want to hold You to what You said." The Bible says, "Are any among you sick?...prayer offered in faith will heal the sick, and the Lord will make them well" (James 5:14-15). How can any Bible-believing Christian argue with that?

The reason the majority of people in Nazareth didn't believe in Jesus was because they had known Him and His family for decades. They knew He was a very good person, but they had no idea that He was God's Son. They refused to believe in Him, even though they had heard about His miracles in other places and heard Him speak before them with great wisdom. Thankfully, however, there were a few people in Nazareth who apparently had some faith, but who, as the original Greek indicates, had only minor ailments. Jesus laid His hands on them and healed them. But for the majority of people in Nazareth, Jesus was "amazed at their unbelief" (Mark 6:6).

 Q. How do you think Jesus feels about the lack of faith in people today?

A. He is probably amazed at everyone who doesn't believe in Him because of the overwhelming evidence that He was a historical person whose life story is accurately recorded in the Bible. However, Jesus once wondered if anyone would have any faith when He returns, saying, "When the Son of Man comes, will He find faith on the earth?" (Luke 18:8, NASB).

Application: Could it be that you may have hindered Jesus from working more in your life by your unbelief? In prayer today, ask the Lord is this is so, and if it is, ask Him to help you grow in faith.

Jesus Heals a Lame Man at the Pool of Bethesda
John 5:1-15

Praise God for what Jesus did for this lame man at the pool of Bethesda! He had been suffering for thirty-eight years from his sickness, and perhaps had been unable to walk all that time. But he still had hope of being healed. He'd heard that an angel of the Lord would occasionally stir the waters at the pool of Bethesda. Afterwards, whoever stepped into the water first was healed of whatever ailed him. So the lame man joined many other sick people who sat around the pool each day, watching and waiting for the troubling of the waters. He had been present a number of times when the waters were previously stirred, but others who had more mobility reached the water before he did. So he kept on waiting for another opportunity, and hoped that the next time the waters were stirred, someone would care enough to help him be the first to get in.

Angels, of course, don't work independently of the Lord, and so we can be sure that the only time an angel stirred the Bethesda waters was when God sent him. So why didn't God send an angel every five minutes to stir the water so that everyone could be healed? Can we conclude from this story that it wasn't God's will for everyone there to be healed?

Actually, all the sick people at Bethesda could have been healed without ever stepping into the pool of Bethesda, because God promised health for every obedient Israelite in His covenant with them. God said in Exodus 23:25 (NASB), "But you shall serve the Lord your God, and He will bless your bread and your water; and I will remove sickness from your midst." In Deuteronomy 7:12-15, God promised the Israelites that, if they obeyed Him faithfully, He would remove all sickness from them. If any of the sick people at Bethesda had believed what God had promised, acting in faith, they would have been healed. Even if they had been disobedient to the Lord, thus not meeting the conditions of their covenant with God, they could have repented, received forgiveness, and then received healing. Anyone who disagrees with that is saying that God is a liar, and that His promises can't be trusted. It's true: *He promised health to obedient Israelites!*

By occasionally sending an angel to stir the waters of the pool of Bethesda, perhaps God was also trying to stir up His people by way of reminder that He was still in the healing business. Every time someone was healed, God was sending a message to all Israel that He'd spoken centuries earlier to their ancestors: "I am the Lord who heals you" (Exodus 15:26). Surely God didn't want all those sick people waiting at the pool to think His mercy was limited, or that His love was greater for sick people who were more watchful and mobile than other sick people. Surely He wasn't trying to encourage a selfish competition that would make the majority of suffering people continual losers. No, the God whom the Bible says shows no partiality (see Deut. 10:17; Rom. 2:11; Gal. 2:6) wanted His covenant people to know that He was their healer. And He was not choosing to heal specific ones and choosing not to heal specific others, because *anyone* who got into the water first was healed. Individual responsibility was a factor.

The same God who occasionally sent an angel, sent His Son one day to the same pool. And just as when the angel visited, only one person was healed that day as well. Did Jesus want to convey to the sick people present that He loved only one person enough to heal him? No, like His Father, He was trying to show them that He had the power to heal them all, hoping that all would trust Him for their healing. Numerous times in the four Gospels, we can read about Jesus healing *everyone* who came to Him requesting healing. This healing at the pool of Bethesda was an advertisement for Jesus and an encouragement for the rest to trust Him and be healed. This healing should encourage us today, because the Bible says that "Jesus Christ is the same yesterday, today, and forever" (Hebrews 13:8).

Q. Was this lame man at the pool of Bethesda healed through his faith? A. No, this man, unlike so many others whom Jesus healed, was not healed through his faith. Here is the evidence: First, the man was not seeking Jesus, rather, Jesus found him. Second, Jesus said nothing to him about his faith healing him as He often did with others. And third, the lame man had no idea who Jesus was, even after he'd been healed. When he first conversed with Jesus, he wasn't looking to Him as someone who could heal him. In his mind, Jesus was no different than any other person present.

This healing, then, is an example of a "gift of healing" working through Jesus. Gifts of healings operate as the Holy Spirit wills (see 1 Cor. 12:11), and faith is not necessarily a requirement for the sick person to be healed. It is a sovereign act of God.

Q. Jesus later told the man He'd healed, "Stop sinning, or something even worse may happen to you" (John 5:14). What can we learn from that statement?

A. We can learn that sin can lead to God's judgment. If the healed man didn't repent and quit sinning, there was the possibility that he might wind up worse than he previously was. God is a loving God, but He is also holy. He will punish evildoers. We must be careful, however, that we don't conclude that all sick people are being punished for their sins. Then we would be guilty of passing judgment.

Application: The people of the world often need signs from God to open their hearts to the gospel. Let's pray today that God would mercifully grant that more signs and wonders would be shown to the unbelieving world. Also that even people who have no faith would be healed, that more attention would be given to the good news of Jesus Christ.

Jesus' Special Relationship with God the Father
John 5:16-47

Rather than rejoicing over the healing of a man who had been lame for thirty-eight years, the Jewish leaders found fault with the man who had been healed, claiming that he was breaking the fourth commandment by carrying his pallet on the Sabbath. They also began harassing Jesus, accusing Him of also breaking the Sabbath by healing someone that day.

Jesus responded by truthfully and clearly stating that God was His Father, thus He was God's Son. Although God is perfect in holiness, some of the commandments He's given to human beings don't apply to Himself. For example, your parents might have a rule that you be in bed by nine o'clock each night, but you can't accuse them of doing wrong if they go to bed later than nine! Some of their rules apply only to you, and not to them.

The same is true of God. He commanded the Israelites to offer animal sacrifices on a regular basis, but that is not something God does! And no one can rightfully accuse Him of sinning because He doesn't offer sacrifices. By the same token, although God commanded the Israelites not to work on the Sabbath, that didn't mean it would be a sin for God to work that day! Because Jesus was God, He could work on any Sabbath He chose. That's why He responded to the Jewish leaders by saying, "My Father never stops working, so why should I?" Although God rested on the seventh day after the six days of creation, perhaps He hasn't rested since!

The Jewish leaders recognized that Jesus, in calling God His Father, was claiming to be equal with God, and hated Him all the more. But Jesus didn't back down from His claim. Rather, He expanded on it, showing that He had a unique relationship with God the Father that no one else ever had or ever will have.

Unlike any other person who had ever lived, Jesus perfectly obeyed God the Father. He was acting as the Father's perfect representative on earth, and they shared an intimate relationship. It was the Father who gave Jesus the ability to teach with amazing wisdom and work miracles, and those signs proved to all that He was God's Son.

God the Father, who is the only one who can give physical or spiritual life, determined and decreed that it would be only through Jesus that anyone could receive new physical life and be resurrected after he had died. Jesus will one day exercise His God-given authority to raise the dead by resurrecting everyone who has ever lived. Also, by the Father's decision, only through Jesus can anyone receive spiritual life and be born again. And just as physically dead people will one day be resurrected when Jesus speaks, so spiritually dead people are hearing Jesus' words and being spiritually reborn.

The Father has also appointed Jesus as judge of all people, and one day everyone will stand before Him to give an account of his or her life. He will determine who goes to heaven and who goes to hell. His judgment will be perfectly just because it will be in perfect accordance with the Father's judgment. Obviously, as Jesus said, God the Father wants Jesus to be equally honored with Himself. In light of such incredible claims, we can only conclude that Jesus was either God's divine Son or He was a very deranged and evil man.

In light of His amazing teaching and the miracles that God did through Him, however, the only intelligent choice of the two alternatives is that Jesus was indeed God's only Son!

Q. Jesus said that the Scriptures pointed to Him (see John 5:39), and specifically referred to the writings of Moses (see John 5:46). Can you think of any scriptures in the first five books of the Bible that speak of Jesus?

A. First, the entire system of sacrificing animals to atone for sins pointed to Jesus' sacrificial accomplishment on the cross as the Lamb of God. Second, the establishment of a high priest who stood between God and man, interceding on behalf of sinners, points to Jesus as our High Priest who reconciled us to God by His death. Third, God promised in the first books of the Bible that the Messiah would be a descendant of Abraham, Isaac, Jacob and Judah. And fourth, referring to the Messiah, Moses spoke prophetically of another prophet of great authority whom God would raise up (see Deuteronomy 18:18-19; John 1:21; Acts 3:22-23).

Application: Jesus plainly stated that anyone who listens to His message and believes that God sent Him has eternal life. When people do believe, they will pass from the realm of death into the realm of life, and will not be condemned for their sins (see John 5:24-25). That's good news! Does it apply to you?

Jesus Sends Out His Twelve Apostles
Matthew 9:35-10:39

Because Jesus' love was so great, He wanted to serve everyone. He was limited, however, because He was only one human being. There were so many sick and demon-possessed people, and so many who needed to hear the good news and repent of their sins. So Jesus instructed His disciples to pray that God would send out more workers, and God answered their prayer by sending them!

Before Jesus sent them out to minister throughout the towns of Israel, He supernaturally equipped them for their job, giving them authority to cast out demons and heal every kind of disease and illness. He specifically commanded them to heal the sick, raise the dead, cure those with leprosy and cast out demons. Jesus knew that miracles would get people's attention to listen to His disciples' message, just as in His own ministry (see Luke 9:6).

Their message was one of repentance (see Mark 6:12-13), which is not always a popular message, but nevertheless is an integral part of the gospel. Jesus knew that many people would reject His disciples, and He didn't want them wasting their time trying repeatedly to reach unreceptive people. If a town or village didn't receive them, they were to shake the dust off their feet and journey to another one. If God loves everyone, why should anyone have two opportunities to receive Christ until everyone has had at least one?

Jesus' disciples weren't allowed to take any money or extra provisions with them. That would teach them to rely on God to supply their needs, and also provide motivation for them not to stay long in places where their message wasn't received, places where no one would feed or shelter them.

Jesus knew that His disciples would face the same persecutions He'd encountered. They would be slandered, hated and even killed. Some would face martyrdom because their own family members would betray them. We have no record in the Bible of this happening to any of the twelve, so perhaps it occurred after Jesus' ascension into heaven. With the exception of Judas and John, it is thought that all of Jesus' disciples died a martyr's death.

Perhaps the most challenging words in Jesus' commission were the standards He set for every one of His followers. He expects our fully committed allegiance. Our loyalty to Him should supersede the loyalty we have for the people we love the most, including our parents and children. Jesus knew that as a result of His coming, some households would be divided over Him. Unbelieving family members would turn against believing members.

But true believers will not compromise their faith just to please their loved ones, because they love Jesus the most.

Incidentally, if Jesus wasn't God, He was a horrible person, because only God would have a right to demand a higher love and devotion to Himself than what we show for our own families. Jesus said, "If you cling to your life, you will lose it; but if you give it up for me, you will find it" (Matthew 10:39). He wasn't talking about physically dying as a martyr, but of giving up our own agenda in order to obey Him, another way of describing repentance. If anyone refuses to repent, he will miss out on experiencing life as God intended and miss out on eternal life. But whoever will give his life to Jesus, submitting to Him, that person will experience a life that he was created to live, one that is enriched by God forever. Aren't you glad you've given your life to Jesus?

Q. Jesus instructed His disciples to avoid preaching to Gentiles and Samaritans, ministering only to Jews (see Matthew 10:5-6). Why is that? Doesn't God love non-Jewish people?

A. We don't know the answer for sure, but we can be certain that it wasn't because God didn't or doesn't love non-Jewish people. Jesus loves everyone and died for the whole world. Perhaps Jesus sent His disciples to minister to Jews because they would most likely be more receptive than other groups, having a faith in the Old Testament that promised them a Messiah. They would also be more likely to receive a message from Jesus' Jewish messengers. God wants everyone to hear the gospel, and the quickest way for that to happen is to win the most receptive people who can then reach others. Jesus followed this strategy in His own ministry, ministering to Jews and then sending out some who believed. Later, Jesus commissioned His disciples to preach to all the ethnic groups of the world (see Matthew 28:19).

Q. Jesus said that we are to acknowledge Him before others, also saying that if we deny Him publicly, He would deny us before the Father. Does that mean there is no hope for us going to heaven if we, under pressure, say that we don't know Jesus?

A. No, because God is merciful. No true Christian would deny Jesus at a time when he wasn't under pressure, but a true believer might yield to the temptation to deny the Lord if his life was in danger. Under pressure, Peter denied the Lord three times, but Jesus forgave, restored and used him greatly afterwards.

Application: Today there is a need more than ever for workers to be sent into the harvest, as the world's population is more than six billion people. That is five billion, eight hundred million more people than the number that lived on the earth when Jesus sent out His apostles. Pray today that God will send out more laborers who are supernaturally equipped to spread the gospel.

John the Baptist is Martyred
Mark 6:14-29

Herod Antipas, the man who ordered the execution of John the Baptist, was the son of a murderer. His father was Herod the Great, who had once killed his own wife and two of his sons to preserve his power. It was Herod the Great who had also ordered the killing of all the male babies in Bethlehem in an attempt to kill Jesus. With such an example set before him as a child, it is no wonder that Herod Antipas was a wicked man. He had fallen in love with his half-brother's wife, Herodias, who also happened to be his niece, and she had fallen in love with him. So she divorced Herod Antipas's brother and married him.

John the Baptist, a preacher of righteousness, had declared that what Herod and his new wife had done was a sin. Herodias hated John as a result of this and wanted him killed. But Herod's conscience would not allow him to order John's execution, and so he only had John put in prison as a favor to his selfish wife. He was under conviction for his sin and knew that John did not deserve to die.

Herod, however, made a foolish public oath to Herodias's daughter, offering her anything she desired after she pleased him with a dance during his birthday party. Her mother instructed her to request John the Baptist's head on a tray. Herod was trapped by his promise, and so he reluctantly ordered John's beheading. A Roman soldier immediately carried out the gruesome task, and gave Herodias's daughter John's head on a tray. She in turn gave it to Herodias. What a sickening sight! Think how evil someone would have to be to desire such a thing!

Although this is a sad story, for John it had a happy ending, because he was in heaven, enjoying God's presence, even before Herodias had possession of his head! The people I feel sorry for are Herod and Herodias, who, unless they experienced a repentance the Bible doesn't record, have been in hell now for almost two thousand years.

Q. Is it possible for murderers to get into heaven?
A. Yes, but only if they repent and are saved by faith. Remember that Moses, David and Paul could all be considered murderers. However, any

murderer who dies without repenting will spend eternity in hell. The apostle John wrote, "You know that murderers don't have eternal life within them" (1 John 3:15).

Q. At present, the United States government says that it is legal for women to murder their babies before they're born. Because it's legal, does that make it O.K.?

A. No, because God has always said that murder is wrong. Murder is perhaps the highest expression of selfishness that exists, and murdering one's own child is the most debased murder a person could commit. There are millions of mothers and fathers in America who are child-murderers. Their only hope of escaping hell is to repent and believe in Jesus. Praise God that He offers them forgiveness.

Application: Herod Antipas grew up having a murderer for a father. Herodias's daughter grew up with a mother and stepfather who were murderers. Aren't you glad you were born into your family? You are blessed to have parents who love Jesus and who are teaching you right from wrong.

Jesus Multiplies Food for Five Thousand People
Mark 6:30-44

Can God use kids? According to John's record of this same story, the five small barley loaves and two small fish that Jesus multiplied belonged to a young boy (see John 6:9). Perhaps it was his lunch. Regardless, I'm sure that boy never forgot the day when his few loaves and fish fed five thousand men.

This story shows us that God can take what little we have to give and make it into something that can bless a lot of people. We may think, like that little boy, that we don't have very much to offer. But God can multiply what we have. In so doing, it is He, not us, who is rightfully made to look better in other people's eyes.

I've always wondered what it would have been like to see this miracle. Specifically, I've wondered when the food actually multiplied. Did it multiply only in Jesus' hands, or did it also multiply in His disciples' hands? It seems reasonable to conclude that it was both, due to the fact that so many thousands of people were fed. Remember that there must have been many women and children besides just the five thousand men who were fed.

I think it is also very likely that the bread and fish continued to multiply in the hands of the people sitting in the groups. If so, that could be how they all knew that a great miracle had just taken place (see John 6:14). Wouldn't that be something to see—food multiplying in your own hands? Regardless, this story is one more proof that Jesus was God. At least five thousand people witnessed what happened, and there is no record in history that anyone at that time even attempted to claim that it didn't happen.

This story also shows us how much God loves people. Jesus and His disciples were trying to get away from the crowds just to rest for a while and eat a meal without interruption. So they journeyed by boat across the Sea of Galilee to a desolate spot. But when they arrived at their destination, a vast crowd was waiting for them. Amazingly, Jesus displayed no aggravation, but rather, He felt compassion for them and ministered to them by teaching and healing (see Luke 9:11). Then, late in the afternoon, He was concerned that the people needed food to eat, so He provided a meal for them. Our God cares about us. He wants to supply our needs. We shouldn't ever feel that we're bothering Him. He loves us dearly!

Q. Once, a modern Pharisee who didn't believe in the miracles of the Bible, attempted to disprove Jesus' miracle of the feeding of the five thousand. He claimed that back in Jesus' time, the loaves of bread were very large. How do we know that wasn't true?

A. Because the loaves belonged to a young boy. There is no way he could have carried five loaves that were large enough to feed five thousand men. Keep in mind that the women and children who were fed that day weren't even counted, so it's possible Jesus fed more than twenty thousand people. Also, the boy's two fish fed everyone as well. Unless those fish were multiplied by Jesus, they must have been *extremely* large fish to feed so many people! Finally, the disciples picked up twelve baskets of what was left over. One young boy couldn't have carried even a fraction of the leftovers.

Q. Why do you suppose Jesus instructed the disciples to collect all the leftovers?

A. Perhaps so everyone would see that food had been multiplied. Also, Jesus stated that He didn't want any of the food to be wasted. God wants us to be good stewards of what He gives us as well, not wasting things unnecessarily. (Also, God doesn't want us to be litterbugs!)

Q. What do you think Jesus did with the leftovers?

A. I would guess that He gave some to the little boy whose loaves and fish He multiplied. He may also have given some to designated people in the crowd to distribute to the poor. And He may have kept some for His disciples and Himself to eat later.

Application: Has God given you a gift? Offer it to Him to be used as He sees fit, and He'll use you to bless other people.

Jesus Walks on Water
Matthew 14:22-36

Do you remember the story we read a few days ago when Jesus and His disciples were caught in a violent storm in a boat on the Sea of Galilee? After He rebuked the wind and waves, Jesus rebuked His disciples for their lack of faith. They had been filled with fear, even though Jesus was asleep and had clearly said they were going to the other side. He expected them to believe His Word. In the similar story we just read, there was one thing that was different from the start: Jesus was not in the boat with them. This time they were on their own!

Certainly the disciples were in the center of God's will that night, rowing across the Sea of Galilee. They were just following Jesus' orders. And certainly God knew they would encounter threatening winds on their journey. He must have been giving them another opportunity to exercise their faith. From this story, we can learn what we should do when we face opposition that is hindering us from fulfilling God's will.

According to John's record of this same story, Jesus' disciples had rowed about three-and-a-half miles when the wind and waves grew menacing (see John 6:19). Jesus, after spending time praying high on a mountainside, saw that "they were in serious trouble, rowing hard and struggling against the wind and waves" (Mark 6:48). They had been rowing for hours, and now it was the middle of the night. They were sleepy and their muscles were aching. They were probably yelling directions at each other to keep their boat from capsizing. In their own strength, they were trying to make it to shore, but it looked impossible.

There is no indication that any of them even tried to exercise any faith. No one suggested that they pray. No one said, "Let's stop rowing and start praising God that we are going to make it to the other side, because we've been sent by Jesus to do just that." No one attempted to rebuke the wind, imitating Jesus.

Jesus, after waiting until three o'clock in the morning, finally stepped out onto the water and began walking toward the same destination as His disciples. When they saw Him walking by, they were terrified, not recognizing Him in the darkness, thinking He must be a ghost! But Jesus tried to calm their fears by telling them who He was. That is when Peter requested that Jesus command him to walk on the water.

Jesus actually said only one word to Peter: "Come!" Before then, Peter had nothing to stand on but water, and had he stepped out of the boat, he would have immediately sunk. But once Jesus spoke, Peter could stand on the Word of God. By faith, he stepped out of the boat and began walking toward Jesus on the water. He was literally walking by faith. When did Peter begin to sink? It was when he doubted. And why did he doubt? Because he began looking at the high waves around him, becoming fearful.

This is a great illustration of how we can walk by faith. When we have a promise from God to believe, it makes no difference what our circumstances are saying to us. God's Word is always true, and if we'll believe in spite of our circumstances, we'll experience the blessings God promises. If we doubt, however, we may well begin to go down, just like Peter.

Peter almost made it all the way to Jesus. When he began to doubt and sink, he cried out for Jesus to save him, and Jesus mercifully did. Praise God that even when our faith is failing, Jesus still loves us and will help us in our troubles.

Clearly it was Peter's doubts and lack of faith that caused him to sink. Proud people would rather find something else to blame, and amazingly, they often blame God for their failures, claiming that failure must have been God's will. I wonder what Jesus would have said if He had overheard Peter, once he was back in the boat, saying to the other disciples, "The reason I sank, of course, is because it wasn't God's will that I make it all the way to Jesus!"

Q. Jesus apparently wasn't initially planning on rescuing His disciples from their predicament, because Mark's Gospel said, "He started to go past them" (Mark 6:48), walking on the water right by their boat. Why do you suppose Jesus did that?

A. Perhaps because Jesus is so polite. He won't get involved in people's business unless they invite Him. This is a picture of many Christians. In the midst of life's storms, they try to make it in their own strength, and Jesus walks right by, wishing they'd ask for His help. Have you invited Jesus into your boat?

Q. When Jesus and His disciples arrived on the shore of their destination, people soon began bringing all their sick to be healed. The Bible says that all who touched the fringe of Jesus' robe were healed (see Matthew 14:36). What does this teach us about faith?

A. It was obviously God's will for everyone who was healed to be healed, but each sick person had to exercise faith to receive what God wanted him to have. People who have faith will demonstrate their faith by their actions.

Application: Have you begun to sink in some area of your life because you've been doubting God? If so, look again at God's promises regarding your situation, and get back up on the water by faith!

Jesus Compares Himself with Food
John 6:22-71

After Jesus had miraculously fed five thousand people, He sent the multitudes back to their homes in the evening. That night was when He walked on water and rescued His disciples as they all journeyed to the other side of the lake. The next morning, the same crowds Jesus had fed searched for and found Him. Unfortunately, they were not motivated by their hunger for spiritual truth; rather, they were hoping for some more free food.

This greatly disappointed Jesus, so He exhorted them to seek not for what temporarily sustains *physical* life, but for what was vastly more important, the *eternal* life that only He could give them. One reason Jesus had supernaturally provided physical food was because He was hoping the people would see Him as their source for true spiritual food.

Jesus then explained that God's spiritual food is far superior to any physical food. All that physical food can do is keep a person's body alive, and it can only do it for a limited amount of time because everyone eventually dies. The spiritual food that God is offering, however, gives life to our spirits, the part of us that the Bible calls the "inward person." That inward person will live forever, but unless he eats some of God's spiritual food, he will be forever sinful and destined to spend eternity in hell. But if he eats God's spiritual food, he will be reborn and spend eternity in heaven.

Not only that, but God's spiritual food will one day affect his physical body as well. On the last day, God will resurrect everyone's body who has believed in Jesus, making them into "glorified bodies" that will never become sick, grow old or die! What physical food can't keep alive for more than a few decades, God's spiritual food will resurrect and keep alive forever! That's why Jesus said that when we eat God's spiritual food, we will never hunger or thirst again. He meant that His gift of eternal life, once received, was sufficient for all eternity. It's not something that needs constant replenishing. One meal is good forever!

God wants *everyone* to eat His spiritual food, and Jesus told the people that they could eat by simply believing in Him. They, however, were still much more interested in physical food, and, hoped that He would again provide free bread. They requested a sign that would convince them to believe in Him. Because it was food they were after, they mentioned how Moses had miraculously provided bread for the people of Israel, the manna they gathered each morning from the ground.

Jesus explained that it wasn't Moses who provided the bread, it was God. Now the same God was offering everyone "true bread," the spiritual food that could give them eternal life. Jesus then stated that He was God's true bread sent from heaven, indicating that what people really needed was for Him to come inside their spirits.

But His audience began to murmur over what He said. They knew He had been born like any other person, so how could He claim to have come from heaven? They didn't know, of course, that Joseph wasn't actually Jesus' father, and that Jesus had come from heaven via Mary's womb.

Finally, continuing to expand on His comparison of Himself to food, Jesus revealed what would uniquely qualify Him to offer eternal life to the world, and what people must believe in order to receive the eternal life He offered: He would die, offering Himself as a sacrifice so others could have eternal life. Jesus said, "This bread is my flesh, offered so the world may live....I assure you, unless you eat the flesh of the Son of Man and drink his blood, you cannot have eternal life within you. But those who eat my flesh and drink my blood have eternal life, and I will raise them at the last day. For my flesh is the true food, and my blood is the true drink" (John 6:51, 53-55).

Of course, no one can, and neither does Jesus want anyone to actually eat His flesh and drink His blood. But Jesus wants us to receive Him into our spirits, just as we receive physical food into our bodies. And He wants us to believe that He died for us, pouring out His blood and giving His body so we can have eternal life. In Jesus' comparison, eating represents receiving and believing. Eating Jesus, God's true bread, means believing in Him. It means becoming one with Him, just as Jesus said, "All who eat my flesh and drink my blood remain in me, and I in them" (John 6:56).

Many people who were listening that day didn't like what they heard. They took what Jesus said literally, not figuratively as He intended, and just as any sincere person would have taken Him. They really didn't want to understand because they didn't want to believe what He was saying about Himself. So they left Him. But Peter, a sincere believer, confessed that he believed Jesus alone had the words of eternal life and that He was "the Holy One of God" (John 6:69), the Messiah. Even if he didn't fully understand all Jesus said, he and the rest would be staying with Jesus, as all true believers would.

Q. Jesus said that people can't come to Him unless they are drawn by the Father. Does this mean that God is only drawing certain people to Jesus?

A. No. Jesus said that if He was lifted up on the cross, that He would draw everyone to Himself (see John 12:32). So Jesus is drawing *everyone*, but unless He and His Father drew people, none would come to Him, because all are so blinded by sin and hard-hearted.

Q. Did you see any correlation with what we read today and the church's practice of taking communion?

A. When we eat the bread and drink the grape juice, it represents eating Jesus' body and drinking His blood. That sounds like Christians are cannibals! However, we're not! I hope you realize now that partaking of the communion elements represents our becoming one with Jesus and reminds us of His substitutionary death for us. Just as the bread and grape juice go into our stomachs and then nourish every cell in our bodies, so Jesus, by His Holy Spirit, has come into our spirits and given us eternal life. Just as we become "one" with the bread and grape juice, so we've become one with Jesus. He's in us and we're in Him. That's why it's called communion, because what we do symbolizes our communion with Jesus (and each other). Also, communion reminds us that our oneness with Jesus was made possible by His sacrificial death, when His body was broken (like the bread is broken) and His blood was shed, represented by the grape juice.

Application: Some of what we read today was difficult to understand, just as Jesus' disciples expressed to Him. However, we have a good idea of what Jesus meant in general. And, like Peter, even if we don't fully understand everything Jesus said, we know He's the only One who has the words of eternal life. So we'll keep right on following Him! Someday we will understand what we don't understand now.

66

Jesus Teaches About Inner Purity
Mark 7:1-23

Has your mother taught you to wash your hands before you eat? Now you can tell her that Jesus is against her rule, right? Wrong! The Pharisees washed their hands before eating, but not to cleanse themselves of germs, because they didn't know about germs two thousand years ago. They washed their hands to obey their tradition, believing that if they ate with unwashed hands, they would become defiled and unacceptable to God. That small error in their thinking wouldn't have been so bad, except that their misconception about what made them acceptable or unacceptable to God extended much farther. Some of the traditions they kept actually *violated* God's Word. Thus, as Jesus said, they rejected God's specific laws and substituted their own traditions. Obeying man-made rules, they disobeyed God's rules.

One example of this was their breaking of the fifth commandment: "Honor your father and mother." The Pharisees taught that a person didn't have to help his needy parents if he vowed to give his money to God. Because they were lovers of money (see Luke 16:14), this tradition was probably designed to increase their own personal wealth. The Pharisees wouldn't have to spend their money supporting their elderly parents, plus, other people vowed to give their money to the Pharisees to support "God's work" rather than help their parents. This was just one of many examples of how the Pharisees broke God's law in order to protect their own traditions.

Many churches today are guilty of this same sin—exalting their own traditions above God's laws. As a result, people who keep the traditions think they're acceptable to God, even though they break many of His commandments. They attend church every week, say the right things at the right times during the service, receive communion, and think that makes them acceptable to God. But the rest of the week, they lie, steal and take God's name in vain. They're full of lust, hatred and pride. And just like the Pharisees, they'll spend eternity in hell unless they come to their senses, truly repent and begin to follow Jesus. When they do, their lives will change dramatically.

Jesus went on to explain that what a person eats is not what makes him acceptable or unacceptable to God. It is what a person does and says. Unfortunately, even some Christians have fallen into deception in this regard, over-emphasizing the importance of what we eat, and sometimes even claiming that we must follow the dietary laws of the Old Testament. Thinking they are more pleasing to God, they look down on other Christians who don't also restrict their diets. But today we read that Jesus declared that every kind of food is acceptable to eat (see Mark 7:19). Let's be careful that we don't become sidetracked by minor things. God wants His people to live according to His, not our, standards of holiness.

Q. Because Jesus declared all foods are acceptable for us to eat, does that mean it would be OK for us to subsist on a diet of candy bars and Cokes?

A. When Jesus lived on the earth, there were no such things as candy bars and Cokes. In fact, there were not any foods that were processed like the many foods available to us today. In their natural state as God created them, all foods are acceptable for us to eat and contribute to our physical well-being. But foods that have been altered and stripped of their nutritional value are in a different category. There are many nutrients that are essential for our bodies to remain healthy, and a wise Christian will see that his diet contains all the nutrients he needs.

Q. Have you ever met someone who thinks they're holier than you because they keep certain rules that can't be found anywhere in the Bible? What do you think Jesus would say to them?

Application: Like the people in yesterday's reading, the Pharisees of today's reading were more concerned with physical rather than spiritual things, and concentrated more on external rather than internal things. Without neglecting the physical and external, God wants us to be more concerned about the spiritual and internal.

A Gentile Woman Persists in Faith
Matthew 15:21-31

This first story has always been a difficult one to fully understand, because Jesus doesn't act like we'd expect Him to act. We view Him as always kind, compassionate and impartial, but He seems to be uncaring and prejudiced as He relates to this Gentile woman. So how are we to interpret this story?

Some believe that Jesus, in order to teach His disciples a lesson, was at first pretending to act like the average prejudiced Jew. That may well be the correct interpretation, because Jesus did ultimately grant the woman her request, revealing His true compassion for her and her daughter.

Others have suggested that Jesus was simply testing her faith, again by acting as if He didn't want to heal her daughter. Would she persist in believing or would she give up? Was her faith genuine?

And others think that Jesus was being honest in everything He said to her. That is, He was truly sent by His Father to help only the lost people of Israel, and not Gentiles.

This third interpretation is difficult for me to accept for several reasons. First, because if Jesus was sent by His Father to help only the lost people of Israel and not the Gentiles, why then did He apparently disobey His Father by ultimately healing the woman's daughter? Second, why did He help other Gentiles, such as the Roman centurion? Third, why did He die for the sins of every Gentile in the entire world?

Beyond that, Jesus apparently referred to the woman as a dog, a common, derogatory term that prideful Jews used to describe Gentiles. It's difficult for me to believe that Jesus really felt this woman was worthy of such a demeaning title and more undeserving than Jews of receiving God's help. I can't believe that Jesus didn't feel as much compassion for her plight as He did for anyone else's plight, just because she was a Gentile. Chances are that practically every family reading this devotional is a Gentile family. Is this how Jesus feels about us?

For these reasons, I prefer a combination of the first two possible interpretations. Jesus' own disciples expressed no concern for this poor woman, and requested that Jesus send her away, complaining that her begging was bothering them. This could hardly be considered a commendable action on their part. Christian virtue requires a higher standard than that. So perhaps Jesus wanted to teach them a lesson about God's love of non-Jewish people. I wonder if Jesus was looking right at them when He pronounced the woman's daughter healed. I wonder what they were thinking when He did!

Also, we note that Jesus commended the Gentile woman for her great faith, proven by her persistence, and then immediately announced that her daughter was healed. No one can rightfully say that her faith wasn't severely tested, as it seems that even Jesus tried to discourage her. But her persistent faith paid off.

Finally, perhaps there was more to this story than what we realize. Possibly Jesus knew something about this Gentile woman's private life that truly disqualified her from having any right to approach Him. She may have been a devoted idol-worshipper. Perhaps it was some very perverted and sinful thing she did that provided an avenue for her daughter to become demon-possessed. By ignoring her, Jesus may have been initially sending her a message of her need of repentance.

Regardless of what we don't understand about this incident, the ending makes perfect sense. Jesus, the compassionate Son of God, healed the woman's daughter instantly! God's love is so great!

 Q. What do you think would have happened if the Gentile woman had not persisted in faith?

A. Her daughter would not have been healed, even though her healing was obviously God's will. As I've said previously, proud people don't like to hear such things, because they don't want to take responsibility for their unbelief and would rather blame God for their prayers that have gone unanswered. Most of us, like Jesus' twelve disciples, have doubted and failed in our faith. Let's be humble enough to accept responsibility, and wise enough to continue building our faith by feeding it with God's Word and exercising it. Our faith can grow! And praise God that, although He may be disappointed in our lack of faith, He never condemns us for it.

Q. When Jesus returned to Galilee, "a vast crowd brought him the lame, blind, crippled, mute, and many others with physical difficulties, and they laid them before Jesus" (Matthew 15:30). Matthew wrote that Jesus "healed them all" (Matthew 15:30). What does this teach us about God's will for healing?

A. It teaches us that God loves every sick person and it is His will to heal them all. If you had been lame, blind, crippled or mute and had been brought to Jesus that day, you would have been healed. Jesus didn't say to anyone, "I'm sorry, but it is not God's will for everyone to be healed, so I have to turn you away." No, everyone who came requesting healing was healed. Thus, it is certainly safe to assume that seriously ill people who didn't come that day could have been healed if they would have come. But because they didn't believe, they didn't come, and they weren't healed, even though it was God's will for them to be healed.

Application: There is no doubt that our faith is sometimes tested. What we are believing for often doesn't seem as if it's going to come to pass. But we should be encouraged by the Gentile woman we read about today. Her persistence paid off, and so will ours.

Jesus Feeds Four Thousand
Mark 7:31-8:10

When someone is deaf, he normally will have difficulty speaking clearly and in an understandable way, even if there's nothing wrong with his mouth or vocal cords. The reason is because we learn to talk by comparing what we hear ourselves say with what others say. If we can't hear, we can't learn to talk. And if a hearing person becomes deaf, his speech will gradually become more difficult for others to understand, since he can no longer hear himself speak and thus judge how clearly he is speaking. This was perhaps the case of the deaf man with a speech impediment about whom we read.

We don't know why Jesus put His fingers in the man's ears or why He spit on His own fingers and then touched the deaf man's tongue, but we assume He was being led by the Holy Spirit. The wonderful thing is that the man was instantly healed. Can you imagine his joy? Think of how blessed you are if your hearing is good.

This man was only one of the many Jesus healed when He returned from the region of Tyre. As we read yesterday, He healed many who were blind, deaf, mute and lame. From today's reading, we can conclude that Jesus didn't heal them just to prove He was the Son of God. He told the crowd not to tell anyone about His miracles, indicating that He healed because He loved people, not because He was trying to prove His deity or advertise Himself. This should encourage those of us who need healing today, because Jesus is just as merciful now as He was when He walked on the earth. Too many people think that Jesus healed only during His earthly ministry to prove He was God in the form of a human being, and then conclude that He won't heal them since His deity was well-established two thousand years ago.

Today we also read how Jesus once again multiplied loaves of bread and fish. This time there were seven large baskets of food left over, showing how gracious God is—Jesus provided more than they even needed. We should expect that God will do the same for us. Let us not forget, however, that the people who were miraculously blessed with food were not those who were sitting at home, but those who had sought to be with Jesus. God has promised to supply all our needs *if* we will live for Him and make His kingdom our primary concern (see Matthew 6:33).

Q. How many people did Jesus feed in today's story?

A. This is somewhat of a trick question! Mark's Gospel says that Jesus fed four thousand people (see Mark 8:9). So you may have answered four thousand. However, the same story is found in Matthew's Gospel, and Matthew specifies that Jesus fed four thousand men, "in addition to all the women and children" (Matthew 15:38). If every man was married and had four children, Jesus fed twenty-four thousand people that day!

Application: We should look to Jesus not only as our Savior, but as the one who supplies all our needs. God is the one who created us with a need to eat, drink, sleep and be clothed, and so we should expect that He will take care of all those things for us.

The Faith and Doubts of Jesus' Disciples
Matthew 16:1-20

As we continue reading the life story of Jesus, we'll learn that He faced a growing opposition from the Pharisees and other religious leaders. Those men who were supposed to be servants of God hated God's Son with a passion, and wanted to ruin Him. Ultimately they succeeded in killing Him, but that only lasted for three days!

Today we read about the Pharisees and Sadducees asking Jesus for a miraculous sign in order to prove His claims. This was at least the second time they'd made such a request (see Matthew 12:38). They had no doubt heard the reports of the many people who were healed; in fact, some of them actually had been present to see Jesus heal (see Luke 5:17-25). So they were probably asking for something really spectacular, like fire falling from heaven.

Their request revealed how evil they were, and Jesus responded by saying so. The Pharisees and Sadducees could read the weather signs in the sky, but they couldn't read the obvious signs that proved Jesus was their promised Messiah. He had already provided more than sufficient proof that He was God in the form of a human being. Their request of a sign was an indication of the hardness of their hearts, and Jesus promised them only one sign on the magnitude of what they were seeking, calling it "the sign of the prophet Jonah." Of course, Jonah's expulsion from the fish's stomach after three days foreshadowed Jesus' own resurrection.

Obviously, anyone who followed the teaching of the Pharisees or Sadducees was doomed, as Jesus later warned His disciples as they once again crossed the Sea of Galilee. Unfortunately, they completely misunderstood what He meant when He said, "Beware of the yeast of the Pharisees and Sadducees" (Matthew 16:6). They thought He said that because they had forgotten to bring any bread with them in their boat, since yeast is a primary ingredient in bread. Knowing their thoughts, Jesus rebuked them. Why would they have ever thought that He, having recently multiplied bread twice, would be the least bit concerned about having no bread in the boat? Their thoughts revealed their lack of faith in Him, and He told them so.

However, in the final part of today's reading, we learn that Jesus' disciples weren't entirely lacking in faith. Peter, likely speaking as a representative for most of the twelve, confessed that he believed Jesus was the Messiah, the Son of God. Thus in one section of Scripture we have examples of the faith and doubts of the same followers of Christ. This clearly shows us that we may well believe that Jesus is the Son of God, but doubt that He will provide for our other needs, as is the case with too many of us. Sometimes we need to be reminded, like the disciples, of what God has done in the past to provide for our needs.

Like the disciples, all of us have faltered in our faith and failed. That, however, is not a reason to be discouraged, give up, or feel condemned. Jesus kept on working with His disciples, and He will keep on working with us!

 Q. Jesus said to Peter, "You are Peter, and upon this rock I will build my church, and all the powers of hell will not conquer it" (Matthew

16:18). What is the rock Jesus mentioned?

A. Peter had just declared his faith that Jesus was the Messiah and Son of God. The foundation upon which the church is built is the belief that Jesus is God's Son, and the church grows as more people believe it. The rock Jesus referred to was the fact of Him being God's Son and people's faith in that fact.

Q. What did Jesus mean when He promised Peter the keys of the Kingdom of Heaven?

A. Keys represent the means of opening something that is locked. In this case, Jesus promised to give Peter the means to unlock heaven while he was still on the earth. Heaven, in a sense, is locked to all sinners. But it can be opened to sinners if they are made righteous. The key that opens it to them is the gospel of Jesus Christ. Jesus was promising Peter that He would entrust him with the gospel, so that he could open the entrance to heaven for people. Likewise, Peter could boldly declare that heaven was shut to anyone who refused to believe the gospel.

Application: Like Peter, we're blessed to know and believe that Jesus is the Son of God, because so many people don't know or believe it. We're now part of a worldwide church that, as Jesus said, the powers of hell will not conquer. We're on a winning team!

Jesus Foretells His Death, Resurrection and Glorification
Matthew 16:21-17:9

Peter was convinced that Jesus was the Messiah and Son of God, but when Jesus announced to His disciples that He would soon die in Jerusalem, Peter politely took Him aside to correct Him. Surely Jesus was mistaken! What good would it do for God's Son to die? Obviously, Peter didn't yet understand the main reason why Jesus became a man—to die for our sins. Jesus rebuked him sternly, wanting to make a lasting impression on Peter and the rest of His disciples. *It was God's will for Him to die.* It would be no accident or twist of fate, and Jesus was certainly not mistaken. He had been born to die.

Obviously, Jesus was not playing games and was fully committed to His cause. He was paying the highest price possible to redeem humanity. And just as He was giving His life for the people He would save, He expected those He saved to give up their lives for Him. He wasn't requiring that they all die physically as martyrs, but He was calling all of them to die to their selfish desires and live for Him. That is what He meant when He said, "If any of you wants to be my follower, you must put aside your selfish ambition, shoulder your cross, and follow me. If you try to keep your life for yourself, you will lose it. But if you give up your life for me, you will find true life" (Matthew 16:24-25).

Although the price might seem high, any other course would be foolish. By seeking after your own selfish desires, you might, as Jesus said, eventually own everything that can be bought, but you would spend eternity in hell. Jesus Christ is the one who will one day judge all people according to their deeds, and only those who were submitted to Him will be permitted entrance into His eternal kingdom. So no matter what the cost, the only smart choice is to die to selfishness and live for Jesus.

Jesus went on to say that there were some present who would not die before they would see Him coming in His kingdom. His promise was fulfilled just six days later, when Peter, James and John saw Him transfigured and glorified before them. "His face shone like the sun, and his clothing became dazzling white" (Matthew 17:2). That is how our Savior and God will look when we see Him in His kingdom! That is how Jesus will look when we stand before Him to give an account of our lives. Imagining that day should provide all of us with ample motivation to serve Him with all our hearts while we're on the earth.

Q. When Jesus was transfigured on a high mountain before Peter, James and John, Moses and Elijah appeared and began talking with Jesus. Does this teach us anything about what happens to people after they die?

A. This proves that people's spirits live after their bodies die. Some people think that when people die, they die like an animal, ceasing to exist. Some cults teach that when people die, they cease to exist until God resurrects them. The error that both are making is that they are not acknowledging that human beings have spirits. When their bodies die, their spirits live on, and go to heaven or hell. One day everyone's body will be resurrected and rejoined with his or her spirit. But in the meantime, their spirits are very much alive. The spirits of Moses and Elijah must have come from paradise to meet with Jesus that day on the mountain. One day they, like us, will receive new, glorified bodies.

Q. Why do you think that Moses and Elijah were chosen by God to meet with Jesus that day?

A. Nobody knows for sure because the Bible doesn't say. Perhaps it was to make an impression upon Peter, James and John's minds that Jesus' future kingdom would include all the redeemed people of the ages, including the great men of the Old Testament. Or, maybe God wanted them to be certain that Jesus was not Moses or Elijah, because we know that some people thought Jesus was Elijah (see Matthew 16:14). Or perhaps Moses and Elijah made a request of God to meet with His Son! Regardless, we'll all someday have the same privilege as they had.

Application: Peter, James and John never forgot what happened that day on the mountain. Peter later wrote about it in a letter, saying, "For we were not making up clever stories when we told you about the power of our Lord Jesus Christ and his coming again. We have seen his majestic splendor with our own eyes. And he received honor and glory from God the Father when God's glorious, majestic voice called down from heaven, 'This is my beloved Son; I am fully pleased with him.' We ourselves heard the voice when we were there with him on the holy mountain" (2 Peter 1:16-18). What we've read about today really happened, as did everything else we can read about Jesus in the Bible!

Jesus Casts Out A Demon His Disciples Couldn't
Mark 9:14-29

Jesus, Peter, James and John were just coming down from the mountain where Jesus had been transfigured when they found the other disciples engaged in an argument with some religious teachers. A man had brought them his son who was possessed by an evil spirit, but they had failed to cast it out.

We know that, prior to this, Jesus had given His disciples authority to cast out demons (see Matthew 10:1; Mark 3:14-15; Luke 9:1). And, prior to this, they had successfully cast out demons (see Mark 6:13). So why, this time, did they fail? When they later asked Jesus that very question, according to Mark's Gospel, He told them it was because that particular kind of demon could only be cast out through prayer. However, Matthew recorded Jesus' response as being: "You didn't have enough faith" (Matthew 17:20). Both Matthew and Mark were inspired by the Holy Spirit to write their books, and so we must conclude that Jesus gave both reasons as to why the disciples failed.

Lack of faith seems to have been the primary reason for their failure, because as soon as Jesus heard they'd failed, He lamented, "You stubborn, faithless [or, *unbelieving*] people! How long must I be with you until you believe?" (Matthew 17:17). Also, when the boy's father asked Jesus to help him if He could, Jesus responded, "If I can?...Anything is possible if a person believes" (Mark 9:23).

Even though the disciples had God-given authority to cast out demons, their authority didn't work unless they exercised faith. Again, this is proof that God's will doesn't always automatically come to pass in our lives. We must believe what God has said, or else we may not experience what God has promised. As Jesus said, "Anything is possible *if* a person believes" (Mark 9:23, emphasis added). Notice that what is possible depends upon each individual's faith.

In previous times when the disciples had successfully cast out demons, they must have had sufficient faith. Had their faith grown weaker? Probably not. I would be more inclined to think that this particular demon required stronger faith to expel than any demon they had previously dealt with. The reason is because this demon manifested itself in some very dramatic ways. It would take more faith to cast out a demon when it was making someone fall to the ground in violent convulsions, foam at the mouth and grind his teeth than it would to cast out a demon from a calm-looking person! Faith requires disregarding the contrary circumstances, and when the contrary circumstances are greater, greater faith is needed. It takes more faith to move a mountain than a molehill!

Perhaps that was why Jesus also said that this demon could only come out through prayer. Spending time in prayer can't increase anyone's authority over demons, but it can increase his faith in the authority he already possesses as he meditates on God's promises.

Possibly this demon put on the same show for the disciples as it did for Jesus, robbing them of their faith. But Jesus' faith didn't waver during His encounter. He was not afraid, and immediately upon hearing of His disciples' failure, commanded that the boy be brought to Him. As soon as the evil spirit saw Jesus, it immediately threw the boy to the ground in a violent convulsion, making him writhe and foam at the mouth. It was probably hoping to scare Jesus, stealing His faith, and thus continue to torture the boy. Jesus, however, was not moved by what He saw, and confidently commanded the demon to come out of the child and never enter him again. It reluctantly obeyed, screaming and throwing the boy into another convulsion as it came out. Finally, the boy was motionless, and the unbelieving crowd thought he had died. Jesus, of course, wasn't thinking such thoughts, and, taking the boy by the hand, helped him to his feet. That was one happy boy, one happy father, and one amazed crowd!

 Q. Jesus asked the boy's father how long his son had been afflicted. What does this reveal to us about Jesus?

A. First, it reveals His compassion. As Jesus saw the boy's agony, He began wondering how long the boy had been suffering to such a degree. It also reveals to us, once again, that Jesus was not all-knowing, even though He was divine. He stripped Himself of omniscience when He became a man.

Q. The demon-possessed boy's father told Jesus that his son had suffered since childhood with his affliction, and the demon had often thrown his son into fire and water, trying to kill him. What does that tell you about demons?

A. It tells us how evil and wicked they are. This particular demon took a perverted pleasure in making a little boy suffer for years, torturing and trying to kill him.

Application: Thank God that Christians don't have to be afraid of demons or the devil, because Jesus has delivered us from their power. Because we have Jesus inside us, now they're afraid of us! We can learn from today's reading that when the devil puts on his best show to discourage us or fill us with fear, that means he is scared!

Jesus Pays His and Peter's Temple Tax
Matthew 17:24-27

The Temple tax was one that all Jews were supposed to pay once a year for the upkeep and maintenance of the Temple in Jerusalem. It wasn't a large tax, but it wasn't a small one either, equivalent to about two days' wages for a working man. Because the Temple tax, like most taxes, was unpopular, special tax collectors were assigned to certain areas, and were responsible to see that as many people as possible paid. Perhaps knowing how influential Jesus had become in Galilee, several tax collectors approached Peter to find out if Jesus endorsed and personally paid the tax. Confident that Jesus was a very upright person (to say the least), Peter assured his questioners that Jesus did pay the tax, but then went to talk to Jesus about it. He was perhaps fearful that he had misrepresented Jesus, or he may have been planning on asking Jesus for the money to pay the tax while the tax collectors waited outside.

In a small way, Peter *had* misrepresented Jesus, and this becomes clear as we read Jesus' and Peter's conversation. As Peter entered the house where Jesus was, before he could ask Him about the Temple tax, Jesus asked Peter a question about who kings normally tax. Unfortunately, if you've been reading the *New Living Translation* as I suggested, you missed something significant that Jesus said. In the *New American Standard Bible*, Jesus' question to Peter is recorded as, "What do you think, Simon? From whom do the kings of the earth collect customs or poll-tax, from their sons or from strangers?" Peter responded, "From strangers," to which Jesus replied, "Consequently the sons are exempt" (Matthew 17:25-26). Jesus did not, as the *New Living Translation* says, contrast citizens of a kingdom and foreigners, but as kings's sons and his subjects.

What difference does this make? A lot. Jesus was not implying that He, being a citizen rather than a foreigner, was exempt from paying the Temple tax. Rather, He was implying that He, the Son of the King of all creation, was exempt from paying a tax on a house that belonged to that King! He was, once again, claiming to be God's Son!

Although He really didn't have a responsibility to pay the Temple tax, Jesus didn't want to offend the tax collectors, indicating that they probably were waiting outside for His money. So He gave Peter instructions for getting enough money to pay the tax for both of them. All Peter had to do was walk to the shore of the Sea of Galilee, throw in a line, and the first fish he caught would have a coin in its mouth that would exactly pay their tax!

Let's use our imaginations to picture what happened next. Peter walks out of the house and says to the waiting tax collectors, "I'll have the money for Jesus' and my tax in just a minute—I just need to go pick it up. Please follow me." Together they walk to the shore where Peter picks up his fishing rod and casts a line into the water. In a second or two, he has a fish on his line and reels it in. He takes the fish off the hook, opens its mouth, reaches in to pull out a coin, and hands it to the astonished tax collectors! I wonder if they had any more questions for Peter after that! I wonder if they became followers of Jesus themselves!

Q. What is it that made this story so miraculous?
A. God may have created a coin for a fish to pick up, but I think that's unlikely because it would make Him a counterfeiter. Therefore, He must have directed a fish to a coin that had accidentally fallen into the water from someone's purse, hand or pocket. So God had to know the exact whereabouts of a lost coin under the water, direct a fish to put it in its mouth, and have that same fish bite Peter's bait at a precise time! On top of all this, God had to let Jesus know in advance what was going to happen so He, in turn, could instruct Peter about getting their tax money!

Application: Although God rarely supplies our needs through coins in the mouths of fish, He often surprises us by using unexpected sources. That way, we are more likely to realize that He is the supplier. He cares about His children, and He loves to provide for them as they trust and obey.

Jesus Teaches His Disciples
Mark 9:30-48

As the time of His death drew nearer, Jesus began avoiding the crowds in order to spend time teaching His disciples. He knew that they would be the ones to carry on His work after His ascension, and He had a limited amount of time to get them ready.

If they were to succeed in doing Christ's work, it was of foremost importance that they have a correct view of themselves and other believers. God won't use people who think they're somebody important or who want to be somebody important. Proud or selfish people who want positions of respect disqualify themselves from Christ's ministry. Jesus wants us to consider ourselves servants, and see everyone else as being more important. Yet the disciples had been secretly arguing over who was the greatest! Jesus told them what we should all keep in mind: "Anyone who wants to be the first must take last place and be the servant of everyone else." In God's eyes, what makes people great is servanthood.

Jesus also needed to remind His disciples of the proper view they should have of other believers, especially "lesser" ones. God loves all of His children, and so all should be valued by us. Jesus took a little child in his arms, a person that very few others would even have noticed was present, and talked about how valuable he was. Children and other so-called "insignificant" people are often pushed aside, but according to Jesus, they shouldn't be. Jesus said that if we, as His representatives, take notice of and welcome a little child who believes in Him, we are actually welcoming Him. *We are called to love people as God loves them, and this is the heart of being a follower of Christ.*

On the other hand, because God loves people the world deems insignificant and unimportant, we are guilty of a great sin if we don't value them as God does. Jesus said that if anyone causes a child who believes in Him to lose faith, it would be better for that person to be thrown into the sea with a large millstone tied around his neck! Why? Because that would be a better fate than what will actually happen to the person who causes a believing child to lose faith—he will spend eternity in hell! That shows us how much God loves "unimportant" people.

John told Jesus about a man who was using Jesus' name to cast out demons, but because he wasn't part of their group, the disciples told him to stop. This gave Jesus another wonderful opportunity to continue adjusting His disciples' view of others as they prepared to take over His work on earth. Too often, we're looking for what makes people different from us so we can exclude them. Jesus, however, is looking for what is similar so He can include them! He told His disciples that they shouldn't have stopped the man from using His name to cast out demons, explaining that, "No one who performs miracles in my name will soon be able to speak evil of me" (Mark 9:39). We should adopt this same attitude, working to include people rather than exclude them, because that is how God feels. Jesus said that God will reward anyone who shows even a little support for one of His followers!

Q. Jesus said, "If your hand causes you to sin, cut it off. It is better to enter heaven with only one hand than to go into the unquenchable fires of hell with two hands....And if your eye causes you to sin, gouge it out. It is better to enter the Kingdom of God half blind than to have two eyes and be thrown into hell, where the worm never dies and the fire never goes out" (Mark 9:43-44, 47-48). Did He really mean that people should cut off their hands and gouge out their eyes?

A. No, He must have been using a figure of speech we call hyperbole, or exaggerating to make a point unforgettable. Jesus couldn't have meant that people whose hands and eyes have caused them to sin should cut them off and gouge them out, because we all have hands and eyes that we have used to sin. If everyone literally obeyed Jesus on this, everyone in the world would be without hands and eyes. What Jesus was saying is that it is sin that sends people to hell, and so there is no price too high to pay to avoid sin. We should do what is necessary to avoid temptation, and if something is causing us to stumble, we need to remove it from our lives.

Application: Are you guilty of valuing other believers based on their age, their profession, their skin color or where they live? Is there anyone that you've been convicted about undervaluing? Will you change?

The Value of Children
Matthew 18:10-14; 19:13-15

The first part of today's reading is a continuation of what we read yesterday, when Jesus was teaching about the value of little children who believe in Him. Today we again learn that it's wrong to despise little believers because God places such a high value upon them. He cares about them so much that He has specially-assigned angels that watch over them. That tells us how God values them. People on earth hire guards to watch and protect only what is valuable to them, and God is the same. Also, those specially-assigned angels are not second-string angels who have nothing else to do, and thus God makes them watch children just to keep them busy. They are not angels who are low-on-the-totem pole angels, who live in the most re-mote places in heaven, far from the action. No, the angels who watch over God's little children are angels who are very close to God, constantly in His presence.

Some children believe in Jesus, but are led astray, just like a sheep might wander away from its flock. Jesus said that is was not the will of His Father that a believing child would ever go astray and ultimately perish, and He will go to great lengths to seek and rescue that child. So we should have the same attitude towards younger believers. Did you realize how special and important you are to God?

This is why your parents are taking time each day to teach you God's Word. You're very important to God, and no matter what other important things your parents have to do, the most important thing they can do is what they're doing right now.

Unfortunately, just one chapter later, we find that as parents were bring-ing their children to Jesus for Him to lay hands on them and pray for them, the disciples were telling the parents not to bother Him. Why? Simply be-cause they didn't think that such children were worthy of Jesus' time. But Jesus corrected them sternly. Jesus treated kids like most people only treat politicians, company presidents and movie stars!

Q. So you're a kid and now you know how much God values you. Should you now strut around like a proud peacock, expecting people to treat you like a president or movie star?

A. No, God wants you to be a servant, considering others as being more important than yourself. He loves you a great deal, but not more than any-one else.

Application: It's wonderful to know that God loves all His children very much, young and old. That is why we should love each other, and not overlook anyone who believes in Jesus.

What To Do When a Fellow Christian Wrongs You
Matthew 18:15-35

Jesus wants His followers to love one another as devoted friends. But sometimes, through thoughtlessness or misunderstanding, two followers of Christ are divided. What should you do if that happens to you? In most cases, you should simply overlook other people's thoughtlessness, knowing that if they knew better, they'd do better. But when a fellow believer sins against you so that your relationship with him is severely damaged, you should follow Jesus' instructions about how to work out your problem.

First, you should privately confront the believer who has offended you. It should be done gently and lovingly for several reasons. One, because you yourself are imperfect, and your imperfection gives you less of a right to be critical of others. Two, because upon confrontation, you may discover that you are the one to blame for the problem once you hear the other person's side of the story. Often people discover that their disagreement was nothing more than a misunderstanding.

If the other believer did actually sin against you, the large majority of the time he will ask for your forgiveness when he's confronted. Occasionally he won't, and there can only be two possible reasons. Either he is stubborn and unrepentant, or he really hasn't sinned against you as you think. So at that point, you need the help of a few other believers. Jesus said you should take one or two of them with you to confront the offender again. Of course, you'll have to convince those you want to take with you that you are right and the other person is wrong. They may, at that point, help you to see that the fault actually does lie with you, and if they do, then you should be the one asking for forgiveness and seeking reconciliation.

But let's say that your one or two helpers agree that you've been wronged, and with you, confront the offender for the second time. Either one of two things will happen. Either the offender will acknowledge his guilt or maintain his innocence. Most times, under the influence of several others who agree with you, the person will admit his guilt and ask your forgiveness. You, of course, are obligated to forgive him according to what we read today in Jesus' parable of the unforgiving servant. And thus your relationship will be restored.

If the offender still refuses to admit guilt and ask for forgiveness, then the matter should be taken before the whole church. (Keep in mind that for the first three hundred years of Christianity, most churches met in homes and consisted of no more than twenty-five people.) This is the final way of making certain that you have truly been sinned against, as the church considers your story and the evidence. If they decide you are right, they should confront the offender one last time. When he realizes that the whole church agrees with you, he should be persuaded of his sin and ask your forgiveness, thus restoring your relationship as you in turn forgive him. However, if he still refuses to repent, then he should be put out of the church and treated like an unbeliever, because he is obviously not a true follower of Christ. Jesus said that the church has heaven-given authority to do such a thing (see Matthew 18:17).

Jesus' instructions provoked Peter to wonder how many times he was obligated to forgive a fellow believer, suggesting that seven times was a good limit. Jesus, however, said that there was no limit, and then He told a story that explained why God expects His children to be so merciful. We've been shown so much mercy from God that it would be wrong for us to refuse to give mercy to others. In fact, if we refuse to forgive a fellow Christian who asks for forgiveness, God will reinstate our formerly forgiven sins. That is serious!

We must keep in mind that God offers forgiveness only to those who admit their guilt. Those who don't admit their guilt aren't forgiven, although God mercifully and patiently waits for their confession because He wants to be reconciled to all who have sinned against Him. We should follow His example. God expects us to forgive anyone and everyone who asks for our forgiveness, and He expects us to be merciful to those who don't ask for our forgiveness. In the parable of the unforgiving servant, notice that the first man *asked* for forgiveness, and his fellow servant also *asked* for his forgiveness, but he refused to give what he had received. That is what made the king so angry. In a sense, forgiveness can't be given until it's first requested. Jesus once said, "If another believer sins, rebuke him; then *if he repents*, forgive him" (Luke 17:3, emphasis added). Notice in what we read today that there is no forgiveness offered to the unrepentant man who was found guilty by the whole church.

 Q. If a fellow Christian doesn't say hello to you in church, do you think you should begin the process Jesus outlined in Matthew 18:15-17?

A. No. You should work on becoming more like Christ yourself and less like a little baby who is offended so easily. Mature Christians overlook many things that offend others.

Q. How many times do you think God will forgive us when we ask for His forgiveness?

A. He will forgive us an unlimited amount of times, because that is what He expects of us. He certainly wouldn't expect more from us than He does from Himself!

Application: Is there any fellow Christian with whom your relationship is not right? In light of what we've read today, what can you do to begin to work toward reconciliation?

Jesus' Forbearance With Unbelievers and His Expectations of Believers
Luke 9:51-62

When we read the story of Jesus' meeting with the Samaritan woman at the well, we learned that Jews and Samaritans generally hated each other. Samaritans were a mixed race of Jews and Gentiles, considered impure by other Jews. Jesus, of course, was a Jew, but He loved everyone because He was also God. And, unlike most Jews who traveled from Galilee to Judea by taking a long route that bypassed Samaria altogether, once again we read of Jesus journeying right through the heart of that region.

On His way, an entire Samaritan village refused to accommodate Him and His disciples only because they were Jews on the way to Jerusalem. This infuriated the two brothers, James and John, who consequently asked Jesus if they should call fire down from heaven on that Samaritan village, just as Elijah had once done upon a band of enemy soldiers. They felt the Samaritans should die for their offense.

Jesus rebuked both brothers for their attitude, saying (according to some manuscripts), "You don't realize what your hearts are like. For the Son of Man has not come to destroy men's lives, but to save them."

Like James and John, we sometimes think that God should immediately kill sinful people, and wonder why He doesn't. The reason is because He is so merciful and longsuffering. God is so merciful that He wants to give them plenty of time to repent. He knows that their fate is permanently sealed at death, and that hell awaits the unrepentant. Certainly Jesus wasn't pleased by the hatred of the people in that village, but He knew that they were acting just like most Jews acted toward Samaritans. In fact, His own disciples were no different than the unaccommodating Samaritans. If the Samaritan villagers deserved to be burned with fire for their prejudice, so did James and John!

In the second portion of today's reading we learn that, just like today, there were many people in Jesus' time who wanted to follow Him on their own terms. And, like today, those people disqualified themselves from being Jesus' true followers. Luke related three examples of such people.

The first man claimed he would follow Jesus no matter where He went. Jesus warned the man that he was making a vow that might be difficult for him to keep, because He had no place of His own to sleep each night. He and His disciples slept out in the open or relied on the hospitality of sympathetic friends. Of course, followers of Jesus today don't need to literally follow Him from place to place, but they, too, should first count the cost before becoming His disciples. Too many people want to follow Jesus as long as it doesn't inconvenience them. Consequently, they may think they've become His disciples, but they really haven't.

The second man agreed to be Jesus' disciple, but requested that he first return home to bury his father. It seems unlikely that his father had just died and that he just wanted to attend the funeral. More probable is that his father was elderly and could die at any time. So he wanted to delay his decision to follow the Lord. But the decision to delay following Jesus is a decision not to follow Jesus, because Jesus is calling everyone to follow Him now.

The third man also agreed to follow Jesus, but requested that he first say good-bye to his family. There is, of course, nothing wrong with saying good-bye to your family, but it seems Jesus knew this particular man was actually hesitating to follow through on his decision to become a follower and wanted to think about it for a while with the help of his family. The man had "put his hand to the plow" in the field, about to begin plowing, but was looking back toward his home, asking himself if he really wouldn't prefer to head back there and rest. Jesus expects that people who pledge allegiance to Him will follow through with their commitment.

Q. Jesus obviously expects us to be more devoted to Him than to anyone else, even our family members. What does this tell us about Him?

A. It tells us that Jesus is God, because only God has a right to expect us to be more devoted to Him than to our own families! It also tells us that we had better be more devoted to Him than to anyone else.

Application: All three men we read about today verbalized a commitment to follow Jesus. But the real mark of a follower of Jesus is not what he says, but what he does. Those who aren't willing to make any sacrifice for Christ's cause, or who indicate that they will follow Him in the future, or who hesitate in following through with their promise are fooling themselves.

Demons Must Obey Christ's Followers
Luke 10:1-24

Today we read about Jesus sending out seventy-two of His disciples to preach in towns He planned to visit. His instructions to them were very similar to those He gave His twelve disciples when He sent them out to preach. The seventy-two were also sent out in pairs, so they must have ministered in at least thirty-six towns. Jesus knew that some of the preaching pairs would be unwelcome where He was sending them. However, He sent them anyway, so that no one in those towns could accuse God before His judgment seat, saying, "You never sent anyone to tell me how I could be saved." The seventy-two were fully authorized as Jesus' messengers, just as much as Jesus was God the Father's authorized messenger. He told them, "Anyone who accepts your message is also accepting me. And anyone who rejects you is rejecting me. And anyone who rejects me is rejecting God who sent me" (Luke 10:16).

When the seventy-two returned from their missions, they were thrilled to report to Jesus that they had not only been able to heal sick people as He had promised them, but they had also been able to cast out demons in His name. They were amazed that demons, whose power had previously awed them, so quickly obeyed, as if they were powerless.

Jesus, however, wasn't surprised at all. He knew that Satan and his demons were no match for God's power, and told the seventy-two about something He'd witnessed ages ago. Before the world was created, Satan tried to exalt himself, but was cast out of heaven by God. When he was, he could put up no resistance, because God is infinitely more powerful. Satan fell from heaven *like lightning*. One second he was in heaven, and BOOM!, the next second he was on the earth! God the Father had given Jesus authority over everything (see Matthew 10:22), including the devil and demons, and Jesus in turn had given the seventy-two disciples authority "over all the power of the enemy" (Matthew 10:19). Demons are no match for God and for those who have God-given authority over them.

As happy as the seventy-two were about their authority over demons, there was something else Jesus said they should be even happier about— that their names were registered in heaven. Just thinking about how God had revealed the truth to those who were childlike, like the seventy-two who had just returned from their missions, moved Jesus to begin thanking His Father. As He later remarked, His disciples were so privileged to witness His ministry, something that Old Testament prophets and kings longed to see. How privileged *we* are to be able to read about Jesus' life and ministry. How blessed we are to know Him and His Father! And how thankful we should be that our names are also recorded in heaven in "the Lamb's Book of Life" (Revelation 21:27)!

Q. From whom does God hide the truth?

A. From those who think they are wise and clever (see Luke 10:21). Those are people who are proud. That's why it's a good idea regularly to admit that you need God to enlighten you, because there's a lot you don't understand. Proverbs says, "With humility comes wisdom" (Proverbs 11:2).

Q. Jesus told the seventy-two that He had given them authority over all the power of the enemy and that they could "walk among snakes and scorpions and crush them" (Luke 10:19). Did He literally mean that they could crush snakes and scorpions?

A. That is unlikely, and we certainly don't have a biblical example of any of Jesus' disciples doing such a thing. More probable is that Jesus was referring to demons when He spoke of snakes and scorpions. Most people are afraid of those two creatures, and they're also afraid of evil spirits. But those who follow Jesus have authority over them and have no good reason to be afraid. According to what Jesus said in Mark 16:17, all believers in Him have authority to cast out demons.

Application: Just as Jesus sent out the seventy-two, so we have been sent out by Him to be His representatives. The New Testament says that we are "Christ's ambassadors" (2 Corinthians 5:20). And just like the seventy-two, we are fully authorized by Jesus. He said in John 13:20, "Truly, anyone who welcomes my messenger is welcoming me, and anyone who welcomes me is welcoming the Father who sent me." Are you acting like Jesus' representative, doing what He would want you to do in every situation?

Jesus Invites Weary People to Rest
Matthew 11:28-30

In today's short reading, Jesus helps us to understand salvation. By using a *metaphor*, He explains what He's offering us and what we need to do to receive it. What is a metaphor? A metaphor is a comparison of things that are basically not the same, but which have some striking similarities. For example, I might say, "That man is like an oak tree." What is similar between the man and an oak tree? I probably mean that he is very big and strong. I don't mean that leaves grow on him or acorns fall from him each September!

Jesus used metaphors that the people He was teaching could easily understand. He first spoke of carrying heavy burdens and being weary. All of Jesus' listeners could understand what He was talking about because they didn't have cars and trucks in their day to help them carry things. People carried most things on their backs if they didn't have a donkey or a cart. Can you imagine having to carry your groceries all the way from the supermarket to your home on your back? You'd be pretty worn out by the time you got home!

The burden Jesus was talking about was the burden of sin and guilt that unsaved people carry with them all the time. Some people do a good job of ignoring the weight of that load, but their weariness is evident from the looks on their faces. Jesus wants to remove that load of guilt, giving them rest from it. He wasn't talking about a *physical* weariness and rest, because He promised rest for their *souls* (see Matthew 11:29). Once a person has received forgiveness, a great load is removed from his mind and his conscience.

Jesus made it very clear that, in order to be saved, people first must recognize and admit that they are burdened and weary. Second, they have to *want* to be unburdened. Then they must come to Jesus, which means they must recognize that He is the One who can help them.

Jesus also said that He had a yoke He would place on those who came to Him. A yoke is a big piece of wood that is placed around the neck of an ox, attached by ropes to a plow or wagon. When a man places a yoke on an ox, it means he has work for that ox to do, and it means that he is the owner and master of the ox. This tells us something very important about salvation that many people unfortunately don't understand. When we come to Jesus, we are making Him our owner and master; we are ready to go to work for Him. Being saved means being submitted to His will. It means listening to and learning from Him, being His disciple.

Many people have supposedly "accepted Jesus" as their Savior, but never have submitted themselves to obey Him. They still want to control their own lives, and they demonstrate no evidence of any submission to Jesus. Even though they may think they are saved, they really aren't.

Although Jesus wants to be our owner and master, He assures us that He will not be a harsh one. He won't whip us or drive us mercilessly! Rather, He said that He is a master who is humble and gentle. He loves us dearly, a million times more than any man ever loved his ox! The yoke that He puts on us "fits perfectly" (Matthew 11:30). That is, it's custom-made by His loving hands so that it won't scratch our backs or hurt us in any way. And the burden He gives us to pull is not heavy. We won't strain under His load. When people say that they don't want to become followers of Jesus because it would be too hard, we should remind them of what Jesus said here. His burden is *light*.

 Q. If a person claims to believe in Jesus but never attends church, reads his Bible, or listens to Bible teachers, is he really saved?

A. Probably not. Jesus said that those who come to Him must allow Him to teach them (see Matthew 11:29). If a person isn't interested in learning from Jesus, he hasn't really submitted himself to Jesus yet.

Q. When an unsaved person says that he doesn't have any guilt or doesn't need to be forgiven, what does that tell us about him?

A. It tells us that he is fooling himself and ignoring what he knows to be true. Everyone who is unsaved feels guilty whether he admits it or not, because God has placed a conscience inside everyone that convicts them when they do wrong. Until a person can admit his guilt, he can't be saved, because Jesus is offering him something that, in his own mind, he doesn't think he needs.

Application: What does it mean to be saved? According to what we read today, it means becoming one of the blessed, beloved oxen that belong to Jesus. Have you taken His yoke upon you?

Jesus Teaches About Prayer
Luke 11:1-13

Like most teachers, Jesus sometimes repeated to one group what He'd already taught another group. Some of what we read today Jesus taught during His sermon on the mountainside (see Matthew 6-7), so we'll only consider what is new to us.

Teaching about prayer, Jesus used an illustration about a man who was visited late at night by a friend. Unfortunately, he didn't have any food to feed his guest, so he walked to another friend's house to ask if he could borrow three loaves of bread. The problem was that it was midnight, and the friend and his family were already in bed. Naturally, it was a bother for him to get up and give the man three loaves of bread, and he even said so.

If you've been reading from the *New Living Translation*, the translators have, I believe, taken a little too much liberty at this point in the story. They make it sound as if the man who needed the bread ignored his friend's excuse and continued to knock on his door until he finally got up and gave him what he wanted. But the original Greek actually says that his friend got out of bed and gave him bread because of his *shamelessness*. That is, he was very bold to make such a request, expecting a favor so late at night. It took a lot of nerve to do what he did, and it showed that he had great faith in the kindness of his friend. His friend felt obligated to live up to what was obviously expected of him, and so he got up and gave the man what he wanted. Even the *New Living Translation* says that the friend gave the man what he wanted so his reputation wouldn't be damaged. That is, he wanted the man to continue to think that he was a true friend and a kind person.

Jesus' point is not that we should continually repeat our prayer requests to God so that He'll eventually give us what we want. In fact, Jesus taught during His sermon on the mountainside that we shouldn't continually repeat the same words in prayer, because God knows what we need before we ask (see Matthew 6:7-8). Rather, Jesus was encouraging us to have boldness when we make our requests. People who have faith ask boldly, just like the man in Jesus' story. In everyday life, people who get what they want are people who expect to get what they want. People who expect little get little, and they don't ask, seek or knock. The same thing is true in prayer. People who expect little of God get little from God. But people who expect much of God boldly ask Him for what they want and get it. They have an "I don't take 'no' for an answer" type of attitude, and persist in faith.

To further encourage us in prayer, Jesus used an illustration about children making requests of their fathers. Kids are world-famous for boldly asking their parents for many things. Jesus said that if fathers grant their children what they ask for, how much more will God give His children the Holy Spirit when they ask Him. This indicates that one of the things God expects us to request boldly from Him is the Holy Spirit. And it teaches us that we should shamelessly make our requests to our heavenly Father just as we do with our earthly fathers.

Q. Do born-again Christians who already have the Holy Spirit living inside them have any business asking God for the Holy Spirit?

A. Yes, they do. Jesus' promise that God would give the Holy Spirit was given to people who can call God their heavenly Father. They could only be people who are already born again, otherwise God is not their Father. And people who are born again already have the Holy Spirit living in them because they're born of the Spirit. So, Jesus' promise definitely applies to those who are already born again. The New Testament tells us that God wants to baptize His children in the Holy Spirit in order to empower them for service and witnessing, but they must boldly ask Him.

Q. If you are born again, have you shamelessly asked your heavenly Father for the Holy Spirit?

◎ Application: Are you, like so many people, waiting for opportunity to knock on your door? Or are you, as Jesus encouraged us, boldly knocking on opportunity's door? Are you expecting much from God? Does it show by your bold requests and acts of faith?

Jesus Criticizes the Religious Leaders
Luke 11:37-54

Although the Pharisee we first read about today may have wanted to appear as if he was a hospitable person, you can be sure he wasn't being motivated by kindness when he invited Jesus to share a meal at his house. Rather, he was hoping to find fault with Jesus in order to report it to his fellow Pharisees. And it didn't take him long. He was amazed to see that Jesus "sat down to eat without first performing the ceremonial washing required by Jewish custom" (Luke 11:38).

Knowing the Pharisee's thoughts, Jesus used the occasion to illustrate the basic flaw of all the Pharisees. They were primarily concerned with outward cleanliness at the neglect of inward cleanliness, making themselves hypocrites. Jesus said that God made both inside and outside, so both were important, but the Pharisees' insides were full of greed and wickedness. The only way for them to become inwardly clean was to repent, and Jesus said that the way to repent of greed was to give to the needy what the Pharisees greedily possessed.

Also, for the sake of outward appearance, the Pharisees majored in minors. That is, they emphasized the least important things and neglected what was most important. For example, when they picked some of their garden herbs, they would be careful to take a tenth of them and give them to the priests, because the Law of Moses required the Israelites to tithe on their increase. Jesus endorsed their tithing, but criticized them for neglecting other much more important things, like teaching people about and sharing God's love, or defending those who were treated unjustly.

The final proof of the outward show of the Pharisees' religion was their love of the seats of honor at the synagogue and the respectful greetings they received from people in the marketplace. They were not the kind of people who gave secretly to the poor or who prayed behind closed doors. Everything they did was a show so that people would see how holy they supposedly were. They loved it when they were honored by others for putting on their act!

In the same category were the religious teachers who considered themselves experts in the Law of Moses. They taught the common people their own strict interpretations of what God required, putting burdens on them that God never intended for them to carry. They made it next to impossible for people to please God. Jesus said they were no different than the evil religious leaders of the Old Testament who persecuted and killed the prophets whom God sent. In fact, Jesus predicted that they would persecute and kill future prophets and apostles whom God would send, one of them, of course, being Himself. Both Pharisees and religious teachers were very religious people who, unless they repented and believed in Jesus, would spend eternity in hell.

Q. Why do you suppose Jesus said that the generation of His day would be held responsible for the murder of all God's prophets from the creation of the world, from Abel to Zechariah? Is that fair? Will He not hold responsible the actual murderers?

A. Jesus knew that His generation would be responsible for His own death, and certainly, as God's only Son, Jesus was much more valuable than all the former prophets combined. They were men created in God's image and sent by God, but Jesus *was* God! So perhaps He meant that His generation would lay up more guilt by killing Him than if they had been responsible for the death of every prophet God had sent since the creation of the world.

Application: All of us, and especially Christian leaders, can become guilty of being Pharisaical. Here are some healthy questions that we need to ask ourselves from time to time: Does my religion consist mainly of outward conformity to a few aspects of the Christian faith, such as going to church once a week and paying my tithes? Am I living for Christ every hour of every day, spreading God's love, giving to the needy and defending those who are treated unjustly? Do I act more holy when I'm in church than I do at home? Do I do any good deeds privately, proving that my Christianity is not just an act to gain the praise of others?

Jesus Warns Against Greed
Luke 12:13-21

When an unmarried person dies, all his possessions usually become the property of other people, based on the instructions in the deceased person's will. If the deceased person has children, his possessions are usually divided equally among them. When possessions are not divided among the children equally, problems occur, because if one child gets less than another, he feels cheated. This must have been what happened to the man who asked Jesus to tell his brother to divide their father's estate.

Although God knows everything, and Jesus is God, Jesus voluntarily stripped Himself of that ability to know everything when He became a man. Therefore, because He didn't know all the facts, He wasn't able to make an instant judgment in the matter, as God the Father could have. We don't know, and neither did Jesus, if the man had *really* been cheated by his brother. It seems unlikely that he had received absolutely nothing while his brother had received everything. More likely, he'd received close to half of what his father owned, but felt his brother got the "bigger" half. The situation required a judge who would carefully examine the facts, appraise the value of the estate, and then determine if it had been divided fairly. Jesus, being perfectly fair, refused to make a judgment without knowing all those important facts.

However, Jesus did detect that the man was in danger of allowing himself to be gripped by greed. This man was so dominated by the desire for his fair share that he interrupted Jesus' sermon to make his request, foolishly hoping that Jesus would make a judgment so he could hastily possess what he thought belonged to him. Jesus seized the opportunity to warn us all against the sin of greed, a sin that manifests itself in many ways in people's lives.

Using an illustration of a rich man who became richer, Jesus explained that greed is basically a selfish attitude toward material things. The rich man's land was very productive, and his barns couldn't store all his crops. Rather than realizing that his abundance came from God, obligating him to share it, he built bigger barns to store it all so he could retire early and live a life of ease. He didn't think of those who had no food, and said nothing about giving a tithe to the Lord. He was rich in material things, but did not have, as Jesus said, a "rich relationship with God" (Luke 12:21). Otherwise, he would have acted differently.

Jesus said the man was a fool. The reason is clear: Although he was prepared for retirement, he was unprepared for eternity. He died the very same day that he made his selfish decision, making that decision his *final* decision.

No one knows the day he or she will die, but one thing is certain: everyone will die one day. And everyone will have to stand before God to give an account of his life. Our actions on earth will be what God uses to determine our eternal destiny, because our actions reveal what is really in our hearts. *The most important thing in life is to have a rich relationship with God.* If we do, we'll let God direct us in what we do with the material things He gives us. A little later, in this same sermon, Jesus instructed His followers, "Sell what you have and give to those in need. This will store up treasure for you in heaven! And the purses of heaven have no holes in them. Your treasure will be safe—no thief can steal it and no moth can destroy it. Wherever your treasure is, there your heart and thoughts will also be" (Luke 12:33-34).

 Q. Was Jesus telling us that it is wrong for us to own any material things?

A. No, He Himself promised in this same sermon to provide for our material needs (see Luke 12:31). He wouldn't give us something that was sinful for us to have. He was warning us against a selfish attitude toward what we own, and of placing a higher priority on material things than our relationship with God. The best way to guard against greed is to give away a portion of what God gives you regularly.

Q. What do you think Jesus would say about the kid who brings his parents a toy catalog and tells them, "I want everything on pages twelve through forty-one!"

A. He would probably say that material things were much too high of a priority for that child.

Q. What do you think Jesus would say to a child who told his mother, "Please take part of what you'd spend on me for Christmas presents this year and give it to a native missionary"?

A. He would probably say that He is pleased with that child's unselfishness.

 Application: Are you guarding against greed from gripping you? How are you doing it?

Jesus Tells His Followers to be Ready for His Return
Luke 12:35-48

The old Boy Scout motto, "Be Prepared," should also be a motto for every follower of Christ. Boy Scouts are supposed to be prepared for whatever might happen, but Christians should be prepared, above everything else, for the return of Jesus. He said He will come when "least expected" (Luke 12:40). Thus, there exists the potential for people to be caught off guard. Some will be very surprised and completely unprepared.

What is it that will determine who is prepared and who is unprepared for Jesus' return? Those who are obeying Jesus will be prepared, and those who are not obeying Him will be unprepared. Jesus said we should wait for Him as a servant waits for his master to return from a wedding feast. This once again teaches us that, although we are saved through our faith in Jesus, real faith manifests itself in obedience. If Jesus is truly our Savior then He is also our Master, and we are His servants.

Unfortunately, there are many people who think they are Christ's servants but who prove they aren't by what they do. Specifically, Jesus mentioned people who oppress His other servants (see Luke 12:45). At another time, Jesus said that love for one another is the mark of His true disciples (see John 13:34-35). Those who oppress and hate Christians definitely aren't Christians. Jesus also specifically mentioned in today's reading that some of the unprepared will be partying and getting drunk. The Bible plainly teaches that drunkards will not get into heaven (see 1 Corinthians 6:10).

According to Jesus, at His return the unprepared will be treated just like unbelievers (see Luke 12:46), with one exception. They will be punished even more severely because they knew their duty, but refused to do it. Those people who are found to be disobedient at Christ's return but who didn't know much about what He expected of them will be punished less severely. This indicates that the "unprepared" of whom Christ was speaking are probably professing Christians, supposed servants of Christ who have some knowledge of the Bible, but who are not really saved. Both the knowledgeable unprepared and the ignorant unprepared will be banished to hell, although their punishments will vary there. This means that it would be much worse to be the child of Christian parents and only a "church kid" who has no real relationship with Jesus than an ignorant pagan who knows little about Jesus. Both will spend eternity in hell, but the "church kid" will be punished even more severely there.

Jesus said that the servants whom He finds doing His will when He returns will receive a special favor and reward. Amazingly, Jesus said that He would reward His obedient servants by serving them a meal! God foretold through the prophet Isaiah of a fabulous meal that He would prepare for His people: "The Lord Almighty will spread a wonderful feast for everyone around the world. It will be a delicious feast of good food, with clear, well-aged wine and choice beef" (Isaiah 25:6). We can also read in the book of Revelation about something called "the wedding feast of the Lamb" and how blessed are those who are invited to it. If you are a true follower of Jesus who is prepared for His return, you're one of those blessed ones!

Q. Kids of Christian parents often outwardly conform to their parents' standard of behavior while they're growing up, but once they grow old enough to leave home, their lifestyles change dramatically for the worse. What does this tell us about those kids?

A. They were perhaps never really saved in the first place. That is why parents should not only teach their children about what is right and what is wrong, they should teach them *why* certain things are right and certain things are wrong. And even more importantly, they should teach their children about Jesus and who He is, so that their children's good behavior results from their personal relationship with Him and their desire to obey Him—not just a temporary outward conformity.

Q. Jesus compared Himself to a burglar in today's reading. At other times He compared Himself to a "thief in the night." Why would Jesus ever use evil people to describe Himself?

A. Both comparisons teach us the limitations of comparisons and the foolishness of trying to find too much meaning in Jesus' parables and metaphors. Remember that a metaphor is a comparison of things that are basically *not the same*, but which have some striking similarities. The only similarity between Jesus and a burglar is that people are not expecting either, and are caught by surprise when they come. That is where the similarities end.

Application: If Jesus returned at this instant, are you ready this instant?

Jesus Warns People to Repent
Luke 13:1-9

We are sometimes tempted to think that people who suffer some tragedy are more wicked than most people, and that God is punishing them for their sins. Surely, it is with *those* people that God is angry. In today's reading, however, we gain Jesus' perspective of such things, and because Jesus is God, we can be sure His perspective is correct.

Two tragic things had recently occurred in Jerusalem. The first was Herod's murder of some people from Galilee as they were sacrificing in the Temple. We don't know any details of what happened, but can be sure it was the talk of all Judea and Galilee for some time. The second was the accidental death of eighteen men who were killed when a big stone tower toppled over onto them. In both cases, many Jews of Jesus' day had assumed that God was punishing them because of their wickedness. They also assumed that because they were alive, they themselves must not be deserving of such a fate, and they, unlike those who died, had God's approval.

Jesus said, however, that the people who died were not greater sinners than anyone else, and warned the living that unless they repented, they would also perish. In other words, from God's perspective, the survivors were just as deserving of a tragic death as those who perished. The survivors, however, had simply received more time to repent. So, the question people should have been asking was not, "Why did those people die?" Rather, they should have been asking, "Why are any of us still alive?"

Jesus answered that question using an illustration of the unfruitful fig tree. The man who planted the fig tree was tired of waiting for the tree to produce figs and decided that the tree should be cut down because it was wasting space in his garden. His gardener, however, persuaded him to give the tree one more year, promising to give it more fertilizer and special attention. Then, if it didn't produce any figs after that year, he would cut it down.

Those who survived the contemporary tragedies of that time were like the fruitless fig tree that deserved to be cut down. God, however, had mercifully decided to give them more time to repent and produce the fruit of obedience in their lives. The people who died couldn't complain over their fate, because they'd received only what they deserved. In fact, they, too, had doubtlessly deserved to perish long before they did, but also received undeserved mercy.

Although God didn't cause the Tower of Siloam to fall on eighteen men and kill them, and although God didn't inspire Herod to murder the Galileans, no one can intelligently say that God didn't *permit* both tragedies to occur. Jesus said that both served as warnings to the living that they needed to repent. Those warnings, too, were indications of God's mercy to the survivors, who really didn't even deserve to be warned!

Q. If everyone died on his or her eightieth birthday, and no one died before then, how do you think that would affect the way people live their lives?

A. Most people would lead very sinful lives and then, as the time of their eightieth birthday drew near, would become very holy! But, because everyone knows that death can occur at any time, and because we are constantly reminded of that fact by the tragic, unexpected deaths of so many people, smart folks are motivated to repent immediately. That way they're ready to stand before God's judgment seat at any time.

Q. Was it fair that God allowed some people to die in those two tragedies and allowed others who were equally deserving of death to live?

A. It was not really a matter of fairness from God's standpoint since everyone deserved to die before he did. For example, suppose there were two murderers in prison who had both killed many people and who were sentenced to die. One is scheduled to be executed on Monday and the other on Tuesday. What would the prison warden say to the Monday murderer if he complained of unfair treatment? He would say, "You have no right to complain of unfair treatment, because you deserved to die a long time ago. Fairness for you is not something that is an issue at this point. And did you treat the people you murdered with fairness?"

Application: People have been asking for ages, "Why do bad things happen to good people?" Their question reveals their ignorance about God's holiness and humanity's sinfulness. Jesus said that no one is good except God alone (see Mark 10:18), so that disqualifies every person from being classified as "good." In light of our sinfulness and God's holiness, the question people should be asking is, "Why does anything good ever happen to such bad people?" The answer to that question would be, "Because God is so merciful."

Jesus Heals a Crippled Woman on the Sabbath
Luke 13:10-17

When faultfinders want to find faults, they find them! Right before this synagogue leader's eyes, a woman who had suffered for eighteen years was instantly healed. And what did he see? He didn't see a woman who was healed, he saw a man who sinned by "working" on the Sabbath, performing a healing. His words revealed what was in his evil heart and his actions exposed his hypocrisy. Jesus said that everyone takes care of the needs of his animals on the Sabbath day, doing things that could be classified as work but nevertheless are considered unavoidable responsibilities. If it is acceptable to take care of animals on the Sabbath, is it not all right to take care of people on the Sabbath? Certainly it is. Just as in our day, some people of Jesus' day placed a higher value on animals than on people!

By the same token, some modern Christians seem to want to take all the enjoyment out of Sundays on the basis that we should "keep the Sabbath holy." They demonstrate a similar attitude to that of the synagogue leader. Certainly our Sabbath, which most Christians practice on Sunday, not Saturday, is a special day in which we can focus even more on spiritual things. But to forbid children to play on Sunday afternoons, or to say that it is a sin to fix a meal on Sunday to serve hungry people, is not what God had in mind when He gave the Sabbath commandment.

Q. What should have been the response of the synagogue leader?
A. He should have begun to praise God with the woman who was healed, and then fall on his face before Jesus, repenting of his sins and asking for forgiveness.

Q. Jesus said that Satan had held the formerly-crippled woman in bondage for eighteen years. What does this tell us about the source of sickness and God's will concerning healing?
A. It tells us that Satan is the real source of sickness. This also provides additional proof that God wants us well, since the devil is His enemy and the Bible says that Jesus came to destroy the works of the Devil (see 1 John 3:8).

Application: Can you imagine being bent double for eighteen years, unable to stand up straight all that time? Think of how excited and thankful this woman must have been when Jesus healed her. For us, this story is one more proof that Jesus is the Son of God, and it should encourage us to look to Him to grant us the miracles we need in our lives. He is full of compassion.

Jesus Teaches About the Narrow Door to Heaven
Luke 13:22-35

The main reason why Jesus became a human being was to die for our sins so we could be forgiven. Jesus was the "Lamb of God," and it was God's will that He die in Jerusalem during the Passover feast with all the other Passover lambs. As Jesus made His final journey from Galilee to Jerusalem, He taught in towns and villages on the way, and one day someone asked Him a very important question: "Lord, will only a few be saved?"

Using different words, Jesus restated what He'd taught during His sermon on the mountainside, revealing that only a minority of people would be saved, while the majority would go to hell: "You can enter God's Kingdom only through the narrow gate. The highway to hell is broad, and its gate is wide for the many who choose the easy way. But the gateway to life is small, and the road is narrow, and only a few ever find it" (Matthew 7:13-14).

In this instance, Jesus told His questioner that many people would try to enter heaven, but they would be kept out for one reason—because they were evildoers. Some people will even claim that they ate and drank with Jesus and listened to Him teach in their streets, which will be true of many people who were alive when Jesus walked the earth. However, their association with Him won't be enough for them to be saved. It's not being just *associated* with Jesus that gets a person into heaven, it's believing with an obedient faith that He is the Son of God. If a person only *associates* with Jesus, he obviously doesn't believe that Jesus is the Son of God, otherwise he would give his life to Him in obedient service, and no longer be categorized as an evildoer. He may believe that Jesus is a nice person, a good teacher or a faithful friend, but that is not enough. Are you a part of the minority who will enter heaven through the narrow gate?

Jesus also made it plain that there are only two places people will go after they die: heaven or hell. There is no purgatory as some think, a place where people pay for their sins and then are eventually released into heaven.

In the final part of today's reading, we read of Jesus lamenting over Jerusalem. Take note that although He knew He would soon be crucified in that city, He wasn't feeling sorry for Himself. Rather, He was feeling sorry for the people of Jerusalem because He knew the consequences they would suffer for rejecting Him. Within forty years, their city would be destroyed, and tens of thousands of the inhabitants would be crucified by the Roman army. Worse than that, those who rejected Christ would spend eternity in hell.

It was God's perfect will that all the people of Jerusalem be saved, expressed by Jesus when He said, "How often I have wanted to gather your children together as a hen protects her chicks beneath her wings" (Luke 13:34). But why wasn't He able to do what He wanted? Jesus explained: "But you wouldn't let me." It won't be God's fault that anyone is in hell.

Q. Jesus said that in the future, when His kingdom comes, there will be people who are despised now but who will be greatly honored then, and there will be some who are greatly honored now who will be despised then. About what kinds of people do you think He was speaking?

A. For the most part, those who are devoted followers of Christ are not being honored by the world, but are being despised as fanatics and fools. They will be honored by God in His kingdom. On the other hand, there are many unsaved people whom the world presently honors, but who will be despised by God when they stand before Him.

Q. In today's reading, Jesus quoted from Psalm 118. We can read in that same psalm these words: "The stone rejected by the builders has now become the cornerstone" (Psalm 118:22). What do you think the writer of that Psalm was talking about?

A. According to Jesus and Peter, Jesus is the rejected stone that became the cornerstone (see Matthew 21:42; Acts 4:11). If you don't know what a cornerstone is, ask your parents.

Application: Jesus promised in today's reading that people from all over the world would be citizens of His future kingdom. This proves that Jesus died for everyone and that God loves every member of every race and nationality. He is not prejudiced at all. When you think of people of other races or nationalities, are your thoughts like God's thoughts? Christians, above all people, should not be prejudiced.

Jesus Teaches About Humility and Servanthood
Luke 14:1-14

Just the fact that the only fault the Pharisees could find with Jesus was that He healed on the Sabbath tells us that He must have been a very good person. (We know that he was sinless). Jesus wasn't content to let them think that He was guilty of even one little sin, so He explained that the fault they'd found in Him wasn't a fault at all. Rather, they were criticizing Him for a virtue. He was helping someone who needed help on the Sabbath, just as they would do for their sons or animals if they were in need on the Sabbath. So Jesus proved that their only criticism of Him was unjustified. He was sinless.

As we've previously seen, the religion of the Pharisees was mostly just a show. They worked hard at looking good on the outside, but their inward motivation was all wrong. They were seeking the praise of men rather than the praise of God, something that usually characterizes religious people who are not born again. Jesus saw through them, and noted that their desire to be honored before others was evident even in how they seated themselves to eat a meal together. Each one tried to sit near the head of the table where the most "important" people sat, and Jesus seized the opportunity to teach a lesson about humility. When we exalt ourselves, we run the risk of being humbled, just like the man who takes a seat of honor at a wedding feast. It's much better and more pleasing to God if we will humble ourselves. If we will, we're more likely to be exalted.

Humble people are always thinking, not of themselves, but of others. For that reason, they have a servant's attitude, looking for opportunities to be a blessing. However, just because someone serves others isn't sure proof that he's a true servant. Many people outwardly seem to be kind and generous, but often they are just acting in order to gain people's favor. They are hoping to personally benefit in the long run. For example, people sometimes give gifts in order to make others feel indebted to them. That is one reason Jesus told us to give secretly. Secret gifts are motivated by pure love.

That is also why Jesus told the host of the dinner not to invite his friends, brothers, relatives and rich neighbors when he gave a dinner. They could and would repay him for his kindness. A higher, more godly love would be demonstrated by giving a dinner for those who could not repay him. Jesus told him that if he would give a dinner for people who could not repay him, such as the poor, crippled, lame and blind, *God* would reward him at the resurrection of the godly.

This doesn't mean that it's wrong for us to show love to our friends, brothers, relatives and neighbors. But our love for them could be just self-ishness disguised as love if we have hidden motives. God is calling us to a higher love, one that is pure like His. He wants us to show love to those whom most people neglect, ignore, and even hate.

Q. What do you think God would say to a person who wants to look good in the eyes of others when he humbles himself with the hope of being exalted?

A. God would say that person is guilty of *false humility*. True humility has no plans for being exalted by other people. It only desires the praise of God.

Q. How do you think God feels about social cliques, small groups of exclusive people who look down upon or don't associate with those who don't meet their standards for acceptance?

A. He's against them, because they are held together by selfishness and convey hatred toward people He loves.

Application: Is there anyone you know that most people ignore, a person who receives very little love from others? It may even be someone in your school or church who is a little different from everyone else. In light of what Jesus said, what do you think He wants you to do? Will you?

A Feast For Everyone
Luke 14:15-24

This important story was told by Jesus while He was dining with a group of Pharisees. Just after He had said something about the resurrection of the godly people, one of the diners expressed what a privilege it would be to share in the Kingdom of God. The man was, perhaps, conveying the heart-felt feelings of everyone present, and Jesus recognized His opportunity to tell them who will and who will not be one of those privileged people.

Amazingly, the point of Jesus' story is that it is *not* God who determines who gets into His kingdom. People themselves determine their destiny. God has sent an invitation to everyone, but unfortunately many are making excuses to decline His offer.

Their excuses, as Jesus so wonderfully illustrated, make no sense to anyone with good sense. One man in Jesus' story had just purchased a field and wanted to inspect it. Not only was he rude for declining the invitation, but his reason for declining was insulting to the host. He considered the inspection of his field, something he could do at any time, to be more important than his invitation to the feast, which he would never have another opportunity to attend. He also appears foolish not to have inspected his field before he bought it.

The second man was equally insulting, conveying that he would rather spend time with his new oxen than with the host and his guests.

The third man stated that he'd just been married so he couldn't attend. Perhaps this man represents the person who lets other people make his decisions for him, in this case, a wife.

The wealthy host was angry when his servant returned, informing him how his invitations had been denied. So he instructed his servant to go to the streets and alleys of the city and invite the poor, the crippled, the lame and the blind, and all of them gratefully accepted his invitation. But there was room for still more, so the host instructed his servant to go to remote places where few people lived to urge anyone he could find to come to his feast. He wanted his house to be full. He was obviously a very gracious man. He clearly represents our God, who has extended His salvation invitation to everyone.

Q. Many of the people of Jesus' day considered the poor, the crippled, the lame and the blind to be cursed by God, assuming they were deserving their of plight because of their sinfulness. As a result, they had little compassion on such people. What does Jesus' story teach us about that viewpoint?

A. It teaches us that it is entirely wrong. Although we may not understand why some people are born with birth defects, or why some people suffer tragedies in their lives, we should never assume that it is because they are greater sinners than the rest of us. God loves every one of them, and He wants them to accept His invitation to be saved.

Q. Jesus wanted to point out in this story that people who reject God's salvation invitation are very foolish. What could be more foolish than refusing eternal life and living forever in heaven, and choosing to spend eternity in hell? Can you think of any foolish excuses that people use today to decline God's invitation?

Application: The wealthy host in today's story finally told his servant to go to the remote, less-populated areas to invite people to his feast. God loves people in far-away places, and all Christians should be involved in helping those kinds of people hear about God's invitation. We can do that by praying for God to send people, by giving money and praying for those who are taking God's message to far-away places, or by going ourselves. Are you like the servant of the wealthy host?

The Cost of True Discipleship
Luke 14:25-33

By studying almost everything that the Gospels record about the life of Jesus, we have an advantage over daily devotionals that only consider random portions of Scripture: we don't avoid or miss anything that God wants us to know about Jesus. The only record we have of Jesus' life is found in the writings of Matthew, Mark, Luke and John. The Holy Spirit inspired them to write exactly what they did, so all of it is important, and we shouldn't neglect any part.

Today's reading is one of those portions that some people avoid, because what Jesus said seems too demanding of them. But ignoring what Jesus taught doesn't do away with what He said! Everyone needs to face up to what we've just read.

Jesus was very plainly teaching that there is a cost to be His disciple. He expects our highest devotion, and He couldn't have made His standards more clear.

First, we must love Him even more than the people we love the most: our fathers, mothers, spouses, children, brothers and sisters. In fact, Jesus said we must love Him more than our own lives. True disciples of Jesus are sold out to Him. Jesus is not just a *part* of their lives, He is the *center* of their lives.

Second, Jesus said that we must carry our own cross in order to be His disciples. What did He mean? He wasn't saying, of course, that His followers must literally carry a cross on their backs wherever they go. The carrying of the cross that Jesus talked about must be symbolic of something.

In Jesus' day, when crucifixion was a common means of punishment, the expression He used was probably common. It would have meant, "Do the thing that you would naturally not want to do," or "Deny your selfish desires for a greater cause." Those who are Christ's true disciples have done just that. The most important thing in their lives is no longer pleasing themselves, but pleasing God.

Third, we must love Jesus more than any material thing if we are to be His disciples. Jesus owns us and everything we own. Therefore, He should have control over everything we possess, and we should do with it as He directs.

Unfortunately, too many people decided to become followers of Christ without first considering what it might cost them. When they do realize the cost, they change their minds. For example, a person might decide to follow Christ, but when he does, all his friends abandon him. So, in order to gain back their friendship, he stops obeying Jesus. Or a new follower of Christ who didn't count the cost might be required by his employer to lie to customers or lose his job. In order to keep his job, he stops following Jesus.

Have you considered the cost of following Jesus? It seems like a contradiction, but it's true: Salvation is a gift that could cost you everything!

Q. Can someone be a Christian without being a disciple of Christ? A. Not according to the Bible. Neither Jesus nor any of the apostles taught that a person could be a believer in Christ without becoming a follower of Christ. There are not two classes of Christians, the uncommitted who believe in Him and the devoted followers. Those who truly believe in Jesus become His disciples.

Q. Is it possible for a person to be a disciple of Jesus, but not give away any of his earnings to support the spread of the gospel or help the poor? A. In light of all that Jesus said about our responsibility as His followers pertaining to money, it seems highly unlikely that such a person could actually be a true follower of Christ.

Application: A major problem in churches today is that many people claim to be Christian, but they really aren't. They think they're going to heaven just because they prayed a prayer to receive Jesus, even though their lives are no different from that of non-Christians. They are unwilling to sacrifice anything for the sake of following Christ, such as their time, their selfish pursuits, their money or their reputation. Those kinds of people are going to be very surprised when they are condemned to hell. We need to tell them the truth.

God's Lost and Found
Luke 15:1-32

Today we read of another fault the Pharisees and religious teachers found in Jesus: He spent time with sinful people. This once more strengthens our belief that Jesus was sinless, because the only faults anyone could find in Him weren't faults at all, they were virtues. Jesus explained why He spent time with sinners: they were valued by God, just as a lost sheep is to a shepherd and a lost coin is to a woman who owns ten coins.

The Pharisees who criticized Jesus were self-righteous, and were actually just as lost as the people they condemned as being sinners. Jesus considered everyone to be a sinner who needs to be saved, but those who didn't think they were sinners could never be saved, because they thought they already were!

The story of the lost son was really a story about the bad attitude of the older brother, who represented the Pharisees. The younger son was definitely guilty, but he repented before his father, who received him back with rejoicing and a feast. His son had been lost, but was back home where he belonged. The older brother became angry when he saw how gracious his father was toward his brother. He had always obeyed his father and never had received a similar party. To him it didn't seem fair.

Every time I read this story, I always feel myself siding with the older brother. If my father did what his father had done, I would probably react the same way. But when I put myself in the shoes of the father, I'm sure I would do just what he did for his repentant son. There were two different perspectives in the matter, and we must realize that our God has the father's perspective. He loves all of His own, so we should adopt His attitude and rejoice when He blesses someone who has recently repented after committing big sins, even if we feel like God is showing favoritism. Of course, God shows no favoritism, but like the father in the story, He can't help but express His love when a repentant son returns home.

Q. If the younger brother was so graciously received and restored when he returned home, was there any advantage for the older brother to have stayed home, remaining obedient to his father all those years?

A. Absolutely. Everything the father owned was divided between his two sons. The younger of the two had wasted his entire inheritance, but the older brother still possessed all of his. That is why his father reminded him, "Everything I have is yours" (Luke 15:31b). The wayward son, although blessed to be restored, would regret all his life what he did with his inheritance. He would never have another opportunity to receive it again. And the older brother could use his inheritance to have as many feasts with his friends as he wanted.

Q. How do you think Jesus feels about Christians who look down on sinful people who are not Christians?

A. He knows they are guilty of spiritual pride. All of us were sinners at one time who needed a Savior. We were no different than the sinful people we now look down upon, except that we heard and believed the gospel and God forgave and changed us. We need to be merciful toward sinners as God is.

 Application: Did you notice the father's love for his repentant son in today's final story? When the returning son was still a long distance away, his father saw him coming. He had been hoping and longing for his son's return, always looking into the distance. He didn't wait for his son to make it to him. Rather, he ran to his son, filled with love and compassion. When they met, he didn't wait for his son's confession, but immediately embraced and kissed him. When his son confessed his sin, he didn't scold him to make him feel worse, but immediately called for the finest robe, a ring for his finger, sandals for his feet and a great feast in celebration. Does that help you understand God's loves?

90

The Story of the Shrewd Money Manager
Luke 16:1-14

Jesus' story of the shrewd money manager is one that many people have difficulty understanding. However, if we first consider the lessons of the story that Jesus shared at its conclusion, it's easier to understand how the story leads to those lessons.

Jesus mentioned at least three lessons His story teaches, and all of them revolve around the use of and our attitude about money. The last of the three is, "No one can serve two masters. For you will hate one and love the other, or be devoted to one and despise the other. You cannot serve both God and money" (Luke 16:13). Jesus does not want money to be our highest priority as it is for many people. *Every* aspect of some people's lives revolves around money. For example, when faced with a decision about choosing a career, the most important question they ask themselves is, "What can I do that will make me the most money?" A servant of God, considering the same question, would ask, "What does God want me to do?" Those whose god is money are literally controlled by money, as it directs their every decision. And that was the case with the shrewd money manager. He deceived and cheated his master, sinning against God, because money was his highest priority. It was his god. By their actions, the Pharisees also proved they loved money more than God.

The second lesson was about trustworthiness. Jesus said, "Unless you are faithful in small matters, you won't be faithful in large ones. If you cheat even a little, you won't be honest with greater responsibilities" (Luke 16:10).

Trustworthiness is something that must be earned, and it is first earned by proving yourself trustworthy in small things. The shrewd money manager in Jesus' story was found unfaithful, and that was why he lost his job. God is testing everyone's faithfulness by watching what we do with what He's given us, including our money. Christians who don't give anything when they're making only a little money are proving they wouldn't give anything if they made a lot of money, in spite of what they may claim. So why would God bless them with more money? Christians who waste money that God gives them are also proving themselves untrustworthy and provide no reason for God to entrust them with more.

This is more important than many Christians realize. How we spend our money is a primary indicator of our spiritual lives. In fact, it can reveal whether we are truly saved or not. Jesus said, "If you are untrustworthy about worldly wealth, who will trust you with the true riches of heaven?" The shrewd money manager in Jesus' story proved, by his mishandling of his master's money, that he was not truly devoted and obedient to his master. So his master rejected him, just as God will reject those who, by their use of their money, prove that they aren't truly submitted to Him.

The third lesson is perhaps the most difficult one to understand, especially if you are reading from a translation other than the *New Living Translation*. Jesus said, "I tell you, use your worldly resources to benefit others and make friends. In this way, your generosity stores up a reward for you in heaven" (Luke 16:9). The shrewd money manager made friends out of his master's debtors by lowering their debts. Because he'd helped them save money by cheating his master, they'd feel obligated to help him once he lost his job. Jesus, of course, doesn't want us to make friends by cheating anyone, but He does expect that we will assist our brothers and sisters in Christ who are in financial need. And we, like the shrewd manager, will ultimately benefit from helping them when we are rewarded in heaven.

Q. Do you think what we've read today has any application to kids?
A. If they receive any money, either by earning it or receiving it as a gift, it certainly does. They should demonstrate their obedient faith in Jesus by what they do with their money, and it doesn't make any difference how little money they have. In fact, by proving to God at a young age that He can trust them with a little money, kids can ensure themselves a better financial future.

Q. Many people think it's O.K. to tell "little" lies, as long as their lies don't hurt anyone. And they claim they would never tell a "big" lie. How do you think God feels about that?
A. God knows they're lying about not lying! When they're faced with a small temptation to tell a small lie and yield, God knows they'll tell a big

lie when faced with a big temptation. God never tells any lies, big or small, and neither should we.

⊙ Application: When you are faced with a decision, are the financial consequences more important to you than the spiritual consequences? Say, for example, that you have just enough money to buy a certain thing you've wanted for a long time. However, you haven't given away any portion of that money yet, to someone less fortunate, to your church or to a missionary. What is the proper thing to do?

The Rich Man and Lazarus
Luke 16:19-31

Jesus told this story of the rich man and Lazarus directly after He told the story we read yesterday of the shrewd money manager. Both stories teach us something about how God expects us to view and use money.

The final conclusion of yesterday's story was, "No one can serve two masters. For you will hate one and love the other, or be devoted to one and despise the other. You cannot serve both God and money" (Luke 16:13). The rich man in today's story was a perfect illustration of this truth. Money was obviously his god, not because he was wealthy but because of what he did with his money. He repeatedly ignored the pathetic plight of a diseased and starving beggar lying at his doorstep, who became too weak to even chase away the dogs that licked his open sores. The rich man could have easily provided food and shelter for Lazarus, yet he showed him no pity until Lazarus eventually died right on his doorstep. The rich man's actions proved that the love of money controlled his life, and not the love of God. The point of this story is not, "Rich people go to hell and poor people go to heaven." There are many wealthy people mentioned in the Bible as being godly and righteous.

The point of this story is that people whose god is money are unsaved people. The rich man's lack of compassion for Lazarus was a telling sin, but you can be sure it wasn't his only sin. In fact, in hell he knew that the greatest need of his living brothers was that they "turn from their sins" (Luke 16:30). If he would have had faith in God during his life, he, too, would have turned from his sins. True faith is always manifested by obedience. But during his life, the rich man served money, not God.

Jesus obviously believed there was such a place as hell, and made it clear that it's a place of conscious torment. Although the rich man had left his body on earth, his spirit was very much alive, and he was able to see, hear, touch, taste and remember. He longed for some relief from the heat of hell's flames. But, because he had previously ignored the plight of Lazarus, now he was being justly repaid for that sin and all his sins. Praise God that those who believe in Jesus and repent on earth are forgiven of their sins because Jesus suffered the punishment they deserved! Aren't you glad you're one of them?

Q. Do you have to be wealthy to be guilty of the sin of loving money? A. No, middle-class and even poor people can be guilty of that sin. However, wealthy people are probably more often guilty of it than others. Studies show that wealthy people generally give a smaller percentage of their money to charities than people with smaller incomes.

Q. Does what we've read today apply to kids?
A. It does if they are followers of Christ and have any money of their own, either earned or received as a gift. A portion of it should be used to help those who are less fortunate. One way to do that is to give to needy people that you know, or perhaps to sponsor a needy child in another country. Many churches give a portion of their income to the poor, and thus, by giving to their churches, people are also giving to the poor.

Application: We sometimes mistakenly think, like the rich man in hell, that if people witnessed a miracle they would turn from their sins. However, God is doing miracles every day for everyone, trying to get their attention. He uses snowflakes and stars, flowers and fruit, babies being born and water turning to ice, but people ignore His call. Beyond that, God is speaking to them through their consciences and His words in the Bible. Still they don't listen. The real problem isn't the lack of miracles, it's the hardness of people's hearts.

Temptation, Sin, Forgiveness, Faith and Obedience
Luke 17:1-10

The most important thing that people can and should do is to obey God. More than anything else, God wants our obedience. He does not want the kind of obedience that the Pharisees demonstrated, an outward obedience to man-made laws; He wants an obedience that springs from a heart that loves Him. Because obedience to God is so important, anything relating to obedience in our lives is also very important. Jesus talked about the importance of several of those related things in our reading today.

First, disobedience usually begins with a temptation, so God is very opposed to anyone who tempts others to sin. Those kinds of people will incur worse punishment in hell than anyone else because they will not only be held responsible for their own sins, but will also be held partly responsible for the sins of others. Many people make their living at tempting others and causing them to sin, such as publishers of pornography and sellers of illegal drugs.

Second, the opposite of one who helps others to sin is the one who hinders other people from sinning. One way God wants us to help others not to sin is by rebuking fellow believers if they sin against us. Of course, a rebuke such as that should be given gently in love. If the fellow believer repents, we are supposed to forgive him or her. If we don't, we are sinning.

Third is the relationship between faith and obedience. Like the apostles, we would like to have more faith, thinking that the primary result of greater faith would be the working of miracles in our lives. Jesus said, however, that even a very small amount of faith can produce a major miracle. *So miracles aren't the evidence of great faith.* In fact, there are instances in the Gospels of people who performed miracles in Jesus' name who weren't even followers of Jesus. They may have had a little faith in Jesus in regard to His ability and power, but they didn't have faith in Him as being the Savior, Lord and Judge before whom all people must one day stand. Thus, the working of miracles is not what proves a person has faith in all that Jesus is. Rather, it is obedience that indicates a person has that kind of faith, which is why Jesus then immediately proceeded to talk about obedience.

Finally, a fourth issue related to obedience to God is the danger of becoming proud when we are obedient. Because pride is a sin, there exists the danger that not sinning can lead to a sin! So, as Jesus instructed, we should always view ourselves as servants who deserve no praise. When we obey God, we are only doing our duty, not going above and beyond our duty.

Q. If a fellow believer sins against you seven times in one day and you forgive him seven times, what should you do if he sins against you an eighth time that same day?

A. You should forgive him. Jesus wasn't placing a limit of seven acts of forgiveness per day per believer. He was saying that there should be no limit to our forgiveness. It is very unlikely that you will ever have an opportunity to forgive one person seven times in one day, and Jesus knew that!

Q. What sin can most easily originate from obedience?

A. The sin of pride. People who don't sin can easily become proud of it, which means they're sinning again!

Application: What is the most important thing in life? Obedience to God! This should be on our minds all the time.

Jesus Cleanses Ten Lepers
Luke 17:11-19

Leprosy is a terrible disease that causes a person's body parts to slowly rot away. Lepers often lose their fingers and toes and eventually the disease kills them. It is very contagious and is spread by touch. For that reason, lepers in Jesus' day were outcasts of society, and no one wanted to be near them. So they hung around each other, and in today's story we find a group of ten who called on Jesus to heal them. From examining the details of the story, it's obvious that they had faith in His healing power.

First, their faith was evident by their calling out to Jesus to be healed.

Second, when Jesus told them to go and show themselves to the priests, they obeyed. Under the Law of Moses, before a cleansed leper could begin normal interaction with non-leprous people, he had to be examined by a priest and declared cleansed of his leprosy. That is what Jesus was requiring the ten lepers to do, and so they started off on a 25- or 30-mile journey to Jerusalem. They must have believed that they would be better by the time they got to the priests, and as they acted on their faith, they were!

And third, Jesus told the one leper who returned to give thanks that it was his faith that had healed him. For this reason, we can conclude that all ten were healed through their faith in Jesus. Where did these ten lepers get their faith? They must have heard that Jesus was healing all who asked to be healed.

What would have happened if they wouldn't have asked Jesus for healing? What would have happened if they wouldn't have obeyed Him, acting on their faith by heading toward Jerusalem to show themselves to the priests? The answer to both questions is this: They would not have been healed, even though we know from reading the story that it was obviously God's will for them to be healed. This once again proves that God's will doesn't always automatically happen regardless of what we do. And it once again proves that unless we believe, God's will may not come to pass in our lives.

 Q. Jesus healed all ten of the lepers. What does this say to us?
A. It leads us to believe, once again, that God wants everyone to be

healed. Many Christians today will say that it is God's will to heal some but not all. But Jesus healed *all* the lepers. And, if they had believed that it was only God's will for a few of them to be healed, none of them would have been healed, because none of them could have had faith for individual healing.

Q. The one leper who returned to give Jesus thanks was a Samaritan. His faith was actually more impressive than the faith of the other nine. Why?

A. Because Jews and Samaritans had no dealings with one another in Jesus' time. Because of that, he, more than the others, would have been tempted to doubt the wisdom of obeying Jesus' instructions to show himself to the priests. He knew the priests would probably have nothing to do with him. But he obeyed Jesus anyway and was healed.

Application: If we believe in Jesus as our healer, let us begin to talk and act like it!

94

Jesus Teaches About the Coming Kingdom
Luke 17:20-37

There are many places in the Old Testament that tell about the time when God's kingdom will rule over all the earth. That promised future kingdom is something the Jewish people anticipated for a long, long time. As Christians, we also are waiting for that day, knowing that Jesus is the One who will then rule the world. It will be heaven on earth.

One day some of the Pharisees asked Jesus when God's kingdom would come. Knowing that they would not be citizens of that kingdom unless they believed in Him, Jesus answered their question by telling them that the kingdom of God was among them. That is, the God of that kingdom, the One who would one day rule the world, was standing right in front of them, offering blessings that would be enjoyed by every one of that kingdom's citizens. In that sense, God's kingdom isn't coming, it's here right now! Although Jesus is not yet ruling everyone in the world, He is ruling over everyone who has submitted his life to Him.

Later with His disciples, Jesus spoke more about the time when He would return to rule the world. He didn't tell us everything we might want to know, but He told us everything He wanted His disciples and us to know.

First, Jesus made clear to His disciples certain things that modern Christians know quite well: He would suffer and die and then be gone from earth for a considerable amount of time. His followers would want Him to come back much sooner than He would. Knowing how much we would long to see Him, Jesus warned us against being deceived by reports of His supposed return. When He comes back, Jesus said we'll know it, because He won't be sneaking back and hiding somewhere! His return will be as evident as lightning flashing across the sky.

Second, Jesus reiterated to His disciples what He previously said to the Pharisees: His return would not be ushered in with visible signs immediately preceding it. People would be caught unprepared and would be living their lives just as they always had.

Third, when Jesus returns to the earth, He will come with judgment. Many people will die, suffering God's wrath, just as they did during the flood of Noah and the destruction of Sodom. Because entire cities and towns will be destroyed, Christ's followers will have to be cautious not to put themselves into danger by joining the ungodly when God's wrath falls upon them. Jesus reminded us of Lot's wife, who died looking back to a city that God was destroying. However, although there is the possibility of one of us making a mistake, there is no danger of God making a mistake. We don't have to worry about Him accidentally killing us, because Jesus told us that two people could be working side by side or even sleeping in the same bed, and one would be taken and the other saved. God knows those who are His, and He won't treat them like the ungodly.

 Q. If you heard a report on the television news that Jesus had recently returned and was living in France, would you believe it?

A. I hope not! Jesus told us not to believe any reports of His return because we'll all know it when it happens.

Q. Let's suppose you are alive when Jesus returns. You happen to be driving home from a vacation and have just about arrived at the outskirts of your city when fire falls from the sky over and on your entire city. Should you drive as fast as you can to get to your house to rescue your prized possessions?

A. No, you should stay away from any area that looks as if God's wrath is falling on it.

Application: All true Christians hope that Jesus will return in their lifetime. But even if He doesn't, at death we get to immediately be with Jesus in heaven. Then, when He does return, we will return with Him. That might be even better than being on the earth and seeing Him return!

Jesus Encourages His Followers to Trust Him for Justice
Luke 18:1-8

In many places around the world over the last two thousand years, Jesus' followers have been persecuted. Some persecution is not too difficult to take, such as when someone lies about you to hurt your reputation as a Christian. But sometimes persecution can be very harsh, for example, if you lost your job for following Christ, or were kicked out of your home, or perhaps were even tortured and martyred for your faith. Any Christian in that kind of a situation begins to question why his heavenly Father is allowing the people who are persecuting him to get away with it. It's not fair, and since God is fair, why doesn't He punish the evildoers and stop their persecution?

Because the world will grow even worse as the time of Jesus' return draws closer, persecution against Christians will increase, and thus more and more of God's people will be crying out to Him for justice "day and night" (Luke 18:7). We know, of course, that eventually God will act in justice against those who persecute His people, but it won't happen as soon as those who are being persecuted would like. They will be tempted to doubt God's justice, give up hope and quit praying. Some may even be tempted to quit following Jesus.

But Jesus wants all of His persecuted people to be encouraged, and that's why He told this story of the persistent widow. Because she didn't give up, but rather, kept persisting in her quest for justice, she got what she wanted from a godless and uncaring judge. Jesus' point is this: If that widow got justice from a godless judge through her persistence, how much more will God's persistent people obtain justice from their perfectly just and caring heavenly Father? He will, as Jesus said, bring about justice for them quickly. Maybe not as quickly as they'd like, but quickly as far as God is concerned.

 Q. Why do you suppose God allows His people to be persecuted for even a minute? Why doesn't He judge persecutors immediately?

A. There may be several reasons. First, He is merciful toward the persecutors and wants to give them time to repent and be saved. Once they die and go to hell, they will never have another chance. When the persecutors experience the love of the Christians they persecute, who return good for evil, they may very well come to their senses and receive Jesus.

Second, God can use persecution to test His people. Those whose faith in

Jesus is fake are exposed when they are persecuted. They quit following Jesus. Perhaps that's why Jesus asked at the end of today's story, "But when I, the Son of Man, return, how many will I find who have faith?" (Luke 18:8).

Third, God can use persecution to help His children grow spiritually and become more like Jesus. Persecution gives us a chance to obey His command to love our enemies and develop the fruit of the Spirit. At the same time, we can prove our love for Him as we endure.

Finally, because God lives in a timeless realm, and because He knows all about the glorious eternity that we will experience, His perspective of persecution is different from ours. He will reward us in His kingdom for the persecution we experience now. When that time comes, we might wish that we had experienced more persecution on earth!

Q. Do Jesus' comments about persistence in prayer apply to every prayer we might pray?

A. No, they don't. We know they apply when we're praying for justice but not seeing immediate answers. However, when someone is praying for salvation, for example, he only needs to pray one time in faith and immediately receive what God has promised. This would be true for other things God has promised as well, such as the Holy Spirit (see Luke 11:13).

Application: If persecutors of Christians don't repent, you can be sure they will be punished fairly in hell when they die. Jesus even promised some persecuted Christians in the ancient city of Philadelphia that He would force their persecutors to bow down at their feet (see Revelation 3:9).

The Pharisee and the Tax Collector
Luke 18:9-14

This story was aimed at the Pharisees, who were generally proud of themselves for their supposed obedience to God and consequently despised everyone else. They were no different than many modern religious people who are proud of their outward conformity to God's law and who look down on others who don't come up to their standards.

The good points that the Pharisee listed about himself were commendable, as all of them indicated some obedience to God. He claimed that he never cheated, sinned or committed adultery. He fasted regularly and tithed. However, he had at least one major flaw: he was very proud. He thought that his good works earned his salvation. He didn't feel like he needed a Savior because he had saved himself!

We know, however, that the Pharisee needed a Savior, if for no other sin than the sin of pride. And most likely, he was guilty of a number of other sins as well. One, to be sure, was his lack of compassion for other people like the tax collector.

Unlike the Pharisee, the tax collector knew he was a sinner who needed forgiveness if he was to be saved. So he humbly admitted his sinfulness and asked for mercy from God. And Jesus said that his prayer was answered. He left his place of prayer saved, whereas the Pharisee left unsaved. To be saved, a person must humble himself, admitting that he is a sinner who needs a Savior. If we think, like the Pharisee, that we don't need a Savior, then we cannot be saved.

Q. Jesus said that the tax collector, unlike the Pharisee, left the Temple justified before God. Do you know what it means to be "justified"?

A. The easiest-to-remember definition of the word *justified* is this: *"just as if I'd* never sinned." When a person goes to court and the judge says at the end of his trial, "You are justified," he means, "I find you not guilty for the crime of which you've been accused." A person who is justified is not a forgiven sinner, he is a person who has not sinned! The Bible teaches us that Jesus bore our sins and gives believers His right standing before God the Father. Because Jesus never sinned, He has perfect standing before God, and that is what we get when we believe in Him!

Q. Would it be possible to have a perfect standing before God apart from Jesus?

A. Only if a person never sinned could he have a perfect standing before God without Jesus. However, since every person has sinned (even so-called good religious people who might be more obedient than the average person), everyone needs Jesus to be saved.

Application: Kids raised in Christian homes are often well taught to do what is right, and consequently they do what is right most of the time. The danger that exists for them is that they might tend to think that their good behavior is what saves them, and they might not see their great need for Jesus to save them. The cure for such a proud attitude is to ask the Lord to show us our sins, especially the ones that are hidden from others, like wrong thoughts, motives and attitudes. Why don't you ask the Lord to reveal to you how much you need Him as your Savior today in prayer?

The Unbelief of Jesus' Brothers and People of Jerusalem
John 7:1-36

According to what John wrote, before Jesus' death and resurrection, His own brothers didn't believe in Him. This teaches us that believing in Jesus means believing more than the fact that He was just a person in history. And it means believing more than the fact that Jesus did miracles. Jesus' brothers certainly believed He was a real person, and they also knew He did miracles. But they didn't believe that He was the divine Son of God, as indicated by how they spoke to Him, scoffing at Him. *In order to be saved, we must believe that Jesus is the Son of God.*

Being members of the same family, Jesus' brothers were perhaps embarrassed by His claims that seemed so outrageous and His growing unpopularity. We are told in Mark's Gospel that on at least one occasion, Jesus' family tried to drag Him back home with them, saying to other people that He was out of His mind (see Mark 3:21). On this occasion that John recorded, Jesus' brothers chided Him for what they perceived as His inconsistency. If He wanted to succeed in His mission, why would He hesitate to go to a well-attended Jewish feast in Jerusalem?

Jesus replied that it wasn't time for Him to go, indicating His obedience to His Father. He knew that, because many people in Jerusalem didn't like His convicting message, there was a growing opposition there that would eventually result in His crucifixion. It was important that He not be crucified prematurely, before the Passover Feast. So, in order not to cause too much of a stir, Jesus went to Jerusalem secretly, separately from His brothers.

Even though at first very few people knew He was there, Jesus was the main topic of conversation at the feast, and the Jewish leaders were on the lookout for Him. People debated about Him. Some thought He was a wonderful man while others considered Him to be a deceiver or even demon-possessed. Some believed He was the Messiah because of all His miracles. Others thought He couldn't be the promised One because they didn't know enough of the Scriptures and assumed the Messiah would simply appear, having no known origin. They knew, however, that Jesus was the son of Mary and (they thought) Joseph, and was from the town of Nazareth. So how could He be the Messiah?

Jesus, as always, answered His critics truthfully. He told them that He wasn't trying to pretend that He had just appeared or that He had no earthly origin. (Such credentials were not required of the Messiah.) And He clearly claimed to have come from God, having been sent as God's representative to bring God's teaching, that He was seeking to honor God, and that He would soon be going back to God. He was claiming to be much more than just a wonderful person or a prophet. He was claiming to be the Messiah, the Son of God!

Q. We read today that the Jewish leaders in Jerusalem tried to arrest Jesus, but no one laid a hand on Him because, "His time had not yet come" (John 7:30). What do you think that means?

A. We find that phrase, "His time had not yet come" and variations of it a number of times in the Gospel of John. As we read in later chapters, it becomes clear that Jesus was referring to the time of His crucifixion, the event for which He had been born. Jesus was predestined to die at the Passover Feast in Jerusalem, thus, when men made plans to arrest Him before then, God somehow prevented it from happening. Jesus would die when it was God's preordained time.

Q. Jesus told the Pharisees that they would not be able to come where He would be going. What did He mean?

A. He meant that they would not be able to enter heaven, joining Him there, because they did not believe in Him.

Application: People today have the same opinions about Jesus as they did back when Jesus walked the earth. The reason John recorded so much of their debate is because the most important thing anyone can do is to decide who Jesus is. Those who believe that He is who He claimed to be are given eternal life, just as John wrote near the end of his Gospel, "[I have written] so that you may believe that Jesus is the Messiah, the Son of God, and that by believing in him you will have life" (John 20:31).

98

Jesus Offers Living Water to Thirsty People
John 7:37-53

Can you imagine Jesus shouting to the Jerusalem crowds, "If you are thirsty, come to me! If you believe in me, come and drink! For the Scriptures declare that rivers of living water will flow out from within" (John 7:37b-38)? That would take a lot of nerve to do, unless you were crazy—or you were the Son of God.

Speaking figuratively, Jesus was once again offering what only He can give. He wasn't offering actual water to quench people's physical thirst—He was offering living water that would quench people's spiritual thirst. John wrote that the "living water" of which Jesus spoke was really the Holy Spirit. Jesus gives the Holy Spirit to everyone who comes to Him in faith, and the Holy Spirit lives within every true Christian from the moment of his conversion.

Jesus made this declaration on the last day of a Jewish celebration called *The Festival of Shelters*. It was a feast instituted by God to help the people of Israel remember their wanderings in the wilderness when they lived in temporary shelters after their exodus from Egypt. Each day during the festival, the priests would draw water from the Pool of Siloam and pour it out at the altar in the Temple. It was done in remembrance of the water that supernaturally came forth from a rock that Moses struck. Unfortunately, the Jews of Jesus' day missed the real significance of that original miracle and its yearly commemoration. God gave His people physical life through Moses by providing water when they were once dying of thirst. But much more important, He, through an even greater man, wanted to give living water to everyone who was dying of spiritual thirst. Jesus wanted everyone to know that He was the One whom Moses prefigured, and He was like the water that saved the thirsty Israelites.

As expected, the reaction of those who heard Jesus make His claim was divided. Some considered Him to be the great Prophet whom Moses had predicted. Others thought He was the Messiah. And others, especially the religious leaders, were convinced that Jesus was neither the Messiah nor a prophet because He was originally from the region of Galilee. They knew that the Messiah would be born in Bethlehem and that He would be David's descendant. Too bad they didn't do their homework, or they would have found out that Jesus met those conditions!

Q. When the leading priests and Pharisees learned that the Temple guards didn't arrest Jesus as they had been ordered, they mocked them, saying, "Have you been led astray, too? Is there a single one of us rulers or Pharisees who believes in him? These ignorant crowds do, but what do they know about it?" (John 7:47-49). Does this teach us anything about following religious leaders?

A. Yes, it does. Many people today refuse to think for themselves about spiritual matters, assuming that if something was important for them to know, their learned priest or pastor would surely tell them. That's a big mistake, because many modern "Christian" leaders don't believe that Jesus is the Son of God or the inspiration of the Bible. They are, to borrow one of Jesus' phrases, "blind leaders of the blind."

Q. What kinds of people did Jesus invite to come to Him?

A. He invited thirsty people to come to Him and drink. Only when people realize that they are dying of spiritual thirst do they see their need to come to Jesus.

Application: Jesus spoke of two experiences with the Holy Spirit in this passage. First, He spoke about people coming to Him and drinking. Then He spoke of rivers of living water flowing out from people who drank. God wants us to receive the Holy Spirit, but not just for our benefit. He wants the living waters within us to flow out to others, spreading His life to them.

Jesus Shows Mercy to an Adulterous Woman
John 8:1-11

Because they didn't believe in Him, the Pharisees and religious teachers wanted to prove that Jesus was not from God. So they formed a plan that they hoped would expose Him as a fraud. In the Law of Moses, God commanded that adulterers be stoned to death for their sin, and the Pharisees figured that if Jesus didn't endorse what God's Law required, that would be proof that He really wasn't from God. So, they somehow caught a woman in the act of committing adultery and brought her to Jesus to see if He would say the same thing God said through Moses.

Filled with wisdom, Jesus masterfully turned the tables on the Pharisees. They had passed judgment on Him and the woman they'd brought, but He forced them to judge themselves. "All right, stone her," He told them, "but let those who have never sinned throw the first stones!" (John 8:7). Jesus actually proved that they were guilty of what they accused Him of: not keeping the Law of Moses. In Moses' Law, the one who accused another person of a sin that was punishable by death was required to throw the first stone if the accused person was found guilty. Jesus was simply asking the woman's accusers to obey the Law, and He reminded them of part of the reason God required accusers to throw the first stone at people they helped condemn: When a person is as guilty as the person he's accusing, he has no right to accuse that person, much less throw the first of many stones that will kill that person!

Jesus' challengers got the message, and slowly snuck away, beginning with the oldest. They realized that none of them had the right to throw the first stone.

The only person who had the right to stone the woman was Jesus, because He was sinless. He, however, demonstrated God's mercy, giving the guilty woman a chance to repent and begin following Him. I hope she did!

Q. When she died years later, what would have happened to the adulterous woman if she didn't do as Jesus said, repenting of her sins after He showed her mercy?

A. She would have been condemned to hell forever. Just because God shows a person mercy during his or her lifetime doesn't guarantee that person will receive mercy after death.

Q. What do you think Jesus was writing in the dust with His finger as the Pharisees waited for His answer to their question?

A. No one knows because the Bible doesn't say. However, many have wondered if He wasn't writing the names of the women with whom the accusing Pharisees had committed adultery!

Application: God has treated everyone in the world just like Jesus treated the adulterous woman. All of us have broken God's laws, but He has shown us mercy and given us an opportunity to repent and come to Him. As those who have repented, let us be especially careful that we don't become like the Pharisees, condemning people who are just like we were!

Jesus Makes Amazing Claims
John 8:12-59

As we've often realized from other readings, if Jesus wasn't God's Son, He was guilty of making outrageous claims about Himself. If He was only a man, His claims could be considered blasphemous, because what He said about Himself can only be rightfully said of God. Today's reading contains a number of Jesus' specific claims regarding who He is and only what He can do. As we read them, we realize that there has never been and never will be another person like Jesus. If Jesus wasn't God's Son, He told the biggest tales anyone has ever told. Let's consider some of Jesus' claims that we just read.

Jesus once again declared that God was His Father and that they had a unique relationship. For example, He had come from His Father, having been sent by Him to the earth, and was going back to Him. In a special way, His Father was always with Him, and Jesus said only what His Father told

Him to say. Likewise, He always did what was pleasing to His Father, and so He never sinned. Not even once! Jesus claimed that God wanted to glorify Him and that He knew the Father like no one else. Finally, He declared that He existed before Abraham was born, making Himself thousands of years old. Jesus literally told His Jewish audience, "Truly, truly, before Abraham was, I Am." *I Am* was a name by which God revealed Himself to Moses, and so Jesus was actually claiming to be the eternal God of the Old Testament! When Jesus made that claim, the unbelievers who heard Him decided He was worthy of death for such blasphemy, and they picked up stones to kill Him.

Because Jesus was who He was, He could do what no one else could do. He claimed to be the "light of the world" (John 8:12). Light stands for truth whereas darkness represents ignorance of the truth. Everyone who doesn't believe in Jesus is ignorant of the truth and believes lies, stumbling in darkness, just as Jesus said. But if they'll follow Him, just as a person follows a light in the darkness, He'll lead them to eternal life.

Notice that Jesus didn't claim to be just a small candle or the light of a little town. He claimed to be the light of the *entire world!* What a claim! He was saying that every single person in the entire world should look to Him as *the* source of truth and the *only* way to find eternal life!

This was not Jesus' only claim to be the sole source of salvation for humanity. He declared that anyone who wouldn't believe in Him would die in their sin. That means they would go to hell. However, whoever would believe in Him, He would set them free from their sins. Whoever would obey Him would *never* die.

Can you understand why it is so absurd for people to say that Jesus was a good man, but not the Son of God? Jesus left us no option to believe that He was just a good man. If He wasn't God, He was either a liar or a lunatic.

Why are Jesus' amazing claims so important? Because they force everyone to make a decision to either believe in Him or not believe. And everyone's eternal destiny is determined by what he or she believes.

If a person truly does believe that Jesus is who He claimed to be and that Jesus can do what He claimed only He can do, that person will begin to obey Jesus. That is why Jesus talked about Himself setting people free from their slavery to sin, and why He said, "Anyone who *obeys* my teaching will never die!" (John 8:51, emphasis added). And that is why He said, "You are truly my disciples if you keep obeying my teachings" (John 8:31). Many people make claims of being Jesus' disciples, but aren't, as proven by how they live. Jesus' *true* disciples keep obeying Him.

 Q. When people first believe in Jesus, are they set free from all their sins immediately?

A. No, they are progressively set free from their sins as they learn and grow spiritually. Jesus said that we would be set free by knowing the truth. When we first believe in Him, we gain knowledge of some truth and are set free from some of the more major sins. And as we learn more about Jesus, we grow more like Him, becoming less and less sinful. One day in heaven, we'll all be sinless!

Q. When Jesus promised that people who obey Him will never die, did He mean that they will never die physically?

A. No, because everyone in the Bible who believed in Him died physically. Jesus must have meant that those who display an obedient faith will never die *spiritually*, which is much worse than physical death. Physical death is a separation of the body and spirit, whereas spiritual death is a separation of the spirit from God. When people believe in Jesus with an obedient faith, their spiritually dead spirits are reborn and they receive God's life inside. As they continue in their faith, they never have to be concerned about dying spiritually.

Application: As Jesus said, those who are not born again have Satan as their spiritual father. Because of that, they act like the devil, who is a liar by nature. Those of us who have truly believed in Jesus, however, have God as our spiritual Father. He has caused our spirits to be reborn. Because of that, we act like Him. He always tells the truth, and so should we. People who always lie prove that they aren't saved. The Bible says that all liars will spend eternity in the lake of fire (see Revelation 21:8).

Jesus Heals a Man Born Blind
John 9:1-41

Have you ever wondered why some people are born with what are called "birth defects"? That is, they have something wrong with them physically, like the man blind from birth that we just read about. It doesn't seem fair, because most people with birth defects have to live with their problems all their lives. Why does God allow such things?

The Jews of Jesus' day thought they had the answer to this question, and Jesus' disciples expressed it when they passed a blind beggar. They assumed that God was punishing the man either for his own sin or his parents' sins. But their answer to the question wasn't a very good one. If God was punishing the man for his own sins, then the man must have sinned in his mother's womb, because he had been *born* blind. What could a baby in its mother's womb possibly do that would make God that angry?

And if God were punishing the man for his parents' sins, that would be completely unfair of God. He Himself stated in His own Law that no child should be punished for its parents' crimes (see Deuteronomy 24:16; Ezekiel 18:19-20).

Jesus' disciples were wrong in their assumptions, and He told them so. The man wasn't born blind because of his or his parents' sins. Jesus said it was so the power of God could be seen in him. That is, the man was born blind so that Jesus could heal him.

This still doesn't answer every question we might have because we might wonder why God would have a man suffer blindness for years just so His supernatural power could be demonstrated in him. Something about that doesn't seem right, even though we know God has the right to do anything He pleases. And what about the many people born blind whom Jesus has never healed? Since they don't fall into the category of being afflicted so God's power could be demonstrated in them, why are they born blind?

God has not given us the answers to all these questions, but the one major consolation that all Christians share is the knowledge that Jesus died for everyone. And any person who believes in Him is guaranteed one day to receive a new body that has no defects. And for those Christians like myself who strongly believe in God's healing promises, we take heart knowing that healing is available in this life. We believe that everyone who has been born with birth defects is a potential candidate for God's power to be displayed in them, just as everyone whom God has declared a sinner is a potential candidate to be saved—if they'll only believe. In Jesus' day, every single person who came to Jesus requesting healing was healed if they believed. Our problem today is lack of faith. Unfortunately, unbiblical teaching has fueled our doubts.

Nothing is mentioned in this story about the blind man's faith being the reason for his healing, so his healing probably fell under the category of what the Bible calls "gifts of healing" (see 1 Corinthians 12:9). Gifts of healings are sovereign acts of God that don't necessarily require any faith on the part of the person needing healing. However, notice that the blind man in today's story did have to obey Jesus by walking to the Pool of Siloam and washing his eyes. That required some faith on his part.

John recorded this story, not only to glorify Jesus, but also to show the various reactions to the miracle. Most of the proud Pharisees refused to believe that Jesus was from God, because He performed this miracle on the Sabbath, breaking their interpretation of God's Law! And at first, the healed man thought Jesus must be a prophet. Later, however, Jesus spoke to him privately and told him that He was the Son of Man. Some of the ancient manuscripts of John's Gospel record that Jesus told the man that He was the Son of God. Regardless, the healed man believed in Him. How do we know? Because he confessed his faith in Jesus and then proved his faith by worshipping Jesus. If the man had believed that Jesus was only a prophet, he would have shaken His hand or hugged Him, but he wouldn't have worshipped Him.

Q. Why do you suppose Jesus put mud on the blind man's eyes in order to heal him? Why didn't He just lay His hand on the man, or simply declare him healed?

A. As Jesus said, He only did exactly what His Father told Him to do. So He must have been following the orders of His Father. Perhaps His Father was trying to help people realize that Jesus was not just a prophet, but God. The original human being was made from the soil. Now some new eyes were being made from soil, something that only God could do!

Q. What did Jesus mean when He said, "I have come to give sight to the blind and to show those who think they see that they are blind" (John 9:39)?

A. Jesus was talking about two kinds of blindness, physical and spiritual. Jesus came to give sight to the physically and spiritually blind. To be spiritually blind means to be ignorant of the truth that Jesus is the Messiah and Son of God. The problem is that, unlike physically blind people, spiritually blind people often don't even realize they're blind.

Application: People may be able to argue against your theology or what you believe, but they can't reasonably argue against what has happened to you since you believed in Jesus. That's your testimony. Just like the man in today's story said, "I was blind, and now I can see!" (John 9:25), so you can tell others how God has changed your life. For some people, your testimony could be what sparks their interest in learning more about Jesus!

Jesus Compares Himself to a Gate and a Good Shepherd
John 10:1-21

Jesus was a great teacher, and that's why He used so many comparisons when He taught. In today's reading He compared Himself to a gate and a shepherd. Unlike many of us, the people Jesus taught knew all about sheep and shepherds, however, they didn't initially understand the spiritual truths Jesus was trying to convey. So He explained.

Sheep, like other livestock, are usually confined within fences or walls when they're not grazing in open pasture. Regardless of what confines them, there must be a gate to let them as well as the shepherd in or out.

Jesus said that He was like the gate to the sheepfold. Those who believe in Him are, of course, the sheep. The only legitimate way to be a part of the sheepfold, or to be a part of God's true church and kingdom, is to enter through Jesus, believing in Him. Some try to enter without going through Jesus, but that proves they really don't belong among the sheep. They have an evil motive, usually to harm the sheep and get something for themselves. For example, a thief might climb over a wall to steal a sheep.

Not only is Jesus the gate, He is also the shepherd. When a shepherd wants to lead his sheep out to graze, he comes through the gate and calls his sheep. Even if his sheep are mixed with another flock, only his sheep will follow him out of the gate. Sheep won't be deceived into following another shepherd because they recognize their shepherd's voice. *They know to whom they belong.*

Jesus is like the shepherd who is calling His sheep. Many sheep may hear His voice, but only those who are His, those who believe in Him and love Him, will come out from among the other sheep and follow Him, obeying Him. That is how true Christians are known—they follow Jesus when others don't. When false prophets and false teachers call out to the masses of sheep, leading many astray, true Christians aren't deceived because they know their shepherd and they know what He's said.

Jesus is not comparable to just *any* shepherd. He's a *good* shepherd who is devoted to His own sheep. In fact, He was willing to die for His sheep. He knows them and they know Him. He leads them to green pastures where there is abundant food. He wants them to enjoy His blessings. He cares about each one. There is no better shepherd than Jesus!

Q. Jesus talked about having other sheep that were not "in this sheepfold" (John 10:16), promising to bring them also into His flock. About whom was He talking?

A. Most likely, He was speaking of the Gentiles who would be saved and brought into His kingdom as equal citizens with Jewish believers.

Q. Jesus made it plain that no one could take His life from Him, but that He laid down His life voluntarily. Why is this so important for us to know?

A. Because we otherwise might be tempted to think that Jesus' death was involuntary. That is, we might think He had no choice but to die, having been the victim of unfortunate circumstances. If that were the case, then it couldn't be said that Jesus died for our sins according to the preordained plan of God. He would have died just like any other martyr.

⊙ Application: David wrote, "The Lord is my shepherd; I have every-thing I need" (Psalm 23:1). Before we know Him as Shepherd, we have to know Him as Lord, just like David did. Sheep look to their shepherd, not just as someone to take care of them and lead them, but also as someone to obey and follow. Wandering sheep don't have a shepherd!

Jesus Teaches About Divorce and Remarriage
Matthew 19:1-9

The religious teachers of Jesus' day were divided over the question of divorce. The Law of Moses spoke about a man finding some "indecency" in his wife and giving her a certificate of divorce (see Deuteronomy 24:1). The question was, what qualified as an "indecency"? Some religious teachers taught that if a man found *anything* he didn't like about his wife, that was an indecency and he could lawfully divorce her. Others considered that the only indecency over which a man could lawfully divorce his wife was the sin of adultery. The question that the Pharisees posed to Jesus doesn't reveal which group they were in: "Should a man be allowed to divorce his wife for *any reason?*" (Matthew 19:3).

Jesus first responded by telling them what God had said in the Scriptures. God initially created one man and one woman and joined them together as one. It was His intention that they never be separated, and that is His intention for every marriage. Divorce is not His plan for anyone.

The Pharisees then brought up the issue of the provision for divorce in the Law of Moses. Jesus explained that, because of the people's hard-hearted wickedness, God permitted divorce. He may have meant that because of people's general selfishness, it was inevitable that married people would fight and separate. Again, this was never God's original intention for any marriage, but it inevitably occurs. Therefore, the Law of Moses had a regulation to govern divorce when it happened, part of that regulation being that the man had to give his wife a certificate so she could prove she was divorced.

Jesus also clearly endorsed the fact that adultery was the only indecency by which a man could lawfully divorce his wife. It's possible that when Jesus said that Moses permitted divorce because of the hardness of people's hearts, He meant that Moses permitted divorce when adultery had been committed because of the hardness of people's hearts. That is, a truly loving husband would forgive an adulterous wife who was repentant. If his heart was soft, he would not divorce her.

But what about Jesus' words, "A man who divorces his wife and marries another commits adultery"? (Matthew 19:9). It is my opinion that He must have been talking about a married man who falls in love with a woman who is not his wife, quickly finds some small "indecency" in his wife, divorces her, and marries the other woman. He thinks to himself that he has not sinned, and has kept the requirements of God's Law. What he's done, however, is no different than adultery.

I find it hard to believe that Jesus' words apply to other divorced people, like a person who was divorced before he was saved, and then, after he's born again, falls in love with and marries another Christian. That hardly seems like something that could be considered equivalent to adultery. Nor do I think Jesus' words would apply to a Christian who finds himself divorced from a nonbeliever, and who later marries a Christian. If everyone who has been divorced and is now remarried is living in the sin of adultery, then not one of them is going to heaven, because the Bible plainly says that adulterers will not inherit the kingdom of God (see 1 Corinthians 6:9-10). That fact in itself tells me that what Jesus said has little application to many divorced and remarried people.

It's important that we consider all that God has said when we interpret the few things Jesus said about divorce and remarriage. Some people seem to ignore everything else in the Bible, including the gospel of the wonderful forgiveness that is offered us through Christ, in order to form a theology about divorce! In their minds, God will forgive every sin except divorce or remarriage. If that were true, we'd have to start preaching the gospel differently, telling people, "If you believe in Jesus, all your sins will be forgiven, except if you've been divorced and remarried, because then you're an adulterer as long as you remain married, and adulterers aren't saved!"

Q. What could an unmarried person do to avoid ever getting a divorce?
A. First of all, he should make sure that he is fully committed to Christ. Second, he should make certain that the person he intends to marry is fully committed to Christ. Third, he should not hurry into marriage, but take his time in getting to know his potential mate. Fourth, he should learn to be unselfish and walk in love, and look for those same qualities in a potential spouse. Fifth, he should seek the advice of his parents and friends, getting their perspective about any potential spouse. Finally, he should keep in mind that it is better to be unhappily unmarried than unhappily married!

Application: There is much more that could be said about the subject of divorce and remarriage from a biblical standpoint. However, the most important thing to remember is that God never intends for anyone to be divorced, but when it occurs, He has made provision for forgiveness.

A Rich Young Man Rejects Jesus
Matthew 19:16-30

The first question that the rich young man asked Jesus was, "What good things must I do to have eternal life?" (Matthew 19:16). His question contained his assumption that a person could receive eternal life by doing certain good things. He assumed eternal life was something to be earned by good behavior.

Immediately recognizing the error in the man's thinking, Jesus tried to help him realize that he was a sinner who fell short of God's standards of holiness by saying, "Why ask me about what is good? Only God is good" (Matthew 19:17). If only God is good, then everyone else is bad, including the rich young man, and Jesus wanted him to know it.

Jesus also wanted the man to know that, even though he was a sinner, he could be saved if he repented, which is why He told him he could receive eternal life by keeping God's commandments. He then immediately asked Jesus *which* of the commandments he needed to keep.

Jesus listed six of the Ten Commandments that dealt with how we treat other people. The rich young man claimed to have kept them all, which was very doubtful. He then asked if there was anything else that he must do to have eternal life. And there was. He needed to become a believer in and a follower of Jesus, the only Savior and Lord. That is God's requirement for anyone to be saved.

There were, however, two things standing in the man's way, and Jesus knew it. First, the man didn't believe that Jesus was the Son of God; he only believed that Jesus was a good teacher. That's how he addressed Jesus at first (see Mark 10:17). In order for a person to have eternal life, he must believe in Jesus, and if he believes in Jesus, he will follow and obey Him.

Second, money was the rich man's god. As Jesus once said, it's impossible to serve God and money. If Jesus had been the rich man's God, he would have obeyed Jesus and given his money away to the poor as Jesus commanded him. But the man didn't believe in Jesus, so he didn't obey Jesus. Even though he walked away saddened by what he'd heard, he wouldn't give up any of his many possessions.

As He watched the rich young man walk away, Jesus commented to His disciples, "It is easier for a camel to go through the eye of a needle than for a rich person to enter the Kingdom of God!" (Matthew 19:24). The reason is because so many rich people are just like the rich young ruler. They love money and are unwilling to submit to Jesus, making Him their Lord and the Lord of their money. Jesus expects everyone who follows Him to be generous and share what God gives to them.

 Q. Wasn't Jesus asking the rich man to give up an awful lot in order to follow Him?

A. Actually, it could be said that Jesus wasn't asking him to give up anything, because He promised the rich man that if he gave his money away to the poor, he would have treasure in heaven. If the rich man was giving up anything, it was only temporarily. And what he gave up he would have had to give up anyway when he died, whereas what he gained in heaven would be his for eternity. As martyred missionary Jim Elliot once said, "He is no fool who gives up what he cannot keep to gain what he cannot lose."

Q. In heaven, will anyone regret any earthly sacrifice he made for Christ's cause?

A. No, most will probably wish they had made greater sacrifices and given more when they were on the earth.

Application: Praise God that not all wealthy people are like the rich young man we read about today. Paul wrote to Timothy, concerning wealthy Christians, "Tell those who are rich in this world not to be proud and not to trust in their money, which will soon be gone. But their trust should be in the living God, who richly gives us all we need for our enjoyment. Tell them to use their money to do good. They should be rich in good works and should give generously to those in need, always being ready to share with others whatever God has given them. By doing this they will be storing up their treasure as a good foundation for the future so that they may take hold of real life" (1 Timothy 6:17-19).

The Parable of the Vineyard Workers
Matthew 20:1-16

What was Jesus trying to teach us in this parable? Some think the point is that we'll all have the same reward in heaven no matter how long or hard we work for the Lord on earth. But that can't be right, because the Bible teaches that each person will be rewarded individually, according to his own labor (see 1 Corinthians 3:8).

The best way to interpret this parable is to consider the context in which it was spoken. Notice that Jesus told this parable right after Peter had asked what reward he and the other disciples would receive for giving up everything to follow Jesus. Jesus promised him that they would be abundantly rewarded in heaven for the earthly sacrifices they made for His cause. In fact, He promised that "everyone who has given up houses or brothers or sisters or father or mother or children or property, for my sake, will receive a hundred times as much in return and will have eternal life" (Matthew 19:29).

The lesson of this parable is that God rewards us based upon the opportunities that He gives us. The later workers would have been willing to go to work earlier, but they were not given the opportunity by the employer.

Had you been given a lot of money, you may have been willing to give a lot of money away to the poor. But if God gave you only a little money, you were not given the opportunity to give away lots of money. Still, if you are faithful with the small opportunities that God gives you, God will reward you with just as much as someone who was faithful with large opportunities that God gave them. He is perfectly fair.

Q. Jesus concluded the parable of the vineyard workers by saying, "And so it is, that many who are first now will be last then; and those who are last now will be first then" (Matthew 20:16). In light of the parable, can you describe someone who might be first now but last in God's kingdom, and vice versa?

A. Some who are faithful with the small opportunities that God gives them, now "last" in the eyes of people, might receive more reward than one who is "first" in the eyes of people but who is unfaithful with the bigger opportunities God has given him.

Application: Are you being faithful with the opportunities God has given you?

Jesus Claims to be One With the Father
John 10:22-42

The Jewish leaders who asked Jesus to tell them if He was the Messiah weren't asking so they could consider believing in Him. They wanted to hear Him plainly and publicly state what they knew He had already been claiming using other terminology. Then they could put Him on trial for blasphemy.

Jesus, wise to their plan, refused to grant them what they wanted. However, at the same time, He made a claim that believers would easily recognize as being even greater than a claim to being the Messiah, but vague enough that unbelievers would have a difficult time using it as evidence to prosecute Him for blasphemy. That is, Jesus said, "The Father and I are one" (John 10:30).

We know that when Jesus spoke of the Father, He was speaking of God the Father, and His claim to be one with Him was a claim to be everything that God was. The Jewish leaders who heard Him say it rightly suspected He was claiming to be God and accused Him of it. But it would be difficult to prosecute Him for blasphemy on such a vague statement. That is why they wanted Him to make a clear claim of being the Messiah.

Realizing that they weren't going to get a public statement from Jesus that they could use to have Him legally executed, the Jewish leaders decided to take the law into their own hands by stoning Him immediately. In their minds, His claim to be one with the Father was grounds enough to justify His stoning. To them, it mattered not that they were about to end a ministry that was responsible for the healing of thousands of sick and suffering people, raising the dead and feeding the multitudes. It mattered not how Jesus was able to do such things supposedly without God's endorsement or help. It mattered not that He was sinless.

Jesus even reminded His accusers of a verse in the Old Testament when God spoke of certain leaders as being gods, rulers over their domain. So how could they consider it blasphemous for the one who was sent from heaven to call Himself the Son of God? Jesus' life works and claims were all the proof anyone should need that He was and is the Messiah, the Son of God!

Q. How do you suppose Jesus escaped the hostile crowds of Jewish leaders who had surrounded Him in the Jerusalem Temple with stones in their hands, ready to kill Him?

A. It seems that He must have had God's supernatural help. Either God blinded the eyes of those in the crowd, or somehow hid Jesus, or supernaturally transported Him away.

Q. Jesus promised eternal life to those who follow Him, joining His flock, saying that they will never perish in hell. Moreover, He promised that no one will be able to snatch them away from Him like sheep are sometimes stolen from their flock. Does this mean that once a person is saved he could never become unsaved?

A. According to other scriptures, it's possible for a saved person to become unsaved if he, after truly believing in Jesus, decides in his heart to stop believing. Most people who apparently believe and then become unbelievers probably never truly believed in Jesus in the first place. As true believers in Jesus, we are responsible to continue believing in Him, and as we do, we are assured that we will go to heaven (see Romans 11:22; 1 Corinthians 15:1-2; Philippians 3:17-19; Colossians 1:21-23; Hebrews 3:12-14). We never have to worry about losing our salvation because of God's unfaithfulness or weakness!

Application: In today's reading, Jesus made three incredible claims: (1) "The Father and I are one," (2) "I am the Son of God," and (3) "The Father is in me, and I am in the Father" (John 10:30,36,38). Just like today, many didn't believe Him then. But many did (see John 10:42). And just like to those who believed in Him then, Jesus gives eternal life to those who believe in Him today (see John 10:28).

Jesus Raises Lazarus From the Dead
John 11:1-57

When Jesus heard that His friend, Lazarus, was sick, He stated that Lazarus's sickness would not end in death, but that He would receive glory from it. Jesus, of course, was talking about how He would be glorified when Lazarus was raised from the dead.

Some people, misapplying what Jesus said, talk about how God is glorified by their sickness, thinking that God wants them to remain sick so that He can be continually glorified. But Jesus wasn't claiming to be glorified by Lazarus's sickness! He was claiming that He would be glorified by Lazarus's resurrection. Jesus isn't glorified by our being sick, but by our being healed by His power!

Following the leading of the Holy Spirit, Jesus delayed journeying to Bethany where Mary, Martha and Lazarus lived. God wanted Jesus to perform a miracle that would convince everyone whose heart wasn't hopelessly hardened that Jesus was the Son of God. When Jesus finally did arrive in Bethany, Lazarus had been dead for four days. Thus, no one would be able to intelligently claim that Lazarus had only been unconscious and had simply been revived!

Both Mary and Martha believed that Jesus could and would have healed Lazarus if He had been near when Lazarus was still alive. They didn't realize that Jesus had purposely stayed away so that He could heal *and* resurrect Lazarus, rather than just heal him! Even when Jesus promised Martha that her brother would rise again, she initially assumed He was referring to the general resurrection of many people foretold in the Old Testament.

Then Jesus made another wonderful claim: "I am the resurrection and the life. Those who believe in me, even though they die like everyone else, will live again. They are given eternal life for believing in me and will never perish" (John 11:25-26). Lazarus's resurrection would serve as a proof that Jesus was the one who would be in charge of the promised future resurrection, and it would serve as a foreshadowing of what Jesus would do for everyone who believes in Him.

Notice that even though Jesus supernaturally knew that Lazarus had died, He didn't know exactly where Lazarus's tomb was and asked about the location. This is further proof that, although Jesus was the Son of God, He stripped Himself of omniscience when He became a man. In His ministry, He operated as a man anointed by the Holy Spirit, empowered with gifts of the Holy Spirit that operated as the Spirit willed. Jesus said that He could do nothing by Himself, but only what He saw His Father doing (see John 5:19). What God didn't tell Him by the Holy Spirit, He had to learn like anyone else.

Amazingly, although the leading priests and Pharisees knew of Jesus' many miracles, they refused to believe in Him. Moreover, they were fearful that the whole nation might believe in Him, resulting in political turmoil, an invasion by the Roman army, and the deaths of many people. But Caiaphas, the high priest, rebuked them, saying that the solution was simple. They didn't need to fear that many people would die—if Jesus died instead. Caiaphas unknowingly prophesied when he said it this way: "Let this one man die for the people" (John 11:50). That is exactly what happened, and what God had planned from eternity past!

Q. Why do you think Jesus at first told His disciples that Lazarus was asleep and that He was going to wake him up?

A. In the Bible, Christian death is sometimes described using the word "sleep". The reason is because death is always temporary, like sleep, for those who believe in Jesus. They know their bodies will one day be resurrected, whereas unbelievers view death as a permanent state. Additionally, for God, raising Lazarus from the dead was no more difficult than awakening someone from sleep!

Q. Jesus' disciples were fearful of Jesus' plans to journey back to Judea where the Jewish leaders were waiting to kill Him. Jesus replied, "There are twelve hours of daylight every day. As long as it is light, people can walk safely. They can see because they have the light of this world. Only at night is there danger of stumbling because there is no light" (John 11:9-10). Jesus' words have a natural and a spiritual meaning. What are they and how can you apply them to your life?

A. The natural meaning is plain. When there is light, people are safer, because evil deeds are usually done in darkness. That is when evil people normally get drunk, steal and murder, because they have a better chance of not getting caught. You can increase your chances of not being a victim of someone's crime by staying away from dark places and being extra cautious at night. For example, most people who are killed by drunk drivers are killed at night, so if you must drive after dark, you should be extra cautious. The later it is at night, the more cautious you should be. Jesus knew that He was safe in a dangerous city as long as His enemies knew where He was only during the day. It was Judas who ultimately told the Jewish leaders where Jesus was at night, and that is when He was arrested and tried before the Jewish council.

The spiritual meaning behind Jesus' words is this: When people walk in the light of Jesus and the truth of His word, they are spiritually safe, because Satan and his evil spirits can only work in spiritual darkness. When people don't follow Jesus, the spiritual light of the world, they are walking in darkness, not knowing where they are going and destined to be deceived by Satan, stumble over sin and fall into hell.

Application: In one sense, all of us who believe in Jesus are like Lazarus. With the exception of those who will be alive when Jesus returns, all of us will one day die and Jesus will be glorified as He resurrects our bodies all at the same time! So when you get to heaven, you'll have something to talk about with Lazarus when you see him!

The Greatest Servant Teaches About Serving
Mark 10:32-45

When we read about James' and John's selfish request to sit at Jesus' right and left hand in His kingdom, it makes us realize how much they needed to grow spiritually at that point in their lives. But praise God, they did eventually grow up, although not overnight. James and John should also serve as reminders to us that God is dedicated to our spiritual growth, and He will complete the good work He's begun in us. Additionally, we should be patient with young believers who still have a long way to grow. James and John were like we were at one time, and like some of us still are! But God is patient with us all, as demonstrated by Jesus' patience with His disciples.

There were several problems with the request made by James and John. First, God the Father would only consider granting that kind of honor to those who were equally devoted to Him as Jesus was, and who served others to the degree that Jesus did. So Jesus asked James and John if they were able to drink from the same bitter cup and be baptized with the same baptism of suffering as He was to experience. Jesus was speaking of being mocked, spit upon, beaten, flogged and crucified. Although they probably didn't understand what He was talking about, they claimed they were able. Jesus prophesied to them that they *would* suffer and die for His cause, although again, they probably didn't understand what He meant.

The second problem with the request of James and John is that they were asking for something that Jesus didn't have a right to grant. Jesus explained that it was not His place to decide who sits next to Him in the future kingdom. That is a decision made only by God the Father. This also shows us that God the Father and Jesus are two distinct persons, and not the same identical person as some mistakenly think.

The third problem with the request of James and John is that it revealed their lack of understanding of what God considers the greatest virtue a person can possess. He honors servanthood and exalts those who humble themselves. Conversely, He humbles those who exalt themselves. If anything, James' and John's request got them further away from the seats of honor in which they desired to sit!

The lesson for us? God is not looking for rulers; He's looking for servants. And servants aren't seeking for honor, they are looking for opportunities to serve. Is that you?

 Q. We already know who will be seated at Jesus' left hand from other Scriptures. Do you know who it will be?

A. It will be God the Father, because Jesus is now seated at His right hand.

Q. Jesus will obviously be exalted and honored by His Father in the future kingdom. Will it be only because He is the Son of God?

A. No, it will also be because Jesus is the greatest servant, giving His life for everyone, and because Jesus humbled Himself more than anyone else ever has. Paul wrote, "Your attitude should be the same that Christ Jesus had. Though he was God, he did not demand and cling to his rights as God. He made himself nothing; he took the humble position of a slave and appeared in human form. And in human form he obediently humbled himself even further by dying a criminal's death on a cross. Because of this, God raised him up to the heights of heaven and gave him a name that is above every other name" (Philippians 2:5-9).

Application: In our reading today, Jesus revealed not only that He would die, but also why He would die. He said it was to give His life as a ransom for many (see Mark 10:45). A ransom is a payment made to release someone from captivity. Jesus' death was the payment required by God's own justice to release us from our captivity to sin and our destiny in hell. Jesus' servanthood on our behalf will bring blessing to us for eternity, so we can say that Jesus will be serving us forever, which is one reason we'll be praising Him forever!

Jesus Heals a Blind Man Named Bartimaeus
Mark 10:46-52

Bartimaeus must have heard about Jesus and the many people who were being healed by Him. It sparked a faith within him that he would be healed if Jesus would ever visit Jericho, and when he heard that Jesus was passing nearby, his faith went into action. Bartimaeus began calling out, "Jesus, Son of David, have mercy on me!" That shows how much faith he had. He wasn't embarrassed to request healing publicly. He was certain Jesus could give him what he wanted if he could only get His attention. Even after people around him tried to discourage him, telling him to be quiet, he just yelled all the louder.

When Bartimaeus was told that Jesus had stopped and invited him to come to Him, he knew he would soon be seeing. He threw aside his coat and excitedly jumped up. Some say that blind people back in Jesus' time wore special coats that identified them to everyone else as being blind. If that was the case, Bartimaeus throwing aside his coat was another act of faith. He believed he no longer had any need of a blind man's coat!

With someone guiding him, Bartimaeus made his way to Jesus. Testing his faith one more time, Jesus asked him what he wanted Him to do. Without hesitation, Bartimaeus made his request: "Teacher, I want to see!" Obviously he wouldn't have made such a request unless he believed Jesus could and would grant it. And Jesus gave him exactly what he requested.

 Q. According to Jesus, Bartimaeus was healed because of his faith. What would have happened if Bartimaeus had not believed?

A. He would not have been healed, even though it was obviously God's will for him to be healed. This once again proves that God's will doesn't always automatically come to pass. When people say, "If God wants me to be healed, I'll be healed," they're mistaken.

Q. Was Bartimaeus instantly healed?

A. He was instantly healed once Jesus told him, "Go your way. Your faith has healed you" (Mark 10:52). However, it took some time and persistence before Bartimaeus heard Jesus speak those words. Actually, he was believing even before Jesus visited Jericho, and kept on believing as he continually cried out to Jesus. In that sense, his healing wasn't instantaneous.

Application: We will probably never know the joy that Bartimaeus experienced when he regained his sight. Why not close your eyes for the first five minutes of your next family meal to experience a small sampling of the frustration that blind people face all day, every day? When you open your eyes to finish your meal, think of how Bartimaeus felt when Jesus opened his eyes.

Zacchaeus is Saved
Luke 19:1-10

You may remember that most Jews despised tax collectors in Jesus' time. Not only did they work for the occupying foreign government, Rome, but they also made themselves very rich by overcharging their own countrymen. Zacchaeus was no different than any other tax collector of his day: selfish, greedy and dishonest.

However, he heard that Jesus was visiting his town of Jericho, and people were mobbing this well-known teacher and miracle worker as He walked through. Being short, Zacchaeus climbed a tree down the street so that when Jesus passed by, he could catch a glimpse of Him.

But God had more planned for Zacchaeus than just a glimpse of Jesus. He wanted Zacchaeus to know Jesus personally. And was Zacchaeus ever shocked when Jesus stopped, looked up at him, called his name and told him that He must be a guest at his house that day. Zacchaeus quickly climbed down and excitedly led Jesus to his house.

But finding himself in Jesus' loving and holy presence, Zacchaeus became even more conscious of his own sinfulness, and he realized how uncomfortable he would be with pure and holy Jesus as his guest. What would he do? Unlike most wealthy people whose god is money, Zacchaeus decided to change, making Jesus his Lord. Because money would no longer be his god, he immediately changed his attitude and actions concerning it.

This story illustrates a very important point about salvation. Jesus said that salvation had come to Zacchaeus's home that day after Zacchaeus repented. That is, Zacchaeus admitted his guilt and changed his ways. Beyond even that, he promised to make restitution to those he'd wronged.

Repentance is an essential part of salvation. In fact, there is no true salvation apart from repentance. Too many people think they're saved because they've prayed a prayer for salvation, but they've never truly repented, but have continued living their same old sinful lives. How do you think Jesus would have responded if Zacchaeus had said, "Jesus, I accept you as my Lord and Savior. However, I'm going to continue being greedy and dishonest"?

Q. How did Jesus know Zacchaeus's name?
A. The Holy Spirit must have revealed it to Him. That is an example of the gift of the Spirit called "the word of knowledge."

Q. In order to be saved, is it necessary for us to make restitution to people we've wronged, like Zacchaeus did?

A. No. We must repent, which means changing our attitude and actions from that point onward. Usually there is no possible way we could make restitution to everyone we've wronged before our salvation. However, it is a good idea to try to make as much restitution as is reasonably possible, as a way of showing others that you've changed and as a way to gain an entrance to share the gospel with them as well.

Application: The crowds grumbled about Jesus wanting to be a guest at the house of a notorious sinner. But Jesus came to save sinners, and God, knowing the hearts of all people, led Jesus to reach out specifically to Zacchaeus. He knew that Zacchaeus was on the verge of repentance and that a visit from Jesus would be all he needed to nudge him to make the right decision. Let's pray today that God will also lead us to people who are ready to repent.

The Parable of the Ten Servants
Luke 19:11-27

Many of Jesus' followers, including His closest disciples, assumed it would be just a short time before He would do what the Old Testament said He would do: set up God's kingdom on the earth and rule over it from Jerusalem. But the truth was, in less than a week's time, Jesus would die for the sins of the world just as the Old Testament said He would, and it would be at least two thousand years before He would begin ruling the entire world from Jerusalem.

Jesus wanted His followers to understand that He would be leaving the earth for a time but would eventually return. While they waited during the interim, there was something He wanted them to do. And that's why He told them the parable of the ten servants.

In the story, the nobleman who was called away to a distant empire to be crowned king obviously represented Jesus. When He arrived in heaven after His resurrection and ascension, the Bible says that Jesus was "crowned with glory and honor because He suffered death for us" (Hebrews 2:9).

The servants who each received ten pounds of silver from the nobleman represent those who are servants of Christ. The silver or money they were given represents the gifts, talents and opportunities He gives us, by which we can serve Him and others.

The people who hated the nobleman and sent a delegation after him to tell him that they didn't want him to be their king, represent all those who refuse to repent and follow Jesus.

When the nobleman returned, he called his servants in for an accounting. The first two had used the money they'd been given to make more money for the nobleman, so he rewarded them by giving them cities over which to rule. But the third hadn't made any profit, having hidden his money. The nobleman was enraged at the unfaithful servant. At least he could have put the money in the bank and made a little interest on it! There was no excuse for what he did. Not only did he not receive a reward as the others had, but what he did have was taken away from him.

Whom does this unfaithful servant represent? He represents a profess-ing servant of Christ, who, by his actions, proves he is not a true servant. True followers of Christ will produce some fruit, even if it's only a little. If the third servant had produced even a little profit for the nobleman by depositing his money in the bank, he would have received a reward and would not have been reprimanded and punished. But he was, as the noble-man said, "unfaithful" (Luke 19:26). That is, he had no faith and didn't be-lieve what the nobleman said. True faith is always manifested by actions.

Finally, when the nobleman was done dealing with his servants, he dealt with his rebellious subjects who didn't want to submit to his lordship. They were immediately executed. When Jesus returns, it will mean swift judg-ment upon all those who refused to believe in and follow Him.

Notice that everyone in the story, believers and unbelievers alike, were judged by their works, just as the Bible teaches in other places. We are saved by God's grace through our faith in Jesus, but, as the apostle James wrote, "Faith is dead without good deeds" (James 2:26).

Q. The unfruitful servant described the nobleman as being "a hard man to deal with, taking what isn't [his] and harvesting crops [he] didn't plant" (Luke 19:21). Is that an accurate description of what Jesus is like, since the nobleman in the story represents Him?

A. No, that is not an accurate description of Jesus. It was just the third servant's opinion, and it describes the opposite of what Jesus is. He is not hard to deal with, but is the most merciful person who's ever existed. He doesn't take what isn't His and He doesn't harvest crops He didn't plant.

Q. The money that was taken from the unfaithful servant was given to the most faithful servant, and some people complained about it. They thought the first servant was already blessed enough. How did the nobleman feel about that?

A. He didn't agree at all. He wanted the most faithful servant to be rewarded the most.

Application: There are two applications of today's parable to our lives: First, let's make certain we're proving ourselves to be true servants of Jesus by how we live our lives. Is God getting a return on what He's invested in us? And second, let's be diligent to produce as much fruit as we can for our Master. One day, we'll be rewarded for all of it.

Jesus' Triumphal Entry Into Jerusalem
Luke 19:28-44

Jesus had finally made it to Jerusalem, the capital city of Israel, the place where He knew He was destined to die on a cross in one week's time. Many of Jesus' followers, in spite of what He said in the story of the ten servants that we read yesterday, believed that Jesus would immediately set up His kingdom, and they gave Him a king's greeting as He entered Jerusalem. But the story was anticlimactic. His triumphal entry ended with His looking around the Temple and then leaving the city to sleep overnight in the nearby town of Bethany (see Mark 11:11). So what was the point of Jesus' dramatic entrance into Jerusalem?

Although Luke didn't mention it in His Gospel, Jesus actually fulfilled an ancient prophecy as He entered Jerusalem on a colt. Matthew and John both recorded what the prophet Zechariah had foretold: "Tell the people of Israel, 'Look, your King is coming to you. He is humble, riding on a donkey—even on a donkey's colt'" (Matthew 21:5).

That was not the only miraculous aspect of Jesus' entry into Jerusalem. Jesus knew that there would be a colt tied in a certain place, and He knew that when He sent some of His disciples to get it, the colt's owners would object to their taking it. Jesus also knew that if the disciples told the owners that He had need of the colt and would return it, they would allow it to be taken. Additionally, Jesus knew that the colt had never been previously ridden. And amazingly, the colt allowed Him to ride on its back, not bucking Him off! These are just more proofs that Jesus is the Son of God.

Jesus' great mercy for the people of Jerusalem was revealed as He wept over the city, grieving for the calamity they would face in the future. In about forty years, the Roman army would come and destroy the city, and thousands of people would die violent deaths, many by being hung on crosses. Why would God allow such a thing to happen? It was an act of judgment upon them for their rejection of Jesus, as Jesus said, "Because you have rejected the opportunity God offered you" (Luke 19:44). In this we see both the love and holy judgment of God. God's love is seen in Jesus' weeping over the city, and His holy judgment is seen in His predicting and allowing the future disaster to occur. Those who reject God's love have no choice but to suffer His judgment. Aren't you glad you've received His love?

Q. The hard-hearted Pharisees, as they witnessed the crowds shouting and singing praises to God for the miracles they'd seen, requested that Jesus quiet His followers. Jesus replied, "If they kept quiet, the stones along the road would burst into cheers!" (Luke 19:40). What do you think He meant?

A. He must have been speaking in *hyperbole,* defined as "exaggeration for effect." Jesus meant that what His followers were doing was the only appropriate response to what was happening. Those who were not rejoicing and praising God were the abnormal ones who were out of order. The situation *demanded* praise to God, so much that if people wouldn't praise God, something else would.

Application: Jesus didn't try to stop anyone from treating Him like a king as He entered Jerusalem, even to the point of allowing people to spread their garments on the road before Him, creating a long carpet on which His donkey could walk. Jesus knew He was God and acted the part. It would be sinful for anyone else to accept such favored treatment, honor that God alone deserves.

Jesus Curses a Fig Tree and Clears the Temple
Mark 11:12-25

Keep in mind that we are reading about the final week before Jesus' crucifixion. The Holy Spirit must want us to know more about that week than any other week of Jesus' life, because the four Gospel writers, Matthew, Mark, Luke and John, devoted almost one third of their combined writings to it. It was the most important week in human history.

The incident of Jesus cursing the fig tree has raised some questions. First, why did Jesus, upon seeing the fig tree from a distance, need to get close to see if it had any figs? If He was God, why didn't He automatically know the tree was fruitless, since God knows everything?

The answer, as you hopefully already know by now, is that Jesus stripped Himself of omniscience when He became a human being. Any knowledge He possessed that could be categorized as supernatural was given to Him as God might give it to any of His servants—through the Holy Spirit's gift of the word of knowledge. Unless God revealed something to Jesus, He had to obtain information like anyone else. It was too early in the fig season for figs in the region of Jerusalem, and Jesus discovered that the fig tree was fruitless.

So why did He curse a fruitless fig tree that was fruitless because of the season? You can be certain Jesus wasn't angry at the tree and certainly wasn't holding the tree responsible for its fruitlessness. Trees aren't people, and God isn't holding them accountable for their actions!

Some people think the fig tree was representative of fruitless Israel, and that Jesus cursed it as a foreshadowing of God's soon-coming curse. Perhaps that's true, but the Bible doesn't say. More likely, Jesus was using the fig tree to teach His disciples a lesson about faith. The next day, they were amazed that the fig tree had withered, and Jesus explained to them the power of faith in God. If they would believe and not doubt in their hearts, they could speak to mountains and make them move! Jesus went on to explain that faith was an important key to answered prayer.

We must understand that faith can only be born from God's promises, and unless we have a promise from God that He wants an actual mountain moved, we couldn't have faith to move it. But there are many "mountains" for which we do possess promises, and, with faith, we can move them by speaking to them. The key is not to doubt in our hearts, even when it appears as if our mountains aren't moving. They *will* move if we believe God's promise.

When Jesus cleared the Temple of those who were buying and selling there, it was the second time He did so, the first being about three years earlier (see John 2:13-17). Again, He was angered that a place that God had intended to be a place of prayer had been turned into a marketplace dominated by dishonesty. With a right only God possesses, Jesus acted as if He owned everything and cleaned house. That's our Jesus—not just loving and compassionate, but holy and righteous.

Q. When we trust God to keep a promise, does what we believe for always come to pass instantly?

A. No, not always. According to Mark's Gospel, the disciples didn't notice that the fig tree had withered until about twenty-four hours after Jesus had cursed it.

Q. If we want our prayers to be answered, according to Jesus, what is even more important than having faith?

A. It is more important that we first forgive others, otherwise we have no assurance that God will forgive our sins.

Application: Jesus is still cleansing temples today, purifying them of sin and making them pleasing to God. Has He cleansed your temple?

The Stories of the Two Sons and Evil Farmers
Matthew 21:23-46

Today's reading contrasts Christ's reception by the common people with His rejection by the religious leaders. When the leading priests demanded that Jesus tell them by what authority He had driven out the merchants from the Temple, He responded by asking them a question: Had God commissioned John the Baptist or did John act on his own initiative and power? Jesus knew the religious leaders would have trouble answering publicly, because He knew they really didn't believe John was commissioned by God, otherwise they would have repented at his preaching. However, Jesus also knew that the majority of the common people felt that John was a God-sent prophet, and the religious leaders would be taking a great risk to say otherwise publicly. They were trying to force Jesus to say something in public that they could use to discredit Him, but by His question, Jesus put them in that same place! Afraid of the people, they wouldn't give an honest answer, and their fear also prevented them from openly arresting Jesus later on, because so many people considered Him to be a God-sent prophet.

Then Jesus told the parable of the two sons to illustrate the difference between the religious leaders and the sinners who had repented. The first son, when told by his father to work in the vineyard, said, "No, I won't go." But he later changed his mind and obeyed. He represents those who were previously in rebellion toward God, but who repented.

The other son, when told by his father to go and work in the vineyard, said, "Yes, sir, I will." But he never followed through on what he promised. He represents the religious leaders who always talked about obedience to God's commands, but who never really obeyed. Jesus reprimanded them, saying that the worst sinners of their day, tax collectors and prostitutes would get into heaven before them because they repented when they heard John the Baptist preach.

Incidentally, notice that it wasn't their repentance that saved them; it was their belief in John's message that the kingdom of heaven was at hand. Because they believed John's message, they repented, proving that they really did believe. Salvation works the same way today. We are saved by God's grace through a faith that moves us to repent and begin a life of obedience. True faith always produces fruit.

The story of the evil farmers is easy for us to understand, but the religious leaders apparently missed its meaning at first. After hearing it, they unknowingly pronounced their own judgment when they condemned the wicked farmers who killed the vineyard owner's son. And once they understood that they were the wicked farmers in Jesus' story, they still refused to repent, fulfilling the scripture in the Psalms that talks about the builders rejecting a stone that would become the chief cornerstone. The chief cornerstone was the first and most important stone in any significant building in Jesus' time. Every other stone in a building had to be properly related to that most important stone, by being lined up with it. Those who aren't properly lined up with that stone are destined for trouble. As Jesus said, "Anyone who stumbles over that stone will be broken to pieces, and it will crush anyone on whom it falls" (Matthew 21:44).

 Q. If a person is unsaved, is he more likely to become saved if he's self-righteous or if he's a horrible sinner?

A. He is more likely to become saved if he realizes he needs to be saved. Self-righteous people often don't think they need a Savior, because they assume they have saved themselves by their good deeds. That's why horrible sinners are more likely to be saved, and that's why tax collectors and prostitutes were saved when John the Baptist preached while the religious leaders remained unsaved.

Q. In the parable of the evil farmers, the owner of the vineyard sent representatives and finally his own son to collect some of the fruit. What did the fruit represent? What does this tell us about what God desires from us?

A. The fruit represents acts of obedience, which is what God expects from His people.

Application: It's good for us to read sections of Scripture that contrast the reaction of believers and non-believers, because it helps us evaluate which category we are in. With whom did you identify in today's reading?

The Parable of the Wedding Guests
Matthew 22:1-14

Here is another parable Jesus told that was packed with significance for both believers and unbelievers, modern and ancient. However, when we interpret any parable, we must realize that every parable is an *imperfect* comparison, and we need to discern which details are significant and which details have no significance at all in illustrating spiritual truths.

This parable is about the kingdom of heaven, and Jesus compared it to a great wedding feast prepared by a king for his son. Just like a wedding feast, heaven is going to be a place of celebration, fun and enjoyment. Like a wedding feast, it won't be a pointless party. It will be a place to honor God's Son.

Jesus may have also used the marriage feast illustration because the Bible speaks of those who believe in Jesus as being His bride (see Ephesians 5:25-32; Revelation 19:7-9). Marriage is a good illustration of our relationship with Jesus, because true believers are inseparably joined with Him in an intimate, trusting and devoted relationship. As husband and wife become one in God's eyes, so we have become one with Jesus. True Christians are not just Christ's neighbors or acquaintances, they are married to Him!

Many guests were invited to the wedding feast but refused the invitation. The king mercifully sent his messengers with invitations more than once, but they were ignored and even mistreated. The invited guests were more interested in other things, illustrating the attitude of so many people who hear and ignore the gospel.

Eventually, however, the king's patience ran out, and he became furious with those who spurned his kindness. Consequently, he sent his army to destroy them. This teaches us that although God is love, He will not be merciful forever with those who ignore Him. Judgment is coming.

Then the king sent his servants out again to invite anyone they could find to attend the wedding feast. If this part of the parable has any significance, it represents the gospel invitation that was rejected by the Jews and offered to the Gentiles.

Of course, even those on the street corners who were invited had a choice to accept or reject the invitation. Unfortunately, one man tried to accept the invitation but not abide by the rules of the king. In Jesus' time, wealthy people often provided special wedding robes for their wedding guests. In Jesus' parable, the wedding robes may well represent the "robes of righteousness" spoken of in the book of Revelation (see Rev. 19:8). The man who was caught without a robe was either lacking Christ's righteousness, something that is given as a free gift to every believer in Jesus, or he was lacking any personal obedience, the fruit of real faith. Consequently, he didn't belong in heaven.

Jesus' primary point, as He summarized in the conclusion of the parable, was, "Many are called, but few are chosen" (Matthew 22:14). That is, many are invited to the kingdom of heaven, but *the invitation doesn't guarantee salvation.* Only those who truly believe are chosen to attend God's great wedding feast.

Q. What does this parable have to teach us about the idea that some people are predestined by God to be saved while others are predestined by God to be unsaved?

A. This parable teaches that everyone has a choice in the matter of his salvation, and that God has not predestined certain ones to be saved and certain ones to be unsaved. This parable shows us that it is God's will for people to be in heaven who will not be there.

Q. In Jesus' story, once the man at the wedding feast was discovered to be without a wedding robe, he was cast out. Is Jesus trying to tell us that some people who don't really belong in heaven will be mistakenly allowed in and then later be cast out and thrown into hell?

A. No, and this is where we must draw the line in trying to find significance in every detail of the parable. Jesus was only illustrating the fact that, even though the invitation is so freely extended to everyone and so many people do apparently accept the invitation, there will be those who will try to accept the invitation on their own terms and who ultimately will be rejected. The man who was cast out represents a false believer. He accepted the invitation but didn't do what the king required.

Application: The most important thing in life is accepting God's salvation invitation and then doing His will the rest of your life. If you've done that, you're on the right track and have a happy future indeed!

Jesus Answers Two Trick Questions
Mark 12:13-27

In Jesus' time, Israel was under the domination of the Roman Empire, led by a king named Tiberius Caesar who lived in Rome. In Israel, one of the men who represented the Roman government was Herod Antipas. Among other things, he was responsible to see that the Jews under his jurisdiction paid their appropriate taxes to Rome, taxes that every Jew resented having to pay.

One day, some Pharisees came to Jesus, bringing with them some of Herod's supporters. They hoped to trick Jesus into saying something that would get Him in trouble with the Roman government. That way, He'd be arrested, tried and maybe executed. So they asked Him if they should pay taxes to the Roman government, hoping Herod's supporters would hear Him say that they shouldn't. They figured they had Jesus trapped, because they knew He always told the pure truth. Surely He wouldn't endorse paying unjust taxes to a cruel, dominating foreign power, a tax that everyone who would hear Him resented paying.

But Jesus saw through their trickery, and answered in a way they didn't expect. The Bible teaches that us that all government has been established by God (see Romans 13:1-2), and so our government deserves our respect and obedience—as long as our government doesn't require us to sin against God. On the other hand, some people look to governmental leaders as if they were God, giving them praise, honor and devotion that only God deserves. We, as Jesus said, should give to Caesar what belongs to him and give to God what belongs to Him.

Next, a religious group called the Sadducees stepped up to ask Jesus a difficult question. They didn't believe that there was life after death or that people would one day be resurrected, even though those truths were taught in the Old Testament. (No wonder they were *sad, you see!*) So they posed a ridiculous question, hoping to make Jesus look foolish as He tried to defend the doctrine of the resurrection. Their question was about a woman who had been widowed seven times. Whose wife would she be when they were all resurrected, since she'd had seven husbands?

Jesus replied that she would be no one's wife, because in heaven, no one will be married. That is why, at Christian weddings, couples promise to be husband and wife only until death. In heaven, there will apparently be no exclusive relationships. We'll all be deeply devoted to one another and, of course, to the Lord.

Jesus then furnished scriptural proof that people live after they die, citing God's conversation with Moses at the burning bush. God said to Moses, "I am the God of Abraham, the God of Isaac, and the God of Jacob." Notice God spoke using the present, not the past tense, indicating that all three men were still alive right then, long after they had physically died. The Sadducees had made a serious error in their understanding.

 Q. If our government makes a law saying it is illegal to worship Jesus Christ, should we obey that law?

A. Although the government is an authority over us, there is a higher authority: God. If the lower authority tells us to disobey the higher authority, we shouldn't obey the lower authority.

Q. Why is it, as Jesus said, such a serious error not to believe that people live after their bodies die?

A. Because if there is no life after death, there is no judgment and no heaven or hell. If that is the case, there is no need to be saved and so there's no need for Jesus to save us. And there's no ultimate reason to obey God in this life. That is why believing in the resurrection is so important.

Application: If Jesus had ever answered someone's question by saying, "I'm sorry, but I just don't know the answer to that one. You've stumped Me," we'd be tempted to think that He wasn't God in the form of a human being. But Jesus never was stumped by anyone. One day, we'll get to ask Him all the questions for which we don't presently have answers. In the meantime, we can thank God for what He has revealed to us, and ask Him to help us understand everything He wants us to know in this present life.

Jesus Answers and Asks a Difficult Question
Mark 12:28-37

Because Jesus was God in the form of a human being, He had a right to judge which commandments were the most important. No one else has this right, yet even Christians sometimes seem to think they have that right. They take one commandment, verse, subject, or principle in the Bible and emphasize it above everything else in God's Word. In so doing, they unknowingly are saying that Jesus' judgment is wrong. Although He clearly stated which commandments were the most important, they've supposedly found more important ones.

There is nothing more important than loving God with all our heart, soul, mind and strength, and loving our neighbor as ourselves. These are the two things on which we ought to be focused. It is sad indeed when Christians greatly emphasize other biblical concepts to the point of neglecting or even violating the greatest commandments. For example, some Christians emphasize a certain Bible translation, a certain dress code, or a favorite doctrine, and refuse to fellowship with those who don't agree with them. They are, in effect, saying to Jesus, "What You said is most important is not most important." Everything that God says is important, but God Himself said that part of what He said is the most important.

Having been asked a series of questions, Jesus decided to ask a question of His own. He, of course, knew the answer to His question, but He wanted to provoke people to think about God's Word and what it said about Him. The religious teachers of His day correctly believed and taught that, according to the Old Testament, the Messiah would be a descendant of David, which, of course, Jesus was through His mother Mary. However, neglecting or not understanding other messianic prophecies, the religious leaders were anticipating a Messiah who would be only a human being, and not God Himself. Hoping to help them realize that the Messiah would not only be David's descendant, but also God, Jesus posed a question about David addressing the Messiah as his Lord. How could the Messiah be David's descendant if David himself called Him his Lord? The only way that would be possible was if God became a man through the agency of one of David's descendants, and that is what Jesus wanted everyone to understand about Himself. He was more than a descendant of David, He was the Lord Himself!

Q. Jesus told the teacher who asked Him what the greatest commandment was, "You are not far from the Kingdom of God" (Mark 12:34). This indicates the teacher, although close to God's kingdom, was not actually in it yet. What did he need to do to enter?

A. Although he recognized what the two most important commandments were, he needed to realize how much he had broken those two commandments. Then, he needed to repent and believe in Jesus, recognizing that Jesus was the only One who could save him from his sins.

Q. Some Christians emphasize faith and how it works in a believer's life more than anything else. How do you suppose God feels about that?

A. He considers it unbalanced. Taking his cue from Jesus, Paul wrote that love is greater than faith (see 1 Corinthians 13:13).

Application: Because Jesus told us what are the most important commandments, it would be a good thing to ask ourselves this question all the time: "Am I loving God with all my heart, soul, mind and strength, and loving my neighbor as myself?" If we are, it will be reflected in how we live our lives.

The Parable of the Good Samaritan
Luke 10:25-37

Like the religious teacher we read about yesterday, the teacher in today's story also understood that the most important commandments were to love God with all our heart, soul, mind and strength, and love our neighbor as ourselves. If a person did those things, he would, according to Jesus, inherit eternal life. The religious teacher in today's story obviously felt guilty for not loving his neighbor as himself. He wanted to justify his lack of love by embracing a very narrow definition of what a neighbor is. If God was speaking of us only loving our next-door neighbor, then perhaps this teacher could justify his lack of love and even hatred for so many other people. So he asked Jesus, "And who is my neighbor?" (Luke 10:29), and Jesus told him the story of the Good Samaritan.

The lesson of the story is that anyone and everyone is our neighbor by God's definition, even people of other races or religions who are usually despised by those with whom we identify. As you probably remember, in Jesus' day, Jews and Samaritans hated each other. But the Samaritan in Jesus' story showed love to a Jewish man, probably saving his life, while other Jews showed him no love at all.

When Jesus asked the religious teacher, "Now which of these three would you say was a neighbor to the man who was attacked by bandits?" (Luke 10:36), his hatred of Samaritans surfaced in his answer. Not wanting to admit that the one who obeyed God's second most important commandment was a member of a race he despised, he simply replied, "The one who showed him mercy" (Luke 10:37). Jesus then told him, "Go and do the same" (Luke 10:37). This seems to indicate that he had not been showing mercy to those who needed it, thus not loving his neighbor as himself. Now he was confronted with his own sin and need for repentance.

Q. In the story of the Good Samaritan, why do you suppose that two very religious people, the priest and the Temple assistant, didn't help the dying man?

A. Because they were religious but not actually saved. They were hypocrites, claiming to be followers of God's law, but breaking His second most important commandment. They no doubt justified their actions in some way, because everyone who sins justifies his actions in order to salve his conscience.

Q. If Jesus told this same story today in the United States, do you think He might change the identities of the characters in the story? If so, how?

A. He would probably use characters that would be more applicable to the prejudices of our own society. Perhaps the two who passed by the dying man would be pastors or Sunday school teachers. Perhaps the dying man would be black or white, depending on the color of Jesus' audience.

Application: In many ways, Jesus was like a good Samaritan to us. We were attacked by the devil and demons, robbed of the truth, and left spiritually dead and destined to die physically. No religion or person could save us, but Jesus felt compassion for us and saved us from death. Praise God for His love for us!

Jesus Warns the Religious Leaders
Matthew 23:1-36

What we read today was certainly not the only time Jesus strongly rebuked the Pharisees and religious teachers. In fact, we've previously read in Luke's Gospel of a time when Jesus spoke some of the very same words while dining in a Pharisee's home (see Luke 11:37-52)! Because He was God, Jesus had every right to make such a critical judgment. Moreover, His criticism could be considered an act of love, because He was only telling them what they will hear Him say in the future when they stand before His throne of judgment. Jesus' warning was spoken when the religious leaders still had time to repent and be saved from their eternal fate in hell.

Just like the religious leaders of Jesus' day, modern Christian leaders also face the same temptations to abuse their authority. Because people often think more highly of Christian leaders than they should, these leaders are often tempted to take advantage of the people they lead. However, if Christians and their leaders will simply do what Jesus said, a problem that is widespread in the church will end.

The solution is two-fold. First, Christians should be careful how they view their leaders, respecting but not revering them. God is the only Person who should be revered. Too many Christians are focused more on human leaders than they are on God, giving them even more praise than God! Jesus said we should avoid using any titles when we speak of our leaders, such as "Teacher," "Father," or "Master," because we should consider God alone to be all of these to us.

Second, Christian leaders should be careful how they view themselves. They should not allow those they lead to give them titles, teaching their followers that, as Jesus said, we're all equal brothers and sisters in God's family. God should be the One we're focused on, not any man who has been gifted by God. Personally, I discourage people in the church I pastored from calling me "Pastor David" for the same reason I wouldn't allow them to call me "Teacher David," "Father David," or "Master David." God alone is our Shepherd, which is what the word *pastor* means. I wanted the people of my church to consider God to be their only Pastor and consider me to be only His servant. The word minister means "servant," and that is how all Christian leaders should view themselves, just as Jesus said in today's reading, "The greatest among you must be a servant" (Matthew 23:11). I told my congregation that if they wanted to attach a title to my name, they should call me "Slave Dave."

All of us, not just leaders, should monitor our own lives for hypocrisy. If our private lives are different than our public lives, if we preach what we don't practice ourselves, if we interpret or bend God's Word to fit our own lifestyles, if we emphasize what is minor and neglect what is most important, then we're hypocrites just like the Pharisees. Outwardly, they appeared holy and clean, but inwardly they were filthy, just like whitewashed tombs. Jesus called them blind guides, snakes, sons of vipers and sons of hell! We don't want to be one of them!

Q. Jesus promised the religious leaders that He would send them prophets, wise men and teachers whom they would persecute. How is this statement an indirect claim to His being God?

A. Only God sends prophets, so Jesus' claim that He would send prophets was a claim to be God.

Q. Kids sometimes make a promise to a friend, but because they had their fingers crossed behind their backs when they spoke, later claim that they don't have to keep their promise. How do you think God feels about that?

A. He would feel the same way about that as He did about the Pharisees claiming that they could break an oath if they swore "by God's Temple," but were obligated to keep an oath if they swore "by the gold in the Temple." Lying is lying.

 Application: Today is a good time to examine ourselves. We all need to make sure our insides—our motives, thoughts and desires—are just as clean as our outsides. Why not ask the Lord to show you if you are in any way guilty of an inward sin so you can purify yourself from it?

A Poor But Generous Widow
Mark 12:41-44

People who love God will show their love by how they live their lives. One area in which their love for God will be manifested is how they spend their money. If how they spend their money isn't affected by their relationship with God, they probably have no relationship with Him.

For example, parents love their children, and their love shows when they use their money to take care of their children's needs or buy them gifts. If a parent never spent any money on his children, we would doubt his love. People love their friends, and their love shows when they, among other things, spend money to show hospitality to, or help their friends. People love their dogs, and their love shows when they spend money on their dogs.

By the same token, when people love God, it affects their pocketbooks. Unfortunately, many people who claim to love God actually prove by their actions that they love their dogs more!

Of course, there is no way to give God money or any material thing directly. The only way we can give to God is to support what He is interested in, and He is primarily interested in His kingdom and the advancement of it. He wants people to be saved and discipled. So we can show our love for God by supporting our church, missionaries and other biblical ministries.

As today's story clearly illustrates, God is not so impressed by how much we give, but by how much we give in proportion to how much we have available to give. It's easy for a millionaire to give a thousand dollars to God's work, but in God's eyes, a poor person's gift of one dollar could be a bigger gift. This is something for us to consider in our own lives. Every Christian should regularly be giving a portion of his income to God's work, but those who have more should be giving a larger percentage—if they want their gifts to be equivalent to the smaller percentages that poorer Christians are giving.

Q. Is there a biblical percentage of income that is the minimum that every Christian should be giving? If so, what is that percentage?

A. In the Old Testament, God commanded all of His people to give ten percent of their income to His work, regardless of how rich or poor they were. It would seem reasonable to conclude that God does not expect less of His people under the new covenant, and so giving ten percent is a good place to start.

Q. Let's say your parents give you an allowance of five dollars a week and you give it all to a missionary. Would that be the same as your parents giving away all of their weekly income?

A. Your giving would be commendable, but your parents' giving would be a much greater sacrifice. This is not because the amount of their gift was greater, but because they gave what they had to live on for a week, something you really didn't do. You probably didn't need any of your money to buy food, pay electric bills or purchase clothing for your kids!

Application: Because God knows everything, He views things differently than we often do. What impresses us might not impress Him, and vice versa. Jesus once said, "What this world honors is an abomination in the sight of God" (Luke 16:15).

Jesus Talks About Jerusalem's Destruction and the End Times
Matthew 24:1-28

If you were giving Jesus a tour of your city and pointed out the city hall, public library and largest old stone church, and He told you that the time was coming when those buildings would be completely destroyed, you'd probably want to know when! That is how the disciples felt when Jesus predicted that the massive Temple buildings in Jerusalem would be destroyed. They knew that if the Temple was to be demolished, a building that took forty-six years to build, it could only be for one of two possible reasons. Either a highly motivated enemy would destroy it during a major war, or God would destroy it. In either case, to the disciples, such an event would surely be a sign of the end of the world. So they asked Jesus when this would take place, and what signs would signal His return and the end of the world.

We know from history that Jerusalem and the Temple *were* destroyed about forty years later by the Roman army, and Jesus told His disciples what would happen immediately preceding that disaster so they could preserve their lives. However, only Luke recorded that portion of what Jesus said: "When you see Jerusalem surrounded by armies, then you will know that the time of its destruction has arrived. Then those in Judea must flee to the hills. Let those in Jerusalem escape, and those outside the city should not enter it for shelter. For those will be days of God's vengeance, and the prophetic words of the Scriptures will be fulfilled. How terrible it will be for pregnant women and for mothers nursing their babies. For there will be great distress in the land and wrath upon this people. They will be brutally killed by the sword or sent away as captives to all the nations of the world. And Jerusalem will be conquered and trampled down by the Gentiles until the age of the Gentiles comes to an end" (Luke 21:20-24).

History tells us that Jerusalem was surrounded by Roman armies around A.D. 70, but for a short time they were drawn away to fight elsewhere, and that is when all the Christians escaped, obeying Jesus' words. When the Roman armies returned to besiege the city and destroy it, not one true follower of Christ was harmed during the siege, while tens of thousands of nonbelievers lost their lives.

Matthew, whose record we've read today, seemed to focus more on Jesus' predictions that related to His return and the end of the age. Notice that Jesus first talked about things that would *not* be signs of His return and the end of the world. False christs, wars, famines and earthquakes would be many, but they are not signs that the end is near. Neither are severe persecution, false prophets or rampant sin and selfishness indications that Jesus will soon come back.

However, Jesus did give us two signs that will occur within a short time before His return. First, when the gospel has been proclaimed to the whole world, the end will be near. As I write this, as many as half the people in the world have not heard the name of Jesus. However, that looks like it is changing as the church takes Christ's command to preach the gospel to every person more seriously.

The second sign is something that Daniel predicted about 2,500 years ago, what Jesus called "the sacrilegious object that causes desecration standing in the holy place" (Matthew 24:15). We don't have the space to explore this in detail, but one day a man whom the Bible calls the antichrist will walk into the new Temple in Jerusalem and proclaim that he is God. Paul wrote to the Christians in Thessalonica about that man, saying, "He will exalt himself and defy every god there is and tear down every object of adoration and worship. He will position himself in the temple of God, claiming that he himself is God" (2 Thessalonians 2:4).

That event will be a sign that the end of the world and Christ's return are very near. Many Bible scholars believe that, according to other scriptures, that event will precede Christ's return by three-and-a-half years. It will be a time of terrible distress for people in Jerusalem and around the world, what the Bible calls the "great tribulation," of which we can read in the book of Revelation. God's wrath will be poured out upon the inhabitants of the earth like never before. At the end of it, Jesus will return in a way that no one will miss seeing Him, lighting up the entire sky like a flash of lightning does for only a split second. And although the world will consider that to be the end, we will consider it to be another beginning!

Q. The Jerusalem Temple that was destroyed in A.D. 70 has never been rebuilt. Does this mean that Daniel, Jesus and Paul were mistaken about the future antichrist walking into the holy place of the Temple to proclaim himself as being God?

A. No, you can be sure that Scripture will be fulfilled. Obviously a new Temple will have to be built before the antichrist can fulfill Daniel's, Jesus' and Paul's predictions. Therefore, when we hear that a new Temple is being constructed in Jerusalem, this will be a sign to us that the end is drawing closer. Think about this: It wasn't until 1948 that the Jews repossessed the region of ancient Israel as their homeland for the first time since A.D. 70, and it wasn't until a short war in 1967 that they repossessed Jerusalem as their own city. These are two relatively recent events that were both necessary before the Jerusalem Temple could ever be rebuilt.

Q. When God's wrath is poured out upon the earth during the tribulation period that the Bible tells us about, will true Christians be punished along with nonbelievers?

A. No, they will not. Some Bible scholars believe that all true Christians will be taken up to heaven *prior* to the tribulation period. This is called the "rapture," and Paul wrote about it in 1 Thessalonians 4:13-18. There is no doubt that it will happen; the only question is when it will happen. Those who think the rapture won't happen until some point during the tribulation period or at the end of the tribulation period agree that Christians will be protected from God's wrath upon the ungodly, as this is what God has always done in the past. They will not, however, be necessarily spared from the persecution of the anti-Christ.

Application: It sure is good to know that we have nothing to dread about the future. We will not have to suffer God's eternal wrath like those who don't follow Jesus. And any trials we face on the road to heaven are only temporary.

Jesus Exhorts Everyone to be Ready for His Return
Matthew 24:29-51

Today we continue reading Jesus' response to His disciples' question about the signs that will precede His return and the end of the world. After a time of terrible, worldwide tribulation, there will be some unmistakable signs that Jesus is just about to return. The sun will be darkened, and the moon, because it only reflects the sun's light, will not shine. The stars will fall from the sky. Can you imagine seeing that? It will terrorize those who are unprepared. Isaiah predicted this almost three thousand years ago, writing, "The land will be destroyed and all the sinners with it. The heavens will be black above them. No light will shine from stars or sun or moon.... The heavens above will melt away and disappear like a rolled-up scroll. The stars will fall from the sky, just as withered leaves and fruit fall from a tree" (Isaiah 13:9-10; 34:4).

Then Jesus will return, shining brightly in a black sky, in clouds of God's radiant glory. All who are alive on earth will see Him and mourn, for they will have no doubts then that their eternal fate is sealed because they rejected Him. A great trumpet will sound, and God's angels will gather His people from the farthest ends of the earth and heaven.

That will mark the beginning of Jesus' reign over all the earth, and people would be foolish to be unprepared for such a momentous event. Jesus therefore admonished us to be ready by watching for the signs He predicted and by living obedient lives. Although no one knows the exact day or hour of His return, everyone should be able to recognize when the time is near. The signs He described will not be spread out over centuries of time.

Unfortunately, multitudes *will be* caught unprepared, living their normal lives right up until the day when Jesus comes back. In spite of the distress that will exist during the time just prior to Jesus' return, people will be working, eating and partying right up until the end. In some cases, they will be working right alongside people who have come to believe in Jesus, and will see them disappear when Jesus sends His angels to gather His people. The unsaved will be completely caught off guard.

Those who are ready for Christ's return will be those who believe in Him, and naturally, their faith will be evident by their lifestyles. When Jesus comes back, they will be doing His will. Those who are selfishly living for themselves, always partying and getting drunk, prove that they don't believe in Jesus or His promise to return. And, as Jesus said, they will be banished to hell.

Are you ready?

Q. We read today about some major changes that will one day occur to some things most people think are permanent: the sun, moon and stars. Jesus also mentioned a major change in something else people consider permanent. What is it?

A. Jesus said that one day the earth would disappear (see Matthew 24:35). Don't be alarmed, however, because God will create a new one right after He destroys the present one (see Revelation 21:1)!

Application: In today's reading and throughout Scripture, we are told that every material thing we presently own will one day disappear. For that reason we should view material things from a spiritual perspective. We should, as much as possible, use material things for spiritual purposes, to serve God and others. Our use of material things is a test of our Christ-likeness, and one day we'll be rewarded for every unselfish act.

Ten Bridesmaids and Three Servants
Matthew 25:1-30

Today's reading is a continuation of Jesus' response to His disciples' questions about His return. The first parable of the ten bridesmaids is a little difficult for us to understand unless we know something about the wedding customs of Jesus' day.

Back then, people didn't get married in churches, but in their own homes. With his friends, the bridegroom would walk from his house to the house of the bride. From there he would take her back home in a wedding procession, and the wedding guests would light their way through the darkened streets with oil lamps. The ten bridesmaids in this story were either stationed at the bride's home, waiting for the bridegroom to arrive, or at his house, waiting for both bride and bridegroom to arrive.

The important point of the story is that, because the bridegroom was delayed, five of the bridesmaids ran out of oil to fuel their lamps and had to go and purchase more oil. When they returned, they couldn't gain entrance into the wedding feast that was by then in progress.

We should be very cautious about searching for significance in every detail of parables such as this, otherwise we'll become confused. Every parable is an imperfect comparison that usually serves to make one major point.

We don't need to wonder what the oil represents, what is the significance of the number of bridesmaids, or why the five foolish ones were excluded from the wedding feast just because they arrived late. The obvious point of this parable is that we need to stay ready for the return of our bridegroom, Jesus, even if it seems He's delayed. People who are spiritually asleep will miss out on a great eternal wedding feast.

The story of the three servants is very similar to the parable of the ten servants we read in the nineteenth chapter of Luke's Gospel. Notice that in this parable, the unfaithful servant was cast into "outer darkness, where there will be weeping and gnashing of teeth" (Matthew 25:30), obviously hell. We can be sure he wasn't a Christian. So what did the one bag of gold he was entrusted with represent? It represented either his life, a gift given to him by God, or it represents gifts, abilities and opportunities that God gave him. When he had to give an account at the final judgment, he had nothing to show for what God had given him. He was considered to be lazy, wicked and useless by God (see Matthew 25:26, 30). The least he could have done would have been to invest his master's money in the bank and earn a little interest for him. A true believer would have at least produced a little fruit in his life. But this man had none.

The other two servants represent those who, by their obedience, prove their faithfulness. (The reason they had been given more money than the other servant was perhaps because they had already proven themselves faithful with one bag of gold). As God finds us faithful, He entrusts us with more responsibility. This is true in this life and the next one.

The primary point of this parable is that every person is accountable to God for what God entrusts to him. Those who prove to be completely faithless will suffer eternally, but those who prove themselves faithful to serve God with their gifts will be rewarded. Again, this parable teaches us that true believers are identifiable by their deeds.

Q. If Jesus visited the earth for the first time today, do you think He would tell people the same parable of ten bridesmaids as He did two thousand years ago?

A. He probably wouldn't, because it doesn't fit our modern customs. He would probably adapt it to fit modern weddings or use an entirely different story to illustrate the same truth. Perhaps He would talk about a man who was late for his job interview and who wasn't hired, or a young lady who arrived late for her college entrance exams and was consequently prohibited from entering the room where the test was being taken.

Q. How do you think Jesus might change the parable of the three servants to fit our modern culture?

A. He might change the wealthy master into an employer who, upon leaving for a business trip, gave his employees certain assignments according to their abilities. Upon his return, he would discover that one employee, to whom he gave the easiest task, had accomplished nothing. That employee would be fired. Or Jesus might tell a story about a mother who gave her three children jobs to do while she went grocery shopping. When she returned earlier than expected, she found out that one child had been watching TV the whole time. Because of this, his mom grounded him for a week!

 Application: What did we learn today? Stay ready, and be faithful. If Jesus returned right now, would you be ready to meet Him?

Jesus Talks About the Final Judgment
Matthew 25:31-46

Continuing to answer His disciples' questions about His return, Jesus concluded by telling them what would happen soon after He did come back. That will be the time when He will judge everyone on the earth, ultimately allowing them to remain in His kingdom or be cast into hell.

The question most asked about this portion of Scripture centers on the criteria used by God to determine who is saved and who is not. If we are saved by grace through faith and not by works, then why are people's works the determining factor in their salvation or damnation? The answer is that our deeds show if we believe or don't believe in Jesus. The Bible often declares that every person will be judged according to his or her deeds. The reason is because deeds alone reveal the faith a person possesses or doesn't possess.

True believers in Jesus love others who believe in Jesus. Jesus Himself said, "Your love for one another will prove to the world that you are my disciples" (John 13:35). The apostle John wrote, "If we love other Christians, it proves that we have passed from death to eternal life" (1 John 3:14). Love is manifested in deeds, and that is why the saved in today's reading were the ones who gave food, drink, hospitality and clothing to their needy brothers and sisters, cared for them when they were sick and visited them when they were in prison. That is what true believers do, and when they show their love for the brethren, they show their love for Christ.

On the other hand, unbelievers could care less about Christians who are suffering. In fact, they are often glad because of it. And when they show their hatred for Christians, they show their hatred for Christ. Again, the apostle John wrote, "Anyone who hates another Christian is really a murderer at heart. And you know that murderers don't have eternal life within them" (1 John 3:15).

Q. Today's reading gives us another indication that God wants everyone to be saved. What indication is that? (Clue: It has something to do with for whom hell is prepared.)

A. Jesus said that hell was prepared for the Devil and his demons. That could indicate that is wasn't originally intended to be a place for human beings. God's will is for everyone to be saved, even for those who will spend eternity in hell. The unsaved forfeit what God wants for them by their unbelief.

Q. Jesus said that His kingdom was prepared for saved people from the foundation of the world. Does this prove that God has predestined only certain people to be saved?

A. No, that would contradict what He said about salvation being offered to everyone. God planned from the foundation of the world that anyone who would believe in His Son would inherit His kingdom. The kingdom has been prepared from the foundation of the world for all who will believe the gospel.

Application: The most important question any of us could ask is this: Is my love for Jesus Christ evident in how I treat fellow Christians? More specifically, what needy Christian have I served or am I serving?

Jesus Talks Again About His Impending Death
John 12:20-33

Jesus knew that He would be crucified in Jerusalem during the Passover festival in just a few days. He had already predicted His death on several occasions to His disciples, but now He wanted them to begin to understand the purpose of His death.

First of all, Jesus didn't consider His death to be an end, but a beginning. He said, "The time has come for the Son of Man to enter into his glory" (John 12:23). That is, it was time for Him to go to heaven. The death of any Christian should also be viewed as a beginning. However, Christians enter into God's glory when they die, not their own glory, as did Jesus.

Second, Jesus' death was not an accident or twist of fate. It was God's intention that He die. In fact, it was the main reason Jesus became a human being and lived on the earth (see John 12:27).

Third, the result of His death would be new life for a lot of people. Jesus compared Himself to a kernel of wheat that dies and is planted in the ground. The result is new life for many more kernels of wheat that grow from that single seed.

Fourth, Jesus explained what we must do to reap the benefits of His death, saying, "Those who love their life in this world will lose it. Those who despise their life in this world will keep it for eternal life" (John 12:25). Before a person can be saved, he must come to the place of despising his life, recognizing that he is a sinner trapped in his sins, and is displeasing to God. Then and only then will he be motivated to come sincerely to Jesus, repenting of his sins and seeking a new life that is pleasing to God.

Fifth, Jesus' death would glorify God (see John 12:28) because it would reveal the greatness of His love for humanity.

Sixth, Jesus' death would be the beginning of the end of Satan's rule over the millions of sinful people in the world (see John 12:31). The reason is because God has allowed Satan to hold everyone who is a sinner in captivity. But once the penalty for people's sins was paid, those who were made righteous by believing are released from Satan's captivity. Moreover, one day only righteous, redeemed people will be living on the earth, and then Satan will have no authority whatsoever. He himself will ultimately be cast into hell. And it will be due to Jesus' sacrificial death.

Seventh, Jesus' death would, more than anything else He did, draw people to Him as they learn of His great sacrifice on their behalf (see John 12:32). His death on the cross is the central part of the gospel.

Q. People often "accept Jesus" for different reasons. For example, some people hope God will give them a better edge in their business or enhance their relationship with others. Are these valid reasons for becoming a Christian?

A. No, according to Jesus, they're not. A person must despise his life in this world if he wants eternal life. People who supposedly "accept Jesus" to help them become more successful in life aren't meeting the requirements Jesus laid down. They are those, who, as Jesus said, love their lives in this world, and don't recognize their pathetic condition—rebellious, lost, and hell-bound.

Q. We read today about God speaking in an audible voice to Jesus so that the crowd who was listening to Jesus heard it. Everyone heard the same thing, but not everyone who heard God's voice agreed about what they'd heard. Why do you suppose they disagreed?

A. Because everyone in the crowd was more or less receptive to the truth, either believing or doubtful. The less receptive ones didn't want to admit that anything supernatural had happened, so they explained God's voice by saying it was thunder. The more receptive ones thought an angel had spoken. However, all of them knew that Jesus had just addressed His Father in prayer, but none of them were apparently receptive enough to believe that God Himself had spoken.

Application: The problem is not that people can't believe, it's that they won't believe because of the hardness of their hearts. Here is a modern example of the same kind of unbelief Jesus encountered, found in an article in Popular Mechanics magazine that explains how Jesus was able to raise Lazarus from the dead:

> "Dr. Gerald A. Larue, professor emeritus of biblical history and archeology at the University of Southern California and president of the Committee for the Scientific Examination of Religion (CSER), a secular humanist organization, says it's possible Lazarus was either in a coma or a catatonic state....Larue says that a person in a catatonic state shows few signs of a heartbeat or breathing. The biblical account leads him to suspect Lazarus was actually in a coma, since in this condition hearing is often the last sense lost. "Assuming Jesus had a loud voice, and he called out 'Lazarus,' the man may have heard him and come out of the coma," Larue says. (Popular Mechanics, Vol. 173, No 12, p. 42).

What do you think?

Jesus Again Claims to be God
John 12:34-50

When Jesus told the crowd that He would die by being lifted up on a cross, they were confused. How could He claim to be the Messiah if He was going to die? Didn't the Old Testament promise that the Messiah's kingdom would have no end?

The problem was their limited understanding of the Old Testament messianic predictions. Yes, the Scriptures did promise a never-ending messianic kingdom, but they also revealed that the Messiah would die for our sins.

Jesus emphasized that His remaining time on earth was limited, and encouraged His audience to take advantage of the opportunity that would soon be gone. Comparing Himself to a light that was about to be shut off, He told them to walk in His light and believe in it. Light is symbolic of truth, and that is all Jesus spoke. In fact, He Himself was a revelation of God's truthfulness, because He was the Savior God promised to send. Those who walk in His light, that is, base their lives on what He said, and believe in Him, become His spiritual offspring, members of His family, or as Jesus said, "children of the light" (John 12:36).

Perhaps anticipating that some of his readers might wonder why so many Jews rejected Jesus if He was their long-awaited Messiah, John mentions that Isaiah the prophet foretold Christ's rejection. Thus Jesus' widespread rejection is not reason for readers to doubt He is the Messiah; rather, it is even more reason to believe He is the Messiah.

Unfortunately, the *New Living Translation*, in translating John's paraphrase of Isaiah's prophecy, makes it seem as if God hardened people's hearts so that they could not believe in Him even if they wanted to. However, other translations leave room for varied interpretations of Isaiah's words. It would certainly seem strange and unfair if God expected people to do what He made it impossible for them to do! Paul wrote that it is *Satan*, not God, who blinds the minds of the unbelieving (see 2 Corinthians 4:4).

In the final part of today's reading, Jesus again repeated His often-made claims, clearly conveying that He was nothing less than God. To believe in Him was to believe in God. To see Him was to see God. He was the sole source of truth in the world. He had come to save the world. He should be obeyed. The truth He had spoken would be the standard by which every person will be judged on the last day. His words were actually the words of God the Father, and they were the words that could bring eternal life. Anyone other than God who would make those kinds of claims would be guilty of blasphemy!

Q. Although many people rejected Jesus, according to John, many people also believed in Him, including some Jewish leaders. However, John told us that they wouldn't admit their faith to anyone for fear that the Pharisees would throw them out of the synagogue. Does that mean that they weren't true believers?

A. No, it just means they were timid believers. John criticized them for loving the praise of men more than the praise of God. When we are hesitant to confess Christ openly and boldly, we are guilty of the same fault.

Q. According to what we read today, Jesus expects people to believe in Him and obey Him. Which is more important?

A. That was a trick question. They are equally important, and, in fact, the two can't be separated. If a person believes in Jesus, he will also obey Jesus.

Application: Jesus, although obviously the Son of God sent from heaven, is still rejected by the majority of people. Because of the hardness of their hearts, they refuse to believe in Him. As the saying goes, "The majority is not always right." Be glad that you're a part of the minority who is right!

Jesus is Twice Anointed
Matthew 26:1-16; John 12:1-11

To a casual reader, it might seem as if Matthew and John were writing about the same incident. The two stories, however, contain details that differ significantly. Mary anointed Jesus *six days* before the Passover, and the unnamed woman anointed Him *two days* before the Passover. It seems Mary anointed Jesus while He was visiting her, her sister Martha and her brother Lazarus in their home; the unnamed woman anointed Jesus in the home of a man named Simon the Leper. Mary anointed Jesus' feet and wiped them with her hair; the unnamed woman poured her perfume on His head.

Both women were expressing their love for Jesus in a costly act of worship, spending the equivalent of a year's wages in a few minutes of adoration. Both women obviously believed Jesus was God! He was worth it.

Both women were rebuked for what they did, the unnamed woman by Jesus' disciples, and Mary by Judas Iscariot. This gives us some more insight into Judas's evil character. The disciples' rebuke of the unnamed woman was motivated by concern for the poor, certainly a worthy motive. Still, Jesus rebuked them, correcting their perspective. Four days later, they again watched as another year's wages was spent on Jesus' feet. Even after being among those rebuked by Jesus four days earlier, Judas still grumbled about it. Beyond that, John informs us that Judas really wasn't concerned with the poor. He often stole money from the box where Jesus kept money that was to be given to the poor, and he wanted the perfume to be sold only so there would be more money for him to steal.

Judas was a classic example of someone whose true god is money. Anyone who enriches himself in ways that are sinful or unethical proves that money, and not the Lord, is his god. People have often speculated what Judas's motive was in betraying Jesus for thirty pieces of silver. The answer is that he saw an opportunity to make a large sum of money easily.

Q. Let's pretend that your parents spent thirty thousand dollars in one day on your sister, buying her all kinds of expensive and unnecessary things. Let's also pretend that you complained about it, saying that the money could have been spent on a much more worthy cause, perhaps given to the poor for the basic necessities of life. If your sister responded as Jesus did, essentially saying that she was more important than all the poor people who could have been helped, what would that say about her?

A. It would prove she had a huge ego and was incredibly selfish.

Q. Then what about Jesus? Didn't His answer prove the same about Him?

A. No, because Jesus was God. He is infinitely more valuable than all the people of the world, rich and poor, combined. It would be impossible for Him to think a thought or say a word that could be considered egotistical. He has no equals and couldn't do anything that could rightfully be considered selfish. Selfishness is a sin that can only be committed by a human being.

⊙ Application: When Mary anointed Jesus' feet with her expensive perfume, the house was filled with the fragrance. Likewise, when we sincerely worship Jesus from our hearts, there seems to be a heavenly fragrance of God's Spirit that fills the place where we worship.

The Last Supper
Luke 22:7-20

Today we've read about a portion of Jesus' final full day on earth. Thousands of Jews from all over Israel had journeyed to Jerusalem for the weeklong Feast of Unleavened Bread, which began with the Passover celebration. On that day, every Israelite family would kill a year-old lamb, commemorating the time when the angel of death, who killed all the firstborn in Egypt, passed over their homes on the night of their exodus from Egypt. The Bible refers to Jesus as the Lamb of God because He came to fulfill what every previous Passover lamb prefigured—His substitutionary death for the sins of the world.

Jesus and His disciples had been staying each night in the nearby town of Bethany. On this particular day, Jesus sent Peter and John before Him into Jerusalem to prepare the Passover meal so Jesus and His disciples could eat it together. The instructions Jesus gave them for the preparations were amazing. Just as they entered through a gate in Jerusalem's wall, they would meet a man carrying a pitcher of water. They should simply follow him to a house he would enter. Then they were to say to the owner of that house, "The Teacher asks, 'Where is the guest room where I can eat the Passover meal with my disciples?'" He would take them to a large upstairs room that was already set up for them.

Apparently, the owner had some prior knowledge that Jesus wanted to use his upper room for a meal with His disciples, but how he knew that, we don't know. Either Jesus had previously made arrangements with him, or God had somehow informed him. The man, whom Peter and John followed, was on an errand to bring a pitcher of water to the house they needed to find. He wasn't specifically waiting for Peter and John at the Jerusalem Gate, but just "happened" to be walking there at the same time they entered the city. God had arranged the circumstances so that they were all at the right place at the right time. If He desires, God can slow us down or speed us up to make sure that we're in the right place at the right time as well. For example, God might arrange for a slowpoke driver to be ahead of your car to help you avoid an accident in which you would otherwise be involved.

Once Jesus and His disciples had gathered for the Passover meal, Jesus made it very clear that it would be the last time He would eat the Passover meal until it came to fulfillment in the Kingdom of God (see Luke 22:16). Either He was speaking of the time of His thousand-year reign on the earth, indicating that He would join people then who would celebrate the Passover in commemoration of His sacrifice, or He was speaking of celebrating the Passover in a spiritual sense with every person who would believe in Him.

Although Luke didn't record it, as Jesus shared the cup of wine with His disciples, He said, "This is my blood, which seals the covenant between God and his people. It is poured out to forgive the sins of many" (Matthew 26:28). God couldn't simply forgive people's sins by a decree of forgiveness; otherwise He would be compromising His own holiness and justice. As the Creator and moral Judge of all humanity, He must punish all sin. Amazingly, Jesus was willing to suffer our deserved punishment, dying as our substitute. His blood being poured out speaks of His violent and painful death. And like all ancient covenants that were ratified by blood being shed, God has entered into a covenant with us, promising to forgive all our sins. That covenant is ratified by Jesus' shed blood.

Just as the wine Jesus shared represented His blood, so the bread He broke and shared represented His body. Our eating and drinking what represents His body and blood is symbolic of our becoming one with Him. We're in Him and He's in us. Our sins have been paid for in full by the One who now lives in us by His Holy Spirit.

 Q. Did Jesus tell us how often we are to share in what is now called Communion or the Lord's Supper?

A. No, He didn't. He just said that as often as we do it, we should do it in His remembrance.

Q. Is the Lord's Supper something we can only celebrate in a church service officiated by an ordained minister?

A. No, not according to the Bible. When Jesus broke bread and drank wine, He did something that was extremely common in His day. People broke and ate bread at practically every meal of their lives. Wine was the most common beverage other than water. For this reason, some Christians believe that every meal we eat can be viewed as Communion, blessed at the beginning, done in Christ's remembrance and serving as a reminder of our oneness with Him.

Application: The author of Hebrews wrote, "We have become partakers of Christ" (Hebrews 3:14, NASB). One of the greatest truths of the New Testament is that Jesus lives inside of everyone who truly believes in Him. Now Christ in us wants to live through us. Our job is to allow Him to do just that.

Jesus Washes His Disciples' Feet
John 13:1-17

In Jesus' time, foot washing was a common practice. People wore sandals, and their feet would often become dirty from traveling dusty roads and paths. Upon entering a house, the first order of business was the washing of feet. If a person were wealthy enough to have a servant, his servant would wash his feet and the feet of visiting guests.

By washing His disciples' feet, Jesus was doing what an ordinary servant would do. What made His act so extraordinary is that He was their Lord and Teacher. In their society (and ours) no one of any stature would stoop to such a lowly level of servanthood. But Jesus wanted to demonstrate to them what true greatness was in God's eyes. In God's kingdom, the greatest person is the one who serves others. Jesus, of course, is the greatest servant there ever was—He gave His life for us all.

If Jesus visited you and wanted to teach the same lesson, He probably wouldn't wash your feet, but would do something more culturally relevant. He would perform some equivalent lowly and undesirable task to demonstrate true servanthood. Perhaps He would wash out your garbage cans or clean your toilet. If He was visiting your church on Sunday, He might work in the nursery, changing diapers. Then He would say, "I have given you an example to follow. Do as I have done to you" (John 13:15). God wants His children to serve each other in practical ways. The question is: *Are we?*

Peter was at first very reluctant to allow Jesus to wash his feet, feeling that it wasn't the Lord's place to be kneeling before him, performing such a humble task. But Jesus responded by saying, "If I don't wash you, you won't belong to me" (John 13:8). He must have been speaking of the spiritual cleansing that Jesus gives us when we're born again. Peter replied, "Then wash my hands and head as well, Lord, not just my feet!" (John 13:9). He knew that his hands and head were in more need of cleansing than his feet, for his hands had done sinful things and his head had harbored sinful thoughts.

Jesus then compared Peter to a person who had recently taken a bath. He might need his feet washed if he'd walked somewhere, but the rest of him was still clean. Peter had already been cleansed of his sins but, like all Christians who commit a sin, needed a partial cleansing. Perhaps a better analogy for our day would describe the washing of hands rather than feet. Even the cleanest people need to wash their hands occasionally. When they do, it doesn't mean they're a dirty person; it only means they have dirty hands. When we sin as Christians, it doesn't mean we're sinful. It means we've dirtied ourselves somewhat. We need to go to Jesus, the One who has already cleansed us entirely, and request a partial cleansing.

Q. What could you do to obey Jesus' command to wash the feet of others in regard to your relationship with your brothers or sisters? (Hint: they will be lowly tasks that you would probably rather not do!)

Q. Even though Jesus knew that Judas was going to betray Him, do you think Jesus washed his feet as well?

A. Yes, Jesus did wash Judas's feet. By doing so, Jesus demonstrated something else that He preached: loving our enemies. Can you imagine what Judas must have been thinking as the One he was about to betray unto death knelt before him and humbly washed his feet?

Application: Jesus said that the path of blessing is the path of servanthood. Families whose members serve one another are truly blessed. Is your family on that blessing path?

Jesus Predicts Judas's Betrayal and Peter's Denial
John 13:18-38

Jesus knew from the beginning that Judas would betray Him (see John 6:64,70-71), and of course God knew it from eternity past. In fact, it was predicted in Psalm 41:9 that the Messiah would be betrayed by one with whom He would share His food. Jesus revealed to Peter that Judas was the betrayer, and in so doing proved His foreknowledge of what was about to happen.

Was Judas really responsible for what he did? Didn't someone have to betray Jesus in order for prophecy to be fulfilled? And doesn't Satan really bear the responsibility, since the Bible says he entered Judas? And what about Jesus? Wasn't He partly responsible for His own betrayal, since He instructed Judas to do quickly what he was about to do?

The answer to those questions is that Judas bore most of the responsibility for Christ's betrayal, Satan bore some and Christ bore none. The Scriptures only *foretold* what God knew would happen, so we shouldn't think that someone *had* to betray Jesus or that Judas was predestined to do it. Judas decided to betray Christ on his own (see Matthew 26:14-16).

The Bible does indicate that Satan was involved in tempting Judas, so he also bears some guilt. However, his tempting of Judas didn't remove Judas's guilt in the matter. Satan didn't force Judas; he only tempted him. Judas still had to decide whether or not he would yield to the temptation.

Finally, when Jesus told Judas to do quickly what he had planned, we shouldn't think Jesus was encouraging Judas to betray Him. Judas had already made up his mind what he was going to do; Jesus was revealing to Judas that He knew he was about to betray Him. Jesus' words should have made it more difficult for Judas to follow through on his plan, since he certainly didn't want Jesus to know what he was about to do, but now he knew that Jesus knew.

Jesus also realized that His time with His disciples was very short. He would soon be in heaven. So He took His final opportunity to share what was most important with those who would carry on His work. They would be the ones who would lead the church, and the one thing that could ruin them before they got started was strife. However, if they would love one another, they would remain unified and strong. So Jesus commanded them to love one another, saying that their love would be the identifying mark that they were His disciples.

Unfortunately, either this truth hasn't sunk into the hearts of many Christians, or many people who claim to be Christians are just fooling themselves, because they don't display what Jesus said would mark them as being His. Sitting in church once a week is not the identifying mark of a true Christian, neither is prophesying, possessing Bible knowledge, going on youth retreats, nor playing on the church softball team. True followers of Christ love each other.

Q. Why did the chief priests need someone to betray Jesus? Why didn't they just arrest Jesus when He was teaching in the Temple each day?

A. Because they were afraid that the people would riot if they arrested Jesus in a public place. So they needed someone to inform them of Jesus' whereabouts when He would be alone or with only His twelve disciples (see Matthew 26:3-5; Luke 22:6).

Q. Jesus not only knew Judas's plans, He also knew what Peter would do: denying Him three times after boasting that he was ready to die for Him. Can you think of a spiritual principle that describes what happened to Peter?

A. "Pride goes before destruction" (see Proverbs 16:18).

Application: Jesus didn't suggest that we love one another. He commanded it. And the standard by which He said we should measure our love for one another is by His love for us. That means we should really love each other, from our hearts, proving our love through our words and actions.

Jesus Comforts His Disciples
John 14:1-31

As Jesus' disciples listened to Jesus talk after their Passover meal, their hearts became troubled. He had told them that He would be leaving them very soon, and that they would not be able to go where He was going (see John 13:33). Keep in mind that they had been with Him for over three years, so the thought of being separated from Him was traumatic. Jesus told them not to be troubled, and gave them at least five good reasons why they shouldn't be.

First, He said He was going to prepare a place for them in His Father's house, a house in which there were many rooms.

Second, He promised that He would ultimately come back for them to take them with Him to His Father's house. Then they would never be separated from Him again.

Third, during the time they were apart, He would send them another Helper, the Holy Spirit, who would never leave them. The Holy Spirit would lead them into truth, teaching them and reminding them of what Jesus had said.

Fourth, soon after His departure, they would see Him again for a time after His resurrection and be assured that He was alive forevermore. Once they saw Him raised from the dead, they wouldn't entertain the idea that He was dead and gone.

And fifth, He would give them peace in their hearts, His own peace, as a gift. They only needed to tap into it. What more could they ask?

In today's reading, Jesus made several claims, most of which only God could rightfully make. He claimed to be the way, the truth and the life (see John 14:6). That is, He is the only way to heaven, the only One who knew and revealed spiritual truth, and the only One who could give eternal life. He claimed to be one with the Father, to the extent that anyone who saw or knew Him could say they'd seen and known the Father.

He claimed that His words were His Father's, and His ability to do miracles came from the Father. As I've written before, Jesus didn't leave us the option to think of Him as just a good man or a prophet. His claims were too outrageous. If He wasn't God, He was the biggest liar who has ever lived.

Finally, Jesus made it very clear who His people are. They are those who love Him and who prove their love by their obedience to Him. And those are the people whom God indwells by His Holy Spirit. Isn't it great to be one of them?

Q. Near the end of today's reading, Jesus said, "I don't have much more time to talk to you, because the prince of this world approaches. He has no power over me, but I will do what the Father requires of me, so that the world will know that I love the Father" (John 14:30-31). Who is the "prince of this world"?

A. Satan.

Q. What did Jesus mean when He said that the prince of this world was approaching?

A. He was referring to how Satan was orchestrating His imminent betrayal, arrest, and crucifixion. Jesus implied that Satan was only doing what God was permitting him to do, and, unknowingly, was playing right into God's hands. By motivating men to kill Jesus, Satan was setting the stage for Jesus to fulfill God's preordained plan for His Son to be sacrificed for the sins of the world!

◎ Application: Jesus said, "For I will live again, and you will, too" (John 14:19). For Christians, death is not something to be feared. It's the beginning of a new life. We have that promise from someone we can trust, someone who knows what He's talking about, and someone who's crossed over the line of death and come back to life!

We are Branches in Jesus' Vine
John 15:1-17

Using the analogy of a vine, Jesus explained what a true Christian is: he is a person who, as a result of being joined to Jesus, produces fruit. Fruit, of course, represents the good things that we do. It includes our actions, attitudes, words and answers to our prayers. We can only produce that fruit if we are connected with Jesus.

Notice how Jesus emphasized fruitfulness, stressing its great importance. Whether a person produces fruit is what determines his eternal destination. Those who don't produce fruit are like worthless branches on the grapevine—and they are destined to be burnt by fire, spending eternity in hell. God prunes those who do produce fruit so they may become more fruitful.

If you've believed in Jesus, then you are already producing some fruit. But God will not be satisfied until you are just like Jesus. So, like a gardener who prunes his grapevine so it might produce more fruit, God will work with us, cutting off what is displeasing to Him. He is dedicated to our spiritual growth.

Our job, according to Christ's command, is to remain in Him (see John 15:4). To "remain in Jesus" means to continue to believe that He is the Son of God and thus continue to follow and obey Him. If we will remain in Him, He'll remain in us and we'll produce much fruit.

Jesus also instructed His followers to remain *in His love* (see John 15:9). That's the same thing as remaining *in Him*, because the proof of a person's remaining in Jesus' love is the same proof as that of a person's remaining in Jesus: his obedience. In today's reading, Jesus stressed the importance of our obeying His commandment to love one another. He expects us to love one another just as He loves us. He literally laid down His life for us, and wants us to give sacrificially of ourselves to one another. John wrote, "Let us stop just saying we love each other; let us really show it by our actions" (1 John 3:18). Have you demonstrated your love for a fellow Christian recently?

Q. Jesus talked about the branch that was cut off from the vine because it wasn't bearing fruit. Does this prove that a person can be joined to Christ but produce no fruit?

A. As with every parable and comparison, we must be careful about searching for significance in every detail, because at some point, the similarities in the comparison end. We shouldn't necessarily conclude, just because the fruitless branch was connected to the vine, that it's possible for a person who doesn't produce fruit to be connected to Christ. That might be reading more into His analogy than Jesus intended. The way a person becomes connected to Jesus is by faith, and the Bible tells us that "faith without works is dead" (see James 2:26, NASB). For that reason, it seems unlikely that Jesus was trying to teach that a person can be joined to Him yet remain fruitless. In fact, Jesus said that fruitlessness is what results in being cut off from the vine.

Q. For those who do remain in Him, Jesus has given tremendous promises regarding their prayers. He said, "But if you stay joined to me and my words remain in you, you may ask any request you like, and it will be granted!" (John 15:7). Does that mean we could ask for all our enemies to be killed in car crashes on the same day?

A. People who remain in Jesus and who allow Jesus' words to remain in them would never make such a prayer request, because Jesus said in another place that we should bless our enemies and pray *for* them, not *against* them! We can pray with assurance for anything that God has promised us in His word, and we should only want to pray for what is His will.

Application: Jesus is our Lord and Master, but He's not a distant master who only cares about our obedience and doesn't care about us. He's our Friend. But don't forget that He's only our Friend if He's first our Master and Lord. Jesus plainly said that those who obey Him are His Friends (see John 15:14). Too many people want Jesus as their friend but not their Lord. But Jesus does not offer such a relationship to anyone.

133
Jesus Warns His Disciples of the World's Hatred
John 15:18-16:4

Keep in mind that Jesus would be gone in less than twenty-four hours. This was the final opportunity He would have to speak with His disciples before His crucifixion.

Jesus knew that unsaved people would hate His disciples just like they had hated Him, and He wanted to prepare them for what lay ahead. The hatred they would experience would tempt them to fall away from their faith in Him. They would wonder, as all persecuted Christians are tempted to wonder, why God would allow them to suffer at the hands of evil people. But because Jesus has forewarned all of us, we shouldn't doubt God when we're persecuted. He told us it was coming. Jesus even told us that some of us would be killed for our faith in Him, but that doesn't change His love for us.

The apostle Paul wrote, "Everyone who wants to live a godly life in Christ Jesus will suffer persecution" (2 Timothy 3:12). Rather than be concerned when we *do* suffer persecution, we should be concerned if we *aren't* suffering some persecution. Although we aren't persecuted nearly as much in our country as Christians are in other places in the world, anyone who takes a stand for Christ anywhere will be talked about and hated by others. We should expect that. Jesus said, "Woe to you when all men speak well of you" (Luke 6:26, NASB).

Pre-teens and teenagers, perhaps even more so than older adults, want to be accepted by others. But if you are going to be a true follower of Christ, you'll have to be willing to face some rejection. The place to receive love and acceptance is from your family and other fellow believers in Christ. Their love for you should more than counterbalance the hatred of the world.

Jesus also explained the reason the world hates us. It is because they hate Him and His Father whom we serve and represent. We are not the main target of the world's hatred. It is actually God Himself. We are just being caught in the crossfire.

The amazing thing is that it is often people who claim to be Christians who persecute those who are born again. Jesus said, "The time is coming when those who kill you will think they are doing God a service" (John 16:2). These kinds of "Christians," however, aren't really saved, as proven by their hatred for true believers. John wrote, "If someone says, 'I love God,' but hates another Christian, that person is a liar; for if we don't love people we can see, how can we love God, whom we have not seen?" (1 John 4:20).

 Q. When non-Christians express their hatred for us, what should be our response?

A. We should show them love in return. Jesus said, "Love your enemies. Do good to those who hate you. Pray for the happiness of those who curse you. Pray for those who hurt you" (Luke 6:27-28). The love we show our persecutors can have a profound influence upon them, softening their hearts toward Jesus.

Q. Can you think of a reason why God rarely seems to stop persecution against His own people?

A. One reason is because He's so merciful to His enemies. He is acting toward them the same way He expects us to act, loving them in spite of their hatred. He's hoping that during the time He's showing them mercy, they'll come to their senses and repent. He knows that if they die without repenting, they'll suffer eternally. That is only one reason, among others, that God allows persecution against His people.

Application: Do you know of anyone who doesn't like you, or who has said something derogatory about you because you are a follower of Christ? If so, what has been your response?

Jesus' Final Words to His Disciples
John 16:5-33

As we read today, we realize what an advantage we have over Jesus' disciples, because we understand what they didn't. Unlike them, we know exactly what Jesus meant when He said, "In just a little while I will be gone, and you won't see me anymore. Then, just a little while after that, you will see me again" (John 16:16). Because we do understand that Jesus was speaking of His death and resurrection, let us not overlook the amazing fact that Jesus foretold what was about to take place. How did He know? Only God could know or reveal such knowledge.

Even though Jesus was going away, He would not be leaving His disciples alone. He would send them the Holy Spirit, and amazingly, that would actually be better for them than if He remained. Jesus was limited to being in one place at a time, but the Holy Spirit could indwell every one of His followers, and He would help them. One of the ways the Holy Spirit will help us is in spreading the gospel and leading people to Jesus. He is the One who convicts people of their sin of not believing in Jesus, and of God's righteousness and the future judgment. When we talk about those things with unbelievers, we can be certain that the Holy Spirit is helping us and convicting those with whom we speak.

Another way the Holy Spirit would help Jesus' disciples would be by teaching them. Jesus said that He had many other things He wanted to tell them, but they weren't ready to receive it yet. However, the Holy Spirit would pick up where Jesus left off. That is why, in the New Testament, we have the many letters written to the churches. They contain truths, given by the Holy Spirit to the apostles, which build on Jesus' teaching.

To further comfort His disciples about His leaving them, Jesus emphasized that they had a special relationship with the Father who loved them dearly. They could go directly to Him in prayer using Jesus' name, so Jesus' departure wouldn't mean the end of their communication with God. Jesus assured them that His Father wanted to answer their prayers so that their joy would be made full. The Father feels the same way about all His children, not just Jesus' original eleven disciples. He loves us dearly!

Q. Some Christians refer to the Holy Spirit using the word "it," speaking as if the Holy Spirit is a term for God's power. Is this correct?

A. No, the Holy Spirit is not just a power and shouldn't be referred to as "it." Jesus always spoke of the Holy Spirit as a person, using the personal pronoun "He." The Holy Spirit can be referred to as God, just as much as Jesus and the Father. To have Him live in us is to have God live in us!

Q. When the Holy Spirit wants to tell us what He has heard from Jesus or the Father, how does He communicate with us?

A. According to the record of what happened in the early church, the Holy Spirit can communicate with us in a number of ways. He can speak to us in dreams, visions, through the gift of prophecy or by using an audible voice. He can also speak to us by impressions within our spirits where He lives, and this seems to be the most common way He communicates with us. It may not be as spectacular as a vision or an audible voice, but it is just as supernatural. Our job is to learn to listen and remain sensitive to His leadings.

Application: Why not make a decision to try to be more sensitive to the Holy Spirit who indwells you for a specified period of time, perhaps for a few hours or a day, and see what happens? Do you think you'll act more or less like Jesus?

Jesus Prays for His Disciples
John 17:1-26

Although Jesus knew that He would die an excruciatingly painful death in just a few hours, His mind was not on Himself. Rather, He was primarily thinking about those who did and would believe in Him. Jesus' great love and concern for them is made obvious in the prayer we just read.

As Jesus stated in His prayer, He told His disciples everything the Father had told Him to tell them. As a result, they had come to believe in Him, and Jesus considered them to be gifts from His Father. Unlike the majority of people, those eleven men believed that Jesus was sent from God, and Jesus was so proud of them, he called them His "glory" (John 17:10).

Now, as Jesus returned to His Father in heaven, they would remain in a world that hated them, a world ruled by a spiritual leader who would love to destroy them and their work. While in their presence, Jesus had provided for their spiritual protection, so that none of them, except Judas, was led astray. Now He prayed that the Father would keep them safe in His absence, so that none of them would be divided or led astray by Satan or false doctrine. Jesus prayed that they would be unified and would be pure and holy. He prayed that they would reach out to the world in a convincing way.

Did you notice that Jesus also prayed these same things for you? Jesus said, "I am praying not only for these disciples but also for all who will ever believe in me because of their testimony" (John 17:20). All of us who believe in Jesus have done so as a result of the passed-down testimony of the original eleven disciples.

It seems that more than anything else, Jesus desired and prayed for our oneness, indicating that our unity is a major key in convincing the world that God sent Jesus. When the world looks at the church and sees us disagreeing, fighting and dividing, it certainly doesn't help convince them that God sent His Son. Our unity should be based on our common belief in Jesus and our common goal of making disciples of all nations. Anything else that we disagree about is not important enough to divide us. But, by and large, the church has been divided over hundreds of issues that fall into this secondary category, even giving themselves identifying titles that advertise their separation from other Christians. All who believe in Christ should share one title: Christian. Anything beyond that demonstrates disunity.

Q. What do you think would happen if all the churches in the world that truly believe in Jesus would remove their present titles and unite with the rest of the body of Christ under the one name of Christian for the common cause of spreading the gospel to the whole world?

A. It would make a lot of people angry because they are more loyal to their brand of Christianity than to Christ, but it would also result in the world hearing the gospel.

Application: Today, as Jesus did, pray for the unity of those who believe in Jesus so that the world will believe in Him.

Jesus is Arrested
Matthew 26:36-56

It was the night before His crucifixion. Having counseled, comforted and prayed for His disciples, there was nothing left for Jesus to do but wait for His arrest, trial and execution. Jesus decided to wait in a grove of olive trees called Gethsemane, just outside of Jerusalem, a place where He and His disciples had often met. Judas would know right where to find Him.

Anticipating what He was about to endure, Jesus was "filled with anguish and deep distress" (Matthew 26:37). He told His disciples that His soul was "crushed with grief to the point of death" (Matthew 26:38), and even prayed that, if possible, the cup of suffering might be taken away from Him. It was not, however, just the thought of being beaten, whipped and crucified that disturbed Jesus so much. He was about to bear the sins of the world as He hung on the cross. He knew He would suffer God's holy wrath, as had no other human being. Jesus would become the guiltiest person who ever lived, having no guilt of His own, but taking the guilt for our sins. The anguish Jesus would experience would be the combined anguish of every sinner at the moment of His condemnation, and the "cup" that Jesus requested be taken away if possible was the cup of God's wrath spoken of in other places in the Bible (see Isaiah 51:17; Jeremiah 25:15; Revelation 14:10; 16:19). By the time He was led away from Gethsemane by the soldiers, Jesus had fully resolved to take what was due us. He responded to Peter's defending Him from arrest by saying, "Shall I not drink from the cup the Father has given me?" (John 18:11).

John recorded in his Gospel that when Judas arrived with soldiers and Temple guards in Gethsemane, Jesus stepped forward to meet them and asked, "Whom are you looking for?" (John 18:4). They replied, "Jesus of Nazareth." When Jesus said, "I am he," they all fell backward to the ground! They got a small taste of God's power when God speaks! John also revealed that it was Peter who cut off the ear of the high priest's slave, and Luke revealed in his Gospel that Jesus immediately healed the man! That was the second miracle in Gethsemane witnessed by the mob who came to arrest Jesus. Still they arrested Him.

One of the most significant statements we read today was what Jesus said about His being able to call for thousands of angels to protect Him from arrest. This makes it ever so clear that Jesus didn't have to die. His death was not an accident or twist of fate. It was God's plan. And the only possible reason such a thing could be God's plan was because Jesus' death would accomplish something good. We know, of course, that Jesus' death is what satisfied the requirements of God's justice on our behalf. If Jesus hadn't died, we would have to spend eternity in hell, enduring the punishment we deserve for our sins.

Praise God for Jesus! Praise God that we've had the privilege of knowing about what we've read today!

Q. Jesus prayed essentially the same prayer three times in Gethsemane. Does this teach us that we should follow His example, repeatedly making the same requests?

A. No, because Jesus was not praying a prayer of faith, that is, a prayer based on one of God's promises. In fact, He knew what He requested was *not* God's will. His was actually a prayer of consecration, submitting to God's will. To ask continually for what God has promised us is to doubt Him.

Q. When Peter cut off the ear of the high priest's slave with his sword, do you suppose he was aiming for the man's ear?

A. More likely, Peter was aiming for the man's neck, and the man ducked in the nick of time. I almost wish the man hadn't ducked so that Jesus, rather than healing a severed ear, could have healed a severed head! That would have been considered one of His greatest miracles!

Application: When Jesus was arrested, the mob apparently tried to arrest Jesus' disciples as well (see Mark 14:51-52; John 18:8). Yet they all escaped, deserting Jesus, fearing for their own lives. Jesus had predicted this, and the Old Testament had foretold it as well (see Matthew 26:31). But when He was resurrected, Jesus received and restored deserters and then used them to build His church. This shows us how merciful Jesus is. In the world, deserters are rarely given a second chance. In God's kingdom, there is abundant grace available.

Jesus' Trial Before the Jewish Council
Matthew 26:57-75

It was probably very early in the morning and certainly still dark when Jesus was arrested in Gethsemane. This was the plan of the Jewish leaders so that most of the people wouldn't know about what was happening to Jesus. From Gethsemane, He was taken to the home of the high priest, where the Jewish council gathered for His trial. The plan of the majority was to find Him guilty of blasphemy and have Him executed, but according to the Law of Moses, they needed the consistent testimony of at least two people. Those witnesses who agreed to lie about Jesus were found inconsistent, making their testimony invalid. This shows us that there must have been some sense of true justice among at least a few members of the council who were holding the rest accountable.

Those who were dead set against Christ were unable to find anyone who would say he'd heard Jesus directly claim to be the Messiah and Son of God. So they gathered witnesses who heard Jesus say things that could be considered claims that implied those things. Finally they found two witnesses who said they'd heard Jesus claim that He could rebuild the Temple in three days if it were destroyed. That was the best evidence they could come up with to find Him guilty of the charge of blasphemy. Was this claim not a claim of deity?

We know, of course, that it was indeed a claim of deity, and also a prediction of Jesus' death and resurrection! The Jewish council was about to help fulfill that very claim!

Jesus kept quiet during His trial, a silent testimony of the absurdity of what was happening. Finally, in desperate frustration, the high priest directly questioned Jesus in a customary manner by which Jesus was obligated to respond. Was He the Messiah and Son of God?

Jesus replied that He was, and even quoted an Old Testament messianic prophecy as being a reference to Himself. Finally they had what they wanted. He was indeed guilty of claiming to be divine, and they found Him guilty of blasphemy, just as the majority had hoped. They hated Him passionately. As if in celebration of their victory, they began mocking, hitting, slapping, and spitting on Him. They had found God guilty of claiming to be Himself!

Peter, who had followed at a distance behind the mob who arrested Jesus, then gained entrance into the courtyard of the high priest's house. He was questioned three times by bystanders about his association with Jesus. Each time Peter denied knowing Him. Close to daybreak, he denied Jesus the third time, just as a rooster crowed. Although he had declared a few hours before that he was ready to die for Jesus, his words proved to be only boasts, just as Jesus had predicted. When Peter realized what he'd done, denying his Lord, he went away, crying bitter tears. Jesus knew Peter better than he knew himself.

Q. Why didn't the Jewish council, upon reaching their verdict of blasphemy, immediately execute Jesus by stoning Him, as Jewish law required?

A. The Jews were under the authority of the occupying Roman government. Although they were permitted by the Roman government to put their own people on trial and punish them, they were not permitted to execute anyone without Roman permission (see John 18:29-31). Had this not been the case, they would have stoned Jesus immediately. We know, however, that the Old Testament predicted that the Messiah would die by crucifixion rather than stoning.

Q. What was it that made some of the bystanders suspicious that Peter was one of Jesus' disciples?

A. His accent revealed that he was from Galilee, the region where Jesus lived most of His life. Jesus, too, probably spoke with a Galilean accent.

Application: Jesus obviously believed that He was the Messiah and Son of God, because He was willing to die for His belief. Had He denied it at His trial, He probably would have escaped crucifixion. This destroys the foolish theory that Jesus was only playing a game, pretending to be someone He knew He wasn't. Had that been the case, Jesus would have declared an end to the game at His trial before it cost Him His life.

Judas Commits Suicide
Matthew 27:1-10

When Judas agreed to betray Jesus' whereabouts to the chief priests and elders, he apparently didn't anticipate that it would result in Jesus' crucifixion. When he realized that he would be partly responsible for the death of a man he knew was innocent, he was filled with remorse. In a vain attempt to reverse what he'd done, Judas went back to the chief priests and elders with the money he'd received from them. He was planning to return it, perhaps hoping his act would spark some remorse in them so they might release Jesus. But Judas the betrayer soon realized that they had betrayed him. Although they previously treated him as an important partner, he had served their purpose, and they could now care less about him, his money or his guilty conscience. And they certainly didn't want to hear anything that would tempt them to feel guilty for their part in Jesus' death.

Realizing that he had been their pawn, Judas angrily threw the thirty pieces of silver onto the floor of the Temple. He knew he was guilty of a great sin, and to keep the money, profiting by his betrayal, would make his sin even greater. But getting rid of the money didn't alleviate his guilt. Jesus was still going to die and Judas couldn't reverse what he'd done. Utterly in despair, he committed suicide.

Why did Judas hang himself? He saw death as a solution to his problem. We don't know, however, what problem Judas hoped to solve by killing himself. Did he think that death would end his guilt? Or did he think that by dying he could somehow atone for his sin? One thing we can be certain of is that Judas did not believe he could receive forgiveness from God for what he'd done, although the Bible leads us to believe that he could have. Had Judas believed that, he would have asked for and received it, and then acted like he was forgiven; thus he wouldn't have killed himself.

Suicide is never a good solution to any problem. His taking his own life didn't lessen Judas' guilt. Nor did he atone for his sin by his act. What Judas needed was faith that Jesus was the Son of God. If he had possessed such faith, he would have never betrayed Jesus in the first place. Had he gained such a faith after betraying the Lord, he would have believed that Jesus could forgive him.

Judas went to hell when he died, not just because he betrayed Jesus, but for the same reason anyone else goes to hell: he was a sinner who didn't believe in Jesus. Judas was set apart from everyone else in hell because he was guiltier than the average sinner, having lived with Jesus for three years and having seen His many miracles. His unbelief is almost unbelievable.

Matthew highlights the hypocrisy of the chief priests and elders who wouldn't put the returned money in the Temple treasury because it was unlawful to accept donations earned by doing what they had just paid Judas to do! And after they'd condemned an innocent man, the very Son of God, they wanted to do the right thing before God with the returned betrayal money. So they purchased a field owned by a potter to be used as a place to bury people from other countries who died while in Jerusalem and naturally didn't own a burial place of their own. In doing so, they helped prove to everyone since then that Jesus was the Messiah, unknowingly fulfilling one of Jeremiah's prophecies that the thirty pieces of silver used to betray the Messiah would be used to purchase a potter's field!

Q. Was Judas the only person responsible for Jesus' death?

A. No, many others were responsible, including the chief priests and elders. The truth is, we're all responsible for Jesus' death, because Jesus died according to the preordained plan of God for our sins. If none of us had sinned, Jesus wouldn't have needed to die. In that sense, we're all like Judas. Thank God we've received the forgiveness offered to us.

Q. Is feeling sorry when you've done wrong the same as repenting?

A. No, a person can feel remorse without repenting. Repenting means at least attempting to change your actions from then on. Remorse is usually a temporary emotion. Many people feel sorry for what they've done only because they've been caught or suffered some consequence, and not because they know they've disobeyed God. Christians, on the other hand, feel remorse when they've done wrong because they know they've offended God and in many cases hurt another person. Their remorse leads them to repent.

⊙ᵔ Application: When people commit suicide, there is something wrong with their thinking. If they knew and believed the truth, they would solve their problems in a different way rather than by taking their own life. People think they are ending their problem by committing suicide, but, like Judas, they're getting into a bigger problem from which they'll never escape.

Jesus Stands Trial Before Pilate
John 18:28-19:16

During Jesus' time, Israel was under the domination of the Roman Empire, and although the Jews were permitted to conduct judicial proceedings and punish criminals, they were forbidden to punish anyone by death. Consequently, the chief priests and elders needed the agreement of Pilate, the Roman governor, if Jesus was to be executed as they hoped. So early in the morning, they brought Jesus to him.

Knowing that Pilate would not consider the crime of blasphemy to be worthy of death, they accused Jesus of opposing the payment of taxes to Caesar and claiming to be a king (see Luke 23:2). Such crimes were capital offences against the Roman government.

Pilate knew that it was out of envy that the chief priests wanted Jesus dead, because they were threatened by His growing popularity (see Mark 15:10). So he ordered Jesus to be brought to him inside his palace where he could privately question Him. Jesus made it clear to Pilate that He was indeed a king, but that His kingdom was not an earthly one. His kingdom was in heaven because it was only there that everyone gave Him allegiance. The reason He had left His heavenly kingdom was to bring truth to the world, but it was only those who loved the truth who recognized the truthfulness of His words.

Pilate realized that Jesus was not a dangerous threat to the stability of his kingdom, and to his credit, he did practically everything he could to spare Jesus' life. First, he boldly announced to the chief priests and the crowd outside his palace that Jesus was not guilty of any punishable crime. They responded by telling him that Jesus had been stirring up crowds all over

Judea, having already done the same in Galilee (see Luke 23:5). Seeing an opportunity to pass the decision of Jesus' destiny to someone else, Pilate had Jesus sent to be examined by Herod, who happened to be visiting Jerusalem, because Jesus was under Herod's Galilean jurisdiction. So Jesus was taken to Herod, and was again accused by the chief priests of crimes worthy of death.

According to Luke's Gospel, Herod had wanted to see Jesus for a long time, hoping to see Him perform a miracle. But even though Herod questioned Him extensively, Jesus did not respond to any of his questions. After mocking Him, Herod sent Jesus back to Pilate dressed in a royal robe (see Luke 23:8-11).

Once again Pilate was faced with the crowd of Jewish leaders who were demanding Jesus' death. Apparently there were other Jews at his doorstep who wanted him to release one prisoner, as was the custom every Passover. Seeing another opportunity to obtain Jesus' release, Pilate offered them a choice: Did they want him to release a murderer named Barabbas or Jesus? Surely, given the choice, the crowd that now consisted of others besides the chief priests and elders would pick Jesus. But the chief priests and elders were able to persuade the crowd to request Barabbas's release and cry out for Jesus to be crucified.

Pilate's second attempt to release Jesus had failed, and pressure was mounting on both sides. Not only was the growing crowd becoming more boisterous, but also according to Matthew's Gospel, Pilate's wife sent him a message, saying, "Leave that innocent man alone, because I had a terrible nightmare about him last night" (Matthew 27:19).

Wanting even more to release Jesus but facing the pressure of a large crowd that included many Jewish leaders, Pilate offered a compromise: he would punish Jesus and then release Him. He ordered that Jesus be flogged with a lead-tipped whip, a brutal punishment that ripped a person's back to shreds and often resulted in death. The soldiers who performed the flogging also mocked Jesus, placing a crown of thorns on His head and hitting Him. Before presenting Him to the crowd, Pilate again declared Jesus' innocence, and then brought Him out, beaten and bloody, to be seen by all, hoping the sight of His suffering would compel them to have some compassion. But the crowd continued to call for His crucifixion.

In desperation, Pilate cried out, "You crucify him...I find him not guilty" (John 19:6). The Jewish leaders, realizing that Pilate would not be persuaded that Jesus was guilty of breaking Roman law, appealed by revealing their true charges against Him. Jesus had broken Jewish law by claiming to be God's Son. Now Pilate knew more of the truth, and it frightened him. He took Jesus back inside his palace to further question Him, but Jesus did not answer.

It had been a long morning, and it was almost noon. Having exhausted his resources, Pilate finally caved in to the crowd. In one final, symbolic act, he washed his hands in front of them and declared, "I am innocent of the blood of this man. The responsibility is yours!" (Matthew 27:24). Then he turned Jesus over to his soldiers to be crucified.

 Q. Although Pilate declared his own innocence before the crowd, was he completely innocent before God?

A. No, because he could have stood his ground against the crowd, regardless of what it cost him. Jesus told him that he was guilty of sin (see John 19:11). People often claim their innocence by putting the blame on others. For example, people who write and produce sinful TV programs and movies often justify what they do by saying that they are only giving people what they want. But that is not an acceptable excuse before God. Some people justify their lying by saying that their boss requires it. But they could quit their job. The most important question we could ask is, "What does God think about what I'm doing?" He is the one to whom we must ultimately answer to.

Q. When Pilate said to Jesus, "Don't you realize that I have the power to release you or to crucify you?" Jesus responded, "You would have no power over me at all unless it were given to you from above" (John 19:10-11). What did Jesus mean?

A. He meant that Pilate would not have any authority to decide Jesus' fate unless God had allowed him to have such authority. God is the source of all authority, and no one possesses any authority without His permission. Pilate could not have been a Roman governor unless God had allowed it.

Application: We're all like Barabbas in today's reading. We deserved to die, but Jesus took our place. I wonder what Barabbas was thinking when he was saved from his fate and released, and then watching Jesus, an innocent man, being led away to be crucified?

Jesus' First Three Hours on the Cross
Matthew 27:32-44

According to John's Gospel, Jesus initially carried His own cross on the way to Golgotha, but at some point the Roman soldiers forced a man named Simon, visiting from northern Africa, to carry Jesus' cross. Due to

His physical condition, Jesus must have been unable to carry it Himself. Remember that He had endured several beatings and had been mercilessly whipped by the Roman soldiers, no doubt losing lots of blood.

Once at Golgotha, just outside the walls of Jerusalem, Jesus was offered wine mixed with bitter gall by the soldiers. It would have considerably lessened the excruciating pain He was about to suffer, but upon tasting it, Jesus refused to drink. Because He was paying for our sins, Jesus knew that it was God's will that He suffer to the full degree. So He refused what would have made Him less conscious as the nails were pounded through His wrists and feet.

The soldiers then stripped Jesus of His clothing so He was completely naked, nailed Him to the cross as it lay on the ground, and then raised it upright. Amazingly, according to Luke's Gospel, Jesus prayed that His Father would forgive the soldiers because they didn't know what they were doing (see Luke 23:34). To them, Jesus was just one more condemned criminal. It was their responsibility to remain stationed at Golgotha until all the condemned men were dead, lest someone rescue them from their fate. In some cases, it took days for people to die by crucifixion. Jesus had been so abused prior to being crucified that He died in six hours.

John reported in his Gospel that as the four soldiers waited for death to claim its victims, they divided Jesus' clothing into four shares. However, because His robe was seamless, woven in one piece from top to bottom, they didn't want to tear it. So they drew lots to decide who would get it. This fulfilled exactly what David had predicted in Psalm 22:18: "They divide my clothes among themselves and cast lots for my garments," proving again that Jesus was the Messiah.

John also reported that the words on the sign posted above Jesus' head which read, "Jesus of Nazareth, the King of the Jews," were Pilate's idea and were written in Hebrew, Latin and Greek. Normally, the crimes of crucified individuals were written on signs above their crosses so that everyone would know why they were being executed. The leading priests complained to Pilate about the sign, requesting that he change it to read, "*He said,* I am King of the Jews'" (John 19:21, emphasis added). But Pilate refused. It was his small way of showing his contempt for them and to gain some revenge for the way they had pressured him into condemning Christ.

Many people came to watch Jesus hang on the cross. Some came because they loved Him and others because they hated Him. Those who loved Him may have been hoping to witness His being miraculously delivered. According to John's account, two of those people were Jesus' mother, Mary, and His one disciple, John, who were standing together. Apparently, Jesus' stepfather, Joseph, was dead by this time, and Jesus was concerned for His mother's wellbeing. So He said to His mother, "Woman, he is your son," referring to John. And to John, Jesus said, "She is your mother" (John 19:26-27). From then on John took Mary into his home to take care of her. This was before any of Jesus' brothers believed in Him, and so it's probable that after they became believers they took responsibility for caring for their own mother. It also indicates that Jesus' four half-brothers may have alienated themselves from their own mother, perhaps due to her faith in Jesus. Jesus had predicted that families would be divided over Him, and His own certainly was.

According to Matthew and Mark's accounts of Jesus' crucifixion, the two thieves who were crucified on either side of Jesus mocked Him. However, Luke reveals that after almost three hours of hanging on a cross, one of the thieves had a change of heart. Perhaps he was moved to repentance by witnessing Jesus' prayer for the forgiveness of those who crucified Him, and that he did not return the insults of the many who mocked Him. Jesus loved those who hated Him. The one thief realized that Jesus was an extraordinary person, obviously innocent and holy, and came to believe that He really was the Messiah. He rebuked the other thief for mocking Jesus, saying, "Don't you fear God even when you are dying? We deserve to die for our evil deeds, but this man hasn't done anything wrong" (Luke 23:40-41). Then, without shame, he asked the Lord, "Jesus, remember me when you come into your Kingdom" (Luke 23:42). Jesus promised him even more than he asked for, saying that they would be together in paradise that very day (see Luke 23:43).

 Q. Is it possible for a person who has led a sinful life to be saved right before he dies and go to heaven?

A. Yes, and the one thief on the cross is proof. Because salvation is a gift of God's grace, people can be completely forgiven at any time in their lives, even with their last breath. God's mercy is amazing.

Q. The one thief was saved by God's grace by means of his faith. But like all authentic faith, his had corresponding actions. Can you list any of his actions that proved his faith was genuine?

A. First, he openly confessed that he was a sinner, which is the first step toward salvation. Second, he stated his belief that Jesus was innocent and unworthy of death, defending Him before the other thief. Third, without shame he looked to Jesus as the source of salvation and publicly asked him for it before a hostile crowd.

Application: Those who hated Jesus also made a point of coming to see Him as He hung on the cross. The chief priests and teachers of the law who had condemned Him stopped by to mock Him, calling for Him to come down from the cross if He was actually the Messiah. Unknowing, in their mocking, they declared the reason for His death, saying, "He saved others.... but he can't save himself!" (Mark 15:31). The only way we could be saved was if Jesus didn't save Himself.

Jesus' Second Three Hours on the Cross and Death
Matthew 27:45-56

Although it was now noon, the brightest time of day, we read that there was darkness until Jesus died at three o'clock. We are told very little in the Gospels of what happened during those three hours, but many think that was the time when God's wrath fell upon Jesus in a way that is unimaginable to us. Near the end of that three-hour period Jesus cried out, "Eli, Eli, lema sabachthani?" which means, "My God, my God, why have you forsaken me?" (Matthew 27:46). This gives us some insight into Jesus' emotional state. He felt utterly abandoned by the One with whom He had shared intimate fellowship from eternity past. To Jesus, it hurt more than the nails pounded through His wrists and feet. We must remember, however, that the Father had a reason for abandoning His Son. God forsook Jesus so He could accept us.

Some of those who were nearby heard Jesus' cry, and mistakenly thought He was calling for Elijah. According to John's Gospel, at about the same time Jesus also declared that He was thirsty, so one of the bystanders offered Him some sour wine in a sponge. The rest waited to see if Elijah would come and save Him.

After He drank from the sponge, Jesus said only two other sentences from the cross, probably one right after the other. The first was, "It is finished!" (John 19:30), a phrase that can also be translated, "It has been paid in full!" When Jesus died, the full price had been paid for the sins of humanity. Potentially, everyone could be forgiven.

The last thing Jesus said from the cross was, "Father, I entrust my spirit into your hands!" (Luke 23:46), after which His body immediately died and His spirit departed. But that was not all that happened. As Jesus cried out His final words and then expired, there was an earthquake and that split rocks in the immediate vicinity. Some tombs even opened, and the bodies of many holy people were resurrected. What they saw terrified the Roman soldiers standing guard, to the degree that they exclaimed, "Truly, this was the Son of God!" (Matthew 27:54). Jesus' birth, life, and death were like no other. But the biggest surprise was yet to come in three days!

Q. Some teachers say that Jesus became a spiritual child of Satan on the cross, and, after He died, He went to hell to suffer for three days for our sins. From what we've read yesterday and today, how do we know those two things aren't true?

A. We know that Jesus wasn't a spiritual child of Satan, as unsaved people are, because He spoke to God as being His Father right before He died. We know that Jesus didn't go to hell where unsaved people go when they die, because Jesus told the repentant thief that they would be together in paradise that very day.

Q. We read today that the veil in the Temple was torn in half, from top to bottom, just as Jesus died. What do you think that signified?

A. The Temple curtain that was torn divided the holy place from the holy of holies, which only the high priest could enter once a year, and only with great precaution. God's holy presence remained there, and no human being could get near it without dying. When it was torn, it obviously signified that there was no longer a barrier between God and man, and that through Jesus' substitutionary sacrifice, people now have access to a holy God.

Application: Jesus' crucifixion had been predicted by David in Psalm 22, written hundreds of years before Jesus was born. By inspiration of the Holy Spirit, David wrote, "My God, my God! Why have you forsaken me? ... Everyone who sees me mocks me. They sneer and shake their heads, saying, Is this the one who relies on the Lord? Then let the Lord save him! If the Lord loves him so much, let the Lord rescue him'.... My life is poured out like water, and all my bones are out of joint. My heart is like wax, melting within me. My strength has dried up like sun-baked clay. My tongue sticks to the roof of my mouth.... My enemies surround me like a pack of dogs; an evil gang closes in on me. They have pierced my hands and feet.... They divide my clothes among themselves and throw dice for my garments" (Psalm 22:1,7-8,14-16,18). This is further proof that Jesus was the Messiah, and that it was God's plan for Him to die on a cross.

Jesus' Burial
John 19:31-42; Matthew 27:62-66

When people were nailed to a cross in Roman times, all of their weight was suspended on the nails through their wrists and hands. The muscles in their arms and legs were severely stressed and soon became exhausted, resulting in the dislocation of shoulder bones and a tightening of the rib cage. This made breathing a difficult task, and victims would find themselves attempting to hoist themselves on the nails from which they dangled in order to get enough air into their lungs to stay alive. Because the Jews didn't want three crucified men screaming outside the city walls on a special Sabbath, they requested that Pilate order their legs broken. This would make it impossible for the condemned men to exert any pressure from their legs to hoist themselves for air, and they would quickly die from lack of oxygen.

Pilate granted their request, but when the soldiers arrived to carry out their gruesome task, they found that Jesus was already dead, so there was no need to do to Him what they did to the other two men. This fulfilled what God had spoken to the people of Israel, forbidding them to break any bones of their Passover lambs. As the Lamb of God, none of Jesus' bones were broken either.

One of the soldiers, however, did thrust his spear in Jesus' side to make certain of His death, and John, an eyewitness, said that he saw blood and water flow out. Modern medical authorities tell us this indicates that a ruptured heart was the actual cause of Jesus' death. This incident also offered further proof that Jesus was the Messiah, as it fulfilled a scripture in the book of Zechariah that foretold the Messiah would be pierced (see John 19:37).

Joseph of Arimathea, a member of the Jewish council that condemned Jesus, but one who had not agreed with the council's decision, requested Pilate's permission to take Jesus' body down from the cross. He and Nicodemus wrapped Jesus' body with a long linen cloth along with about seventy-five pounds of embalming ointment made from myrrh and aloes. Jesus' body looked like a mummy. Then they placed it in Joseph's own tomb that had been cut out of rock, like a small cave, and rolled a large stone, also specially cut for the tomb, across its opening. According to other Gospel accounts, a number of women who had come with Jesus from Galilee, including Mary Magdalene and another woman named Mary, watched as Jesus was buried, planning to return at a later date with other spices and perfumes to anoint His body.

By requesting a guard to be stationed at Jesus' tomb in order to prevent His body from being stolen, the chief priests and Pharisees actually helped authenticate Jesus' resurrection. Had there been no guard posted, they could have easily claimed His disciples stole Jesus' body, a simple task to accomplish if there was no guard to prevent it. However, since there was a guard posted, they had to concoct a less believable story, claiming that Jesus' disciples were able to roll away a large stone and steal Jesus' body without waking sleeping soldiers, who by Roman law would have been executed for falling asleep while on watch!

Q. Some skeptics have theorized that when Mary returned to Jesus' tomb on Easter morning, she mistakenly went to the wrong place, finding an empty tomb that was not the one in which Jesus had been buried. How do we know that theory is false?

A. First, because Mary saw exactly where Jesus was buried, and so did a number of other women who returned together on the first Easter morning. If Mary was mistaken, so were the other women. We also know, according to John's Gospel, that Jesus' tomb was very near the place of His crucifixion, making it highly unlikely for Mary and her companions to make a mistake. Others visited the empty tomb also, and no one suggested that they were at the wrong place. Finally, if anyone had wanted to disprove the fact of Jesus' resurrection (and many did), all they would have needed to do was locate the actual tomb, roll away the stone, and pull out Jesus' dead body. But no one ever did because there was no doubt His body was gone, which is why the Jewish leaders had to make up a story to explain where the body went.

Q. Why do you think that Christians often refer to the day of Jesus' death as "Good Friday"?

A. Although the events that surrounded Jesus' death were not good at all, and although Jesus suffered immeasurably, and although His death was a sad thing to His first disciples, we now know that Jesus died for our sins on the cross. And that is the best thing that has ever happened to us!

Application: Although Jesus' body was dead, His spirit was very much alive. He waited for three days in paradise for the moment when He would be reunited with His resurrected body and walk out of His tomb. The world was in for a shock!

Jesus is Resurrected!
Matthew 28:1-15

Matthew, Mark, Luke and John all record the story of Jesus' resurrection, and when we read them without careful comparison, they seem to be contradictory. However, upon closer examination, we see that all four Gospel writers told different details of the same event, and the four accounts can be reconciled.

There were at least three women, and Luke indicates that there were more (see Luke 24:10), who had agreed to meet together to anoint Jesus' body at daybreak on the first Easter Sunday. They apparently did not all arrive at the tomb at the same time, and it seems that Mary Magdalene, either alone or with two other companions, arrived first while it was still dark (see John 20:1). Sometime before they arrived, however, an angel had moved the stone from the tomb's entrance and sat upon it, paralyzing the Roman guards with fear. When Mary and her companions arrived, the angel had disappeared, but it's very possible that the Roman soldiers were still lying unconscious on the ground. If that was the case, Mary may have assumed that they'd been killed.

Upon discovery that the stone had been rolled from the entrance to the tomb, Mary, apparently by herself, ran to tell Peter and John, while her companions remained at the tomb. They entered it and immediately saw an angel, who said to them, "Don't be afraid! ... I know you are looking for Jesus, who was crucified. He isn't here! He has been raised from the dead, just as he said would happen. Come; see where his body was lying. And now, go quickly and tell his disciples he has been raised from the dead, and he is going ahead of you to Galilee. You will see him there. Remember, I have told you" (Matthew 28:5-7). The two women immediately ran from the tomb to find the disciples.

Shortly thereafter, a second group of women arrived and found the same scene. They entered the tomb and immediately noticed Jesus' body was missing and wondered what had happened. But suddenly, two angels appeared to them, clothed in dazzling robes. The women were terrified and fell on their faces to the ground, and the angels said to them, "Why are you looking in a tomb for someone who is alive? He isn't here! He has risen from the dead! Don't you remember he told you back in Galilee, that the Son of Man must be betrayed into the hands of sinful men and be crucified, and that he would rise again the third day?" (Luke 24:5-7). That second group of women also fled to tell Jesus' disciples.

By that time, Mary Magdalene had found Peter and John, and told them, "They have taken the Lord's body out of the tomb, and I don't know where they have put him!" (John 20:2). Both men immediately ran to the tomb and, upon entry, saw the linen cloth that Joseph of Arimathea and Nicodemus had wrapped around Jesus' body lying there. It was an empty cocoon, and John realized then that no one had stolen Jesus' body! He had been raised from the dead. Peter, however, still had doubts (see Luke 24:12). They then went back to where they had been staying, while the other disciples were also being informed of what happened by the women who had seen the angels.

Shortly thereafter, Mary again arrived at the tomb and stood weeping at its entrance, still clueless about what had happened. Finally, she also stooped and peered into the tomb, and saw two angels sitting at the head and foot of where Jesus' body had been lying. This time, either the angels didn't appear as majestic as when the first women had seen them, or Mary was so emotionally distraught that what she was seeing didn't fully register in her mind. They asked her, "Why are you crying?" and she responded, "Because they have taken away my Lord and I don't know where they have put him" (John 20:13). But they didn't respond to her because the Lord Himself wanted to tell her the good news.

Mary glanced over her shoulder as she was still stooped down at the tomb's entrance and saw someone standing behind her. He, too, asked her, "Why are your crying? ...Who are you looking for?" (John 20:15).

Thinking He was the gardener, Mary said, "Sir, if you have taken him away, tell me where you have put him, and I will go and get him" (John 20:15).

Jesus then said, "Mary!" She turned toward Him, and realizing who He was, embraced Him, hardly believing what was happening. Jesus told her, "Don't cling to me, for I haven't yet ascended to the Father. But go find my brothers and tell them that I am ascending to my Father and your Father, my God and your God" (John 20:17). And so she headed back to Jerusalem to tell the disciples the good news. Apparently, on her way, another woman joined her, and Jesus appeared to them both. As they clasped His feet and worshiped Him, He instructed them to tell His disciples to go to Galilee where He would appear to them (see Matthew 28:9-10).

Unfortunately, none of the disciples, with the exception of John, believed the reports of any of the women. They were still mourning and weeping (see Mark 16:10-11) when they should have been rejoicing! But they, too, would soon be convinced that Jesus had been raised from the dead!

Q. Jesus had told the repentant thief that they would be together that very day in paradise. But, three days later, Jesus told Mary that He had not yet ascended to the Father. Did Jesus lie to the repentant thief?

A. No, Jesus never lies. He told His disciples that He would spend three days and nights in the heart of the earth (see Matthew 12:40). Considering other scriptures, it is thought that there must have been a place called *Paradise* in the heart of the earth where Old Testament saints went when they died. It is also thought that Jesus emptied that place when He ascended into heaven. Now, when a Christian dies, he goes to heaven.

Q. The Jewish leaders bribed the guards to spread the story that the disciples stole Jesus' body while they were asleep. What makes that story so difficult to believe?

A. First, why weren't the guards awakened when the stone was rolled away? Second, what were they doing sleeping, when Roman law would execute guards if they were caught sleeping while on duty? Third, if they were sleeping, how did they know what had happened?

⊙ Application: Jesus' resurrection was more than just a miracle. It was God's ultimate proof that Jesus is the Messiah and Son of God, and a sign to us that the penalty for our sins has been fully paid and accepted by God.

Jesus Appears to His Disciples
Luke 24:13-43; John 20:24-31

Both Jesus and the angels who appeared to various women on the first Easter morning had told them to tell Jesus' disciples to go to Galilee. There He would appear to them. However, because virtually none of the disciples believed the report of the women, none of them left Jerusalem for Galilee. Jesus was going to have to convince them personally that He had risen from the dead.

So Jesus appeared to Peter, although we don't know any details of that appearance. Next, He appeared to two of His disciples as they journeyed to Emmaus, a village about seven miles from Jerusalem. God prevented them from recognizing Him at first, and Jesus pretended not to know anything about what had happened in Jerusalem over the past few days. They expressed their sadness about Jesus' death, explaining that they had hoped He was the Messiah, and were wondering about the reports of His resurrection. Finally, quoting many scriptures, Jesus explained to them that the Old Testament had predicted the Messiah would suffer just as He had, and that He would be resurrected. How privileged they were to be a part of that Bible study! It began to dawn on them that the reports they'd heard about His resurrection had to be true, because that was what God had foretold.

The moment God opened the eyes of the two disciples to realize that it was Jesus who was with them, He disappeared. Filled with joy, they hurried back to Jerusalem to tell the eleven disciples and other followers of Jesus what had happened. When they arrived, they were immediately told that Jesus had appeared to Peter! As they related their experience, Jesus appeared to them all!

Jesus' appearances were not visions, or just pictures in the people's minds. Jesus was actually present physically when He made His appearances. He was able to appear and disappear at will and travel from place to place instantly and invisibly.

When Jesus appeared to all His disciples, it frightened them terribly because they thought they were seeing a spirit or ghost. But Jesus proved to them that He really was there in a physical body by allowing them to touch Him, and by eating a piece of fish in their presence. When they realized it was really Jesus, they were elated!

Thomas was not present at that gathering, and when he heard the report, he became suspicious that someone who was impersonating Jesus had deceived his friends. How did they know it was really Jesus they had seen? Two of the disciples spent several hours with Him without recognizing Him. Perhaps it was someone who just looked very much like Jesus.

They probably told him that they were sure it was Jesus because He showed them the nail prints in His hands and the wound in His side. So Thomas stated that he would not believe Jesus was alive unless four conditions were met. First, he had to see Jesus for himself. Second, he had to see the nail marks in His hands. Third, to be certain those nail marks weren't just painted on His skin, he had to put his finger in the holes. Finally, to be sure the wound in Jesus' side wasn't also just the work of an artist, he had to put his hand in the spear hole.

The next time Jesus appeared to His disciples, Thomas was with them, and for several reasons he was immediately convinced that Jesus was alive. First, the doors were all locked, so there was no way for an impersonator to gain entrance. Second, Jesus suddenly appeared right in their midst. He didn't walk in from another room. He was suddenly there. Third, Jesus instructed Thomas to put his finger in the nail holes and his hand in the wound in His side. If He was an impersonator, He was collaborating with the other disciples, because at least one had informed Him of Thomas's previous words. Otherwise, this person was obviously the all-knowing Lord.

The evidence was overwhelming, and Thomas confessed that Jesus was his Lord and God.

Q. Thomas has been nicknamed "Doubting Thomas" for obvious reasons. However, was Thomas any more a doubter than the rest of the disciples?

A. Not really. The biblical record indicates that none of the eleven, with the exception of John, believed the women's reports of Jesus' resurrection, and John believed only because he personally saw the empty cocoon of Jesus' body wrappings. Furthermore, John recorded that when Jesus first appeared to all the disciples, He showed them the wounds in His hands and side, an obvious attempt to convince them that it was really He they were seeing (see John 20:20). So it's really unfair to label only Thomas as one who doubted.

Q. Is there any reason to be glad that Jesus' disciples were so doubtful?

A. Yes. Their skepticism provides fuel for our faith. Because we know they weren't easily convinced, we are all the more certain that their testimony of Jesus' resurrection is the truth.

Application: Jesus promised, "Blessed are those who haven't seen me and believe anyway" (John 20:29). Although we, unlike Thomas and the rest of Jesus' original disciples, haven't actually seen Him after His resurrection, our faith can rest firmly in the testimonies of those who have seen Him, especially since we know that they weren't easily convinced themselves. We're blessed!

Jesus Appears to His Disciples in Galilee
John 21:1-25

Luke tells us that, after His crucifixion, Jesus appeared to His disciples from time to time over a period of forty days, talking to them about the Kingdom of God (see Acts 1:3). Soon after His second appearance, Jesus' disciples left Jerusalem at His orders and went back to the region of Galilee (see Matthew 26:32; 28:7,10; 28:16).

Three years earlier, Peter, Andrew, James and John had left their fishing nets on the shore of the Sea of Galilee to follow the man who did miracles. Now, back in Galilee, Peter decided to go fishing again, and six of Jesus' disciples joined him.

After fishing all night and catching nothing, at dawn, Jesus appeared on the shore. The disciples didn't recognize Him, either because He was too far away, or because God supernaturally prevented them from recognizing Him, just as He had done with the two disciples on the road to Emmaus. However, once they followed His simple instructions and succeeded in catching an amazing quantity of fish, they realized who He was.

Peter may well have had a flashback of his other miraculous catch of fish three years earlier when he first encountered Jesus. This new catch was perhaps a sign that was intended to assure him of Jesus' love, regardless of the condemnation he still felt in his heart for denying his Lord.

Remember that Peter had previously boasted that even if all the other disciples deserted Jesus, he would not, even claiming his willingness to go to prison and die if need be (see Matthew 26: 33-35; Luke 22:33). It was a claim that he loved the Lord more than the others. But his actions proved that his love wasn't nearly as devoted as he'd thought.

Apparently during the other times that Jesus had appeared when Peter was present, the issue of what Peter had done had not been raised. Peter hadn't confessed his sin, and Jesus hadn't mentioned it either, waiting for the appropriate time. He wanted to be alone with Peter so as not to humiliate him. And He first wanted Peter to be assured that His love was unchanged. Peter had to be confronted, but Jesus didn't want the confrontation to crush him. Peter already felt condemned in his heart for what he'd done. He probably wondered if his relationship with Jesus could ever be the same. Would the Lord ever trust him again, or use him in the ministry? The very fact that he had decided to go fishing may have been an indication that he was considering returning to his old vocation, thinking he had disqualified himself for the Lord's service.

So after a breakfast of fish and bread that Jesus prepared and served, again demonstrating His undying love for the disciples who deserted Him, Jesus privately asked Peter a question, to which He, of course, already knew the answer. "Do you love me more than these?" (John 21:15). What were the "these" Jesus was referring to? Probably the other disciples. Jesus was asking, "Do you still claim to love Me more than they do?"

Peter's response, "Yes, Lord, you know I love you" (John 21:15), is better understood if we know something about the original Greek language in which he and Jesus conversed. The word Jesus used that is translated "love" is the word *agapeo*, which is a deep, self-sacrificing love. Peter responded by using the Greek word *phileo*, which is a lesser love of friendship. Jesus asked Peter, "Do you still believe that you love Me with a love that is more self-sacrificing than the other disciples?"

A few days earlier, Peter would have responded with a proud, "Yes!" But now he realized that Jesus knew him better than he knew himself. With a sigh of acknowledgement, he replied, "Yes, Lord, You know the truth. I've proven that my love for You doesn't go beyond the love of friendship." Peter had confessed his pride.

But Jesus didn't condemn Peter as Peter was condemning himself. He knew Peter loved Him more than what Peter now thought. He'd left everything behind to follow Jesus and had repeatedly obeyed Him for three years. Wanting Peter to know that He still believed in him and still had a plan to use him, Jesus replied, "Then feed my lambs" (John 21:15). Jesus was saying, "It isn't My plan for you to be a fisherman for the rest of your life, because I've called you to serve Me."

Jesus then asked Peter another question: "Simon, son of John, do you love me?" (John 21:16). He again used the word *agapeo*, but didn't add the "more than these." This question and its related commandment are perhaps an indication that Peter had indeed decided to quit the ministry. Jesus wanted Peter to realize that he couldn't do that, regardless of whether his love was the agape or phileo kind. Peter's answer was, again, self-condemning: "Yes, Lord, You know that I obviously only possess a *phileo* love for You." But Jesus believed Peter's love was greater than that, and He wanted Peter to believe it too, and so He commanded him, "Take care of my sheep" (John

21:16). Jesus was saying, "Your evaluation of yourself doesn't matter; only Mine does. I believe in you, and to prove it, I'm entrusting My very own sheep to your care."

Finally, Jesus again asked Peter if he loved Him, but this third time, Jesus used the word *phileo*. Jesus, of course, didn't now doubt that Peter possessed a *phileo* kind of love for Him. Rather, He was trying to help Peter understand himself. It grieved Peter that Jesus had questioned his *phileo* for Him, and he objected to the question. "Lord, You know everything," he replied. "You *know* I *phileo* You," defending and yet still condemning himself. The hurt Peter felt at the question would help him to see that he did possess a heart-felt devotion for Jesus. And again, Jesus wanted him to realize that He knew Peter better than Peter knew himself. Jesus' evaluation is all that matters, and His faith in Peter was unchanging. "Feed my sheep," Jesus commanded him.

Concluding their conversation, Jesus, the One who knew that Peter would deny Him three times, the One who knew Peter better than he knew himself, also knew how Peter would die. And in his death, Peter would prove his *agape* love for his Lord. So Jesus told him how he would glorify God by martyrdom, conveying to Peter that his past failure had no bearing on his future.

In the process of a few days, Peter had gone from overestimating his love to underestimating it. Just as Peter's appraisal of himself a few days before had been wrong and Jesus' appraisal had proved to be true, now, again, Peter's appraisal was wrong, and Jesus' would prove true. Peter's pendulum of perception had swung from pride to self-condemnation, but Jesus realigned it.

Q. Jesus gave Peter three commandments in today's reading: 1) Feed my lambs, 2) Take care of my sheep, and 3) Feed my sheep. What do you think He meant?

A. Lambs and sheep represent those who believe in Jesus, some spiritual babies and some more mature in their faith. Feeding them is symbolic of teaching them the Word of God, and taking care of them represents a concern for their wellbeing, spiritually and in every other way. Jesus needs those in His body who will do just that, and He calls certain individuals for that purpose.

Q. Because of what Jesus said to Peter about John, many thought that John wouldn't ever die. Why did they misunderstand?

A. Because they added to what Jesus actually said, making an assumption. We should be careful that we don't make the same mistake, as Christians are often known to do.

⊙ Application: Jesus believed the best about Peter in spite of his failures. And He lifted Peter out of condemnation, showing him mercy and giving him hope for the future. Jesus also knew the sins and mistakes you would commit before you committed them, but He still loves you. And He doesn't want our failures to be stumbling blocks. Rather, He wants them to be stepping-stones. The answer to all our problems is gaining Jesus' perspective.

Jesus' Final Words and Ascension to Heaven
Matthew 28:16-20; Mark 16:15-20

On one of the occasions when Jesus appeared to the eleven disciples in Galilee, He told them what He wanted them to do for the remainder of their lives. It would be their job to make disciples of all the nations. The Greek word translated "nations" could be better translated, "ethnic groups," which is a group of people who are distinct from other groups by virtue of their culture, circumstances, language or the location where they live. For example, many Americans think that all Chinese people are part of the same ethnic group, but there are many different minorities living in China. America itself is made up of many ethnic groups, and God wants us to make disciples among them all. In order for that to happen, someone from one culture has to purposely cross over a cultural line, showing love for people who are different. At present, there are thousands of ethnic groups in the world without a single Christian among them. No one is trying to reach them with the good news of Jesus Christ. If a person within one of those un-reached groups wanted to find out about Jesus, *he* would have to cross a culture to find out. Our prayers and money should be directed toward those un-reached groups of people. And if God sends us to one of them, we should go.

Notice also that Jesus doesn't want just converts made; He wants disciples. Disciples are true believers in Christ; thus they are obedient followers. Jesus said they should be baptized, which would be the first indication of their true faith, and that they should be taught to obey His commandments. Of course, one of those commandments which they should teach their disciples was the commandment Jesus gave for disciples to make disciples. Every true believer in Christ should be doing what he can to make disciples. That is not a job that God has given only to pastors.

From Mark's Gospel we learn that there should be certain supernatural signs that follow those who believe. Jesus listed five. The first one is that they will cast out demons in His name. Every believer has the authority to cast out demons if the need arises.

Second, Jesus said that believers would speak in new tongues. According to the pattern found in the book of Acts, speaking in tongues is something every believer should expect to experience when he is baptized in the Holy Spirit.

The next sign Jesus mentioned was the safe handling of poisonous snakes. He certainly did not mean that Christians should pass around poisonous snakes during church services, because that would be the same as testing God, and there is no record of such a thing being done by the early church in the book of Acts. However, Luke did record that Paul was once accidentally bitten by a deadly snake and suffered no harm. That is more likely the kind of thing Jesus had in mind. He knew that snakes might bite those who would be carrying the gospel to remote places.

The fourth sign Jesus mentioned is probably in the same category. Jesus promised no harm to believers who drank poisonous liquids. As they take the gospel to other places, believers might accidentally drink something poisonous, or unbelievers might intentionally poison their water. In those cases, believers could claim Jesus' promise.

The fifth sign that should follow believers is the healing of others as they lay their hands upon them. This does not mean that every single sick person upon whom a believer lays his hands will be healed. But it does indicate that God wants to use all believers in healing others. In the context of Jesus' command to preach the gospel to everyone, this fifth sign should also be considered an aid to effective evangelism. Divine healing can get people's attention to listen to the gospel. We read in the very last verse of Mark's Gospel that God worked with the first disciples by confirming their words with miraculous signs. No doubt many of those signs were the five that Jesus listed, and the record of the book of Acts proves this to be so.

Q. Jesus promised His disciples that He would be with them always, even to the end of the age. Soon after He made that promise, He left them to sit at the right hand of God the Father. Did He break His promise?

A. No, Jesus didn't break His promise. He only departed physically. However, spiritually He now lives within every believer. That is why Paul wrote, "I myself no longer live, but Christ lives in me" (Galatians 2:20). Besides that, God is omnipresent, which means His presence is everywhere. In that sense, Jesus is always with us as well.

Q. In Mark's Gospel, we read that everyone who believes the good news about Jesus and is baptized will be saved. Does this mean that a person who believes in Jesus but who dies before being baptized goes to hell?

A. No, it does not. However, it does indicate to us that true believers in Jesus will want to obey Him, and since He commanded all who believe in Him to be baptized, people who profess to believe in Him but who refuse to be baptized prove their faith is not genuine.

Application: As believers, our job is not just to wait for the time we'll go to heaven but, our job is to work for Jesus, helping to expand His kingdom. Are you doing something to help?

147

Luke Summarizes Jesus' Final Days on Earth
Luke 24:44-53; Acts 1:1-11

Jesus appeared to His disciples enough times over a period of forty days that all of them became convinced that He had risen from the dead. They were not just having visions, and no one was impersonating Jesus. The apostle Paul informs us in his letter to the Corinthians that Jesus once appeared to over five hundred people at one time (see 1 Corinthians 15:6)!

First, it was Jesus' plan that His disciples would soon begin to take the gospel to the whole world, and He wanted them to begin in Jerusalem and Judea. Because most of the people living in those places were Jews, it was important for Jesus' disciples to understand the many messianic scriptures in the Old Testament so they could prove that He was the promised Messiah. Jesus said that there were things written about Him in Moses' books, the first five books of the Bible, as well as in the books of the prophets and Psalms. He then opened their minds to understand those many scriptures.

Second, it was important that Jesus' disciples proclaim the message Jesus wanted proclaimed. So He made it very clear to them. They should tell people that He had suffered, died and risen three days later. Now, forgiveness of sins was being offered to anyone who would repent of his sins, and believe in Him. That is the message Jesus still wants us to proclaim.

Finally, Jesus knew His disciples needed supernatural help to be successful in proclaiming the gospel and making disciples. So He promised to send them the Holy Spirit so they would be filled with power. Just a few days later, the Holy Spirit came suddenly upon one hundred and twenty of Jesus' disciples, and they all began speaking in foreign languages, speaking of the wonderful things God had done. This was a sign that got the attention of a lot of people in Jerusalem, and as a result, three thousand people turned to the Lord, many of whom were foreign visitors. This miracle of speaking in other languages was also probably a reminder to Jesus' disciples that the Holy Spirit was being given to them because God loves every different ethnic group, and God wants the gospel taken to all of them.

The story of Jesus' life and ministry certainly doesn't end with His ascension into heaven. In fact, Luke began the book of Acts by stating that his Gospel was only an account of everything Jesus "began to do and teach" (Acts 1:1, emphasis added). Jesus continued to work after His ascension by using His people. Jesus is still working today through everyone who believes in Him, and the most wonderful thing in the entire world is to be used by God.

Q. Jesus' disciples asked Him, "Lord, are you going to free Israel now and restore our kingdom?" (Acts 1:6). What were they hoping for and why were they hoping for it?

A. It was foretold in the Old Testament that a time would come when the Messiah would rule over Israel on David's throne. During that messianic age, Israel would become an exalted nation, but when the disciples asked Jesus their question, Israel was under the domination of the Roman Empire. Because the disciples believed that Jesus was the promised Messiah, they expected that Jesus would soon usher in the promised age. Jesus, however, knew that the kingdom age was still a long time away. There was still much to be done before then. Because Jesus' kingdom was not a political but a spiritual kingdom, it was first necessary that people submit to Him, the King. That would occur as the disciples proclaimed the gospel. Then, according to God's predetermined plan, Jesus will one day rule the world from Jerusalem.

Application: Two angels promised Jesus' disciples that He would return to the earth just as He had departed from the earth. That promise hasn't been fulfilled yet, or you can be sure we'd know it! But it will come to pass! We should live every day of our lives in anticipation of that day.

Some Final Words

Yesterday was the final day of our 147-day study of Jesus' life. I hope that you and your children enjoyed our journey together, and that you all grew closer to God and to one another. I also hope that your family has established a practice that will continue for many years, and I hope that I can be of further service to you. I haven't had time to write a family devotional that covers the rest of the New Testament, but I have written a general devotional that takes readers through the New Testament chronologically in one year by just reading one Bible chapter every weekday. That devotional, called *HeavenWord Daily*, can be used for family devotions, and can be ordered from our website at HeavensFamily.org/hwd. It is also available through weekday emails that you can start receiving in your inbox by signing up at HeavensFamily.org/devotional.

We've also produced a high-quality 7-minute daily video devotional that we call *HeavenWord 7* and a 30-minute weekly video devotional called *HeavenWord TV*. You can view those devotionals at our *HeavenWord TV* website, and there you can also subscribe to the podcasts or subscribe to receive the devotionals by email. Visit us at HeavenWord.tv.

Finally, I invite your participation in the ministry of *Heaven's Family*. Our hope is to be your love-link to the "least of these" among Jesus' world-wide family, as we strive to meet their pressing needs together.

May God bless you as you and your children continue to follow our Lord Jesus Christ!

In Him,

David

Also by David Servant...

Through the Needle's Eye
An Impossible Journey Made Possible by God

In this book, David Servant considers everything that Jesus, as well as every author of the Old and New Testaments, taught in regard to stewardship. His conclusions are not easy to disregard. Although impossible by pure human effort, the journey through the needle's eye is possible with God! (ISBN 096-296-2592, 269 pages, Paperback, $17.95)

The Disciple-Making Minister
Biblical Principles for Fruitfulness and Multiplication

David Servant has been ministering to Christian leaders in conferences around the world for over two decades. From his experience of speaking to tens of thousands of pastors in over forty countries, he has compiled biblical teaching in this book that addresses the most important issues that Christian leaders are facing today. (ISBN 096-296-2585, 489 pages, Paperback, $19.95)

Forgive Me for Waiting So Long to Tell You This

Searching for a respectful way to share the gospel with a friend or loved one? Give them a copy of this book. In an easy-to-understand style, David Servant presents a convincing and biblical viewpoint that provokes readers to look at themselves, Jesus Christ, and their eternal destiny. (ISBN 096-296-2503, 132 pages, Paperback, $6.95)

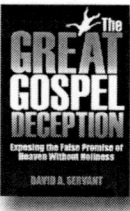

The Great Gospel Deception
Exposing the False Promise of Heaven Without Holiness

In this eye-opening book, David Servant takes a close look at what the New Testament actually teaches about saving faith, God's transforming grace, and "the holiness without which no one will see the Lord" (Hebrews 12:14). (ISBN 096-296-2578, 240 pages, Paperback, $17.95)

CPSIA information can be obtained at www.ICGtesting.com
Printed in the USA
BVOW041635240213

314001BV00002B/8/P

RADISHES AND
RED BANDANAS

RADISHES AND RED BANDANAS

Speak out against injustice & love fiercely

Trudy Knowles

Trudy Knowles

Larone Family Press
Westfield, MA

Hardcover: ISBN: 979-8-9867248-2-9
Paperback: ISBN: 979-8-9867248-0-5
Ebook: ISBN: 979-8-9867248-1-2

Cover design: Scott DeNino
Cover photo: Christine Blacke

Larone Family Press
Westfield, MA

www.trudyknowles.com

To Melissa Anne, my love child

I felt amazed at the choosing one had to do, over and over, a million times daily—choosing love, then choosing it again, how loving and being in love could be so different.

Sue Monk Kidd, *The Mermaid Chair*, p. 322

Times filled with tragedy are also times of greatness and wonder, times that really matter, and times truly worth living through. Whatever the future holds, and as satisfying as my life is today, I miss the sixties and always will.

Tom Hayden, *Reunion*, p. 507

PROLOGUE

Criminal Court—New York City
December 2012

Matt approached the judge, his waist-long dreadlocks pulled back from his face, a black bandana hanging from his pocket.

"Thanks for always supporting me," Matt said to his dad and me moments earlier.

I gave him a hug. "That's what families do." *Biological or chosen,* I thought.

Matt was in court for his arrest during an Occupy Wall Street protest a year ago. Today the judge must rule.

"Is the prosecution ready?" the judge asked.

"Yes, Your Honor."

"What are the charges?"

"This young man was arrested when he refused to leave the sidewalk after orders were given. He is charged with resisting arrest, refusing to disperse, trespassing, blocking traffic, and intent to harm an officer."

"Those are serious charges, young man," the judge said. "How do you plead?"

I tightened the grip on my husband's hand. I thought of another time, another courtroom, forty years ago. I heard the

1

chants. *What do we want? Peace. When do we want it? Now! Hey, Hey, LBJ. How many kids did you kill today? The Whole World's Watching.* I heard the plea. *"Not guilty."* I heard the judge pass sentence.

"Not guilty," Matt said.

I cried both times.

PART ONE

FRESHMAN YEAR

1967-1968

Chapter 1
"The Times They Are A'Changin'"

I do not like beginnings.

On the first day of first grade, the teacher sent me to the corner for blowing a sheet of paper around the table I shared with three other girls. Standing in the corner, I wet my pants.

On the first day of fifth grade, I tripped up the stairs to school, skinning both my knees. The boy I loved, because we shared the same initials, laughed at me.

At the beginning of middle school, I got my first period. The blood soaked through my skirt.

At the beginning of high school, a friend of mine died after falling off a horse. Three months later, President Kennedy was assassinated.

I really do not like beginnings.

It was September 1967. I stood at the window in my dorm room at Lake Forest College, thirty miles north of Chicago, and watched my mom and dad in the parking lot below. I wiped my eyes with the Kleenex my mom gave me moments before, "Always use Kleenex brand. No cheap imitation will do," she said. My mom had a way with metaphors. She was telling me to be my best and only accept the best.

My dad took my hands. "Don't forget to be yourself," he said. Dad was direct. He didn't need metaphors.

As I watched them drive away, I wanted the beginning to be over, to have it be the middle, to know what the end would be.

I chose Lake Forest College because of the name. It sounded like the perfect place to spend the next four years of my life—a half-mile from Lake Michigan on a hundred-acre campus covered with a forest of trees.

More importantly, Lake Forest College was 400 miles away from my hometown and I needed to get away from home. I loved my mom and dad, but I had to figure out who I was.

Before I arrived, my roommate came and went, leaving the ashtray on her desk full of cigarette butts. I was on my own to find my way across campus to registration. I took a deep breath, left my dorm, and headed to the tables on the patio outside of the student center, known as Commons. Orientation week. Four days of discussions, testing, and getting to know what college was about.

I got in the line marked H-M. "Rebecca Jamison," I told the upperclassman sitting at the registration table. He searched through the box, gave me a name tag and an information packet, the name of my advisor on the front—Tom Garson, Sociology Department.

"You're lucky," the upperclassman said, as he passed me the packet. "Garson's the best." I released the breath I held.

"Great. I need all the help I can get." I pushed the bangs out of my eyes. I started growing them out after high school, but they weren't long enough to stay tucked behind my ears. In *Teen Idol* magazine Patti Boyd, George Harrison's wife, said it was time for her to develop a more mature look, so she was growing out her bangs. If it was good enough for a Beatle wife, it was good enough for me.

He pushed the hair out of his eyes too and said with a grin, "Don't worry, you'll figure it out."

6

"Thanks." I walked away. "By the way." I turned back but he was already assisting the next person in line. For some reason, I wanted him to know I go by Becky.

* * *

Our orientation group met in the shade of a sprawling oak tree on the lawn outside of Commons. Dr. Tom Garson wore blue jeans and a corduroy sports coat. His long wavy hair covered his ears, a dark out-of-control mustache covered his top lip. Garson looked us over, perused the name tags we wore, glancing down at his advisement list and matching names to faces He finally said, "I'm Tom Garson. Please call me Tom. I'll be your advisor for this year at least. I teach in the Sociology Department. We will spend the next four days getting to know each other, figuring out class schedules, talking about what college means, and discussing the life-altering implications of our freshman book, *Catch-22*."

I knew it well, having read it over the summer. Best book I ever read and the first book that made me laugh out loud.

"We'll start discussing it tomorrow. Today, three questions. Who are you? What event in high school shaped your life philosophy the most? Why did you choose Lake Forest?" Garson turned to me. "You first."

Of course. I never won raffles or lotteries or door prizes. But when it came to the stuff you didn't want to win, like going first, I always won.

I took a deep breath. "I'm Becky Jamison from Rogerstown, Kentucky. I chose Lake Forest College because I loved the name and I love Chicago." I didn't want to reveal that I also wanted to escape my dad's reputation. In addition to teaching at the local junior college, he was a minister and gave the 'don't have sex until marriage' talks at high schools all over Kentucky.

7

"Most significant event?" Garson asked.

"President Kennedy's assassination during my freshman year in high school. It transformed the way I viewed the world."

"In what way?"

"I fell in love with everything he stood for, particularly the part about giving back to the world. The world seemed pretty bleak after he died."

A guy sitting across from me rolled his eyes.

Garson went around the group asking questions. Most significant event? Getting elected cheerleader. Winning the state baseball championship. Being valedictorian. Flunking out of Phillips Exeter and going to public school.

"You're next, Joe." Garson pointed to that eye-roller across from me, dressed like an athlete on game day in high school—loafers with no socks, blue casual pants, a long-sleeve dress shirt open at the collar, sleeves rolled up to the elbow, a tie with the knot loosened.

After he introduced himself as Joe Scott, I couldn't help thinking that his last name could be his first. Joe Scott. Scott Joe. Like Benedict Arnold. He became Joe Scott Joe.

Joe Scott Joe pulled a Marlboro out of the hard pack he kept in the pocket of his shirt and lit it. He inhaled, exhaled dramatically. "The summer before my junior year I went to Martha's Vineyard for vacation and developed a true appreciation for alcoholic beverages. I guess you could say my first drunk was the most significant event in my life." I rolled my eyes back at him. I detested his type

He went on. "I'm here because of Garson's name on my registration packet." Joe Scott Joe laughed. No one laughed with him. "Seriously, I figure if I stay in college I won't have to go to Vietnam. Not that I'm against the war. I'll leave protesting to the long-hairs. I don't want to get hurt or killed."

"If you're not willing to do something to stop it, why shouldn't you have to go?" Garson asked.

Joe Scott Joe didn't respond. Instead, he looked over at the one person who hadn't talked yet, a guy with a red bandana around his head, wearing an army jacket, sitting up against a tree, his arms wrapped around his legs, eyes lowered. On his left arm was a hook where his hand should be. His orientation packet sat on the ground beside him. "You against the tree. Your turn," Joe Scott Joe said. "By the way, you ever kill anybody with that hook?"

The guy slowly unwrapped his arms from his legs and stood up, leaving his orientation packet on the ground. He glanced around, stepped over Joe Scott Joe, and patted Garson's shoulder with his good hand as he passed. He never looked back. As he walked away, Garson said, "Dennis McKinney, Vietnam veteran."

"Shit. He probably did kill someone." Joe Scott Joe grinned. He put out his cigarette on the ground and left the butt there.

"Shut up, Scott," one of the guys in the group murmured. I wish I said it.

Joe Scott Joe said, "He shouldn't have gone to Vietnam."

"Maybe he didn't have a fucking choice," Garson said to no one in particular. "See you tomorrow."

My dad never said fucking. He never wore blue jeans. No student ever called him by his first name. Times were changing. I looked at Garson. He caught my eye and smiled. I liked him already.

I watched Dennis McKinney, Vietnam veteran, walk away until he entered one of the two men's dorms next to Commons. Joe Scott Joe walked toward the same dorm, his arm draped around a girl, an unlit cigarette in his mouth.

* * *

9

The next day I took placement tests in Math and English and registered for classes. I wrote a check for $96 at the bookstore in the basement of Commons for books, a college pennant, and a sweatshirt. Walking back to my dorm, carrying two bags of books, it happened.

Just past where our orientation group gathered, halfway to my dorm, a guy jumped out of a tree in front of me. He somersaulted to his feet, rubbed the leaves and dirt off his brown leather jacket with the Kawasaki patch on the sleeve, and said, "Under that baggy shirt is a body I would love to get to know."

If my two hands had not been carrying bags of books, I would have grabbed my shirt to hide whatever was under it. Nothing would ever be the same again.

His eyes, like magnets, focused on mine. Mine, the metal, couldn't pull away.

"Tonight. Commons. Snack Bar. 7:30." As he walked away, he must have sensed me watching him because he turned back, grinned, and nodded his head.

My roommate lit another cigarette, dropping the ashes into the already full ash tray. "You're crazy to go. You don't even know his name," she said.

Why did I go? Throughout high school, I dated a few times but never had a serious boyfriend. I knew it would never happen because of my father's speeches. The guy who jumped out of the tree? Here was my chance. I wasn't going to let it pass me up.

When I arrived at the snack bar, he was sitting at a table halfway across the room, leaning back in his chair, his arms crossed over the brown leather jacket, a slight grin on his face. When he saw me, the grin turned into a smile. I walked over to the table.

"Hi, I'm Jeff Ledford."

"Becky Jamison."

"I wasn't sure you would come."

"My roommate told me I was crazy, but I figured I'm safe in a room full of people."

He smiled. "I'm glad you did, otherwise I would have had to eat the éclair I got you." He handed me a plate. "I don't even know if you like éclairs."

"I'm a fan of anything sweet," I said. The éclair he gave me changed my life.

I was always easily changed. When the Beatles came to America, my life changed. When I worked at a camp for children with disabilities the summer before my senior year in high school, my life changed. When I was selected with twenty-four other young people in Kentucky to develop a conference on juvenile delinquency, my life changed. My life changing over an éclair wasn't out of the question.

He caught my eyes and held them there. "I'm a second semester junior, transferred from Northeastern in Boston."

"Why did you transfer?" I took a bite of the éclair, licking off the cream that squirted out the other end.

"I'm going to tell you, but first you have to promise you won't leave. Promise you'll hear me out."

"Promise," I gave him the scout salute, although I never was a Girl Scout. I wanted to join in fifth grade because I thought the scarves were cool. The boy next door, who I vowed to marry when I was older, told me he hated girls in Girl Scouts, so that was the end of that.

"I was kicked out of Northeastern University on a drug charge."

I inhaled sharply. I didn't know much about drugs. In high school, while drinking a five-cent cherry coke at the downtown drugstore, a friend warned me to watch out for cigarettes with twisted ends. My dad warned me about LSD and broken chromosomes. I believed them, but after reading about the hippies who flooded San Francisco during the 'Summer of Love' I was curious.

Jeff sensed my uneasiness, reached over and took my hand, sticky from the éclair and oozing cream. "I promise you'll like me by the time I'm done." I believed him. Something about those eyes.

Jeff continued. "I'm not a doper or a hippie. It was a freak thing. I was in the wrong place at the wrong time."

"What am I doing sitting here eating an éclair with a guy who got kicked out of college on a dope charge?" This éclair affair was getting out of control.

He leaned back in his chair again, crossed his arms over his brown leather jacket. "Just passing time, I guess." He grinned. "Tell me something about you."

"I come from a small town in Kentucky. My mom's a third-grade teacher. My dad teaches at a junior college. I have two brothers."

"Now tell me something that would make me want to turn and run like you wanted to when I told you about my drug charge."

"My dad's also an ordained minister."

Jeff chuckled and at that exact moment I knew I was in trouble. I had bad luck with guys in high school. Partly it was my dad's 'don't have sex until marriage' speeches. Partly it was just my lack of luck.

My first love was my older brother's best friend. The first time he came by our house to hang out with my brother I was in the eighth grade and he was a sophomore. I fell in love on the spot, but he always treated me like a little sister, teasing me, joking with me. My love was unrequited. He joined up the summer after his freshman year in college. He died in Vietnam eight months later.

12

I liked a guy from my church youth group. We went out a couple times but he moved to Virginia.

There was the guy I met at that camp for children with disabilities that changed my life. Don't know if it was the camp or him. He was the first guy I kissed. As luck would have it, he lived eighty miles away.

I knew nothing more about guys.

"So, Miss Jamison. Anything else I need to know about you?" Jeff took a bite of his éclair and stared at me as he very slowly licked the cream that squirted out the end. My stomach took a flip.

"I've never done drugs, never really tasted alcohol. I graduated first in my class. And I'm not trying to hide anything under this shirt. That's about it but if you need to know something else, ask away."

"That's all I need to know."

I kept talking. "My parents are teetotalers. Dad always told me alcohol tasted like water left in the bottom of a boat for three days. The only alcohol I ever tasted was from a tiny bottle he got on an airplane. I agreed with the boat thing."

Jeff laughed and leaned back in his chair. He looked me over. "You are unbelievable."

"Yeah, I know." I finished my éclair and reached over to the adjacent table for a napkin. I wiped the cream off my lips and fingers and took a drink of coke.

"Why did you come?" It was his eyes. Hypnotic. They immobilized me.

I wasn't very well going to say that so when I said, "Maybe it's your eyes," I wanted the ground to open and swallow me whole. "Anyhow, Jeff, I'm not your type. I better go." I stood up to leave.

"I haven't got a type." Jeff got up and walked towards me.

I pushed back my bangs. "Growing out my bangs since graduation. My mom hates hair in the face. I guess you could call

13

it my first bit of family rebellion. If they don't grow out soon, I swear I'm going to cut them. They're driving me crazy."

Jeff took my chin in one hand, licked the fingers on his other, slicked back my bangs, and still looking me in the eyes, said, "I'll see you around."

U.S. Soldier Body Count: 16,461

Chapter 2
"Glad All Over"

Classes started Monday: Biology, Journalism, English, Intro to Sociology, Calculus. In the afternoon, I wandered around the extra-curricular fair on the patio outside Commons. The Young Republicans' table was filled with bowls of candy and decked out in red, white, and blue bunting. They would never convince me to go over to the dark side with candy alone. I had been a Democrat ever since my mom and dad told me they voted for Kennedy.

I walked by the Fencing Club table. Two students dressed in gloves, jackets, and masks parried on the grass. There were tables for the photography club, yearbook, drama club, tutorial project, foreign language club. Each group of students tried to convince me that their club was the one I needed to join.

A girl with long dark hair, bangs all grown out, sat behind the school newspaper table playing guitar and singing with a voice like Joni Mitchell. She stopped when she saw me. "Welcome to '*The Forester*,' our weekly campus newspaper. I'm Ginger, Assistant Editor this year." She leaned the guitar against the table and stood up.

"Hi, I'm Becky. I'm majoring in journalism." I picked up a sample newspaper from the table.

"Great. We need help. Sign your name and mailbox number. We'll send out a notice of our first meeting."

I signed the paper latched to the clipboard then said to Ginger, "Great voice. Great guitar."

"Thanks. Do you play?"

"Got me through high school sane. My guitar was my salvation." I bought my first guitar from my sister for $30 after she decided she didn't want to play anymore. It was a Gibson small-sized Sunburst guitar. We were inseparable. At our high school graduation party, my friends got Ambush perfume and I got Bob Dylan records. My friends got blenders for their new apartments, and I got guitar strings. Ambush perfume vs. Dylan? Dylan wins every time.

"I understand. I can always count on my guitar," she said.

I smiled at Ginger. "Recommend any other clubs?"

She pointed across the patio where a "Peace Now" banner flapped in the breeze. "If you're against the war, talk to them."

I headed across the patio. The guy who handed me my orientation packet on the first day tried to tie the banner to the table legs while simultaneously brushing the dark hair out of his eyes. A stack of pamphlets blew off the table. He reached for them, holding on to the banner and losing the battle of the bangs. I picked up the pamphlets and put them on the table under a small rock.

"Let me help." I took one end of the banner and tied it to a table leg.

"Thanks." He tied down the other end then stuck out his hand and introduced himself. "Hi, I'm Marty and this is Lake Forest College Students Against the War."

"Hi, I'm Becky."

"I remember you from registration, although you were Rebecca then. How was Garson?"

"He didn't convince me to major in sociology, but I enjoyed discussing *Catch-22* from his perspective."

"Best book ever written."

"I agree." I picked up a flyer that announced leafletting and a march in downtown Lake Forest on October 21st in solidarity with a protest in Washington, D.C. sponsored by the National Mobilization Committee to End the War in Vietnam.

"We're having our organizing meeting Wednesday night, seven o'clock, Bradley Hall on North Campus. It's the men's honor dorm. We'd love to see you there."

I felt a tug on my braids. "Signing up for anything?" I turned to face the brown leather motorcycle jacket. Jeff smiled. God, he unnerved me.

"Maybe," I said.

Jeff shook Marty's hand. "Just don't get involved with this guy." He patted Marty on the shoulder.

I signed my name to the list and promised to be at the meeting on Wednesday.

So it began, my life in the anti-war movement. My life at college.

Jeff put his hand on the small of my back, leaving it there only long enough for me to remember how I wanted to feel all those nights in high school when I cried into my pillow wishing for a boyfriend. "Another éclair?" he asked.

"I'm meeting my roommate in a half hour to walk to town."

"It won't take a half hour to eat one éclair."

"Although I do have a fondness for éclairs, I'll pass. I could use a coke."

"Bet you filled up with candy from the Republicans." He returned his hand to my back and guided me to the door of Commons.

"I will never sell my soul for some sweets."

17

"What will you sell your soul for?" Without waiting for my reply, we went into Commons. "Sure you don't want anything to eat?" Jeff asked. He ordered two cokes and a large fries at the snack bar.

"Absolutely sure."

Jeff poured a huge glob of ketchup on the side of the French fry plate and picked up a coke. I picked up the other. Jeff led me to a small room adjacent to the snack bar with a brass sign outside that said Hixson Lounge.

He pushed open the French doors to Hixson. I wondered who Hixson was and what you have to do to get yourself a lounge. "Are you sure we can be in here?" It looked like one of those fancy rooms at my dad's college that served as a faculty center or a place to entertain anyone wanting to give a big endowment to the campus. But there was no "Faculty Only" sign on the French doors.

Hixson Lounge was unique. Victorian style couches with flowered upholstery and curved backs and arms. Carpeted. A grand piano against the back wall. Easy chairs. Coffee tables of rich dark wood. Floor to ceiling bookcases filled with old editions of campus yearbooks. There was nothing casual-looking about the furniture in the room, yet the students sitting in there made it seem casual.

"This is Hixson Lounge," Jeff said. "The place to be on campus."

Hixson Lounge had been appropriated by the hippies. A couple folks strummed guitars. Four or five bell-bottomed, beaded, tie-dyed t-shirted folks read, chatted, or ate ice cream sundaes. The thought went through my head that maybe I would see one of those cigarettes with a twisted end in an ashtray.

"When did you turn against the war?" Jeff put the fries on the coffee table in front of the couch.

"I never thought much about the war before last spring. I had to write a paper for Senior English class defending our support or opposition to the war."

"I'm guessing you did a lot of research and came out against the war."

"Nope. Since I was going to graduate in a couple months, I didn't much care, so I took the easy way out and wrote in support of the war. I cited treaties I'd read about in the paper and did no more research. I got an 'A'."

"What you're telling me is that you sold your soul for a grade?" He took a fry, dipped it in the ketchup, sucked off all the ketchup, dipped it again before eating the fry.

I took a drink of coke. "My dad saw the paper on the dining room table and ripped into me about war and how I didn't deserve an 'A' on a paper that glorified killing. He told me I needed to pay more attention."

"That seems pretty harsh."

"That's my dad. I love him but he has definite views about things. Dad's a pacifist. Told the draft board he refused to carry a gun during World War II, so he served as a chaplain. My older brother's best friend died in Vietnam a week after I handed in my paper. I was secretly in love with him, so I was devastated. I've regretted writing that paper ever since. My dad was right. I started paying attention. We're sending young men to fight in Vietnam for no reason. There's so much violence and death, body counts on TV every night. I was stupid to write that paper. I learned my lesson."

I stole a fry from his plate. I dipped it in ketchup and stuck the whole thing in my mouth.

"I get it and I agree." He sucked the ketchup off another fry. "You sound like you have a pretty good family."

19

"They're the best. I'm worried my brothers might get drafted. How about your family?"

"I'm an only child. I missed out on all that sibling rivalry. Two weeks after I got kicked out of school my parents died in a car accident."

The thought of not having my mom and dad in my life brought tears to my eyes. Who would be there if I couldn't figure out life? Who would be there to steer me when I went off course? How can anyone survive that? I leaned over and took his hands in mine. They felt warm, cozy, even familiar. "I'm so sorry."

"Doesn't matter. They were drunk. They never cared much about what I did."

"Every parent cares."

"They didn't. My parents sent me to boarding school in seventh grade. They also left me a shitload of money when they died. Lucky me."

Jeff let go of my hands, reached over with a napkin, and wiped the tears off my cheeks. "I'm sorry," I said again.

With the back of my hand I dried what the napkin missed and took a deep breath. "So why Lake Forest?"

"They accepted me. Probably the money." He paused. "And I guess I knew you'd be here."

There it was again, that stomach flipping thing, that twitching down there.

I took another fry from his plate. I didn't know what to say. Some things were beyond my ability to understand. Not caring about your parents was one of them. Parents not caring about their kids was another. What to do about this twitching feeling that wouldn't stop when I thought about Jeff was the third.

I looked at my watch. "Much as I enjoy this fry eating adventure, I have to go. Thanks for the coke and fries, Jeff. Maybe I'll see you at the anti-war meeting." We both got up.

"First of all, I didn't get you fries. Remember? You weren't hungry. You stole them." Jeff walked to my side of the table.

"You didn't stop me." I smiled at him and started to walk away.

Jeff touched me on the shoulder, turned me to face him. "Second of all, maybe I will see you at the anti-war meeting. Third of all." He put his hands on either side of my face. His lips gently caressed mine. "See you around, Becky."

That evening I lay in bed in my dorm staring at the ceiling. The air was filled with the foul smell of stale smoke left over from my roommate. She was at a party in a frat house. I heard laughter coming from the halls, dormmates running up and down, eager to go out with the new guy they met.

I thought of my dad's list. He never actually said these things but they were his expectations. Don't have sex. Don't drink. Don't drive too fast. Don't break curfew. Don't slack off on your studies. Don't use drugs. Do help other people. Do be kind and generous. Do right in the world.

I had no idea what to do next. Dad on one side of my mind. Jeff Ledford on the other.

U.S. Soldier Body Count: 16,529

Chapter 3
"I'm a Believer"

The sounds of *If I Had a Hammer* greeted me as I entered Bradley Hall for my first anti-war meeting. Ginger led the singing. I wished I'd come sooner. The songs rolled over me like gentle waves of familiarity. I knew them all having cut my teeth on Bob Dylan and Peter, Paul, and Mary. Jeff waved from the other side of the room. Marty sat at a table handing out information.

The leader of the group took the floor, the overhead light reflecting in his wire-rimmed glasses. "I'm Jake Stedman and together we've got a lot of work to do to end this war."

Jake spoke with authority and charisma. "Most of us grew up feeling 'my country right or wrong.' We said the Pledge of Allegiance every day and felt our country was always on the right side of history. In recent years we have seen our country go very wrong." There was complete silence in the room except for Jake.

He continued, "Our government says we are defending freedom in Vietnam. They say if we don't fight in Vietnam, Communism will reach the shores of California. How is fighting in Vietnam a defense of my freedom right here?" By then there were murmurs in the crowd.

A chant started. I didn't see who started it. "What do you want?" "Peace." "When do you want it?" "Now." With each "Peace" I got louder. With each "Now" I raised my fist.

My parents were pacifists and fierce defenders of equal rights and social justice. My mom gave me the button she wore when they heard Martin Luther King at a rally at the state capitol in Frankfort on March 4th, 1965. It says, "March Fourth for Justice." The same year my mom quit buying grapes in support of migrant farm workers in California.

My dad, with seven of his colleagues, forced the integration of the movie theater in town. A sign on the ticket booth said, "Whites only downstairs—$1. Colored balcony only—50 cents." The balcony, where the seats were broken, the floor sticky, and the bathrooms didn't work. Every Saturday night for two months they went to the theater and asked for tickets to the balcony. Saturday after Saturday the manager said, "I can't sit you in the balcony. You don't even want to go up there."

All eight walked away.

The movement grew and the owner finally relented. During that whole time, Dad wouldn't let me go to the movies. "Not until everyone can sit together," he said. He was right.

As Jake talked, I saw my brother's best friend, in our living room, throwing sunflower seeds at me. I saw him at the swimming pool doing a double flip off the diving board and splashing me with water when he came up the ladder. I saw the moment my brother told me that he died in Vietnam and asked if I wanted to go to the funeral.

My first love didn't have to die. None of those boys had to die.

Now was my time. My regret at writing the essay supporting the war stared me in the face. I would redeem myself. I would work to end this war, dedicated to my brother's best friend.

Jake's timing was perfect. He let the chants die down, then continued. "All across the country, the movement is growing. It's not just a protest movement, it is a movement that goes deep to the core of American values. It is a movement to support the young men who refuse to go and the young men who feel they have no choice. It is a movement that says we will not tolerate more body bags. It's a movement to change the world."

The room exploded in cheers and applause. Jake gave his big finale. "If it requires civil disobedience. If it requires we put our bodies on the line, so be it. Our lives, our future, the future of the entire world depends on it."

By the time Jake was done, I would have walked through fire for him.

It took an hour for the group to decide on projects for the year. An information table in Commons every day during lunch. Leafletting and a march in downtown Lake Forest coordinated with the National Mobilization to End the War. A Be-In during the spring semester. A letter-writing campaign. Jake and Marty handed around clipboards and people signed up for what they wanted to help with.

I signed every list. Here was my grape boycott, my movie theater, my English essay rewritten. I wouldn't let it pass me by.

I lingered as people left. Marty reintroduced himself. Jeff came over and the three of us moved furniture and gathered up the clipboards. "What's Jake's story? He's pretty convincing." I handed Marty two of the clipboards.

Marty smiled. "That he is. He's a senior, big man on campus, president of the student government." We moved a couch to the center of the room. "Government major. Wants to be a lawyer. In love with Ginger."

I looked over at Jake hugging Ginger. "I see."

"What's he doing about the draft when he graduates?"

"He was granted his conscientious objector status last summer. He's going to work in a state hospital outside of Chicago instead of going to Vietnam. Ginger is a junior."

We moved a couch perpendicular to the first. "What are you doing about the draft, Marty?"

"Hoping we end the war before I graduate in three years. I'll apply for CO status but it's never a given." Marty said.

"How about you, Jeff?"

"Haven't figured that one out yet. Maybe I'll stay in college for the rest of my life."

We moved the last couch into place. "Sign up for anything?" Marty asked.

"Everything."

"I need someone to help staff the table tomorrow, twelve o'clock."

"Perfect. I'm out of bio class at eleven forty-five."

"Great. I'll see you at Commons."

"Can I walk you to your dorm?" Jeff asked. He put his hand in mine.

I looked down at our hands locked together. "Guess the answer is yes."

U.S. Soldier Body Count: 16,680

Chapter 4
"Where Have All the Flowers Gone?"

The next day I joined Marty at the anti-war table. "What brought you to Lake Forest?" he asked.

"The name."

"The name? Really?"

"That's the truth. My dad gave me a list of about fifty colleges that have a tuition exchange with the college where he teaches. I chose based on the name."

Marty stopped to give someone a pamphlet and tell them about our next meeting. He turned back to me. "Where does he teach?"

"A small junior college in Kentucky."

Marty grinned. "Kentucky. Known for bluegrass, fast horses, and beautiful women. Or is it beautiful grass, blue horses, and fast women?"

I laughed, trying not to blush. "I think it's fast grass, beautiful horses, and blue women."

Marty leaned back in his chair. "Blue as in the color or blue as in sad?"

"Either one. The important piece is the beautiful horses."

Two girls stopped at the table and sifted through the pile of buttons we sold for ten cents each. One took a button that said,

"Bring them home now." She gave Marty a dime. "My brother just shipped over."

"Let's end this war and bring him home where he belongs," Marty said. He handed them information about our next meeting.

"What brought you here?"

"I grew up in Springfield, Illinois, and wanted to go to school near Chicago. My guidance counselor steered me to the Government Department at Lake Forest. I plan to go to law school after college. I'm also a White Sox fan."

"I am a die-hard Yankees fan. My dad says the only way to make it to heaven is to be a Yankees fan."

Luckily someone came up to the table. Beautiful friendships have been ruined over baseball rivalries.

As we boxed up materials when lunch hour was over, Marty said, "This spring we'll turn our attention to next year's presidential election. We need to elect an anti-war candidate."

"President Johnson's a lock for the Democratic nomination and he loves this war. My birthday is on election day next year, November 5th." I handed a pile of pamphlets to Marty.

He put the pamphlets in a box and closed the top. "We're practically twins. My birthday is November 8th."

"Except for the fact that we were born on different days, in different years, in different cities, to different mothers, I agree. We're practically twins," I said.

Marty thought for a moment. "If we were born practically on the same day, then we were conceived practically on the same day in February. Let's have a conception party."

I'd been to my share of parties in my life: birthday parties, surprise parties, slumber parties, come-as-you-are parties. I had never been to a conception party. Never even considered a conception party. I didn't want to think about how I was conceived.

27

"Valentine's Day," Marty suddenly said. "We were probably both conceived on Valentine's Day. Perfect day for a party. Deal?"

He stuck out his hand. Without thinking much more about conceptions, I shook it. "Deal."

So far, I liked this beginning.

U.S. Soldier Body Count: 16,768

Chapter 5
"There But For Fortune"

Dennis McKinney stopped by the anti-war table three weeks from the day he walked out of my orientation group. I didn't think he'd been listening during orientation. Apparently, he had because he said, "Becky, Kentucky, liked the name, Kennedy's assassination."

"Dennis McKinney. Vietnam Vet," I said back to him. "I know nothing more because you walked away."

"That would be me." He put out his good hand. I shook it.

I never saw his face that first day. What a shame. It was the most perfect face I ever saw. Like a Greek statue I thought. I'd never been to Greece or seen a Greek statue, but I assumed Dennis McKinney was close to looking like one. Perfectly formed nose and mouth. Eyes so dark they almost looked black. Honey blonde wavy hair held back by a red bandana.

What wasn't perfect about his face was the look. A bit angry, a bit mocking, a bit 'I don't give a shit.' I didn't know how to react to that look.

"Surprised you remembered my name," I said to him.

"I had a little help. I saw you with Jeff Ledford the other day in the snack bar and asked about you. He lives in the room across the hall from me." He said all that without letting go of my hand.

Dennis McKinney, a Greek God, asked about me. Jeff Ledford talked about me. Life was getting complicated.

"I just met Jeff. We had a couple of éclairs and some fries together. Nothing more."

"Jeff told me to keep my hands off you. I reminded him in my case it would be hand off." He held up his hook and smiled.

Dennis sorted through the buttons and chose a small peace sign. He handed me a dime. I wondered how he could pin such a small button to his jacket with just one hand and a hook. I wondered how he lost his hand. I wondered what it was like to be in Vietnam. I wondered why Jeff told him to keep his hands off me.

"Thanks," Dennis said. Then he leaned in inches from my face, hook and hand on the table. "It's a pleasure to meet you face to face." He turned and walked away. He looked back and said, "It don't mean nothin' anyway." When he got to the door, he raised his hook and smiled.

U.S. Soldier Body Count: 16,853

Chapter 6
"Respect"

Ginger and I sat in the snack bar in Commons editing my article for 'The Forester.' "I love the way you start with the details of our meeting but then bring in the reality of the war: deaths, injuries, ages of the soldiers, men drafted. I'm impressed." She marked the article with things to clean up.

"Marty and Jake helped with the statistics. Every time I see Marty, he's watching the news or reading a newspaper." I became aware of a whispered conversation between two girls at the table behind us. One girl was crying.

"I don't know what I am going to do," the girl said between sobs. Ginger looked over at the table.

"We'll figure it out," the other girl said.

"How? It's not fair. I only did it once."

I wasn't sure what they were talking about. "What are they talking about?" Ginger put her finger to her lips.

"He was leaving for Vietnam. I wanted to prove I loved him. What am I going to do?" With that, I knew what the 'once' was all about. Obviously, she never heard my dad's speeches.

Ginger stood up. "I'll be right back. Keep working on the edits." She walked over to the table and sat down. The three of them talked for about ten minutes. Ginger wrote something on a piece of paper and handed it to one of the girls.

"I can't thank you enough," She hugged Ginger.

"You don't have to thank me. I know what it's like." The two girls left, arm in arm.

"What was that all about?" I asked. I slid the edited articles over to her.

"She's pregnant." She watched the girls walk away.

"I got that."

"I gave her the address of a doctor in Chicago who performs abortions." Ginger gathered up the articles and put them in a folder.

"Isn't it illegal?"

"Yes, having an abortion is illegal but she doesn't have much choice, does she?" I had not really thought about being pregnant and what someone does when she's pregnant and doesn't want to be.

"What's going to happen? What if she gets caught?"

"I'll tell you what's going to happen. She will catch the train into Chicago, go into some cheap hotel room this doctor rented, lie on a folding table, and hope and pray he sterilized his instruments. He's going to give her some kind of sedative and wait about fifteen minutes. Then he's going to give her an abortion." Ginger took the folder with the edited articles and stuffed it, a little too harshly, into her book bag. "If she's lucky she'll live and be able to have children later."

I gathered up the coffee cups and plates.

"Nice job on the edits by the way," she said.

I watched her walk away while my dad pushed his way into my brain. "Wait until you're married," I heard. I guess Dad was right. If she had waited.

U.S. Soldier Body Count: 16,982

Chapter 7

"You're The Best Thing
That Ever Happened To Me"

My roommate left college after a month. "I can't stand being away from my boyfriend at home," she told me. "I can't concentrate on my classes when I'm thinking about him."

That was fine with me. She smoked too much and supported the war, so we didn't have much in common. I was alone in a room meant for two. First thing I did was open the windows to get rid of the cigarette smell that always lingered. I spread my books and papers out over the two desks. I bought some pillows and made her bed into a couch.

When I had research to do, I studied in a small room attached to the library, my books, papers, and a pack of five-flavor Life Savers on the desk next to me. I was never without Life Savers. I got that from my mom. In addition to Kleenex, she always carried three kinds of Life Savers in her purse: wintergreen, peppermint, and cloves. They kept the three of us quiet at church.

I reached for another Life Saver. A hand beat me to it. "Cherry, my favorite."

"Mine too."

"We have a lot in common," Jeff said. He put the Life Saver in his mouth. "How does your social calendar look for the last weekend in October?"

My social calendar is clear. It will probably be clear for the rest of my life. That's one thing that's clear.

Instead of saying what I thought, I said, "Why are you asking?" I reached for the Life Saver pack, noticed the orange one on the table and the pineapple gone, my second favorite flavor. "Do you like pineapple too?" I asked.

"It's my second favorite flavor."

"We do have a lot in common." I opened the entire pack and found the last cherry one.

"Would you go to the homecoming dance with me?" Jeff asked. "It's October twenty-eighth."

"I'm not much of a dancer." I took dance lessons in junior high school from the Hall School of Dance with pretty much everyone in my class. We learned the basic waltz, two-step, and jitterbug, ending each class with a ten-minute dance. I was always the last chosen by the boys to dance. I was also the last to receive my Master Jitterbug Basic award. Having that award didn't prove I could dance.

"Everyone can dance," he said. He stood me up, put my left hand behind his back, my right hand in his. "Just relax and follow." He hummed a Beatle song as he moved from side to side.

"That's my favorite Beatle song," I said. He did a quick turn to the right. His hold on me tightened as he wormed his way deeper into my head. He was pushing my dad right out of there.

"Mine too," he said.

"Yes," I told him. "I'll go to the dance with you."

During the next week, I saw Jeff dash into dinner a few times, grab a tray of food, and sit alone at a back table. I saw him twice across the green. He waved but never stopped to talk.

Maybe he forgot about asking me to the dance.

* * *

34

A student approached. "You're wrong. You should support the government." He walked away, didn't give us a chance to respond.

"What was that all about?"

Marty taped up the last poster. "I don't know how anyone could be in support of the war." Without pausing to take a breath, he said, "Would you like to go to the homecoming dance with me?"

I was never asked to a homecoming dance in high school. Not once in four years. And now two guys asked me.

"Jeff asked me to the dance," I said. "I'd love to go out sometime though."

"Deal." The awkward silence began.

Jake came with a new stack of posters and spared us from our silence. "Got time to hang these?" he asked.

"I'm heading to class," Marty said. He picked up his book bag. "See you around, Becky. Jake, catch you later."

I watched him go. I turned back to Jake. "Sure." He handed me the stack of posters.

"I sure appreciate you helping Marty at the table every day."

"I wish I could do more. I hate this war."

"Me too. Thanks again, Becky." As Jake walked away, I saw him talking to Dennis McKinney who headed my way.

35

I had seen Dennis around the past couple of weeks at anti-war meetings or going to class. He always smiled when he saw me. That 'angry, mocking, I don't give a shit' look that marred his perfect face was changing.

Dennis nodded towards the poster. "You going?"

"Wouldn't miss it for the world. How about you?" I put the posters on the table and reached for the Life Saver pack I had in my pocket.

"Probably."

"Want a Life Saver?" I held the pack out to him.

"Only if the next one is cherry," he said.

"I think cherry is everyone's favorite." I found the cherry one and handed it to him. "I've never met anyone who liked green the best."

He put the Life Saver in his mouth. "I think green tastes like the stuff my mom mops the kitchen floor with."

"How would you know?"

He laughed. "I haven't had a Life Saver from a five-flavor pack since I was a kid. Did you ever get one of those ten-roll Life Saver boxes for Christmas?" he asked.

"Every year. I always ate them all in two days except for the butterscotch. I hated those."

"I loved the butterscotch ones."

Joe Scott Joe appeared. I hadn't talked to him since orientation. "If it isn't Becky from orientation." He casually put his arm around me.

I shook it off and wanted to say, "If it isn't that jerk Joe Scott Joe." Instead, I said, "What are you doing here?"

He put his arm back around my shoulder and said, "I've come to convince you to quit hanging out with these anti-war hippies and go out with me."

I shook off his arm again.

36

"Friday night. Keg party. My dorm," he said.

"No thanks. I don't drink."

Joe Scott Joe put his arm around me a third time and pulled me close. "Maybe it's time to start." He saw Dennis standing there. "What's up, Hook?"

I never heard anyone call Dennis 'Hook' before. Wasn't sure it was appropriate. Granted he did have a hook on his left arm, but did that give people the right to call him Hook?

"Name's Dennis. Told you that the other day." Dennis turned to walk away.

"I heard your friends call you Hook." Joe Scott Joe said to Dennis's back. He still had his arm around my shoulder. I tried to break free, but he held tighter.

Dennis turned back to face him, "Who said you were my friend?"

"I'm as good as they get." Joe Scott Joe let go of me and spread his arms wide as though he were everyone's gift. I had an urge to slug him in the stomach. I am a lover of non-violence but something about Joe Scott Joe rubbed me the wrong way.

"Fuck you, Joe," Dennis said.

"No, fuck you, Hook. You're not getting any sympathy from me."

"I didn't ask for your sympathy."

Joe Scott Joe continued. "Why did you even go to Vietnam? You could have done what the other long hairs do, go to Canada or jail."

"You're not worth it, Joe. Someday they'll call your number. Although I don't wish this on anyone," Dennis held up his hook, "you'll get what you deserve."

"By the way, Hook. You ever kill anyone over there?"

I heard enough. "Shut up, Joe. And get lost," I moved between him and Dennis.

37

Dennis smiled at me. He put up his hand as if to tell me he could handle this on his own. "None of your goddamn business, Joe. And by the way, you're no friend of mine."

"I'm the best there is, Hook."

"Lay off him, Joe," I said.

Joe Scott Joe patted me on the head. As he left, he said, "Friday night. Keg party. My dorm. See you there."

I turned back to Dennis. "Sorry, Dennis. He's a jerk. I hope I never see him again. In fact, I think I'll go out of my way to never see him again."

"Thanks for trying to help, Becky." He paused and smiled. God, he was gorgeous. "By the way, my friends call me Hook."

* * *

6:30 a.m. Friday. October 20, 1967. At the train station, Jake stood in front of the fifteen of us who volunteered to talk to commuters as they boarded trains to Chicago. "Today and tomorrow are National Days of Protest. Anti-war groups all around the country are leafleting commuters." Jake held up the morning newspaper. An article on the front page announced the national effort and warned commuters they would be 'accosted by Viet Cong sympathizers' while going to work. It advised commuters to lower their eyes and walk by. "Are we going to let the Chicago newspapers dictate who we are? No. So, let's go get 'em."

"Ready, Becky?" Ginger said. She handed me a bag of doughnuts. I pulled out a chocolate frosted one.

"I'm scared as hell. I hate walking up to people and talking to them. Put a guitar in my hand. Let me write an article. Anything but this."

"Don't worry," Ginger said. "You'll be fine. Do you know if Jeff is coming?"

"He said he was. I have no idea where he is."

"The key is to tell the truth." Marty walked up beside me and handed me a pile of leaflets.

I glared at him. "That might be the stupidest thing anyone could say right now. It's freezing out and I'm about to do something petrifying."

"One way or other this war will touch every person on every block in every city in this country," Marty said.

"My God, Marty. It's 6:30 in the morning." I pulled a glazed doughnut out of the bag and gave it to Marty. "Here, eat another doughnut." He could be overly pious at times.

Bleary eyed commuters sauntered warily onto the platform. The first commuter silently took the pamphlet I held out. The second passed me by, eyes lowered. The third said, "Go get a haircut." My hair was tucked under a knit hat so he had no idea what it looked like. One commuter said, "Go get a job." Another said, "Thank you. Keep up the good fight."

I was drawn to a commuter talking to Hook. "Move to Russia if you don't like this country."

All my fear left me at that moment. Start on my friends and you're in trouble. I moved between the commuter and Hook and said, "He's a Vietnam vet. Have some respect."

Hook put his hand on my shoulder. "It's okay, Becky. I can handle this."

"It's not okay," I said to Hook. I turned back to the commuter. "You can say that to me, but you can't say that to a veteran. He lost his hand in Vietnam."

The commuter turned and walked away. I moved in front of him again. "If you like this war so much, why don't you enlist?

Lose your hand in service to this country. Lose your life for all I care."

Marty walked over and pulled me out of harm's way. I jerked out of his grip and turned back to the commuter. "You move to Russia," I yelled at him.

Marty took my arm again and pulled me farther away. "It doesn't do any good to yell at them."

I tried to jerk free from his hand. He held on tight. "It doesn't do any good to not yell at them either. Let go of me." I jerked again and his hand dropped.

"Calm down," Marty said.

"Shut up, Marty."

Hook was still engaged in a conversation with the guy. When the train came, he shook Hook's hand and boarded the train to Chicago.

Hook walked over to me, kissed me on the head, and gave me a hug. It was my first Dennis McKinney hug. I was addicted immediately. Hook hugged with his whole body, shoulders touching, chest touching, thighs touching, knees touching. "Thanks for always trying to protect me. I can fight my own battles." The hug lingered.

We stayed on the platform until 8:00. Students imploring. Commuters ignoring, briefcase in one hand, cup of coffee in the other. They were in a hurry. They had jobs to go to and families to feed, threatened by cries for peace.

The cold apathy of the commuters did not deter us. It enraged us. It goaded us. It pushed us, made us hungry for change, made us feel powerless. Powerlessness made us strong.

We gathered at a café after the leafletting. "Sorry I told you to shut up, Marty," I said.

"Forgiven. Sorry I pulled you away so forcefully."

"Forgiven."

"Does that mean our conception party is still a go?"

"Absolutely."

Jeff showed soon after. "Sorry I'm late. I forgot to set my clock and overslept."

More than a tenth of the 1,200 students at Lake Forest College showed up for the march at 10:00. Added to the tenth of the entire population of the United States in rallies around the country, the movement was massive.

We marched around the square in the center of Lake Forest carrying signs—*Escalate Peace, War on Poverty Not People, Peace Now, Bring Our Boys Home*. Hippies in frayed denims and fringed leather moccasins marched next to fraternity guys, cheerleaders, professors, sorority girls, and a few local people. My sign said, *"Out of Vietnam."*

Jake led the march with his bullhorn. "What do we want? PEACE. When do we want it? NOW." Another chant started farther down the line. "Hey, Hey, LBJ. How many kids did you kill today?"

Some townspeople urged us to go back to Russia where we belonged. A few held signs. *God Yes—Communism No. Support Your Country.* I noticed Joe Scott Joe among them holding a sign that said *Love it or Leave it.* I walked over to Joe. "You're on the wrong side of this, Joe."

"Missed you at the keg party." I didn't respond.

We walked for an hour, Jeff by my side, Jake leading the chants with Ginger by his side, Hook in his army jacket with the peace button pinned on the pocket, the red bandana around his head. He walked the line encouraging the chants, occasionally stopping to chat with someone walking by.

I don't know if we changed any minds that day, but that day changed me. It energized me and boosted my confidence. I made my voice heard like my dad when he helped to integrate the theater in town, like my mom when she boycotted grapes. It was a beginning.

* * *

The Forester
Contributor Column
Becky Jamison

Fifteen Lake Forest College students gathered at the train station at 6:30 am on Friday to leaflet commuters and talk to them about the war. Despite a few hostile interactions, most of the commuters ignored the students altogether.

Later more than one hundred students and a couple dozen townspeople marched through downtown Lake Forest in support of a march in Washington, D.C. the following day. The Lake Forest College Students Against the War organized both events. The group thanks the administration for canceling morning classes so students could attend the march.

More than 100,000 people marched in Washington D.C. and 35,000 marched to the Pentagon. The police arrested eight hundred protesters there.

President Johnson said, "We are inflicting greater losses than we're taking. We are making progress." Yet, since the beginning of October, more than 700 young men have lost their lives in Vietnam with more than 4,000 injured.

The Lake Forest College Students Against the War meets every Wednesday in Bradley Hall at 7:00. Come help end this war.

Officials called the march at the Pentagon a riot. Protesters called it their right to assemble. Government infiltrators threw bottles and called the movement violent.

* * *

Jeff managed to not oversleep for the homecoming dance, and it was magical. The dance lesson he gave me in the library was all I needed. The slow dances made me tingle, gave me goose bumps, started that twitching. After that weekend, Jeff and I became an item. I had never been an item before. I was sort of an item with the first guy I kissed when I was sixteen, but, because he lived eighty miles away, I don't think that counts.

Pretty soon I wondered what my dad meant in those speeches he made. I had fallen for Jeff and needed to get my dad out of my head.

U.S. Soldier Body Count: 17,522

Chapter 8
"Birthday"

November 5. My birthday.

As I waited in Hixson Lounge for Jeff, Marty sat down and handed me a brown paper bag. "It's your present. Happy Birthday."

"Thanks. Can't believe you remembered."

"How could I forget? You're my twin."

Inside was a white candle.

"Reminded me of you. Innocent. Pure. There aren't many like you around." I leaned over and kissed him on the cheek. The sweetness of his skin surprised me.

Later that afternoon, Jeff and I stood on the edge of Lake Michigan looking out over the water. At that moment, the angle of the sun made the water look like stripes of gold.

"I bought you a present," Jeff said. He pulled an orange out of his pocket, peeled it, broke off a segment, and put it in my mouth. His finger stayed. I licked it, sucked off the juice.

Jeff rubbed sticky fingers over my cheeks. He broke off another segment and put it in his mouth.

"I want to know more about you," I said. My dad popped into my head telling me to back off. Should I really be hanging out with a guy who was kicked out of college because of drugs? Those eyes.

His finger in my mouth. The heat of his hand on my back. The gentle touch of his lips on mine. I inhaled and pushed Dad away.

"Ask me anything. But I get to ask you back." We sat down in the sand.

"Favorite color."

"Blue. Yours?"

"Yellow."

"Why yellow?" He sifted a handful of sand between his fingers.

"Reminds me of daffodils that grow in our backyard. Your turn."

"Favorite song," he asked.

"Any Beatles song. Yours?"

"Anything by the Rolling Stones."

"They come in second to the Beatles. Favorite movie."

"That's easy," he said. "*Cool Hand* Luke."

"Me too. I love that movie."

At the same time, we said, "I can eat fifty eggs." We laughed and Jeff leaned over and gave me a kiss. The kiss deepened. I don't know who pulled back first.

"Favorite book."

"*Catch-22*. Yours?"

"*Cat's Cradle,*" he said.

"We're reading that in my freshman English class."

"You'll love it," Jeff said.

"Favorite baseball team." This question was very important.

"I love to play but I don't watch baseball so don't have a favorite team," he said.

"That's too bad. I can't hang out with someone who doesn't love to watch baseball." I looked at Jeff. His eyes held a hint of laughter, a hint of gentleness, a hint of melancholy. They sucked me in.

Eating an orange by the lake, sharing the superficial things of life, an extraordinary, unexpected, perfect moment.

We walked back to campus in silence, Jeff's arm around me. At my dorm he kissed me. My skin tingled. My stomach flipped. My palms sweated. I wanted the kiss to go on forever.

The next Wednesday night at our anti-war meeting we surprised Marty with a cake and twenty candles. After Marty made a wish, he winked at me. "You get the first piece, twin," he said.

U.S. Soldier Body Count: 18,217

Chapter 9
"Eve of Destruction"

With finals in ten days, my parents decided it would be best for me to stay on campus for Thanksgiving. I ate a plate of turkey and mashed potatoes in the college dining room with my friends. I missed my family but was thankful for what I had.

That afternoon, heading to Jeff's room, I ran into Hook. We walked down the hall together. Jeff greeted me at the door with one of those twisted ended cigarettes in his hand. I was ready to try it. I'd gotten drunk the week before. It was a terrible experience. I threw up behind the science building and had a hangover for two days. Jeff promised me this would be different.

"Care to join us, Hook?" Jeff raised the joint.

"I'll pass, but thanks." Hook looked at me and back at Jeff. "Don't forget what I told you the other night, Jeff."

"What did you tell him?" I glanced back and forth between the two of them.

Hook spoke. "I told him he better not ever hurt you or he would have to answer to me."

I walked over to Hook and leaned in to kiss him on the cheek. "Don't worry. He won't."

Hook put his arms around me in one of his hugs. "Be careful, Becky. Promise me."

"I promise." I turned and went into Jeff's room. I looked back at Hook right before the door closed. He raised his hand in a slight wave.

"Why does Hook think you would ever hurt me?" I took off my jacket and threw it on the bed.

"I think he's jealous and maybe a little bit in love with you." Jeff held up the joint.

"Hook has to know I love you." That was the first time I mentioned love to Jeff. It came out of my mouth unexpectedly.

Jeff smiled and held up the joint. "You ready for this?"

"I'm trusting you," I said, not sure if I really trusted him after the getting drunk debacle.

"It's not anything like getting drunk. I would never do anything to hurt you." Then he looked at me. God damn eyes. They did it every time. "You should never pass up the opportunity to try something you've never done before."

"I'm sure there are some opportunities worth passing up, like cannibalism."

"Not this one," he said. He took a book of matches out of the pocket of the leather jacket he always wore, even inside. Jeff lit the joint and inhaled slowly, held it in, and slowly exhaled.

He handed me the joint while his hand found its way under my shirt. My body ached for Jeff. "Inhale slowly and hold it in as long as you can."

I could hear my dad. It was like having the angel and the devil on my shoulders. The angel said, "Tell him to stop. Don't inhale. Leave." The devil said, "You want him. Inhale. Stay." They argued back and forth.

The devil won. I inhaled and coughed it out.

"Try again," Jeff said.

Each time I held it longer.

We finished the joint and Jeff went to roll another. "When will I start to feel something?" As soon as I said that I felt it. "Whoa, that's kind of nice."

Jeff came back with the second joint, lit it, and handed it to me. He slid my shirt over my head. I didn't resist. My body arched towards him.

This thing opened in my head. My dad's speeches didn't matter anymore. I was completely at peace with what was happening. Jeff put the unfinished joint in the ashtray, turned off the light, took off his jacket and shirt.

He moved me to the bed and my world changed. That night I fell in love with dope and hopelessly over the edge for Jeff. Once you taste the good life, there's no going back. I was ready to spend the rest of my life with this man.

* * *

"I didn't even think about birth control. What should I do?" I asked Ginger.

"Pray," she said.

"This isn't funny."

"I know. You can't do anything now except wait."

"How could I have been so stupid?" I reached for a Kleenex on her desk to wipe the tears from the corners of my eyes.

"My guess is you think you're in love and whatever magic he did, it was hard to resist."

"I was stoned. That was my second mistake."

Ginger took both of my hands. "None of it was a mistake. What you did was normal."

"Normal? I spent my life hearing my dad say I should wait until I'm married. Seems he's been right all along. On Thanksgiving Day of all days."

"Your dad was neither right nor wrong."

"It can't be both."

"You have to decide for yourself. It's not your dad's choice. It's yours."

"Seems I made a stupid choice. What if I'm pregnant?"

"We can deal with that." Her eyes caught mine. She smiled. "Trust me. I know."

"Like that girl in Commons? Is that what you mean? Send me to Chicago and do something illegal? Maybe die? Maybe never have children?"

"Becky, this isn't the end of the world."

"Of course it's the end of the world. Nothing could be worse."

"There's a war out there, Becky. Twenty thousand U.S. soldiers have died.'

"Shut up about the war, Ginger. This isn't the war. This is my life, my future, everything."

Ginger walked over to where I sat. She put her arms around me and held me close. "All you can do is wait," she said.

Jeff tried to lure me back into bed. I told him no. "This is your fault," I said.

"What's my fault?"

"You get me stoned. You seduce me. You don't protect yourself. And I have to worry about whether I might be pregnant."

"No one gets pregnant the first time," he said.

"Of course someone can get pregnant the first time. Don't be stupid, Jeff."

I walked away. I didn't ever want to see him again. My body ached for him. I wanted his kisses. I wanted him to disappear.

My period was always on time. It was due three days before my last final. Would I go home pregnant? Would I have to lie through Christmas? Would they notice something different about me?

I wanted my period to come early. Maybe sex does that, changes your cycle. I prayed it would. My prayers weren't answered. A day passed and then two. Every time I went to the bathroom, I said a prayer. Why wasn't God listening to me? Was it because I sinned? Was it because there wasn't a God after all?

I took my English final, head muddled, writing an essay that didn't sound like me. Another day, another final, no blood.

The deadline crept towards me slowly. I couldn't sleep. I couldn't study. I went to the bathroom every hour. Nothing. Hour after hour. Nothing. Another day. Another final.

One more final to go, biology. Two days to study. Maybe I should have listened more in class. Maybe I should have studied more about how amoebas procreate or paid attention to the fetal pig we dissected. Maybe I should have simply listened to my dad. I woke up in dread. This was the due date and I couldn't feel anything wet in my underwear. I always felt it the first thing when I wake up, the moisture starting to come. This day, nothing. My worst fears come true.

Tears formed in the corner of my eyes. I put on a bathrobe and shuffled to the bathroom down the hall. I shut the stall, pulled down my pants, and sat down. I didn't look. I couldn't. I knew the answer. There would be nothing there. I have to look. I can't. I have to know the truth. If nothing was there, it was over for me. I can't. I have to. There, in my underwear, scarlet, a few drops, but there, announcing loudly for the world to hear, "I'm not pregnant."

Who cries over a period? I do. Sobs. There, sitting on the toilet in a communal bathroom, a girl brushing her teeth at the sink.

"You okay in there?" Someone asked.

"Perfect. Thanks."

Ginger was the first person I told. Jeff was second. "I'm sorry I got angry at you and ignored you. It was my fault as much as yours. I was scared."

He put his arms around me, rubbed my back, and kissed my neck. "I'm sorry for not protecting you. I'm ready now." He pulled a condom from his pocket. "I want to wake up with you in my arms. You know I love you." That was the first time he said it.

"Ginger's going with me to get on the pill. Can't we wait?"

"I don't want to wait. The condom will protect you until then. Besides you can't get pregnant during your period."

"Are you sure?" I wanted him to say yes. I wanted him more than anything.

I never wanted to go through that again, the waiting, the guilt, the fear. I also knew, without a doubt, that what I wanted more than anything was to feel Jeff on me again, to feel him in me, to let him know that I loved him.

"I can trust you?" I asked as he entered me.

"With every fiber of your being." It may have been a mistake to do so.

 After my last final, Ginger drove me to the doctor so I could get on the pill. In the waiting room, she put a small button in my hand, about the size of the peace button I wore on my jacket. It said, 'Wet and Wild.' I needed a good laugh.

* * *

While all that was happening, while I lost a roommate, danced at homecoming, ate Life Savers with Hook, marched around the square and handed out leaflets, got drunk and stoned, had sex, was afraid I was pregnant, went on the pill, took final exams, while all that happened, the war went on. The powerlessness turned into a hopelessness and, as hopelessness often does, it turned into rage. Does absolute powerlessness corrupt as much as absolute power?

Around the country protesters bombed ROTC offices and took over administration buildings. JFK predicted we'd be out by 1965 but he was dead. The war kept going, getting uglier, more deaths, more napalm, more young boys in body bags.

By the end of 1967, 486,000 troops had been sent to Vietnam. More than 20,000 were dead. My generation was disappearing, one boy killed at a time. You see, politics, policies, and treaties aside, war is plain and simply about death.

U.S. Soldier Body Count: 20,057

Chapter 10
"Universal Soldier"

It was good to be home for Christmas. My brothers were there and for two weeks we laughed, played games, wrapped presents, made cookies, decorated the tree we cut down on a farm outside my hometown, sang carols, and told stories.

Christmas vacation was also a time of omission. I didn't lie to my family. I simply omitted talking about sex, drugs, and alcohol. I couldn't tell them I threw up because I drank too much. I couldn't say that when I got stoned, I had unprotected sex and was afraid I might be pregnant. And I certainly couldn't tell them I went on the pill.

When they dropped me off at the airport for the flight back to Chicago, Dad hugged me tight and said, "Remember who you are. I love you."

Mom hugged me with tears in her eyes. "I always miss you when you're gone."

* * *

Second semester started. I sat on a couch in Hixson Lounge strumming my guitar. Hixson Lounge was my second home. In between classes, that was my place to study, play my guitar, or simply hang out. Hook sat down next to me and handed me a box.

"My Christmas present?" I asked.

"Open it."

I stared at the medal in the box.

"I'm a hero. Bronze Star to go with my Purple Heart. I'm sending it back." Hook shifted uneasily.

I picked up the medal. It was the same one my uncle got in World War II. He displayed it in the china cabinet in his dining room. My uncle told me stories of the war. It seemed glorious. It wasn't.

I looked at Hook, the medal still in my hand. "You can't send it back. You earned it. When you lost your hand, you still saved two of your buddies."

"Anybody would have done the same thing."

"Not true." I put the medal in the box.

Hook took the box from me and snapped it shut. "The recruiters promised glory. They lied. All I got was a stainless-steel hook and this piece of cheap jewelry." He put the box in the pocket of the army jacket.

"You got a good jacket out of the deal." Hook always wore his army jacket and a red bandana around his head. I loved the look.

"You want to know the worst thing I did in Nam?"

I knew he was going to tell me, and I wasn't sure I wanted to hear.

"One day, about seven months in, I'm outside at the airfield on base smoking a cigarette near a couple of fifty-five-gallon drums of fuel."

"I didn't know you smoked," I said.

"Quit when I got back. As I stood there the fumes in those drums made me sick to my stomach."

Hook sat still, looking down at the floor. I slipped the guitar strap over my head and balanced the guitar against the couch.

Hook continued, "An airplane landed and forty guys in clean fatigues got off. I yelled to them, 'Get the fuck back on that plane. Go home.' They couldn't hear me. It wouldn't have mattered. It was too late."

"In front of me, on the other side of those drums of fuel, were four bodies waiting to be boarded on that same plane. They were in these black body bags with white name tags hanging from them. It was fucking hot out there. It was so goddamn humid. I saw the heat rising off the asphalt. And there was the smell of the fuel." Hook's voice lowered. I leaned in to hear the rest of the story. He still wouldn't look at me.

"The person guarding the bodies asked if I'd keep watch over them while he finished the paperwork." Hook glanced up at me. "What were those bodies going to do? Get up and run away?" He looked down again. "I walked over to those four dead bodies next to the fifty-five-gallon drums of fuel, smoking my cigarette. I needed to know who I was guarding. I picked up the tag on the first body. Michael, twenty. Then the other three. James, twenty-one. Andrew, twenty. David, nineteen. I remember those names as though it happened yesterday. Fuck, I thought. They were my age. What were they doing dead? I looked at the fifty-five-gallon drums of fuel, at those four dead bodies, at the new recruits in their clean pants."

Hook glanced up at me again. "The worse thing I did in Nam? I wanted to throw my cigarette in those drums of fuel and burn up those bodies. I wanted them to disappear. I wanted them to go up in flames. God, I hated those bodies."

I was silent. Our eyes locked.

"Sometimes when I close my eyes, I feel the heat. I smell those drums of fuel. I see those four dead bodies with the white tags. Michael. James. Andrew. David. They don't know I hated their guts and wanted them to disappear. Their families don't know I wanted to burn them."

I reached out for my guitar and pulled it into my lap. The guitar steadied me.

"I planned on reenlisting. I left my buddies there. I'm not keeping the damn medal."

Hook got up to leave. He leaned down, kissed me on the top of the head, and tugged my braids with his good hand. "Thanks for listening. It don't mean nothin' anyhow."

"That's what you keep telling me."

He stopped for a moment and grinned. "See you later."

I thought about Michael, James, Andrew, and David. They had mothers and fathers, girlfriends, wives, children, brothers, sisters, uncles, cousins, dentists, aunts, Sunday school teachers, friends, scout leaders, next-door neighbors. They could have been my friend, my lover, the father of my children. They were simply four dead bodies in four black plastic bags with white tags next to two stinking fifty-five-gallon drums of fuel. Goddamn war.

U.S. Soldier Body Count: 21,462

Chapter 11
"The Birds and The Bees"

The Forester
Contributor Column
Becky Jamison

On January 30, the Viet Cong shattered their own ceasefire in coordinated attacks all over South Vietnam. This Tet Offensive, named after the Vietnamese New Year, surprised the South Vietnamese and U.S. forces. Many who believed President Johnson when he said the enemy was being defeated now predict an escalation of the war.

More than 11,000 U.S. troops died in Vietnam in 1967. With these new developments, we can expect this number to increase in 1968.

The LFC Students Against the War meets every Wednesday, Bradley Hall, 7:00. All are welcome.

Who is the enemy and what is victory in war but the systematic and random murder of the losers?

* * *

The Saturday after Valentine's Day, Marty and I held our conception party in the living room of his dorm. I arrived with Jeff, my arms full of bags of potato chips and popcorn. "Happy Conception Day, Marty," I hugged him. "You look about half-drunk already."

"I am and I intend to be full-drunk before the night is over."

"Don't get so drunk that tomorrow you will have forgotten our first conception party."

"I'll never forget it or you."

Marty brought out gallon jugs of Pisano wine and bags of cookies. We moved couches back, put tables against the wall, set up the record player with piles of LPs.

The room filled and we danced. Someone put a glass of wine in my hand, someone passed a joint.

About an hour in Jeff said, "I'll be right back." He kissed me and I kept dancing. It was the Rolling Stones. I wasn't stopping for anything.

Ginger saw Jeff leave. "Where's he going?"

"Don't know. Said he'd be right back."

"He disappears a lot," Ginger said.

"No, he doesn't."

"Yes, he does." She didn't say anything else. I was glad. She was right. I didn't want to admit it. I had no idea where he always went.

Hook cut in and we danced to the Beatles and the Dave Clark Five. At one point he took my hand and started to say something.

"What?" I asked.

"It's nothing," he said.

"It's never nothing."

The conversation ended as Marty, now completely drunk, called for attention. "Welcome to our conception party." Marty put his arm around me. "We share November birthdays so from

59

this day forth we declare the nearest Saturday to Valentine's Day our conception date." He held up a bottle of wine. "To conceptions."

"To conceptions," the crowd responded. They kept on drinking and dancing.

Marty whispered in my ear, "I love conceptions."

I noticed Jeff had returned and was leaning against the wall, his feet crossed, arms folded across his chest. He was grinning. I gestured for him to come join us, but he shook his head no.

Marty said, "You make sure he doesn't hurt you."

"He would never hurt me."

Marty grabbed my arm to steady himself. "I'm serious, Becky. You're too good for him. He better not hurt you."

I put my hands on his shoulders. "Marty, he's a good man and you don't have to worry about me. Now go sit down. You're drunk."

"I worry about you every day." He grabbed hold of me. Maybe it was for a hug or maybe because he couldn't stand up anymore. "You're about my best friend in the whole wide world."

That was probably true. Marty and I spent a lot of time together at the anti-war table. I knew more about him than I did Jeff. I led Marty to a couch and sat him down.

"I mean it. You're not just my conception twin, you're my best friend."

"You already said that, Marty."

He leaned his head back against the couch and was out. I kissed him on the forehead. Jeff watched the entire scenario with a peaceful grin on his face.

When all was said and done, the guitars put away, the record albums back in their covers, and the food eaten, we declared the party a success. Jake and Jeff helped Marty to his room but not before I kissed his cheek and vowed again to make our conception party a yearly tradition. I don't think he heard me.

* * *

Jeff and I spent as much time as we could curled up on his single bed in his single room. We smoked dope, made love always with the lights off, slept, laughed, talked, read Robert Frost poetry to each other, listened to music. Sometimes I missed class. It was hard to focus on conjugating French verbs, combining two chemicals, analyzing social structures, or comparing poetic elements when I knew the next joint awaited me. On the other side of that joint, the lights were going out.

U.S. Soldier Body Count: 23,618

Chapter 12
"Cruel War"

Vietnam was a civil war—mothers against children, fathers against sons, workers against students, a war for the soul of the country. Society continued to fragment. The endless, hostile, undeclared war in a faraway land split the country apart and spilled its blood. This bitter war also held a generation together. Cemented by Kennedy's assassination, we became the tasters and seekers of a new world, a powerless powerful majority.

Protests continued all winter, not only of an illegal war but of an inequitable and immoral government policy. A policy gone awry, a disenchantment, authority viewed as illegitimate, arbitrary. My country 'tis of thee, sweet land of misery. Sweet land of tyranny.

The Forester
Contributor Column
Becky Jamison

The presidential election is eight months away. Because of his opposition to the Vietnam War, The Lake Forest College Students Against the War has endorsed Senator Eugene McCarthy in his challenge to unseat President Lyndon Johnson for President of the United States. Jake Stedman, the group's leader, said, "McCarthy has a clear vision about U.S. involvement in Vietnam. He was correct when he said, 'The entire history of this war in Vietnam, no matter what we call it, has been one of continued error and misjudgment.' We support McCarthy's efforts to put this country back on the right course."

If you want to learn more about McCarthy or become involved in the campaign, join the LFC Students Against the War, Wednesdays at 7:00, Bradley Hall.

* * *

On March 12, with 42% of the vote, McCarthy came close to beating a seated President in the New Hampshire primary. Four days later, Bobby Kennedy entered the race.

The war was out of control. I wanted someone to restore order to the chaos. In one week, five hundred and forty-seven Americans died in Vietnam. I thought of the black asphalt, the smell of fifty-five-gallon drums of oil, the heat, the humidity, five hundred and forty-seven black body bags with white nametags.

All spring I campaigned for Eugene McCarthy, addressing envelopes at the campaign office in Chicago, looking up telephone numbers for pollsters. I put a McCarthy bumper sticker on my dorm room door and wore my McCarthy button.

I was for McCarthy, but I also loved Bobby Kennedy. I loved him when he was Attorney General and played football on the White House lawn with his brothers. I loved the way he rolled up the sleeves of his shirt. I loved the way he talked with his thick Boston accent. I loved how he pushed back his hair with the palm of his hand. It reminded me of Marty. I loved the Kennedys. But

I didn't support Bobby Kennedy for president. I wanted the war to end. McCarthy was the man to do that

On the last day of March 1968, Ginger called. "President Johnson is about to make an important speech. Come watch."

"I've got an article due tomorrow. Tell me what happens."

"Tell her I bought Oreos," I heard someone yell.

"Was that Marty and did he say Oreos?" I asked.

"Yes. Jeff just got here. Bring your guitar."

When I arrived at Bradley Hall, Jeff was on a couch chatting with Jake. Hook paced back and forth. Marty sat on a couch in front of the TV, his elbows on his knees, hands on his face, telling Hook to get out of the way every time he wandered in front of the TV. Ginger and I played and sang until the speech began.

Jake had a notebook in front of him to write down every important thing LBJ said even though we knew the entire speech would be in the paper tomorrow. I put my guitar away and joined Jeff on the couch. He fed me Oreos.

Oreos reminded me of summer evenings at the elderly couple's house across the street from where I grew up. Every summer I became best friends with their grandchildren. We played hour-long games of croquet and, when it got dark, bowls of Oreos and glasses of milk appeared on their front porch. We chased fireflies and put them in jars with pierced lids. Life was easy then, in 1960, when I was ten going on eleven. Oreos, milk, croquet, fireflies in jars. It was the best of times. That was before all this. Back before the fireflies died.

"What happened to fireflies?" I asked Jeff as we waited for Johnson's speech to begin.

"What?" he asked.

"I was thinking about how when I was ten, we used to catch fireflies. I haven't seen a firefly in a long time. Where did they go?"

"Maybe you caught them all. Oreo?"

I took an Oreo and wondered what happened to those times when the world was easy to understand.

Johnson told us what we already knew. They attack. We attack. "LBJ, tell us something we don't know."

Marty talked to the TV. Jake wrote. I ate Oreos.

Johnson announced a unilateral bombing halt on North Vietnam. "What the fuck do you mean?" Marty asked the TV. "You're going to decrease bombing and increase napalm? You're going to pretend you care about ending the war and you might win the nomination?"

Jeff turned to me, "Be back in a second." He got up to leave. As he passed Marty, he patted his shoulder. "Hey man. You're talking to the TV. People are going to think you're crazy." Marty didn't even look at him.

Jeff walked out the front door. Ginger glanced my way and gave me a questioning look. I looked at Hook. He looked back. I shrugged my shoulders. I didn't know where he went.

The speech droned on. LBJ told us how noble our country was because we wanted to end the war if Hanoi would talk to us. Marty said, "It would be noble to get out."

"Marty, hush." Jake kept writing.

Johnson talked about the budget, taxes, and prosperity. I couldn't follow his train of thought. Must have been all the Oreos I was eating or the fact that Jeff was back and, while he was feeding me Oreos with one hand, the other was moving up and down my leg.

LBJ said there would be peace in Southeast Asia one day, but they had to want it. "It will come if we get the hell out of there." Marty stood and gestured towards the TV.

"Sit down, Marty. You're blocking the TV." Jake stopped writing

LBJ told us to quit being so divisive. If we would just unite.

"Fuck you, Johnson," Hook said gesturing with his hook.

"We aren't the ones being divisive," Marty said.

"We are united, Johnson. You're not," Ginger said.

Jeff didn't say anything. He watched the TV with a grin on his face while rubbing my leg. I didn't say anything. I had a mouthful of Oreos.

"Be quiet, everyone," said Jake, "He's not finished."

I was only half listening when, at the end of his speech, President Johnson said, "Accordingly, I shall not seek, and I will not accept the nomination of my party for another term as your president."

"No way," Marty said. That summed it up. We just won our first battle.

* * *

During this whole time, the military was covering up the slaughter of close to five hundred innocent South Vietnamese civilians in the town of My Lai. It would take more than a year and a half for the story to break. Don't let anyone tell you war is about national honor. It's not. It's about despair, helplessness, and ugly, senseless murder.

U.S. Soldier Body Count: 24,942

Chapter 13
"We Shall Overcome"

Four days later. Thursday. April 4, 1968, 7:30 p.m. I was in my dorm room when Ginger called. "King's dead," she said. It didn't register.

"What?"

"Martin Luther King was killed in Memphis. He went there to support striking sanitation workers. Someone shot him. He died about a half hour ago."

"It can't be true."

"It is."

The hope for a country free of segregation and discrimination lay dead on a balcony at the Lorraine Motel in Memphis, Tennessee. We gathered at Bradley Hall as I knew we would. There is comfort in community.

Marty was pacing when I showed up, mumbling under his breath, his fists clenched by his side. He picked up a pillow and slammed it against the couch. "What the fuck is wrong with this country?" he said. The pillow slammed once, twice, a dozen times. "We pass Civil Rights legislation and nothing changes. We protest the war. Nothing changes." Bam. Bam. Bam. "My brother was destroyed. King is dead. Fuck." Bam. Bam Bam. One can only hit a pillow for so long. One can only cry for so long. Grief sets in. Disbelief. Numbness. Anger. Or does the anger come first?

We watched the news coverage, over and over. King's speech the night before, his premonition. "Like anybody, I would like to live a long life. But I'm not concerned about that now. I've seen the Promised Land. I may not get there with you. But I want you to know tonight, that we will get to the Promised Land. I'm happy tonight; I'm not fearing any man. Mine eyes have seen the glory of the coming of the Lord." How did he know his end was near?

The image, on the balcony, the men over the dead body, pointing to where the shots came from. Bobby Kennedy's words at his campaign rally in Indianapolis, telling the crowd, who hadn't heard that Martin Luther King was dead. "What we need in the United States is not division, what we need in the United States is not hatred, what we need in the United States is not violence and lawlessness but is love and wisdom and compassion toward one another."

See what happens to non-violent resistance? See what happens to a dream? It dies violent. It dies ugly. It dies dead. Riots broke out in major cities around the country. It wasn't surprising. Two years before, King said, "A riot is the language of the unheard." In the streets of Chicago, the unheard spoke, demanding a change that wouldn't come. The rage of the people continued, unabated, for forty-eight hours.

Chicago Mayor Daley instituted curfews, authorized the use of tear gas, and closed roads. He ordered police "to shoot to kill arsonists, shoot to maim looters." It triggered the unbridled aggression by Chicago police.

* * *

The Forester
Contributor Column
By Becky Jamison

The entire Lake Forest College community was shocked by the assassination of Martin Luther King in Memphis last week. Dr. King dedicated his life to ending segregation through non-violent means. In the end, it cost him his life.

Dr. King's body was flown to Atlanta for burial. Tens of thousands of people lined the streets as his body was carried in a mule-drawn wagon to Ebenezer Baptist Church for his final good-bye.

The Lake Forest College Students Against the War will be walking the streets of Lake Forest this weekend asking for donations of money, food, or clothing for those displaced by the riots in Chicago.

If you would like to join the effort, meet in front of Bradley Hall at 10:00 a.m. on Saturday.

Please pray for the family of Dr. King and for all those affected by the riots. While we continue our work to end the war in Vietnam, we must dedicate ourselves to ending segregation in this country.

The people of Lake Forest were generous.

U.S. Soldier Body Count: 25,156

Chapter 14
"Blowing In the Wind"

BE-IN
Saturday, April 27
1:00 – 7:00
Bring your frisbees, bubbles, blankets, chalk, dancing shoes, and friends.
Music by the Unknowns.
Box dinners served by Commons.
Sponsored by the Lake Forest College Students Against the War.

By 1:00 the platform was up outside of Commons. We strung cloth banners between trees. One banner was decorated with flowers and said, "War Is Not Healthy for Children or Other Living Things." One said, "Peace" next to a blue and gold peace sign. The third, "Make Love. Not War." Jake didn't like that one. He wanted something like, "Don't Be Guilty of the Complicity of Silence."

By 2:00 the Frisbee game began and across the sidewalk on the green, a softball game. That day I fell in love with softball on the Lake Forest College green.

Hook leaned against a tree. "We could use one more in the field," I called to him. He raised his hook and shook his head. I never thought of Hook as being incapable of doing anything.

70

Most of the time I forgot he had a hook. So, he leaned against the tree, the red bandana tied around his head, high fiving everyone who scored.

Blue-jeaned, bleary-eyed folks decorated sidewalks with colored chalk; a hopscotch game, flowers, a sun the entire width of one sidewalk square, peace slogans, peace signs. Soon the entire patio of Commons and all the sidewalks leading up to it from three directions were colored. Bubbles reflected rainbows; the faint scent of marijuana filled the air. Blankets were scattered throughout the lawn.

When the game was over Jake took the stand. "Much as I like the music, dancing, frisbees, and softball, we are here because of a deadly serious war. Every month this war goes by, more than five hundred of our troops lose their lives. The average age of the U.S. soldiers who die is twenty. That's all of you." Jake paused. There was power in his pauses.

I looked around at the students, listening silently to Jake. On the fringes were a few students holding pro-war signs. Joe Scott Joe held his "Love It or Leave It" sign. I headed that way.

"Still on the wrong side, Joe."

"And you still haven't come to a keg party with me." I walked away. He was a hopeless case.

Jake continued. "More than 10,000 soldiers died in Vietnam in 1967. On one day this year, more than two hundred and forty soldiers were killed. We're set to beat last year's total. Can we accept that from our government?"

In my mind I saw 10,000 black body bags, 10,000 white tags, 10,000 Michaels, Jameses, Andrews and Davids. 10,000 mothers, 10,000 fathers. A million tears.

The chants started. *1-2-3-4 we don't want your fucking war. Hey, hey, LBJ, how many kids did you kill today?*

"Let's end this war. Please sign the petitions circulating. We're sending them to the president. Every day during lunch we have a table outside the dining room. Come help. Whatever you do, speak out."

He left the stage and the chanting increased. God, he was magical. With his passion and our energy, we could stop this war. He walked away; his arm draped around Ginger. She wouldn't lose him to Vietnam. His CO status assured that.

It rained the next day. Chalk peace signs and slogans only a memory.

U.S. Soldier Body Count: 26,133

Chapter 15
"Abraham, Martin, and John"

I had five days of finals before going home for the summer. Instead of studying, I joined friends in Bradley Hall to watch the California Democratic primary returns. We held high hopes for McCarthy.

Polls closed at 10 p.m. Chicago time. It was now close to 2 a.m. and I drifted in and out of sleep, curled up with Jeff on the couch. Ginger, as usual, softly strummed her guitar. Hook, as usual, alternated between pacing and standing against a wall, arms crossed. Jake and Marty, as usual, strategized. They were planning our trip to the Democratic National Convention in August. Chicago was never going to know what hit it.

I wanted to give up. The Oreo bag was empty, and I had an 9:00 final the next morning. "I'm leaving. Someone tell me how it turns out."

"Stay until 3:00 and if nothing's final by then, I'll walk you back to your dorm," Jeff said.

It became final, very final, long before. Fifteen minutes later the newscasters projected Kennedy the winner. "Shit," Marty said. "I was sure McCarthy was going to pull this one out." I sat stunned, tears rolling down my face as I stared at the celebration on the screen.

Bobby Kennedy came to the stage with his wife and gave the peace sign to the crowd. They cheered as he gave seven minutes of thank yous. To his dog. To the pitcher for the Dodgers. To everyone standing there. I didn't want to watch but I couldn't pull myself away. I felt so sad. At the same time, this charismatic man, whom I loved, won the primary, would win the nomination, would win the election, would be the next president of the United States.

Kennedy's speech continued. "I think we can end the divisions within the United States. We are a great country, a selfless and a compassionate country. The country wants to move in a different direction. We want to deal with our own problems within our own country and we want peace in Vietnam." Maybe he could do it. Maybe he could stop the war.

"We didn't do enough," Marty said. "We fucking didn't do enough."

"Knock it off, Marty," Hook said. "You worked your heart out. Move on."

Hook was right. Enough was enough. I walked over and sat next to Marty, my hand on his knee. Kennedy finished. "So, my thanks to all of you and now it's on to Chicago and let's win there." He gave a thumbs up and a peace sign. Then Kennedy's right hand moved to his head where he brushed back his hair.

"Marty, you do that just like Kennedy," I said.

"Do what?"

"Brush back your hair."

"No, I don't."

"Watch him sometime. You do it almost exactly like him."

Marty turned back to the TV trying hard not to push the hair out of his eyes. We stared as the crowd screamed, "We want Bobby! We want Bobby!" Kennedy left the podium, shaking hands and smiling, scratching the back of his head as he disappeared backstage. That was it. That was the end of it all. That was the end of Eugene McCarthy. That was the end of Bobby Kennedy.

I squeezed Marty's leg and stood up. "God, I'm tired," I said. I glanced back at the TV. Kennedy's advisors left the stage. Marty didn't move. He stared at the TV, at the crowd of supporters mulling around the ballroom floor not wanting to leave their celebration.

While I gathered empty cookie bags and Jake and Jeff moved couches back against the wall, Marty stayed glued to the TV and the crowd yelling, "RFK! RFK! RFK! RFK!" None of us said a word. Hook stood against the wall; his arms crossed over his chest.

I sat down next to Marty again. "It's over, Marty. McCarthy lost." The crowd on the TV turned silent.

Marty looked at me, then back at the TV. "Something's happened."

"What do you mean?"

"Look."

The people near the stage were no longer celebrating but looked towards the door where Kennedy exited. They seemed confused, frantic. A woman on stage put her hands to her mouth and appeared to cry. Advisors pushed, trying to see what was going on. I heard someone on the TV say, "What happened? Do you know?"

I grabbed Marty's hand.

Two people came to the microphone, shocked looks in their eyes. "Please stay back. Everybody please stay back. If there's a doctor come right here." Jeff sat down next to me and took my other hand. Hook moved from the wall to a chair next to the TV. Jake and Ginger stopped what they were doing. A series of people took the microphone calling for help, calling for people to leave.

"Is there a doctor? Would a doctor come right here? We need a doctor right here at the microphone immediately." Frantic movement on the stage. Confusion. Chaos. "Please stay back. Please stay back. Is there a doctor? We need a doctor. It's very important. Quiet please. The best thing everybody can do here is, in an orderly way, leave. Would you please do that? Please, in an orderly way clear the room." They kept saying it over and over and over again. *Leave the room in an orderly way. Leave the room in an orderly way.* What was going on? Why do you need a doctor? Tell us something. "Would you please do that? Would you please do that for us? Would you move out quietly?" Tell us what is going on.

Stephen Smith, Kennedy's brother-in-law, took the stage and in a calm voice tried to get everyone to leave. "We don't know what's happened, but all of this noise and confusion is not going to help." It didn't work. Nobody was leaving. They wouldn't tell anybody what happened. People clung to each other crying. A young man wearing a sweater and jacket took the microphone and said, "Ladies and Gentlemen. Ladies and Gentlemen. We have a doctor now. Will you please clear the room? And offer your prayers at this hour." Prayers for what?

It had been seven minutes since Kennedy left the podium and all anyone said was *Clear the room. Please clear the room. Please clear the room. You can help us by clearing the room. You can help us most by clearing the room. Please clear the room. Please clear the room.* It became a mantra. We didn't move. We couldn't clear the room. No pillow slamming. No talking. Silence as we watched.

Someone said to the crowd, "If you do not leave the room, we cannot get medical aid to the Senator so would you please leave or would you rather stand and cause confusion."

Medical care? What happened? *Are there any more doctors? We need more doctors.* It must be serious. *Proceed to the exits.* Tell us something. We don't want to leave until we know what's going on. The police took the microphone and asked people to clear the room. The press cornered people to ask what happened. Nobody commented. Nobody knew.

Calling for a doctor. Please somebody help us.

Finally, a voice of a newscaster. "Indication now is that Senator Kennedy himself has been wounded." He told us two doctors were helping the Senator, but he didn't know any more than we did at this point. Something terrible had happened. *Leave the room. Leave the room.* Aides were still not saying anything. *I can say nothing. I can say nothing. Are there any more doctors in the house? If not, could you clear the room and find some?*

A group of men huddled on the stage talking face to face with each other. One stood up. "This is Terry Drinkwater, CBS news. We've had indication of clarification of exactly what has happened back there." What does that mean, "indication of clarification?" Just say it. He did. "Senator Kennedy was involved in a shooting. And a newsman was involved, and one other man was involved. There are now three doctors back there caring for them." *A lot of blood. They are taking ice into the room.*

They interviewed someone who said there were several shots fired and there was panic. They brought out an injured woman and put her on a table so doctors could tend to her.

Another woman said she saw them put Kennedy in the ambulance. *He was unconscious. Not moving.* Another man said he gave the senator a pair of rosary beads and Kennedy looked straight up. *I said the act of contrition. I am sure he heard it. He was alive.* The man said he thought Kennedy was shot from the rear of his neck and that it was a male who did the shooting. Time crept by, seconds moved slowly. *Clear the room. Clear the room.* We were silent.

The words came at us, chaotically, quickly. I couldn't make sense of them. *Here's what we know. Six shot revolver. Hit in the head.*

Hit in the hip. Surgery needed. Color good. Assailant white. Three others shot. Unidentified man. A woman. A boy. Good Samaritan Hospital. Intensive Care. Good enough condition to be moved. Rosey Grier, bodyguard with New York Giants, apprehended the assailant. Small caliber revolver. Definitely hit more than once. Fell to the ground. Cognizant. Awake. Wife came to his side and talked to him. He was on the floor. Packs of ice. They've given him last rites. Shrieks. Pandemonium. Remembering 1963. Remembering another Kennedy.

We watched for forty minutes. We watched for an eternity. I want to go back in time. I want to go back to when the fireflies were alive. Back when the world was easy, when the world made sense.

In the end, one bullet lodged near the base of his neck, another atomized in his brain, a third out his chest. Marty put his hand on his head. The tears rolled down his cheeks. He broke the silence. "Fuck," he said, almost to himself. "King. Now Kennedy. Fuck."

I showed up for my exam a few hours later. It reminded me of taking my exams the semester before, worried I might be pregnant. I couldn't concentrate on Totalitarian Regimes Throughout History. Every time I tried to write something down, I heard, *"Can you please clear the room. Kennedy's been shot."*

After my exam, I tried to study for my next exam, but it was no use. I watched the news all day: the shooting, John Kennedy's assassination, John and Bobby's wives, stoic, composed, a model for how we all should act. Fuck that.

The victory speech. The hair pushed back. The peace sign. "On to Chicago and let's win there." The walk to the pantry. The shots. The 17-year-old busboy handing him a crucifix as he lay on the floor. Those staring, hopeless eyes.

I was asleep in my bed when Bobby Kennedy died at 1:44 a.m. the next morning. My professor cancelled the exam.

* * *

The Forester
Contributor Column
By Becky Jamison

The Lake Forest College community has been shocked by the second assassination of a major figure this spring. Bobby Kennedy died on June 6 after being shot following his California primary victory.

Kennedy's body was flown back to New York City where he lay in state so those who loved him could pay their respects. The young, the old, the poor, the black, and the disenfranchised came by the thousands to walk past his coffin lying at the great high altar at St. Patrick's Cathedral.

Bobby Kennedy will be remembered for the passion with which he fought for civil rights. He desegregated the justice department and sent U.S. Marshals to protect the first black student at the University of Mississippi. He was instrumental in getting the Civil Rights Act of 1964 passed.

We remember Bobby Kennedy and pray for his family.

* * *

We watched his funeral, this noble and decent man who would be President. Bobby Kennedy's brother, Teddy, gave the final goodbye. "My brother need not be idealized or enlarged in death beyond what he was in life, to be remembered simply as a good and decent man who saw wrong and tried to right it, saw suffering and tried to heal it, saw war and tried to stop it." Teddy paused, a catch in his voice. "As he said may times in many parts of this nation to those he touched and who sought to touch him, 'Some men see things as they are and say why. I dream things that never were and say why not.'"

There was no 'why not?' There was only an ugly 'why.'

The door to the cathedral opened as the strains of the Hallelujah Chorus filled Fifth Avenue. Kennedy's coffin was taken for burial by train on a slow ride to Washington. Mobs of people lined the length of the tracks from beginning to end.

"Maybe something good will come out of this. After President Kennedy died, Congress passed Civil Rights legislation to honor him."

"A lot of good that did, Becky. Civil Rights legislation didn't end segregation. King is dead and we still have discrimination in this country. Nothing good will come out of this." Marty said.

"Maybe it will, Marty. Maybe Congress will end the war to honor Martin and Bobby. Maybe segregation will end."

"Don't count on anything good to come out of this," Marty said. "Don't count on anything to ever be good again."

The hope that comes from new beginnings began to fade. The pain was deep. I didn't know it could go deeper.

U.S. Soldier Body Count: 28,374

Chapter 16
"Do You Want To Know A Secret?"

We celebrated Jake's graduation at a white, wooden farmhouse in the country five miles west of Lake Forest that Marty rented for the next year. Jeff and I were moving into the attic room. Ginger was taking the first-floor bedroom. Marty was in one of the second-floor bedrooms. He hoped to find someone to take the other room on the second floor. Marty invited Hook but he chose to rent a small apartment in town.

We started the celebration by throwing random flower seeds in the back yard of the farmhouse. Then we went inside and toasted Jake. Marty started. "Jake, you have been my mentor for two years. When my brother got injured in Vietnam, I was angry at the war and what it did to him. You took my anger, shaped it, and gave it purpose. What will we do without you? Thanks, man."

My turn. "Jake, you had me hooked with that speech nine months ago in Bradley Hall. Your heart, spirit, passion, dedication, intelligence. I can't imagine you not being here. What am I going to do without your guidance and wisdom? Thanks for being true to who you are. Thanks for reminding me to always be true to who I am." I glanced over at Ginger then finished, "By the way, I am going to love having Ginger all to myself next year."

"Except for nearly every weekend when I come visit or she comes down to Chicago." Jake grinned.

"My turn," Hook put his arm around Jake. "This is the man." He patted Jake's chest with his hook.

"Watch it with that thing," Jake laughed.

"When the rest of the campus couldn't figure out what to do with me, Jake was there. 'Expect to see you are the meeting.' 'We're handing out literature to commuters.' 'We need someone to sit at the table.' The guy wouldn't shut up. And because of him I found all of you. I love you, man."

Jeff was next. "I started going to anti-war meetings because I knew Becky was going." He grinned and put his arm around me. "But then the movement seduced me, and, in the process, I got some amazing friends. Good luck next year, my friend. We're only thirty miles away."

"The anti-war movement is in good hands with all of you." Jake lifted his glass in a toast. "I have no doubt you are going to do great work next year. I promise to come back for any event or action you plan."

"We'll hold you to that," Jeff said. The toasts were over. The party ended. We said our goodbyes.

My final hug was from Hook. He held me. "You take care of yourself, Becky. If you need anything over the summer, call." He gave me a card with his mom's phone number on it. "Promise me you'll be careful."

"I promise."

Jake was moving to Chicago to start his two years of alternative service. Ginger would stay with him for the summer. Marty was spending the summer in his hometown working parttime bagging groceries. Hook was heading home to Cleveland to stay with his mom. The garden seeds were left untended.

"How will I survive three months without you?" I said as Jeff drove me to the airport. I was heading home to work again at the summer camp for children with disabilities. He was heading to

Boston to take care of his parents' estate. We would meet back in Chicago the end of August for the Democratic National Convention.

* * *

Jeff promised to write every day and as promised, every day I got a brightly colored green, neon envelope. Every day I wrote back. In July he moved in with old friends from his days at Northeastern University.

"I finished with my parents' estate. Hoping to get a job for the rest of the summer. It will give me something to do."

I hated Sunday. No mail call. I hated July 22nd. No letter. I hated July 23rd. No letter. I hated July 24th. No letter.

The letters simply stopped. I didn't hear from him again until the last letter. I didn't know it was the last one. I waited for another.

All it said was, "Quit my job today. I'm transferring back to Northeastern for my last semester. They're willing to take me back. It's been fun. Stay cool." Signed Jeff. I read it again, hoping I missed some words. It said the same thing the second time, the third time, the fourth time. Each time it said exactly the same thing.

He wasn't coming back. Not ever. Not, I still love you and we'll keep in touch. Just I'm not coming back. Never.

There were two more weeks of camp. I woke up my campers, took them to breakfast, did exercises on the lawn, hiked to the edge of the forest, taught swimming, sang around the campfire. It was torture. All I kept thinking about was Jeff. All that went through my head was, "I'm transferring back to Northeastern. It's been fun. Stay cool."

My dad wrote my mom every day when they were in college. She still has all the letters. They are bound together in a crimson ribbon. I was going to save all the letters Jeff wrote, tie them up in a florescent yellow ribbon, and put them in a box in my closet so our daughter could read them one day like I do with my parents' letters.

I wrote back. "We can work this out." I didn't hear from him. I had to get to Boston so we could figure it out.

Camp dragged on and on. Campfires, s'mores, and hikes. Swimming, canoe rides, and sing-alongs.

Time goes by. Step by step it passes. Excruciatingly slow when we want it to go fast. Too fast when we want it to slow down. Finally, on August 17th, the campers left. I drove home, packed the car my parents bought me knowing I'd be living off campus, and said goodbye. I drove, possessed, to Boston. I intended to drive until I couldn't go anymore. Sleep in a cheap motel. Finish the trip the next day. All thousand miles of it.

The odometer clicked off the miles. Mile one. Mile two. Mile three. Three point one. Three point two. Relentless clicking. Mile four. Mile five. I got caught in a traffic jam in Cincinnati. The Reds baseball game just ended. I was stuck on the highway with fans honking horns and waving pennants. I didn't care about the Reds. I cared about, "Northeastern has taken me back for the last semester. It's been fun. Stay cool."

The traffic stopped. "Fuck you, Jeff." I yelled at no one in particular, hoping the ten-year old girl in the car in front of me waving her pennant out the window couldn't hear. "You can't do this to me. I gave you everything. You can't just say, 'Stay cool.'" He did.

I couldn't allow myself to cry. If I cried, I wouldn't be able to drive and I had to drive.

By the time Cincinnati cleared out I'd been on the road for four and a half hours and gone one hundred and twenty miles of a thousand-mile trip. I was twelve percent of the way there. At this rate I'd never arrive. I'd never find out. I'd never know.

By eleven o'clock that night, I couldn't drive another ten yards. I found a cheap motel, got the key to room eight, ripped the paper off the toilet that told me someone had sanitized it for my personal use, and crashed on the bed without changing my clothes or brushing my teeth. I was halfway there.

I woke up as the sun came up, splashed cold water on my face, and rinsed the awful taste out of my mouth. My toothbrush was somewhere in my suitcase in the car.

Five hundred more miles, ten more hours. I should be there before dinner. Jeff and I could have a nice dinner and talk things out. If need be, we could do that long distance thing, stay together with calls and letters, visit during vacations. Then he could transfer back to Lake Forest.

In Clarksburg, West Virginia, I passed a sign pointing north to Pittsburgh, one hundred miles. My eyes filled with tears. I pulled over to the side of the road. My mom grew up in Pittsburgh and my parents married there. I needed to feel my parents' love affair. I needed to believe that I had the same kind of love affair, that it would work out, that it would be okay. I slammed my fists into the steering wheel. Then I opened the door of the car, walked to the passenger side, pulled down my pants and peed. I didn't give a damn if the whole world watched.

I got back in the car, put three lifesavers in my mouth, one cherry, one pineapple, one orange. I took a deep breath, wiped my eyes, and pulled back onto the highway. The road to Elmira disappeared in the rearview mirror as I drove east.

About a hundred miles out of Boston I stopped at a Texaco station to fill up. On the rack next to the bathroom was a map of

Boston for sale. I circled the street where Jeff lived and mapped out the shortest route.

I reached Boston at four. Bad timing. The whole world was heading into or out of Boston. The whole entire world. The cars moved at snail speed. "Damn, damn, damn. Get out of the way," I yelled at no one in particular. I passed Fenway Park going a mile an hour. At that rate I could pull off the highway, go to a ballgame, and not lose any time. It was tempting. I love baseball.

I finally exited the highway, turned down a side road, and pulled over to look at the map again. I was still miles away through back streets. An hour later I found a parking place. I walked up to the house where Jeff lived. I could hear the Rolling Stones. I took a deep breath and knocked on the door.

A very stoned looking girl wearing a long, peasant skirt answered. She didn't say anything. "Hi," I said.

She stared at me. I looked behind her into the living room. The curtains were drawn, and it was dark. I didn't see Jeff.

"Is Jeff around?" I asked.

She stared at me. "Huh?" She grabbed onto the doorframe to steady herself.

"I said, is Jeff around?"

"I know you." She poked me in the chest. "You're that girl of his. I recognize you from the pictures in his room." She turned towards the living room. "Turn the record player down. I can't hear myself think." Nothing happened. "Hold on a minute," she said as she went into the dark living room and turned down the music. She still hadn't invited me in.

She came back to the door. "Now what did you say you wanted?"

I was getting impatient. Her hand on the doorframe blocked the way in. "I'm looking for Jeff. Can I come in?"

She moved out of the way and gestured with her arm. "Be my guest." The only light on in the house was a 40-watt bulb in the hallway. It took a second for my eyes to adjust. This is where Jeff lived. A tattered red chair with only one arm, an old couch with a blanket and sheet thrown over the back, a beanbag chair on the floor with someone asleep in it, a coffee table with ashtrays overflowing with cigarette butts and what was left of those twisted ended cigarettes, plates, bottles, cups on every surface. The room was filled with smoke and smelled of incense, cigarettes, marijuana. I hate the smell of incense.

I turned towards the woman who answered the door. "Is Jeff here? If not, do you know when he'll be back?"

She stared at me. "Well, I'm not quite sure where he is right now and I'm pretty sure he's not coming back." She took a pack of cigarettes out of the pocket of her skirt, put one in her mouth, and lit it. She offered me one. I declined.

"Why? Did he move?"

She inhaled, put her head back, exhaled, and laughed. "Nope. Jeff's dead. He overdosed a couple days ago."

All I could get out of my mouth was, "What?"

"I said Jeff's dead. He overdosed a couple days ago. Do you want to go through his stuff?"

Nothing worked in my brain. I needed to sit down before I fell. I walked over and sat on the red chair. She followed me. I sensed something was terribly wrong here, terribly, terribly wrong. "What did you say?"

"Look. We could really use his room. Someone's been sleeping on the couch at night. Do you want to go through his stuff?"

I looked up at her and said as calmly as I could, "What are you talking about?" Overdosed on what? He doesn't use drugs like that. I wanted to run out of there. To not face the truth, another truth that someone was dead.

She looked down at me and spoke loud and slowly as though I didn't speak English. "I don't know how I can be any clearer. Jeff is dead. Do you want to go through his stuff?"

My brain went numb. I couldn't feel. I couldn't think. Thank God for that. If I'd been able to realize the truth at the moment, I wouldn't have been able to do what I had to do. "Yes, I would like to go through his stuff." I followed the girl.

"Here's his room. Good luck."

I went in and shut the door behind me. Enough light came through the window that I could see what Jeff had been here, who he had been. An old, dirty, double mattress on the floor with a crumpled-up sheet half-on, half-off the bed. A caseless pillow with stained blue and white ticking. A pile of clothes in the corner. A dresser against one wall with every drawer pulled out a little, except the bottom one. An ashtray on the floor by the bed filled with cigarette butts and the remains of joints. Another on the dresser. Jeff never smoked cigarettes. Did he? Here? Why? A small table under the window with a folding chair under it. On the table a half-filled pad of green, neon paper and a box of matching envelopes. A pile of papers stacked on the edge of the table. Dirty dishes on every surface, rotten fruit.

I couldn't make sense of the room. I wanted Jeff. I wanted to feel him again. I wanted him to cup my chin in his hand and kiss me. The woman kept telling me he was dead, but he had been here. He had been alive here. He slept here and wrote me letters here.

I walked to the table. On the top of the pile of papers was the last letter I'd written, unopened.

I looked around the room ever so slowly. I sat on the mattress, grabbed the pillow, and held it to my face, hoping to have one last smell of him. The pillow didn't smell like him. It smelled dirty and musty. And then I cried. Finally. Jeff was the first boy who ever said he loved me. He was my life, my future, my everything. I couldn't breathe. I looked around the room again. I wanted something to hold onto, something that made sense. Something that didn't smell musty and dead. The brown leather jacket was on top of the pile of clothes in the corner. I crawled over to it, dragged it back to the bed, put it on, laid my head on the musty, mildewed pillow that held his head, and fell asleep. When I woke up, it was dark.

Jeff was still dead.

I stood up and found my way to the wall, feeling for the light switch. A lone 100-watt bulb lit up the room. On the wall, next to the light switch, were two pictures, each held up with one tack, both hanging at a slant. One was a picture of me with my hand on my hip reaching for the camera to get him to stop taking pictures of me. The other picture was of both of us taken by the school photographer during a softball game. Jeff hit a home run. I met him at home base and jumped into his arms. We both had our heads thrown back and we were laughing. It appeared in the campus newspaper the next week. I took the picture of both of us off the wall, sticking the tack back in the wall. I held it to my chest and slid down the wall to the floor, tears flooding.

I didn't want to move but I had to do whatever it meant to go through his stuff. I put the picture of us in the inside pocket of the brown leather jacket I still wore, went over to the top drawer of the dresser, pulled it out and poured everything on the bed. "Everything" wasn't much. Most of his stuff was packed in boxes, left in a small room in the basement of his dorm. For a guy who claimed he had a lot of money from his parents' estate, he sure had a pile of junk. There were three pairs of underwear, two pairs of socks, four pencils, the pocket watch that I remembered him telling me belonged to his dad, a blue ceramic pipe, a smaller wooden pipe, a pack of rolling papers, and a bag of marijuana. I pocketed the watch, the two pipes, and the papers. I left the bag of marijuana. I have no idea why.

I emptied the second drawer and then the third. I found the olive-green long sleeve t-shirt with three buttons at the neckline. It was my favorite shirt. I threw the stuff I wanted to keep on the mildewed pillow. I found a similar dark blue shirt with holes in the elbows. It went in the keep pile.

Suddenly I desperately wanted his well-worn leather belt. It reminded me of him, of us. I went through all the clothes in the dresser, all the clothes in the corner. It wasn't there. I jerked all the clothes out of the closet. The thought crossed my mind that maybe he was wearing it when he died. I would have to go to the morgue to find it. I needed it. Then I saw the belt in a pair of pants under the window. When I went to pull out the belt, I saw a piece of rubber tubing next to a needle on the floor.

My stomach lurched. I ran out of the room. Most of the vomit made it into the filthy toilet, the rest on the seat. I didn't worry about cleaning it up. When I came out of the bathroom, that woman stood there in the hall, the 40-watts of light reflecting off her face. "You okay?" she asked me.

I stopped. "Who are you anyway?" I asked.

"I'm Linda. Are you okay?"

I walked up to Linda and stood not more than six inches from her face. "You fucking bitch," I said to her. "This is all your fault. He'd never choose to live in a dump like this."

"He called me. He was desperate. Said he knew I could help him. Could he move in."

"Help him with what? He didn't need you. He needed me."

"I was the one who made him write to you every day. We'd shoot some stuff together. I'd hand him a piece of that neon green

90

paper. 'Write to Becky. Tell her the truth.' He'd write and probably say sweet nothings. Never told you the truth, I'm guessing."

"You turned him into a user."

She took a puff of a cigarette and blew the smoke in my face. "Believe what you want. Jeff was an addict for as long as I have known him, probably longer. And believe me, I have known him."

"Shut up," I yelled at her. "You're lying. I knew him. You didn't know shit about him." I tried to get by her. I wanted to finish 'going through his stuff' and get out of there.

She grabbed my arm and put her face close to mine. Her breath had the acrid smell of sleep and decay combined with marijuana, cigarettes, and booze. "Did you ever see his arms? Did you ever see him wear anything but a long sleeve shirt? Did he ever even take that jacket off?" She grabbed hold of the collar of the brown leather jacket.

I slapped her hand. "Don't ever touch this jacket."

Linda laughed, an evil laugh. "Did he ever just not show up? Did he ever just leave? Think about it. Your boyfriend lived and died an addict."

The acid churned in my stomach again. I ran to the bathroom, retched, and knew that was all there was. Next time it would be pure, acidy bile. I picked up the seat because it had vomit all over it and stooped over the bowl to pee. I left it there without flushing. I splashed some water on my face, rinsed out my mouth, and finger-brushed my teeth with the last squeeze of toothpaste from the tube I found on the corner of the sink. I looked at my reflection in the mirror. It wasn't me, but it was. It was me without him.

I left the bathroom and brushed past Linda. I didn't give a shit about her anymore. I didn't give a shit about her bathroom or vomit on the toilet seat or empty toothpaste tubes or cleaning up the dirty dishes in Jeff's room. I wanted out of there.

I went back in the room. I was angry. At Linda. At heroin. Mostly at Jeff. How dare he do this to me? How did he expect me to go on living? I frantically looked through all his clothes trying to find a short sleeve shirt, an undershirt, anything to convince me Linda was wrong. Why didn't I ever notice? I spent many nights in his arms and never noticed. Or I didn't want to notice.

Jeff had been an addict all along. He was a fucking addict. Everything he told me was a long list of addict lies. In the fourth drawer I found a small baggie with white residue stuck on the side and a small box I was afraid to open. I left them in the drawer.

I had to get out of there. I had to. I couldn't. I had to. Fuck him. Fuck her. What could I do? I had to get out of there. My eyes focused on a backpack in the corner of the closet. I grabbed it. I stuffed in the green and blue long-sleeved shirts, the belt.

I looked at the pile of papers on the table. Was there something important in there? An electric bill? Who cared anymore? Turn off the damn electricity. His homework? Unfinished Psychology paper? Who cared? His transcript would be incomplete. I picked up the unopened last letter I wrote him. Maybe he saved all the letters I wrote to him. Maybe I could tie them in a florescent yellow ribbon and put them in a cardboard box in my attic. With my right arm I swept everything off the desk to wherever it landed on the floor. I threw the unopened letter on top. "Fuck you, Jeff," I yelled. Let Linda clean up this shit. Let Linda deal with his stuff.

I noticed a dog-eared copy of *Catch-22* on the floor by the bed. I had a copy but needed his. I took his wallet from the pocket of the pants. In it were his drivers' license, $17, and a picture of me. In the other pocket of the pants was a half-eaten package of five-flavored lifesavers. I put it all in the pocket of the brown leather jacket.

This was it. The last look of him. The last vision of where he was, where he lived, where he died. I couldn't afford any more tears. I couldn't afford any more vomit. I had to get out of there. I opened the door, turned off the light switch, and, at the last moment, ripped off the picture of me on the wall hanging there with one tack. I needed to remember how he remembered me. I closed the door of his nasty, dirty, mildewed, musty, moldy room without saying goodbye. That was the end of Jeff Ledford. I missed him fiercely.

"You deal with his stuff," I screamed to Linda. I walked out the door.

It was five in the morning when I got to my car. There was a ticket on the windshield. I didn't care. I ripped it up and threw it on the ground. I opened the front door of my car and threw the backpack on the passenger seat. Then I sat down, pounded the steering wheel, and screamed. The screams turned to tears. Nobody was around. They couldn't have done anything anyway.

I stopped at the first, open 24-hour a day 7-11 store I found. I spent the entire $17 on a package of NoDoz, two bags of Oreos, three packages of crackers and peanut butter, a cup of coffee, and five rolls of lifesavers: two five-flavored, one wintergreen, one peppermint, one cloves. I needed Mom with me. As I walked to the register, I saw packages of chocolate covered peanuts. When I was young, my dad and I had this thing for chocolate covered peanuts. Every now and then he'd wink and say, "Let's pretend we're depressed and go buy some chocolate covered peanuts to make us feel better." This time I really was depressed, about as low as I could get. I bought two packages. I needed Dad with me. I couldn't make it back to Chicago alone. I left Boston.

One thousand miles. At 50 mph it would take twenty hours. Add in a few gas stops, a few pee stops, I'd be in Lake Forest by 5:00 the next morning. I couldn't do it. I had to do it. I couldn't do it. The trip to Boston had been a thousand miles. I couldn't do another thousand. I had to. I had to get somewhere. How in the world was I going to travel a thousand miles on two hours of sleep and a huge hole in my heart?

I headed out I-90. I wanted to leave Massachusetts. If I left Massachusetts, things would be better. For some reason I believed the farther I drove, the easier it would get. It wasn't true but it kept me going. Another mile and I'll be all right. Another ten miles and it won't hurt so much. I drove like a maniac, high on NoDoz, coffee, Oreos, lifesavers, and a fierce determination to be where it seemed safe. Demon possessed, wanting to be home.

I followed the Erie Canal through New York. To keep awake, I sang a song I'd learned in fifth grade. *"You'll always know your neighbor; you'll always know your pal if you've ever navigated on the Erie Canal."* Maybe that was the problem. I hadn't navigated the Erie Canal, so I didn't know Jeff. It didn't make any sense. Nothing made any sense. I stopped for gas and to pee, bought another coke, took another NoDoz, and kept going.

The longer it went, the harder it got. Every hour I stopped to run around and breathe some fresh air. Every couple of hours I got another cup of coffee. At a rest stop outside of Cleveland, I closed my eyes and slept for a half hour. I replenished the Oreos, chose a cheese sandwich from a refrigerator in a convenient store, and bought another bag of chocolate covered peanuts. I turned the radio on loud, opened the windows, and pushed on through. I'd been on the road forever. I promised myself I would never drive through the night again.

It was just past 5:00 a.m. when I arrived at the two-story, white, wooden farmhouse where I was living this year. A porch with a swing filled the entire front of the house. Trees covered the front yard. I walked to the back of the house. In the garden grew a myriad of zinnias, marigolds, and other flowers in the hodgepodge way they'd been planted at Jake's graduation party. I knelt by the flowers and picked a pink one, an orange one, and a purple one.

I fell asleep on the porch swing, my hand still holding the three drooping flowers. Two hours later a slamming screen door woke me. I opened my eyes. A long-haired, bare-footed guy in faded blue jeans frayed at the cuff walked down the front stairs, followed by a small, brown and white wiry haired dog. The guy's hair came to the middle of his back in soft, wavy, light brown curves. The dog's hair looked more like a Brillo pad.

I looked around. I was here. Jeff was dead. I didn't know what to do. I couldn't breathe because of the crushing weight of his absence.

The dog returned, bounded over to me, stuck her nose in my hand dangling off the porch swing, and demanded a pat. I was scratching the dog behind the ears when the bare-footed guy came up the stairs, his hand full of radishes. He pulled a radish out of the pile, rubbed off the visible dirt, and handed it to me. I reached out to take it and looked into a gentle pair of deep brown eyes, compassionate eyes, benevolent eyes, silent eyes.

"Thanks." I tried to become a fan of radishes in high school the summer I headed to the hills of Tennessee with my church youth group to help build a church in the mountains. Local folks fed us lunch every day and fresh radishes were plentiful. I decided I would learn to love radishes that summer. I did learn to tolerate them but never love them. Today was different. When the silent guy handed me a radish, the ragged hole in my heart filled a tiny pinhole bit.

I bit into the radish. The barefoot man without a name went into the house. The dog stayed for one more scratch and then trotted through the still-open door. As they went in, Marty came out.

"Welcome to Chicago," Marty said, sitting on the swing next to me. "I see you met our newest housemate, Peter, and his dog, Suki."

"He gave me a radish. He didn't say anything." I finished the radish and threw the green top off the porch.

"Periodically Peter quits talking. He calls it a voice fast. Transferring junior, been in school for a while. Still has his student deferment. Not for long though."

"Where's Ginger?" My eyes filled with tears, the breath labored in and out. I wiped the tears away, but they wouldn't stay away. "I need Ginger."

"She's in Chicago with Jake. When's Jeff getting here?" Marty put his foot down to start the porch swing swinging.

"He's not coming." I looked around frantic. "When is she coming back? I need to talk to her."

Marty stopped the porch swing and turned to me, "What do you mean he's not coming? Becky are you okay?"

"I'm fine," I started the porch swing swinging again. "I need Ginger is all. When is she going to get here?" I threw the three, drooping flowers off the porch next to the green, leafy part of the radish.

He stopped the swing with his foot. "Becky, she'll be here in a couple days. Are you sure you're okay?"

I turned to Marty. I didn't know what to say. I didn't want to hear I told you so. I didn't want to hear I'm so sorry. I didn't want to hear time would take way the goddamn pain. I didn't want to hear it would eventually be all right. I didn't want to hear that everything happens for a reason. Nothing I said would make any sense and nothing Marty said would make any difference. I started the porch swing swinging.

I tried to speak but the words wouldn't come out. They stopped halfway up. I jumped off the swing, bolted off the porch, and vomited the last twenty-four hours onto the top of the radish greens and the three flowers. When there was no more, I said to Marty standing at the edge of the steps, "He's dead." I sat down in the grass. Marty came down, wiped off my mouth with the red bandana he always had in his belt loop, picked me up, and carried me into the house. He laid me on the tattered couch and covered me with a blanket. I turned to face the back of the couch, closed my eyes, and fell asleep.

I woke crying. Ginger was next to me. Hook sat in a chair across the room. Jake sat at the counter in the kitchen talking with Marty. Peter was cooking something at the stove. Everyone was there.

"You came," I said through my sobs. Then I looked at Hook. "You came." He smiled and raised his hook.

"I'm not going anywhere. None of us are going anywhere," Ginger said, handing me a cup of tea.

"Thanks," I took the tea and felt the warmth go down my nasty tasting throat. Ginger picked up her guitar and quietly began to play. It was what I needed. Tea and music always brought comfort.

Peter handed me a fork and plate of brown rice. "Thanks," I said again, not knowing if I could even keep anything down.

I didn't want to tell anyone what happened to Jeff. No one asked. I didn't want Ginger to say she noticed how Jeff disappeared. I didn't want to hear Marty say he made me promise that I would never let Jeff hurt me.

Hook sat next to me on the couch. "Don't say a thing," I said to him. I didn't want to hear Hook say he warned me to be careful, that he told Jeff if he hurt me he would have to answer to him. He took my hand and held it without saying a word. When I cried, he took the red bandana off his head and wiped my eyes with it.

Red bandanas saved me that day. Maybe it wasn't the bandanas. Maybe it was the people.

During those long nights, I slept on the couch. Someone always slept on a sleeping bag on the floor next to me. When I woke up in the middle of the night in a panic, not able to breathe, someone was there.

It went on for five days. One day I said, "He overdosed. He stuck a needle in his arm and shot too much heroin into his vein and he died. I had to go through his stuff." That seemed the important piece, that I had to go through his stuff. "Someone is going to have to go through the stuff he left at his dorm." Throughout the day bits and pieces of the story came out. The letter I got at camp, the drive to Boston, finding the house, meeting Linda, finding out he was dead, cleaning out his stuff, the drive to Chicago. My friends listened and never once, not once, not ever, not the whole time did anyone say, "I warned you about him." Never. They loved me and sat with me and fed me.

Marty and Hook went through his stuff in the small room in the basement of his dorm. There wasn't much. They donated most of it. Marty brought me the oversized sweater Jeff and I fit in together. "This sweater reminded me of the two of you together. Either Jeff wore it, or you, or both of you together." A nice gesture. It brought no comfort.

U.S. Soldier Body Count: 31,618

Chapter 17
"Summer in the City"

On August 26, my friends woke me up, made me take a shower, and took me into Chicago for the anti-war protests at the Democratic National Convention. I wanted to stay on the couch with the covers pulled up over my head. I wanted to stare into space, pick flowers, and eat Peter's radishes. I wanted to forget the war, forget the election. I wanted to die. I didn't give a damn. They wouldn't let me. We took the train to Chicago and gathered at Jake's two blocks from Grant Park.

A fragmented nation came to Chicago for the convention: the angry, the disenfranchised, the young, the poor, the black, the elite, the delegates, the candidates, and me. Ten thousand demonstrators confronted by twenty-three thousand police. The country and the convention were fraught with divisions. Eugene McCarthy captured the hearts of the anti-war movement. Bobby Kennedy captured a bullet. Hubert Humphrey captured the delegates. Chicago was about powerlessness and hopelessness, about the disaffected saying; *You can kill Kennedy. You can kill McCarthy's candidacy. But you can't kill our rage, our despair, or our dreams.* For me, Chicago was about being able to scream because Jeff was dead and always would be.

Hook never left my side as we marched in the streets of Chicago. At night, we gathered at the apartment where Ginger played her guitar. I tried to sing with her. The words stuck. Peter cooked meals. Marty and Jake made plans.

Violence erupted on day three. "Fuck you, pigs," I yelled at the police officers who dragged protestors through the park. I walked up and down the line of cops screaming obscenities at them. "You deserve to die, you jerks." Hook stood nearby, ready to pull me out of trouble.

Tear gas filled the air. "Shit." I covered my mouth with my hands. Hook tried to pull me from the melee. "I'm not leaving," I said, coughing, my eyes burning from the tear gas.

He handed me his red bandana. "Tie this over your mouth." The bandana helped me breathe and I could still yell at the police. I didn't care what I yelled. As long as it was loud I was sure it would get the rage out of me, get the sadness out of me. The tear gas let me cry.

I saw brutal aggression by the police. They beat protestors and kept tear gas flowing. We linked arms. "The Whole World's Watching. The Whole World's Watching." In view of millions watching on TV, police clubbed photographers, smashed cameras, and confiscated film.

It was what I needed. "Fuck you, pigs." It was the only thing I could think of to yell. I pushed forward and refused to disperse. Something hit a police officer on the face and the surge began with the police swinging nightsticks. Inside the convention hall, a nomination took place. The world didn't watch the convention. They watched us. The police surged forward. We didn't retreat. They started hitting. We stood our ground. I didn't care if I got seriously hurt.

Six police officers stepped out of a van in complete riot gear. Hook said, "Let's go Becky." I couldn't go, wouldn't go.

"Disperse now," a police officer said.

I took the bandana off my mouth so the officer could see it was me talking. "You disperse, asshole." I couldn't move out of the way of the nightstick as it smashed into my arm. It rose and smashed a second time. Then again, barely missing me, smashing into the head of the guy next to me. When the news stations announced that there had been a "display of naked violence in the streets of Chicago" they were talking about the guys in blue, public officials, paid by taxes to serve and protect. They weren't serving and they weren't protecting.

Blood streamed down my arm, staining my shirt and my pants. I screamed, "You fucking assholes. We're here to stay and the whole world is watching!"

Hook grabbed me and carried me away to an empty spot where he encompassed me in a hug, holding every single part of me. I cried and cried. If he let go, I would have fallen but he held me completely, the blood from my arm smearing his shirt. In his holding, I knew that someday I would come out of this fog, this grief, this anger. I didn't know how. I didn't know when. I only knew I would.

When the convention was over Hubert Humphrey, the Democratic nominee for President, was left to pick up the fragments of a broken society and mend a party. The antiwar effort was left with a legend. I was left with a four-inch, bloody gash on my bruised arm and a great big, jagged hole in my heart filled with unbridled rage, deep despair, and somewhere way down, a bit of hope.

U.S. Soldier Body Count: 31,752

101

OCCUPY WALL STREET ENCAMPMENT
OCTOBER 14-15, 2011
Zuccotti Park and Times Square
New York City

They were the occupiers, almost two hundred strong, many continuing their parents' legacy, fighting against injustice, working for peace.

These occupiers reclaimed public space to protest economic inequalities, corporate corruption, and greed. Since September 17, 2011, they lived in tents pitched in Zuccotti Park in the Wall Street financial district in lower Manhattan. The tents surrounded the kitchen that served hundreds of meals a day with food donated by thousands of supporters. On one side of the park was a media tent and a library with 5,000 donated books. On the other was a fully equipped medical tent.

Every day, along with throngs of supporters, occupiers walked the streets of New York City confronting the police and Wall Street about the one percent who owned the majority of wealth in our country, more than 40 trillion dollars.

Every evening the occupiers gathered for General Assembly. Matt stood on a stone wall, the first to speak. "Mic check," Matt said. Since it is illegal in New York City to use amplified sound on public property without a permit, five people standing near him repeated his words so the crowd could hear.

"Mic check," Matt said again. His human microphones echoed, "Mic check." His words echoed through the crowd. "We will not be deterred (echo) by the illegal actions of the police yesterday (echo). Our jailed comrades will receive legal representation (echo) by The National Lawyers Guild (echo). Tomorrow we march again to let the cops know (echo) we will not be intimidated by their brutal tactics (echo). We are not afraid (echo). The Direct Action group will meet following General Assembly (echo) at the northeast corner of the park (echo). Check the board by the library for the list of other working groups (echo) and for updates about the march tomorrow (echo)."

Matt stepped off the wall. As he walked away, he heard the next announcement. "Mic check." "Mic check." "The library group needs help (echo) cataloging the new books that arrived yesterday (echo). Meet after General Assembly by the Library (echo)."

Matt headed to his tent. He lay down on his sleeping bag, put his hands behind his head, and closed his eyes.

The hypnotic beat of drums startled Matt awake. General Assembly was over. He took a drink from his bottle of water, poured some on his black bandana, and used it to wash the sleep out of his eyes. He slipped the bandana through his belt loop.

Matt headed to the northeast corner of the park. As he walked past the kitchen, he took one of the remaining chocolate chip cookies donated by a local restaurant. Matt sent a text to his mom. "Choc Chip Cookies not as good as yours. Marching tomorrow. Will send details."

* * *

Matt tied the black bandana across his face and walked with hundreds of comrades through the streets of New York City.

"Whose streets?" someone yelled.

"Our streets," he replied.

A drum kept the beat as the group chanted.

"We are the 99 per cent. We are the 99 per cent."

They walked down the middle of the street towards Times Square, through the immobile cars. Drivers honked in support. Taxi drivers gave high-fives to the marchers. Tourists and curious onlookers watched from the sidewalks. The police kept a lookout from the sides, thousands of them, in full riot gear, battle-ready, hands on nightsticks.

"No justice. No peace. No justice. No peace," the marchers chanted. "Banks got bailed out. We got sold out."

The marchers were stopped by metal barricades. Matt walked up to one of the barricades, the black bandana across his mouth. "Do not go over the barricade," he heard a police officer say in a Brooklyn accent. Matt never moved his eyes from the officer in front of him.

A young man crossed over the barricade, and, in a flash, three cops threw him down, one pushing his face into the asphalt road, another ramming a knee into his back. The third cop pulled the protester's arms back sharply to handcuff him with zip cuffs. "The cuffs are too tight," the man yelled. The police dragged him to a waiting car, not loosening the cuffs.

A police officer yelled, "Off the street!"

Matt raised his arm. "Whose streets?" Matt yelled at the officer.

"Our streets." The nightsticks came out to the ready.

A police officer grabbed a woman and threw her to the ground, dragging her into the street by the straps of her backpack.

"She didn't do anything," Matt yelled. "Let her go." He pointed his camera phone at her.

Police on motorcycles advanced from the back. The motorcycles behind and the barricades in front pushed the protesters off the street and onto the sidewalks. Many ran down side streets, back from where they came, or forward, on the sidewalks. The brute force of the police stopped many from moving.

"Shit! Get off my foot," Matt heard a fellow comrade say. The motorcycles kept rolling.

"This is a peaceful protest. What you're doing is wrong," Matt said to the police officers in front of him who were looking anywhere but at him. "Your job is to protect and serve the people, not Wall Street," Matt said to a young cop. "This is about justice. You should be on our side," Matt said.

The cop made eye contact with Matt. "Walk over the line," Matt said to him. He didn't.

ARRESTS: 92

PART TWO

SOPHOMORE YEAR

1968-1969

Chapter 18
"What Becomes of the Broken Hearted?"

Another beginning. A beginning without Jeff. I wanted this one to be over, to have the pain stop.

I took possession of an empty place inside of me that wasn't there when Jeff was. And I took possession of the attic room. It became my refuge. My arm slowly began to heal. My heart took longer. I wasn't sure I would ever forgive Jeff or stop missing him.

I furnished the room with a Salvation Army mattress, a table scratched at one end that wobbled without a folded-up piece of paper under the back leg, a green folding chair with a cushioned seat, and a three-drawer dresser not big enough for my clothes. The rest of the clothes were in a pile in the corner or hanging on the row of five nails pounded into the wall to the left of the door. The window above the bed faced the side yard. The other window above the table faced the garden where I could watch the flowers turn brown and die.

On the wall to the right of the door next to the light switch I tacked the two pictures I took off the wall at Jeff's. A single picture of Jeff taken during that same softball game sat on top of the dresser. He was rounding third and heading for home, laughing, his arms waving above his head. A perfect moment.

Over the bed to the right of the window I tacked up a poster with a vase of flowers that said, "What If They Gave A War And

Nobody Came?" On the opposite wall, above the nails that held my clothes was a psychedelic drawing of four children playing on a swing set. It said, "War Is Not Good For Children And Other Living Things." Two McCarthy for President posters filled the remaining walls.

* * *

Fall, 1968. Vietnam escalated out of control. Our dream of a president who would stop the war was as dead as Bobby Kennedy lying on that hotel floor. The choices weren't choices at all. They rarely are.

That's how the fall semester of my sophomore year started. I was numb.

One morning, Peter came into the kitchen while I ate breakfast at the counter that separated the living room from the kitchen. He said, "Hi." That was the first time I ever heard him speak.

"Hi," I said back to him. "Thanks for the radish."

He smiled at me and poured some granola in a bowl covering it with milk. He turned to me. "I'm sorry about Jeff." That was it. Two sentences, if you call 'hi' a sentence.

It was nice to have Peter talking. He didn't say much but what he said meant something. Unlike me. I vomited words to fill the quiet, to fill a hole too big to fill.

Dr. Garson helped me register for classes. "I was so sad to hear about Jeff, Becky. He was one of the good ones."

"He was an addict. He died of an overdose." Maybe talking about it would help me get through the pain. Maybe letting it out would help. Probably not. Tears filled the corners of my eyes. "Sorry. I'm struggling to deal with it."

"Let's pick some classes for you that won't be too challenging."

I smiled. "Thanks."

"I'm teaching a Sociology of Politics class," he said. "We'll be talking about how politics, the war, and the civil rights movement inform each other."

Perfect. Add to that second semester French, World Lit, Intro to Art, and Abnormal Psychology to maybe find out why Jeff did what he did.

I survived the first few weeks of the semester with a lot of help from my friends. My housemates gave me normalcy. Every morning someone woke me up. Otherwise, I would have slept through the alarm.

They took me to campus. In between classes, I sat in Hixson Lounge and tried to do homework. When that failed, I strummed my guitar endlessly. They took me to anti-war meetings. They assigned me tasks to do, and I did them. At night, we sat around the living room studying, drinking wine, jamming on our guitars. Slowly, ever so slowly, the world began to make sense again. I held on to the memory of Hook's hug in Chicago.

Ginger was editor of the school paper that fall. One night after dinner, two weeks into the semester, she said, "Becky, you need to start writing again. I want you to write an article about Jeff. You knew him better than anyone."

"I can't write about Jeff. I'm too angry at him."

"You want to be a journalist? You have to write what's hard."

That night, I went up to my room, put a piece of paper in the typewriter, and typed, "Jeff Ledford died this summer. I hate him for leaving me like this. I will never forgive him for dying." I ripped out the paper and rolled in another. "Jeff Ledford lied to me for an entire year." I ripped it out and tore it up. It took me four days, but I submitted the article by the deadline, the only obituary Jeff would ever get. He deserved more.

* * *

The Forester
Contributor Column
By Becky Jamison

Jeff Ledford, class of 1969, died this past August in Boston, Massachusetts, in an apartment he shared with friends from his years at Northeastern University. He will be missed by the entire Lake Forest College community. Although he was only here a year, Jeff touched everyone who knew him. His love of music, his love of softball, his love of life, and his passion for ending the war in Vietnam were the hallmarks of Jeff's incredible spirit. He was preceded in death by his parents. He leaves behind dear friends who cherish the short time they had with him.

Bullshit.

* * *

Hook's apartment became my second home. His demons became mine. Mine became his. Fifty-five-gallon drums, dead bodies in black bags with white nametags, heat, humidity, asphalt, swamps, explosions, dead friends, rubber tubing, needles. I could make it with time and space and that's what Hook gave me. We poured wine and played cards.

"I hate Ripple," I told him as I took a sip of wine and dealt out the cards.

"Best wine there is," he said.

"Gin." I put down my cards.

"That's nine in a row." Hook shuffled and dealt another hand. "How do you keep winning?"

"I practiced. My dad told me if I could beat him in gin, he'd buy me something. It took me months and I finally won." I picked up a card and discarded a jack.

"What did he buy you?"

"A tether ball set for the back yard."

Hook laughed. "Anything you wanted and you chose a tether ball set?" He picked up the jack and discarded a seven of spades.

That filled in my straight. I picked it up. "Any eleven-year-old would choose a tether ball set. Anyhow, he gave me good tips. Like, never pick up a card from the discard pile unless it fills in a set or run of three." Hook moved his hand from the discard pile and drew one from the deck.

I loved Slap Jack with him most of all. Try beating a hook slapping down on a card. Gets the adrenaline running.

* * *

I read an article about grief for my Abnormal Psych class. It said people usually grieve a month for every year they were with someone who died. If you lived with someone for twenty-three years, you grieved for twenty-three months. It wasn't true. I was with Jeff for less than a year. It had been a month. My grieving should be over. It lingered. Maybe because he lied to me all fall. Maybe because I know I should have listened to my dad, and I didn't. Maybe because of all the good ones I could have chosen, I chose the addict who jumped out of the tree. The sadness wouldn't last forever. It felt like it at the time.

The third week of September I sat strumming my guitar under the tree Jeff jumped out of and thought about how he seduced me with his eyes and éclairs. How could I have been so stupid? Marty sat down beside me. "Want to go get some lunch?" he asked.

I stopped playing, looked at Marty, and smiled. I put the guitar on the ground next to me and asked, "Why didn't you ask me out last year?"

"Homecoming last year. I asked you out. We were hanging up posters for the march in Lake Forest and I asked you out."

"Seriously, Marty. That's the best you got? As I recall, you asked me to the dance, and I said that I already had a date but that I would love to go out sometime. You never asked me again. If you had asked me again, everything would be different. Why didn't you?" I strummed my fingers across the strings of the guitar lying in the grass. I looked at Marty. "And don't you dare say you warned me about Jeff."

"I would never say that." Marty smiled at me. "I never got a chance to ask you out again. After the homecoming dance you and Jeff were pretty much a pair."

"If I had cancelled my date with Jeff and said yes to you, everything would be different now. I wouldn't have fallen in love, and it wouldn't hurt so much every single time I take a breath."

I took a breath. It hurt.

I looked at Marty. "He died, Marty."

Marty picked up my guitar. He didn't play often. He had TV to watch, newspapers to read, strategizing to do, plans to make, a movement to lead. But that day, under that tree, he took my guitar and played. I sat with my arms around my knees, my head lying on them, and listened. Like when I was young and scared at night and my mom sang me lullabies.

I don't know how long we sat there. He laid the guitar in the grass next to me. I looked over at him and smiled. "Thanks, Marty."

He leaned over and kissed me on the forehead. "Any time, Becky. I know this sounds stupid, but you'll make it through this."

"I know. I just don't know how do to it."

Marty grinned. "With one foot in front of the other." He got up and put out his hand to help me. "Let's go eat."

* * *

There were more moments of normalcy scattered in between my grief, moments when I forgot Jeff was dead, when anger and denial took a back seat. One Friday night I curled up on the couch reading. Peter cooked brown rice and vegetables in the kitchen and washed the radishes we always had at dinner. Ginger and Marty walked in the back door and Marty tossed a pile of papers on the coffee table in front of me. "Ideas for the teach-in. It's in a month. We need to start thinking." My God, Marty never stopped. I think if he stopped, the earth might screech to a halt.

Ginger said, "I think our focus needs to be on getting Humphrey elected. It's our only hope of stopping the war."

"I disagree." I closed my Psych book and put it on the table. "Most of the students here can't even vote yet. The only states that allow eighteen-year-olds to vote are Georgia and Kentucky. We need to keep the focus on the war."

"By the way, have you applied for your absentee ballot?" Ginger scooped up a pile of rice, covered it with vegetables and poured soy sauce over the whole thing. "You're from Kentucky."

"I don't have the energy to. Doesn't matter anyway. It's only one vote."

"Every vote matters," Marty said. "I'll make a deal with you." I didn't trust deals. Deals were always broken. "I'll call and order you an absentee ballot, put it in front of you, give you a pen, show you where to sign it, and then I'll mail it. Deal?"

"You have to buy the stamp."

"Deal." We shook on it.

It felt normal. Planning teach-ins was normal. Eating brown rice was normal. Making deals with Marty was normal. Ginger's notetaking was normal. Marty's pacing was normal. Peter's summarizing it all into a neat package was normal. It was as it should be.

"I think Hook should tell his story. If we want to get the students fired up, we need to put a face to what they see on TV," I said.

"I bet Jake would come and speak about his CO status," Ginger said.

I missed having Jake around campus. There was that thing about Jake being true to who he was, always being genuine. There was that thing about how he made me want to be genuine. I know I wasn't me right now. Having him come for the weekend might help. Maybe that would bring me back to myself.

"I agree with Becky," Peter put down a freshly popped bowl of popcorn. "Keep the focus on the war."

Marty paused, his hand in the popcorn bowl. "Sounds perfect." In the end, we decided that October's teach-in/be-in would be a two-day affair. A teach-in on Friday, classes cancelled. A be-in on Saturday, music, games, food.

I felt normal and alive.

When I woke up the next morning, Jeff was still dead and that dark hole engulfed me again. I couldn't understand why I could be so normal one moment and so empty the next. I wanted to pull the blanket over my head and slip back into the darkness. I picked

116

up the joint I always kept on the nightstand by my bed then dropped it back into the ashtray. This hole was too deep. Nothing would help me crawl out of it this time. Not wine. Not dope. Not anything. Nothing except the fact that I really had to pee.

I dragged myself to the bathroom, hoping I wouldn't encounter any of my housemates along the way. I didn't want to hear, 'good morning,' or 'there are pancakes on the table,' or 'the coffee is brewing.' I wanted to pee, get back in bed, and pull the blanket over my head.

I didn't encounter anyone on the way to the bathroom. I encountered something far worse. I got up from the toilet and turned the water on in the sink to wash my hands and rinse out the horrible taste I had in my mouth. I looked in the mirror. I stared back at someone I didn't recognize. She told me that it was time to pull myself together and get over it.

"Shut up," I told the person in the mirror. "You can't tell me how long I get to grieve. I can grieve the whole rest of my miserable life if I want to."

She looked back at me. She didn't look scared, alone, and miserable. She kind of looked like a sixteen-year-old me, when I had my first kiss, when I felt like a woman for the first time because I figured out how to use a tampon. She looked like me when I heard I had been accepted into Lake Forest.

"Leave me alone," I told the mirror. "I am not that person anymore." I lifted my arm to throw a paper cup at the mirror when she smiled at me. I knew that smile. That was the smile I had when Jeff taught me how to dance in a small room off the library after we shared five-flavored lifesavers, when we shared sticky orange segments at the lake.

That smile didn't fool me. I turned the water back on and splashed it on the face I knew was mine. When I looked back in the mirror, I was gone. It was just me with my horrible tasting mouth, stringy hair, and water dripping off my chin. I knew that me. That me would leave me alone.

"Good riddance." She wouldn't come back until I was ready. I had to go deeper, go darker before I found her again.

I stayed in bed until noon. Marty sat at the counter eating yogurt and fruit with granola on top when I emerged. He looked up at me. "God, you look terrible."

I gave him a sneer. I felt terrible. I was terrible. "Will I ever feel normal again?" I picked up an apple from the fruit bowl.

He looked up and smiled. "You never were normal." I threw the apple at him. Lucky catch. "Seriously. Your life is forever changed but you will feel okay again. I promise you."

On warm afternoons, Hook and I often walked to the beach, hook in hand. It was crazy, I know, but I felt comfort holding on to his hook. It was solid and steady, and it couldn't die.

One day we stood on the edge of Lake Michigan. Jeff's face, streamed in gold, flashed through my mind. I picked up a flat stone and tossed it in the water. It skipped twice.

"That was pathetic. I could do better with the hook." Hook put a stone in his hook and tossed it, five skips.

The stones always sank. Healing came slow.

We'd go back to Commons to eat ice cream sundaes. Hook put dimes in the juke box and pressed A7, "All You Need is Love." It was the worst of times.

* * *

Joseph Heller, author of *Catch-22*, was coming to campus the day after the election to talk about the life-altering implications of the book we discussed during freshman orientation. It seemed so long ago. It would be a great birthday present.

One night I picked up Jeff's dog-eared copy of *Catch-22*, crawled into bed, and started to reread it. As I read the best first line of any book ever written, "It was love at first sight," a piece of green neon paper folded into quarters fell out. I turned it over and saw my name written on the front. I started to open it up then stopped. I was still angry at Jeff. "Fuck him." I threw the note in the trash. I crawled back into bed, picked up the book, and read, "It was love at first sight." Then I read it once more.

"Love at first sight?" I thought. "Never has been, never will be." I'll never know why I put the book down, got up, walked over to the trash, pulled out the bright green paper folded into quarters, opened it up, inhaled sharply, and started to read. But I did.

"If you're reading this note, it means I didn't make it. It also means you came to Boston. I knew you would after you got that last letter. I needed you here. I needed you to convince me to come back to Lake Forest. Most of all, I needed you to help me." *Why didn't you write to me and tell me you needed me? Why did you only tell me you weren't coming back?* I kept reading.

"I ran out of time, though, shot too much, I guess. I tried all last year to beat this thing. I couldn't do it. It had me too hard. I didn't give up, but it wasn't enough. One more time, I'd say, and then I'll quit. It was always one more time. I'd stop for a day but then my brain would tell me I just needed a little bit, not much. I was too scared to tell you. I was afraid you'd leave me."

"I knew if you got to Boston and I was gone, you would take the book and find the note, my last love letter to you."

"I am sorry it ended like this. I wanted more than anything to get clean and go back to Lake Forest and spend the rest of my life with you."

I couldn't read any more. I couldn't stop.

"You have to know that you were the best thing that ever happened to me." *Shut up, Jeff.* Tears spotted the neon green paper. "I lied a lot to you last year." *No shit.* "But this is not a lie. I loved you completely with every part of my heart."

"Don't spend too much time missing me. Find someone else to love. You are the most incredible person I have ever met. Love forever, Jeff."

I wrinkled up the neon green paper and threw it on the floor under the table. I couldn't breathe. Every inhale was painful. I was convinced I was going to die. I crawled to the door, opened it, and tried to yell. Nothing came out. I kicked at the door, anything to make a sound. I kicked harder. God, please, somebody hear me. I don't want to die. I don't want to give him the satisfaction of destroying me like this. I gave up, curled up, and prepared to die.

Ginger found me in the doorway breathing hard and fast but not getting any air. "Marty, bring me a paper lunch bag fast," she yelled down the stairs. By then the lack of air turned into panic. Marty appeared and Ginger put the bag to my mouth. "Breathe," she said. I obeyed. My whole body hurt. "What happened?" I pointed to the green neon paper.

Marty picked up the wrinkled piece of paper, straightened it out, and read it. "Son of a bitch." Once I started breathing normally again Marty carried me downstairs. I leaned my head against his shoulder and cried. He put me on the couch and Ginger covered me up with an afghan her grandmother made.

Ginger read the note. "Goddamn Jeff," she said. That said it all. He dies and then reminds me of it. Just when I was beginning to have a good day every now and then. Just when I was starting to feel normal again Jeff reminds me of how much he claimed to love me, a love filled with lies. Fuck him.

The darkness took hold of me again and turned into a deep, black sadness. I walked around but it wasn't me walking around.

I couldn't shake it. Hook walked me to the lake to throw stones. That didn't help. He played gin with me. That didn't help. Ginger made tea. The deep dark blackness held on tight. Peter fed me brown rice, vegetables, and radishes while Suki lay on the couch next to me, her head in my lap. It hung around. Marty drove me to school, to classes, and to anti-war meetings. I took my guitar to Hixson Lounge on campus and played. It didn't help. I needed a bag of chocolate-covered peanuts. I needed a lifesaver. I needed my mom and dad but even talking to them on the phone didn't help. I was too ashamed to tell them the truth about Jeff.

U.S. Soldier Body Count: 32,219

Chapter 19
"Like A Rolling Stone"

Jake arrived the night before our big weekend. He pulled me up into a tight, long hug. It helped.

The administration cancelled classes Friday. We scheduled workshops throughout the day. A dozen professors conducted sessions about the economic, political, and historical implications of the war. Jake talked about his CO status. Hook told his story.

The be-in began at 3:00 on Saturday with Ginger singing. I sang with her on "Blowing in the Wind" and "Five Hundred Miles." For those few minutes, I forgot about Jeff being dead.

I saw Joe Scott Joe holding the same sign that said, "Love It or Leave It." I walked over to him. "Go back to your dorm, Joe. Quit embarrassing yourself." I walked away before he could respond.

I joined the softball game. I tossed my shoes and the brown leather jacket under a tree. Hook leaned against the tree and watched. I wore Jeff's olive-green, long sleeve shirt. My braids were intertwined with beads, my bangs long enough to fit into the first twist of my braids. Every ball pitched to me I blasted over the shortstop's head. I never made it past first, but I often made it home. I was home.

The game ended as the evening sun began to fade and the pink, polluted Chicago sky gave us one last look at its beauty. We sat on blankets and the band began to play. I wrapped Jeff's jacket around me a little tighter. A joint came my way. I toked and handed it to Marty. He passed it on. He always passed it on. I wondered why?

"Who wants to dance?" I asked. Marty shook his head, got up and walked over to the literature table. Hook shook his hook and took another drink of wine out of the cup he carried around most of the night. Ginger and Jake cuddled under a blanket. Peter was nowhere to be seen. I danced alone.

The lead guitarist was a goddamn good guitar player. He put the guitar over his head, turned his back to the audience, and played amazing rifts. He put the guitar up to his mouth and played with his teeth. He caught my eyes, held them there, my stoned eyes, my stoned, dead soul. He winked.

It was dark when the band finished their set. I had to get out of there. "I'm going to get some air," I said to Hook.

"We're outside," Hook said. "Air is everywhere."

I leaned down and took his hand and hook. "Come take a walk with me. I can't sit here any longer."

"I'm too drunk to move. But you be careful."

I kissed him on the head. "Why should I?"

I walked behind Commons not quite knowing where I was headed. I found myself at the coffee house, a small building behind Commons where folks gathered to drink cider, eat donuts, and play guitars. I hadn't been there all fall. It was dark. I reached for the doorknob knowing it was probably locked. The door opened. I turned and looked around to make sure no one was watching and walked into the darkness. Across the room I could see the end of a cigarette glowing in the dark.

"Who's here?" I felt maybe I should turn around and leave. The danger made me stay.

"Just me," I heard a voice say, low, dark, husky. "Care to join me?"

"How did you get in here?" I asked. I still couldn't see who it was but, as my eyes adjusted to the dark, I saw a path to where he sat in a metal folding chair, his feet up on the chair in front of him.

"I got in here the same way you did, through the door." He pulled a chair out from the table and patted the seat. "Want a cigarette?"

"I don't smoke nicotine," I tried to get a good look at him. I pulled a joint from my pocket, lit it, toked, and handed it to him.

"Thanks," he said as he handed the joint back to me. "I'm R.J."

"What does R.J. stand for?"

"Rob Jackson, same name as my dad. Very inconvenient. Folks have always called me R.J." He had the same initials I had, sort of like the guy I liked in the fifth grade who laughed at me when I fell up the stairs the first day of school. I also couldn't help thinking that he had one of those names that could go either way, like Joe Scott. His last name could be his first. Rob Jackson, Jackson Rob, who cared?

From the glow of his cigarette, I began to make out his face and realized he was the lead guitar player. "Becky Jamison. By the way, you are a damn good guitar player." I took back the joint.

"Thanks. Been playing since my dad gave me a guitar for my tenth birthday. You're a damn good dancer."

That's when I decided I would love to make out with his face. I still took my birth-control pills with the twisted idea that maybe Jeff wasn't dead and one day he would walk through the door. I needed to be ready. So, I was ready. R.J. looked dangerous and I needed dangerous. He looked rugged and I needed rugged. He looked sexy and I needed sex. I needed something to help me forget and R.J. might be the ticket.

I stifled the urge to take off my clothes and maybe feel normal again. "I don't know what the hell you're doing in here or how the hell you got in here. I do know that you have the same initials I do, because my first name is really Rebecca, and that's got to count for something." I looked around to see if I could find something to eat. I found some apple cider and a bag of day-old glazed doughnuts in the refrigerator. It would do.

"I learned how to pick locks at fifteen. It's the most important skill I know."

"Except for typing," I said. "I bet typing is more important."

R.J. put out his cigarette and the joint in the ashtray on the table in front of him. "Well, the lock picking got us both in here." With that, R.J. stood up and walked over to where I stood with the doughnuts. He took them from me and slipped my arms out of the brown leather jacket. He slid my shirt over my head. I reached down to undo his belt when he pushed me against the refrigerator. Pants off, he lifted me up, covered my mouth with his, entered me, pushed into me hard. We came, standing up, against a cold refrigerator in a darkened room we weren't supposed to be in.

There wasn't any love in the lovemaking. It didn't matter. It helped me forget for a few minutes.

I put on my pants, shirt, and the leather jacket. "That was about the most fun I've had since last June." The last time I saw Jeff alive. "I've got to get back or I'll lose my ride home."

R.J. took my arm as I started to walk away. "If you dare, my place tomorrow night. 9:00. Basement of Blackburn. Room 4."

"I'll be there." As I got to the door, I turned back. I could see the glow of R.J.'s cigarette across the room.

The next night I knocked on R.J.s door at five minutes after nine. He lived in a single room almost directly underneath where Jeff's room had been. He opened the door. "You're late," he said.

125

A bed, dresser, desk, a guitar stand in the corner with two guitars on it, and a poster on the wall with a big green peace sign and the words, "Make Love Not War" over the sign. I intended to do just that.

I looked at his collection of pipes on his dresser. I picked up a black ceramic pipe. "Do you ever think about going to Nam?"

"I figure if the war lasts that long, I'll go underground."

"What if they catch you, the Army, I mean?" I put the pipe back and walked over to him, ready.

"They'll never get me."

We weren't there to chat about Vietnam or look at posters. I wanted to keep on forgetting. He wanted to keep on getting laid.

I threw the brown leather jacket on his desk. The rest of the clothes landed wherever they happened to land.

I thought passionless sex might help. It never does, not in the long run. If God doesn't exist, then Jeff's gone, and I'll never see him again. Time doesn't heal. The lake doesn't heal. The dope doesn't heal. Sex doesn't heal. When a hole the size of your fist is ripped out of your heart, it never heals. It stays forever and every time you remember a little bit, a piece of your soul rushes out. If I lose my soul I may as well be dead. I may as well be dead anyway.

* * *

When R.J. wasn't there, I stayed stoned, particularly on dark and cold nights. That's when I missed Jeff the most. That's when I saw his face in the streams of light that filtered through the window. After all these weeks, Jeff was still there. With R.J.'s help, maybe I could fuck him out of my mind.

U.S. Soldier Body Count: 33,182

Chapter 20
"Lucy in the Sky with Diamonds"

Election day and my birthday arrived. I sat in front of the TV with Ginger waiting for results to come in. "It's nice having you here without R.J."

"It's hard when he's not around. My mind fills with Jeff."

"Do you think someone like R.J. is the answer?

"He helps me forget is all."

"Maybe you shouldn't be forgetting. Maybe you should feel it and get through it. You can't let Jeff win."

"There is nothing to win or lose here. Jeff is dead in case you forgot. Besides, what do you even know about pain, Ginger? You have no clue what I'm going through. Go to hell." I got up, intending to go upstairs, pull the covers over my head, and sleep, forget about dinner and birthday cake. Ginger blocked my way.

"I saw my dad beat my mom to an inch of dying right before he walked out on us. Two years later, I watched my mom die in front of my eyes. I was fifteen years old. One of her many bad boyfriends got her pregnant. She died on a table in some dirty motel room. The doctor's knife slipped trying to get that baby out of her. She bled to death and I couldn't do anything for her. What mother takes her fifteen-year-old daughter to a motel room to watch an abortion? Pain? You don't own it."

Ginger kept talking, wouldn't let me respond. "You think Marty didn't feel that pain when his dad died in Korea and his brother almost died in Vietnam? He relives it every time he visits him. When Jake was seven, he watched his four-year-old brother die of leukemia. We love you, Becky. But enough is enough. Pull your shit together."

Peter walked in from the kitchen carrying a tray with bowls of food and a carob birthday cake. He saw the tears streaming down my cheeks and handed me a napkin. "Ginger, now's not the time. Eat, Becky." That's all he said.

I didn't know why it wasn't the time, or when the time would be, or what time even had to do with it. Time wasn't helping. I wanted to eat and get this whole election and birthday thing over with.

Marty walked in, hugged me, wished me happy birthday, took a plate of food, and planted himself on the couch in front of the TV.

I scooped up a spoonful of brown rice, smothered it with soy sauce and topped it with a few alfalfa sprouts. Peter had taken to growing sprouts in a jar on the counter. He tried to convince me that I could physically live on sprouts. Emotionally I needed chocolate to balance it out.

I ignored Ginger. I didn't want to fight her. To scream at her. To admit she was right.

"Thanks for dinner, Peter," I said. He sat next to me on the couch and put Suki in his lap. She was due to litter any day.

"You going over to R.J.'s?" Marty asked.

"Why do you care? You have a world to save," I said. I don't know why I acted like that to Marty. He hadn't done anything except hug me and wish me a happy birthday. "And no, I'm not."

"You're better off," Marty said.

"What does that even mean, Marty?"

128

"It means what I said. You're better off without him." Marty scooped up some more rice from the bowl on the coffee table.

"Fuck all of you." The whole world was against me. Except Peter. He never seemed to be against me.

Marty stopped eating long enough to tell me that rice and alfalfa sprouts were a complete meal and, combined with carob cake, you couldn't get much better than that so why didn't I shut up.

"Shut up, Marty," I said back to him. I hated him at that point.

The phone rang. It was Hook.

"Happy Birthday, Becky. Watching election returns?"

"Yes. Why aren't you here? Everyone is being a complete jerk."

"Sorry. I had a paper to write. I finished it and am killing cockroaches. Come over if you want to help."

I grabbed the leather jacket and headed to the door. I really didn't care about who won, about Marty or Ginger or anybody else. Rice, alfalfa sprouts, and election returns have a way of doing that to me.

Ginger touched my arm as I walked towards the door. She had tears in her eyes. She put her arms around me. "I love you, Becky. Remember that."

I walked out the door without saying a word.

I knocked on Hook's door. He opened it; the red bandana tied around his head. I could hear the TV in the background.

"They were giving me shit." Hook gestured for me to come in. I took a toke of the joint burning in the ashtray.

"Where's R.J.?" he asked.

"Had to be someplace."

"You're better off," Hook offered me a glass of wine.

"Don't you start too." I thought, *Better off than what? Better off than being alone? Better off than sitting in my attic room obsessing about Jeff?*

Just what was I better off of?" I didn't ask him. I didn't want to think about it anymore.

"I hate Ripple," I said. I took a drink of wine.

"You already told me that. I love it," Hook said.

Before I got there, Hook had been stabbing cockroaches with his hook. He invited me into the kitchen to join him. "I have learned a lot about the art of cockroach stabbing," he said handing me a fork. "First, be very quiet and wait. When I say 'Now,' attack."

"Wait for what?"

"Hush and wait." Slowly a cockroach appeared up through the drawer and started walking across the counter. "Now," he said. We both stabled at the same time, he with the hook, me with a fork. I could have lost a finger except neither of us were fast enough to do any damage. Cockroach stabbing is an art and, apparently, we didn't have the talent.

"What do you think of the election returns?" I put the fork in the sink after we tired of our adventure, hoping Hook washed it before using it.

"Disappointed but not surprised. I figured Nixon would win." Hook walked over to the cupboards and opened them up. "I don't have much to offer in the way of a birthday celebration," he said, looking back at me. "How about graham crackers?"

"Got any frosting to go with them?"

"Best I can offer you is peanut butter." We finished off the box of graham crackers and played a couple games of cards. I beat him twice at gin. He beat me at Slap Jack. Something there is about that hook.

The clock struck midnight and my birthday ended. "Mind if I sleep on your couch?" I asked him.

"Take my bed. I'll take the couch." How could I resist? He walked me into the bedroom and gave me a hug. That was the real birthday present. That's why I came. And that's how I spent election night and my birthday, 1968.

* * *

Joseph Heller came to campus the next day. *Catch-22* was still my favorite, laugh-out-loud book. I loved the part about how if you're having fun, time seems to fly and life, therefore, goes by fast. It's better to be bored because when you're bored, time goes by slowly and life lasts longer. I was caught in a time warp. I believed time would heal me. Why was it going so damn slow?

Heller convinced us that we were all caught in a Catch 22. You had to be crazy to support this illegal war. If you opposed it, you weren't crazy and since you weren't crazy, you could be drafted. If you supported the war, you were crazy so you wouldn't be drafted. That was crazy because if you supported the war you wanted to be drafted which was crazy and they didn't draft you.

After Heller spoke, I went up to him with Jeff's copy of *Catch-22*. "Best book I ever read," I said. I handed Heller the book.

"Whom should I sign it to?" he asked.

"To Becky and Jeff," I said. Jeff would have loved it.

* * *

Ginger apologized. I forgave her. It was hard to remember what our argument was about. It took me longer to forgive Marty, but I finally did, not in time to wish him a happy birthday the next Friday. Peter hadn't told me what that time thing was all about. I went on. I couldn't stop. Something inside had broken and I wasn't sure it would ever fix itself.

U.S. Soldier Body Count: 33,816

131

Chapter 21
"Mr. Tambourine Man"

The guitars came out every night, Ginger on one chair in the living room, me opposite so I could see the chords she played. Marty sat on the couch, papers spread around him, organizing, writing the next petition, planning the next meeting.

I loved those times. Music healed. Jeff's face left the neighborhood of my mind for a little while Dylan, Pete Seeger, and Simon and Garfunkel took his place. I felt normal, alive, and happy.

Jeff eventually moved back in, and I needed R.J. to take over the rent. I needed R.J. so I could forget. I needed the dope and the cheap wine and the sex. That's what I saw in R.J.

One night, Ginger and I were figuring out an arrangement to "Mr. Tambourine Man." She played the first few lines. She stopped playing and looked at me. "I'll always be here for you. You know that don't you?" I counted on that. I shook my head yes.

"By the way, Becky," Ginger said. "I need one more article about the anti-war group before the end of the semester."

Besides music, my passion was writing. Despite everything, I hadn't missed a deadline. Ginger understood what it meant to have someone live in your head who needed to move out. Like her mom, Ginger had a string of bad boyfriends before she found

Jake. I figure every boyfriend ends up bad except the one you end up with at the end.

"When do you need it?" I asked.

Before she answered, Peter called from his bedroom where he went moments before. "Suki's having her puppies."

Within the hour, Suki's puppies were born, four flopped-eared, wiry haired mutts. Peter promised three of them already. When the fourth came out, we knew we had to keep her. She had one white ear and one tan and a pink nose like an elementary school pencil eraser. She became known as Racer.

Peter loved those puppies. He loved all living things. Peter was the real-deal hippie, not the beaded, flowered, bell-bottomed, tie-dyed, fringed moccasins, free sex and drugs hippie. He owned two pairs of blue jeans, both frayed at the cuff and thin in the butt. He had a denim jacket he wore over a series of plain colored, faded t-shirts. He went barefoot most of the time. When the cold hit, he put on pair of wool socks and scuffed boots. He kept the denim jacket and added a sweater underneath, a knit cap on his head, and a pair of thick, wool gloves. I never saw him take a toke. Peter was gentle with people and animals. He didn't eat meat. He lived his life in those faded blue jeans and denim jacket, taking care of his dogs, caring about people, and eating radishes.

Those puppies adored Peter, followed him around the house, slept on the floor next to his bed. Every morning he carried them downstairs and put them in front of the warm fire. Every evening he carried them back upstairs. Suki trusted him.

I trusted Peter too. When he spoke, he always told the truth. He was the most genuine person I ever met. A couple days after the puppies were born, Peter and I were alone at home playing with the pups.

"You going out tonight?" he asked. He picked Racer up and put her next to him on the couch.

"R.J. might call later. He's at some practice or gig or something." I reached for the glass of wine on the table in front of me. I already had a joint in the ashtray to keep my mind vacant, to let me sleep deep and dreamless, a sleep free from terror, free from sadness.

"Good," he said. He extinguished the joint in the ashtray. "It's time."

"What does that mean? Time for what?"

"He doesn't care for you, Beck. You know he's using you."

"Maybe I'm the one using him."

"You can't get through your pain this way."

"What do you know about pain? You and your dogs and your talking fasts and your radishes. You're full of shit, Peter." I got up and started to walk away. I didn't want to fight with Peter.

"Nineteen sixty-six. Southern California. I'm doing acid with my girlfriend and a bunch of friends on a boat in the Pacific. We felt invincible. She fell off the boat and they never found her body. No one ever held me responsible. I was. So shut the fuck up." He picked up the four pups and disappeared upstairs. That was the first time I ever heard Peter say fuck.

I knew I was in bad trouble.

U.S. Soldier Body Count: 34,718

134

Chapter 22
"I Go to Pieces"

"Big party at Stinson's tonight. Want to go?" R.J. asked me the next Friday night.

"Who the hell is Stinson?"

"New Sociology professor. He's a cool dude. Promise."

"Is he as cool as Professor Garson? When Garson talks about the connections between the war and civil rights, it's mind-blowing."

"You want to blow your mind? Try this." As we walked to Stinson's house about a half-mile south of campus, R.J. pulled out some hash he scored straight from Turkey, the type of hash that got you stoned looking at it. Take a toke and you were more than stoned. Take a few tokes and you were way beyond stoned. I toked and handed it to R.J. He toked and handed it back. I kept smoking and was way beyond stoned by the time we got to Stinson's. Way way beyond stoned. Way 'dizzy the world is tilting' kind of stoned. 'Everything has a hazy glow around it' kind of stoned. 'I might fall on my ass if I'm not careful' kind of stoned.

We entered the side door of Stinson's house. Incense burned on every counter in the kitchen. Six people were gathered round the kitchen table. I could see another half dozen people in the living room on the couch or on one of the beanbag chairs scattered on the floor. I sat down at the table next to R.J.

"That is the biggest jar of Vitamin C I ever saw in my life." Seven hundred and fifty chewable tablets, multi-berry flavor. "What's up with that?" The jar glowed.

The guy next to me said, "Some scientist guy said Vitamin C was the answer to everything. Stinson said if we were going to smoke dope, we had to eat a C." I opened the jar and picked out a red one. It didn't taste like a lifesaver.

The guy across from me lit up a couple joints. The girl next to him took a joint and smiled. She had huge teeth. Panther teeth. She inhaled and the teeth disappeared. The other joint went the other way. I was smart enough to know that they were going to get to me about the same time. I was so smart I could hardly believe it. One came to me as I finished sucking on my Vitamin C and I toked. The joint was in my mouth when the second one came from the right. I handed the first to R.J. and savored the second for a couple of tokes. What was I doing? I was already beyond stoned.

Sitar music came from the stereo in the other room. "I want the Beatles," I called out. R.J. put his hand over my mouth to keep me quiet.

Someone handed me a bowl filled with glowing round cookies. I put one in my mouth. "Damn, that's good." I took ten of those cookies and placed them in a line on the table in front of me. I put them in my mouth whole, one after another.

"Where is Stinson?" I asked.

I almost forgot I asked the question when the girl across the table, who now had a pink halo around her head, said, "He disappeared a long time ago. Told us to make ourselves at home."

"Where did he go?" I asked.

"Who knows?" she said. She smiled again with those panther teeth; the pink halo turned green.

"Who cares?" R.J. had his hands all over me, down my pants, there at the table, in front of everyone. My body arched and I wanted him. His fingers entered me. I moaned. "Oh my God, R.J. Don't stop." Everyone knew and saw what R.J. was doing to me.

"I need you now," I said to R.J. "More. Harder."

"Go get her, R.J." someone said. Everyone laughed.

"Now," I said. "I can't wait any longer."

R.J. carried me into the living room. He took my pants off. Then he was inside of me. "Harder," I yelled as the world watched. I grabbed him and pulled him towards me. He couldn't get close enough. He wasn't pushing hard enough. I wanted more. "Don't stop," I yelled. He came as I passed out.

As the sky lightened, I woke, still curled up in a fetal position on the beanbag chair, my pants on the floor next to me. I had to pee. I stood up, grabbed my pants, and stepped over two bodies on the floor. I walked to the bathroom, peed, put on my pants, splashed some cold water on my face, and rubbed some toothpaste on my teeth with my finger.

I walked back in the living room to look for R.J. He was one of the two bodies on the floor, entwined with that girl with the panther teeth, both with their pants off, both fast asleep. I was the only one awake in the whole house.

I kicked him. "Wake up." He moaned and put his arm tighter around the girl. "I said wake up." I kicked him harder.

"Shut up. We're sleeping," someone said from the couch.

"I don't give a fuck what you're doing," I turned back to R.J. "What's this all about?" I pointed to the naked girl next to him.

He looked up at me, still half asleep. "You passed out on me," he said. "What was I supposed to do?"

"What were you supposed to do? You weren't supposed to fuck someone else when you're my boyfriend,"

The guy from the couch again said, "Shut up."

"Fuck you," I said back to him.

"Don't get so bent out of shape," R.J. said.

I leaned down close to R.J. "I can't believe you did this to me."

He grabbed my leg as I stepped over him. "Come on, Becky. It was a one-time thing. You know you're my gal."

"Let go of me," I shouted.

"Let's have a quick fuck and talk this over."

"You think a quick fuck will solve this?"

"You'll be back," he said. "You'll never get a fuck as good as the one I can give you."

I turned around and left. The sun wasn't up over the houses yet, but it was light enough to see my way.

My heart raced. My breath came in ragged gasps. *It was a mistake to leave. What am I going to do now? How will I keep Jeff out of my brain?* I panicked. *I should go back and have a quick fuck with R.J. We can talk it out, work it out. It was only one time. I'll promise not to pass out on him again. He's the only thing helping me to forget. I need him. I can't go on without him.*

I turned to walk back to Stinson's house. I took a step. I tried to take another step, but my leg wouldn't move. Something stopped me. At that moment, the sun peeked over the house on the corner. The sky around it turned a brilliant pink. I froze, watching the sun rise, watching the new day dawn. The sun didn't know I had violated everything I ever believed in. It didn't know I wanted to go back and fuck R.J. The sun simply rose above the house and shone on my face. It spoke to me, that sun. Maybe it was the leftovers of the hash I smoked that spoke. Doesn't matter. I stood there and listened. *Maybe if you quit chasing the pain with cheap wine and dope like Ginger said. Maybe if you quit thinking you can fuck Jeff out of your head. Maybe if you did what your dad and Jake told you to do and stayed true to yourself. Then you could heal, and the pain will slowly go away.*

138

The sun blinded me with its light. I stood, motionless, feeling its warmth, feeling the love of my friends, feeling my parents' love. Jeff's face flashed before me in streaks of gold. I saw his smile, heard his laugh, felt his hand in mine. It didn't make me sad to see him. I heard him say, "You can do this, Becky. You can keep living. I believe in you."

At that moment, I changed. I always was easily changed.

I got in my car on campus to head home. I needed sleep. I was surprised ten minutes later to find myself knocking on Hook's door, tears flowing down my face. It was 6:55 a.m.

U.S. Soldier Body Count: 34,074

Chapter 23
"Time Is On My Side"

Hook answered the door wearing only his boxer shorts, hook off. I'd never seen him without his hook. "You were right," I said through my tears.

"About what?"

"About everything. About Jeff. About R.J. About the fact that gin is all about luck. About the fact that using a fork is not an efficient way to kill cockroaches. About the fact that I am not very good at skipping stones. About the fact that to win at slap jack you have to have a hook."

"I never said that last thing." He took my hand and led me into the living room. I took off my jacket and sat down on the edge of the easy chair.

He left and came back wearing jeans and an undershirt, a glass of water and a red bandana in his hand. He handed me the water and wiped the tears off my face with the bandana. "Keep it," he said. "You might need it again. I have another."

Hook always knew just what I needed.

He let me cry, didn't ask what happened.

When the tears were done, I put on the brown leather jacket and headed for the door, the red bandana in my hand. "Hook, you're my best friend and I love you. I am so sorry I've been such a mess since Jeff died. Something happened a half hour ago and

I've got a lot to figure out. Thanks for being here." I put the red bandana on the bookcase by the door.

Hook stopped me and put me in a whole-body hug. I let him hold me. I felt all of him hugging all of me. "Don't leave. Tell me what happened. Let me help you figure it out however long it takes. I'll be here."

I pulled back. "Look at me. How did I get everything so messed up?"

"Jeff died, Becky. That's what happened. Underneath all that mess is the real you. You'll figure it out." He took me in his hug again. "Please don't leave."

"You're going to think I'm crazy, but the sun spoke to me. Told me I needed to feel my pain to get through it. I don't know how to do that, Hook."

"First of all, I don't think you're crazy. We hear what we need to hear when we're ready to hear it."

"The sun talked to me, Hook. How can you not call that crazy?"

"Whatever the sun said, it was what you needed to hear."

"What's second of all?"

"Second of all. You get through it the way we all get through it, by holding on to your friends."

"Make love to me, Hook," I said.

"Now's not the time, Becky."

"Why does everyone always say that to me? What does it even mean? When is the time? I need to be loved by someone who really loves me."

"You are," Hook tightened his embrace. "You hungry?"

"Starving."

He let go.

We found crackers, a half-jar of peanut butter, one brown banana, a rotten carrot, some applesauce with mold growing on

141

the top, two slices of baloney, and some left-over macaroni and cheese. "Interesting breakfast," I said to Hook. We tossed the banana, carrot, and apple sauce into the trash and put the macaroni in a pan to heat up.

"I'll make it up to you. I promise. I'll cook you a perfect dinner tonight."

What happened that morning was about a friend helping me get through the pain, about finding those perfect moments of beauty and joy where you are. It was about beginning to figure out what's next, about the things that keep us going because we put one foot in front of the other.

Late that morning I headed home to clean up. Water was boiling on the stove when I got there. Peter and I drank tea together on the couch with Suki and the pups.

"You look different somehow," Peter said.

"I am," I replied. I paused and looked at Peter. "You were right about R.J. I'm sorry I've been so hard to live with this semester."

"You were doing what anyone does who ever lost someone they love."

"Were you that crazy when your girlfriend died?"

"I left home when I was sixteen because my dad disagreed with every choice I made in life. One day he told me that if I didn't cut my hair I could find a new place to live, so I did."

"That's brutal."

"It felt like that at the time. The only thing that got me through was my grandmother. She supported everything I ever did. Still does. When my girlfriend died, I didn't talk for four months. Then I found this starving, mangy dog wandering the streets of San Francisco. She saved my life." He scratched Suki behind the ears and put his arm around the puppies. "You'll get through all of this, Becky. Let's never talk about R.J. again." I

142

got back to Hook's house in time to see him cook dinner. I leaned against the counter and watched him chop, sauté, stir, season, wearing an apron and chef's hat. I felt content. "I didn't know you could cook. By the way, I like the hat."

"Thanks. I found it in the baked goods aisle at the grocery store." He reached up and rearranged the hat on his head.

"It's not quite as sexy as a red bandana but attractive in its own way."

"I gave the bandana to someone who needed it." It still sat on the bookcase by the door. He put a chopped carrot in my mouth.

"I know you have another."

After dinner, he gave me a foot massage while we listened to Dylan on the record player. "How come I didn't know you gave such great foot massages?"

"I am a man of multiple talents. You haven't even begun to discover everything I can do," Hook massaged between the big and second toe.

He stopped massaging my foot. "You ever been in a place where something happened, you knew your life could be over, and some kind of miracle saved you?"

I thought for a moment. "I was hiking along the cliffs above Norris Lake right outside my hometown. I slipped and was heading down the cliff when I saw a tiny tree branch growing out of the rocks. I grabbed it and it stopped my fall."

"That's exactly what I'm talking about. I don't know how I survived Vietnam except for those small miracles." Hook picked up my other foot. "I drop my canteen, stoop to pick it up when sniper fire goes over my head. I'm four minutes late to a place that just blew up with a land mine. My buddy dies because he's a foot away from me. I don't get why I'm alive right now. What's the purpose?"

I put my hand over his. I wanted to somehow let him know that I was glad he was here, alive, massaging my feet, being my friend, helping me heal. I guess that was the purpose. "Maybe it was because somehow, somewhere, someone knew I would need you some day. You had to stay alive for me."

Hook squeezed each of my toes, patted my foot. "Someday I'll give you a one-handed back massage. That's my ultimate purpose. I give amazing back massages." It didn't surprise me. I could sense it in his hugs.

Reluctantly I put on my socks. "Is it the time now?" I smiled at him.

"Patience, Becky. We have all the time in the world." he replied.

"Well, then, I better go. I have a full day of classes tomorrow. I am so behind. Can I see you tomorrow?"

He handed me my jacket and gave me a hug. "Tomorrow afternoon after classes, stone skipping. Tomorrow night I'll show you my magic tricks."

Hook made six skips at the lake the next afternoon. I never got more than three. That night he gave me magic. "I used to be great at sleight of hand card tricks but I kind of lost that ability." He held up his hook. With his other hand he pulled a quarter from behind my ear.

"I can still do one card trick." Hook spread a deck of cards on the coffee table. "Pick one," he said. He told me to double the number, add three, multiply by five, and add either one, two, three, four depending on what suit it was. "What's your number?"

"Ninety-seven."

"You drew the eight of diamonds."

There was nothing magic about it, but I was still impressed. That was it for the card tricks. "You lured me over here for one card trick? I was promised a night of magic."

"Yep," he said. For a moment I thought he was going to kiss me. That's what I wanted. To be kissed by perfection. To be kissed by loveliness. To be kissed into loveliness. To be loved by loveliness. Instead, he leaned over and gently caressed my cheek with his thumb.

"Why didn't you stop me from being crazy?"

"You're here now. That's what matters. Shit, what you did doesn't even compare to some of the crazy stuff I did back home. The only crazy thing you did was love someone."

I reached over and took his hand. I brought it to my lips. "Tell me everything."

"I will. First let me get some popcorn." I let go of his hand. Letting go of his eyes was harder.

Hook handed me the bowl of popcorn. "In high school I got on my skateboard and grabbed on to the bumper of a car stopped at a light. When the light changed, they pulled me through the city, not knowing I was there."

"Not smart," I said.

"Once I rode drunk on the hood of a pick-up truck through a field of cows. I ended up sliding off the hood right into a cow. I drove drunk at two o'clock in the morning on the fourth of July, I guess it was the fifth by then, waving lit sparklers out of the window."

I laughed. "Shit, Hook. You could have killed yourself," I took a handful of popcorn, washed it down with a drink of coke. "I'm beginning to feel better about myself. Tell me more."

"When I was a senior in high school, four of us got drunk and sneaked into the chemistry lab at school at night. We caused a small explosion."

Hook told me crazy story after crazy story. Once he climbed to the top of a tree and jumped from the branches to the roof of his house, found his way across the roof to an attic window that

145

he pried open. Another time he created a Tarzan rope swing in an oak tree. At the highest point of the swing, he let go, trying to land in the leaf pile he raked below.

Laughter came easy. With every moment that passed I healed a little. Time became my friend.

Finally, I had to go. I had an early class and needed to spend the rest of the day working on a paper. "Come over tomorrow night." He said goodbye with a hug and a gentle kiss.

"I will."

The next night when I arrived, he said, "I've got something to show you. Remember when I told you I was sending back my medals? I did. Look what I got in the mail today." He handed me a box. It held his purple heart and bronze star.

"The letter said, 'The United States Government does not accept medals of any kind and, therefore, we are returning yours forthwith.' I can't even get rid of these damn things."

I looked at the medals. Looked at Hook. I started to laugh.

"This isn't funny. I want them to go away."

"Throw them in the damn trash can," I said.

"I want the government to know I'm throwing them away. They won't know if I throw them in the trash can."

"So now you're being particular about the disposal of these medals that you are dying to get rid of."

That's sort of how the conversation went except that we both laughed so hard as we talked that it was difficult to understand. Every time I opened that box it started all over again. I pinned one to my sweater. "What do you think?"

"It looks great. I bequeath it to you. Now it's yours to get rid of."

I felt completely alive.

I took a breath. "I am sorry I laughed at you. It's like you try to do the right thing and the world won't let you do it." I took the medal off my sweater and put it back in the box and put the box on the counter. "I am unbequeathing it to me."

He leaned over and kissed me. Then he looked me in the eyes. He started to say something and stopped.

"What were you about to say?" I asked.

"Doesn't matter."

"Listen, my friend. You can say that about Vietnam. You know the old, 'It don't mean nothin'. But you can't say that about us. What were you going to say just now?"

His right hand tucked the stray hairs back in my braids. "It's not important. The important thing is that you are here. Do you want something to drink?" He turned and walked towards the kitchen.

"Everything you say is important. Wine?"

"You hate Ripple and that's all I have. I'll heat up water." He opened the cabinet and pulled out a couple boxes of herbal tea. "Peppermint or lemon?" He turned back to look at me and started to say something again.

"Peppermint," I got two cups out of the cupboard and turned back to Hook. "Spill it."

He hesitated. "How come you never loved me like you loved Jeff or R.J.?"

"I didn't love R.J. I used him. I may have loved Jeff, but I don't know. You? I loved you the first time I saw you at the table in Commons. Maybe even before that when you walked away from our orientation group."

"But not in that way. Not in the way that counts." He put a teabag in each cup and wouldn't look at me.

"You were always my best friend. Doesn't that count for something?"

"It counts for everything. But I'm damaged goods." He held up his hook and smiled. "When I take it off there's only a stump. And it's not very pretty."

"I've seen your stump and it doesn't matter."

He slid his shirt over his head and took off the harness that held his hook. He stood there in his undershirt, the hook on the table.

I picked up his handless arm and kissed it. "You are the most gorgeous man I ever met in my life. Inside and out. Hand and stump. You are perfect."

Hook put his hand on one side of my face and the stump on the other. He lifted my face to his. He was the most gorgeous person in the world. Hands down.

The week gently rolled by. No wine. No dope. No sex. Just Hook giving me time. Just me healing and waiting for the time. Just stone skipping at the lake, lunch in Commons between classes, guitar-playing in Hixson Lounge, ice cream sundaes at the snack bar while listening to "All You Need is Love" on the juke box, games of gin and slap jack, dinner and easy conversation, long sustaining hugs, and deepening kisses.

On Saturday, we took the train into Chicago to visit the Museum of Science and Industry. We stood holding hands for more than an hour to watch a baby chick hatch, neither of us saying a word, sensing the miracle. We caught the late train back and walked from the station to his place.

As we walked, Hook said, "You never told me what brought you to my place last week at 6:00 in the morning."

"Doesn't really matter anymore. Besides, it was closer to seven." I looked at his face, reached over and touched his cheek, rubbed my fingers on his lips. "When I first met you, you had the scariest look on your face."

"I was pretty fucked up at the time. I don't know why you even bothered to become friends with me."

"I had no choice. We kept running into each other. You always seemed to be standing in the hall when I went to visit Jeff. You stopped by the anti-war table every time I was there. And besides, like I already said, you have the most gorgeous face I ever saw in my life."

"Me being in the hall when you came to visit Jeff was no accident. I would ask him, 'Becky coming over tonight?' He'd say, 'Yeah.' I'd say, 'What time?' and he'd tell me. I would be waiting for you. I needed to make sure you were safe and happy."

"You knew he was an addict, didn't you? Why didn't you tell me?"

"I wanted to so many times. I am so sorry I didn't." He took my hand and kissed it. "I thought it should be his choice not mine. I regret it and hope you can forgive me."

"I wrote a paper in high school in support of the Vietnam War. That's a bigger regret than your regret. I forgive you for not telling me."

"I forgive you for that paper you wrote. Anyway, you are wrong about my face. Yours is the most gorgeous." He rubbed his thumb on my cheek.

"Did you ever even look in the mirror?"

When we got to his place, the evening wore on with easy banter. "You don't deserve to be miserable," Hook said, dealing out cards for a game of gin. "I hate Jeff and R.J. for what they did to you."

"I deserved everything I got. It serves me right, what they did to me."

"I'm never going to ask you what happened with R.J., but you don't deserve to be miserable. Don't you ever again say you deserved it. You are amazing." Hook put down a seven of spades. It completed my run.

I looked at him. "I'm not sure that's true but thanks away."

"I will spend my life proving that to you if it takes that long." Hook handed me a Kleenex. He took to buying Kleenex brand tissues after I informed him early in September that his choice of tissues was a disgrace to humanity and if I was going to visit, he would have to replace all his boxes with Kleenex brand. That was my mom speaking.

We were still talking at 2:00 a.m. when Hook suddenly said, "Shit, I forgot, there's one of those cool astronomical things going on tonight, a full moon, with Venus and Saturn both visible. Put your shoes on. We're going out."

I loved astronomy. In fifth grade my teacher built a spaceship in our classroom, floor to ceiling. It was only when I realized that astronomy required math that I gave up my idea of being an astronomer.

Hook put his arm around me. I put my head on his shoulder. We stared at the planets. We were in heaven until the cool November air drove us inside.

Back on the couch I dozed in and out. We talked. I slept. Every time I woke up, Hook was at the other end of the couch looking at me. Once I said to him, "How could you even stand me this fall? I can't figure out how I got so crazy. What happened at Stinson's house, that wasn't even me."

"You going to tell me about it?"

I paused and looked at him. I didn't want him to know, not yet. Someday I would tell him, my final confession. Someday when the healing was complete, if that ever really happens, then I could say, "You'll never believe what happened." Not now. I wasn't ready. We weren't ready.

"Someday I'll tell you when it's funny instead of simply pathetic. Think of it this way. Your story about driving drunk with lit sparklers out the window? That pales in comparison to Stinson's. What was I even thinking?"

Hook rearranged the blanket that fell off my feet. "You were thinking that if you ran hard enough and fast enough the pain would go away. It never works that way."

"What were you like when you got back from Vietnam?"

"I'll tell you someday," he said. "When it quits being so painful to talk or think about."

The next time I woke up it was past 4:30 and there was a bowl of popcorn on the floor next to me. I looked at Hook. His hook was off, on the floor next to him. "Have you slept at all?" I asked.

"I've been in and out. Sleeping will only make this perfect night end sooner."

I reached for Hook and pulled him to me. We rearranged ourselves on the couch, his left arm draped around me. He circled me with one of his hugs and that was more than enough. I was safe and happy.

I woke up when Hook started to move, trying to move off the couch without waking me. "What time is it?" I asked.

"Shortly after seven. I'll put coffee on then I'm taking a shower. I'll make you breakfast when I'm done."

I was on the couch drinking a cup of coffee when Hook came out of the bathroom, jeans on, undershirt on, harness and hook on, hair washed and combed back, freshly shaved.

"God, that harness is sexy on you," I said.

Hook walked over and kissed the top of my head. "Didn't think I'd ever hear someone say the harness is sexy."

"Well, it is. Turns me on a little bit."

Another lazy Sunday playing cards, laughing, reading jokes out of the 'Saturday Evening Post,' stabbing cockroaches, doing homework, editing articles for the school newspaper.

We took a break in the afternoon to walk to the lake knowing that in a couple weeks winter would hit Chicago.

I tossed a stone. "Four skips," I cheered.

"Pathetic. I do four on a bad day." I ran to him, jumped up on his back, my feet wrapped around his waist, my arms around his neck.

"I challenge you to five skips with me hanging here." He tossed the stone that was in his hand. Eight skips.

"I'm trying to make it skip forty-six times."

I slid off his back. "Why forty-six?"

"That's the year I was born."

Back at his place, I worked on a paper while he cooked me dinner. "Dinner's ready," he called. In the kitchen Hook leaned against the cabinet; his arms crossed over his chest. He had an amazing grin on his face. I could tell he was truly happy.

That night I slept in Hook's bed, Hook next to me, his arm draped around me. I woke up the next morning when Hook sat down on the bed. He handed me a cup of coffee. "I've got to go soon to catch the train into Chicago for a VA appointment. I'm going to shower. Doughnuts in the kitchen."

He found me in the kitchen drinking coffee and eating doughnuts. We drank and ate and looked at each other as the minutes ticked by.

Hook said. "I've got to go. Don't want to miss the train. Stay as long as you want."

"One more doughnut," I handed him a glazed one from the bag. I didn't want him to leave. He took it.

It was time. We stood at the door holding each other. I didn't want to let go. I never wanted to let go again. I needed his hug to hold me throughout the day, throughout my life. I thought back to the hug Hook gave me at the Democratic National Convention. It was the hug that made me know that one day I would be okay again. One day I wouldn't be so sad. Here was that day.

How long did we stand there? I'm not sure. Long enough to know that it's never long enough. Long enough to know that something perfect happened and it would be with me forever. Long enough to know that being with him was magic. He looked me in the eyes and said, "I'll see you later." I watched him go, my heart full, the hole in it so tiny, smaller than a pinprick.

I washed the dishes and cleaned the apartment a bit. I brushed my teeth with his toothbrush and left it drying in a cup. I wrote a note that I left on the counter. "Give me a call when you're home."

I walked out the door. When I shut it behind me, I stood holding the doorknob. Sometimes things in life are perfect.

U.S. Soldier Body Count: 35,523

Chapter 24
"All You Need Is Love"

In my Sociology of Politics class, we discussed the relationship of redlining to poor schools to race disparities in the military. Our assignment was to research how the draft unduly penalizes the black and poor. I was convinced before I took the class. I had the pleasure of watching Garson work his magic and win over the rest of the class.

I worked on the newspaper after lunch and got home early afternoon. I didn't feel tired. I felt different. I washed up the dishes left from the night before. They weren't even mine. I didn't care.

Peter walked up and said, "You look happy." I smiled at him. He took a dishtowel and started drying. Nothing needed saying.

The phone rang. We ignored it. Marty could answer or they could call back. This was more important. This being with Peter.

I sensed Marty's presence behind us. He was silent. I turned and looked at him. "Who was it?" I asked.

He didn't say anything. His teeth and fists were clenched, like they were the night King died.

I stopped what I was doing, a rinsed plate poised above the drain tray. "Marty, is something wrong?"

"I don't know how to say this." He looked at Peter, imploring, asking for help with his eyes.

"Say what?"

"That was Hook's mom." He hesitated.

"How did she get our number?"

"Hook gave it to her in case she couldn't get him at his place."

"What did she want? Is she looking for Hook? He had a meeting at the VA in Chicago this morning."

Marty looked at me, looked at Peter, tears clouding his eyes. "What did she want?" I asked again.

"There was an accident on I-94."

My heart started beating hard. I didn't want to hear what I was afraid I was going to hear. "What are you trying to tell me?" I still held the dish with my rubber-gloved hand.

Marty walked over to me and put his hand on my shoulder. He looked at me gently, but I saw the tears in his eyes. He looked at Peter.

I looked at them both. "What?"

"Becky, Hook's dead."

The plate crashed to the floor. I quickly followed. Peter and Marty surrounded me. They didn't know that for the last week Hook made me laugh and loved me into some kind of loveliness. They didn't know that I healed a bit, that I thought I could never find gentleness again, but I had. That I thought I didn't deserve goodness anymore, but I did. They didn't know that the beautiful, gorgeous man with one hand held me in a full body hug and said, "I'll see you later." They didn't know I was waiting for him to call. That I was waiting for it to finally be the time.

Without letting go of me, Peter asked, "What happened?"

"A drunk driver. Three people died and two more are in the hospital. The police called her. She called us."

"It wasn't him. I know it wasn't him. He told me he was taking the train in. It wasn't him." I tried to get up. I wanted to go outside and run and run and never stop but at the end of the run, the truth would still be there. I didn't want to hear the truth, to feel the truth, to know the truth. I was afraid of what the truth might do.

"Becky," Marty said without letting go. "They found his license and college I.D. It was him."

I choked. "It was my fault. He was late because of me. He missed his train because of me. We ate doughnuts. We drank coffee." For some reason I had this idea that if I kept on talking, if I just kept on talking, I wouldn't have to feel what I was going to feel. I wouldn't have to admit the truth. "I gave him another doughnut. I made him stay and have another doughnut. That made him late, so he had to drive instead of taking the train in. He missed his train because of me. Then he took his car and he died because of me. Everyone dies because of me."

Marty stroked my hair. "It wasn't your fault. The entire system was down for a couple of hours because of electrical problems. No trains headed into Chicago this morning. He drove because there were no trains."

"It was a glazed doughnut. He ate it. Then he hugged me for a long time. If he left ten minutes earlier, it wouldn't have happened. Or if he left ten minutes later. Or one minute. But he left when he did because of me. If I hadn't given him another doughnut. But I did. I gave him another doughnut. If he hadn't hugged me for so long."

I jerked away from Peter and Marty and forced myself to get up. I took off the rubber gloves and threw them on the floor. I ran outside barefoot in the November cold screaming as loud as I could. I ran until I couldn't run anymore. I stopped, leaned over to catch my breath. The world seemed bleak, and my feet were frozen. I didn't know what to do.

I did the only thing I could. I went inside. I sat on the couch. I put the blanket from the back of the couch around my feet and I stared at nothing. Peter brought me a glass of water. I drank it.

I didn't know what else to do. Marty sat next to me and put his hand on my leg. It brought a strange sense of comfort. I couldn't forget they loved him too.

I turned to Marty. "I gave him another doughnut."

"I know." Marty pulled me close and we cried together.

Ginger came home as soon as she heard. Within a couple of hours Jake showed up.

"How could God have taken someone we loved so much? Hook was the best person in the world. What are we going to do? How do we get past this?" I looked around at my friends, all Hook's friends. We'd been here before, last August, before I really knew Peter, before I knew R.J., before I knew loveliness. They'd been here when Jeff died. We would heal together.

Tears came and went. Stories came and went. Laughter came and went. We tried to eat. It didn't go down easily.

I couldn't be alone in my attic room at night staring at my posters, seeing his face, feeling his hug. I couldn't let this take me down. I had come out of that deep well of sadness and couldn't go back into it. I crawled into bed with Marty. I said to him, "He loved me into loveliness." That's all I said. Marty held me all night.

I couldn't stay in Marty's bed forever. The next night I went up to my attic room and lay on the bed, my comforter pulled up around my shoulders, staring at the ceiling, not seeing anything because it was too dark to see anything, but seeing everything because it was all so open and raw and painful and sad. My body twitched. I tried to calm my legs, will them to stop twitching, but they wouldn't stop. I couldn't lie there anymore.

I put on my shoes and walked quietly down the stairs. I didn't want to wake anyone up. I didn't want to worry anyone. I could get through this. I got through Jeff. Hook's hug in Chicago gave me hope and helped get me through. The problem was, I didn't have Hook to help me get through him. I didn't have his hugs to sustain and hold me. I would never have his hugs again.

I opened the back door and closed it behind me without making a sound. I walked to the garden plot behind the house where Peter planted winter vegetables. I picked a leaf of kale and took a bite. It was bitter and raw, like me. I leaned down and touched a winter squash, cradled it in my hands. It was living. Maybe it would help me live. "God damn it," I said to the squash, to the stars, to anyone who would listen. "I didn't tell you about Stinson's party. You didn't tell me about Vietnam. I didn't show you my magic trick. You didn't give me a one-handed back massage. Why did I give you the doughnut? I am so sorry." My heart beat hard, my breathing shallow. I couldn't endure the pain anymore. I couldn't put one foot in front of the other anymore. I picked the squash off the vine, stood up, and threw it as far as I could.

Then gently, ever so gently, a breeze circled round me, embracing my body. It circled round my feet, my thighs, my chest, my arms, then around my head, caressing my cheeks. The breeze covered me and held me. Hook. He would never leave me. Never.

The next day Jake and Marty went into Chicago to identify the body. I didn't go. I gave up the chance to see him one last time.

We went to Hook's apartment. Once again, I had to take care of stuff.

I didn't know how I would be able to go back into his apartment. The red bandana would still be on the shelf by the door where I left it that first morning. The dishes would be in the drain tray. His toothbrush would be in the cup where I left it to dry. A note would be on the counter: "Give me a call when you're home." He wouldn't be there. I had to go. Maybe I could find some little part of him there.

I walked around the apartment aimlessly, touching everything, rubbing my hand across the top of the dresser, picking up the pillow on his bed and putting it to my face. It didn't smell musty and mildewed. It smelled like him. On his dresser I found the small peace button he picked out that day in Commons so long ago. I pinned it on my jacket.

Marty, Peter, Ginger, and Jake didn't know how to start. I was the only one with stuff experience. "Let's start with the bedroom," I finally said. I opened a drawer and took out his shirts. I noticed that he had no shirts with buttons. I never noticed that before. I leaned against the wall, holding the shirts. Then I slid down to the floor with his shirts held tightly to my chest. I cried until I was dry. They let me.

Peter found a bottle of Ripple in the cupboard and poured five glasses. For Hook, I drank the Ripple. For Hook, I raised a glass.

We piled up the clothes. After the dirty things were washed, Jake would find people who could use them. We left the furniture.

Marty took the poster on the wall above the bed—a psychedelic peace sign. In the corner Hook wrote, "It don't mean nothin'." It meant everything. Jake took the other poster that said, "Fuck the draft." Ginger took a strand of beads. Peter was satisfied with his memories. I took the red bandana. We'd send the personal items to his mom. I was going to hand deliver his medals to her in Cleveland on the way home for Christmas break.

Thanksgiving was somber that year. While we ate, Hook's body was at the morgue ready to be shipped to Cleveland by the government for proper burial. The next Monday we gave him his final good-bye at Commons. The snack bar was full. Hook touched everybody in his own special way.

Professor Garson spoke first. "I met Dennis McKinney the night before orientation. He walked away from my orientation group after only an hour and never returned. He often came by my office, and we chatted about life, the war, college, what he was going to do next. It took him a while to forgive what the war did to him. But he did. He was one of the kindest people I have ever met."

Don't make me cry, Garson. I need to be stoic, like the Kennedy wives.

Fuck that. I cried.

Jake talked of Hook and the anti-war movement. "I bribed him into coming to the first meeting. Can't even remember what I promised him and I'm sure I didn't pay up. I remember him saying that he didn't want to be the symbol of the protest. I am so grateful he decided to come. He was a true friend."

Marty told about how I tried to protect Hook from the commuter at the Lake Forest train station. "By the time the train came, Hook was best friends with the guy. The shook hands and probably exchanged phone numbers."

Ginger said, "Most of you don't know that Hook had a killer voice." How come I never knew that? Masseuse, chef, magician, singer. "He generally didn't sing when there were a lot of people around but sometimes, I lucked out. He'd find me sitting under a tree somewhere on campus and join me. Those are the days I will always remember."

I put two quarters in the juke box and pressed A7 six times. "All You Need Is Love." "This was Hook's song," I said. "It was our song." That's all I could get out. I could hear the hook beating out the beat. Love is never enough. The Beatles had it wrong.

My friends were afraid that Hook's death would destroy me. His love was too strong for that. He brought me back to life.

Ginger gave me four days to write an article about Hook for the school newspaper. "You can do this," she said. I stood before her shaking my head no.

"I don't want to write any more tributes."

"No one else can do this, Becky. It's your story."

I met my deadline.

* * *

The Forester
Contributor Column
By Becky Jamison

Dennis McKinney hugged. We loved him for a lot of things, but the hugs stood out. If you never had a Dennis McKinney hug you missed out on one of the most amazing experiences you could have in life.

These arms come around you and you feel his strength around your back. Your shoulders touch and you feel like you are melting into his body. Every inch of your chest becomes part of this hug, then the hips, the thighs, the knees. Before you know it, you are surrounded by this metaphysical force, and you never want to leave.

That's a Dennis McKinney hug.

Dennis was in my freshman orientation group for an hour before he walked away, never to come back. I thought I wouldn't see him again, but he showed up at the anti-war table in Commons one day at lunch and we forged a friendship that will never be broken, even in death.

Here's what you might not know about Dennis McKinney.

He was a chef, masseuse, and magician all wrapped into one. He could chop a carrot with flare, massage a foot until it felt completely alive and relaxed at the same time, and stun you with his card tricks.

Dennis was opinionated. He knew what he believed and he said it with conviction, humility, and kindness. "No doubt about it," he said one day at an anti-war meeting. "This war is immoral, and we must do everything we can to stop it." He never wavered and worked until his death speaking out against the war.

Dennis was a procrastinator. He always did what he said he would do, but it never came in early. I can still hear Dennis say, "Why did I wait until the last minute to do this paper?"

Dennis was drop dead gorgeous. Maybe that's not the right thing to say about someone in the newspaper but with Dennis, how could you not? The red bandana he wore around his hair brought it all out.

Dennis was funny. Get him talking about how to stab cockroaches with a hook and within minutes you wouldn't be able to breathe.

Dennis would die for his friends, and he almost did. Even after he lost his hand, he put himself in danger pulling two of his buddies out of a swamp in Vietnam. There was nothing that Dennis McKinney wouldn't do for me.

In the end, Dennis lost his life because of a drunk driver. He died knowing he was loved beyond compare. He is missed every single day.

By the way, his friends called him Hook.

U.S. Soldier Body Count: 35,614

Chapter 25
"I Shall Be Released"

The week after Hook died, I ran into R.J. as I walked into Commons. We both stopped.

"Sorry about Hook," he said.

"His name is Dennis." I pushed by him. He grabbed my arm.

"You can't shut me out, Becky."

I stopped and turned. I looked into his eyes and for some reason I felt a deep sadness for him. I was surprised at how calm I felt. Kennedy wife calm. Hook was doing his magic, surrounding me.

I paused and looked around. "R.J., you are the best damn guitar player I ever heard. Don't blow it." I turned and walked away.

I never saw R.J. again. He left Lake Forest after that semester.

* * *

Fall semester was over. I hit the road to spend Christmas at home, detouring through Cleveland to give Dennis' mom the medals and his army jacket. Dennis was all she had. Her husband left without a word when Dennis was little.

Mrs. McKinney greeted me with a hug that only the mother of Dennis could give. It was good to feel a Dennis hug again.

"It is so nice to meet you, Mrs. McKinney," I said as she invited me in.

"Any friend of Dennis is always welcome."

Mrs. McKinney took me to the living room and went into the kitchen. I walked over to the fireplace. On the mantle were three framed pictures. One was of Dennis and his mom when he was about two years old. He had a giant ball in his hands and a grin that covered his entire face. I picked up the picture as she arrived with a tray. "He sure was cute," I said.

"That he was," she replied. "He was also quite a pistol." My mom described my little brother that way, but I never heard anyone else use that word.

"We called him Hook."

"I know. He loved it."

I picked up the second picture, high school graduation. His hair was growing out and he had that sexy grin. "I bet the girls loved him."

Mrs. McKinney smiled. "He was never without a date. His special girlfriend, Sarah, broke his heart when she went away to college and told him they should break up so they could both meet new people."

The third picture was a 3 X 5 photograph of Dennis in fatigues with his arm around his buddy grinning at the camera. "I found that one in his stuff after he got back from Vietnam. That's the buddy who died in the swamp when Dennis lost his hand."

I picked it up. "He looks so happy."

We sat down on the couch, and she served me coffee and cookies. On the tray with the cookies was the Christmas present Dennis made for her in the first grade. "Isn't this adorable?" She handed me a blue felt frame with sequins glued around the outside and a picture of him standing by his desk smiling. "This picture of

Dennis has been hanging on the bulletin board by the telephone ever since first grade."

I smiled at her. How in the world could she be so composed? How could I be so composed? What we both wanted to do was scream at the world, pump our fists at heaven, and ask why such a good person could be taken. It was the Kennedy wives' thing again. They showed us how to grieve gracefully.

We looked through a scrapbook she had on the table by the couch. "This picture was taken in the third grade when he had the role of the shoemaker in 'The Elves and the Shoemaker.' He took the role so seriously that we took a trip to a shoe repair shop. The owner showed Dennis all his tools and gave Dennis the tool that's in that picture."

"Here he is playing Little League Baseball in the sixth grade. He played catcher."

"He never told me that."

"He loved being in every play of every inning." She showed me the baseball they gave her when he hit his first homerun the next to last game of the season. He signed it, "To Mom. Love Dennis."

"Here's the ribbon he won at the science fair in the ninth grade for his display on the impact of flood and drought on farmland. One night after dinner he said his science project was due the next day and he didn't know what to do. All I could think of was to make something with a salt dough mixture. He came up with an idea of a field with gullies on the flood side and cracked earth on the drought side. I couldn't believe he won second place." She smiled at me.

"And waited until the last possible minute to do it."

"Always was his weakness."

She turned the page. It was the program from the state championship football game and the newspaper article when he won Most Valuable Player. "That's his trophy," she pointed to the bookcase in the corner. "He played football from the time he was in seventh grade. He was a smart kid but all he wanted to do was play sports. Even though he struggled with his grades, he wasn't stupid."

I walked over to the bookcase and picked up the trophy. The inscription on the bottom said 'Dennis McKinney, Most Valuable Player.' I touched his name. "You're right. Not only was he smart but he had an opinion about everything."

"Opinionated and stubborn."

I held the trophy to my chest as the tears rolled down my cheeks. "Thank you for sharing him with me, Mrs. McKinney." I put down the trophy and walked over to her, took hold of both of her hands and we cried together. It was still too raw. We didn't want to be composed. We weren't the Kennedy wives.

"Now Becky. I cannot have you call me Mrs. McKinney. It's too formal."

I laughed as I wiped the tears out of my eyes. "I do have a name for you. Dennis was very generous with your care packages of homemade cookies and brownies. When I saw him with one of your packages, I'd say, 'What did Mama McKinney send today?' That's who you always were to me."

"It's perfect," she said. She picked up the box with the two medals in it, fingered each one. "He hated these things." She looked at me. "I begged him not to enlist. I always felt guilty for being happy when he was injured. I know the injuries tormented him. But he was coming home."

I walked to the mantel and picked up the picture of Dennis and his buddy. I touched his face. "When I first met Dennis, I was scared of him. It didn't take long to realize he had a heart of gold. He was my best friend." I put the picture down and went back to the couch.

"He talked about you all the time in his letters. You helped him come alive again." She looked at me then took both my hands. "I think he was in love with you."

I smiled. "I was in love with him too."

"I have something for you." She walked over to the end table under the window and picked up a box. In it was a framed picture of Dennis and me walking down the sidewalk outside Commons. The picture was taken from the back. I was holding on to his hook and we were looking at each other laughing.

"Where did you get this?" I looked up at her.

"The public relations department at the college sent me a number of pictures of Dennis a couple of weeks after he died along with a beautiful card. I had this one framed for you."

I looked at her, overwhelmed by a sense of grief and gratitude. I held the picture to my heart. "Thank you," I said. I looked down and then back up at her. "I am so sorry I let him go into Chicago that day. I should have stopped him from going."

"It wasn't your fault, dear. No one ever knows what's going to happen. He died happy. I know that."

"I was with him that morning before he went into Chicago. We were eating doughnuts at his apartment. If we ate one less doughnut or one more. If I kept talking for five more minutes or if I let him go the first time he said he had to go, it wouldn't have happened."

Mama McKinney took one of my hands, patted it, and held it in both of hers. "You loved him. That's what's important."

"Thank you so much for the picture. I will cherish it. I carry his red bandana with me everywhere."

"That infernal bandana," she laughed. "When he got back from Vietnam, he made me tie that bandana around his head every day. He was so proud when he learned to tie it himself."

I didn't want to leave but had to get further down the road. I'd be back.

"I want you to take some cookies for the road and I want you to keep his army jacket." She handed me a bag of cookies. I put the jacket on, and Mama McKinney gave me another Dennis hug. She said, "You give all those wonderful friends of Dennis a hug for me."

"I will."

"Promise me something." Anything. "Promise me you won't forget him. Promise me that." I promised. Cross my heart hope to die. I would never forget Dennis McKinney. "And end this damn war."

* * *

It was good to be home with my family for Christmas. We made cookies. My mom had the best collection of cookie cutters. We frosted them red, green, blue, yellow, white. For some reason, my younger brother always made the reindeer blue. We decorated the cookies with colored sprinkles, red cinnamon drops, and silver balls. We covered the tree with decorations we'd made throughout the years.

I lay in bed one night wondering what happened to me. My dad's only piece of advice had been to be myself. Where had I gone off the path?

Jeff. He seduced me with his eyes. I got caught up in the wine and weed, the kisses and caresses. Is it all part of growing up? Does everyone go through it? Losing yourself to find yourself? I loved Jeff. I loved Hook. They died. Will everyone I love die? Can I love and have it last? Why did I ever think R.J. could make it better?

I survived. I could think of Jeff and smile. He taught me to live life full-out, not be afraid. It still hurt to think of Hook. But whenever I thought I couldn't stand it anymore, when the missing was the fiercest, I felt him hold me.

I told my family stories about Dennis, about playing gin and slapjack, walks to the lake and stone skipping adventures. I told them about the medals he won and wanted to get rid of. "One is the same medal Uncle Jim has in the cabinet in his living room." I told them his story about Vietnam. No one in the family moved except to refill glasses of Diet Rite Cola and bowls of chips. They let me talk until way past midnight. I don't know why I didn't share more with my parents when Jeff died. It would have helped the healing.

When I was done, I cried. My mom reached across the table and took hold of my hand. "I was in love with him, Mom."

When my mom was four, her six-year-old sister died. No one told my mom what happened. Her sister simply disappeared. When mom took my hand, I knew she knew. The pain of love is deep. Love heals that pain.

U.S. Soldier Body Count: 36,956

Chapter 26
"Dedicated To The One I Love"

When I arrived back in Lake Forest, Jake was on the couch in front of the fire, his feet on the coffee table, reading a book. I put my suitcase and the box with the picture in it next to the door. "God, it's good to see you," I said. He gave me a long hug. "I didn't expect you here."

"I figured I could use your help planning a wedding."

"What?" I pulled away from the hug and looked around as Ginger came out of the bedroom.

She came over and held out her hand. "My Christmas present."

I looked at the diamond ring and then at her. "All I got was a new blanket."

Ginger took both of my hands in hers. "Would you be my maid of honor?"

"Of course," I said.

"Welcome back," Peter said as he came in the living room followed by Suki and Racer. The other puppies made great Christmas presents for three lucky kids. Peter walked over and hugged me.

If I got enough hugs it might add up to one Dennis hug. That's what I was counting on. That I could live with. "How is Suki doing without her pups?"

"She's hovering over Racer most of the time. Hungry?"

"Always."

The back door flew open. "You're back." Marty bounded into the room, his nervous energy intact. I bounded into his arms. We were all there. I wanted this moment, this place, these people to last forever.

Peter made dinner. Always and forever brown rice. Always and forever alfalfa sprouts. Sautéed vegetables, most of which grew in the small greenhouse Peter constructed the past September. A side cabbage salad. Carob brownies for dessert.

While we sat around eating, I told them all about the visit with Mama McKinney.

I cried. They cried. I cried some more. "Sometimes it hurts so much I don't know how I can keep on living. Then I feel him there. It's strange. I never felt that with Jeff."

"I know what you mean," Marty said. "It's like he's hovering."

"I miss his hugs," I said.

"They were the best," Ginger said. Everyone nodded. Hook wasn't stingy with his hugs.

"He learned it from his mom. Mama McKinney asked me to give all of you a hug from her," I said. I did.

"I have something to show you," I got the box with the picture in it. "Mama McKinney gave it to me."

I handed the picture around. Speechless. Peter summed it up. "It is so perfect."

That night I looked through my drawers for something I knew was there, the white candle Marty gave me for my birthday my freshman year. I took the sliver of a candle out of a wine bottle I had by my bed and put Marty's candle in. Lit it. Got in bed. Pulled the covers over me and looked at the picture. Hook and me laughing. It was the only picture I had of him. I held it, feeling warm, feeling sad, feeling complete, feeling empty. I cried. I

171

laughed. I didn't know how I felt. I didn't want to share this moment with anyone else. I would carry his gentleness and his love. His love touched me deeply and made me lovely. I missed him more than I could even imagine and yet at the same time he surrounded me. I could breathe. Love always lets you breathe. I fell asleep holding the picture, convinced he died knowing I loved him.

* * *

The second semester of my sophomore year began. I kept myself busy during the day with classes, my work study job in the library, studying in Hixson Lounge, and writing for *The Forester*. Nights were the hardest. With Hook everywhere around me and with the help of my friends, I could make it.

Richard Nixon was inaugurated as the 37th President of the United States.

* * *

The Forester
Contributor Column
By Becky Jamison

The administration cancelled classes last Monday so that students could watch the inauguration of President Richard Nixon and Vice President Spiro Agnew. In his speech, Nixon made a "sacred commitment to peace." He asked the American people to "lower our voices" because "we cannot learn from one another until we stop shouting at one another, until we speak quietly enough so that our words can be heard."

The inauguration was not without controversy. A thousand anti-war demonstrators, including former Lake Forest College student, Jake Stedman, participated in an anti-inauguration march. More than eighty arrests were made. It was only the second time a presidential inauguration has been protested. The first was a protest of unemployed workers at Franklin Pierce's inauguration in 1853.

Join the LFC Students Against the War. The meetings are held in Hixson Lounge, Wednesdays at 7:00.

U.S. Soldier Body Count: 37,496

Chapter 27

"Everlasting Love"

It was near time for our annual conception party. "Maybe we should cancel this year," I said to Marty a week before Valentine's Day. I put a pot of brown rice on the stove to cook.

He walked over to me and put both his hands on my shoulders. "We have a deal. We agreed we would do this every February on the Saturday closest to the 14th."

I laughed. "I am surprised you remember what deals we forged last year. You were drunk before the party even started."

"That I was." He chopped vegetables to sauté. "Anyhow, Jake is coming up. It will be the five of us."

We had our party. It was Peter's first conception party and he promised it wouldn't be his last. He and I concocted what we called our *Cornbread Surprise* for dinner. Cornbread split it in half, covered with black beans, salsa, and cheese, and then the top half of the cornbread. Add that to the vegetables and we had a perfect meal for a celebration.

As conception parties go, it was the best so far. We sang, danced, ate like kings, and drank cheap wine.

"Sometimes I miss him so much I feel like I'm going to stop breathing," I said when there was a lull in the music.

"I know what you mean," Ginger said. "In Hixson, at our anti-war meeting last week, I looked up and expected to see him

174

leaning against the back wall, his arms across his chest, that red bandana holding back his hair, ready to say the one thing that put us all going in the right direction."

"I think about him every day," Jake said. "I can feel him behind me, pushing me."

"He's everywhere," Marty said.

Peter poured wine into our empty glasses and raised a toast. "To Hook," he said.

Midnight came and we declared conception day over. I walked over to Marty and hugged him tightly. "We're connected, you know," I said. I pulled back and looked him in the eyes. "No matter where we end up in our lives, you and I are connected."

He kissed my forehead. "There's no one else I'd rather be connected to."

U.S. Soldier Body Count: 38,727

Chapter 28
"Bring 'Em Home"

Easter weekend, April 5th. Celebrating the resurrection of the movement, we gathered again in Chicago, almost a year to the day since King's death, to march in support of the GIs National Day of Action Against the War. King's death wouldn't silence our voices. Kennedy's death wouldn't silence our voices. Raw violence in the streets of Chicago wouldn't silence our voices. Nixon's election wouldn't silence our voices. We weren't going away.

Twenty thousand gathered in Chicago. More than a quarter million marched throughout the country. Led by a large sign that said *GIs for Peace,* we marched and chanted. I carried a sign that said, *Bring the Troops Home Now.* Underneath I wrote, "Dennis McKinney, here in spirit." I tied the red bandana around my head.

Jake's sign said, *Fuck the draft.* Underneath he wrote. "This one's for you, Hook."

Marty walked without a sign, strategizing the whole time.

I looked at the signs in front of and behind me. *Vietnam Veterans for Peace. Get the Hell Out of Vietnam. GIs Against the War in Vietnam. Stop the Bombing Now. BRING OUR GIs HOME NOW.* Vets pushed their wheel-chaired buddies the whole parade length.

I walked by police officers lining the road. One of them had hit me on the arm with his nightstick during the Democratic National Convention and bashed in the head of the guy standing

176

next to me. I approached the police line. I looked each one in the eye as I walked past chanting, "Nixon, Nixon hey, hey. How many kids did you kill today?" They were statues, well-trained, shoot-to-kill trained. Their eyes didn't move. Their faces passive, stoic, stone. I stopped in front of one of them momentarily. Our eyes connected. "Was it you who hit me with your billy club last summer and bashed in the head of the guy next to me?" I asked, not expecting an answer. I leaned in close. He didn't blink.

"They don't have hearts," I said. Ginger carried a sign that said *End the War Now.*

Ginger smiled. "They're just doing their job."

"Their job is to serve and protect." I turned back to the police officer. "If you were doing your job, you'd march with us."

A quarter million didn't do the trick. The war went on.

* * *

The Forester
Contributor Column
By Becky Jamison

The anti-war movement is alive and well. All around the country students are demanding that their colleges and universities divest themselves of all financial and political involvement in the war. They are protesting ROTC programs and other policies tied to the military. Thousands are boycotting classes and taking over campus buildings.

At Lake Forest College, thanks to the tireless work of Professor Garson and his committee, President Coleman has instituted reforms that put students at the center of the governing process. Any student who wishes to address the faculty at their meetings should contact President Coleman's secretary. The Board of Trustees has also invited Student Government officers to attend and speak at their meetings.

Join our efforts. Lake Forest College Students Against the War meets every Wednesday at 7:00 in Hixson Lounge.

* * *

It felt good to be alive again. At the end of this semester Ginger would marry and move out. She was the person who understood me and accepted me no matter how ugly it got, the person who made great music with me and made me a better journalist every time she edited my articles. She would leave. Before she did, we were going to sing, plan a wedding, publish a newspaper, and talk about politics.

One night in May we sat on the couch studying. I turned to her. "I never told you how sorry I was about the way I behaved on election day."

"That was a long time ago, Becky. A lot has happened since." She closed her book and looked at me. "I understand."

I swallowed hard trying to muster up the courage to say what I needed to say. "I am so sorry about what happened to your mom. After you told me, I never said anything."

"My mom was not a good person. My dad was even worse."

"That can't be entirely true. Look how you turned out."

"I was fourteen when I got my first bad boyfriend. He was nineteen. My mom told me to stay away until 9:00 p.m. I was walking down the side of the road eating an ice cream cone and he picked me up on his motorcycle. What kind of mother does that to a fourteen-year-old?" She reached for a Kleenex. "After him it was one boyfriend after another. They only lasted long enough to get me in bed and maybe rough me up a bit."

178

"Where did you live after your mother died?"

"I went to live with my mom's sister. They hadn't seen each other for ten years. That's when I started writing a journal. The more I wrote, the more I realized I was like my mom. I didn't want to be like her. I hated her. I owe my life to Aunt Jane and Uncle Ed."

"I am so sorry." I reached over and took hold of her hand.

"It's okay. Look where I ended up."

"I can't believe it's going to be over in a few weeks. You're going to marry and move in with Jake. God, what am I going to do without you?"

"Chicago is only thirty miles away." She squeezed my hand.

Life leveled out. The pain of losing faded away. The laughter came back. In the next two years before I graduated new people would come into my life and others would drift away. Through it all, I would get by. My friends would make sure of that. But Ginger? I would miss her when she left.

U.S. Soldier Body Count: 41,663

Chapter 29
"The First Time Ever I Saw Your Face"

That summer of 1969, the war escalated and three thousand young men were given a free, all-expenses-paid trip to Vietnam.

I spent the summer working as an intern at the local newspaper. Marty worked in a law office. Peter raised vegetables, some of which he sold at a stand by the side of the highway, some of which filled our refrigerator and our plates. We pooled our money. It would get us through the next year.

July 20, Peter, Marty, and I gathered on the couch, a plate of carob brownies on the coffee table in front of us. That night, man would walk on the moon. That's if all went well. Armstrong, Aldrin, and Collins. Armstrong, Aldrin, and Collins. I knew those names like the back of my hand. That's all anyone talked about since they launched four days earlier.

"Why are we spending so much money going to the moon when there is so much poverty here?" Marty picked up another brownie and ate it in two bites.

"It's cool," I said.

"That doesn't seem like a good enough reason to spend all that money."

"Don't you think it's a little bit exciting, Marty?"

The newscaster repeated the sequence again. Armstrong and Aldrin would move to the lunar module, Eagle, and separate the command module. Collins would keep orbiting and, if all went well, the lunar module would slowly make its way down to the moon's surface.

"This is scary," I said. Suki and Racer jumped up on the couch to join me. "What happens if something goes wrong?"

"What kind of question is that?" Marty asked. "If something goes wrong, then something goes wrong. They die and Collins flies all the way back to earth by himself, leaving his dead friends. Their wives will forever look at the moon and know that their husbands are up there dead. That's what's going to happen if something goes wrong."

"You're scared too, aren't you?" I said to Marty. I could always tell Marty's emotions. Any minute I expected him to start talking to the command module.

"Am not." He poured himself another glass of wine from the gallon jug of Pisano on the counter. "Anyone want wine?"

"Not me," I said. "I want to be sober when they land. If something goes wrong, I want to be ready."

"Ready for what?"

"I don't know. I always need to be ready. Too many bad things have happened to me in the last two years. If I'm ready and something bad happens then I'll be ready."

"Becky, that makes no sense. If you're ready, of course you'll be ready."

"Marty, let her be ready," Peter said.

"Thanks, Peter." If they crashed on the moon, I could be ready to cry. Or if they actually made it to the moon and walked on the moon and made it back to the command module, I could be ready to celebrate. I turned my attention back to the television set.

"Three minutes to landing," the announcer said. I grabbed Marty's hand and held on for dear life. "Going for landing, going for landing. Go. Go. Go. Go. 3,000 feet." They sounded so in control. So sure. I didn't hear fear. I didn't hear hesitancy. "Go. Go. 2,000 feet. Still looking very good." I realized I was holding my breath. I exhaled, inhaled, and held it again.

"1,600 feet. Eagle looking good. 540 feet. 220 feet. Moon getting closer. 100 feet. 75 feet. Looking good. Sixty seconds. Picking up some dust. Drifting to the right."

"Oh no," I said. "Go left. Go left."

"Thirty seconds." It went dark. "We copy you down Eagle." *Where are you Eagle? Where are you?*

Then the voice, "Houston." A pause. *What? What? What?* "Tranquility Base here. The Eagle has landed."

We breathed. They breathed. Everyone breathed. When I let go of Marty's hand, he shook it. "Shit. You've got a grip." I gave him a kiss on the cheek.

Later, Neil Armstrong took the first step on the powdery surface of the moon, "One Small Step for Man. One Giant Leap for Mankind."

"Now that that is over, maybe the government could get back to solving all the problems we have here," Marty said.

"Marty, if we can make it to the moon, we can do anything."

The world rejoiced as three men traveled 480,000 miles, landing on the moon and returning safely. That summer, in a small country in Southeast Asia, two thousand five hundred soldiers died with little fanfare.

* * *

On August 9th, Peter, Marty, and I rode the train into Chicago and converged on Jake and Ginger's apartment. They were getting married the next day and we had one more night to party. While Peter and Marty took Jake out for a night on the town, Ginger and I practiced the song she would sing to Jake, "The First Time Ever I Saw Your Face." I didn't know how she could ever get through a song while looking at the one she was going to spend the rest of her life with.

As she practiced, Jeff's face flashed before me. The first time I ever saw him was when he jumped out of that tree and stood in front of me, dared me to come see him that night at Commons. The last time I saw his face was when he drove me to the airport on my way to working at summer camp. I still missed him. Then I saw Hook's face. That's when the tears came. The first time I saw his face was at orientation. I didn't see how gorgeous he was until he came to the anti-war table three weeks later. The last time I saw his face was after I fed him a doughnut and he gently kissed me before walking out the door.

"I don't know how you'll be able to do this, Ginger. I'm crying and I'm not even the one singing to my future husband."

"I need you to carry a Kleenex in case I need it."

"You know I always carry Kleenex."

"That's one of the things I've always loved about you."

We hugged, held on to each other for a long time. "How will I survive without you, Ginger? Who will I do music with? Who will be there when I fall apart?"

"You'll get another roommate."

"But it won't be you."

"Every time you think you can't stand it, pull out the guitar, sing a little Bob Dylan, and think of me. If you really can't stand it, get on the train and come visit."

"It won't be the same." I couldn't stop crying.

"Sometimes I wish we could freeze time and stay in one place forever," Ginger said.

"What time would you freeze?"

"Jake's graduation party. Planting flowers. Being there together."

"I'm so happy for you but the selfish part of me wants you to stay in Lake Forest."

Later that evening, when the men returned, we drank a little wine, reminisced, talked about the future, laughed, and promised we would never lose touch with each other.

"I hear there's a music festival in New York starting next weekend. You all should go. Your last bash before school starts. The lineup is incredible," Jake said.

"We talked about it," I said. "We decided that the drive was too long and none of us can take that much time away from our jobs. We're down one roommate so need all the cash we can get to survive the year. We're going to Cleveland on Friday to visit Hook's mom and his gravesite. She said the gravestone is finally up."

The next day, Jake and Ginger married in a quiet ceremony in the courtyard at the hospital where Jake was completing his alternative service. Ginger wore the beads she took from Hook's room.

Barefooted, Marty walked me in, one hand in mine, the other brushing back the hair from his eyes. Peter handed a daisy to everyone who came. Parents and family. A few college friends. A few childhood friends. A few administrators and colleagues from the hospital.

I looked around the crowd as Ginger sang her love song to Jake. Not a dry eye in the house. Ginger had tears flowing down her face, but she made it through the song with her crystal voice and without the help of a Kleenex.

They wrote their own vows.

"Ginger, I love you. I have loved you for a long time. You are my past, my present, my future. I am not perfect but my love for you is. Now. Forever."

"Jake, I love you. You are my soul, my rock, my very best friend. I have loved you from the first moment I saw you. You are my everything. Now. Forever."

The hospital chaplain pronounced them man and wife. They kissed. We sang and danced the night away.

I didn't want to say good-bye. My time with Ginger had changed. She would be a phone call away. A train ride away. But away.

* * *

We left Suki and Racer with a friend and the next Friday we drove to Cleveland. As we left the Chicago area, the news came on the radio at the half hour. "The roads are clogged heading to the Woodstock Music Festival in Bethel, New York. The police are closing the roads and urging people to stay away."

"We should go," I said.

"They are telling us to stay away," Marty said. He always was the one to think things through.

"That's why we should go." We didn't.

U.S. Soldier Body Count: 44,467

Chapter 30
"In My Life"

We arrived in Cleveland late afternoon. The site under the oak tree was shaded from the heat of whatever summer heaviness lingered. Not a cloud in the sky. A slight breeze from the west. All the stone said was "Dennis Joseph "Hook" McKinney. June 12, 1946—November 25, 1968. Beloved son and friend." That's what Dennis would have wanted on his tombstone. He didn't need anything about how God took the best ones first. Or that he was a soldier in a war he didn't agree with. Or that we missed him and he enriched our lives.

I placed fresh daisies on his grave and traced his name with my finger. "I miss you every day, Hook. I'm sorry I gave you one last doughnut to eat." I took his red bandana out of the belt loop where I always carried it and used it to dry my eyes as he had dried them for me. It still held him holding me.

Peter placed a bouquet of dandelions next to the daisies and stood in silence.

Marty rubbed the tombstone and whispered. I couldn't hear what he was saying. When he finished, he brushed back his hair, catching a tear.

I started slowly singing, "All You Need is Love." Using the tombstone as a drum, Marty sang with me. I will always carry Hook's love.

We went to visit Mama McKinney hoping to find a piece of Hook there. She gave us each a McKinney hug, some iced tea, and a slice of chocolate pie. We talked about our time with Dennis, laughed at stories about him, cried together. The missing would never go away.

We spent that night in a cheap motel room on the outskirts of Cleveland, taking advantage of the ice machine, the hot water, and small bars of soap, calling for extra towels. "What would I ever do without you two?" I wrapped my wet hair in a towel and chose a donut from the dozen we bought on the drive, a chocolate doughnut filled with lemon cream. Boston cream.

"I guess you'll find out next year when we're gone," Marty said. He headed to the shower.

I stood at the sink in front of the mirror and yelled at him through the door. "Gone where?"

"Who knows?" He turned on the shower. I could barely hear his next words. Something like graduation. The draft. Vietnam.

I was left looking in the giant mirror. I caught Peter's eye in the reflection. He shook his head. I was drowning.

Down Interstate 90, through Ohio, across Indiana. Marty talked about plans for National Moratoriums in the fall to protest the war. "We shut down the country for one day in October and two days in November. If the government doesn't respond, three days in December."

"Marty, you know Nixon won't listen to us anyway. No matter what we do this war isn't going to stop until he's ready." I opened the bag of potato chips we bought at the 7-11 on our last stop. I took a handful and handed the bag to Peter in the back seat.

"Can't I dream?" Marty asked. "Hand up the chips when you're done." Peter handed me the bag. I put it beside Marty.

"Dreams die, Marty. Or they turn into nightmares. Dreamers die too. I don't think anything we do makes a difference."

"We have to do it anyway."

Marty turned silent.

We picked up the dogs and rolled up to our small white house in the country. It was two and a half weeks before classes started. My junior year. Their senior. I didn't want to think about it.

U.S. Soldier Body Count: 44,497

OCCUPY WALL STREET ENCAMPMENT NOVEMBER 14-15, 2011
Zuccotti Park, New York City

"We've been ordered to evacuate," Matt said to his friends. They sat drinking warm tea and eating oatmeal raisin cookies donated by a local restaurant. He preferred the chocolate chip. Reminded him of home. "The mayor says it's a health issue and ordered us to evacuate the park. They're saying we can return when it's clean. Sounds like BS to me. I doubt they'll let us back."

Matt stood up and stretched. He took one more cookie. "I'm beat. Catch you later."

Matt went into his tent, slipped into his sleeping bag, zipped it up around him, and was instantly asleep. He woke up to the sound of police officers. Matt looked at his phone. One o'clock in the morning. He climbed out of his tent.

The officers descended on the park, pushing people who got in their way. As the police came closer to the center of the park, Matt heard occupiers yelling at the cops. "Shame on you! Shame on you!"

A police officer said through a megaphone, "If you do not leave now, you will be subject to arrest."

Matt heard the crack of a nightstick against bone. He pushed his way through the crowd as the cops continued their onslaught. They violently ripped tents apart, destroyed everything they saw. They filled dumpsters with sleeping bags, mats, tents, clothes, shoes. They destroyed the people's library. Five thousand books donated, read, thrown in the dumpster.

"Fuck you," Matt yelled. He saw a group gathering at the kitchen area near the center of the encampment. They chained themselves together. Matt pushed his way through the melee to get there.

"You're blocking pedestrian passage," a police officer said.

"We are the pedestrians. We're not blocking anyone." Matt kept moving.

Where was the press? Barricaded two blocks away and not allowed to record the destruction. The occupiers had their cell phones and made sure the whole world would see.

Matt made it to the kitchen area and chained himself to his friends. They sat; arms linked. Matt texted his parents. "Getting arrested. Don't worry. Mom, you need to tell this story."

"This is our home," Matt said to the cops who brought in bolt cutters.

The cops cuffed Matt with zip ties, too tight, and dragged him across the park to the waiting paddy wagon.

Matt's mom won a Pulitzer Prize for her reporting on the destruction.

Arrests: 192

PART THREE

JUNIOR YEAR

1969-1970

Chapter 31

"San Francisco"

I walked gingerly into the beginning of my junior year, not wanting it to begin but once it did, wanting it to last. At the end of this beginning, Marty and Peter might be gone.

I had a job set up in the college library ten hours a week. I would also be assistant editor for the school paper, responsible for editing articles, piecing together lay-outs, reporting on anti-war events, and getting the paper ready for publication. My life elevated and the war escalated. America the land of the free and the home of the brave continued to be the home of the grave.

* * *

"Do you want to take over Ginger's room?" Marty asked. "It's warmer in the winter."

"I'll keep the attic." I couldn't imagine leaving it. "We do need to find another roommate. Preferably not a senior so I'll have someone to live with next year, and preferably a female to even out the odds."

Later that week Marty came home with a proposition. He waited to tell me when my hands were in dirty dishwater so I couldn't pummel him. "How about a twenty-nine-year-old sociology professor, male, unmarried?"

I turned to look at him, rubber gloved hands still in the water. The right glove had a hole in the thumb. "I asked for a junior female, Marty. I did not ask for a 29-year-old male. I definitely don't want to live with a sociology professor."

"You'll like this guy." He took a towel and dried the dishes. "He's coming from San Francisco."

"That's supposed to make a difference? I don't care where he comes from. I don't want to live with a sociology professor or be stuck with one when you graduate. Have you met him?"

"Not exactly. I ran into a professor on campus who told me their new hire was looking for a place to live. I called the guy and he said he'd be willing to pay a higher portion of the rent because we're all students." Marty wiped a dish then threw the towel on the counter.

"Now this is about the money?"

"No. It's not about the money. Although it would be nice not to have to eat boxed mac and cheese for the entire last week of every month because we're out of money."

"So, it is about money."

"You exasperate me, Becky. I said it's not about money. It's about finding someone else to live with us."

"There are a lot of people who would love to live here. No sociology professors. Period." I washed the last few pieces of silverware in the bottom of the sink.

"You don't know anything about him or about sociology professors. You're not a sociology major."

I turned to face Marty. "I know a lot about sociology professors. In two years, I have taken four sociology courses."

"That makes you an expert?"

"I'm not done, Marty. Tom Garson was my advisor. Remember? Like everyone else, he deserted me, and I need a new advisor. That's what sociology professors do."

194

"You can't blame Garson. He got a great job at a research university. You have no argument." Marty put the last fork in the drawer still wet.

"It isn't just Garson. R.J. was a sociology major. We went to a party at Professor Stinson's house once. I learned everything else I need to know about sociology professors there."

"You can't judge sociology professors by Stinson. He only lasted a year. I took his Sociology of Politics class, and he was crazy."

"You should have taken Garson's Sociology of Politics class. Changed my life." I said. "You're assuming this guy will be like Garson. What if he's not? How do you know this guy isn't like Stinson?" I pulled the plug from the sink, took off the rubber gloves and drained the right one. I dried my hands on the towel hanging over the refrigerator door handle. It needed to be washed.

I sat down and put both hands on the kitchen table. "Let me tell you about sociology professors. It will change your mind about having one live here and then we can look for a junior female."

Marty poured boiling water into our teapot that played "Tea-For-Two" when you picked it up, provided you remembered to wind it beforehand. The teapot was silent. Marty handed me a cup of hot water with a peppermint teabag in it, a mason jar full of honey, and a wooden honeycomb. "Enlighten me."

"My job as a journalist is to observe and investigate so here's what I saw at Stinson's. Apparently, all good hippies major in sociology, and their professors think it's groovy to interact with them and find out what makes them tick." I poured honey into the tea straight from the jar, ignoring the honeycomb.

"You actually expect me to take this conversation seriously when you just said 'groovy'?" Marty reached for the honey.

"It's a sociological experiment. The professors search for the hippie ideology and I don't want them searching here."

"Whatever that means. Go on."

"These hippie sociology majors sat around Stinson's house putting down some dope. I don't think I've ever been at a party with that much dope." I blew on the tea and took a drink.

"That's saying something. I saw you put down some dope last fall."

"Beside the point. In the middle of the kitchen table, Stinson had the biggest jar of Vitamin C I ever saw. Something about Vitamin C depletion and marijuana. I don't think there's a shred of truth in it. By the way, and this point is important, throughout all of this, Stinson is nowhere to be seen."

"So now you're all stoned and Stinson is nowhere."

"That's the point. He is nowhere and we're in his house. I got really stoned. Actually, I was stoned before I even got there but that's also beside the point. Everyone had pink halos around their heads and R.J.'s ears were green, I think. I can't remember exactly who had what color of what. Incense burned in weird Buddha statues on every counter."

Marty laughed. "Stop right there. Having a sociology professor live here does not mean that people will have pink halos around their heads. That's the dope you smoked and not the professor. I happen to like Buddha."

"The point is that they did it at the professor's house and I don't particularly want a bunch of sociology majors with pink halos smoking dope and hanging out in our house all the time."

"You have a lot of points and I'm still not convinced."

"The incense made me nauseated. God, I hate incense." I thought of the incense burning in Jeff's apartment in Boston. It made me hate incense even more. "Sitar music played on the record player. I remember wondering why they weren't listening to the Beatles. I know the Beatles got into sitar music but I'm not talking about Beatles sitar. I'm talking about sitar sitar, twangy with no real tune. God, I hate sitar music even more than I hate incense. Can you imagine constant sitar music playing on our stereo with raspberry smelling incense filling the house?" It was then I realized that I was telling Marty about what happened at Stinson's house. If Hook were still alive, I'd tell him, and we would laugh about it.

Marty looked at me, drumming his fingers on the table. "Becky, back to sociology professors."

"I am talking about sociology professors. They play sitar music. The only good thing was the gallon of Pisano. They don't drink Ripple. Everyone smokes cigarettes or joints. The room is filled with smoke. I don't want cigarette smoke in my house all the time. And I hate incense."

"You already said that."

"I know. But I want you to know how much I hate incense. It gives me a headache. Over in the corner there's a big water pipe, probably bought on a research trip to Turkey. There must have been two dozen jars filled with various nuts and grains on the shelf in the kitchen."

"Nuts and grains are good for you. You haven't convinced me yet."

"Okay. This will get you. They eat Vanilla Wafers." I walked over to the counter that separated the kitchen from the living room and picked up the Winnie-the-Pooh cookie jar. I took it to the table and pulled out five Oreos. "Can you imagine Winnie-the-Pooh filled with Vanilla Wafers? It would be sacrilegious."

"Still not convinced." Marty put an Oreo in his mouth whole and got up to pour more water into the teapot.

"This will do it. Everyone is stoned and making out or having sex on the couch or on the bean bag chairs on the floor in the living room."

"That doesn't have anything to do with sociology professors." Marty stopped and looked at me, the teacup half-way to his mouth.

"It does because it's what happens at their houses that's important. Do you want all that happening here?"

"Stick to Stinson. I don't need to hear what you and R.J. did there when you were stoned."

"That's the point. Stinson let it happen. What professor in their right mind would allow people to smoke dope in their kitchen and have sex on their living room floor? Do you want weird sociology majors coming over here to hang out with this guy from San Francisco who you know nothing about? They smoke dope, eat sunflower seeds out of mason jars, down Vitamin C, and then make out."

"Like I said. I don't need to hear what you did with R.J. on the couch."

"I told you before. It isn't about the couch. It's about the weird people at Stinson's house. Anyhow, it was on a bean bag chair not the couch."

"I told you I don't want to hear about you and R.J." Marty stood up and paced back and forth behind the table, his hands stuffed in the pockets of his jeans.

"Calm down, Marty. I'm only giving you a warning. If a sociology professor lives here all sorts of weird things will happen right in front of your eyes."

Marty looked at me. "In fact, I don't really give a shit about R.J. at all." There was an edge to his voice. He was beginning to piss me off.

I looked at Marty. "I told you a million times, this has nothing to do with R.J."

"By the way, someone told me he got shipped off to Nam."

"Who told you that?"

"Can't remember. Why do you care?" Marty glared at me.

"Cool your jets, Marty. He was my friend for a while. He got me through some tough shit."

Marty slammed his hand down on the table and leaned across so that he could look at me eyeball to eyeball. "You call that man your friend? That man almost destroyed you. I hope he dies in Nam."

I pushed my chair back so hard it fell over. I stood up but didn't pick up the chair. "That is cruel. Why do you even care what I did with R.J.? It's none of your damn business. I don't ask you what you do when you go out with someone. I don't give a shit what you think about R.J. and me having sex on a beanbag chair in Stinson's living room. This isn't about him anyway. It's about sociology professors."

"Shut up about R.J."

Marty had crossed the line. I hated R.J. for what he did to me or what I allowed to happen, for who I was when I was with him. That wasn't the point. It was none of Marty's business. I walked over to the other side of the table and stood in front of him. He wanted eyeball to eyeball, I'd give him eyeball to eyeball. "Yeah, we had sex right there in front of everybody. Maybe we had sex two or three times in front of everybody. Maybe it was a big orgy and I had sex with everyone at the party. Why do you even care who I have sex with?"

Marty wouldn't answer. He turned to walk away. "Don't you walk away from me, Marty. You started this."

He turned towards me. "I told you to shut up about R.J."

I wanted to hurt Marty in some way. I don't know why. Why was I even defending R.J.? "You shut up about R.J. He was the best damn guitar player I ever heard."

"What does that have to do with anything?"

"It has everything to do with everything. You don't have a clue what I went through last year."

Marty picked up the first thing on the table his hand touched, the "Tea-For-Two" teapot, and slammed it down. The last three notes of "Tea-For-Two" played. "I lived with what you went through last year. I know every second of what you went through. R.J. didn't help."

"How do you know if he helped or not? Are you God? Do you know everything about everybody? By the way, where were you when I was going through all that shit last year? If you remember, I lost the love of my life. R.J. was the only one who got me through."

"I was here, Becky. All along."

"No, you weren't. You were stopping wars and campaigning for people and writing letters and getting petitions signed. You weren't here. Fuck you, Marty. And no sociology professors."

The fight was up. I had no more in me. I ran up to my attic room and slammed the door. It wasn't true, of course. Marty was there for me every day in every way. But right now, I wanted to pound his face. I wanted to put my fist through the wall. I didn't give a shit about R.J. That wasn't the point. I couldn't quite figure out what the point was.

Thirty minutes later there was a knock on the attic door. I opened it. No one was there but on the floor was a plate of Oreos. We never mentioned that conversation again.

* * *

Peter and Marty outvoted me. Twenty-nine-year-old sociology professor Rick Barton moved in. A few early grays peppered his full beard and the long dark hair braided down his back. When Rick Barton sat, he didn't just sit. He set. He plopped himself down as though he meant to be there for a while. They do that a lot in the South. He didn't come from the South, but he knew how to set. Wherever he was, he belonged there for a long time, even if it was only for a moment.

An incurable pot smoker and lover of incense, Rick quickly placed a jar of Vitamin C in the middle of the kitchen table and insisted everyone take one every morning, dope or not. Pretty soon I learned to tolerate incense. I never grew to love it, but I did grow to love Rick Barton.

Rick came to Lake Forest College after receiving his doctorate from one of the University of California campuses. Childhood memories of the Midwest brought him to Chicago.

Rick moved all his stuff into the downstairs bedroom the week before school started. All his stuff is what he could fit in his VW van for the trip from the West Coast. A new stereo system, a bunch of big pillows, a great batch of records that he put on the board-and-brick bookcase that held our entire collection, some serapes he'd picked up in Mexico, a bean bag chair, a couple boxes of clothes, and lots of books. Best of all, he brought in the third seat of his VW van. We used it as an extra couch.

* * *

"There's nothing to eat." I stood in front of the refrigerator, door open, light on. Rick pointed out the carrots, cabbage, radishes, celery, sprouts, apples, oranges.

"I want food. Pie, crackers, a hunk of cheese, some luncheon meat, peanut butter and jelly." I looked at the mason quart jars on

201

the shelf above the sink, each filled with a different grain, seed, or nut. Barley, sprouted wheat, alfalfa seeds, popcorn.

Damn sociology professors. I knew this would happen. Peter strolled into the kitchen and opened the refrigerator door. "Great job shopping, Rick."

* * *

Over Pisano wine, marijuana, and the nauseating smell of incense, we spent the last few days of summer talking about Berkeley, Haight-Asbury, free speech, campus takeovers, and student strikes. One night, Rick handed me a *Life Magazine*. I opened it up to faces of the week's dead in Vietnam.

"Oh, my God." I touched each picture. "They're all my age." Page after page of faces. Two hundred and forty-two faces. Yearbook pictures. The war wasn't hundreds dead or thousands dead. It was one person dead over and over and over again. Russell and Charles. Elmer and John. Keith and Michael. Robert and James. That person and this one. All had a family who loved him. One by one, individuals, each once a living breathing human being. Each one dead. Two hundred and forty-two black body bags with white name tags.

U.S. Soldier Body Count: 45,935

Chapter 32
"Piece Of My Heart"

"Rick, convince me to shift my major from journalism to sociology." I was eating a vegetable lasagna and listening to Janis Joplin.

"Sociology is a worthless profession. Stick to journalism."

"Should I enroll in your American Subcultures course next semester?"

"It's going to be great."

"Would I get an automatic 'A'?"

He grinned. "Not on your life. But you will learn how we divide ourselves into groups based on shared ideology or lifestyle and how those groups can bring us together or tear us apart."

"I'm convinced."

Easy banter filled the dinner hour. Finally, Marty made his move. "Hey, Becky. Want to go to the homecoming dance with me November first?" he asked.

"Sure." It came out of my mouth without a thought.

"Far out."

Later that night in my attic room I thought about Marty. *Oh, my God, I don't want to fall in love with Marty. If we become lovers, it will ruin our friendship. He'll die and I'll inherit another jacket. I don't need another jacket. I have Jeff's brown leather one and Hook's army jacket. I can't risk another jacket. I can't risk ruining our friendship. I have to tell him no.*

On the other hand, he is my best friend and it is only a date. It's not like we're getting married or anything. He only asked me to the homecoming dance. He didn't ask me to be his girlfriend.

What if he wants more than I can give? What if he thinks that I want more? What if things get awkward in the house? What if he dies?

I picked up my history book but couldn't concentrate. I tried to fold my clean clothes. I folded one t-shirt and threw it back in the corner. I picked up my guitar figuring I could strum my way out of this. I put the guitar back in the corner. I couldn't get Marty out of my head.

"A glass of wine," I thought. *"That will do it."*

That's where I met Marty. He sat at the counter in the kitchen, tearing an anti-war pamphlet into tiny pieces, drinking wine out of a quart mason jar with a gallon of Pisano on the counter in front of him.

He looked at me as I walked in. "Hey." Marty held up his quart mason jar. "Want a drink?"

"That's why I came down." He got a clean jar from the drain tray, filled it halfway up with wine, and handed it to me.

"What are you doing here in the kitchen tearing up an anti-war pamphlet into little pieces?" I took a drink of wine.

"I am tearing an anti-war pamphlet into little pieces." He downed the rest of the wine in his jar.

"I hear that's what people who are anti-anti-war people do when we hand them a pamphlet. Are you trying to tell me something?" This conversation was going nowhere. I needed more wine. I finished up the half mason jar and held it out to Marty for more.

"When I get really rich or even a little bit rich or even just have a real job, I am going to buy myself some good wine. This really doesn't taste very good." Marty filled up his jar again almost to the top.

"It's terrible," I agreed. "Ripple is worse and that's what Hook drank all the time."

"I actually do my best thinking while drinking bad wine."

"What were you thinking about before I interrupted you?"

"That is a very interesting question." He pushed all the tiny pieces of the anti-war pamphlet into a pile. "I was wondering what would happen if everyone in the whole world jumped at exactly the same time. I believe there is enough power in the entire three and a half billion of us that we could literally change the course of history with a single jump." He picked up the tiny pieces of the pamphlet, held them at eye level, let go, and watched them float down to the counter.

"How could you get everyone in the whole world to jump at the same time?"

"I thought about that too. I happen to be a brilliant thinker, you know." He looked at me, smiled, and pushed the hair out of his eyes. "We would advertise in all the major newspapers in the world and on all the most popular TV shows."

Marty poured more wine into his mason jar. I slid his jar out of reach. He didn't notice.

"When the time came, the entire world would count at the same time. One. Two. Three. BAM. We'd jump." Marty hit the table.

"God. You scared me."

"See, it will work. All it takes is One. Two. Three. BAM." He hit the table again. "Everyone jumps at the same moment, and everything is different. We would shift the world. No more war. No more draft. No more poverty. No more segregation. No more death. No more pain. What do you think?" He looked around for his jar of wine.

"I think it has potential."

"How did my wine get all the way over to the other side of the counter?" he asked. "See, I told you it works. One. Two. Three. BAM. And suddenly my jar of wine is somewhere else. I know it will work. It's the way to end the war." He leaned over, got his wine, and drank.

"I'm sure if three and a half billion people all jumped at the same time something would happen. I'm not sure we can make it happen."

"Oh, ye of little faith." Marty got up. "I'll show you how it works. One. Two. Three." Marty tried to jump but stumbled into the counter, knocking over his jar of wine. I grabbed a towel and threw it over the spilled wine before it had a chance to drip to the floor. "See. All I had to do was jump and the jar falls over. Just think of three and a half billion people jumping."

Marty sat back down. "God, I'm drunk." He put his head down on the little pieces of anti-war literature on the counter.

"Let me help you to bed." When he looked up at me, he had tiny pieces of paper stuck to his forehead. I picked them off, pulled him up, put my arm around him, and helped him up the stairs. When we got to his room, he looked at me.

"I love you, you know," he said.

"Yeah, I know."

"No, I mean, I really, really love you."

"I know."

Marty collapsed back on the bed. I took off his shoes and covered him with a blanket. Before he passed out, he said, "I love you for real."

* * *

I woke up the next morning and knew I had to get to Ginger. Drinking wine with Marty and listening to him solve the problems of the world by jumping hadn't helped. There was still the problem of the homecoming dance.

I took the 2:00 p.m. train into Chicago. When Ginger answered the door all I could say was, "I can't fall in love with Marty."

Ginger sat me down at the kitchen table and gave me a cup of coffee. "He asked you to the dance, Becky. That's all."

"What if we have a good time? What if he decides he wants to date me? What if we make love and then he decides he doesn't like me anymore? What if he dies?" I couldn't breathe.

Jake walked into the apartment and saw me sitting at the table. "Becky, what brings you into Chicago?"

"Marty asked her to the homecoming dance," Ginger said.

"It's about time." Jake poured a cup of coffee and joined us at the table.

"What do you mean by that?" I asked.

"He's been in love with you for two years, ever since you came to your first anti-war meeting."

"Shit." It seemed like an appropriate response. It didn't really solve my problem though or deal with the issue at hand. "He can't fall in love with me, Jake. It will ruin everything. He'll probably die."

"He's not going to die, Becky. Besides he doesn't need to fall in love with you. He's already in love with you." Jake stood up. "I'll let you two talk. Let me know if you need my advice."

I looked at Ginger. She smiled. "You would be crazy not to know that he likes you, Becky."

"Shit," I said again.

"Saying shit is not going to help."

"What am I going to do? Besides you, he's my best friend. I couldn't stand it if we weren't friends anymore."

"He's been your best friend for a long time, Becky. See what happens."

"Maybe I should tell him I changed my mind. Maybe I shouldn't go."

"Go, Becky. It's just a dance."

I had a hard time falling asleep that night. The pull-out couch in the living room was lumpy and this fear thing took hold of my brain. I relived the fight Marty and I had over Rick moving in. What if we became enemies and fought all the time? I would have to find some place to live, move out, leave Marty, leave Peter and Rick, leave the dogs.

When I fell asleep, I dreamed of Hook for the first time. He stood on the beach far away. He tossed a flat stone into the water. It skipped forty-six times. He turned towards me and yelled, "Did you see that?"

I yelled back. "How in the world did you do that?"

"You can't skip it forty-six times if you don't toss the stone."

I ran down the beach towards him but the more I ran, the farther away he was. Right before he disappeared, I heard him say, "Toss the stone, Becky. Toss the stone."

I woke up crying. Ginger heard me from the kitchen. She sat down on the bed next to me and handed me a cup of coffee.

"I dreamed about Hook," I told her. "He told me to toss the stone."

"Hook always had good advice," she said.

"What does it even mean?"

"You'll figure it out."

* * *

208

The homecoming date remained unspoken. An uneasiness lingered.

I begged Ginger and Jake to come visit the next weekend. "I can't stand it anymore, Ginger. I was playing my guitar last night. Marty was on the couch looking at me. He didn't say anything, didn't drum the table like he usually does. He simply looked at me. I finally went upstairs."

They came and everything seemed normal again. As we sat in front of the fireplace after dinner, Jake said, "Draft lottery in December. You ready?" The first draft lottery since 1942. Birthdays, drawn out of a bowl to determine the order of who gets drafted. The lottery would determine the fate of males born between 1944 and 1950. How could anyone get ready for that? You're number one, you die. You're number three hundred and sixty-six, you live. Marty shifted uneasily in his chair.

"You ever read that story called *The Lottery*?" I asked. "I read it in a high school English class. Every year this town has a lottery and the person who wins gets pelted with stones by the whole town until they die. We had a lottery in my class. The person who won had to do what we said. Like bring a piece of gum for everyone. Wear your shirt backwards for a day. Stuff like that. The freshman class football star picked out the Black X. He basically said he wasn't going to play and that was it." It was like if they gave a war and nobody showed up.

Marty stood up. "Why didn't people in the town just say no?" He leaned down and cleared the coffee table with one sweep of his arm, walked out of the room and up the stairs. We watched him go and twinged when we heard his door slam.

"What was that all about?" Rick finally said.

"I don't have a clue." I picked up the magazines that landed on the floor next to me. "Somebody should go talk to him."

I looked around the room and realized everyone was staring at me. I shook my head no. They shook their heads yes.

I went upstairs and knocked on the door. No answer. "I'm coming in."

Marty was staring out his window into the darkness, twirling a pencil in his fingers. He turned around when I walked in, snapped the pencil in two with the fingers of his right hand. He threw both pieces, one by one, towards the trashcan in the corner. They ended up on the floor.

I picked up the pencil pieces and threw them away. "I didn't think the story was that bad," I said.

Marty walked over to his desk, picked up a piece of paper, and handed it to me. He still hadn't said anything. He hadn't said whether he liked the story or not or why he cleared the coffee table or broke the pencil in one snap.

"Your application for CO status has been denied," I read. "If you have questions about this decision, please contact your local draft board." I looked up at him.

"Why?" I asked.

"How do I know? I pretty much said the same thing that Jake did on his application. What am I going to do?"

"You can appeal. Contact the draft board and tell them you disagree with their decision."

"They're not going to listen to me, Becky."

"You won't know until you try."

"You are the eternal optimist, aren't you? While I appreciate your positive attitude, I think this is the end for me." Marty kicked the trash can and knocked it over. The broken pencil pieces rolled onto the floor.

I put the paper back on his desk and picked up the trash can and the two pencil pieces. I took hold of Marty's hands, held them until he looked in my eyes. "Maybe you'll be lucky with the lottery."

"Maybe I won't."

"Maybe you will."

Outside, the Milky Way filled the night sky with its infinite stars. Our eyes stayed locked. "You are amazing," Marty said. He kissed me soft and deep and long. I kissed him back. I felt lucky. It was a perfect moment.

* * *

The kiss remained unspoken.

The night after Ginger and Jake left, Marty and I sat at the counter drinking milk and eating cookies.

"Becky, the Turtles are playing a concert Friday night before homecoming. Want to go?" Marty stood up and started humming, tapping his fingers on the counter.

"What's your favorite Turtles song?" I asked.

"Imagine."

"That's not the name of any song I know."

"Me and you." Marty moved towards me, humming. "I do."

Toss the stone, I heard in my mind. *No*, I said back. Then it was more insistent. *Toss the stone, Becky.*

"Happy together," he said. Or sang. I'm not sure which. "That's my favorite Turtles song."

He looked at me while he sang. We had a kiss, one kiss, that's all. What does a kiss mean after all? He was upset. I comforted him. What do I do now? He's my friend, for God's sake.

He walked right by me, still humming, put on the album, moved the needle to the song. "The girl you love," he sang.

The eyes, the humming, the words, something welling up inside me. I'm scared, I thought. Everyone I fall in love with dies.

211

You can't skip it forty-six times if you don't toss the stone.

Marty took my hand and pulled me off the stool. He put his right hand on the small of my back, just tight enough so I felt secure, just light enough so I wanted more. I put my left hand on his shoulder, my fingers on his neck. He put his left hand in my right hand and slowly we moved, eyes connected. His fingers on my back tapped ever so slightly to the beat. My fingers on his neck did the same. *"Please don't die,"* I thought.

We stopped moving except his fingers and my fingers. It was me and him and him and me. The song ended and we stood there. I was still rubbing his neck with my fingers. He was still caressing my back. "Happy Together," he said.

"Yes. I'll go to the concert with you." The stone skipped forty-six times.

* * *

In all my amazing fantasies, I could never imagine I would be going to homecoming with the guy who two years before at freshman registration brushed the hair out of his eyes and told me Garson was the best.

In high school, I created amazing stories in my head to deal with my loneliness. Paul McCartney wandered down the street of my hometown, saw me lying in a hammock in my back yard, and vowed to wait for me until I turned eighteen. Nothing was as fantastic as reality.

The next Friday night we saw the Turtles. Marty held my hand throughout the entire concert. Saturday, we went to the football game. I don't remember who won. Then we went to the dance. Holding hands with Marty and dancing. When a slow song played, holding Marty and dancing.

I felt almost whole. The edges of that tiny hole in my heart for Jeff and Hook weren't ragged anymore. They were smooth like stones tossed and skipped.

When we got home from the dance Marty said, "Want a cup of tea?"

A cup of tea? I thought. *A cup of tea?* I didn't want a cup of tea. I wanted him. Desperately. That's what I wanted. Him, wet and wild, against my body. I said, "Sure, chamomile."

He put a kettle of water on the stove, put two chamomile tea bags in the "Tea-for-Two" teapot, and wound it up. He walked back to the stove and turned around. "I want to tell you about my brother."

That was the last thing I expected. All I knew about his brother was that he came home from Vietnam after being shot in the spine.

The kettle whistled. Marty poured water into the teapot. He picked it up to bring it to the table. *Picture-Me-Upon-Your-Knee.*

Marty poured tea into two cups and pushed the honey over to me. I poured some into my cup and pushed the jar back to him. He sat there not taking the honey, not drinking the tea.

"What I first remember about my big brother Billy was sitting on his lap at my dad's funeral. I was four years old. We sat in this graveyard on grey, metal folding chairs. Mom had a black veil over her face. Someone started shooting guns. Billy held me tight on his lap so I wouldn't run towards the guns. He kept saying to me, 'It'll be okay.' I idolized him. He read me bedtime stories when my mom couldn't, those little Golden Books. He played games with me: Candy Land, Cootie, Chutes and Ladders. He let me win most of the time." Marty got up from the table and paced.

"As we got older, Billy bossed me around and I got in his way. I remember once when he was about twelve and I was nine. He went out to play basketball with his friends. Mom told me not to bug them, but I did anyway. I snuck over to the park and told Billy I wanted to play. 'Go away, brat,' he said. I ran home crying."

Marty ran his fingers through his hair and rubbed his eyes with the palms of his hands. He sat back down and took a sip of tea. "Damn, that's hot."

"When Billy was thirteen, he caught a foul ball at a White Sox game and had it autographed by his favorite player, Nellie Fox. When he left for college, he gave me the ball for safekeeping." Marty walked over to the bookcase where he displayed the ball on a wooden stand. He brought it back to the table and turned it over and over in his hands.

"I remember his first real date. He was fourteen. It took him forever to get ready. They went to the movies. Mom drove. After he came home, Billy woke me up to tell me he was in love.

Marty put the baseball on the table and took a drink of tea. "Billy grew more tolerant of me as he got older. He became my hero. I could count on him for anything. He went away to college at Southern Illinois University in Carbondale when I was a sophomore. During vacations he came home and told me stories of college. I couldn't wait to go." Marty wiped a tear from his cheek and sat silent.

"Marty." He looked up at me. "You don't have to go on."

"No, I do. I want you to know. I don't know why he enlisted. Everything was going great for him in college. But that summer after his junior year, the summer I graduated from high school, he came back one day from town with his papers and told me he joined up. I asked him why and all he could say was, 'I figure I might as well get it over with. When I get back they can pay the rest of my way through school.'"

Marty poured more tea. The teapot played *Me – For – You – And – You – For – Me*. It ground to a stop. Marty poured honey in his tea and stirred.

I took hold of his hand. "I think the honey is well-mixed."

He smiled. "Billy went to basic training and in October I get a call at Lake Forest that he's being shipped to Nam but he's got a few days leave. I head home for the weekend. Billy and I smoke dope and talk. He's scared. He doesn't want to go. He remembers more than I do when he heard Dad was dead. I tried to reassure him that it would be fine, but I didn't believe it either. He told me that when he was at college in Carbondale he saw a recruiting poster. There was a marine in his dress white uniform, yellow braids on his shoulders, a gold-handled sword by his side, saluting the flag in the distance. He enlisted because of that damn poster. Billy said, 'Basic training was never like that. Nothing was ever like they said it would be. I want to get out but I think it's too late.' I'll never forget his face at that moment. The face of fear."

"The dope had its effect and we both crashed. I got on the bus back to Lake Forest the next morning and that was it." Marty stood up and got the cookie jar from the counter. He took out four cookies and handed the jar to me. I pulled out a Vanilla Wafer and bit off a tiny piece.

"He wrote regularly, mostly to Mom, but she forwarded the letters to me. Six months later I got a call from Mom that a bullet shattered his spine. Billy remained in the hospital for four months. He came home the summer after my freshman year."

I put the rest of the cookie in my mouth. I had to do something to stop myself from crying. It didn't work. I picked up a cloth napkin from the basket in the middle of the table and held it to my face, pressing it against my eyes.

Marty continued, "I was there when the military jet landed at the airport in Springfield. They wheeled him off the plane. There was Billy, staring straight ahead. The marines who wheeled him out said to my mom, 'Your son is a hero. You should be proud of him.' Billy looked at them and said in a voice almost too low to hear, 'Fuck pride. I'm no fucking hero so shut the fuck up.' Mom pretended not to hear."

"When we got him home, he wheeled himself into the downstairs bedroom in front of the window that looks out into the back yard and didn't say a word."

Marty stopped and drank some tea, cold by now, took another cookie and chewed aimlessly. "He's been home for more than two years. The VA did some counseling with him. They said that in addition to his spinal injuries he had combat fatigue, shell shock. Later they decided that since he didn't get better in six months, his so-called combat fatigue was really a pre-existing condition and they wouldn't give him counseling anymore." Marty looked straight at me and asked, "What is wrong with the U.S. government anyway?"

"That's my brother. Billy still has nightmares and reacts to every loud noise. His anger consumes him. He stays in his room day after day and reads. He sits at the dinner table with Mom but doesn't say very much. She wheels him to the local Memorial Day or Fourth of July parades and people clap for him." Marty stopped again and looked at me. "Sometimes I think it would have been better if he had died."

"You don't mean that." I knew he did. Sometimes death is sweet release.

I went to Marty, sat in his lap, put my head on his shoulder, and cried. When the tears stopped, he took me by the hand, walked me to his room where we held each other until we fell asleep.

U.S. Soldier Body Count: 46,339

Chapter 33
"Hair"

The following Wednesday, Marty gave me daffodils for my birthday. "It's not even daffodil season," I said. *Favorite color? Yellow. Why? Because of the daffodils that grow in our backyard.* "How did you know? Where did you get them?"

"I was in Chicago yesterday and saw them in a flower shop. They reminded me of you." I was moved by the gift, by his knowing.

* * *

The next weekend Marty took me to Springfield to celebrate his birthday and meet his mom and brother Billy. They sat at the dinner table when we walked in. Billy looked up. "Well, if it isn't golden boy with his girlfriend." I wanted to say that I really wasn't his girlfriend, at least I didn't know if I was or not. Did one kiss constitute a girlfriend?

"Nice to see you too, brother." Marty patted Billy on the shoulder.

I walked over and held out my hand. He offered his, looking somewhat surprised. "Hi, Billy. I'm Becky, a friend of your brother." Billy winked at me. He didn't believe the 'friend' thing for a minute.

"It is very nice to meet you, Becky. I look forward to getting to know you this weekend."

After a dinner of Mom Olsen's famous spaghetti and meatballs, Billy said, "While it certainly has been a pleasure eating with you, particularly you, Becky, I'm not sure I can stand much more small talk." He took a brownie from the plate in the center of the table and rolled away from the table turning back to say, "Becky, I hope you enjoy your stay in Springfield." He disappeared into his bedroom.

Mom Olsen looked at Marty. "I don't know how much more I can stand, Marty. You saw his attitude. He's rude or doesn't talk at all. All day he sits in his room."

"Give him time, Mom. He's been through hell."

"It's been two and a half years. Isn't that enough time?"

"Apparently not."

I folded my napkin and put it on the table. "If you don't mind, I'm going to go get acquainted with Billy." The wink invited me.

"Good luck," Marty said. I smiled at him.

"What's the worst that could happen?"

I knocked on Billy's door. "I'm coming in." Billy sat in his chair tossing a baseball up and down in his right hand, looking out the window to the back yard. It was dark out. He said nothing. "Do you mind?"

He nodded. "Be my guest."

I put my leather satchel on the bed and looked around. I walked up to the five-drawer dresser that stood against the wall by the bed. "Looks like this dresser has a lot of history." I rubbed my hand over his name carved in the top drawer next to where he carved 'Chicago White Sox.' "I bet your mom was mad as hell when you did this."

He grinned. "Mad doesn't even being to describe it. She grounded me."

"And you obeyed?"

"Except when I crawled out the window and ran around the block. I crawled back in before she even knew I was gone."

I laughed. "I got in trouble for screaming at my little brother when he followed me around the house singing this one note. He wouldn't stop. My dad grounded me. I sneaked out the window, climbed a big tree in my back yard, sat awhile, climbed down, and sneaked back in. We have a lot in common."

I pulled a joint out of my satchel, lit it, took a toke, and walked it over to Billy. "Thanks, it's been a long time. In fact, I haven't had any weed since Vietnam." He took a toke, held it for a second, and took another before handing it back.

"Shit, that's a long time." I toked and handed it back.

"I couldn't very well ask my mom to go buy me some marijuana, could I?"

I laughed. "It might get a bit complicated." I walked back to the dresser and rubbed the Chicago White Sox bumper stickers that covered every inch of the third and fourth drawers and the psychedelic swirls painted on the sides.

"Did those in high school. Mom stopped being mad about the dresser by then. She would have had a fit if she knew what I hid in the drawers, though."

"Like what?"

"Cigarettes. Condoms. The typical things."

The joint came and left.

"Why did you give Marty your Nellie Fox baseball?"

"I have no fucking clue. Doesn't a day go by when I wish I had it back."

"I could probably steal it for you. It's on the bookcase in our living room. He'd never notice. Nellie Fox wasn't half bad for a second baseman. Nothing compared to Bobby Richardson." I lit a second.

"Of the Yankees?"

I sat down on the bed. Billy was still in his chair by the desk.

"1961 Yankees. Best team that ever played. In junior high, I cut out every Yankee box score and tacked them to the wall of my bedroom."

"Must have been a real turn-on for those junior high school guys."

I threw a pillow at him. He threw the baseball at me. I caught it and tossed it back.

"Bobby Richardson and Tony Kubek were the best double play team in baseball. Hands down. No argument," I said.

"1961 White Sox. Luis Aparicio. One of the best infielders ever lived. He and Nellie Fox were unbeatable, better stats than Richardson and Kubek."

"I doubt it. 1961. That's the year Maris and Mantle had their homerun battle."

"1961. That's the year Don Larsen pitched for the White Sox."

I didn't know who was winning the argument. "Later he pitched a perfect game in the World Series as a Yankee."

"Yeah, well." Billy had no comeback.

"Yeah, well. I win. The Yankees won the series that year. Where did the White Sox end up?"

"Don't have a clue, but do you have a baseball signed by Bobby Richardson?"

"Do you have a baseball signed by Nellie Fox? No, Marty has it. We're even."

He tossed me the baseball again. I caught it with one hand. "Not bad," he said.

"Best ball player on my high school softball team."

Billy paused then gestured towards the door. "Are they out there talking about me?"

"That's why I left."

"It's the same thing every time. Mom says, 'I don't know how much more I can take.' Marty says, 'Give him time.' Then Mom says, 'It's been two years.' Was that about how it was going?"

"Something like that. So how long are you going to be miserable in this little room with your high school dresser?"

"I don't know. Maybe the rest of my miserable life."

"That's completely messed up, Billy. The only thing wrong with you is that your legs don't work. Get off your ass and do something."

"In case you didn't notice, it's pretty difficult for me to get off my ass."

"Sometime ask Marty about the shit I went through last year. What I learned was that you just have to feel the pain and get through it."

"That is the stupidest thing anyone has told me. Like that's going to motivate me or something."

"Worth a try. What will motivate you?"

"Right now, food. I'm starving."

From my satchel I pulled out a package of Oreos and Vanilla Wafers. "Which one?"

"Oreos."

"I knew you'd choose Oreos."

"You had no idea which one I would choose."

I held onto the packages of cookies. "No, really I did. I've been doing this experiment. The intelligent, abstract, sociology types pick the wafers. The down-to-earth real folks pick the Oreos."

"Are you telling me that I'm not intelligent or abstract?" He reached for the package. I pulled back.

"Sort of. Most of all I'm telling you that you are real." He reached for the package again. "Isn't it tragic for you that I control the cookies?"

The wheelchair spun around, was next to me, and the package of Oreos was out of my hand before I knew what happened.

"How did you do that?"

"I haven't had much more do to for the past two and a half years but practice my chair moves. I figured that someday I'd have to get something quick. I needed to be ready."

"So, the past two and a half years haven't been a total waste."

"I got the cookies, didn't I?" He opened the bag and pulled out seven Oreos. "Which are you choosing?" he asked. He saw the twelve Vanilla Wafers I pulled out. "Intellectual type?"

"No, I like the taste of them." I may have gone over to the dark side.

"How did you meet Marty?"

"The first day at school I went up to a table to get my orientation packet and there's this cute guy sitting there."

"You actually think my brother is cute?" Billy laughed as he put another cookie in his mouth.

"Adorable. Anyhow, I gave him my name, he brushed the hair out of his eyes with the palm of his hand and gave me my packet. It was the hair that got me."

"He keeps cutting it so it never gets long enough to stay put."

"I get it. I had bangs problems too, but I let them grow."

"He should do that or cut the damn hair."

"I agree."

"Let's grab him, tie him down, and cut it off."

"He can outrun you. You'll never catch him."

"You saw how fast I was with the chair."

Billy got going. I couldn't stop him. "Ever hear the story about the tortoise and the hare? The hare lost. And there's the story of

Rapunzel. 'Marty, Marty, please for God's sake, grow out your golden hair.'"

By then I was laughing so hard I couldn't breathe. I hit Billy with the pillow, told him to stop. He wouldn't. "Sometimes he makes my hair stand on end. Maybe he'll end up on Broadway."

Billy started singing songs from the Broadway Play *Hair*. Although I've always thought that everyone could sing but not everyone had a good voice. Billy could not even sing. He imitated that move of Marty's where he pushes back his hair.

"Marty's going to make my hair turn gray or at least make me want to tear my hair out." I got the hiccups from laughing so hard and my ribs hurt.

"Stop it, Billy. I beg you."

"Marty, why don't you wear some flowers in your hair."

I grabbed the pillow and smothered his face. It didn't stop him. "They couldn't stop me with a bullet. You think you can stop me with a pillow?"

A knock on the door. "You okay in there?" It was Marty.

"Hush," Billy said. "He'll know we're in here."

"Nobody's here," I said.

A second knock. I stood up. Straightened my face, opened the door, and hiccupped. Marty stood there with his hand in his hair. "What's going on . . .?"

That was all he got out before I shut the door in his face and rolled back on the bed in hysterics.

Marty opened the door and closed it quickly behind him. "What is going on in here?"

I swallowed, trying to stop the hiccups, but one escaped. "I'm getting to know your brother. You didn't tell me he was such a great singer."

Billy took the pillow that was still in his lap and covered his face to try and control his laugh. It didn't work.

Marty picked up the two roaches in the ashtray. I wish I had eaten them to hide the evidence, not that everything wasn't completely evident.

Billy threw the pillow at Marty, who ducked. It landed on the floor behind him. Marty picked it up and tossed it on the bed, glancing from Billy to me.

"Well, my brother with the beautiful hair. For the first time in two and a half years someone treated me like a human being. Hang on to this one. She's for real."

"Despite the Vanilla Wafers," I said.

Marty tackled me on the bed and whispered in my ear, "I think I might keep you." Then he looked at Billy. "Have you been telling lies about me?"

"Au contraire, brother. I told her the absolute truth."

"I know absolutely everything there is to know about you." Marty was still on top of me.

"If you don't mind, brother, I'm going to take her to bed."

Billy grinned at both of us. "Try to be quiet so you don't bother Mom. Or me. Your bedroom is right above mine."

I took the pillow off the bed and hit Billy with it again, "He doesn't mean that." But he did.

Billy brushed pretend hair out of his eyes. I gave him a quick hug. "Thanks for the fun. I haven't laughed that much in a long time."

He squeezed me back. "Me neither."

Marty took my hand as we walked up the stairs to our separate bedrooms. As we got to his door, Marty pulled me in with him, closed the door, and took me in his arms. What happened next was slow and gentle. Marty, my closest friend, was now my lover.

I snuck into Billy's old room early in the morning before Mom Olsen woke up. It was pretty much as he left it. A desk under the window. I could practically see it covered with hamster cages, an

224

aquarium, a baseball glove, baseball cards, model cars, rocks, snake skins, plates filled with crumbs from midnight snacks. Some of the remnants remained. A trophy from his Little League baseball tournament. The model ship I'm sure took him an entire summer to put together. Cans filled with pens and chewed on pencils.

Sunday morning after breakfast, I pulled the red bandana out of my belt loop. It was the one thing I had that belonged to Hook. I was ready to give it away. I tied it around Billy's forehead. It looked perfect. "This belonged to a Vietnam Vet I probably was in love with. He didn't live long enough for me to find out. Died in a car accident a year ago. Had a hook where his hand used to be." I told Billy the story of the 55-gallon drums of fuel and the four dead bodies.

"I get it," Billy said. "And you know what? It don't mean nothin'."

I leaned down and kissed his cheek. "That's what I hear." I gently touched the red bandana. "You look great."

He took my hands and looked me in the eyes. "Thanks."

* * *

The Forester
Assistant Editor's Corner
By Becky Jamison

Americans woke up this week to gruesome front-page pictures of the killing of hundreds of civilians in My Lai, Vietnam. Five hundred innocent people, including children, were rounded up, slaughtered, and left to bleed and die. The

U.S. government covered up this horrific massacre for eighteen months.

In his inaugural speech, Richard Nixon asked America to call forth "the better angels of our nature" such as love, kindness, decency, and goodness. We hold Nixon responsible and will not forget what happened at My Lai.

Be part of the efforts to stop this war. On October 15, there will be an anti-war march in Chicago. On November 14th and 15th, the Lake Forest College Students Against the War will observe two days of actions against our government's policies in Vietnam. Join them on the 14th in the chapel to read the names of all the U.S soldiers killed in Vietnam. Join them again on the 15th for a peace rally in Chicago. They will be chartering buses for both events in Chicago. Sign up in Commons.

U.S. Soldier Body Count: 47,276

Chapter 34
"War"

The October Moratorium marches had been peaceful. In dozens of cities, including Chicago, Los Angeles, Denver, Boston, Milwaukee, Dallas, New York City, Seattle, and San Francisco, churches, stores, restaurants, businesses, and colleges closed for the day to express concern for American involvement in Vietnam. Nixon hid away at Camp David, plotting the seeds of his own destruction.

The November Moratorium wasn't so peaceful.

Friday, November 14, 1969, was a memorial to the dead.

Michael Volheim, Robert Layman, Roy Clark, James Hickey, Mario Lameize, Roy Robertson, Cleveland Browning, Charles Fleek, Matthew Lozano, Melvin Green, Robert Randall, John Rosemond, Warren Nix, Terry Clark, David Tiffany, Isaac Saap, Forrest Smith, Calvin Cooper, William Smith, Thomas Bliss, Clovis May.

Starting at 6:00 a.m. we began to read. At one per second, it took fourteen hours to read the names of the almost 48,000 American soldiers killed in Vietnam. We remembered them all. They were my generation. How can a government create a policy that takes 48,000 of the youngest and best, and sentences them to death without a judge or jury?

That same day, Pete Conrad, Richard Gordon, and Alan Bean shot off from Cape Kennedy for the second landing on the moon. I wonder what they thought when they looked down at the tiny planet suspended in space, embroiled in war.

Saturday, November 15, 1969. Half a million people gathered in Washington D.C. for the largest war protest ever. At the same time, a hundred thousand gathered in Grant Park in Chicago for the march to the Civic Center Plaza. It was staged as a non-violent protest against the war machine.

Rick, Peter, Marty, and I took the early train into Chicago and gathered at Ginger and Jake's apartment. While the guys strategized, Ginger and I ate blueberry pancakes. "Looks like you tossed the stone." Ginger pushed the Log Cabin syrup over to me. "It's good to see you both happy."

"I needed that nudge from Hook to see what was in front of me all along. It's only been two weeks. A lot can happen."

"He's not going to die, Becky." Ginger could always read my mind.

The week before, I had a nightmare. Marty and Hook walked on the beach tossing stones into the water. I tried to run but my feet were glued to the sand. Marty and Hook slowly disappeared.

When I told Marty about my dream he said, missing the whole point, "I had a dream about Hook last night too. We were on the beach, and he put small stones in my hand. 'Toss them,' he told me." Marty put his arm around me. I lay on his shoulder listening to his breath and feeling his heartbeat. "We almost shared a dream." Maybe he hadn't missed the point after all.

We marched near the front of the crowd. There were probably fewer than a thousand people in front of us, almost one-hundred thousand behind. The air was festive. The bell-bottoms and long hairs marched side-by-side with business folk and the elderly.

Chants rolled up and down the crowd as drummers beat out the beat. *Nixon, Nixon, hey, hey, how many kids did you kill today?*

Then, without warning, the atmosphere changed. Someone yelled, "The police are beating people with clubs up there." Someone one else yelled, "They dragged that guy across the plaza by his hair."

Peace now. Louder. Peace now. Louder. Peace now.

Marchers surged. Why? The rage of the war. The rage of My Lai. The rage of powerlessness, hopelessness, and despair. When no one listens, you yell louder. Cheers became jeers. *Nixon, Nixon, Hey, Hey, how many kids did you kill today? Nixon, Nixon, Hey, Hey, how many kids did you kill today? What do we want? Peace. When do we want it? Now. Peace Now Peace Now Peace Now. 1, 2, 3, 4, we don't want your fucking war. 1, 2, 3, 4, we don't want your fucking war. Pigs suck. Down with pigs. Down with pigs. Pigs suck. Nixon, Nixon, Hey, Hey, how many kids did you kill today?* Peace now. Peace now. No peace now.

Police attacked. On both sides of the barricades, it was war.

Keep singing. *We shall overcome. We shall overcome. We shall. We shall.*

Pigs suck. Pigs suck. Run. "It's tear gas. Don't let go of my hand, Becky." *Down with pigs. 1, 2, 3, 4. We don't want your fucking war.*

What do we want? Peace. When do we want it? Now. Louder. Louder.

"I can't breathe, Marty."

A surge pushed us closer to the barricade, farther into the tear gas, nearer to the swinging billy clubs, People ran in every direction to get away. We were stuck in the mass. Hysteria grabbed the crowd. *Peace Now Pigs. Peace Now Pigs. Down With Pigs. The whole world's watching. The whole world's watching. The whole world's watching.*

There was no peace anywhere.

We got separated from the rest. I was no longer linked to Ginger. Marty was no longer linked to Rick. I couldn't see Jake or Peter.

"Where is everyone? We have to find them."

"Don't let go, Becky." Marty held my hand tighter and pushed his way through the crowd.

I yelled for the others. They were gone.

"We have to find them, Marty."

"Don't let go."

The crowd pushed and retreated. Panic set in. Be calm. Be calm. *We shall overcome. Peace now. Make love not war. Run for your life, they've got more tear gas. They're bringing in the hoses.*

What happened to the peace generation? What happened to the flower children? When did they get so powerless? Kennedy, King, and Kennedy died. The war kept happening.

The police beat us down. Did anybody see? The whole world was watching but did anybody see?

We got stuck in the crowd being pushed, punched, pummeled. It took us two hours to find our way back to Ginger and Jake's apartment. They had just arrived. Peter showed up, silent, an hour later. We waited for Rick. Then the call came.

Rick ended up on the front lines trying to restore order out of chaos. Instead of stopping the police, they stopped him. A billy club to his arm, a trip to the hospital to set the break, a night in jail, all charges dropped against him. No one was holding the police liable. We would. We would be back.

Up in space, Conrad, Gordon, and Bean were sent news from earth. They received no word of the hundreds and thousands of demonstrations in moratorium actions across the country. We had the technology to conquer space but we couldn't conquer war.

Organizers planned a rally for the next Saturday. *We will keep marching until we can do so without fear. The Constitution, Mayor Daley, gives us the right to assemble. We will keep coming back.* Mayor Daley was pressed to okay the parade passes. He knew the whole world was watching him.

"I don't want to go back," I told Marty the following Friday.

"We have to. We can't let them beat us."

"They already have."

The group was smaller, maybe 20,000. We wore our uniforms: bell bottoms or faded and torn blue jeans, worn at the knee, worn at the butt, frayed at the cuff, red cotton bandanas through belt loops, fringed moccasins, peasant blouses, t-shirts with slogans, long hair, parted in the middle covering eyes, hair bands, beads. We smeared Vaseline on our faces to prevent the tear gas from stinging, the bandanas to cover the mouth.

Organizers with bullhorns prepared us for the worst. "We are determined to make our voices heard. We will continue to march until we are heard. Are you with us?" "Yes" "Are you with us?" "Yes." "ARE YOU WITH US?" "YES."

On to the Civic Center. *What do we want? Peace! When do we want it? Now!*

We marched peacefully from the park to the plaza. The speakers we hadn't heard last week spoke as much to the police as to the crowd. "You will not intimidate us. You will not take away our voices. Chicago. The world is watching you."

How can we stop a war overseas if the police beat people in the streets of America? How can we solve our problems if the people hired to protect us brutalize us instead?

We were tired when we got back home. Not tired from the march. Bone deep tired. Discouraged tired. Angry tired. Fear tired. Hatred tired. War tired. Nothing was getting better tired.

We sat around the living room trying to make sense of it. Rick with his arm in a cast, Peter with the dogs on his lap, Marty with his hand in mine, and me.

What is so hard about wanting peace? How did peace get so violent?

"I don't get it," I said. "We come in peace and they bash our heads in."

"There's nothing to get," Rick said. "The war is not going to stop until they want it to. It doesn't have anything to do with us."

"Then why are we doing what we're doing?" Marty asked.

"Because we have to." Peter said. He was right.

Three days later was the first anniversary of Hook's death. The hurting was less but it would never go away. I would always keep the promise I made to Hook's mom. I would always remember Dennis McKinney.

U.S. Soldier Body Count: 47,975

Chapter 35
"Hello, Vietnam"

The country continued to polarize. Black against white. Old against young. Hawk against dove. Nixon spoke to the 'silent majority,' calling for the nation to bring itself together. Vice-President Agnew pulled it apart when he said, "When the President said, 'bring us together,' he meant the functioning, contributing portions of the American citizenry." He went on to call college students an intellectual group of effete snobs.

The war went on. My life went on. My heart went on. I moved into Marty's room.

December 1, 1969. Live from Washington, D.C. Lottery night. Like the story from my high school literature book, if you win this lottery you die.

Jake and Ginger came for the event. Someone's number was going to be drawn first. It might be Peter or Marty. My older brother. Someone. Not me.

Marty and I played "Lie Detector" waiting for the lottery to begin. It was like electronic Clue, complete with suspect cards, arrest and summons cards, and secret information cards. The lie detector machine indicated if the testimony was true or false. Our task was to find the guilty person out of twenty-four suspects.

The 'bank president' gave his testimony. "The request for a loan might not have been signed with the applicant's real name—

but I couldn't mistake that LARGE NOSE." I put his card on the machine and inserted the small wand through the hole in the card. BUZZ. The needle indicated the testimony was false. So far, all the evidence pointed to the trombone player. The 'schoolteacher' said the suspect had a moustache. BUZZ. I looked at the 'Secret Information' cards I held in my hand. I must be interpreting them wrong. On his next turn, Marty made an arrest. "The gas station attendant." GUILTY. How could I have been so wrong?

"That's three in a row," Marty said. "So much for your investigative journalism expertise."

"One more," I said. I hoped if we kept playing, the lottery wouldn't start, and we wouldn't have to know. Who would be first?

Marty looked at his watch. "Don't think we have time. I want to be ready." *Ready for what? We're talking about Marty's life here. And Peter's. And thousands of other young men. Maybe if I'm ready for this nothing bad will happen.* I was ready. I wasn't even close to ready.

Marty had two number two pencils, a pen, and paper. One sheet listed every day of the year. It took him an hour to make it. My job, he told me, was to write the lottery number on the correct birthday. I was glad to have a job, something to occupy my mind. Marty's task was to write down, on another sheet of paper, the numbers in order with the birthdays after. All we needed to know was whether Marty or Peter or any of our friends or brothers or friends of our brothers had to go. This writing down kept us busy.

Rick finished the dishes and brought in a plate of crackers, cheese, radishes, and sliced apples. He put it on the coffee table, sliding over our Lie Detector game to make room.

"Eat up," he said. The food stayed untouched.

Peter sprawled on the beanbag chair, Suki and Racer in his lap.

In addition to Marty and Peter, 849,994 other young men watched somewhere, their hearts beating a little too fast, their teeth clenched a little too hard.

The lottery was supposed to level the playing field. No longer would the poor and uneducated bear the burden of fighting the war. Those smart enough or rich enough to get a student deferment, those 'effete snobs' that Agnew talked about, would pay the price, too.

No one should suffer for a sick, arrogant, unjust government policy.

Suddenly, live from Washington D.C. "Good evening. Tonight, for the first time in twenty-seven years, the United States has again started a draft lottery."

The night began with a prayer. *Dear God. Tonight, we are going to draw little capsules out of a jar and serve as judge, jury, and executioner to the young men who we will send to fight a war that old white guys orchestrated. Please forgive our sins.*

The prayer did not go exactly like that. It should have, though. Someone should ask for forgiveness. Thousands of those chosen tonight could die in Vietnam, dehumanized, merely numbers drawn out of a glass jar.

Males born between 1944 and 1950 were eligible to play that night. If your number was drawn, BUZZ. You lose. They called it a 'random selection sequence.'

I adjusted the vertical hold on the television set. Television lights glared in the small auditorium room in the Selective Service building in Washington.

"Just get on with it." When the going got rough, Marty talked to TV sets.

They weren't going to get on with it that easily. First the rules. The 366 days of the year were written on small strips of paper, and each put into a plastic capsule. These capsules were dumped

235

into a big glass jar. A capsule would be taken out of the glass jar, broken open by the woman at the desk who would hand the piece of paper to a man, who would announce the date and hand it to another man in front of the list of numbers. He would stick the date up by the corresponding number. Those numbers determined the order that young men would be drafted. For this lottery only, those with student deferments could keep them. Once their deferment was up, they were on their way. Well-crafted and completely sick. It was expected that you weren't safe if your number was under 200.

We watched for the ceremonial first draw with our hearts in our throats, hands clinched on chairs, on arms, on someone else's hand. "Please, dear God, don't make it November 8." I held on to Marty's arm. "Please don't ever make it November 8. Please, dear God, make November 8 be lost or forgotten."

The ranking Republican on the House Armed Services Committee drew the first capsule and read the date. And the winner is—I wanted a drum roll, trumpets blaring—September 14. If you were born on that day you die first. I breathed a sigh of relief. All those born on September 14 quit breathing. It didn't stop there. If, by chance, your mother had you on April 24, you die second. December 30. February 14.

"That's Valentine's Day," I said. "You can't do that to kids born on Valentine's Day."

"You can't do that to anyone," Jake said.

October 18. September 6. October 26. September 7. November 22. "That's the day John Kennedy was assassinated. They shouldn't have to go either. That's a holy day."

Peter looked at me. "No one should have to go, Becky."

"I know that. God, I know that." I talked to keep myself sane.

It went on and on in a surreal display of power and death. What a way to die, tiny blue capsules jerked from a fishbowl.

Rick's birthday was the twenty-seventh number called. "Good thing I'm too old."

A commercial tried to convince folks to buy an electric shaver for someone for Christmas. Thank you, Jesus. Can't finance the lottery without a commercial break.

I held Marty's hand tighter. With each number they called I squeezed, he squeezed, and we breathed again. They called another and each time I exhaled a bit. Then it started again. I held my breath. I heard a date. I exhaled. Finally, it came.

Number 97. November 8. Marty's birthday. I squeezed his hand as tears rolled down my face. Marty stared straight ahead and dropped the pencil on the table. "What the fuck am I going to do?"

Number 124. April 13. Peter. He didn't say anything, just held Suki a bit tighter.

Remember when your birthday was the day you celebrated with presents and cake? Today it became your death day.

Why Marty? Why anyone? Why was September 14th drawn first? What about those boys? What about their girlfriends and wives, lovers and friends and siblings, mothers and fathers? One Christmas Eve two lovers conceived a son. The night was cold as snow fell. The lights on the tree reflected off the branches. Quiet music played on the stereo. After hot chocolate and popcorn, the lovers went to bed and made quiet, gentle 'joy to the world' love. Twenty years later their son was pulled first out of a fishbowl.

Why April 24th? Sometime in July, the two lovers spent the day at the lake water skiing. That night they ate cold chicken salad for dinner and drank a glass of white wine. They sat on the porch of the cabin they rented and watched the sun go down. Then they went into the cabin and made love. Little did they know that twenty years later the son they conceived that night would be destined for Vietnam.

If either of those lovers had waited a day or two. Three days after. Two days before. The next day. The day before. Couldn't you wait one more day, Mom?

If I had been male, I wouldn't have had to go. My birthday number was 310. Lucky me. Why couldn't I exchange with Marty? My older brother was 321. At least he was safe. My little brother was too young for this drawing.

"This isn't fucking fair." I'm not sure who said it, I was crying too hard. It might have been Marty. He still stared at the TV set. It might have been Peter, but he didn't say 'fucking' very often. It might have been Rick. There but for the grace of God go I.

It's not my war. My war rages inside me. My war rages against a system that sends its kids to a monsonic jungle. Against a system that lets jungle rot eat away at their feet. Against a system that welcomes back their coffins with pomp and circumstance without questioning why they are dead to begin with. My war rages against the fears and nightmares they will live with for the rest of their lives. All from a game of chance.

Maybe I was the one who said it.

Marty got up and walked out the front door, the screen slamming behind him. I found him on the porch, his draft card burning in his hand. He held it until the fire singed his fingers, dropped it on the porch, and crushed it with his foot. If only it could be that easy. If only he could say, "I'm not going to play," like the captain of the JV football team did in high school when he lost our class lottery.

Marty looked at me. "I am never celebrating another conception day."

U.S. Soldier Body Count: 48,312

Chapter 36
"You've Made Me So Very Happy"

Christmas. Peace on Earth. Good Will to All. Troops rotted in the jungles of Vietnam living with daily fear and excruciating fatigue, fighting mosquitoes, and fighting to survive. While those young men celebrated Christmas with a prayer, 'Let me live one more day,' Nixon began to withdraw troops from Vietnam. For those still slated to die, it was a meaningless gesture.

I spent two weeks with my parents and brothers soaking in family love, decorating cookies, opening homemade presents. I missed Marty like crazy and finally headed back north to meet him in Springfield.

It was late afternoon when I drove up to the small brick house. I honked the horn, got out of the car, and opened the trunk to haul out my suitcase. Marty met me there. Two weeks is too damn long for new love. I held him, kissed him, and looked him in the eye. "God, I missed you."

Billy and Mom Olsen sat at the dining room table. The three had been engaged in a wild game of Crazy Eights to pass the time until my arrival. Billy wore the red bandana, a glint in his eyes, and his cheeks filled out.

I hugged Mom Olsen first. Then I went over to Billy, leaned over and hugged him. "You look great," I said.

"Dinner in an hour," Mom Olsen said. "You kids catch up."
I don't think she meant that we should sneak away to the bedroom
but that's exactly what Marty and I did.

"I'm going to take my stuff upstairs."

"Let me help." Marty took the suitcase from me. Billy grinned.

We made it upstairs in five seconds, out of our clothes in
fifteen. Nine minutes later we were downstairs in time to catch up
with each other.

I sat at the table with Billy and asked him about his life.

"Well, I got me a girlfriend and I'm starting back to school to
finish my senior year. G.I. bill is picking up the cost." He said it
all casually while fiddling with the fork in front of him.

"Halt right there, mister. You can't throw out, 'I got me a
girlfriend,' and then move on like it's something you say every
day." I turned to Marty. "You knew, didn't you?" He shook his
head yes. "Why didn't you tell me when I called?"

"Billy wanted to tell you himself."

"Tell me everything."

"After we saw you in November, I checked myself into the
V.A. I needed help dealing with my anger and I was having trouble
with some of the equipment that keeps me going. There was this
student nurse who worked the floor the day I checked in. The first
thing she said to me when she walked in my room was, 'I love that
bandana in your hair.' It was love at first sight. We talked all day
and when her shift was over, I asked her if she'd be back the next
day. She simply said, 'Not as a nurse.' Wasn't sure what she meant
until she walked in the next day with a box of hot dogs grilled to
perfection and two Sports Illustrated magazines. She came every
day for the month I was there. Her name is Julie, and, for some
reason, she likes me. I tried to discourage her and tell her how
impossible it would be to date someone like me." He paused.

"Keep going. I want you to get to the good part."

"You mean the part that's none of your business?" He grinned and gave me a slight wink. Marty held my hand under the table, rubbing my thigh with his thumb. God, that turned me on.

"Absolutely."

"After I got out of the hospital, she invited me to dinner. Picked me up, took me to this cool Mexican restaurant."

"The restaurant is not important, Billy. Get to the good part."

"She brought me home, rolled me up to the door, put the brake on my wheelchair, came around the front, sat on my lap, put her arms around my neck, and kissed me whole. We've got a lot to figure out but so far so good. Hey, did you hear about my Christmas present?"

"Wait a minute. What the hell does 'kissed me whole' mean?"

"We're going out together tomorrow night. You can ask her all the questions you want."

"Trust me. I will. So, were you surprised at your Christmas present?" He got a car with hand controls.

"Shit, yeah."

"Billy, watch your mouth." Mom Olsen put a bowl of potatoes in the middle of the table.

I got up to help bring in the food. In the kitchen, Billy's mom took both of my hands. "Thanks for what you did for Billy."

"I didn't do anything."

"What you did in that room with him in November was the turning point."

"It would have happened eventually without me."

"But you made it happen then." She hugged me and whispered, "By the way, I do know what you did in Billy's room that night. I raised two boys. I knew what was up. Thank you."

The next night I met Julie. She was beautiful with dark brown hair, halfway down her back. Her real beauty was this rare thing that comes from inside people when they are truly happy. I didn't learn much about Julie's life that night. Maybe she'd never felt pain. Maybe she'd never lost anyone she loved. Maybe she had and made the decision that the pain wouldn't define her life. Whatever the reason, she was truly happy.

"What the hell are you doing hanging out with Billy?" I asked.

She smiled at Billy. "He's funny."

"True." Anybody who can make me laugh until I get hiccups is down-to-the-bone funny.

"He's intelligent, well-read."

"That's all he's been doing for the past two years, reading."

"He's kind and generous to a fault. He would give the shirt off his back if someone needed it."

Then Billy said, "Tell her the real reason."

"What? You're a good kisser?"

"That one and also the one about how I'm about the handsomest man you've ever met."

"Julie, I will warn you about one thing. It may be the deal breaker."

"Tell me now before I get more invested in this relationship."

Billy took her hand. "Too late. You can't go back now."

"He's a terrible singer," I said.

We watched the ball drop in Times Square at 11:00 and celebrated the end of the 1960s by watching it drop again at midnight our time. I kissed Marty. Julie kissed Billy. We toasted with a glass of champagne, reminisced a bit about the past year, and made predictions about the new decade.

The 60s were over. They were fun, exciting, everything a young person could ask for. Drama, passion, love, determination, purpose, meaning. They were also filled with everything no one should have to endure. War, death, assassinations, rage, conflict, hatred, and deep dark holes filled with deep dark pain.

It was 1970. I wanted time to stop right there in the living room at Marty's childhood home. I didn't want January to come. Or February, March, April, May, June when Marty and Peter would graduate and something would happen. The two of them would go somewhere or be somewhere and nobody knew where or when or how.

"Happy New Year," I kissed Marty deep and held him tight.

"I wonder what this new decade will bring," he said. I didn't want to know.

U.S. Soldier Body Count: 48,936

Chapter 37

"Did You Ever Have To Make Up Your Mind?"

Five months until Marty and Peter lost their student deferments. What were they going to do? The choices were endless. There were no choices at all.

"Marty, what if you flunk a couple of courses and don't graduate? That gives you another year."

"It doesn't work like that." Marty was reading some information from the Vietnam Veterans Against the War. "Here's an article about someone who got out of the draft because he was officially obese. I can't think of a better way to get out. A six-pack of beer every night. Doughnuts for breakfast. Bags of Oreos. You're too fat, soldier."

I picked up one of the pamphlets. "Marty, since they didn't accept your request for conscientious objector you could ask for 1-A-O status. That way you wouldn't have to carry a gun."

"They would make me a medic or something. I would stitch people back together or put them in body bags."

Convince the draft board you are the sole support of your widowed mother and your brother injured in Vietnam.

Grow six inches. They'll reject you if you're too tall.

244

Become a drug addict. That didn't work for Jeff.

Move to Canada. You can never come home.

Refuse to go. End up in jail.

What are you going to do, Marty? What in the world are you going to do?

* * *

Time passed, relentlessly. When I wanted it to slow down, it sped up. I could not stop it, so I denied its passing. I denied the ending was coming, that Marty and Peter would have to decide.

Spring break came too soon.

"I can't. I won't do it," I said to Marty. He wanted me to get in the car, turn it on, put it in reverse, turn my head so I could see where I was going, press my foot on the gas pedal, and run over his foot with the car. Just like that.

"It's my way out of Vietnam. You've got to do this for me."

I could hear the bones crushing and Marty scream, see him collapse, never able to walk again. I could hear the sirens of the ambulance coming to take him to the hospital, the paramedics asking me what happened. "I don't know," I would say. But I did know. He wanted me to run over his foot with the car.

Marty smoked a joint and downed two beers. He looked at me. "I'm begging you."

"Let's get it over with," I said. "If I think too much about it, I won't be able to do it."

Marty put on a pair of tennis shoes he found in the back of his closet, the mud shoes, the 'I don't want to ruin a good pair of shoes.'

"Why not go barefoot?" I asked.

"I don't want you to see it when it's done." He kissed me on the nose and went out the back door. I followed.

I got in the car and put the key in the ignition. "I'm ready," he called from behind the car.

"Why me?" I thought. I was the kind of person who caught spiders in the shower and released them out the window. Despite my cockroach stabbing adventure with Hook, I generally brushed cockroaches aside instead of crushing them. I said sorry to every mosquito I slapped, every fly I swatted.

I sat in the car, my hand on the key. "I'm ready," he called again. He didn't want me to see his foot when it was over, but I could see the picture from my anatomy book, all fifty-two bones, all thirty-three joints, all one hundred and seven ligaments, all nineteen muscles, and all the tendons that held everything else together. I could see them bloody and oozing.

Then I saw Marty in his army fatigues, a gun in his hands, running through a swamp, sniper fire all around him.

I turned on the car. I could do this for Marty. The thing he begged me to do. I could do it.

"I'm ready." I could hear the hesitancy in his voice.

"I heard you," I said back to him. "I heard you," I said again, quieter, choking back my tears, choking on the words, seeing the pain, seeing the ooze, seeing the swamp. What was I going to do? "I can't hurt you," I whispered. Jeff's face flashed in front of me. Hook's face flashed in front of me. *If I don't do this, Marty might die. He'll be sent to Vietnam and die. I'll lose him too. If I do this, I'll hurt him. There has to be another way. There has to be.*

"I'm ready," Marty said the fourth time.

"I heard you," I screamed as I turned off the car. I opened the car door, got out, and ran to the back of the car, threw my arms around Marty's neck. "I heard you," I said through my tears. I was sure Marty would never forgive me.

Marty hugged me and kissed my hair. "It's okay. I'll think of something."

* * *

Peter and I were folding laundry thrown in a heap on the Salvation Army couch. It was spring-cleaning time, curtains, blankets, every sheet and towel we owned. In a few short weeks, Peter and Marty would lose their student deferments. Then what? Vietnam? Fort Hood? Jail? Canada? Thrown away like dirty laundry? I tried to make my life boring like *Catch 22,* to make time pass slower, make life last longer. It didn't work.

Folding a blanket was the perfect opportunity to talk to Peter about his plan. "What are you going to do when you graduate?" I asked.

"It'll work out." Peter handed me two ends of the blanket.

"What do you mean, 'It'll work out'? You know as well as I do that the war is not going to work itself out in the next few weeks. You're not going to get a higher lottery number. No one is going to run over your foot with the car, at least I'm not going to." I folded the two ends together, handed them to Peter a bit more aggressively than I meant to, and picked up the other two ends.

"Twenty years from now it will be over one way or another. A hundred years from now we'll be no less dead than those in Vietnam."

"That's stupid."

Peter stopped folding and looked at me. "It's the luck of the draw. My lottery number is low. I have to go. You have two X chromosomes. You don't have to worry what the fuck is going to happen to you." Peter rarely said fuck and he said it with a rare edge to his voice.

247

I wanted to quietly put down my two corners of the blanket and sneak out of the room. He continued. "It doesn't make sense, does it? Why should your fucking birthday be number 310 when you're a girl and it doesn't matter, and I have to fucking worry about whether I'm going to be sent to Vietnam?" Three fucks in one conversation.

I wanted to yell at him that he couldn't blame me, that I suggested months ago that he apply for his CO status and he didn't. I wanted to tell him that my boyfriend had a lower lottery number and that wasn't my fault either. "Fold your own damn blanket," was all I could get out of my mouth as I let go of the ends and headed to the stairs. "And don't blame me."

I stopped and looked at him. "It's not my fault that you got a low lottery number or that I am a female. It's not my fault that this goddamn war keeps going on and on. It's not my fault. I'm as scared as you are."

Peter threw the half-folded blanket on the couch and followed me to the stairs. "What have you got to be afraid of? You're female. This doesn't affect you at all."

"Are you kidding me? Everything about this war affects me." I started up the stairs. Peter followed and when I tried to slam the bedroom door, he stopped it with his foot.

"I'm going to Canada." It came out of the blue. He'd made his decision. He knew and I knew, once he left, he could never come back. I looked at him. Goddamn war. Goddamn stupid war. He turned around and left.

I shut the door. I couldn't bear it. That gentle soul of a man and his dog, that man who helped me heal with his radishes. That man made a choice. He was leaving.

U.S. Soldier Body Count: 50,424

248

Chapter 38
"The Kent State Massacre"

The Forester
Assistant Editor's Corner
By Becky Jamison

Join us on April 22 for the first annual celebration of Earth Day. Local farmers will bring organic snacks. Science majors will talk about the effects of pollution on the planet. The Union of Concerned Scientists will be giving a series of workshops in Commons. At 7:00 p.m. the Paul Butterfield Blues Band will play on the green.

Our anti-war efforts continue but once the war is over, we need to make sure we have a planet worth living on. Come have fun and learn something in the process.

* * *

If Earth Day was a distraction from the war, it didn't stay that way long.

On Thursday night, April 30, I got home from the library to see Rick, Peter, and Marty engaged in a deep and serious conversation. Suki and Racer were both asleep on the floor in front of them. "What's up?" I asked as I greeted each one with a kiss, lingering somewhat on Marty's.

"The shit hit the fan," Marty reached up for a second kiss.

"What fan?"

Rick said, "Nixon announced that American soldiers invaded Cambodia and have been secretly bombing there since March of last year.'

"Why are we invading them?" I asked. "They're neutral."

"Nixon believes 40,000 North Vietnamese troops are at the border," Rick explained. "He's been lying all along."

I couldn't think of a thing to say.

Around the campus and the country, people found plenty to say.

Eight hundred Lake Forest College students joined a spontaneous rally on campus the next day, two-thirds of all students. Marty said to the crowd, "We are asking for an immediate response by our faculty, staff, and administration to the President of the United States, condemning the invasion of Cambodia and asking for a withdrawal of troops."

The chants began. "Right on." "Shut it down." "Occupy the administration building."

Marty continued, "We will not waver. We will boycott classes until they meet our demands."

Rick came out of Commons where the faculty was meeting and took the bullhorn. "The faculty and administration are in conversation as we speak."

"How long do these conversations take?" someone yelled from the crowd.

As long as the faculty went on with their conversation, we stayed on the green. It wasn't an Earth Day celebration feeling, a harbinger of good things to come. It was a shit-hit-the-fan feeling. Marty kept moving, strategizing, organizing. I moved with him, interviewed students for the next edition of the paper, sat with my guitar under a tree and sang. I needed Ginger to keep the music going with me. I missed her and Jake more than ever.

Lunch came and went. Dinner came and went. Students came and went. We still hadn't heard from the administration. What was taking so long? At 8:00 p.m., Rick informed us that they were shutting down for the night and that a small group was working to compose a letter. Delay. Delay. Delay. We weren't leaving. We could wait them out.

We occupied the administration building that night, sleeping on cold tiled floors, barely sleeping at all. The next morning someone from the dining commons brought us coffee, juice, and doughnuts, a perfect ending to a sleepless night.

By 9:00 most of the student body gathered on the green next to a banner that said, "SHUT IT DOWN." They chanted, "1-2-3-4. We don't want your fucking war. 1-2-3-4." "Out of Cambodia now." "We're not leaving."

Marty took the bullhorn. "We demand accountability from the faculty and staff. We will occupy for as long as we need to. We will boycott classes. WE WILL SHUT DOWN THIS COLLEGE."

Five weeks until graduation. I could hear Marty's sense of doom in every word. *Shut it down. Get us out. End this war. Don't make me choose.*

The chants got louder, more aggressive. *SHUT IT DOWN. WE'RE NOT LEAVING. OCCUPY.* It was anger, fear, fatigue, a fierce rage at the war that kept going on and on and on, at the lies and complicity, the injustice and violence.

Someone took the bullhorn. "Where are they? How long does it take to write a letter?" I could feel the energy rising and changing. If we all moved at the same time, we could take over

251

this campus We were strong enough. We were willing. We would put our bodies on the line.

The group parted and grew silent as the president of the college, accompanied by Rick and at least one hundred staff and faculty members, walked through. Marty handed the president the bullhorn. "I am proud to be your president. You have demonstrated your passion and your dedication to making this world better." He read a letter demanding an immediate withdrawal of troops from Cambodia and an end to the war in Vietnam. It was signed by 90% of the faculty and administration. What about the other 10%? Did they not care?

On college campuses all over the country, protests flared. As rage and anger over the deception increased, students rioted, took over college buildings, and demanded an end to any complicity with the U.S. government. The anti-war movement was alive and well. So was the war.

Vietnam didn't own the violence. Cambodia didn't own the violence. It was everywhere. Students had had enough. We tried it non-violently. You didn't listen. Now we will show you we mean what we say.

In the small town of Kent, Ohio, at Kent State University, students held rallies protesting the war, the bombing, and the ROTC training programs on campus. Monday, May 4th. A noon rally was organized to reclaim the campus from the National Guard sent in by the governor. More than forty percent of the student body was there. The guard ordered them to disperse. "You have no right to assemble." No right? Who took away that right? Did they amend the Constitution when I wasn't paying attention? It's our right. It's our duty.

Shots rang out, and when the carnage was complete, four students, Allison Krause, Sandra Lee Scheuer, Jeffrey Glenn Miller, and William K. Schroeder, lay in pools of their own blood, dead, shot by their own guard while peacefully protesting. Nine others were injured. Less than two weeks later, police killed James Earl Green and Phillip Lafayette Gibbs at a protest at Jackson State College in Jackson, Mississippi. The war had come home. We were killing our own.

* * *

The Forester
Assistant Editor's Corner
By Becky Jamison

In response to the horrible events around the country, the college administration has cancelled classes for the remainder of the week. The faculty also voted to allow students to boycott classes for the rest of the year. If you choose that option, you will receive the grade you now have. Professors will be in class for students who wish to continue.

* * *

More than seventy-five percent of the students at Lake Forest boycotted classes following the killings at Kent State. We were angry. We were loud. We felt powerful. In the end, we were powerless. Wars don't end because we yell. Wars end when it is no longer politically or economically expedient for the government to continue. We would keep yelling anyway.

U.S. Soldier Body Count: 50,963

Chapter 39
"Oh, Canada"

I returned home a week after we heard about the bombings in Cambodia and found Peter packing his bags, Marty sitting on the edge of his bed looking at a road atlas. "I'm only taking what I can fit on my back and a few things in a suitcase. You keep the rest," Peter said.

"When are you going?" I picked up Racer and held her tight. I couldn't bear the thought of Peter and his radishes not being part of my life anymore. Goddamn war.

"In the morning." He looked at me "I've got a favor to ask you, Becky."

At that moment I would have promised him my life. I would have gone to Vietnam for him. I would have gone to Canada with him. "Anything."

"Take care of Racer, my radishes, and my jar of guppies."

"That is actually three favors, and I don't really like radishes."

"You never told me that. I thought you loved them."

"I love you, Peter. I only appreciate radishes. The radish you gave me on the porch swing the day I got back from Boston was what I needed. Two years of radishes is enough." I was trying to convince myself to go radish-free, Peter-free.

"What the hell am I going to do with the guppies?" I asked. Marty gave them to Peter for his birthday three weeks before. He caught them in the stream that separates North and Middle Campus,

"Liberate them. Plant lettuce in the greenhouse if you want."

"That's not really taking care of your radishes or guppies, is it?" Tears streamed down my face.

Peter took my hands, pulled me off the bed, and gave me a hug. "I can't imagine life without you, Peter," I said.

He didn't answer. He couldn't answer. There wasn't an answer. There was only Peter and me standing there.

"Will you drive me to the border?"

"That's the fourth favor. What about your truck?" Peter had one of the best pick-up trucks around. 1957 Ford, dark blue with a red bumper on the front, a replacement for an accident that happened before he bought it.

"I signed it over to Marty. I can't drive across the border. The guards are on particular alert."

"How are you getting in?" Don't have an answer, I prayed to myself silently. Tell me that you haven't figured that out so you have to stay a few more days, let it never end.

"I'll walk over and meet up with you somewhere. You're the only one who can get across without a problem."

"You can't just show up in Canada." I knew he could. Peter could be anywhere and be fine. I wanted him to be safe.

"A group of draft resisters, their families, and a few friends live in a small commune north of Winnipeg. They connected me to someone in Pembina, North Dakota, where we'll stay for the night. They'll show me how to get across the border. You'll follow with the car, pick me up and drive me to the commune."

I heard Rick come in the front door. "We're up here in Peter's room," I called.

Rick walked in. He didn't have to ask. He saw the backpack and open suitcase.

"I'm leaving tomorrow for Winnipeg. If I don't go now, I'll never make it. I'm trying to convince Marty and Becky to move up there with me." He turned and looked at both of us. I looked at Marty.

"It's a way out, Marty." I wanted him to say yes so he would not have to go to Vietnam. I wanted him to say no so I could stay in school, get my degree, and become a journalist. I wanted this war to quit ripping my heart out.

Marty kissed my forehead, and said to Peter, "You know I can't go. If I went, I'd never see my mom and brother again."

Never come back. That sounded like a hell of a long time. I knew it was true. Once Peter crossed the border, he couldn't come back. If he did and got caught, he'd be in jail for a long time. If he stayed here and refused, they could throw him in jail for a long time. Neither was the choice of a free man.

Rick went downstairs for food and came back with a tray holding a plate of cherry tomatoes, a box of Ritz crackers, a hunk of cheese, some radishes, a bottle of Pisano, and four glasses. "How are you getting there?"

"Becky's driving me."

Rick poured wine for everyone. "To memories and to us together."

Peter raised his glass and said, "Here's to new beginnings."

"I hate beginnings," I said.

We ate the tomatoes, the cheese, and the entire box of Ritz crackers. Peter finished his packing, we laughed, we cried, we remembered. "When I'm braving the cold Canadian winters, I'll remember this perfect night and who we were in this house together."

Marty was going with me. Rick promised to take care of Racer and liberate the guppies in the stream.

We got on the road by seven with a thermos of coffee, doughnuts, and a lunch Rick made for us. I packed my clothes on top of Peter's in the suitcase in case they checked it. We'd drive to the safe house in Pembina where Marty would stay. Peter would walk over the border with Suki and his backpack. I would drive over and meet up with him, drive him to the commune, and head back to Pembina.

It was a long trip, almost eight hundred miles. We hoped to make it there before midnight.

We passed the first hour silently. Marty drove. Peter sat in the front passenger seat. I sprawled in the back, my head leaning against the door, a blanket pulled up to my shoulders. I wasn't cold. It was security.

"Coffee and doughnuts anyone?" I poured cups for Peter and Marty. They put them in cup holders hanging on the window and put the powdered sugar doughnuts on napkins in their laps. The sun was fully up behind us as we headed west. I looked out the window at the Wisconsin land passing by in a surreal passage of time. I wanted it to stop. Freeze me in it. Time had never been my friend.

Outside of Madison we made our first pit stop. Then, knowing we had fourteen more hours, we sang every Beatles, Monkees, Rolling Stones, Dylan, and war protest song we knew.

North through Wisconsin. Towards Minnesota. At noon we found a rest stop past Eau Claire and feasted on cheese sandwiches with tomatoes and lettuce, a few radishes, grapes, and a bag of Fritos. I ate the radishes. Best I ever tasted.

I took over the driving and began with songs that had a state's name in it. California, Texas, Carolina, Kentucky. We got fifteen.

We played the alphabet game. We kept track of license plates.

We hit Minneapolis at 3:30, Peter asleep in the back, Marty asleep in the seat next to me in the front. On the half hour I listened to the news. "Violence continues to erupt on college campuses across the country. Estimates are that nearly four million students are being affected by student strikes, more than one-third of all college students. Thousands plan to invade Washington D.C. as protests continue against Nixon's bombing of Cambodia." Strange that they called our protests an invasion. The newscaster went on to say that on many major campuses, students occupied buildings. Police beat students. Buildings burned.

"Shit," I thought.

At about eleven, we pulled into Pembina, a town of less than six hundred people, a stop on the Underground Railroad. They've been helping people to freedom for a long time. We located the address and were greeted at the door with hugs, juice, and a pan of cheese lasagna. We would make plans in the morning. That night we slept.

We woke up late the next morning to the smell of fresh biscuits and scrambled eggs. We spent the day planning, taking walks through the small town, waiting. Peter would cross the border the next morning at about four a.m. about three miles northwest from where we stayed. From there, he and Suki would be on their own to find the prearranged meeting spot, a small café four and a half miles up the road on the other side of the border, about a six mile walk from where we dropped him off. He had a hand-drawn map, some written directions, signposts, houses to look for, a small country road to walk down, another field to go through. He would finally hit the main road about five miles up from the border. If he'd done it right. I would be waiting for him there at a small café. If all went well.

We dropped Peter and Suki off shortly after 4:00 a.m. We gave him a flashlight, but the half-moon lit the way. My heart was in my throat. I was scared, sad, angry. I had no idea how Peter felt. He looked calm. I hugged him and told him I'd see him in a few hours. Marty hugged him longer. They both knew. If Peter got caught, he would end up in jail. Either way, they might never see each other again.

We went back to the house to wait, awake, couldn't sleep. Time went slowly, ever so slowly, tick tock tick.

I arrived at the border at 7:00.

"Citizenship?"

"U.S."

"ID."

I handed him my driver's license.

"Where are you headed?"

"The University of Winnipeg."

"You a student there?"

"Hope to be. I'm applying for an internship in anthropology for the summer."

"Good luck." He gave me back my driver's license and waved me on. He didn't check the suitcase. I breathed again.

I found the café five miles up, sat by the front window, and ordered a cup of coffee. Two cups later, I saw Peter walking down the road towards the café. I threw a buck on the table and ran out to hug him. Suki practically jumped into my arms. Peter's crossing had been damp, cold, and flawless. The first thing he did was put on a dry pair of socks.

We arrived in Winnipeg by mid-morning. After hugs and introductions, we toured the place. Fourteen people lived there. A common house held the kitchen, dining area, a big room for hanging out, and a couple of small rooms on the side that served as temporary sleeping quarters for new folks or visitors. Scattered around, but near the house, were small cabins.

Behind the common house was a giant garden plot for the short planting season and an even bigger greenhouse for the winter. Radishes sprouted through the ground.

Peter knelt in the garden, picked up some soil and let it sift through his fingers. He pulled a few weeds from between the radish plants. I knelt beside him, picked a radish, wiped off the visible dirt, and handed it to him. "Welcome home," I said.

He took a bite. "Thanks." He handed the radish back to me. I took a bite. Our private communion service. He picked up Suki, hugging her hard.

"Marty and I could be happy here raising vegetables."

Peter smiled. "Your life is there."

"What is Marty going to do? What are we going to do?"

"His path will become clear." Peter brushed the dirt off his hands, stood up, took both my hands to help me up, and held me.

"You can't ever come back, can you?"

"Not unless they change the laws. Don't worry about me. I'm home."

"You're going to miss everything. Your graduation. My graduation. My marriage. Everything."

Peter wiped the tears off my cheeks with his bandana. "It's okay not to be free to go into a country I wasn't free in anyhow. I'm not angry or afraid anymore." I never knew he was either one.

"I will write you every week. Promise me you'll write back. And I'll be back to visit. I promise." I knelt by Suki and scratched her behind the ears, tickled her nose, and gave her a squeeze. I was going to miss her. She was going to miss Racer. I hugged Peter again and drove away. The leaving left a small hole in my heart next to the one for Jeff and Hook. That's how it is with friends.

You love them for as long as you're with them and then you keep on loving them from afar.

I did the reverse at the border. "Where are you from?"

"The U.S."

"What were you doing in Canada?"

"Visiting the University of Winnipeg." They let me through.

Marty and I ate chocolate covered peanuts and cried the whole way back to Chicago. I feared what was coming next.

U.S. Soldier Body Count: 51,012

Chapter 40
"Let It Be"

Marty's senior year ended with a whimper. We continued our boycott of classes. On graduation day, he dressed in a clean pair of jeans, a black t-shirt, a black band around his arm. He walked across the stage as Mom Olsen, Billy, Julie, and I watched. It was a somber affair. I don't know if it was because of the shadow of Cambodia, Kent State, and Jackson State or if it was the fact that all the young male graduates who won the lottery would get their prize that summer.

After school let out, Rick left for the Rosebud Reservation in South Dakota to do sociological research on how the Lakota people felt about being sent to fight in a war few people support. Marty and I spent the summer digging in the dirt, planting flowers and vegetables for the summer, not saying what we both knew. Marty might not be around to pick the flowers or eat the vegetables.

* * *

"I have to go to court." Marty and I weeded in the greenhouse one Saturday in early August, getting the soil ready for winter planting. Racer dug in the dirt next to us.

I stood up, dirt covering my hands, deep into my nails. "What? When did that happen?" All summer we avoided the conversation. We didn't say we weren't going to talk about it. We just didn't. Kind of like if you didn't talk about it, it wouldn't happen. What if they gave a war and no one talked about it? That's what we did.

He sat down and with his dirty hand pushed the hair out of his eyes, smearing dirt on his forehead. He looked at me, then his gaze shifted down.

I sat down next to him. "About two weeks after graduation I got a letter telling me to report for my physical."

"You never told me."

The day Marty got his diploma was the day his draft status shifted from "2-S—Registrant Deferred Because of Activity in Study" to "1-A—Available for Military Service." Why didn't they call it what it was? "1-A—We Can Send You to Die if We Want." Why the obfuscation?

"I didn't show up," he said.

What a difference a day makes. God, why was he born on November 8th? If we were conceived on the same day, why wasn't he born on my birthday?

"Why didn't I run over your foot with the car?" Then his status would have been "IV-F—Registrant Not Qualified for Any Military Service." In other words, you are safe, young man. You'll never walk again but at least you are safe.

Why didn't we go to Canada? Why didn't he have braces put on his teeth or at least try the drug route? He didn't. He didn't show up. He plain and simply didn't show up.

Marty put a dirt-covered hand in his back pocket and pulled out the letter he received the first week in August. He handed it to me. I wiped as much dirt as I could from my hands and then brushed back the few wisps of hair that escaped from the bandana tied around my head. I took the letter.

"You have been summoned to appear in court for failure to report to your pre-induction physical as required by your selective service notice."

"When were you going to tell me?"

"Right now." He grinned.

"This isn't funny, Marty. You knew all summer that you didn't show up. I didn't know you didn't show up. Now you think it's funny that you have to go to court and we didn't even talk about it?"

"I couldn't face it," he said. "I couldn't worry you."

"We can go to Canada. It's not too late. You could change your name and we could go into the witness protection program."

He laughed. "Like the government will protect me from itself."

"This is not funny, Marty."

He looked at me. "I know it's not funny, Becky. We're talking about my life here. It is not funny."

"Don't show up. They won't be able to find you."

"I don't know what I'm going to do." He crumbled up the letter and threw it in the lettuce. I picked it up in case he decided to go and needed to know when and where.

Marty got up and pulled me up next to him. "I've got to get out of here." He wiped the tears and dirt off my face with the bandana he always had tied to his belt loop. Then he wiped his own. It only smeared the dirt more.

"Where?"

"I don't know. I have to think."

"I'm going with you."

He hugged me again, a sob escaping from his throat. "I've got to do this alone."

"But this decision affects both of us."

"I know that. But I've got to get my head clear, alone."

A shower and an hour later he was in the car. He kissed me through the window. "I won't be long."

I watched him drive away, his hand waving out the window as he disappeared. I understood. It's like when I ran after I heard that Hook died. If you go long enough, maybe at the end it will be different. It never is.

I sat down on the ground and looked around. The world didn't make sense, none of it. We weeded lettuce and then he's in the shower and then he drives away. What was I going to do? Peter was gone. He couldn't help. Rick was on the Rosebud Reservation. He couldn't help. Ginger and Jake were on their way home from a vacation in Vermont. They couldn't help. Hook was the only one who could help me. He couldn't help. I picked up a handful of dirt from the ground next to me and let it sift through my fingers.

I went inside and called Mama McKinney. I cried outright when she answered the phone.

"Hi, it's Becky." That's all I got out.

"My dear, are you okay?"

"No."

"Take a breath, dear and tell me what's wrong."

"Marty has to go to court for not going to his physical. They can throw him in jail if they find him guilty. What am I going to do? I'm not sure I could survive that."

I knew I could. She knew I could. I needed Mama McKinney to tell me I could survive whatever happened. I needed to feel her hug through the telephone wires.

As I lay in bed that night, I noticed a crack in the ceiling that spanned the entire width of the room. The face plate on the light switch was broken. The curtains were frayed at the bottom. The windows creaked when the wind blew. The bed had a lump in the middle. None of that was there when Marty was with me.

Sunday I wandered around the house picking up things and moving them to new places, picking them up, moving them again. Later, I watched Bonanza on TV. Little Joe got his heart broken again by a young schoolteacher who was killed by a random bullet. That always happened on Bonanza. Little Joe fell in love and then the girl he was in love with always died. Little Joe never got a break. When it came to love, neither of us ever got a break, except for our hearts. They broke too often.

I slept on the couch in the living room that night. I couldn't stand to see the crack in the ceiling again or hear the wind moaning.

I went to my internship at the local paper on Monday morning. I wrote an article about a couple's 50th anniversary celebration. I wondered if I'd ever have one.

Marty showed up late Monday afternoon. I heard the horn honk. Racer and I met him at the back door. God, I never wanted to let go of him again. He took my hand and sat me down at the kitchen table. "I'll get us some tea." He turned to the stove.

"Why do you always offer me tea?" I stood up. "It's hot out. I don't need any tea."

Marty came back to the table and gently sat me down again. Racer jumped into my lap. Marty sat next to me, took both hands, and looked straight at me. I was already crying. He let go of one hand and handed me his bandana. I blew my nose in it.

"I thought a lot about this."

I stopped him. "I don't want to hear it. Whatever it is, don't tell me. Let's go to Canada. Let's hide in the woods somewhere."

"Becky, I need to make my statement in court. I need to stand before the draft board and the court and tell them that I won't go, that I won't be complicit with their war."

"What good will that do?" I asked him. "What good will it do to stand before some judge and tell that judge that you refuse to go to Vietnam. No newspaper is going to pick up the story. Nobody will know. Nothing will change."

"I'll know." Marty stood up and walked towards the refrigerator. "Iced tea?"

"Shut up about tea," I said to him. He came back to the table and sat down. I looked at him. "What will happen?" I knew the answer before he told me.

"Probably twenty-five months."

I stopped breathing. I slammed my hand on the table. It startled Racer who jumped down and hid under the table. "1-2-3 Bam. Remember? Let's all jump and change the course of history. 1-2-3 Bam. Well, it didn't work." I needed to run. "All for not wanting to take a gun and shoot someone in the face. All for not being willing to drop napalm on a forest or bombs on a city. Something is wrong with justice in this country. That's not fair." Then I looked at Marty. It was his life. He was the one going to prison.

I put my hand gently on the side of his face. "You know I love you, don't you?"

"More than tongue-can-tell," That's what Marty's mom always said to him. It took him a long time to realize a person named Tunkin' Tell did not exist.

I wiped the tears out of my eyes.

Marty had to speak, to make his voice heard, to make his statement. That's one of the things I loved most about him.

* * *

Time continued to pass relentlessly. Court day arrived. I sat in the courtroom next to Marty, holding his hand, waiting for the judge to call his name. We were all there. Rick finished his research on the reservation early. Billy, Julie, and Mom Olsen came up from Springfield. Jake and Ginger were back from Vermont. Jake had finished his first year of law school. Ginger was six months pregnant. I pulled a package of five-flavor lifesavers from my pocket and handed it around. Marty took the red one. I didn't care. At that point, I didn't care if I ended up with the green one, the one that tasted like the stuff you clean the kitchen floor with.

Even when you're right, there's nothing more demoralizing than a courtroom. It seemed like a good idea when the Bill of Rights was written, speedy trial, jury of your peers. The problem with justice, though, is that a judge or jury get to decide your fate whether they are right or not, whether you are right or not. Marty was right. It didn't make a damn bit of difference when it came to justice.

I heard Marty's name. He leaned over to shake his brother's hand and nodded at everyone. Marty stood up and pulled me with him. He hugged me. I couldn't let go. He wouldn't let go.

"Mr. Olson," the judge said. "Please face the court with your attorney."

I held on tighter. "Let's run," I whispered to him. "There's still time."

Marty smiled and held me tighter. "It's going to be okay, Becky. I love you. Never forget." He let go first. I never would have. He rubbed his thumb over my eyes, taking the tears with him. "More than tongue-can-tell." He kissed me gently, one hand on each side of my face.

Marty stood before the judge next to his attorney. "Mr. Olsen. You are in court because of a failure to appear at your pre-induction physical. How do you plead?"

"Not guilty, Your Honor."

"Can you explain why you think you are not guilty when you obviously did not appear?"

"Yes, Your Honor."

"Care to enlighten me?"

I held onto Billy's hand. "The war is wrong and I won't go," was all Marty said.

Chants ran through my mind. *Hell no, we won't go. Hell no, he won't go.* That means jail. It's easy to chant it, but then you have to live with it.

The judge replied, "You understand that it is against the laws of the U.S. government and Selective Service to refuse induction?"

"I do, Your Honor."

I put a pineapple lifesaver in my mouth, chewing it, not even savoring the taste. *Why do you keep saying 'Your Honor?' There's no honor here.* I gripped Billy's hand so hard he probably thought it was going to break.

The judge said, "Regardless of how I feel about the war, I find you guilty. Do you want to say anything before I pass sentence?"

"Yes, Your Honor."

Stop the 'Your Honor' crap, Marty. Run. Run like hell. Run as fast as you can. Run to Canada. There's still time. I squeezed harder.

Marty turned to us briefly and smiled. He turned back to the judge. "If there is a God, that God does not want me to kill. And whether there is a God or not, what the government is doing in Vietnam is wrong. I will not be, I cannot be, complicit with the evils perpetrated on the people of Vietnam in the name of our government. I cannot serve two masters. I cannot serve the United States government and the morality of my soul. I choose my soul."

The judge cleared his throat and wrote something on a piece of paper in front of him. "You are a courageous young man. I

269

wish there were more like you in this country. If there were, we might see an end to this damnable war."

The judge looked at us. "You should be proud of him," he said. He looked back at Marty. "Despite my feelings about the war, I must follow the laws of this country. I hereby sentence you to twenty-five months in prison." One month more than the obligation of the draft. The gavel fell.

I saw Marty's head drop. Then he turned to us and brushed back his hair. He looked at Billy and grinned. The bailiff gave us a chance to hug Marty before taking him away. I needed that hug to hold me for a long time. He tucked my hair behind my ear and kissed me. My last kiss for twenty-five months. "You've got this," he said. I wasn't so sure.

As Marty walked from the courtroom, hands cuffed behind his back, his hair falling in his eyes, he whispered something to the guard. They both laughed.

He did it. He spoke his conscience. A lot of good that did. God, I would miss him. Relentless time swallowed me again.

Marty's mom touched me on the shoulder. I turned for her hug. Her son had just been sentenced to jail. "He'll be home before you know it."

"It will feel like forever," I said.

I walked over to Billy and leaned down to hug him. He pulled me into his lap. I laid my head on his shoulder while he stroked my hair and let me cry. "You should be proud of him, Becky. He did the right thing for him. That's obvious."

"Proud? Fuck pride. Fuck the right thing. How is he going to survive? How am we going to live through the next twenty-five months?" I wanted to stay in Billy's lap the whole time, to not get up and make my bed and brush my teeth and eat breakfast and sweep the floor and take a shower and go to class and put one

270

foot in front of the other. I was tired of putting one foot in front of the other. I wanted my feet to be rooted for a while.

Billy kissed me on the head. "He'll survive and you'll get through the next twenty-five months one day at a time."

We stayed at the courthouse only long enough to find out details about where Marty would be taken, when we could visit, when we could call, how we could send him care packages. Then we left and went our separate ways.

On the ride back from the courthouse to our little white house in the country, Rick couldn't hear the tears rolling down my face or feel the knot in my stomach, the nausea, the coldness creeping through my veins. He gave me silence. It was a gift I needed.

I stood in the doorway of what used to feel like home, not knowing what way to go. I couldn't go to the bedroom. Too much of Marty would be there. I simply stood. Racer bounded up to me. I leaned down to scratch him behind the ears.

Rick guided me to the stool at the counter and put on water for tea. I pulled the Winnie-the-Pooh cookie jar towards me and picked out two cookies.

Rick picked through the cookies and found a lemon cream one. "The cookie stash has improved this summer."

"That's Marty. One day he said, 'Enough with Oreos and Vanilla Wafers' and he went out and bought four packages of random cookies." I remembered that day. Marty and I sat at the counter and ate one of each new kind of cookie, skipping dinner that night. That memory brought tears.

I stared at the wall, the counter, the ceiling, until Rick placed a hot cup of chamomile tea in front of me. "Why does everyone give me tea when life is falling apart?" I stirred in some honey, grateful for the warmth down my throat until I choked, the words wanting to come up, stopping the tea from going down. "It's my fault he's going to prison. It's always my fault."

"How do you figure that?"

I lifted my head and looked straight at him. He handed me a napkin to wipe the tears off my face. "Everyone I love suffers. Jeff died. Hook died. Marty's in prison. I knew something would happen. If I had not tossed the stone, he'd still be here. He wouldn't have to go away. It's what I do."

"Not tossed the stone? What the hell does that mean?"

I smiled slightly. "In a dream, Hook told me that you can't skip a stone forty-six times if you don't toss it. He told me to toss the stone. I did. I fell in love, and this is what happens. How is he going to survive it? Is prison going to change him?"

"Your love is what's going to get him through."

"Shut up about love. It's my love that did this to him. I never wanted to fall in love with Marty because I knew something would happen. It always happens when I love somebody. My love is poison."

"Becky," Rick said. I stopped him from saying anything else.

"Don't you dare tell me about my love helping him get through this. Don't tell me I'll make it through. You know what's going to happen tonight?" I paced around the counter like a caged panther. "I'm going to get into our bed and lie there staring at the ceiling. I'll notice a crack that I don't see when Marty is next to me. I'll see the broken face plate of the light switch and the frayed curtains. I'll hear the windows creak. I won't be able to sleep because of the lump in the middle of the bed that I can't feel when he's there. I'll grab his pillow and try to inhale a bit of him. Slowly, over time, that scent will disappear. I'll stay awake knowing that for the next, probably close to eight hundred nights, I'll be alone. For the next eight hundred nights, he'll fall asleep alone in a cold prison cell."

I was bone tired. He was gone. Goddamn war. It ripped out my heart time and time again. Maybe I didn't have to worry about being drafted and going to Vietnam, but when the war touched everyone I cared for, it touched me. The touching wasn't that of a lover. It was the touch of sandpaper on raw skin. It hurt like hell.

I stopped pacing and picked up the nearest thing to my hand, a slotted wooden spoon, the spoon Marty always used to stir soup. I never knew why he chose that spoon. Soup doesn't do well with slots. Now I'll never know. For twenty-five months I'll never know. I threw the spoon as far as I could. It knocked over his Nellie Fox baseball on the bookshelf. I picked up the spoon and pounded it on the back of the couch. "Fuck this."

Suddenly he was there, surrounding me. It wasn't Hook's whole-body hug. It was Marty, the pressure of his shoulders against mine, his hand tucking my hair behind my ear, the muskiness of him. In Chicago after Jeff died, Hook's hug told me that someday I would be whole again. Someday I would get through Jeff's death. Marty didn't tell me that I would be alright someday. He held me in his gentle embrace and told me that I was okay right now.

I stood there, feeling him, my gaze on the spoon I held in my hand. I could hear the Turtles singing how we could be happy together. I felt his hand in mine, his arm around my back, swaying to the song. Twenty-five long months. I sobbed until there were no more tears. Rick let me cry.

"I'll be here for you. You know that don't you?"

"I know that. It's just that everyone else is gone. Jeff's gone. Hook's gone. Peter's gone. Jake and Ginger are gone. Marty is gone. Everyone."

"Except you and me."

Sleep came hard, alone, without Marty.

U.S. Soldier Body Count: 52,237

OCCUPY WALL STREET
DECEMBER 17, 2011
Duarte Square

"Hey, Matt. You're on." Matt put a Wint-O-Green lifesaver in his mouth and walked in front of the gathered crowd at Duarte Square in lower Manhattan. After being evicted from Zuccotti Park, the occupiers searched for a new place for their encampment. The empty lot next to Duarte Square seemed perfect, despite the six-foot high chain link fence surrounding it.

"Mic check," Matt said. "Mic check," the people around him echoed. He chewed up the lifesaver and spoke.

"In thousands of cities around the world (echo) people are claiming spaces for sanctuary and free speech (echo). On our three-month anniversary, we claim this empty lot for the people (echo)."

Faith leaders, artists, musicians, lawyers, students, teachers, unemployed, comrades all stood in front of the empty lot owned by Trinity Church, the third largest real estate holder in New York City. The occupiers hoped the church would be sympathetic.

A ladder appeared from behind a yellow banner that said, "Liberate Space." An Episcopal Bishop was the first to climb the ladder and scale the fence, occupying the empty lot. Then one by one, hundreds went over, including Matt.

One man being cuffed said to a police officer in riot gear, "There's nothing to be proud of here. These are American citizens. I did two tours in Nam and this is not a proud moment for you." Matt smiled and thought of his mom and dad.

Matt saw fear in the eyes of the police officers. The occupiers threatened to overpower the cops who were barking orders and pushing protesters. The police pulled down the ladder. Occupiers uprooted the fence allowing people to get out or in.

Matt ran to the uplifted fence and scooted out of the lot. He turned and saw the police dragging someone by the leg across the lot.

Police maintained their line in front of the fence while the occupiers moved back and forth cajoling, mocking, videotaping, photographing. The police stood solid; stone solid. Inside the fence, officers made arrests. Occupiers sat cuffed behind the back, waiting for transport.

"Mic check (echo). General Assembly in ten minutes (echo) to talk about what's happening here (echo)." Slowly, occupiers wandered back to Duarte Square to regroup.

As the sun was setting, the protesters came back to life with a wave of anticipation, like a hive disturbed, awakened. Out of nowhere, the cry spread through the crowd, "March! March! March!"

The crowd left Duarte Square and moved through the streets towards Times Square accompanied by constant drumbeat and police on scooters. "Hey, Hey, Ho, Ho. Wall Street Greed Has Got To Go!" Walking, then running, diverting, turning left, dashing through cars, down the street, on the sidewalk, "We are the 99%!"

The police couldn't control the crowd. The crowd wouldn't be controlled. Matt turned left, right again, evading the police barricades. The cops didn't know which way marchers were going.

275

The police began their systematic arrest of identified marchers. With each arrest, with each marcher grabbed from the crowd, tossed to the ground, surrounded, kneed, and cuffed, the crowd yelled, "Shame, shame, shame! The whole world is watching! You're not getting away with this!" Even with cameras on every arrest, the cops got away with it.

"Back up. Get off the street," an officer said.

"I'm on the sidewalk. You can't get me for walking on the sidewalk."

They did. An officer threw him to the ground. Six officers surrounded him, landed on him, cuffed him, too hard, too tight. "What's your name?" his comrades called to him. "Tell us your name."

The marchers ran into the street and weaved through the traffic as they chanted, "Banks got bailed out. We got sold out. We are unstoppable. Another world is possible."

As Matt walked down the sidewalk, he saw a man in a dark shirt point at him. Matt turned and headed the other way. Four cops stood behind him. He turned to the side. Matt was blocked. The man in the dark shirt grabbed him and threw him to the ground. Matt struggled to get away. The man said nothing. He wasn't in uniform. He didn't say, "You're under arrest," or "I'm a cop." The four cops helped hold him down.

How did they choose who to arrest? Out of the hundreds running in the streets, why did they pick Matt out of the crowd? Maybe they saw him at Zuccotti Park chained to his friends, or in the lot across from Duarte Square. Maybe because he was loud. Maybe it was that at six foot two he stood above the crowd. Maybe it was the black hoodie covering his long dreadlocks.

"We've got ya covered, Matt. We got six cameras on you, dude," Matt heard someone say.

"Stop resisting," the police officer said.

"How can he resist with five cops on him?" someone yelled.

One cop pushed Matt's head into the ground. Matt could feel the concrete dig into his skin, the skin pull away. Another cop sat on Matt's back and rammed his knee into his kidneys once, twice, three times. A third pulled Matt's arms back and put on the zip ties. They pulled off the hoodie and jerked Matt's head up by his dreadlocks, pulled the black bandana off his face, grabbed him under the arms, and dragged him to the waiting police car. Matt heard his comrades yelling, "Shame! Shame! He didn't do anything!"

The police drove Matt to the station to book him. After they uncuffed him and before they took his belongings, he texted his mom and dad. "Arrested."

Arrested because he called for the end to economic inequality. Called for the big corporations to stop their exploitation of the workers. Called for an end to greed and corruption. Called for an end to police brutality. *Called for an end to the war in Vietnam.* That night in jail, Matt and his comrades banged on the walls, chanting in solidarity. They scratched D17 OWS 2011 into the wall of the jail cell so others would know they were there. December 17 Occupy Wall Street 2011.

The New York City police released Matt after thirty-six hours. He left the precinct with open sores on his face from being slammed into the concrete and with his hands still numb from the cuffs. They gave Matt his plastic bag of possessions—a smashed cell phone that wasn't smashed when they'd taken it from him, a key ring with his car keys missing, and his black bandana.

He never saw the text his mom and dad sent back. "We love you and support you. The world will know about this."

ARRESTS: 55

PART FOUR

SENIOR YEAR

1970-1971

Chapter 41
"Love Is Here And Now You're Gone"

Two more weeks before school started. The beginning of senior year is supposed to be joyous, moving towards the end, towards graduation. Instead, this beginning was filled with loneliness, fear, and grief. I was here, Marty was gone, locked up in a prison cell. Fuck beginnings.

Every night for the past ten months I slept by his side, curled up by him, his arm around me. Every night for the past ten months he was the last thing I saw before I fell asleep and the first thing I saw when I woke up.

I slept curled up on his side of the bed hoping to feel a little of him. It didn't help. Before I fell asleep, I saw an empty pillow. When I woke, expecting to see him, he wasn't there. My breath caught going in. I grabbed his pillow in a panic and put it to my face. It didn't smell like him anymore.

I lay in bed and stared at the ceiling. I counted four more cracks. Why hadn't I noticed them before? I noticed stains on the frayed curtains, worn spots in the carpet. The closet doorknob missed a screw. The house was falling apart.

Marty moved sixty-five miles away from me into the Joliet Correctional Center, a building built more than one hundred years ago by the very men imprisoned there. Marty didn't need correcting. There was nothing to correct. He was in prison, plain and simple.

Prison regulations allowed Marty to receive two hours of calls every week and visits on Sunday. Every Sunday for the next twenty-five months I promised to be there.

The first Sunday was the hardest. I sat in the car looking at a fortress, a poor imitation of a medieval castle designed to keep the enemies in or keep them out. I'm not sure which. I could almost imagine Marty on his steed, fully armored, lance in hand, ready to charge. He did that in the courtroom and lost. They ensconced him behind the tall stone walls, took away his steed, his armor, his lance. I prayed they wouldn't take away his fight. I pulled the bandana from my belt loop and dried my eyes. *Here's where Marty is spending the next twenty-five months of his life. Locked behind these walls. What's going to happen to him?*

I walked through the massive front doors, signed in, and waited. Then he appeared, in front of me, all of him. I didn't want to cry. *Kennedy stoic,* I thought. I walked up and hugged him, kissed him gently. The guard cleared his throat and said, "No touching."

"You got an hour," the guard said, posting himself next to the wall, arms crossed, eyes scanning the prisoners and their visitors, ever cautious, looking for infractions. Like lifeguards at the pools in the summer, eager to blow a whistle for the slightest thing. It was the power inherent in a whistle. We couldn't hold hands during the hour but under the table I felt the pressure of his shoes against my flip-flopped feet. I missed him completely.

"What do you do all day?" I asked him that first Sunday.

"I wake about 6:30 to some kind of air-raid siren alarm, the kind they had when we were kids and had air raid drills at school."

I remember the drills. When the siren went off, we dropped under our desks and put our hands over our heads. Drop. Duck.

Cover. It wouldn't protect us from a nuclear attack, but it kept us in line.

Marty continued. "The siren means we have ten minutes before they unlock the cell and we go to the courtyard for fifteen minutes of calisthenics. Then breakfast. I sit with someone different every day. I have to live with these guys for the next two years. I might as well get to know them. Thirty minutes later we go to our workstations."

I moved my foot up inside his pants and felt skin against skin. I glanced at the guard. He wasn't looking our way.

"I'm on laundry duty now. That's where they put all the newbies. Hoping to get switched to the print shop or library sometime. We work until lunch. Break for an hour. Workstations for another couple hours. Dinner. Evening recreation. Then bed where I lie and think of you."

"What do you do when you think of me?" He grinned but didn't answer.

His days sounded like mine. Wake up. Stretch a bit to get my body going. Eat breakfast. Go to work until noon. When school starts, go to class. Eat lunch. Back to work. Go home. Take a walk or weed the garden. Watch TV. Lie in bed and think of Marty. Day after day for twenty-five months.

* * *

I took the next week off work to visit my family. I needed Mom's tuna-noodle casserole and Dad's chocolate-covered peanuts. I needed to play cards with my younger brother and convince him to file for CO status now, before it's too late. He promised he would.

"Twenty-five months," I said to Mom and Dad. "How am I going to live through it?"

Dad looked at me. "Time goes by one day at a time. That's how you'll get through this, one day at a time." Dad took a chocolate-covered peanut from the bowl and handed it to me. "That, and chocolate-covered peanuts."

By the time I left on Wednesday to head back north, Marty was five days closer to coming home.

I stopped in Springfield. I needed Mom Olsen's home-made spaghetti and brownies. I needed to sit with her and look at scrapbooks of Marty as a child. I needed to hear Billy talk about the pranks they pulled when they were young. I needed to sit on the front porch with Billy and Julie after Mom Olsen went to bed, smoke a joint, and eat more brownies. I needed to sit in Billy's lap and have his strong arms tell me that it was going to be all right, that Marty would come out the other end and so would I.

Mostly I needed Marty. Mostly I needed to put one foot in front of the other and go on. I did.

* * *

Kentucky Fried Chicken with sides of mashed potatoes and gravy, coleslaw, and biscuits. Comfort food. My favorite meal. Rick walked in and insulted my choice of food. He preceded to take some mashed potatoes, covering them with gravy.

"I got a call from a woman who is looking for a place to live. Sounds like she'll fit right in. Her name is Ronda," I said.

"Who is she and how did she get our name?"

"She teaches at Lake Forest Academy. She ran across someone who teaches at the college who gave her our name and number." I poured a bunch of gravy over the mashed potatoes, broke off a huge hunk of white meat, dipped it into the gravy and potatoes.

Rick stopped eating. "No way."

"Why not? The house is too big for the two of us. She seems nice and I could use another female. Against the war and all that."

"If you're worried about covering the rent, I can handle it."

"It's not about the money." Same argument I had with Marty when he wanted Rick to move in."

"Listen, Becky. She works at Lake Forest Academy, an elitist school for rich prep school kids."

I almost choked on the chicken in my mouth. "You teach at an elitist college for kids who went to expensive prep schools."

Rick stood and took his plate into the kitchen. He turned back to me. "No. She'll bring her snooty attitude, her English literature, her pants suits, her high heels. She'll bring steak and Wonder Bread."

"What the hell are you talking about? You don't know anything about her."

"I hate the name Ronda."

"This is why I didn't want you moving in. You are an arrogant, self-righteous jerk." I put another piece of chicken in my mouth.

"I don't want some snotty rich chick moving in. Especially one I don't know anything about."

"Did you just call her a chick?"

"I did. Ronda. The elitist American Literature chick from Lake Forest Academy."

I wanted to throw something at him but the only thing within my reach were tubs of mashed potatoes and gravy, two biscuits, and a plastic spoon. So instead, I yelled at him, "She teaches history, Rick. She doesn't teach American Literature. How do you know she wears pants suits?"

"It will change everything having her here."

"You changed everything having you here. I'm going to call her up and say yes. In the meantime, you need to get laid, Rick."

"My sex life is none of your business," Rick said.

I started to laugh, remembering the argument I had with Marty before Rick moved in.

"What's so funny?" Rick asked.

"Marty and I had a huge argument before you moved in."

"What did you argue about?"

"I didn't want a sociology professor moving in here because I knew what would happen. Incense, pot, mason jars full of grains. You turned out okay."

"I never knew you didn't want me."

"I didn't want you real bad." I thought about Marty in his cell, wondered if he was pacing. Wondered if he was pushing back his hair. Wondered if he was thinking about me the same time I was thinking about him. I missed him at that moment. At every moment. The argument was over. "I was wrong about you, Rick. I'm glad you're here. Let's meet her and decide."

When Rick saw her peasant skirt, bare feet, and beaded headband, he said yes. Ronda moved into our little white house in the country.

* * *

The class of 1974 showed up on campus. They missed the entire 60s. Rallies. Protests, Marches, Campaigns. Raw violence in the streets of Chicago. Occupations. Assassinations. Lotteries. Missing the 60s was like missing it all.

It seemed a lifetime ago that I went to my first anti-war meeting in the men's honor dorm, when I got seduced by a movement, sucked in by Jake, held in by the rest. It seemed a lifetime ago that Jeff died, Hook died, Ginger and Jake married. Now, I just had to make it through the next nine months to graduation and the rest of Marty's twenty-five months.

286

Ronda moved into Peter's second floor bedroom. She grew up in Great Neck, New York, on Long Island. In high school, she was head cheerleader and was voted most popular by her senior class. She wanted to be an airline stewardess, but her parents insisted she go to college. They paid the bills, so she enrolled at Columbia. It changed her. Maybe that's why we connected so deeply. We both changed easily. She donated her wardrobe to the Salvation Army and bought bell-bottoms, peasant skirts, and fringed moccasins. She majored in history with a minor in secondary education. After she graduated, she spent a year in San Francisco and finally decided she needed to head back home. When she saw a job advertised at Lake Forest Academy, she applied. Chicago was halfway home.

Once again, the small white house outside of Lake Forest filled with life. Plotting, planning, scheming, laughing, jamming, singing, playing cards until early in the morning.

Rick and Ronda argued often. "You've got to be kidding me, Rick. You really think that if you just tell people they can't do that, they'll stop?"

"Do what?" I asked. "Stop what?" They ignored me.

"Ronda. Your approach is based on the philosophy of 'Do your own thing.' Free float through the universe and hope the rest of the world catches up with you. The world doesn't work that way." Rick turned to stir the soup on the stove.

"You are not being fair," Ronda said. "You make it sound like all I care about is me. And please move, I need to get the bread out of the oven."

"When will the soup be ready?" I asked Rick. He ignored me. "What are you two even arguing about?"

They both looked at me and didn't say a word.

"Well, you sound like that most of the time."

The argument lasted through dinner. I never figured out what it was about. Who did what and where they did it and who tried to change what and how. I chimed in from time to time but mostly the two of them argued about who was the most right about the things they both agreed on anyway. I loved them both and couldn't imagine them not in my life.

We finished dinner and the music started. I brought out my guitar. Ronda used the coffee table as a drum. Rick took to playing a flute he got while visiting the Rosebud. The music filled the house. Filled my soul. Filled my time.

While all this was happening, the war went on. The deaths continued. Fewer soldiers were sent, but that didn't mean that the ones who died were any less dead. Who would be the last American soldier to die in Vietnam? What would that be like?

Things calmed down on college campuses. Summers have a way of doing that. Fewer occupations, less violence. Colleges and universities adapted to demands and many divested in companies that supported the war effort. Hit them in the pocketbook. That's the way to end this war. Maybe.

U.S. Soldier Body Count: 52,667

Chapter 42
"Draft Dodger Rag"

Stranger things entered the refrigerator, slimy white cubes that shook when you poked them, exotic fruits, things that looked like hamburgers, almost tasted like hamburgers if covered with enough ketchup, but weren't even distantly related to hamburgers, jars of wheat germ, raw goat's milk. Ronda continued Peter's alfalfa sprout production. In my room, I had my private stash of chocolate-covered peanuts and lifesavers. All was right with the world.

"I'm afraid prison is going to change him." I said one night at dinner. I chopped an already tiny piece of tofu into smaller pieces until it crumbled beneath my fork. I put down the fork and leaned my face into my hands, elbows on the table. "I don't want to lose him." I scooped more salad onto my plate and poured Thousand Island dressing on top of it.

Ronda handed me a glass of papaya juice and said, "You're mad at him, aren't you?"

"I am royally pissed off at him. I hate that he chose prison. We could have gone to Canada or Sweden or underground. Why didn't I fall in love with some rich prep school frat guy who could buy his way out of Nam? Like Joe Scott Joe. Although it didn't work for him. He got shipped out."

"Who in the world is Joe Scott Joe?" she asked.

289

"Doesn't matter."

"How am I supposed to follow this conversation if you throw out names like Joe Scott Joe?"

"I met him my freshman year. A jerk who only cared about booze and himself. He always showed up at rallies carrying a sign that said 'Love It or Leave It.' I guess he flunked out of school after sophomore year. I never saw him again."

"Why would you want to fall in love with him?" Ronda took another piece of cornbread and poured honey on it.

"The real question is why do I lose everyone I fall in love with?"

Rick walked in the door, grabbed a plate, and joined us at the table. "Thanks to whoever made this salad."

We ignored him. "Don't blame Marty, Becky," Ronda said.

"Blame him for what?" Rick asked.

"Hush, Rick. We're not talking to you." Ronda didn't look at Rick. "He didn't have a choice. The only thing he ever did was follow his conscience."

"And fall in love with me. That was his fatal mistake. My love is toxic." I put the last bit of slimy tofu in my mouth.

"That's ridiculous. You know that don't you?"

"I don't know that. Look at my record."

* * *

The Forester
Editor's Corner
Becky Jamison

The Lake Forest College Students Against the War will be holding a weekend of fun and education October 9th and 10th. Join us Friday in the dining hall as we listen to true stories about how the Vietnam War is affecting young men in this country. Then stick around for a party.

Saturday October 10ᵗʰ, the Vietnam Veterans Against the War will provide draft counseling in Commons for all draft eligible males.

President Nixon has promised to reduce troops in Vietnam, but the war continues. Get involved. The LFC Students Against the War meet every Wednesday night at seven o'clock in Hixson Lounge.

* * *

Friday night I took the microphone before a packed room, something I could not have done three years ago. "Welcome Lake Foresters. What do we want?"

"Peace."

"When do we want it?"

"Now!"

"Come on, Foresters. You can do better than that. Let me hear you! What do you want?"

"Peace!"

"When do you want it?"

"NOW!"

"Thanks for coming out. Tonight, we have stories that I hope will scare you into action. You men out there should be scared. The government wants to send you to fight in a war we have no business being in. 52,000 have died in that war so far. Two years ago, I lost my best friend in a car accident. This jacket was his. He came back from Vietnam with a hook where his hand had been. He never got rid of the demons that haunted him. I wish he were here tonight to tell you about those demons, of seeing his best buddy die right next to him. Of dragging dead soldiers out of the

291

swamp. Of seeing body bags lined up at the airport on base ready to be shipped home. I wish he could tell you himself."

I took a red bandana from my belt loop. I wiped my eyes. I wasn't going to let my tears stop me from telling the truth, from scaring them into action.

"Tonight, you'll hear stories from Jake, conscientious objector, from Peter, who went to Canada, from Marty, who chose to go to prison instead of being drafted, and from Billy, member of the Vietnam Veterans against the War."

"All you women out there should be scared too. Don't think this war doesn't affect you because you won't be drafted. Take it from me. This war hurts like hell. It hurt like crazy when Peter went to Canada. He may never be able to come home. It hurts because my boyfriend, Marty, is in prison for twenty-five months for refusing to show up at his physical. It hurts because my boyfriend's brother, Billy, is in a wheelchair, his spine shattered by a bullet." I looked at the faces of the young men eager to figure out their lives, the young women who love them.

"First, from Forester class of 1968, Jake Stedman. Jake spent two years at a hospital in Chicago doing alternative service. Please welcome conscientious objector, Jake Stedman."

Ginger, due to deliver in two months, gave Jake a kiss as he came to the stage. I handed him the microphone. The crowd was silent as he talked about how he made the decision that he couldn't fight in the war. "If any of you are considering applying for conscientious objector status, I'll be here all day tomorrow. Stop by and see me. I've got forms and information."

After he finished, he read Peter's letter. "This is a letter written by someone who chose to go to Canada.' The letter ended, "*I know I may never be able to come home again. But Canada ain't half bad. I've got my greenhouse. I've got my friends. You're welcome here anytime. Love and peace from the land up north.*"

I took the microphone again. "When Peter sneaked into Canada, I had the job of driving over the border, meeting him at our designated spot, and driving him to the commune where he lives now. I miss him every day of my life."

I wiped the tear from my eye. Partially because I missed Peter and his gentle quietness. Mostly because I missed Marty.

"My boyfriend, Marty Olsen, can't be here tonight because he is in Joliet Prison for refusing to go to Vietnam. I can visit him once a week for an hour, no touching, and he's allowed two hours of phone calls a week." I took Marty's letter out of the pocket of the army jacket. *"Hey Lake Foresters. I wish I could speak to you in person. Catch me in a couple years and we can talk."* The tears rolled down my face. Damn. Ginger walked up on stage next to me, took my hand, and whispered, "You can do this. Take a deep breath."

I moved the microphone back in front of my face and read again.

"Each one of you has to decide about what you are going to do when the draft comes for you. Only you can figure that out. When I had to make the decision, I didn't consult the person I love most in the world." I took a deep breath. *"In the end I had to live with myself, so the decision was mine alone."* I got to the ending, *"I'm free here in prison because I did what was right for me. My only regret? Leaving the people I love. Listen to your conscience. Don't be complicit with the evil perpetrated by the U.S. government. One last request, please take care of Becky for me."*

I blew my nose into the red bandana. "Let's end this war, okay?"

Someone in the audience yelled, "What do we want?" "Peace!" "When do we want it?" "Now!"

I took a deep breath and introduced Billy. "Our last speaker is Marty's brother, Billy Olsen. Billy is a Vietnam veteran, returned from Vietnam in 1967. A member of the Vietnam Veterans Against the War. Please welcome Billy Olsen."

I lowered the microphone as Julie wheeled Billy up to the stage. I gave him a hug. "Give 'em hell, Billy."

No one made a sound. Billy talked about a frontless war with a faceless enemy, about the fear, heat, jungle, chaos. Then he talked about his injury. "We walked through the jungle towards a hamlet where we were told Vietcong soldiers hid. I heard a shot and turned. My buddy behind me was down. I ran to him. He died in my arms. I was alive simply because I was five steps in front of him. At that point, I felt an incredible pain, shot in the spine by the same sniper who shot my buddy. The next thing I remember was waking up in a hospital room. It took me a long time to recover physically and even longer to recover emotionally." Everyone in the room cried. Billy continued. "Come for draft counseling tomorrow no matter what your lottery number is. If you don't have to worry about the draft, come in support. This war is wrong, and we must speak out until we get out of Vietnam." With a Semper Fi, he was done.

The intensity in the room was palpable. People lingered, surrounded Jake, surrounded Billy, wanting someone to tell them what to do.

I think every male in the freshman class came for draft counseling the next day. They got information on immigrating to Canada, on physical and mental deferments, on what might happen if they didn't show up. They learned how to file for conscientious objector status. Every female was there, supporting the males in their lives because there was nowhere else to be. All because the United States engaged in an immoral war that very few people supported anymore.

U.S. Soldier Body Count: 53,220

Chapter 43
"Unchained Melody"

The next day I visited Marty. "I broke down reading your letter. When you said that you'd see everyone in two years, I lost it." My eyes filled with tears.

"I'm okay, Becky. I am going to survive this. You can too."

"I don't want to survive anymore. I'm tired of surviving."

"What's the alternative?" he asked.

"The alternative is that we all jump at the same time, 1-2-3-bam, and the world changes. The war is over and you're with me and I can sleep again. I can breathe again. I can live again."

Marty moved his chair out from under the table in front of him and patted his legs. "Come here."

I looked over at the guard who smiled and looked the other way.

"Come here," he said again.

I got up and sat in his lap, put my head on his chest. He put his arms around me and stroked my hair. "I couldn't survive without you," he said. No other words were needed. The guard let us be for a good fifteen seconds. He came over and cleared his throat.

Marty smiled. "Alex, we could really use a room."

Alex laughed. "I can see that. Unfortunately, we have no vacancies. I need you to separate."

When I got to the prison the following week, Alex, the guard, came up to me in the waiting room. "Follow me," he said.

"Is everything alright?"

"Marty is in the infirmary. You have permission to visit him there."

"What happened to him? Is he okay?"

"I am not at liberty to say." We walked down a dirty prison hallway to a door at the end. He opened the door and winked at Marty seated in a chair. "You've got fifteen minutes max."

"Thanks, man." The door closed.

The next thing I knew, Marty had me in his arms in that dirty, filthy prison room with no windows, only two folding chairs, and a desk filled with papers. Marty kissed me and I kissed him back. He slid my shirt over my head. Soon we were there, naked, together. He pressed me against the dirty prison wall. Who knew what germs lingered there? I didn't care. He lifted me up and my legs went around his back. Then he entered me and the world righted itself.

We slid down the dirty prison wall with its green paint chipping off and landed on the dirty prison floor filled with more germs. I didn't care even more. We sat entwined and satisfied.

"How did you manage this?" I asked when I could speak again.

"I learned that if you are nice to people, they'll be nice back. After you visited last week, Alex said he'd try to work out the room situation for us. Had to be a perfect set of circumstances, the right people doing the right shifts on the right day, and here we are."

We sat silently. A rap on the door "Two minutes."

He kissed me again and we got dressed.

296

A light knock again and the door opened. I stayed and Alex took Marty into the visiting area to wait for me so we could finish our visit sedately in public.

When Alex came back, I asked, "You like chocolate chip cookies?"

"The best," he said.

"I happen to be famous for my cookies. I'll bring you some next week." I knew how long to bake cookies so they had that chewy feeling to them.

"Sounds like a bribe." He smiled at me.

"No, just payment for the best birthday present I ever received."

"Today's your birthday?" he asked.

"Close enough. Mine's the 5th. Marty's is the 8th." The cookies wouldn't be close to payment enough for what Alex did for us.

Marty's birthday came. No more back rooms. No more green paint peeled walls. Just Marty. That was enough.

U.S. Soldier Body Count: 53,561

297

Chapter 44

"Mrs. Brown, You've Got a Lovely Daughter"

Nine weeks down. Ninety-one to go.

On the dining room table I found a registered letter from Brown and Associates Law Firm in Boston. I put down my books, took off my coat, got a glass of water, sat down at the table, and opened the letter. "Our firm represents the estate of Jeffrey Ledford, deceased, August 1968. We only recently became aware of his death. You are one of the inheritors in his will. Would you please contact our office as soon as possible so we can make arrangements for you to come to Boston for the reading of the will?"

I felt the bile rise in my throat. I thought I'd gotten rid of it all in Boston. I inhaled sharply. Is this a sick joke? Jeff had been dead for more than two years. I held onto the table and shook my head to get rid of the fuzziness. I went outside and took a walk around the house. Then I jogged around the house. I went into the greenhouse, pulled a radish, wiped off the dirt, and ate it. It brought sanity. I grabbed a hoe and weeded. I paced. I panicked. I couldn't get clear. Ronda arrived as I was ready to go over the deep edge.

"Damn son-of-a-bitch," she said after she read the letter. That was exactly my sentiment. Ronda went to heat water for tea. When the going gets rough, it's always tea.

"What should I do?" I couldn't drink. Whatever went down was coming back up. Clear liquids included.

"Call Jake," she said.

Jake was the closest thing I had to a personal lawyer. I explained the situation. "I'll call as your 'legal consultant'," Jake said. It sounded impressive.

Jake called back two hours later. "All they told me was that they recently found out about Jeff's death and were making arrangements with those involved in the settlement of the will so they could close his account. Sounds like you might be inheriting something."

I didn't want to go to Boston ever again in my whole life. I didn't want to see Fenway Park. I didn't want to relive his death or anything surrounding it. I didn't want to see Linda. I didn't want to hear how he died or any of that. "I already have his jacket and *Catch-22*. I don't want to go."

"Give them a call," Jake said. That was the advice from my legal consultant so I promised I would.

"How's Ginger doing?"

"Not long now."

"You better call me the second she goes into labor."

"You can bet on it. We want you here."

When I called, someone from Brown and Associates said, "We have contacted a Mrs. McKinney and she will be coming in next weekend. Her son, Dennis McKinney, also is an inheritor in the will. He was a friend of Jeffrey Ledford."

"I know who Dennis is. And his name isn't Jeffrey. His name is Jeff," I said more aggressively than I should have. Nothing made sense.

When all was said and done, they arranged to pay for the trip, the hotel room, the food, and I would have a chance for a McKinney hug. Why not? I desperately needed a hug.

I flew to Boston on Friday arriving at Logan Airport at 6:42 p.m. A car waited to take me to the hotel. A McKinney hug and dinner later, I lay in bed wondering why in the world I took this trip. Maybe because I really hadn't finished my "Jeff life." I never said goodbye or went to a funeral or a memorial or said some prayers or sang some songs after he died. I got stoned, depressed, and crazy. Maybe, in some strange way, now I had my chance to tell him goodbye.

A car picked us up at the hotel in the morning and drove us to the law offices of Brown and Associates. I wore Hook's army jacket. He'd be there if I needed him. Someone escorted us to a room where we found a pot of coffee and a pitcher of water sitting on the table. "Help yourself," he said.

"Mama McKinney, would you like a cup of coffee?" I poured myself a cup and added too much sugar to it. I probably wouldn't drink it. "Or water?"

"Water, please. Thank you."

Ten minutes later someone came in. He didn't introduce himself.

He started. I stopped him. "Who are you?"

"I'm so sorry. I am Attorney Walter Brown. I represented the Ledford family for many years. I am so sorry for your loss."

What loss? Jeff died two years ago. What did Mr. Brown know about my loss? Why is he bringing up my loss? My loss had been lost a long time ago and I didn't need it to be found. So be quiet about my loss. I couldn't focus.

Mr. Brown looked weird. I think he was supposed to be bald, but it looked like he had a hairpiece. I wondered if he had any kids and what they looked like. Maybe Mr. and Mrs. Brown had a lovely daughter, like that Herman's Hermit song. I liked the Herman's Hermit. They were kind of cute. I bet they have cute daughters. No way that Mr. Brown could have a lovely daughter.

His brow was too furrowed. His ears were too low on his head. *Focus, Becky, Focus.*

Mr. Brown continued. "Jeffrey Ledford had no close living relatives after his parents died. A few weeks before he died, he came to our office with a will written on a scrap of paper. We typed up the formal will and contacted him to come in and sign the papers. We never heard from him again."

"Are you telling me that you didn't hear from him so you dropped it? You didn't take the time to find out where he was? You let it slide for two years? What kind of law firm are you?"

"I do apologize, Miss Jamison. We only recently became aware of his death. He dated and signed his name to the scrap of paper so, it was determined to be a legal document. We would like to share that with you today." Attorney Brown shuffled some papers in his hands.

I stood up. "Where's the bathroom please? I need a minute." I held onto the sink, the only thing holding me up. I splashed water on my face, drank some from my hand. I looked at myself in the mirror. Thank God, I looked sane. It looked like me. I could do this.

When I returned to the conference room, I apologized to Mama McKinney and sat down.

Mr. Brown began again, reading from the will. "As the sole inheritor of the estate of my parents, I would like to make known my wishes in the event of my death. This document is to be considered legal and valid." The letter impressed me. I had no idea Jeff could speak legalese. Why did he write a will? Did he have a premonition he was going to die?

Mr. Brown read the specifics of the will. "The following organizations are to be given twenty-five percent of my estate divided evenly among each of them." The lawyer read off a list of organizations. He read so quickly I couldn't quite follow. The only names I caught were Lake Forest College, Northeastern University, and the National Mobilization Committee to End the War in Vietnam. "Those organizations have been contacted concerning this inheritance."

"To my friend, Dennis McKinney. While living across the hall from you at Lake Forest you became my best friend. Thanks for being my sounding board, my support, and for keeping my secret."

Hook was loyal to a fault. If he made a promise, he kept it. I forgave Hook for keeping that secret. He forgave me for writing my pro-Vietnam essay in Senior English class. Maybe things would have been different if he told me. *Listen, Becky. Focus.*

"To Dennis, I bequeath twenty-five percent of my estate." Attorney Brown looked at Mama McKinney. "In our investigation, we discovered, of course, that Dennis McKinney is also deceased and we brought you here as next of kin." He handed Mama a certified check for $369,097.19. She looked at the check, looked at the man, looked at me, and clutched the check to her chest. Tears rolled down her cheeks. She would never have to worry or struggle again. I hugged her as she whispered to me, "I wish I had known him."

"Finally, to the light of my life, Becky Jamison. You are the best thing that ever happened to me. Please believe me when I say I loved you with my entire being. I bequeath the remaining fifty percent of my estate to you. I want you to live joyously and without regret." That was it, that was the end. The lawyer handed me a check for $738,194.38.

I sat in stunned silence: numb, angry, sad, guilty. I put the check in the inside pocket of the army jacket. I left the office in a daze; I was rich. Jeff and Hook were dead. Marty was in prison.

"I miss Hook," I said to Mama McKinney as we waited for the car to take us to the airport.

"I do too. I know he loved you, Becky. He died feeling loved." She gave me a McKinney. "You and Marty are my family, Becky. Always."

"Always," I said.

I flew back to Chicago, spent the night at the airport hotel, arrangements made by the law firm of Brown and Associates. The next day I got my car out of parking and drove to the prison to see Marty. I pulled out the check and put it on the table in front of him. "What are you going to do with that?" he asked.

"Buy your way out of prison."

"It doesn't work like that."

"It should." I folded the check neatly and put it back in my pocket. I knew I couldn't buy his way out. It would have been nice. Marty leaned across the table and kissed me. Alex smiled. The check went in the bank.

U.S. Soldier Body Count: 53,956

Chapter 45
"He Ain't Heavy, He's My Brother"

The small sign on the door to the library caught my attention. "Interested in Communal Living? Meet in Hixson Lounge, Thursday, December 10, 7:00. For more information see Rick Burton, Room 214." I ripped the sign off the door and went to room 214 to see Rick Burton.

"Thanks for telling me about this." I tossed the flyer on his desk. "We live together and you don't tell me that you're planning on moving to a commune?" I was angry and hurt. "I am trying to make it through the next twenty-five months and you do this?"

"Twenty-two," he said. "You've made it through three."

"What were you going to do? Just leave?"

"You hold your horses, Missy." Rick never called me Missy. "You graduate this May anyway and you'll move out."

"You have no idea what I am going to do in May."

"Nevertheless."

"Don't you nevertheless me, Rick. I deserved to know."

"Nevertheless," he said again. "Ronda has been researching communes for a while. When she presented the idea to me, it made perfect sense."

"So, Ronda is in on this, too? This is all Ronda's fault?"

"Don't blame Ronda, Becky. I had also been thinking about what direction I wanted my life to go."

"This isn't about whether you live on a commune somewhere. It's about the fact that neither you nor Ronda told me about it."

Rick dropped his head then looked up at me. He stood, walked around the desk, and hugged me. "I am sorry. I wasn't thinking. I got caught up in the idea of moving to a commune. There's always a place for you until Marty is released."

"How could you not tell me?"

"I know. Come to the meeting." Then he tilted my chin up and looked me in the eye. "We are not going to abandon you."

"I know."

"You'll be fine," he said. "We'll all be fine."

* * *

The next night I got the call that Ginger was in labor. It was the 24th of November, one day before the second anniversary of Hook's death, two days before Thanksgiving. I drove into Chicago.

"How's she doing," I asked Jake.

"So far so good, but it's still early. She wanted me to send you back when you arrived. I'm going to eat something while I can."

Ginger was still early in her labor but when a contraction came, she stopped, looked me in the eye, and breathed, never losing eye contact. She was determined to have the baby naturally.

When Jake came back, I left and fell asleep in a chair in the waiting room. At 7:30 a.m. Ginger had been in labor for more than twelve hours. I got a cup of coffee from the pot in the corner of the waiting room. When I turned around there was Jake, a huge grin on his face. "Come meet our child," he said. Ginger and Jake's baby was born on the second anniversary of Hook's death.

I hugged him. "Congratulations, Dad. Boy or girl?"

"Ginger wants to tell you."

I walked into the room. Ginger held out her baby to me. "Meet Dennis McKinney Stedman."

I took Dennis in my arms, looked up at Jake and Ginger looking at me. The tears came. "Hello, Dennis," I said to the baby asleep in my arms. "Welcome to this world. You are a very lucky little boy." I touched his face, kissed his head. "Thank you," I said. I'm not sure if I said it to baby Dennis or to Ginger and Jake. It didn't matter.

"Are you going to nickname him Hook?"

"Not on your life. We will tell Dennis all about his namesake."

On Sunday I drove to the prison to see Marty. Time would pass and I would watch Dennis grow, but for the next twenty-two months, Marty wouldn't. I could show him pictures, but he wouldn't hold Dennis or sing to him. He wouldn't laugh at the funny faces Dennis made or get excited when he took his first step. The baby would be walking before Marty got out. He would be talking, saying mama and dada.

Marty wouldn't do or see any of that. He was in prison. Behind bars. Because of a damn war. Life goes on. Death goes on. He goes on. I go on.

* * *

Two weeks later I walked into the commune meeting in Hixson Lounge. Ronda reported on some of the research she did about functioning communes. She found a small farm about thirty miles north of Lake Forest. Twenty-five acres of tillable land. Ten acres of hills and woods. A large farmhouse with five bedrooms. A barn in disrepair.

The conversation went on for two hours. What will the structure of the commune be? How will we share the workload

306

and finances? What can we do to make money? How do we get more bedroom space? Should we have a communal eating space?

"We can work in surrounding towns to make enough money for the year, pool our resources, and when we have enough, like man, we quit and enjoy the land and plant crops, and wow, dig it man, groove on the sunrise, you know." I wasn't sure I wanted to live with the guy who said that. I had nothing against 'wow, dig it man, groove on the sunrise.' I loved the sunrise. I loved grooving. I wanted normal.

The amount of work needed to develop a commune far exceeded anyone's expectations. Most people thought all you had to do was buy a plot of land, move onto it, and groove on the sunrise. It's a hell of a lot of work. I'm not sure I was up to it. Maybe they'd let me live with them until Marty got out and I wouldn't have to milk goats and weed gardens.

"I'm still mad at both of you," I said to Ronda and Rick after the meeting. "We already have a commune. Why do we have to move?" I thought about Peter in Winnipeg. Each letter he sounded happier. "Let's go visit Peter before school starts in January," I said.

"It's damn cold in Winnipeg this time of the year," Ronda said.

"I know. But we get to see Peter, you can find out how their commune works, and I bet we can see the Northern Lights."

"What will we do with Racer while we're gone?" Rick asked.

"Let's take him with us. Peter and Suki would love to see him."

U.S. Soldier Body Count: 54,909

307

Chapter 46
"Light My Fire"

Soon it would be 1971. The year I would graduate. The year I would wait for Marty to get out of prison. The year I would figure out how to spend my time, start my career, hang tight. Four and a half months done. Eighteen percent. Eighty-two percent to go.

I visited home for five days over Christmas. It was great to be there, to eat Mom's tuna noodle casserole, to make cookies with my brothers, to sing carols around the piano, to play games around the dining room table. I couldn't stay long. I had to return north to visit Marty.

I drove to Springfield to spend New Year's Eve with Mom Olsen, Billy, and Julie. I sat at the kitchen table drinking a cup of hot chocolate and eating Mom Olsen's famous brownies. She sprinkled half of the brownies with crushed walnuts, the other half with powdered sugar. Billy sat at the end of the table and Julie stood behind him with her arms draped over his shoulders. It took four minutes before I noticed the diamond on Julie's finger. I almost choked on a bite of brownie as I jumped up and grabbed her hand. "Why didn't you tell me the second it happened? Does Marty know? Why didn't he tell me?"

"We wanted to tell you in person. We're going with you Sunday to tell Marty."

I gave Billy a kiss on the cheek and looked at Julie. "Are you sure about this guy?"

Julie leaned down and kissed Billy on the other check. "I'm counting on having you as a sister-in-law. That's why I said yes." Billy turned around and pulled her down for a kiss.

"A year ago Billy said, 'We still have a few things to figure out.' Guess you figured them out."

Julie leaned down and put her chin on Billy's head, her arms again wrapped around his neck. Billy took her hands. "I guess you could say that." Julie blushed.

Five games of Hearts later, the ball dropped in Times Square and Mom Olsen called it a night, kissing us all and telling us not to stay up too late. We were determined to stay up until midnight Central Time. Three handed Hearts was more brutal. I got stuck with twenty-four points once, shot the moon once, and most of the time ended up in the middle.

Right before midnight Billy asked if I wanted to go to Detroit with him the end of January to attend the Winter Soldier Investigation sponsored by the Vietnam Veterans Against the War. Fueled by Lt. William Calley's court-martial and trial for the brutality of the massacres at My Lai, the Vets were gathering to tell their stories.

"There are so many stories to tell. So many atrocities," he said

"Sounds like you've thought about this a lot," I said.

"I have to get rid of this shit I carry with me every day. I'm thinking if I publicly say it, I can put it to sleep."

"You only obeyed orders," I said to Billy.

"That's the problem. The orders were criminal."

"Are you sure you want to do this?" Mostly I asked myself if I could hear it. What could be worse than having a buddy die in your arms? I thought of Hook and his stories. I missed him still, always. He'd go. I could too.

"Absolutely."

"Then I'm in."

Midnight came. I thought of Marty. I knew, if he were awake, he thought of me.

* * *

After a trip to wish Marty a Happy New Year, Rick, Ronda, Racer, and I set off for Winnipeg. We drove halfway, slept in a cheap motel outside of St. Paul, Minnesota, and arrived at the commune about 6:00 p.m. the following day. It was damn cold there.

Suddenly, there he was. How I had missed Peter. We hugged. "Got any radishes?" I asked him. He laughed and held me tighter. Racer ran to Peter, licked his hand, stayed for a few scratches behind the ears. Suki nudged Peter away and licked Racer's face. They tumbled together and ran circles around the room.

Peter seemed at home. A beautiful woman walked into the house. Peter introduced Susie and tenderly put his hand on her belly. "And baby makes three." I looked around the house that Peter built on communal land. A handmade crib stood in the corner. A rocking horse lacked only the varnish. Fresh bread cooled on the counter. Susie and Peter looked at each other.

"I'm jealous," I said. "You're never coming home."

Peter kissed me on the forehead. "I am home, Becky. I'm right where I belong."

We shared a dinner of bread, soup, and fresh radishes. We told Peter about Marty and the trial, a trial of tears. I showed him pictures of baby Dennis.

"Those two years with you were some of the best of my life," Peter said. "I will always cherish them."

I cherished it too, the people I lived with and the things we went through. I could not have made it without them.

Generations went through war and depression before, dust storms and dance crazes. But Vietnam? Kennedy? King? Kennedy? Kent State? Revolution on college campuses? Riots? Police brutality? Segregation? Boycotts? Strikes? Death? I wondered if future generations will ever understand or care. When they look back, what will they say? You tried, but you didn't finish the job?

Ronda, Rick, Racer, and I spent three days exploring the commune, touring the green house, and learning about the communal farming that produced enough food for the season. Everyone had a place to go while I was suspended in space waiting for Marty, waiting for my life.

* * *

Marty made the best of his situation in prison. Although I took cookies every couple of weeks, we never got back to that gritty room with the green chipped painted walls.

I told Marty about commune plans and our visit to Peter's. "What do you think? I could build us a house with the money I have. When you get out, we could move into our little house and never leave."

"That sounds like an idea," he said as my feet went up his pants leg and his hand grabbed mine. "God, I miss seeing you every day. When this is over, I am never leaving your side."

"I'm right there with you." The hour ended.

When I got out to my car I dropped my head on the steering wheel and cried. Why is time going so damn slow? It's *Catch-22* boring right now.

By the time I got back to the house a blizzard raged outside. I hoped someone had built a fire and put a pot of tea to warm on the stove. That's what I wanted to see. That's what I expected to see. Instead, I saw Ronda and Rick cuddling on the couch. When I walked in, Ronda jumped up. Not soon enough.

"You have got to be kidding me." I looked back and forth at the two of them. "How long has this been going on?"

Ronda said, "Oh, about three hours."

Rick grinned from the couch. "It's been going on a bit longer for me."

"Me too, actually," Ronda said.

"You didn't want her to move in," I said to Rick.

"That was before I met her. I fell in love with her the first time I saw her."

"That is not true," I said. "You two bicker night after night." I turned to Ronda. "I am not giving up late-night music jams for anything, bedroom or not. Furthermore, how come I didn't know you were even slightly interested in Rick? You always told me he irritated you."

Rick said, "You talked about me? How sweet."

"It wasn't sweet at all, Rick. She detested you. This relationship is doomed from the start." I turned to Ronda again, "How could you keep this from me?"

She grinned. "I wasn't keeping anything from you."

Rick interrupted, "I was."

"Quiet, Rick. This isn't about you."

"This morning we drove out to the piece of land. We came back, ate lunch, and played some music. He suggested coffee. I got up, he got up, and then, I'm not exactly sure what happened, we accidently bumped into each other."

"On purpose," Rick said.

"I said quiet, Rick. Ronda is telling the story."

"He rubbed against my arm. It all became crystal clear in that one moment. The rest is history."

"Rick, It's your turn. What's your side of the story?"

"It's pretty much as she told it except she left out the part where I've been trying to bump into her for a while now.'

"You two are the most unlikely couple I know. Ronda and Rick don't even sound good together. Two names that begin with the same letter. That's not allowed." I looked back and forth at the two of them. They looked so happy. "Are you moving up or is he moving down?"

Simultaneously Rick said 'up' and Ronda said 'down.' "Guess we should talk about it, huh?" Ronda said. I loved new love. I was jealous.

Eventually, Ronda moved down to Rick's room and the second-floor bedroom stayed empty. When I felt lonely on the second floor, I went up into my old attic room, lay on the bed, and looked around. The nails to hold my clothes were still in the wall. I could see the tack holes by the light switch where I hung the pictures I took from Jeff's room. One McCarthy poster still hung on the wall. Paint had peeled off where I hung the other posters. That was a long time ago. It didn't make me sad anymore, but when I felt sad missing Marty, for some reason that place surrounded me.

U.S. Soldier Body Count: 55,149

Chapter 47
"We Gotta Get Out of This Place"

My last semester began the third week in January. I dropped my job at the library. I had too many other things on my plate. I signed up for Rick's Advanced Social Structures class, a history class about totalitarian governments around the world, one journalism class, and a paid internship to complete my major. I was editor of the student newspaper and chief organizer of the Lake Forest College Students Against the War. I was also the girlfriend of a guy in prison, sleeping alone every night. I was eager for this beginning to be over with, to get on with it, to have time pass.

The next weekend Julie, Billy, and I headed to Detroit for the Winter Soldier Investigation. It was the only time I broke my promise to Marty, the only time I couldn't visit him on a Sunday. Mom Olsen went in my place.

We checked into the Howard Johnson Hotel, and I called Marty. We talked for a half hour, and I gave the phone to Billy. I'm not sure what they talked about but by the time they were done, Billy was laughing so hard he could hardly talk.

At the registration table, Billy waited for his nametag. "God damn. If it isn't Billy Olsen. I thought you died." We looked up. On the other side of the registration table was a big guy with dark hair down to his shoulders and a headband around his hair. He practically jumped over the table to get to Billy.

"If it isn't Karge Christiansen. Semper Fi, man." They locked hands, hugged, looked at each other. I could see the tears in both of their eyes.

"Really man. Once we put you on that helicopter, we didn't hear about you again. I had no idea whether you were dead or alive. I can't believe it. What's the story?"

"The bullet destroyed my spine. I stayed in the hospital for a while. Then they shipped me home. I've been on a long journey back." Billy looked over at Julie and took her hand. "Forgive my manners. This is Julie, my fiancée."

"Shit, Billy Olsen's getting married. I would never have expected it." Karge held out his hand to Julie. "Karge Christiansen. Billy and I were in Nam together. Are you sure about this guy?" Karge patted Billy on the shoulder.

"Pleasure to meet you. I am absolutely sure."

Karge held out his hand to me. "Karge Christiansen."

"Becky Jamison."

"Becky is hopefully my future sister-in-law," Billy said. "My brother is serving twenty-five months for refusing to be inducted."

"Far out. I wish more guys did that." He looked at me. "He'll be out before you know it. And he'll be alive." Karge gave me a hug. "Hey man, a few of us from the unit are getting together for a drink and to take a pleasant stroll down memory lane. If you got the time we can head over there now."

Julie kissed Billy on the cheek. "See you later. Becky and I are heading over to the bar to pick up some cute guys."

The event started the next day in a packed basement room with concrete posts and no windows, the local press lights shining on the participants. One hundred and nine veterans and sixteen civilians went to tell their stories. For three long, emotional, excruciating days.

One story after another, one hundred and twenty-five times. Was anybody listening? How many times does the government turn its head pretending it doesn't see? How many stories does it take until they listen?

"My testimony covers the maltreatment of prisoners and a convoy running down an old woman, with no reason at all."

"My testimony concerns the leveling of villages for no valid reasons, throwing Viet Cong suspects from the aircraft after binding them and gagging them with copper wire."

No reasons. No reasons at all.

"My testimony involves the burning of villages of civilians, the cutting off of ears, cutting off of heads, torturing of prisoners, calling in of artillery on villages for game, corpsmen killing wounded prisoners."

Billy, Julie, and I listened to the testimonies until I was numb with disbelief, grief, sadness. I looked over at Billy who was seemingly unaware of the constant stream of tears running down his cheeks.

"My testimony will consist of eye witnessing and participating in the calling in of artillery on undefended villages, mutilation of bodies, killing of civilians, mistreatment of civilians."

Courage to speak. No reasons at all. No reasons.

"My testimony includes killing of non-combatants, destruction of Vietnamese property and livestock, use of chemical agents and the use of torture in interrogating prisoners."

They call your number. You do what you're told. Killing, mutilating, raping, pillaging. Is this what they call civilization? We did it because all around us were the faces and sounds and the jungle and the heat and the noise and the 55-gallon drums of fuel and dead bodies in black body bags. We did it because we were ordered to do it. We did it because we had no orders. We did it to survive.

No reasonable reasons. No reasons at all.

The national media largely ignored the event. How many voices does it take? Obviously more than one hundred and twenty-five.

It was finally time for the Third Marine Division to give their testimony. Karge rolled Billy up to the head table and sat next to him. Billy worried all morning about what to wear and settled on a blue, pin-striped button up shirt, a Vietnam Veterans Against the War button, the red bandana tied around his head. The emcee announced his name, "William Olsen. Your testimony concerns the murder of innocent civilians."

Billy cleared his throat and spoke into the microphone. "William Olsen, Third Marine Division. My testimony concerns the murder of innocent civilians for no reason at all." He stopped and looked around the room. He focused on Julie and then turned to Karge. "I don't think I can do this." Karge patted him on the back and whispered something in his ear.

Billy continued with a catch in his throat. "I am petrified to tell this story." He looked out at the crowd.

Billy took a drink of water. "We were in a village, burning houses, laughing as the people tried to get away. A little boy, maybe eight years old, ran with his sister away from the village towards a grove of trees on the other side of the field. His sister reached the trees just as the boy fell, shot in the back."

Billy Olsen, Third Marine Division, stopped, looked over at Karge who said something to him again. Billy turned back to the crowd, took another drink of water, looked at Julie, and continued.

"I grabbed their mother as she ran towards her daughter and her dead son. I threw her to the ground. I held a gun to her head and then, at the last minute, turned my rifle up and shot it in the air, leaving her there. I hadn't gone five steps when I heard a shot

317

and turned. The soldier behind me got her. Her daughter made it to the woods alone. The mother and boy got put on the Body Count board. I don't know what happened to the girl. I don't want to know."

Tears ran down my face. Tears ran down Julie's face. Billy wiped at his eyes, daring the tears to come. He looked at Julie and mouthed the words, "I'm sorry." I grabbed Julie's hand and she squeezed as though her life depended on it. "These weren't people we killed. They were targets, Viet Cong. All of them. We played a game of who could kill the most. I became an animal. We all became animals. An entire generation of animals. Why didn't I stop it? What were we doing over there in the first place? Why are we still there?" Courage to speak.

When the Third Marine Division finished their testimony, Billy wheeled himself back to Julie. She sat in his lap and they cried. Marty would have been proud. Fuck pride.

* * *

The Forester
Editor's Corner
By Becky Jamison

This past week the Vietnam Veterans Against the War sponsored the "Winter Soldier Investigation" in Detroit to expose the atrocities occurring every day in Vietnam. Following the event, Senator Mark Hatfield from Oregon, Senator George McGovern from South Dakota, and Representative John Conyers from Michigan called for an investigation, asking that the entire testimony be part of the Congressional record. Hatfield stated that if the testimonies were true, the United States would be in violation of the international laws of war and would suffer the moral consequences of their actions.

The war continues. Get involved. Join the Lake Forest College Students Against the War. Meetings every Wednesday at 7:00 in Hixson Lounge.

Maybe the testimonies helped. Lt. William Calley was convicted on March 29 for his role in the murder of innocent civilians at My Lai and sentenced to life in prison. Maybe they didn't help. Three days later Calley was released to house arrest by orders of President Nixon.

U.S. Soldier Body Count: 55,860

Chapter 48
"Give Peace A Chance"

Ronda bought the land for a commune. She and Rick planned to move there during the summer. I continued visiting Marty every Sunday, sleeping alone in our room every night. I didn't know what I would do come graduation.

As winter turned to spring, opposition to the war became widespread.

January 1969. Operation Dewey Canyon I, a five-day Marine incursion into Laos.

February 1971. Operation Dewey Canyon II, a seven-day South Vietnamese invasion into Laos.

April 1971. Operation Dewey Canyon III, a "limited incursion into the country of Congress" by thousands of veterans from the Vietnam Veterans Against the War. For a week, they gathered in Washington along with the Gold Star mothers, wives, vets from other wars, and friends. I took a week off of classes to attend.

Sunday, Billy, Julie, Mom Olsen, and I visited Marty and then flew to Washington, D.C., where we met Mama McKinney. She embraced Billy and touched the red bandana he always wore.

"It was your son's," I heard Billy say to her.

"I know. It fits you perfectly."

We went to the Mall to set up Julie and Billy's tent. I would stay with the two moms in a hotel near the Mall.

We found the Winter Soldiers sign and watched as Billy reconnected. I looked around at the vets, a raunchy looking group of men dressed in blue jeans and combat jackets with long hair, bandanas, beards, and the sweet smell of weed floating through the air. If the U.S. government wouldn't listen to the millions of Americans against this war, surely they would listen to those who fought in the war.

All week, the veterans lobbied, marched, and protested. The Supreme Court said the vets couldn't sleep on the Mall near the Capitol building. They did anyway. They pitched tents and cooked Campbell's Soup over camp stoves. One group headed to the Supreme Court and asked that the court rule on the constitutionality of the war since it had never been declared by Congress.

Gold Star Mothers, friends, families, and a thousand vets in fatigues marched across the Lincoln Memorial Bridge to Arlington Cemetery to visit graves. The gates were locked. As they stood there, Mama McKinney walked up to every Gold Star mother, spoke softly, and gave each a full-body McKinney hug.

Friday, April 23rd, we headed to the Capitol. In a show of defiance, vets returned their medals to the United States government. That's why I went to Washington, took a week off classes, handed the weekly newspaper duties over to the assistant editor. Julie walked next to Billy as he rolled his wheelchair up to the steps of the Capitol Building. I walked hand in hand with Mama McKinney and Mom Olsen. In the "final act of contempt for the way the executive branch is forcing us to wage war," one by one the vets hurled their medals over a barricade that had been erected in front of the capitol: their purple hearts, bronze stars, silver stars, citations for bravery.

Mama McKinney opened her leather purse and pulled out the boxes that held Hook's bronze star and purple heart. Tears rolled down her face. "He hated these things. They reminded him of everything that was wrong in Vietnam."

Billy rolled over to Mama McKinney. "You don't have to do this," he said. "Dennis earned those medals."

Mama McKinney leaned down, put her arms around Billy, touched the red bandana, and pulled him close. They were silent. "He tried to get rid of these. Called me the day he sent them back to the government. Called me the day they returned the medals to him, two days before he died. That was the last time I ever spoke to him. He didn't want them."

We walked up the steps with two vets. Mama McKinney turned towards me, turned back, and quietly said, "This is for you, Dennis." Almost reverently, she took the two medals and threw them, one at a time, hearing them clink against the cold stone of the Capitol sidewalk. She put the empty boxes back in her purse and hugged the two veterans next to her.

I stood for a minute looking at his medals lying against the stone-cold marble. "We finally got rid of your medals, Hook," I whispered. I smiled at the thought of him.

Julie handed Billy his medals and two vets carried him up the stairs. He paused, gave the finger, and yelled, "Fuck you and your war." He threw the medals. The vets carried him back down and put him in his chair. Veterans threw more than seven hundred medals over the barricade that day.

When the vets took down their encampment, they left the Mall clean. The occupation had been peaceful.

Saturday thousands joined the veterans in Washington: students, teamsters, meat cutters, hospital workers, electricians, nurses, teachers, union leaders, union members, mothers, fathers, children, friends. Three hundred, four hundred, five hundred thousand, the official count didn't matter, reminding the President that we were the majority, and we were not silent. The government was merely deaf. The line of protesters stretched from the White House to the Capitol Building for most of the day.

After the Winter Soldiers' Investigation Karge called me and asked if I would introduce Billy at the rally. The idea petrified me as I knew that thousands of people might be there. Three and a half years earlier, I leafletted commuters with no idea what to say. Now look at me. Could I do it? I knew, with Marty around me, with Hook looking over me, the answer was yes.

I sat on the stage looking out at the banners. 'Remember Kent State—Remember Jackson State.' 'Stop the War.' 'Engineers for Peace.' 'Third Unitarian Church for Peace.' 'Bring Them Home Now.' 'Radical Women for Peace.'

Up in trees. Down Pennsylvania Avenue. Past the White House. Babies on the backs of their dads. Older folks with canes. Thousands upon thousands of people. *"Give Peace a Chance"* we sang. Why was that so hard?

Suddenly I was standing in front of the microphone, the press recording every word. "I'm here to introduce a very special member of the Vietnam Veterans Against the War." I talked about my friendship with Hook, told his story about the worse thing he did in Vietnam, about his mother finally being able to return his medals to the government. I told them that my friend Jake Stedman served twenty-five months as a conscientious objector working in Chicago. I told them that my boyfriend, Marty Olson, was currently in prison for refusing to show up for his physical. "Young men in this country should not be forced to lose life, limb, mobility, or sanity to fight a war that makes no sense. They should not be put in a position to have to make a choice. Let's end this war! Now I'd like to introduce my boyfriend's brother, a proud Vietnam Veteran, a proud veteran against the war, Billy Olson."

He told his story, the one he told in Detroit.
The war raged on.

U.S. Soldier Body Count: 56,168

Chapter 49
"Wonderful World"

Vietnam. It was as much a part of my growing up as Wonder Bread, lilac bushes, Kool-Aid popsicles in the freezer, hide-and-seek games with the entire neighborhood, Oreos, and chasing fireflies. I was only five years old when the United States became involved in Vietnam, starting slowly by providing training and equipment for South Vietnam. By the time I was a senior in college, more than 55,000 U.S. soldiers had been killed in fighting there.

I'd been to the last anti-war event of my college career. My activism started four years earlier helping a guy with hair in his eyes hang a banner at a table during the extra-curricular fair. Four years later, he was in prison. In those four years I picketed, canvassed, marched, yelled, taught, spoke, demanded. I saw raw violence in the streets of Chicago and marched peacefully on those same streets. I spoke before hundreds of thousands of people in Washington D.C. With the help of two vets, I learned that 'it don't mean nothin' meant everything.

I pretty much figured out my life after graduation. I was going to buy the white house in the country with some of the settlement money I got from Jeff. The rest of the money would stay in the bank until Marty got out. I planned on working at the local newspaper for a while. In the fall, I'd look for more roommates. My other friends would scatter, but never be gone.

Rick and Ronda were moving onto the property they bought. Ronda was pregnant and they planned on marrying sometime during the summer. I would build a small cabin there, a place to go to when I was lonely and sad. Jake, Ginger, and their baby boy, Dennis, would stay in the Chicago area. Billy and Julie put their wedding on hold until Marty got released. Every week, month in and month out, I would visit Marty.

That's how it went. That's how it was going to go. I'd keep going to events at Lake Forest College, march in their marches, protest at their protests, attend their lectures and symposiums. I'd go home to Kentucky a few times. I'd head down to Springfield to visit Mom Olsen, sit and talk about Marty, miss him together. I'd take a trip or two to Cleveland to sit under the trees and talk to Hook and get a hug from his mom.

Things never go as planned of course. So, of course, my story didn't go as planned. Thank God. Somebody wrote a better script. A script of perfect endings.

I heard the whole story later.

The prison released Marty after seven and a half months. Universal opposition to the war, overcrowded prisons, and a sympathetic parole board were his ticket out. It cost the government too much to keep him in.

Instead of a one-way ticket to Vietnam, they gave him a one-way ticket to Lake Forest. He got off the train, found a pay phone, and called the house. No one answered. He walked the half-mile to campus to find me or someone to drive him home to me.

He first checked the newspaper office. It was locked. He stopped at the softball game on the green. I wasn't there. He checked Hixson Lounge. I wasn't there. What he didn't see was the dog-eared copy of *Catch-22* next to a glass of Coke on a table in front the couch. I was in the bathroom. In that minute, he came and went.

Marty checked Rick's office. He wasn't there. Then he saw Rick teaching class in one of the rooms down the hall from his office. Marty felt a sense of ease, a sense of coming home, a sense that everything was okay. He said, from the back of the classroom, "Sorry for interrupting class, but I'm looking for a ride home."

Rick looked up and saw Marty standing in the back of the room, a bag casually tossed over his shoulder. Rick paused, adjusted his glasses to make sure he saw what he thought he saw, and said two things. "Far out" and "Class dismissed."

He pushed his way through the students and the desks to the back of the room and embraced Marty in a bear hug. Then he lifted him off the ground and hugged him some more. "Why didn't you tell us you were getting out?" He put Marty down to take a good look at him.

"I didn't want to get anyone's hopes up. Too many guys have been denied parole. I lucked out."

Rick looked at him again. "You look great. Dropped a few pounds."

"All I did was work or exercise. No junk food except the care packages you all sent. Do you know where Becky is?"

"Should be waiting for me in Hixson. We're having lunch together."

"I was just over there. Didn't see her."

"She can't be far." Rick put his arm around Marty and they walked out of the classroom, out of the building, over to Hixson.

They saw me through the French doors, sitting on the couch with my feet up on the coffee table in front of me reading *Catch-22* for the fourth time.

That's what they told me.

Rick said, "Ready for lunch?"

Without looking up I held my hand up to him. "Just a second. I'm almost done with this chapter."

"I don't have a lot of time. Let's go."

That didn't sound like Rick. He always had time. Even when Rick needed to be someplace right away, he always had time. I loved that about him. He set himself down, stopped everything, and was there for as long as he needed. *What's got him in such a hurry?* I thought. *I only need fifteen seconds to finish the last two sentences of the chapter.*

I looked up and started to say, "Give me fifteen seconds," but before I got it out, I saw Marty. It didn't register. It looked like him. It looked like the person who had first been my mentor and my idol. Who became my housemate and best friend. Who became my lover and my future. But what my brain told me about where Marty was supposed to be and what my eyes told me didn't match.

He smiled and pushed back his hair. My brain and eyes connected. I threw the book, bounded over the top of the table, leaped into his arms, both legs wrapped around his waist. He held me tight and twirled me around. Marty was home.

U.S. Soldier Body Count: 56,369

AFTERWARDS
FORTY YEARS LATER
"With A Little Help From My Friends"

Four years. One thousand four hundred and sixty-one days. From the moment he jumped out of that tree and changed the focus of my life to that moment when I realized I was able to live again. From macaroni and cheese dates, tears, and leavings as fast as beginnings. To death and life and suddenly realizing that the person in front of you has been there all along.

It wasn't about the protests and the marches, the chants and songs. Sure, we did all that. We occupied buildings and boycotted classes. But it wasn't about that.

It was about finding love when I thought I was unlovable, when I thought that love was never going to find me again. It was about people holding me up when I was ready to fall and about learning how to not be afraid to fall. It was about silence and puppies, flowers and red bandanas. It was about grains in quart mason jars and radishes when I needed them the most. It was about believing in something so deeply that I finally learned how to speak out even when speaking out was the hardest. It was about finding peace. It was about ordinary moments that became extraordinary, about those unexpected perfect moments.

Oozy éclairs.
Music late into the night.
A dance in the library and five-flavored lifesavers.
Orange sticky fingers by the lake.
Baloney and macaroni and cheese for breakfast.
A week of skipping stones, baby chicks, and magic.
Coffee and doughnuts.
Whole body hugs.
A kiss in the light of the Milky Way.
Oreos and tea.
A moment of laughter when laughter was gone.
The sun shining over the rooftops.
Tomatoes, cheese, and a glass of wine.
Sliding down the green wall of a dirty prison backroom.
Seeing him standing right in front of me.

These are the perfect moments that make up four years. Days well lived. One thousand four hundred and sixty-one of them.

* * *

The four years rolled by.

In 1975, four years after I graduated, I watched the spectacle of the fall of Saigon on TV and tried to put Vietnam out of my life. The Paris Peace Accord had been signed two years before. The draft ended. Lt. William Calley was free, released after serving only three years of house arrest following his conviction related to the massacre at My Lai. I was a journalist. I had the Bicentennial preparations to cover, political campaigns to follow, nuclear power protests to write about.

In 1979, four years after the fall of Saigon, Vietnam came back into my life when I wrote an article about a wheelchair rolling down the middle of a busy Chicago street. The person in the wheelchair was a skinny, tired Vietnam veteran with callouses on his hands, twitches in his muscles, and sweat pouring off his nose. A sweat-stained baseball hat bore the words 'Vietnam Veteran and Proud of It,' his purple heart pinned to the pocket of his army jacket. His pants didn't cover any legs. He was a haunted-eyed veteran who wanted a small business loan so he could keep on living. The article helped. He got his loan. I hoped he would find happiness.

I thought of Billy and Julie, happily married, the parents of two daughters who adored my newborn son. I thought of Peter and Susie who stayed at that commune north of Winnipeg with their baby girl Joy, even though President Carter, on his first day of office, declared amnesty for the more than 100,000 who left the country during the Vietnam War years.

In the fall of 1982, almost four years later, I went to Washington D.C. to cover the dedication of the Vietnam Veterans Memorial, The Wall with 58,193 names.

"You want to walk The Wall with a vet?" I turned and looked at a veteran standing there. "I'm Mickey Coleman," he said.

Mickey and I walked the wall looking for his buddies. As a medic in Vietnam, he put a lot of these soldiers in black body bags with white tags. He never zipped up a bag until he wrote a name in his book. He showed me his little book, pages and pages, now simply names etched on a wall.

"This guy was a scout master before he went to Nam. He had the god-awfullest teeth I ever saw."

"This one got married the day before he shipped out. He never stopped talking about his wife."

"This one left a pregnant wife and never got to see his newborn child."

"This one was a track star in college. He was bound for the Olympics."

Everybody should walk The Wall with a vet.

Four years rolled by ten times. It was 2011, forty years after I graduated from Lake Forest College. I sat with my son in a courtroom in New York City where he faced charges related to his second arrest during the Occupation of Wall Street. The charges for his first arrest had been dropped. These charges were more serious.

I took my husband's hand and held on for dear life thinking of another courtroom, another hand. Matt smiled at us.

"Is the prosecution ready?" the judge asked.

"Yes, Your Honor."

"What are the charges?"

"This young man was arrested when he refused to leave the sidewalk after orders were given. He is charged with resisting arrest, refusing to disperse, trespassing, blocking traffic, and intent to harm an officer."

He handed the judge the papers. "Here is the arrest warrant and the testimony from the arresting officer."

The judge waved the papers away. "I have that here," she said glancing at the papers in front of her. Then she turned to Matt. "These are serious charges. How do you plead?"

"Not guilty, Your Honor."

"Before I rule, do you have anything to say?"

"Yes, Your Honor. I legally walked down the sidewalk during a constitutionally protected protest when a man in a dark shirt attacked me and knocked me down. He never identified himself as a police officer or said I was under arrest. Four other cops held me down. The guy with the dark shirt smashed my face into the ground, a cop pounded his knee into my back. It's hard to disperse when your face is in the ground and a cop is kneeling on top of you." Matt took a deep breath and looked back at us. I nodded.

"Two cops grabbed my arms and pulled them behind my back while another put handcuffs on so tight my hands stayed numb for weeks. It's hard to resist arrest when the cops are holding you down. I'm unsure how I could harm an officer with my hands cuffed behind my back. They put me in jail for thirty-six hours. When they handed me my possessions on my release, my car keys were missing from the key ring and my cell phone was smashed. I am not guilty, Your Honor."

The judge looked at Matt. She asked the prosecutor. "Is the arresting officer here?"

"Yes, Your Honor." He pointed to a police officer.

"Is the arrest warrant accurate?" the judge asked the officer.

"Yes, Your Honor," the officer said without looking at a copy of the warrant.

The judge looked down at the papers in front of her. "Looks clear cut. Do you have a recommendation?"

"Yes, Your Honor. Ninety days in jail."

The judge looked at my son and quietly said, "I find you guilty, young man. While you may believe in your cause, you broke the law."

"Walking down the sidewalk is now against the law?" Matt asked. He knew he wouldn't get an answer.

The judge paused for a second. "The charge of intent to harm an officer is a serious charge. I sentence you to ninety days in jail. Bailiff, take the prisoner." The gavel fell.

Matt's head dropped for a moment. He shook hands with his attorney and came over to hug us.

As he walked away in handcuffs, Matt leaned over to the bailiff escorting him and said something. They both laughed. He looked so much like his dad at that moment.

"Becky, we raised a good son. You should be proud of him."

I watched Matt walk away and smiled. "He takes after his dad." *Fuck pride.*

* * *

The register at the small New York market rang up $19.68. I stopped to buy Matt a book, some Skittles, and a bag of Dove dark chocolate squares, the ones with a message in every wrapper. "Nineteen Sixty-Eight," the cashier said to me.

I handed him a twenty-dollar bill and said, "1968 was an astounding year."

"Sure was. That was the year I was born," he replied. He counted out thirty-two cents and handed me the receipt and change.

I thought for a moment. 1968. One thing after another. The escalation of the Vietnam War. The Tet Offensive. More soldiers killed in Vietnam than any other year. Martin Luther King assassinated. Bobby Kennedy assassinated. Riots erupting in most major cities. Raw violence in the streets of Chicago during the Democratic National Convention. Riots on college campuses. Boycotts. Occupations.

1968? It was about death. The whole ugly dirty war when I was 18 was about death.

More than 58,000 American soldiers lost their lives in Vietnam. How many Vietnamese soldiers? How many civilians? How many children? Half a million? One, two, three million? The living still breathe in the more than eighteen million gallons of Agent Orange sprayed on their land. Generations destroyed.

The veterans continue to feel the effects of Agent Orange. They still die from wounds or illnesses related to combat in Vietnam. When they die, a name is added to The Wall.

Did it matter what we did? The protests, marches, chants, songs, occupations, and boycotts. Did it matter at all?

We still have war, greed, poverty, hunger, racism, discrimination, religious bigotry, homophobia, police brutality, and a dying planet. The job's not done. That's why our son occupied the streets of New York City in 2011.

That's how I came to be lying next to this man in a hotel room in New York City. He said hello. I said hello. He said, "My name is Marty." I said, "My name is Becky." He said yes. I said yes. So it was. So it is.

Marty took me in his arms. I curled up beside him. "He'll be okay," Marty said. "I promise you; he'll be okay." Marty should know.

* * *

So, the story ends. I like endings. I don't like beginnings. For me, beginnings are hard. They are filled with sad leavings, death, and assassinations. But endings? They always signify that something new is coming. That I can handle.

U.S. Soldier Body Count: 58,282

Arrests: Almost 8,000 occupiers were arrested in the U.S. during the Occupy Movement.

AUTHOR'S NOTES

President Kennedy was assassinated during my freshman year of high school. Martin Luther King and Bobby Kennedy were assassinated during my freshman year of college. Those assassinations marred my beginnings and, with the Vietnam War and the civil rights movement, defined my generation. Along with my parents, who were fierce defenders of social justice and peace, those events shaped who I am today. As a result, I was led to march, demonstrate, protest, write letters, get arrested, be jailed, and write this book about speaking out even when it's hard.

Lake Forest College is a small liberal arts college about thirty miles north of Chicago. I chose Lake Forest for the setting of this book because of its nearness to Chicago as well as the amount of activism on that campus during the late 1960s. In the book, I describe the campus as I remember it. There have been changes throughout the years, including the remodeling of Commons that eliminated Hixson Lounge. The green where we played softball, however, is still there.

This book is inspired by true events that took place at Lake Forest, in Chicago, and around the country. I tried to be as true as possible to the events as they happened including, at times, using the actual words spoken. I have taken liberties in condensing and combining some events and in describing the involvement of my characters.

Every male of my generation had Vietnam hanging over his head. Some chose to enlist, feeling it was their duty to give back to their country. Some were drafted and felt they had no choice but to go. Many Vietnam veterans continue to suffer because of that war. Their exposure to Agent Orange has caused untold damage and they are still fighting for their right to health care.

This continues today with the resistance of some politicians to provide health care to veterans exposed to toxic burn pits in Iraq and Afghanistan.

Many in the country were against the war in Vietnam and wanted our government to quit sending young men to fight and die in a faraway country for an undefined reason. By the end of the 1960s, after seeing the devastation, violence, and body counts on the news every night, the majority of people in this country opposed our continuing involvement in Vietnam.

Some soldiers came back from Vietnam knowing what they saw there was wrong. Over 30,000 Vietnam veterans joined protests when they returned, speaking out against the war. At the Winter Soldiers Investigation in Detroit in 1971, veterans had the courage to talk about the atrocities they experienced. In the book, I used some of their actual testimony. Their honesty and words are powerful.

My son helped craft the Occupy Wall Street vignettes from his experiences of participating in the occupation, being arrested, and spending time in jail. The contributions of the occupiers to the national conversation cannot be understated.

Radishes and Red Bandanas is a work of fiction. Becky's hometown of Rogerstown, Kentucky, is fictional as is Norris Lake. Although I have incorporated traits of people I have known, each character is fictional and does not represent any specific person I knew. My children have a hard time separating me from the main character in the book. I remind them that this is a novel.

ACKNOWLEDGEMENTS

This novel was three decades in the making. Throughout those years, many people helped me, supported me, educated me, pushed me, mentored me, and edited me. I thank all of them.

I met Mickey Collins one evening at the Vietnam Veterans Memorial in Washington, D.C. As we walked The Wall, he told me stories of the men he put in body bags as a medic in Vietnam. He opened his heart to me and for that I am forever grateful.

Thank you to all who occupied cities, parks, highways, and bridges in 2011. The Occupy Movement has not gone away. It's still with us, shaping our lives in ways we never imagined. Don't lose faith. You tell the truth. Your voices are heard. I love you.

Except for historical figures, all the characters in this story are fictional. There are attributes of some characters pulled from people I knew.

Karge Olsen taught me about gentle kisses, picnics at the lake, and sweaters that hold two people. He came into my life one day and left as quickly as he came. When I think of him, I smile.

John Geer taught me about passion, great music, and surprises in closets. He was the best damn guitar player I ever knew.

Henry Post lived life completely. He taught me never to be afraid. We jumped over fences together in Athens, Greece, and got caught sneaking into the Parthenon at night. Most importantly, Henry taught me about full body hugs.

I thank them for being part of my life. All three died too soon.

Others shaped my life and this book in ways we didn't know was happening.

Larry jumped out of a tree one day and taught me about love. He changed who I was and I carry his story with me.

Bob had one of those names where the first could be last and last could be first. He gave me magic moments and a trip into

Chicago to see the Chicago 7 trial. Bob was with me when I touched Dustin Hoffman on the shoulder. I hold the magic of those days close to my heart.

Jed spoke out for social justice the first week I was at college and has never stopped. He has always been true to himself.

Peter was the gentlest, most honest person I ever met. When his dog, Guida, had puppies, he trusted me with one of them.

Jim introduced me to Quakerism. Together with his family we protested at nuclear power plants. Jim served as a medic in Vietnam. Some of the stories in this book came from him.

Sera Rivers, writer extraordinaire, was the first person to tell me I had a voice and needed to use it. She encouraged me, supported me, laughed with me, mentored me, taught me, made me wait when I thought I was ready, and told me to go when I was scared to move on. I love her and the belief she has in me.

The rest of the Write Loudly women were there week after week laughing, critiquing, reading, listening, supporting, and telling me I had a story. They read, edited, tore apart, built up, and gave me confidence. You can't imagine how much I love and appreciate them.

My dear friends from my Monday evening and Friday afternoon writing groups gave me advice, encouragement, and laughter. There are too many to list and I'm afraid I'll forget someone. I thank them for being in my life and for supporting me. Many of them read the manuscript and gave feedback.

To my other writing group: Sara, Christine, and Suzanne. I love the times we spend together. Your writing and editing talents amaze me. You made the lockdown bearable and continue to bring joy into my life. Thanks millions.

Scott DeNino volunteered to design the cover. I am so thankful for his willingness to do so and for his vision and talent. Thanks to Christine for letting me use her photo on the cover.

Besides my book club and writing friends, many others read drafts and provided feedback. Thirty-five years ago, my sisters, Nancy and Anne, read the beginnings of this story. The story sat in a box for almost three decades until I picked it up again. Their initial comments helped shape the book as it is today.

Frances was the first to read a draft of the rewritten manuscript and to embrace the story and the characters. Others read and gave feedback: Kevin, Joanne, Jen, Barbara, Nancy, Matthew, Donna, Abby, Sarah, Joan, Pam, Candy, many Inkitt readers, and many I have forgotten, for which I apologize. I want to especially thank Andrea, Ashley, and Becky who were the last to read the manuscript. They gave invaluable feedback for the final edits. A special shout out to H.R. Kemp, an amazing writer, who embraced my story and lifted my confidence.

The Costa Rica Old Ladies Bird Watching Club, Deb, Mark, and Wilma, brought me incredible joy. I promised them a trip to the Bahamas if this book sells.

I am so grateful for my friend, Nancy Doda. She sees me as I am and loves every part of me. My friend, Dave Brown, has been a huge part of my life since we were both at the University of Tennessee. I cherish his friendship.

My family has always supported my writing, my various journeys, and the craziness of my life. I could not have asked for better parents. I thank them for showing me what love is. My siblings, Nancy, Anne, Rex, and Mark are my best friends and know me better than anyone. I love their significant others and their children and grandchildren.

My children are the light of my life. I thank them for their love and support.

Melissa—You are my heart. It was you and me for a long time. You dream big dreams and I love watching you go for them.

Rachel—You are my soul. You have a pure, honest, and gentle heart that weeps at injustice. You find joy in simple places. I love finding joy with you.

Robert—You are my truth. You tell the truth without fail. Sometimes it's hard to hear but it forces me to be truthful too. Thank you for occupying and for helping me tell the story of Occupy Wall Street.

Ariel—You are my laughter. Thank you for allowing me to be Mamoo to your kids and for letting me embrace you in such a big way.

Austin—You are my hope. You see the world in such deep and amazing ways. Thanks for trusting me with part of your journey.

Isaac, Rex, Orion, Denali—Precious ones, you are my future. Thanks for letting me be your grandmother.

For the people who hang out with my kids—Juliano, Jeanna, Jereme, and Jason. You love my children and for that, and much more, I love you.

Throughout my life I have been surrounded by courageous people who speak out even when it's hard. I thank them for making the world a more humane place.

To Dan who plays games with me, encourages me, frustrates me, delights in me, and watches bad TV shows with me. You are my love, the man I've chosen to spend my life with. Thank you for being you.

ABOUT THE AUTHOR

In 1967, Trudy Knowles left her small town in Kentucky and headed to Lake Forest College near Chicago. She attended class, studied, joined softball games on the campus green, hung out in Hixson Lounge, played her guitar under the trees, and became involved in the anti-war movement. In the spring of 1970, Trudy attended the college's study-abroad program in Athens, Greece, intending to return to Lake Forest for her senior year. Instead, she embarked on a trip around the world, traveling with a friend in a VW van. When the van was sold in Kabul, Afghanistan, they continued their travels for two more years using public transportation. The trip transformed her life.

Trudy completed her degree at Centre College in Kentucky, earned her master's degree at the University of Nebraska at Omaha, and obtained her doctorate at the University of Tennessee in Knoxville. She was a professor of education for twenty-five years, retiring in 2016.

Trudy is the co-author of *What Every Middle School Teacher Should Know* and author of *The Kids Behind the Label: An Inside Look at ADHD for Classroom Teachers*. Her essay, "The Miracle Message," appears in *Chicken Soup for the Soul: Miracles and the Unexplainable*. She is also the author of numerous professional journal articles.

As an activist since the early sixties, Trudy still protests, marches, demonstrates, writes letters, and speaks out for peace and social justice. Her life motto comes from a bumper sticker she saw in upstate New York one day, "Dance with Reckless Abandon." She does that every day.

Trudy lives in Westfield, Massachusetts, with her husband. She has five children and four grandchildren who are the lights of her life.

www.trudyknowles.com
Larone Family Press

Made in the USA
Middletown, DE
01 July 2025

77629733R00209